Handbook of Research on Socio-Cultural and Linguistic Perspectives on Language and Literacy Development

Angela K. Salmon
Florida International University, USA

Amparo Clavijo-Olarte
Universidad Distrital Francisco Jose de Caldas, Colombia

A volume in the Advances in Linguistics and Communication Studies (ALCS) Book Series

Published in the United States of America by
IGI Global
Information Science Reference (an imprint of IGI Global)
701 E. Chocolate Avenue
Hershey PA, USA 17033
Tel: 717-533-8845
Fax: 717-533-8661
E-mail: cust@igi-global.com
Web site: http://www.igi-global.com

Copyright © 2023 by IGI Global. All rights reserved. No part of this publication may be reproduced, stored or distributed in any form or by any means, electronic or mechanical, including photocopying, without written permission from the publisher. Product or company names used in this set are for identification purposes only. Inclusion of the names of the products or companies does not indicate a claim of ownership by IGI Global of the trademark or registered trademark.

Library of Congress Cataloging-in-Publication Data

Names: Salmon, Angela K., editor. | Clavijo Olarte, Amparo, DATE- editor.
Title: Handbook of research on socio-cultural and linguistic perspectives on language and literacy
   development / Angela Salmon and Amparo Clavijo Olarte, editors.
Description: Hershey, PA : Information Science Reference, 2023. | Includes
   bibliographical references and index. | Summary: "This volume offers
   global perspectives about language and literacy from international
   experiences working with both children and educators, impacting the
   fields of early childhood and youth literacy, teacher education,
   language education, applied linguistics, and global competencies"--
   Provided by publisher.
Identifiers: LCCN 2022025406 (print) | LCCN 2022025407 (ebook) | ISBN
   9781668450222 (hardcover) | ISBN 9781668450239 (ebook)
Subjects: LCSH: Literacy--Social aspects. | Language acquisition. |
   Children--Language. | Sociolinguistics. | Applied linguistics.
Classification: LCC LC149 .S64 2023 (print) | LCC LC149 (ebook) | DDC
   302.2/244--dc23/eng/20220805
LC record available at https://lccn.loc.gov/2022025406
LC ebook record available at https://lccn.loc.gov/2022025407

This book is published in the IGI Global book series Advances in Linguistics and Communication Studies (ALCS) (ISSN: 2372-109X; eISSN: 2372-1111)

British Cataloguing in Publication Data
A Cataloguing in Publication record for this book is available from the British Library.

All work contributed to this book is new, previously-unpublished material. The views expressed in this book are those of the authors, but not necessarily of the publisher.

For electronic access to this publication, please contact: eresources@igi-global.com.

Advances in Linguistics and Communication Studies (ALCS) Book Series

Abigail G. Scheg
Western Governors University, USA

ISSN:2372-109X
EISSN:2372-1111

Mission

The scope of language and communication is constantly changing as society evolves, new modes of communication are developed through technological advancement, and novel words enter our lexicon as the result of cultural change. Understanding how we communicate and use language is crucial in all industries and updated research is necessary in order to promote further knowledge in this field.

The **Advances in Linguistics and Communication Studies (ALCS)** book series presents the latest research in diverse topics relating to language and communication. Interdisciplinary in its coverage, ALCS presents comprehensive research on the use of language and communication in various industries including business, education, government, and healthcare.

Coverage

- Sociolinguistics
- Forensic Linguistics
- Language Acquisition
- Computer-Mediated Communication
- Dialectology
- Non-Verbal Communication
- Computational Linguistics
- Language and Identity
- Youth Language
- Semantics

IGI Global is currently accepting manuscripts for publication within this series. To submit a proposal for a volume in this series, please contact our Acquisition Editors at Acquisitions@igi-global.com or visit: http://www.igi-global.com/publish/.

The Advances in Linguistics and Communication Studies (ALCS) Book Series (ISSN 2372-109X) is published by IGI Global, 701 E. Chocolate Avenue, Hershey, PA 17033-1240, USA, www.igi-global.com. This series is composed of titles available for purchase individually; each title is edited to be contextually exclusive from any other title within the series. For pricing and ordering information please visit http://www.igi-global.com/book-series/advances-linguistics-communication-studies/78950. Postmaster: Send all address changes to above address. © © 2023 IGI Global. All rights, including translation in other languages reserved by the publisher. No part of this series may be reproduced or used in any form or by any means – graphics, electronic, or mechanical, including photocopying, recording, taping, or information and retrieval systems – without written permission from the publisher, except for non commercial, educational use, including classroom teaching purposes. The views expressed in this series are those of the authors, but not necessarily of IGI Global.

Titles in this Series

For a list of additional titles in this series, please visit: http://www.igi-global.com/book-series/advances-linguistics-communication-studies/78950

A Social-Scientific Examination of the Dynamics of Communication, Thought, nd Selves
Seif Sekalala (Drexel University, USA)
Information Science Reference • © 2022 • 277pp • H/C (ISBN: 9781799875079) • US $205.00

Narrative Theory and Therapy in the Post-Truth Era
Recep Yılmaz (Ondokuz Mayis University, Turkey) and Bozkurt Koç (Ondokuz Mayis University, Turkey)
Information Science Reference • © 2022 • 373pp • H/C (ISBN: 9781799892519) • US $240.00

Handbook of Research on Communication Strategies for Taboo Topics
Geoffrey D. Luurs (Murray State University, USA)
Information Science Reference • © 2022 • 602pp • H/C (ISBN: 9781799891253) • US $295.00

Basic Communication and Assessment Prerequisites for the New Normal of Education
Victorița Trif (University of Bucharest, Romania)
Information Science Reference • © 2022 • 287pp • H/C (ISBN: 9781799882473) • US $215.00

Critical Perspectives on Social Justice in Speech-Language Pathology
RaMonda Horton (Midwestern University, USA)
Information Science Reference • © 2021 • 355pp • H/C (ISBN: 9781799871347) • US $215.00

Rationalist Bias in Communication Theory
Leonard Shedletsky (University of Southern Maine, USA)
Information Science Reference • © 2021 • 355pp • H/C (ISBN: 9781799874393) • US $240.00

Innovative Perspectives on Corporate Communication in the Global World
María Dolores Olvera-Lobo (University of Granada, Spain) Juncal Gutiérrez-Artacho (University of Granada, Spain) Irene Rivera-Trigueros (University of Granada, Spain) and Mar Díaz-Millón (University of Granada, Spain)
Business Science Reference • © 2021 • 319pp • H/C (ISBN: 9781799867999) • US $240.00

Rhetoric and Sociolinguistics in Times of Global Crisis
Eda Başak Hancı-Azizoglu (Mediterranean (Akdeniz) University, Turkey) and Maha Alawdat (Kaye Academic College of Education, Israel)
Information Science Reference • © 2021 • 419pp • H/C (ISBN: 9781799867326) • US $215.00

701 East Chocolate Avenue, Hershey, PA 17033, USA
Tel: 717-533-8845 x100 • Fax: 717-533-8661
E-Mail: cust@igi-global.com • www.igi-global.com

To our families for their love and support.

In loving memory of our friends and mentors Dr. Kenneth Goodman and Dr. Roberta R. Truax

Angela Katiuska & Amparo

List of Contributors

Bittner, Myles / *University of Massachusetts, Amherst, USA* 60
Bratitsis, Tharrenos / *University of Western Macedonia, Greece* 106
Calderon-Aponte, Daniel / *Universidad Distrital Francisco José de Caldas, Colombia* 239
Calle-Díaz, Luzkarime / *Universidad del Norte, Colombia* 363
Castillo, Paula Renata / *Universidad San Francisco de Quito, Ecuador* 41
Castro Garces, Angela Yicely / *Universidad del Cauca, Colombia* 281
Chocontá, Johanna / *Universidad de La Sabana, Colombia* 26
Clavijo Olarte, Amparo / *Universidad Distrital Francisco José de Caldas, Colombia* 239
Evans, Sarah / *North Broward Preparatory School, USA* 323
Fine, Joyce C. / *Florida International University, USA* 93
Fuga, Valdite Pereira / *Pontifical Catholic University of São Paulo, Brazil* 412
Genc, Esra / *Tokat Gaziosmanpasa University, Turkey* 190
Guerra-Lyons, Jesús / *Universidad del Norte, Colombia* 363
Guzmán, Rosa Julia / *Universidad de La Sabana, Colombia* 26
Hernandez, Kelly A. / *Miami Dade College, USA* 343
Hodges, Leanna / *Baylor University, USA* 171
Lasso, Maria Dolores / *Universidad San Francisco de Quito, Ecuador* 153
Liberali, Fernanda / *Pontifical Catholic University of São Paulo, Brazil* 412
López Angel, Silvia / *BaBidiBu Early Childhood Education, Colombia* 1
Lucas, Teresa / *Florida International University, USA* 378
Markowska-Manista, Urszula / *University of Warsaw, Poland* 265
Mazuchelli, Larissa / *Federal University of Uberlandia, Brazil* 412
Medina, Rosa Alejandra / *University of Massachusetts, Amherst, USA* 239
Medrano, Carmen Adriana / *Florida International University, USA* 73
Melliou, Kiriaki / *Greek Ministry of Education and Religious Affairs, Greece* 106
Modesto-Sarra, Luciana / *Pontifical Catholic University of São Paulo, Brazil* 412
Náder, María Clara / *Universidad Distrital Francisco José de Caldas, Colombia* 239
Najera, Kenia / *Florida International University, USA* 302
Ortega, Yecid / *Queen's University Belfast, UK* 216
Pejão, Rafael da Silva Tosetti / *Pontifical Catholic University of São Paulo, Brazil* 412
Pérez-Prado, Aixa / *Florida International University, USA* 389
Ploetz, Michelle L. / *Atlanta Public Schools, USA* 343
Prieto, Kewin / *Universidad Distrital Francisco José de Caldas, Colombia* 239
Rodríguez, Alejandra / *Universidad Distrital Francisco José de Caldas, Colombia* 239
Salmon, Angela K. / *Florida International University, USA* 129

Trigos-Carrillo, Lina / *Universidad del Norte, Colombia* 363
Uzuner, Yildiz / *Anadolu University, Turkey* 190
Vendramini-Zanella, Daniela / *University of Sorocaba, Brazil* 412
Xu, Jiamin / *Florida International University, USA* 302

Table of Contents

Foreword xxi

Preface xxiv

Acknowledgment xxxii

Section 1
Early Literacy

Chapter 1
Emergent Language and Literacy Skills in Early Childhood: A Path to Success 1
Silvia López Angel, BaBidiBu Early Childhood Education, Colombia

Chapter 2
The Didactic in Initial Literacy: Between the Perception and Representation 26
Rosa Julia Guzmán, Universidad de La Sabana, Colombia
Johanna Chocontá, Universidad de La Sabana, Colombia

Section 2
Critical Literacy and Media

Chapter 3
Critical Literacy: Using This Framework in Early Childhood Classrooms 41
Paula Renata Castillo, Universidad San Francisco de Quito, Ecuador

Chapter 4
Early Years Critical Literacies and Rights: A Review 60
Myles Bittner, University of Massachusetts, Amherst, USA

Chapter 5
Teachers Taking the Lead to Help Children Cope With Stress Through the Use of Language and
Cognitive Pedagogical Units 73
Carmen Adriana Medrano, Florida International University, USA

Chapter 6
Encouraging Critical Literacy: Justice and Equity With Children's Literature 93
    Joyce C. Fine, Florida International University, USA

Section 3
Storytelling and Multiliteracies

Chapter 7
Utilizing Digital Storytelling Tools and Thinking Routines for Cultivating Multiliteracies in
Contemporary Classrooms 106
    Tharrenos Bratitsis, University of Western Macedonia, Greece
    Kiriaki Melliou, Greek Ministry of Education and Religious Affairs, Greece

Chapter 8
Crafting Stories of Voice and Influence: Children's Cognitive and Emotional Engagement in
Listening and Telling Stories 129
    Angela K. Salmon, Florida International University, USA

Chapter 9
Integration of Media and New Literacies in Teacher Education Programs: Preparing Teachers to
Adapt to New Literacies 153
    Maria Dolores Lasso, Universidad San Francisco de Quito, Ecuador

Section 4
Multi-Languages

Chapter 10
Maximizing the Impact of Language and Early Intervention on Literacy Among Deaf and Hard of
Hearing Students: A Critical Assessment and Recommendation 171
    Leanna Hodges, Baylor University, USA

Chapter 11
Developing an Inventory to Evaluate Communication Skills of Children With Normal Hearing
and Hearing Loss 190
    Esra Genc, Tokat Gaziosmanpasa University, Turkey
    Yildiz Uzuner, Anadolu University, Turkey

Section 5
Language, Cultural Awareness, and Perspective

Chapter 12
Trans[cultura]linguación: An Intercultural Approach to the Revitalization of Indigenous
Languages 216
    Yecid Ortega, Queen's University Belfast, UK

Chapter 13
Raising Awareness of the City as a Text: Multimodal, Multicultural, and Multilingual Resources for Education 239

Amparo Clavijo Olarte, Universidad Distrital Francisco José de Caldas, Colombia
Rosa Alejandra Medina, University of Massachusetts, Amherst, USA
Daniel Calderon-Aponte, Universidad Distrital Francisco José de Caldas, Colombia
Alejandra Rodríguez, Universidad Distrital Francisco José de Caldas, Colombia
Kewin Prieto, Universidad Distrital Francisco José de Caldas, Colombia
María Clara Náder, Universidad Distrital Francisco José de Caldas, Colombia

Chapter 14
"Twenty-Six Letters of the Forest Alphabet" or Community Social Learning Among the Ba'Aka in the Central African Republic 265

Urszula Markowska-Manista, University of Warsaw, Poland

Section 6
Language, Literacy, and Culture

Chapter 15
Developing Intercultural Awareness Through a Pedadogy of Multiliteracies 281

Angela Yicely Castro Garces, Universidad del Cauca, Colombia

Chapter 16
Development of Language and Identity Through Author's Chair and Draw and Tell in the Context of Storytelling in Early Childhood Classrooms 302

Jiamin Xu, Florida International University, USA
Kenia Najera, Florida International University, USA

Chapter 17
Cultivating Cultural and Global Competence Through Collaboration With Diverse Groups of People 323

Sarah Evans, North Broward Preparatory School, USA

Chapter 18
Sociocultural and Linguistic Assets of a High School Student Named Maria: Amigos y Anime 343

Michelle L. Ploetz, Atlanta Public Schools, USA
Kelly A. Hernandez, Miami Dade College, USA

Section 7
Language and Society

Chapter 19
Literacy Practices for Peacebuilding 363

Lina Trigos-Carrillo, Universidad del Norte, Colombia
Luzkarime Calle-Díaz, Universidad del Norte, Colombia
Jesús Guerra-Lyons, Universidad del Norte, Colombia

Chapter 20
Literacy for Democracy 378
    Teresa Lucas, Florida International University, USA

Chapter 21
Love and Language: Peace Building in the Foreign Language Classroom 389
    Aixa Pérez-Prado, Florida International University, USA

Chapter 22
Funds of Perezhivanie: Creating Cracks in the Walls of Oppression 412
    Fernanda Liberali, Pontifical Catholic University of São Paulo, Brazil
    Larissa Mazuchelli, Federal University of Uberlandia, Brazil
    Rafael da Silva Tosetti Pejão, Pontifical Catholic University of São Paulo, Brazil
    Daniela Vendramini-Zanella, University of Sorocaba, Brazil
    Valdite Pereira Fuga, Pontifical Catholic University of São Paulo, Brazil
    Luciana Modesto-Sarra, Pontifical Catholic University of São Paulo, Brazil

Compilation of References 435

About the Contributors 487

Index 495

Detailed Table of Contents

Foreword xxi

Preface xxiv

Acknowledgment xxxii

Section 1
Early Literacy

Chapter 1
Emergent Language and Literacy Skills in Early Childhood: A Path to Success 1
Silvia López Angel, BaBidiBu Early Childhood Education, Colombia

Studies have emphasized the importance of the first years of life for successful long-term language and literacy development. It is thus crucial we focus on designing appropriate and effective early learning environments with a clear literacy interaction plan that engages learners in their success and helps them advocate for the language skills they need and do not yet have. This chapter will show early natural language and literacy acquisition in children ages 2 to 4 years in a context where youngsters are exposed to a rich verbal, emotional, and experiential environment where thinking is valuable, visible, and actively promoted as a vehicle to language and literacy, and global competency frameworks are leaving the best tools in their backpack for life.

Chapter 2
The Didactic in Initial Literacy: Between the Perception and Representation 26
Rosa Julia Guzmán, Universidad de La Sabana, Colombia
Johanna Chocontá, Universidad de La Sabana, Colombia

This chapter presents reflections derived from various investigations carried out with both children and teachers about the literacy process in school. There is a tendency to extrapolate results from different disciplines such as psychology and sociology, among others, to direct application in the classroom. Teachers follow different trends, without adapting to the teaching and learning needs of reading and writing. The great absence in these discussions is usually didactics, a discipline that deals with studying teaching practices. In advanced research, it has been found that teachers ignore pedagogy, put didactics as an adjective and the activity as a noun; however, although the proposed activities are very interesting, if they are not articulated around an objective that gives them meaning, they do not favor learning. Hence, it is necessary to understand the teachability of reading and writing, which implies didactic knowledge of the content and refers to what is teachable and how it can be taught.

Section 2
Critical Literacy and Media

Chapter 3
Critical Literacy: Using This Framework in Early Childhood Classrooms 41
Paula Renata Castillo, Universidad San Francisco de Quito, Ecuador

This chapter reviews the definition of critical literacy education as well as the benefits of applying this approach. It analyzes the statement that literacy is not a technical skill, but in fact, it is always embedded in socially constructed epistemological notions and power relations in society. The author includes a reflection on how texts are not neutral and the need to encourage children to interrogate what they read and to use language as a way to question inequalities and oppression. The chapter analyzes why this approach has been rarely implemented in early childhood classroom. The author proposes the need for educators to reflect about how their beliefs regarding literacy influence their teaching practices. It argues that children's literature can be a resource to dialogue about identity, culture, diversity, and power relations in society. Finally, it analyzes the importance to build a curriculum based on children´s interests and needs as well as to create spaces for critical literacy in early childhood classrooms.

Chapter 4
Early Years Critical Literacies and Rights: A Review 60
Myles Bittner, University of Massachusetts, Amherst, USA

Critical literacies as a field carries immense potential to provide students tools to build a better, more caring, and just world. This is especially true for students at the earliest years of education as they create the foundations for active citizenship in society. When these tools are connected to discourses that focus on equal treatment of all humans anywhere in the world, there is hope that future generations will actively resist long-standing systems of mistreatment. This literature review seeks to bring together two bodies of work and ponder at how they might work in relation to one another. This literature is then analyzed in relation to the physical location in which they take place to open understandings of how geopolitics, history, and culture impact what can and should be done. Critical literacies and discourses around human rights create complex intersections that share more in common than what might appear at surface level. Educators and educational policies should work to better understand these intersections to support the holistic development of any student.

Chapter 5
Teachers Taking the Lead to Help Children Cope With Stress Through the Use of Language and
Cognitive Pedagogical Units 73
Carmen Adriana Medrano, Florida International University, USA

This chapter will discuss how teachers use and further develop strategies to help children expand their cognitive abilities, improve oral language, and express their emotions. The work presented was done with young English language learners children ages 2 to 3, within a family childcare home (FCCH) setting in Miami Dade County. During the initial stages of the COVID-19 pandemic, teachers from family childcare homes noticed children with stress created by the many difficult situations their families were going through. The author developed a pedagogical unit based on the storybook called Wimberly Worries written by Kevin Henkes. This pedagogical unit used the teaching for understanding framework and visible thinking routines. It is the author's goal to present this work to inspire teachers in the creation of similar pedagogical units.

Chapter 6
Encouraging Critical Literacy: Justice and Equity With Children's Literature 93
Joyce C. Fine, Florida International University, USA

In this chapter, the author explains the difference between teaching critical thinking and critical literacy with children's literature. She suggests ways teachers may select current children's literature that touches upon social justice and equity instead of just reading aloud old favorites that do not stimulate students' thinking about their world. She shares the steps for analyzing student diversity in classrooms and creating classroom libraries that match students' backgrounds and interests. Also, she describes a practical way teachers may prepare to conduct critical literacy discussions using a Classroom Literacy Folio. The folio includes summaries, personal connections, possible ways diversity may be included in selected books, and lesson ideas for how to introduce students to current issues so even young children can think critically. Included is a sample format, a completed Classroom Literacy Folio page, and suggestions for some of the latest children's literacy books that emphasize social justice and equity.

Section 3
Storytelling and Multiliteracies

Chapter 7
Utilizing Digital Storytelling Tools and Thinking Routines for Cultivating Multiliteracies in Contemporary Classrooms 106
Tharrenos Bratitsis, University of Western Macedonia, Greece
Kiriaki Melliou, Greek Ministry of Education and Religious Affairs, Greece

Pedagogies that foster inclusion, diversity, and the celebration of difference are central in contemporary classrooms that are characterized by an ethnically diverse population with multiple learning styles and ranging abilities. A powerful and flexible venue for educators to address the complex literacy needs of all students is incorporating multimodalities into teaching that draw upon a variety of modes including visual, linguistic, gestural, oral, and spatial. The chapter offers theoretical foundations about the pedagogy of multiliteracy through digital storytelling and provides specific examples of tools and strategies such as thinking routines and story element creation tools that are framed within the Harvard's Project Zero's dispositional framework and the StoryLogicNet project. Using these frameworks and tools, the authors seek to contribute authentic examples on developing and advancing young students' multiliteracy skills for inside and outside the classroom.

Chapter 8
Crafting Stories of Voice and Influence: Children's Cognitive and Emotional Engagement in Listening and Telling Stories 129
Angela K. Salmon, Florida International University, USA

The interplay between language, cognition, and the effects of emotions promote language and literacy development. Children have a natural inclination to build on other children's stories, which is the origin of the collective stories of voice and influence discussion. Stories are empowering venues that give children a voice and simultaneously open windows for them to step inside someone else's shoes, make connections, take perspective, and construct meaning. Stories make us human; children become aware of the world around them by listening and sharing stories. This action research project reports the process of children listening to stories and tailoring the telling of a story to a specific audience. Children were cognitively and emotionally engaged in interpreting stories and transmitting their messages through dialogic thinking and boundary objects. The children made their stories visible using a pedagogy of multiliteracies to tell stories in a natural, playful, safe, and engaging way.

Chapter 9
Integration of Media and New Literacies in Teacher Education Programs: Preparing Teachers to Adapt to New Literacies... 153
Maria Dolores Lasso, Universidad San Francisco de Quito, Ecuador

Preparing teachers to meet the challenges of an ever changing and growing multicultural and diverse population of students must become a focus of attention when thinking about the 21st century teacher education. The purpose of this study is to explore how three different teacher education programs are facing the challenge of preparing teachers to incorporate visual texts and diverse forms of literacy as they prepare to become educators. Literature about teacher identity development, teacher education, and teacher literacy education was reviewed to provide an understanding of the notions around the new of incorporation of new literacies as a way to engage future education professionals in the current challenges of the professional practice.

Section 4
Multi-Languages

Chapter 10
Maximizing the Impact of Language and Early Intervention on Literacy Among Deaf and Hard of Hearing Students: A Critical Assessment and Recommendation 171
Leanna Hodges, Baylor University, USA

Deaf and hard of hearing (DHH) children struggle to develop reading success and proficient language. The journey to reading success begins when a child is diagnosed with a hearing difference and receives early intervention services. Access to early intervention services sets the foundation for DHH students' language and reading achievement. If a child cannot achieve fluent language, their reading will follow suit. This chapter explains how DHH children's language impacts their reading development. First, the chapter describes the research related to early intervention, communication modes, and reading in the DHH population. Second, the chapter explains how language affects reading development in DHH children. Lastly, the chapter includes resources and recommendations for DHH children's parents and teachers. The resources and recommendations focus on practical strategies to grow DHH children's language and, therefore, their reading.

Chapter 11
Developing an Inventory to Evaluate Communication Skills of Children With Normal Hearing and Hearing Loss 190
Esra Genc, Tokat Gaziosmanpasa University, Turkey
Yildiz Uzuner, Anadolu University, Turkey

Researchers state that communication skills, which are developed before language acquisition and have very important place in language development, are 1) directing attention, 2) turn-taking, 3) imitation, 4) communicative purposes, and 5) conversation. As in all children, communication skills in children with hearing loss are very important. It is very important to identify children who have problems with their communication skills and to provide appropriate education. Standardized tests are generally used to assess children's language and communication skills in Turkey, but there are no informal tools that allow the assessment of early communication skills. Therefore, in this chapter, firstly, communication skills will be briefly defined and the disadvantages and advantages of formal and informal assessment and evaluation approaches will be discussed. Afterwards, the scope and development process of the informal communication skills inventory (ICSI) based on natural data collection in various contexts will be presented with sample items from the inventory.

Section 5
Language, Cultural Awareness, and Perspective

Chapter 12
Trans[cultura]linguación: An Intercultural Approach to the Revitalization of Indigenous Languages 216
Yecid Ortega, Queen's University Belfast, UK

Learning languages with the intention to understand cultures is the central premise of trans[cultura] linguación. The purpose of this chapter is to describe and reflect on the teaching and learning process of the Quechua language for students in Toronto (Canada) and other participants in the diaspora who wanted to learn more about the Quechua culture or revitalize their heritage language. Deploying a hybrid ethnographic approach to collect data from public online and in-person classes, this research project evidenced a cultural-oriented approach to assert Quechua speakers' identity and to spark curiosity for learning Indigenous languages in international contexts. A Quechua Collective, along with language teachers, used a synergic pedagogical approach to engage students in language learning and appreciation through various online and in-person interactive activities. This chapter sheds light on promising practices that seek to foster a sense of community, well-being, and the promotion of social cohesion and human coexistence.

Chapter 13
Raising Awareness of the City as a Text: Multimodal, Multicultural, and Multilingual Resources for Education 239
Amparo Clavijo Olarte, Universidad Distrital Francisco José de Caldas, Colombia
Rosa Alejandra Medina, University of Massachusetts, Amherst, USA
Daniel Calderon-Aponte, Universidad Distrital Francisco José de Caldas, Colombia
Alejandra Rodríguez, Universidad Distrital Francisco José de Caldas, Colombia
Kewin Prieto, Universidad Distrital Francisco José de Caldas, Colombia
María Clara Náder, Universidad Distrital Francisco José de Caldas, Colombia

In this chapter, the authors explore the semiotic landscape of the city to analyze multimodal, multicultural, and multilingual resources for language and literacy education. In this ethnographic study, teacher-researchers explore urban literacies as social, artistic, political, cultural, and pedagogical practices that connect different community actors, diverse texts, and local realities. Data were collected through community tours, photographs (a corpus of 387 photographs), and semi-structured interviews with graffiti artists and community inhabitants. The findings reveal that semiotic and linguistic landscapes that surround schools can be harnessed to develop critical place awareness and to recognize the audiences and purposes of multimodal texts embedded in the environments. It also leads to the recognition of multicultural and linguistic diversity that is rarely reflected in school-centered curriculum and decontextualized textbooks.

Chapter 14
"Twenty-Six Letters of the Forest Alphabet" or Community Social Learning Among the Ba'Aka in the Central African Republic 265

Urszula Markowska-Manista, University of Warsaw, Poland

The chapter discusses three areas of education for indigenous children from the Ba'Aka hunter-gatherer community in the CAR: public, formal education; private, missionary-run institutions; their traditional, collective education, metaphorically called "the forest alphabet." Children used to be socialized into engaging with the forest-based on the relationship of reciprocal cooperation, protection, and justice. However, this relationship has become incongruent and undesirable in a reality dominated by developmental projects, deforestation, missionary activities, and environmental conservation initiatives. Each undermines indigenous epistemic rights and relationships with and claims to the land. Missionary and state education are shown as posing challenges to indigenous children, while particular attention is paid to forest education in terms of the social learning and engagement of Ba'Aka children in the environment in which they grow up, and in terms of their resistance and adaptation strategies in the face of these developments.

Section 6
Language, Literacy, and Culture

Chapter 15
Developing Intercultural Awareness Through a Pedadogy of Multiliteracies 281

Angela Yicely Castro Garces, Universidad del Cauca, Colombia

The language classroom as a space for reflection, interaction, and enactment calls for language teaching and learning that makes meaning and prepares intercultural communicators who value local knowledge, are sensitive to diversity, and are aware of their global community. This work aims to examine the role of a pedagogy of multiliteracies in the development of pre-service teachers' intercultural awareness. This study was conducted with a group of 12 pre-service teachers at a state university in Colombia. It was based on a pedagogy of multiliteracies, through the knowledge processes, approached from a qualitative interpretive case study perspective. The findings indicate that connecting personal experiences to those of others through global literacies and multimodal tasks helped develop intercultural awareness in relation to issues of ethnicity, gender, physical ability, and social class, thus expanding participants' limited nationalist perspective and taking them to embrace a more intersectional view of others.

Chapter 16
Development of Language and Identity Through Author's Chair and Draw and Tell in the Context of Storytelling in Early Childhood Classrooms 302

Jiamin Xu, Florida International University, USA
Kenia Najera, Florida International University, USA

Storytelling is powerful. Young children use stories to share experiences, cultural beliefs, and thoughts in their early years. This chapter aims to examine the impact of traditional and digital storytelling on language development and identity among young immigrant children. In a study conducted with young children, they were encouraged to tell and share their personal stories with their classmates in a comfortable and engaging environment created by the author's chair and the draw and tell technique. The authors observed and analyzed the children's work in the after-school program over time and saw that they developed social skills and became confident communicating in their newly acquired language by sharing their own stories. The power of language and culture immersion intertwines with stories that encourage young children to freely communicate and share in a safe space, which fosters children's identity and language development.

Chapter 17
Cultivating Cultural and Global Competence Through Collaboration With Diverse Groups of People... 323
    Sarah Evans, North Broward Preparatory School, USA

Can cultural and global competence be cultivated through experiential collaborations with diverse groups of people? There has been a great deal of attention placed on the importance of developing students' cultural competence; however, primary grade teachers often lack the resources and training necessary for thoroughly investigating diversity with young children. To build cultural competence, it is imperative to create meaningful opportunities in which students collaborate on common goals so that children can have positive experiences with people of different cultures. This chapter will explore a research-based method being used effectively in classrooms in the United States, Mexico, and Ecuador to develop students' cultural and global competence through project-based experiences that meet existing curricular needs. In addition to the methodology used to engage students in cross-cultural project-based collaborations, this chapter also includes practical strategies for the evaluation of participants' cultural competence as well as qualitative data that supports the findings.

Chapter 18
Sociocultural and Linguistic Assets of a High School Student Named Maria: Amigos y Anime...... 343
    Michelle L. Ploetz, Atlanta Public Schools, USA
    Kelly A. Hernandez, Miami Dade College, USA

This chapter tells the story of the language learning aspirations and educational experiences of Maria, a high school student from an immigrant family living in a large metropolitan area of the southeastern United States. Her story documents her quest to acquire literacy in a heritage language, Spanish, and to learn other foreign languages, French and Japanese. Her experiences have been shaped by the languages spoken in her home, the respective educational levels of family members and friends who provide academic support to her, the larger multilingual community in which she lives, interpersonal interactions with teachers, and popular culture. Vygotsky's sociocultural theory and other theories derived from this theory were used to analyze her experiences. Stories like hers can serve as a powerful resource for scholars and practitioners of language teaching and learning who seek to inform their practice through greater understanding of many sociocultural factors and linguistic assets that influence the success of language learners at the individual level.

Section 7
Language and Society

Chapter 19
Literacy Practices for Peacebuilding.. 363
    Lina Trigos-Carrillo, Universidad del Norte, Colombia
    Luzkarime Calle-Díaz, Universidad del Norte, Colombia
    Jesús Guerra-Lyons, Universidad del Norte, Colombia

The effects of the pandemic, natural disasters, wars, and economic distress at the turn of the second decade of the 20th century are a call to strengthen peace education around the world. In this chapter, the authors argue that intentional social practices of critical literacies offer opportunities for peacebuilding, understood as a dynamic process which includes the development of harmony in different life dimensions. After providing an overview of peace research and peace education in the Colombian context, the authors provide a conceptualization of critical literacy and its relation to peacebuilding. Finally, the chapter offers a set of practical strategies to promote peacebuilding through critical literacies based on research experiences across the Americas. The strategies include the use of children's literature to understand social reality and to develop empathy, critical literacies to develop critical intercultural awareness, and connecting with families and communities through literacy practices to make peace.

Chapter 20
Literacy for Democracy 378
Teresa Lucas, Florida International University, USA

The world is more literate than ever, but does this literacy lead to a more thoughtful citizenry? The approach to teaching literacy skills governed by the necessity of choosing the "right" answers on multiple choice assessment instruments has the effect of producing literate and competent workers rather than the critical, creative, and ethical citizens required for functioning democratic societies. The fall of the Soviet Union in 1989 was celebrated as the victory of democratic ideals over authoritarian forms of government in many parts of the globe. However, events in the current century point to a trend towards autocracy. This chapter considers how events in the current century in the United States and Venezuela point to a trend towards autocracy and suggests how strengthening educational practices, especially those for engaging children in thoughtful literacy, can result in a return to democracy.

Chapter 21
Love and Language: Peace Building in the Foreign Language Classroom 389
Aixa Pérez-Prado, Florida International University, USA

Language is a necessary tool to understand the world. It can be used as an instrument of hate, harm, exclusion, and dehumanization or as an instrument of love, help, inclusion, and humanization. Language is a component of peace, and the language classroom can be a place where communicative competence is expressed through communicative peace. This chapter will explore the relationship between language acquisition, emotion, critical thinking, and peace building. It will demonstrate how applied peace linguistics can help teachers create empathetic and equitable foreign language classroom environments. The author will describe the characteristics of a language acquisition classroom that encourages both critical thinking and peace building. Strategies for teaching language learners by centering emotion during language activities, encouraging critical thinking, and creating peaceful connections among diverse learners will be suggested.

Chapter 22
Funds of Perezhivanie: Creating Cracks in the Walls of Oppression 412
    Fernanda Liberali, Pontifical Catholic University of São Paulo, Brazil
    Larissa Mazuchelli, Federal University of Uberlandia, Brazil
    Rafael da Silva Tosetti Pejão, Pontifical Catholic University of São Paulo, Brazil
    Daniela Vendramini-Zanella, University of Sorocaba, Brazil
    Valdite Pereira Fuga, Pontifical Catholic University of São Paulo, Brazil
    Luciana Modesto-Sarra, Pontifical Catholic University of São Paulo, Brazil

This chapter discusses the development of funds of perezhivanie in participants of the Brincadas Project, a response to the appalling experiences of COVID-19 in Brazil organized by the Research Group Language in Activities in School Contexts. The project, grounded on critical collaborative research, decolonial studies, and Vygotskian and Freirean's body of works, involves participants' critical, intentional, and engaged actions to individually and collectively recreate ways of "producing life" and research together. The authors focus on two activities for this work: a cine club with the indigenous community Tekoa Pyau and a workshop session on ag(e)ing. Both activities exemplify the development and expansion of participants' funds of perezhivanie while expressing how these resources for "talking back" may significantly impact society.

Compilation of References 435

About the Contributors 487

Index 495

Foreword

CREATING POSSIBILITY THROUGH GLOBAL PERSPECTIVES

As our world grows increasingly interconnected through global mobility and digital technologies, we are also experiencing escalating political divides and tensions. War and conflict, struggling economies, pandemics, and extreme weather have resulted in many countries taking a more conservative political turn and led to deep concerns about the future of our world. A world of unrest and uncertainty leads many people to draw back within their own comfort zones and to close their minds to ways of living that differ from their experiences and beliefs. The challenge is how to resist our tendency to withdraw in the face of uncertainty and instead open ourselves to new possibilities if we are to have any hope of creating a better and more just world.

This book seeks to open minds to the values of linguistic and cultural diversity by sharing the work of educators on literacy and language development in different parts of the world. The authors of these chapters provide real examples of their experiences with teachers and children in thoughtful explorations of cultural and linguistic identities within a multicultural and multilingual world. Their experiences contribute to our knowledge and vision for how to create these opportunities in our own contexts and communities and the deep global divides remind us of why this work matters.

The focus of this book on perspectives is particularly significant in considering the world views we bring to our work as educators. A global orientation must permeate our beings, not be an occasional lens we bring to our work and lives. Hansen (2011) argues that a global orientation is one that balances reflective loyalty to the known with reflective openness to the new. The values and loyalties that lie deep within our hearts and give meaning and purpose to our lives matter--we need that rootedness in the local or "home" to feel secure in reaching out to the new. Reflective loyalty to the known entails closely examining our values and digging deeply to determine which of our loyalties are most essential to our sense of belonging and becoming. That self-examination has a reflective component of criticality in considering whether some of those beliefs include negative biases and cause harm or oppression to others or to ourselves (Freire, 1970).

Reflective openness to the new invites us to take on an attitude of open-mindedness towards global cultures and new ways of thinking and living. This attitude is one of reserving judgement and trying to understand perspectives that differ from our own, instead of immediately reacting with judgement. We also reflect critically on the new, both as a way to understand those whose views differ from ourselves and to consider the possibility of trying on some of those perspectives. This openness provides a means of connecting meaningfully with those whose cultures and languages differ from our own and to continuing to grow our own perspectives and ways of living and thinking.

This definition of a global orientation is reflected in the chapters as authors describe their work with children and teachers. Some of this work involves helping learners engage in self-examination and valuing of their own cultures and languages and other work focuses on opening learners to the new in the lives of classmates and community members.

Another perspective that permeates this book relates to the work of Richard Ruiz (1984) who provides useful distinctions between orientations of language-as-problem, language-as-right, and language-as-resource that "determine what is thinkable about language in society" (p. 16). Language-as-problem is based on the belief that language issues are linked to poverty, low educational achievement, and economic disadvantage, thus creating problems for their speakers and for society. Multilingualism is viewed as leading to a lack of social cohesiveness that makes political and social consensus impossible because people speak different languages. These so-called social problems are resolved through language programs that suppress languages other than the dominant language of that community, such has occurred in the U.S. through English-only laws and ESL programs.

Language-as-right orientations often lead to legislation that protects minoritized languages and the groups who speak those languages within a country. Ruiz (1984) points out this orientation frequently results in groups and authorities invoking their rights against each other and does not challenge societal power structures that continue to prioritize the dominant language. He suggests that, while problem and rights orientations are valid and play important roles, they are insufficient in linguistically diverse communities and societies.

Ruiz (1984) recommends a language-as-resource orientation in which linguistic diversity is viewed as a societal resource valued and utilized by all members of that community, transcending an "us vs them" mentality and highlighting the interests of the entire society. Language is valued as an intellectual, cultural, economic, social, citizenship, and rights resource with multilingualism enriching the sociocultural life of a community and the community members who speak multiple languages regarded as sources of expertise. This orientation of languages-as-resources must be carefully framed in language as identity for the purposes of social justice (Ruiz, 2010).

A language-as-resource orientation is central to this book in that the authors of these chapters view multiple languages and cultures as valuable resources within a community, not as problems. Multilingualism and multiculturalism are thus assets to communities. The chapters provide examples of how this orientation to language, literacy, and culture can be enacted in various contexts.

Finally, these chapters recognize the importance of the narrative imagination so that readers enter story worlds to experience how people live, feel, and think around the world. Through literature, readers immerse themselves into story worlds, providing experiences that go beyond surface-level tourist information to deeper cultural values and beliefs. As readers engage with characters in these story worlds, they develop emotional connections and empathy as well as knowledge about a global culture. They learn from, not merely tolerate, those whose views and ways of living differ from their own. They also come to know their own home cultures better through exploring worlds beyond their homes. These understandings grow out of recognizing the common values they share with those living in other cultural communities as well as the unique differences that distinguish each culture. Experiences with global literature can encourage a stance of reflective openness to how people view themselves, not just how we view them.

Reading globally expands readers' views and encourages the development of empathy and open-mindedness toward cultural ways of thinking that differ from their own. What is often overlooked, however, is that asking readers to read outside their comfort zones holds danger as well as possibility and can establish misunderstandings and stereotypes—how we use books matters (Short, 2019).

Foreword

The significance of story goes beyond written and oral narratives in books and storytelling. Story is a primary act of mind, the way in which we bring meaning to our experiences and make sense of the chaos of daily life. We create stories in our minds in order to be able to understand our experiences. Our views of the world develop as a web of interconnected stories that we keep adding to and rearranging in our minds (Short, 2012). Stories make us human—the nature of a life is that it's a story.

The topics and resources shared in the chapters of this book will be useful to educators as they consider the teaching of language and literacy in their own contexts. More importantly, however, beyond the practical significance are the demonstrations of how to bring a global orientation to our work that is grounded in critical literacy and openness to the new. The perspectives we bring to our teaching and research matter if we want to make a difference and bring about social change as we walk hand-in-hand with learners.

Kathy G. Short
University of Arizona, USA

Kathy G. Short *is a professor and endowed chair of global children's literature in the College of Education at the University of Arizona, where she is Director of Worlds of Words: Center of Global Literacies and Literatures (wowlit.org). She has co-authored many books and articles on inquiry, literature, and inquiry as curriculum. She was President of the National Council of Teachers of English and of the US Board of Books for Young People.*

REFERENCES

Freire, P. (1970). Pedagogy of the oppressed. *Continuum.*

Hansen, D. (2011). *The teacher and the world.* Routledge.

Ruiz, R. (1984). Orientations in language planning. *NABE, 8*(2), 15–34. doi:10.1080/08855072.1984.10668464

Ruiz, R. (2010). Reorienting language-as-resource. In J. Petrovic (Ed.), *International perspectives on bilingual education* (pp. 155–172). Information Age Publishing.

Short, K. (2019). The dangers of reading globally. *Bookbird, 57*(9), 1–11. doi:10.1353/bkb.2019.0025

Short, K. G. (2012). Story as world making. *Language Arts, 90*(1), 9–17.

Preface

The world is experiencing drastic changes that affect humanity. We are witnessing unprecedented human migration, fast advances in technology and increasing social disparity, among other issues that directly affect how people communicate. This is a call for educators to rethink their roles and practices in promoting language and literacy in an interconnected world. This project aims to contribute with research, experiences, and reflections to support the 2030 Agenda for Sustainable Development Goals (SDGs) adopted by the United Nations in 2015. The topics addressed in the books cover SDGs such as quality education, reduced inequalities, peace, justice, and strong institutions, among others, in which language and literacy are built through life and work sociocultural contexts. We are setting the stage to redefine language and literacy development from a sociocultural and linguistic perspective and change literacies in a world on the move.

This book's authors invite readers to inquire and find solutions to these questions: What is appropriate education for 21st century learners? What is appropriate teaching for English language learners, urban and rural citizens, indigenous people, deaf and hard of hearing, and immigrants who do not speak the national language? How can we use language as a gateway to understand and change the world? The upcoming chapters open doors to re-imagine language and literacy for peace, prosperity, and global competence.

This book offers global perspectives about language and literacy from our experiences working with both children of all ages and educators. We curated the chapters of this book based on our research and teaching trajectories in the literacy field. We draw from numerous research-based, progressive experiences developed from thought collectives in the field. We value the learners' socio-emotional, personal, and linguistic stories and their funds of knowledge (Moll, et al. 1992). The chapters offer readers a diversity of voices and experiences from scholars and practitioners about current trends and issues. The book's theme, Socio-Cultural and Linguistic Perspectives on Language and Literacy Development, targets early childhood education, youth literacy, teacher education, language education, critical literacy, multiliteracy, and applied linguistics.

Some authors propose education programs that attempt to integrate new literacies as part of their curriculum. Language and literacy development go beyond the conventional notion of reading and writing, leading us to differentiate the concept of literacies from literacy. The International Literacy Association (ILA, 2022) defines literacies as distinct written and oral language practices evident across varying social circumstances, domains, and classes, for example, school literacy, digital literacy, financial literacy and more. Literacy for the ILA is the ability to identify, understand, interpret, create, compute, and communicate using visual, audible, and digital materials across disciplines and in any contexts. It refers to basic knowledge rather than to anything specific to reading and writing. Another important concept worth highlighting is multiliteracies, defined by the ILA as an instructional framework that supports an

Preface

awareness of how new communications media are shaping the way we use language in a highly diverse and globally connected world.

This book tackles language and literacy from different geographical perspectives and practices through the experiences of professionals in Brazil, Canada, Colombia, Central African Republic, Ecuador, Greece, Northern Ireland, Poland, the United States of America, and Turkey.

This book comprises a series of research contributions, case studies, literature reviews and theoretical discussions that tackle different perspectives on language and literacy development. The research, ideas and practices outlined in the coming pages focus on early literacy; critical and media literacy; storytelling and multiliteracy; multiple languages, language, cultural awareness, and perspective; language, literacy, and culture; and language and society. The chapters in the book are organized under these categories, although most of them fall under two or more categories.

The collective thoughts of the book's authors coincide on critical aspects of authentic language uses (Cambourne, 2009) that emerge from different cultures' practices around the world. They bring a sociocultural and linguistic view of language and literacy development. Freire (1987) claims that learners learn in interactions with their world because they read the world before reading words. The chapters "Raising Awareness of the City as a Text: Multimodal, Multicultural, and Multilingual Resources for Education" and "'Twenty-Six Letters of the Forest Alphabet' or Community Social Learning Among the Ba'Aka in the Central African Republic" are perfect examples of literacy outside the classroom in two different settings.

A sociocultural and linguistic perspective of language and literacy development refers to how and where a language is used as a means of communication for a purpose; in other words, it is the interplay of language and society. It is important, from an educational viewpoint, for educators to reflect on their conception of language and literacy; this is the foundation for the quality learning opportunities that they offer to students. In the chapter "Integration of Media and New Literacies in Teacher Education Programs," the author presents research about literacy that focuses on teaching reading and writing practices that rarely incorporate other ways of communication and information interpretation. Street (1995) considered it necessary to change the pedagogy of literacy to combine the knowledge of schools, home, and the communities to foster reading, writing, and thinking among learners. For the latter, literacy experiences in learners' communities and realities provide meaning to pedagogy and generate local inquiries. Thus, the context in which learners live and experience the world with their family and community constitutes their funds of knowledge. Funds of knowledge for Moll (2019) is a sociocultural approach developed to prepare a community-oriented pedagogy. Families, for him, especially those in the working class, can be characterized by the practices they have developed and the knowledge they have produced and acquired while living their lives.

Early experiences with language and literacy, from which students can listen, talk, read, and write, are predictors of student success. Children build their vocabulary through authentic life experiences, which are essential for their language development. Exposure to the world generates a context in which students can not only develop vocabulary in their first and second language, but they can also learn about the world. Longitudinal studies (Hart & Risley, 2003) are a testament to the importance of early experiences to prevent language disparities. Snow, Griffin & Burns (2005) says that children learn to talk by talking and learn to read and write by reading and writing for authentic purposes.

The chapter "Emergent Language and Literacy Skills in Early Childhood: A Path to Success" approaches language and literacy development from a socially constructed perspective that claims early language experiences connected to children's needs and interests are important. Language and literacy are aligned with children's cognition and emotions. Experiences and stories are powerful provocations to engage children cognitively and emotionally in meaningful conversations about the concepts they are creating about the world. Human cognitive and language development are intertwined for Vygotsky (1978) and Piaget (1977). Children communicate in different ways; they use different sign systems to communicate as they grow, including oral language, drawing, writing, dancing, singing and enacting stories. The chapter "The Didactic in Initial Literacy: Between the Perception and Representation" makes a call to understand the teachability of reading and writing, which implies didactic knowledge of the content. That refers to what is teachable and how it can be taught if they are not articulated around an objective that gives them meaning.

The book brings together different research voices on critical literacy geared to foster intercultural understanding and peace building. It offers critical approaches to the understanding of literacy and how language and literacy are used to shape society. Goodman's (Goodman & Goodman, 2014) legacy sustains that students learn to read through immersion in books. For him teachers' knowledge and skill should respond to student needs, rather than scripted programs and curricula.

Children's books bring the world to children. The different chapters open doors to reflect on the power of children's literature and critical literacy. The technology era is also opening new venues for learning and communicating. The different media for accessing knowledge have created a need for children to develop critical literacy and critical media literacy. Teachers who use critical literacy actively engage children to read in a way that they develop a deep understanding of socially constructed concepts such as power, race, inequality, and injustice in human relationships (ILA, 2022). Children's books and technology are powerful resources to bring the world to the classroom; thus, a need exists for teachers to become knowledgeable and skillful in using these resources to engage the children. Short's (2009) extensive scholarly work suggests that critical literacy is essential to build intercultural understanding through literature.

It is critical for educators to understand the impact of critical media literacy in children in an era of fast advances of information and communication technologies (ILA, 2022). The ILA defines it as an educational response that expands the notion of literacy to include different forms of mass communication, popular culture, and new technologies. It deepens the potential of literacy education to critically analyze relationships between media and audiences, information, and power.

Stories make us human because they help people connect to each other. The use of children's literature as a key resource for language and literacy development and the relevance of intercultural understandings through global literature is a way to recognize the cultures that influence our thinking (Short 2009). The use of both printed and digital literature resources facilitates access to literature works by children, youth, teachers, and parents.

In the chapter "Critical Literacy: Using This Framework in Early Childhood Classroom," the author invites educators to reflect about how their beliefs regarding literacy influence their teaching practices. She sustains that literature can be a resource to dialogue about identity, culture, diversity, and power relations in society.

Critical literacy is an invitation for children to see themselves as authors. Chapters such as "Crafting Stories of Voice and Influence: Children's Cognitive and Emotional Engagement in Listening and Telling Stories" use critical literacy as a provocation to engage children in creating and telling their own stories to influence others. The author shares stories that illustrate how children's books become a provocation to engage them in storytelling. For Goodman & Goodman (2014) writing is a powerful complement to reading rich texts. Young children think in stories and use stories to communicate. Short (2009) says:

Preface

"Through literature, children have the opportunity to go beyond a tourist perspective of gaining surface-level information about another culture. They are invited to immerse themselves in story worlds, gaining insights into how people feel, live, and think around the world" (p 2).

Children's stories are externalized through different sign systems (Gardner, 1980). The authors of "Utilizing Digital Storytelling Tools and Thinking Routines for Cultivating Multiliteracies in Contemporary: Literacy Practices for Peacebuilding" refer to multiliteracy as the ability to identify, interpret, create, and communicate meaning across a variety of visual, oral, corporal, musical and alphabetical forms of communication. Technology, especially digital storytelling, is another way to communicate that is gaining interest from children because it involves them in play. Digital storytelling offers children opportunities to negotiate meanings, think critically, and collaborate in the process of recreating their stories. Digital storytelling is gaining strength as children gain more access to technology. Literacy is a cultural symbol system that conveys meaning. Children use digital and multiliteracy to tell stories through play. Multiliteracy pedagogy facilitates the development of students' individual and collaborative interests and abilities using new digital media, allowing them to interact and collaborate by engaging. This is an inclusive approach that offers children a space to exercise their right to participate (National Convention on Children's Rights, 2022), articles 11, 12, and 30.

The use of critical literacy is an aid, when started at young ages, to help children understand the world where they live, cope with fear, and overcome trauma. In the chapter "Teachers Taking the Lead to Help Children Cope With Stress Using Language and Cognitive Pedagogical Units," the author offers ideas to integrate children's literature in the curriculum to help children face challenging situations.

Some of the trending issues of global significance addressed in the book invite readers to see the power of language as a gateway to facing and influencing problems in a changing world (Boix-Mansilla, 2015). A chapter such as "Cultivating Cultural and Global Competence Through Collaboration With Diverse Groups of People" is an excellent example of communicating in an interdependent world.

Other topics of interest are first and second language acquisition, multiple languages, indigenous languages, and sign language from different contexts. These chapters provide valuable information about translanguage which, according to the ILA (2022), is the process whereby multilingual speakers use their multiple ways of expressing themselves in an integrated communication system. In the chapter "Trans[cultura]linguación: An Intercultural Approach to the Revitalization of Indigenous Languages," the author describes and reflects on the teaching and learning process of the Quechua language for students in Toronto (Canada) and other participants in the diaspora who wanted to learn more about the Quechua culture or revitalize their heritage language.

In another context, the authors of "Linguistic Assets of a High School Student Named Maria: Amigos y Anime" expand our horizons about diversity and second language acquisition in an urban setting. They focus on the understanding of many sociocultural factors and linguistic assets that influence the success of language learners at the individual level.

Educators who attempt to address the difficult question of cultural and linguistic diversity need to understand schooling as the connection between home, community, and education and to embrace language and literacy learning. This book's research-based experiences invite readers to appreciate the dimensions of language and literacy development in authentic contexts that include global perspectives.

The deaf and hard of hearing (DHH) are another community worth understanding. The authors of these chapters bring new perspectives about different language practices in two countries. In "Maximizing the Impact of Language and Early Intervention on Literacy Among Deaf," the author explains how DHH children's language impacts their reading development and describes the research related to early intervention, communication modes, and reading in an American context. In the chapter "Developing an Inventory to Evaluate Communication Skills of Children with Normally Hearing and Hearing Loss," the authors highlight the importance of communication skills to provide appropriate education. They define and analyze the disadvantages and advantages of formal and informal assessment and evaluation approaches in Turkey.

The chapters in language, literacy, and culture focus on the teacher's role to create opportunities that intrinsically motivate learners to externalize their thoughts. The understanding of the interplay between language, literacy and culture is critical for teachers if they are to design quality learning opportunities. Learners are constantly making connections with their prior knowledge to create meaning through talking, reading, listening, and expressing.

The power of language and literacies in diverse social contexts is revealed through the stories of immigrant learners constructing their own identities through language interactions. The authors describe how the learners' immersion in languages spoken at home and in multilingual communities is beneficial, while project-based collaborations provide positive experiences for learning from different cultures for others. The role of teacher-educators reflects the need for preservice language teachers to become sensitive to diversity and to develop awareness of their global community through intercultural awareness. In the chapter "Development of Language and Identity Through Author's Chair and Draw and Tell in the Context of Storytelling in Early Childhood Classrooms," the authors depict stories of immigrant children immersed in a new land and exposed to a new language.

The use of children's books and storytelling helps teachers and students reach a cultural understanding. The author of the chapter "Developing Intercultural Awareness Through a Pedagogy of Multiliteracies" also shares strategies for preservice teachers to work with diverse children using literature.

Language, cultural awareness, and perspective embrace a critical perspective towards languages as social and cultural sites for resistance. They raise awareness towards the need to revitalize indigenous languages, culture, and identity. The invitation is also to understand that languages are represented in different places of individuals' worlds (home, school, community in urban or rural settings). Thus, observing the local communities to analyze the ways languages and cultures are represented engages learners in critical reading of the spaces and fosters cultural awareness and understanding of language as a social practice.

A study of *EFL Learners' Agency Exploring the Sociocultural Landscape of a Public University* by Rodriguez (2021) highlights Pennycook's (2010) claim that "language is part of social and local activity, both locality and language emerge from the activities engaged in" (p. 2). His perspective of language views physical and symbolic spaces as fundamental when constructing language. Comber's (2016) research in Australia with poor and working-class youth, with indigenous children in public schools and with preservice teachers similarly gives a paramount importance to place. Her question "How can teachers make place the object of study in ways that are generative for assembling complex literate repertoires?" (p.xviii) invites teacher researchers to consider inclusive pedagogies.

In observing the languages represented in communities, the presence of indigenous languages is of the greatest importance, given the continuing marginalization of these groups in different parts of the world. This calls for indigenous language revitalization through exploring and discussing how languages are depicted in society.

Critical perspectives of language and literacy are fostered through children's and youth's literature to build intercultural understandings. Short (2009) claims that children have the opportunity through literature to go beyond a tourist perspective to gain surface-level about another culture. Therefore, teacher

Preface

education programs have a responsibility to prepare teachers to connect the literacies available in their surrounding contexts and in literature with a global perspective.

Human beings have multiple means of expression: This is powerful when learners can have a real voice. The realities children experience in their local communities are powerful resources for the language curriculum and teaching that help to create an understanding of the value that the languages and cultures of children and teachers bring from a multicultural perspective. Thus, teachers can help children develop their cultural and linguistic identities to promote multiculturalism, multilingualism, and translingualism so they can thrive in a complex and changing world.

Topics such as peacebuilding, critical citizenry, and participants' critical engaged actions are the goals of some of the chapters in this book. Critical literacy becomes an important tool to build a better, more caring, and fairer world as children grow. Some authors, based on their experiences, reflect on the efficacy of critical literacy to promote understanding of how geopolitics, history, and culture impact what can and should be done. Language also plays an important role in active citizenship in society and participation in issues of global significance. The chapter "Literacy for Democracy" analyzes how events in the current century in the United States and Venezuela point to a trend towards autocracy and suggests how strengthening educational practices, especially those for engaging children in thoughtful literacy, can result in a return to democracy.

In the chapter "Literacy Practices for Peacebuilding," the authors offer a set of practical strategies to promote peacebuilding through critical literacies based on research experiences across the Americas. In the same line, "Love and Language: Peace Building in the Foreign Language Classroom," the author explores the relationship between language acquisition, emotion, critical thinking, and peace building. She demonstrates how applied Peace Linguistics can help teachers create empathetic and equitable foreign language classroom environments.

In the chapter "Encouraging Critical Literacy: Justice and Equity With Children's Literature," the author explains the difference between teaching critical thinking and critical literacy with children's literature. She suggests ways teachers may select current children's literature that touches upon social justice and equity instead of just reading aloud old favorites that do not stimulate students' thinking about their world.

Chapters such as "Funds of Perezhivanie: Creating Cracks in the Walls of Oppression" reflect and inquire on texts using language to question inequalities and oppression; these are also connected to people's emotions.

We hope this publication inspires our readers to rethink and reimagine language and literacy development from a wide scope of experiences and reflections. Each chapter is an eye opener that expands our views; the authors' voices help us see the world of literacy from different angles that nurture our understanding of language and literacy development as users and literacy educators. Thank you!

Angela K. Salmon
Florida International University, USA

Amparo Clavijo-Olarte
Universidad Distrital Francisco Jose de Caldas, Colombia

REFERENCES

Boix-Mansilla, V. (2015). *Finding our way into each other's worlds: Musings on cultural perspective taking*. Retrieved on April 9, 2022, from http://www.pz.harvard.edu/sites/default/files/FINDING%20OUR%20WAY%20INTO%20EACH%20OTHER%C2%B9S%20WORLDS.pdf

Cambourne, B. (2009). Revisiting the Concept of "Natural Learning". In J. V. Hoffman & Y. M. Goodman (Eds.), *Changing literacies for changing times* (pp. 125–145). Taylor & Francis.

Comber, B. (2016). Poverty, place and pedagogy in education: Research stories from front-line workers. *Australian Educational Researcher, 43*(4), 393–417. doi:10.100713384-016-0212-9

Freire, P. (2007). *Pedagogy of the Oppressed*. Continuum.

Gardner, H. (1982). *Artful scribbles: The significance of children's drawings*. Basic Books.

Goodman, K., & Goodman, Y. (2014). *Making Sense of Learners Making Sense of Written Language: The Selected Works of Kenneth S. Goodman and Yetta M Goodman*. Routledge Taylor and Francis Group.

Hart, B., & Risley, T. R. (2003). The early catastrophe: The 30 million word gap by age 3. *American Educator, 27*(1), 4–9.

International Literacy Association (ILA). (2022). https://www.literacyworldwide.org/get-resources/literacy-glossary

Moll, L. C. (2019). Elaborating funds of knowledge: Community-oriented practices in international contexts. *Literacy Research: Theory, Method, and Practice, 68*(1), 130–138. doi:10.1177/2381336919870805

Moll, L. C., Amanti, C., Neff, D., & Gonzalez, N. (1992). Funds of knowledge for teaching: Using a qualitative approach to connect homes and classrooms. *Theory into Practice, 31*(2), 132–141. doi:10.1080/00405849209543534

Pennycook, A. (2010). *Language as a local practice*. Routledge. doi:10.4324/9780203846223

Piaget, J. (1977). The role of action in the development of thinking. In *Knowledge and development* (pp. 17–42). Springer. doi:10.1007/978-1-4684-2547-5_2

Rodríguez, A. (2021). *EFL learners' agency exploring the sociocultural landscape of a public university* [Unpublished Master Thesis]. Universidad Distrital Francisco José de Caldas. Bogotá.

Short, K. (2009). Critically reading the word and the world: Building intercultural understanding through literature. *Bookbird, 47*(2), 1–10. doi:10.1353/bkb.0.0160

Snow, C. E., Griffin, P. E., & Burns, M. (2005). *Knowledge to support the teaching of reading: Preparing teachers for a changing world*. Jossey-Bass.

Street, B. (1995). *Social literacies: Critical approaches to literacy in development, ethnography and education*. Pearson.

Street, B. (2012). Society reschooling. *Reading Research Quarterly, 2*(47), 216–227. doi:10.1002/RRQ.017

UN Convention on the Rights of the Child. (2022). http://www.vofg.org/un-crc

Preface

UN Sustainable Development Goals. (2015). http://www.vofg.org/sdgs

Vygotsky, L. S. (1978). *Mind in society: The development of higher psychological processes Cambridge*. Harvard University Press.

Acknowledgment

This project emerged from years of conversations with colleagues from around the world who perceive language and literacy as a gateway for making a global impact. We are grateful for the lessons learned from our mentors such as Ken and Yetta Goodman, Veronica Boix Mansilla, Luis Moll, Kathy Short, Roberta Truax, and other scholars whose legacies have inspired us to continue our search for new ways of understanding language and literacy in an everchanging world.

We thank the authors of this book who responded to our call for chapters with their valuable contributions. Each chapter helped us expand our horizons in new directions strengthening our view of education through thought provoking and innovative ideas. It was fascinating to hear voices from around the world united by common inquiries and creative solutions. Each of them brought our attention to understanding issues worthy of continued exploration. Our special gratitude is for the peer reviewers for their time, effort, and thoughtful feedback to improve the quality of the content.

We are also very appreciative of our institutions, notably Florida International University and Universidad Distrital Francisco José de Caldas, for their support from the inception of the book proposal to the completion of the project that took over a year.

We especially want to acknowledge our families for their love and continuous encouragement that keep us moving forward.

Section 1
Early Literacy

Chapter 1
Emergent Language and Literacy Skills in Early Childhood:
A Path to Success

Silvia López Angel
BaBidiBu Early Childhood Education, Colombia

ABSTRACT

Studies have emphasized the importance of the first years of life for successful long-term language and literacy development. It is thus crucial we focus on designing appropriate and effective early learning environments with a clear literacy interaction plan that engages learners in their success and helps them advocate for the language skills they need and do not yet have. This chapter will show early natural language and literacy acquisition in children ages 2 to 4 years in a context where youngsters are exposed to a rich verbal, emotional, and experiential environment where thinking is valuable, visible, and actively promoted as a vehicle to language and literacy, and global competency frameworks are leaving the best tools in their backpack for life.

INTRODUCTION

The reader will journey through the analyses of educational frameworks, theories, and study findings, then crystallized in a story where a preschooler's class at BaBidiBu Preschool in Bogota, Colombia, collaboratively constructs a project-based learning experience for Pedagogical Impacts, a term created by the author. The projects mentioned were the result of children's interests and occurred in an educational setting when prompted to take chances and participate in age-appropriate decision-making. At BaBidiBu preschool, in Bogota, Colombia, children grow in an environment where they are prompted to think using what they know (Perkins, 2001), think skillfully for comprehension, and take ownership of their learning and use it. Learning is a consequence of thinking (Perkins, 2001), and we believe children

DOI: 10.4018/978-1-6684-5022-2.ch001

will gain a sense of who they are becoming as thinkers, learners, and globally competent individuals, as a result of their time with us.

TRACING THE ROOTS OF EARLY AUTHENTIC LANGUAGE AND LITERACY EXPERIENCES: MEANINGFUL CURRICULUM AND LEARNING THAT MATTERS

"What is worth learning, Life worthy?" (Perkins, 2016). This question inspires the desire to teach relevant content for the lives preschool children are living now, and the ones they will live in the future (Perkins, 2016). Teaching for Understanding is one of the inspirations from Harvard University's Project Zero. It puts the focus on understanding instead of just knowing. Four central questions regarding Teaching for Understanding, give clear purpose, guidance, and sets an educational journey for preschoolers: What shall we teach? (Generative Topics), What is worth understanding? (Understanding Goals), What should we teach and do for our children to understand? (Understanding Performances), How can teachers know if their children are understanding and how can children develop deeper understanding? (Ongoing Assessment). This instructional map guides can be a valuable guidance in the everyday purpose of any educational setting. (Blythe & Associates, 1998).

It is important for children to understand rather than know. Knowing is just information available everywhere. It's what you can get by repeating and memorizing to passing a test. When children understand, they can use those understandings, make them their own, and apply them to their lives now or the ones they will live in the future. To understand something is in a way recognizing that it makes sense, is meaningful, fully owned, and useful. According to Perkins, (Wiske, 1988), the primary skill worth learning is deep thinking. Understanding is the capacity to think and act flexibly with what one knows (p 40). The flexible and active use of knowledge helps students further scaffold their learning and their passion for doing so. Big understandings include insight, opportunity, ethics, and well-prepared action. (Perkins, 2016). I strongly believe learning should include engagement, and excellence, as Howard Gardner clearly expressed in a conference I attended on good work. Indeed, all learning needs a clear purpose. In our preschool, we teach with the 3 Ps at hand, which I created: (Purpose, Passion, and Persistence). We want our children to understand the value of having a clear plan, then follow that plan with passion and persistence to become good thinkers, self-makers, and autonomous, independent, and empathetic humans.

Teaching means walking by the child's side while he/she is interpreting and learning about the world. Teaching implies focusing on our students and their need, and building opportunities for them to construct and foster their ideas.

Learning is not just about getting the answer right (Perkins, 2009). It is also about making the right connections along with the opportunities that caregivers give children to make them. By working with early ages, educators have invaluable windows of opportunity for teaching youngers how to love learning and how to cultivate dispositions that will remain throughout their emerging lives. This is the time when they are building their character and understandings, unpacking what it means to be a good thinker, a good citizen, a good family member, a good friend, a good neighbor, and what it means to make good decisions and work collectively. This is a time when they learn how to adapt to new circumstances, solve problems and think critically and creatively. This is also the time to reinforce ethics and values, so they understand the importance of being empathetic, stay interested in the world they live in, and are ready to act for its benefit. Children are setting their foundations for life, and they must understand that they are already citizens of the world, a beautiful, but complex one that not only needs them to be curious and interested, but also needs their help to act for its benefit (Boix Mansilla & Jackson, 2013). Our children need to start understanding that their rights begin where other people's rights also begin; that we all co-exist on this planet so we should help each other exhibit our own best selves and work together for collective success. Educators must seek to create a culture of collaboration and relationships that matters when learning together.

Early Childhood professionals, should always seek for high-quality, tough education. This premise also sets the state for excellent language and literacy development. Children's minds remain unlimited whenever they are surrounded by adults that believe in them, their endless capacities, and then set up the best educational scenarios where they can manifest their endless and remarkable potential. Working with Young Children implies assuming the compromise and the responsibility of believing in their endless wisdom, the power of their minds and the transparency of their hearts and souls. Children act on what adults believe of them; in our preschool, we believe in them, set very high expectations for their journeys, and they probe us by showing us their best versions of themselves. They let us peek in their most intimate windows and see their souls, so we can walk beside them and help them construct and transit their desired journeys. Through the years, **BaBidiBu** has become a fabric of opportunities for children to enjoy the magic of learning every day while discovering and interpreting the world through their lenses with joy, wonderment, and awe.

THE POWER OF COMMUNICATING USING PROFOUND SIMPLE INTERACTIONS FOR POSITIVE LANGUAGE ACQUISITION

Li (2018) developed the Simple Interactions approach to help people understand how everyday professionals and families, making simple everyday actions, can have extraordinary moments with their children, when using deep and simple interactions that are far more important than shallow and complex (Li, 2018). Children not only learn key language skills but have developmental impacts and set the core of growing on the inside (Li, 2018).

This Simple Interaction tool has four developmental dimensions: Connection, Reciprocity, Inclusion, and Opportunity to Grow (Li, 2018).

Early educational settings, should pay close attention to these interactions because they predict future integral development outcomes for language and literacy. Starting at 18 months, our young learners are exposed to rich experiences where they have profound, but simple, interactions with their caregivers. There is mutual engaging communication accompanied by clear verbalization by adults of everything they are experiencing with the child that prompts not only communication intention, but also the development of new vocabulary and new ways of verbal interactions: "I am changing your diaper, yes diaper, and it's going to feel so good when we finish because you will feel comfortable and clean, and then, we are going back to see your friends at the park. I'm sure they are all missing you". These are the kinds of phrases commonly heard in our school.

EMOTIONS IN LEARNING, LANGUAGE, AND LITERACY DEVELOPMENT

Emotions play an important role in the acquisition of language as they guide cognitive processing. During their early years, children learn through motivation and engagement and if that learning doesn't have an emotional impact, then the learning cannot thrive. Studies conducted in neuroscience talk about the importance of emotion when learning, and how kids by developing an understanding of how the brain works can better cope with self-regulation and emotional identification (Hans Foundation, 2011). Learning language and literacy is also an emotional journey. It is important to talk to children about tools that will let them become more alert and acquire a sense of agency about their own mental and emotional processes using breathing exercises that help them become more mindful, ready to learn and stay in the present moment.

Children can learn at early ages that if they are not in a positive emotional state, the amygdala becomes an information filter, and will not send the incoming information to the reasoning and thinking brain (prefrontal cortex), where the executive functions take place. Information will stay in the amygdala, and learning cannot thrive. When new information arrives at the brain and enhances emotions, a new synopsis is produced, so children extend their knowledge and keep storing more learning in their memory. The more fun learning is, the more lasting it will be! If learning is not engaging them, they simply won't learn. (Hans Foundation, 2011). It is always rewarding to see children's understanding based on learning in neuroscience findings for how emotions shape behaviors and learning. Starting around the age of four, they often make connections like: "I am happy, that's why I learn". Immondino-Yang & Damasio (2007) sustained that neither memories nor learning happens without our emotions. It is crucial to have this fact in mind and to strive to maintain positive emotional learning contexts so children can keep the love for learning alive.

Indeed, emotions play a very important role in our lives, and especially in language and literacy development in early years. According to Gallingane and Han (2015, para 1), "one of the key objectives of childhood education is to build empathy and understanding in students. Children's ability to comprehend and regulate their own emotions will produce greater learning outcomes and let them have more positive relationships. This benefit leads to more successful social outcomes, as they can feel empathy with the emotions and experiences of others, not just themselves. Every emotion is important since it contains information (Goleman, 2008), and socially, information is highly beneficial. Children little by little start to be aware of their emotions, and then those of others. It is essential to always make profound efforts to provide children with emotional intelligence tools to keep their days balanced with a tranquil learning environment and maintain emotional well-being and happiness. Studies confirm the importance of doing so. As long as children can understand and manage their emotions, they can identify and understand them in others. That's the beginning of learning and of empathy!

Emotions help young children learn new vocabulary while naming new emotions and empower the construction of their emotional intelligence. Studies have found there is importance in teaching children the words that help them identify, cope, and manage their emotions, and offer strategies for doing so, such as reading out loud, recognizing worlds that express emotions in the reading, explaining the meaning, and use the same world in other contexts, (Gallingane & Han 2015). Early childhood teachers should teach ways of expressing emotions; they should also thrive to nurture a trustful and caring relationship with the children and their families, learn the context and culture of the child, and respect and understand the child as an individual, including his or her expectations, emotions, and expressions, as well as their socioemotional intelligence, (Gallingane & Han 2015).

The value and importance of emotions and emotional intelligence in educators and caregivers's teaching journal, is invaluable; for children's creativity, the quality of the relationships they construct, the decisions they will make, the grown-ups they will become, their actions, and their mental health. Guiding our children in their process of self-recognition and self-esteem construction, validating their feelings and emotions, and guiding them so they can regulate them, nurtures their solid journey toward empathy and compassion. Emotions should always be on the radar because, "when we educators fail to appreciate the importance of student's emotions, we fail to appreciate a critical force in student's learning" (Immordino-Yang & Damasio, 2007, p 9).

LANGUAGE AND LITERACY, NATURE AND NURTURE: WHAT NEUROSCIENCE SAYS

Nurture or nature is an often-asked question regarding child development, psychology and education. Language acquisition is no exception. Studies have found that the first year of life is crucial for long-term language and literacy development. The research by Zuk et al. (2021, p 9) explained that "the present findings point towards the significance of brain structure from as early as infancy in providing a scaffold upon which ongoing experience can build throughout development." This study was the first to demonstrate that certain genes, critical for brain development along with the white matter of the brain (which is very receptive to environmental inputs), during the first years of life, will continue to affect children's language and literacy outcomes throughout their development. The neural foundations established in infancy are enriched and further built upon by experiences over time and are what will determine language outcomes. The first years are thus indeed crucial for language acquisition and overall development.

According to Eslava (2014), the function of the brain is to build memory and prints for talking, walking, eating, and everything that precedes action. Engrams are units of cognitive information that are acquired via successive experiences. Our role as educators, therefore, is to make sure that these successive experiences are rich and relevant and so solid that students can learn using all their senses durably and effectively (Eslava, 2014). Once again, neuroscience highlights the immense responsibility and compromise we have with our children to educate and guide them well during their first years of life.

Working with preschoolers, implies being aware of this fact, and everyday aim to carefully construct the most valuable opportunities for them to develop their autonomy and thereby their full potential.

Neuroscience also tells us of the power of conversations and the impact on the brain itself in response to language and literacy skills. Romeo et al. (2018) noted, the importance of talking with your child, instead of talking to your child and also emphasized the value of the interaction, more than the number of words that a child hears in a conversation for creating measurable changes in the brain and for nurturing strong literacy skills in school. Their study proved that early adult-child relationships and interactions shape brain architecture and deeply influence language skills acquisition and future outcomes in life.

Results from Romeo et al. (2018) also show how even from infancy, children can be considered partners for conversations and thus emphasize the importance of conversational turns and the quality of language that the child is exposed to, rather than the quantity of words that are spoken by caregivers in conversation. It is clear that the capacities of these "conversations" are different in toddlers than in 4–5-year old's, as we see every day in our educational setting. With infants, our "Pulgas" (1–2-year old's), it's about giving and taking giggles or coos, repeating intentions, and taking turns with lots of eye contact. With toddlers, our "Enanos" (2-3 years old), we see a lot of repeating and extending of teacher vocabulary and sentences, and with our oldest, "Universitarios" (4-4.5 years), we note they listen with longer attention spans, begin to follow the sequences of stories and ask elaborate questions in search of understanding, such as: what happened? how did it happen? where did it happen? and who was part of the story?.

Regarding the Nurture vs. nature never-ending debate, Chiu (2011) found that a child's ability to read depends mostly on where the child was born, their socioeconomic status, their parents' attitudes about reading, and the educational environment, rather than the child's qualities as an individual. Literacy depends on nurture, the environment, and surroundings, not nature, the child's inherited individual characteristics and qualities, he found.

LANGUAGE AND LITERACY LEARNING IN PRESCHOOLERS

Early language and literacy acquisition should always be on the radar at early ages. Through play, which is the only way in which children can learn, children at early ages should be engage with relevant and rich language and literacy experiences that are both provoking and valuable in content. Presenting new vocabulary that can scaffold good conversations and interactions, and communicating the magic of reading books, are great tools for the endeavor. Starting at 18 months when children don't have a clear oral language yet but have a clear intention of communicating, at our preschool, we try to balance between interpreting what children want to say and inviting them to try to communicate orally before we step in and figure out what they are trying to say. This process helps them with their language development without causing them additional frustration. We start getting ready for language and literacy at very early ages when our children are carefully and consciously exposed to seed the ground for reading and writing. Children start very early to identify basic logos of commercial brands that are relevant to their lives, so these can slowly start promoting their reading processes (see Figure 1).

Figure 1. 18 month old "reading" Brand's symbols

Emergent Language and Literacy Skills in Early Childhood

As they grow older, we actively engage our children in their writing and writing processes, so they can learn how to use these skills in their overall development. The habit of reading is something that should be cultivated emphatically; we recognize a book's invaluable significance in children's educational processes. It stimulates creativity, imagination, language, and literacy acquisition, but also, creates profound bonds in the children's and adults' hearts. Thus, every year we put considerable effort into celebrating our love for books with two very magical Pedagogical Impacts. One is the **Enchanted Nights,** where "Grampa Plutarco", the fairy, and a very naughty elf called "Ping", take children through the most beautiful stories. Parents and children come to school at night in their pajamas and enjoy together every second of this experience very full of fantasy and stories, until most of our children fall asleep in their parents' arms, listening to the last lullaby and enchanted by the magic of this remarkable night (see Figure 2).

Figure 2. BaBidiBu's enchanted nights

Our **Book Faire** is another magical space we have created for children's language and literacy acquisition. A Colombian prestigious book publisher with an excellent children's literature collection every year brings many books our children can explore and then choose the one they want to buy and take home (see Figure 3). The books they buy are not forgotten by our children. These two Pedagogical Impacts are loved by the children, because they encourage their decision-making, give them autonomy and happiness, and offer important tools for their current and future language and literacy journeys.

Figure 3. The school's "book faire"

LANGUAGE AND THINKING GO HAND IN HAND: A CULTURE OF THINKING AND LANGUAGE AS A POWERFUL CULTURAL FORCE

Language is a powerful vehicle for thought that end up in words. Thinking can be taught and learned, as great scholars have found in their investigations. (Costa, 2001; Perkins, 2001). Thinking and Language are two educational fields that have always been an important part of our curriculum. Our children are emerged into a culture of thinking where thinking is seen as valid, visible, and actively promoted, (Ritchhart, Church & Morrison, 2011) that constantly searches for bigger understanding and helps our children become aware of their thinking development, as they make their thinking visible. Our endeavor as educators is to focus on our young students and give them enough opportunities to foster their ideas (Ritchhart, Church &Morrison, 2011). Still, we cannot help them if we don't know what is on their minds. By making their thinking visible, we can better prepare the environment for learning. We can make their thinking visible using Thinking Routing, Documentation, and Study Groups that reflect on our children's thinking (Ritchhart, R &Perkins 2008). A powerful culture of thinking can be created in every educational institute; it is magical thus it also promotes language as one of its key cultural forces.

LANGUAGE AS A CULTURAL FORCE

Language is one of the eight cultural forces that Ritchhart (2015) proposes, sustaining the culture of thinking and thus should be directed and aligned toward effective thinking. Especially with the older

Emergent Language and Literacy Skills in Early Childhood

children in preschools, this complex thinking in language helps elevate the tone of the classroom and prompts these children to undertake more complex thinking and metacognitive processes at a very early age. Some examples are: "you make a connection", "that was a good metaphor", "please describe what's there", "what's your point of view regarding this or that", "let's get to the core of this discussion", etc. By frequently hearing complex conversations and the labeling of their cognitive functions and vocabulary, the children will associate new words with their meaning, internalize them, and then use them personally as new vocabulary.

INQUIRY AS THE TONE OF THE CLASSROOM

As Perkins (2016) stated, there should be a culture of questions in schools rather than answers. The power of well-formulated, open-ended questions that give continuance and flow to great conversations, promote good thinking and deep understandings, it's evident in long term children's outcomes. Questions should simplify, energize, and organize our students' learning processes (Perkins, 2016). Examples of questions that we frequently use with our young students are: What's going on here? What do you think? What makes you say that? What puzzles you about this? What makes you wonder? Why do you think that is happening? How do you know that? Can you explain a little deeper? Can you tell me more? How can you connect this with something you already know? How do you know that, or this? What questions do you still have? "What makes you say that?

These powerful questions let us maintain the flow of the conversations and invite our children to reason with evidence and reflect on their answers. Depending on their developmental level and their age, we can predict which questions can be answered, so we ask them appropriately, while always challenging their amazing minds. Children's thinking processes are very different than adults, so it's important to always try to interpret what they have on their mind, and help construct their questions and understandings within our classrooms, that should always remain positive, encouraging, vivid, loving, and caring. "Most teachers waste their time by asking questions which are intended to discover what a pupil does not know. Whereas the true art of questioning has for its purpose to discover what the pupil knows or is capable of knowing". (Einstein, in Moszkowski, 1921, p 65). Educators should pay close attention not to commit these errors. As mentioned already, the tone of the classroom in a culture of thinking, is not about getting the answer right, but to help our students, so they can arrive at important understandings themselves. (Perkins, 2009).

There is little discussion on the excellent opportunity we have as teachers to scaffold children's language by modeling. Caregivers should model an inclusive discourse, give value to what every child has to say, and give each, time to express themselves. Children's actions and behavior are communication, and their answers sometimes have hidden questions inside, so it is our job to try to interpret. Naming and noticing out loud what children are saying and doing, is part of the Language Force in a Culture of Thinking (Ritchhart, 2015), and this force encourage their efforts for improvement every day.

CHILDREN GROW INTO THE INTELLECTUAL LIFE AROUND THEM: "ENCULTURATING" OUR CHILDREN

Often children will act based on the environment and the context that surrounds them. 21st-century skills are not going to be tested on standardized tests, but will be tested by life itself!! (Salmon 2018), and contexts have a lot to do with these outcomes. A question that should be often asked when working with emerging souls is: "How do we want our children to be when they grow up? and some common answers are: Good people, ethical, curious empathetic, creative, good thinkers, etc. Those dispositions, which Ritchhart called the residuals of education, (2015) are not set in our schedule: Empathic class at 11:00, thinking class at 10:00, decision-making at 9:00, wonderment class at 8:00 am. This simply cannot happen!! What can be done instead, is create the environment and the context where children naturally become empathetic, curious, creative, and good thinkers. Vygotsky (1978) stated that children grow into the intellectual life of those around them. Based on that premise, such dispositions cannot be taught, only enculturated. According to Tishman, Jay, and Perkins (1993), the purpose of an enculturation model of teaching is to provide ideas for the creation of a culture of thinking in the school, where students interact with others and participate in meaningful activities within that created culture.

THEORIES IN PRACTICE: "AMAZING ANIMALS" – A PROJECT WHERE LANGUAGE AND THINKING BECOME VISIBLE

Among the many projects in our preschool, I chose "Amazing Animals", to illustrate our days. An explicit invitation to our children to explore, investigate and understand the special characteristics that make animals amazing, was made. Children investigated different butterflies, frogs and amphibious, strange marine creatures, and animals that camouflage like chameleons, leaf insects, amazing spiders, and tarantulas, to name just a few.

Throughout the project, we place special attention on the interactions that teachers have with our students, the quality of time spent in these discussions, the conversations the children have with each other, and the quality of discussions that occur after each Pedagogical Impact to better achieve their understandings.

In our preschool, we have a clear purpose for our discourse and the types of communications used in our classrooms to give special attention to language. Vygotzqui (1978) theorized that language was the basis of all learning, as it supports reading and writing. Indeed, logic, reasoning, and reflective thinking are possible due to language acquisition. In their language processes, children must feel connected, engaged, and have a sense of belonging and growing during each conversation. Adults should be feeling it too. These conversations are valuable opportunities for teaching and building their knowledge for learning new vocabulary, modeling our students, and having an ongoing assessment of their development. This is what becomes meaningful to them and makes visible the importance of valuable conversations and interactions. In every project, children are engaged in conversations by taking turns where they all can participate. These kinds of learning styles have a more profound impact than having children simply listen to people talking.

Studies by Romero (2018), on the relationship between children's language exposure and verbal skills, found that the quality of talking matters more than the quantity, and parents feel more pressure to engage in conversations with their children and will talk more to them in high socioeconomic backgrounds than in low ones. It also was revealed that the importance of the engagement children has in conversations does prompt higher levels of learning. Romeo (2018, p 706) stated that communicating with children, "is not about learning words, it's about building knowledge, as words bring with them concepts and ideas." Educators should always look for strategies to nurture children's developing minds further. Our children should be growing up in a very intellectual, curious, high expectation context that prompts them to find their path to success.

During our project, our children had different opportunities to understand the topic in greater depth through our Pedagogical Impacts. They refer to children's learning through real-life hands-on experiences from which they can construct their interpretations of the world as valuable opportunities to learn and think skillfully. These are "wow moments", engaging, surprising, significant hands-on experiences that are different from mere activities. They become great scenarios for creating lots of Thinking Routines and offer valuable opportunities for understanding and scaffolding children's thinking dispositions in an emotional happy context. They also help our children interpret the world through their lenses, instead of only the lenses of teachers, parents, or other adults.

A spider's expert's visit, a field trip to a museum, and more, were some of our Pedagogical Impacts for the "Amazing Animals" project they were experiencing, where children could ask big questions that related to the project in search of bigger understandings (see Figures 4 and 5).

Figure 4. Pedagogical impact: interactions with domesticated tarantulas

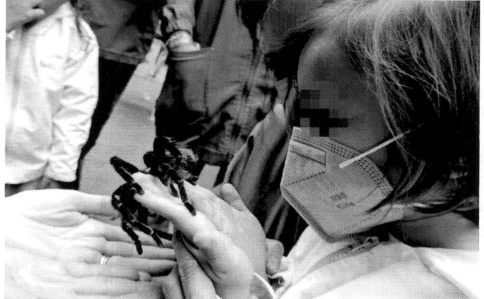

Figure 5. Pedagogical impact: frogs

   In each of our Pedagogical Impacts, children were engaged and were asked about their interest in learning. Lots of questions appeared spontaneously, with the Thinking Routines used. During the month the project lasted, teachers were collecting lots of facts, artifacts, videotapes, pictures, and notes, as the children-built memories and understandings about the topic. The school's physical environment was filled with documentation that was always available to our children and framed their comprehensions via Thinking Routines. Documentation became visual poetry full of metaphors of these days (Rinaldi, as cited in Krechevsky, Mardell, Rivard, & Wilson, 2013).
   Indeed, our walls were talking, telling a story not only for the children to revisit but for visitors, in general, to know what was going on in our classrooms. Thanks to the commitment we have to documentation, we could easily refer to the exact words our children used in their comments, very essential information for writing this chapter. As Perkins (2001) states, the problem with thinking is that is not visible, but with our detailed documentation, we made thinking more visible, so our children could see and follow their thinking processes and teachers, could have an ongoing assessment tool. Documentation simply became a radiography of our children's thinking and of our days together (see Figure 6).

Figure 6. Documentation as a radiography of children's thinking

The power of scaffolding language and thinking in young students its unlimited. Children learn best from what they see adults and caregivers do, rather than from what they are told to do, so parents and educators should be consciously and constantly modeling the expected behavior and the appropriate use of language. Children have 100 languages, as Loris Malaguzzi described, and we as adults need to be prepared and alert for them, becoming interpreters of their necessities, their languages and their processes, and indeed their dreams and their intentions. Teachers have the immense responsibility of observing their actions, their behaviors that are communication, and also their movements, their looks, their laughs, and cries. Their language, verbal and nonverbal, tell valuable stories that must be carefully interpreted, so adults can find the best tools and strategies to teach them appropriately so they can develop their full potential.

Working with young minds it is imperative that we as educators learn how to carefully and empathically listen to our children and let them take the initiative and ownership of their learning processes. Yet knowing that we are their mentors and more experienced ones, we should guide them well. At the end of each project in our preschool, we help our children anchor their understanding and expose them, as proof and personal demonstration of their learning. As a *performance of understanding* (Blythe & Associates, 1998), we undertake our traditional Children's Congress, created at our center a long time ago, where every child has the opportunity to present his or her interests, investigations, and comprehensions on a specific topic from the project to an interactive child and teacher audience. This congress is a perfect scenario for making learning and thinking visible. It is an amazing opportunity for the children to hear feedback for more self-reflection and demonstrate their ability to accommodate and use what they have learned. It also serves as a powerful Ongoing Assessment of their understanding. Overall, it is an example of their courage and ability to prepare and manage a presentation at such a young age to a demanding audience. This experience, without any doubt, will help the children in their future presentations when they grow up and face their professional lives. We received all types of beautiful expositions on the topic (see Figure 7).

Figure 7. Presenting at our children's congress

As a Performance of Understanding (Blythe & Associates, 1998), the children in Lila's class, with Tatiana their teacher decided to create a beautiful storybook. Tatiana always has worked on written language and literacy with them in spite of their young ages. (3.5- 4 years old). She believes in the importance of pushing them a little extra because she recognizes and celebrates their endless capacities. Lots of Thinking Routines have already been done on the topic. Thinking Routines are tools, structures, and patterns of behavior that help children explore, discuss, document, and manage their thinking (Ritchhart, 2015). It also makes their thinking visible by uncovering the thinking moves they are doing to understand, as we already learned earlier here. Children deeply investigated the strange animals they studied during the project, "wrote" about new worlds they learned throughout the project and created a dictionary. All agreed that the most interested animals they studied were the frog and spider, so they decided they would take their project to a more advanced level by creating a Story Book with these characters. In that creation, each one of our children had individual participation. They had a clear plan. First, Tatiana read a storybook naming and noticing the complexities of a well-written story: She emphasized the characters, the sequences (beginning, middle, and end), the illustrations, and the way a storybook usually starts: "Once upon a time…", and ends: "And they all lived happily ever after".

She emphasized the fact that between the beginning and the end, lots of things happen in a book. Then, Tatiana started giving an example of an invented storybook, to model one and help children get ideas for their books. She started to ask questions regarding her story, and they spontaneously and very excitedly, participated. She was making sure the children would understand that books have a sequence. "What's a sequence?" one child asked. "A sequence is when something happens, and then something else comes after, and then something else, and so on. It's like, one, two, three", Tatiana answered. Then she asked the children to name another example of a sequence, and the children immediately started making connections. One said: "When we wake up, then we take a shower and then we go to school". Tatiana happily said: "Perfect! That's called a temporal sequence".

Now they were ready to build their book, and they did. "Mr. Wiki the Savior Frog", was the title proposed by one child. They all agreed on it. Child #2 started: "Once upon a time a spider was climbing a rock and passing a bridge to her house", and Child #3 continued, "the spider got really sad because it was captured, they thought it was venomous", and child # 4 added a new idea, and so did child #5 and so on. The story was going so well that the teacher was documenting and writing everything they were saying. One by one, the children participated in the construction of the book using their imagination and creativity.

Their ideas were amazing, and the children were excited and engaged in the building of this beautiful story. Suddenly, one of the children suggested that the book was getting too long and people could get bored with it, so he decided to end it by saying: "y colorín colorado éste cuento se ha acabado" (and colorin colorado, this book came to an end). My husband, Elliott, is an orthopedic surgeon, and when I told him the story of the child claiming the story was already too long and boring, he proclaimed, "Good for him. He is going to be an Orthopedic Surgeon. Very concrete".

Often children tend to deviate from the main topic and start talking about things that don't connect to the actual conversation. Teachers then have to intervene, so they can connect their ideas and maintain the initial discussion by addressing the fact that they need to keep to a sequence, crucial in all books, narratives, and stories. This time their motivation kept them on track, and their storybook, clearly captured the children's learning and understanding of topics they studied during the school year. They were thinking with what they knew and working collaboratively to produce the specific results targeted in their original purpose.

Since our preschool children are emerged in a culture of thinking, they related this activity to the multiple "beginning, middle, end" Thinking Routine they had done in the past with different topics where they had to invent the beginning, the middle, or the end of a story. After they collected all their ideas and the story was created, Tatiana read them the final product. The children were proud and amazed with their creation and they could identify exactly in which specific part of the book their contributions to the narrative appeared. It was time for the children to "write", to illustrate and print all their ideas and creations. Studies have shown that "all children can develop a strong foundation for literacy and reading development when they are given opportunities to engage in purposeful, meaningful language and early print activities" (Brown, 2014, p 46).

Their pictures were beautiful, full of color and details. Then, they proceeded to "write" their parts of the story. When the children finally saw the final product, they jumped up and down in happiness, called themselves authors, and we're very proud to present their book to everyone. As we saw earlier in this chapter, emotions play a decisive role in learning, and this engaging opportunity for our children was proof of it.

Days later, I went into Tatiana's classroom, saw the book posted on the wall, and asked: "What is this?". They all wanted to talk about it at the same time: Child #1: "Silvia, it's our book, we did this beautiful book". Child # 2: "Silvia we wrote our first book", Child #3 "Yes. We did it alone". Child #4:

"No, we didn't do it alone, Tatis helped us". Child #5: "We also did all the drawings, and in this project, we learned so many new words about amazing animals".

"Wow!!", I exclaimed, and I was truly amazed by the book. I continued, "This book was made with your ideas?". "Yes" they said. Child #2 replied: "Ideas come from the brain".

Another child interrupted: "Brains can think about everything". "And you know how to think?", I asked, "Yes of course. Our brain is very good", one child replied. Another child added: "Tatis guided our writing a little bit, but we did this book ourselves."

I prompted them to explain the vocabulary they used in the book, as it was very advanced for their age, but they ended up questioning me instead. Child #2, "For example, do you know what is metamorphosis?", he asked. and continued, "metamorphosis means change, for example, a change, a transformation in an animal". By this time it was clear to me they had big understandings of the project. Another child interrupted, "For example, frogs and butterflies go through metamorphosis. "We also know about amphibians", another exclaimed". "What is that?", I asked. "Animals that breathe under the water, and also above the water", Child #3 answered. Another one completed the answer, saying "like turtles, and frogs". Tatiana the teacher told me about a discussion they had regarding the crocodile because they couldn't decide if he was amphibious or not. One child interrupted and said: "No, Tatis. The crocodile is not amphibious because he has lungs". Another child completed the answer: "Listen, Silvia, the crocodile is not amphibious because he has lungs, and if an animal has lungs, he cannot breathe underneath the water. Got it?" So, I asked, "If the animal has lungs, it cannot be amphibious?" One child without hesitation answered, "No because they cannot breathe underneath the water because they don't have bronchi and so "se abogan" (he will drown).

As I mentioned before, our children are consistently exposed to rich vocabulary, complex language, and open-ended questions. That's part of the school's culture. Children have learned to respond in complete sentences, and construct well-structured answers via reasoning using both evidence and reflection. "We also talked about animals that camouflage," a child said. "What is camouflage?" I asked. "It means that they camouflage so the predators don't eat them". Another child completed the answer by saying: "They sneak in carefully, so other animals cannot notice they are there". "What is a predator", I asked. "Other animals that can eat them" a child answered. "For example, sharks", another child added. "Wow! Great connections you are all making here", I replied.

Children contently connect their new knowledge with past knowledge, thinking using what they know (Perkings), comparing and contrasting, wondering, arriving at conclusions, and taking into account the viewpoints of others to elaborate on their answers. They continued to name all the animals they had learned that camouflaged. Tatiana, continued to ask key questions: "They are animals that camouflage, but do they start gradually changing color. What does it mean?"

As mentioned earlier, we believe in the power of good questions as prompters of better language and thinking. We believe in the power of children's understanding rather than knowing by only repeating and memorizing. Good questions promote thinking and serve as an Ongoing Assessment of our children's understandings. "Mimic", one child answered Tatianas's question. Next, they proceeded to show me a chart on how animals mimic to protect themselves from depredators. I was very proud of our children's comprehension and their use of very sophisticated vocabulary. They, in return, were also proud of making their learning and thinking more visible and realizing how much they learned during this project.

"There are two mobilizers of education", "curiosity and passion,". Eduardo Caravallo said at a conference. He continued, "Curiosity and passion bring other windows to think and teach differently, in a way that lets children flow with their interests and passions without our own getting in their way" (Caravallo,

Emergent Language and Literacy Skills in Early Childhood

2019). I agree with his statement and saw it appear in our amazing youngsters during the construction of this book. I admire the children's work and told them that I loved the book they created. I have realized that they knew how to read and write, and I was extremely impressed by their abilities at their young ages. After my comment, their faces lit up with pride. I then wanted to ask some final complex questions, so Tatiana and I could see their learning processes and help them see the importance of literacy as a foundation of all learning, and its essential aspect for an individual's life.

"What does reading mean?", I asked. "Reading so we can learn how to read", one child replied. "It's something so we can learn how to write", another child added. "When a person is reading, what is he doing?" I asked, hoping they could describe reading. "Writing", they all said. They were associating reading and writing as a single unit. I then continued, "You are all saying that when you are reading, you are writing, so when you are writing what are you doing? I asked. "When you are writing your name or some animal's name, you are doing the same as what you do when you read a book to go to sleep." One child replied. "Why do you think it's important that people learn how to read? Take a moment to think before you talk," I said. "To have fun", one child said, "And to get sleepy before going to bed", another declared. One child interrupted and said, "Books are made for sleeping", "You made a connection with what your friend just said", I made him notice. Another child jumped in and said, "Reading is important for learning" and still another one added, "Reading is important to learn how to write". "Reading is important to learn how to read better", another stated. "Do you want to learn how to read soon?" I asked. They all said "yes." "Why?" I asked. "To read stories to our children when we grow up" another added. "We want to learn how to read, so we can continue to write", was another child's comment. For all of them, writing and reading went hand in hand.

"Then why is important to write? What are the benefits of writing?", I asked. The children couldn't answer those questions right away, so Jess, the teacher's assistant, helped them with their understanding. "Kids, remember when Easter Rabbit left us some written clues that we had to read to find the eggs?" "Yes", they said. She continued, "What would have happened if Victoria (a girl from the class that already knows how to read) couldn't read out loud the clues?". "We wouldn't have found the eggs", they said. "Then why is it important to know how to read?" I asked, "To find things", one child said. "For telling our children stories", another one commented. "And what happens if we don't know how to write?" Tatiana asked, "We don't know how to read either", they answered. "What would have happened if the rabbit didn't know how to write?", Tatiana asked. "He would have not written the clues and the game was over," another child said.

Again, it was clear the connections they were making between reading and writing.

According to Brown (2014), it is very important that our early learners understand the value of language and literacy and how people read and write, so they are motivated and ready to succeed in their literacy development. By now, all our children were starting to understand the importance of language and literacy as a foundation of all learnings. They were becoming more and more curious about the actual process of reading and writing and why it was crucial for people's everyday lives. As we appreciated, they were very motivated and ready for success in their literacy development.

With adult's help, children can star very soon to understand the value of print. Print awareness, which is very important for reading and writing, was a key factor in the construction of the book. Children understood how prints and drawings also have a sequence that can be read, and also tell stories. "The organization and the basic features of print demonstrate an emerging understanding of spoken words. Syllables and sound demonstrate emergent phonics and word analysis skills and display emerging reading behaviors with purpose and understanding. All of these were "NELP's findings on the key predictors of reading success". TAs cited by (Strickland & Shickedanz, 2009, p 37).

As shown in this experience of storybook creation, our children are motivated by our projects and proposals, where they can display their understandings, their connections with previous knowledge, and open and fearless ways to express their ideas and thoughts, as well as their growth in expressed vocabulary. After this experience, they were ready to formulate and answer relevant questions not only about their project, "amazing animals", but also about the storybook they all created. They were able to compare and contrast the main core of the project and connect it with situations from their personal context and culture, and remarkably they learned a lot of new vocabulary. Children love learning, and every day, they are becoming ready for more complex discussions and new experiences (see Figure 8).

Figure 8. Children explaining their story book: "Don Wiki the Savior Frog."

According to NICHD (2000), language, literacy, and reading acquisition in the kindergartener years or earlier, go through different levels of foundational behaviors and skills that become more polished as the children get older. Key foundation skills have three elements: Phonemic awareness, knowledge of high-frequency sight words and the ability to decode words. Children move through these stages at their own pace, even though most children do use the same process when they are learning how to read. With the right types of early opportunities given to children, we can facilitate these three elements of reading, while they happily play, grow, and learn. According to Zorfass and Urbano (2008), a lack of these foundation skills negatively affects reader outcomes and if this happens, children in middle school will face problems in academic areas that require reading, such as social studies, math, English, science, and language arts. Thus children that are can have significant leaning opportunities from early ages, are preventing these difficulties.

On the other hand, according to Ballantyne, Sanderman and Mc Laughlin (2008), children that are exposed to language and literacy early on and have the opportunity to develop basic foundation skills in these areas are ready to read, write and flourish as readers. Preschool education thus has a fundamental role to play in promoting literacy, preventing reading difficulties, and preparing young children to be kindergarteners. (National Reading Panel, 2000). Teachers and caregivers at our setting believe our children are going to be ready for reading success. This success is indeed another of the tools for life that we pack into their backpacks, so they can crave their pathways in life and make an impact on their world in the near future.

Language and Literacy for a Global Competency Purpose

As children in Tatianas's classroom started to realize that they indeed could "read" and "write", and learned that part of the purpose of language and literacy was to communicate ideas, viewpoints, and even necessities, I had an idea regarding using those new skills our children had acquired, to make a social impact in this world. First, I showed a photo of the families and children refugees as a tool to conceptualize children. Then in appropriate terms, we explained the hardship and difficulties that children were facing in Ukraine and expressed our reflections on empathy and compassion. I then proposed a Global Thinking Routine called the 3 Why's: Why might this [topic, question] matter to me? Why might it matter to people around me [family, friends, city, nation]? Why might it matter to the world? (Boix Mansilla & Jackson, 2013), combined with yet another Thinking Routine, Step Inside, with a big shoe that I invented to have a clear perspective (see Figure 9). (Ritchhart, Church & Morrison, 2011). According to Boix Mansilla, a Global Competent individual will investigate the world beyond their immediate environment, recognize others' perspectives, communicate ideas effectively to a diverse audience, and then takes actions to improve conditions (Boix Mansilla & Jackson, 2013).

Figure 9. Step inside thinking routine

Emergent Language and Literacy Skills in Early Childhood

Finally, we decided to use our writing abilities to send these children a letter with pictures of hope and solidarity to give them some happy moments in the middle of their endless difficulties and show that we care for them and they are important to us and the world.

Children were touched and motivated to help out in this special way. Beautiful reflections and connections came from our discussions and our Thinking Routines where children started to understand these difficult situations: "War is bad, people die" One child said, "and hurts many people", another child commented. "A house got destroyed", exclaimed another one. One child said, "Mothers and children go to another country like France, Paris or Colombia". Why do you think they leave?" asked the teacher. "Because there is no war there", answered another child. "Presidents are fighting because they don't want to share their territories", was the comment of another child. When Tatiana asked how that situation made them feel and how could those mothers and children be feeling?", One child answered fully: "I feel very sad. They must be feeling sad too because they have to leave and be away from their families because they have to fight." "Can we think for a moment what could they do in that difficult situation?" Tatiana asked, "They can come to Colombia to construct other houses," said one child. Another one added, "Here in Colombia we are safe, we don't have a war.". "But we have military and where there are militaries, there are wars", another said. "You made a connection, Rafa", said the teacher. Another child firmly concluded, "but our militaries are good people, not bad people".

After our deep discussions, the children started one by one to dictate their letter to one of the girls of the group. Victoria (4 years old), carefully wrote every sentence while the children were dictating (see Figure 10). After each child signed the letter, Tatiana transcribed the letter that Victoria wrote by herself, and they drew beautiful pictures to complement the letter. In the end, one child realized what had happened and said, "Now that we can "write and read", we can help children in Ukraine". "And make them really happy", another concluded.

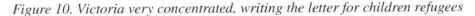

Figure 10. Victoria very concentrated, writing the letter for children refugees

Emergent Language and Literacy Skills in Early Childhood

Here is the children's letter: "Hi, boys and girls from Ukraine, we are children from **BaBidiBu.** Your country will no longer be at war because peace will soon come in. You will be happy because you will meet again with your fathers and will return home. We feel so much love for you. We want you to be happy" (see Figure 11).

Figure 11. The actual letter and the teacher's transcript

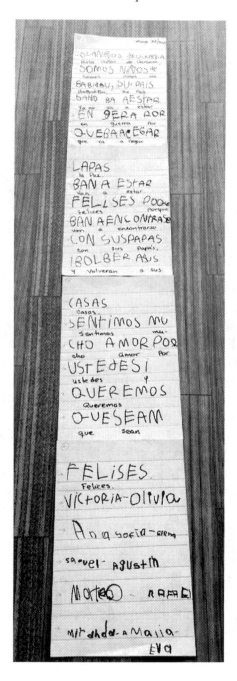

Through this beautiful experience, we not only gave our children the opportunity to once again realize the importance of language and literacy in our lives for communication purposes, but also feel global competency and the goodness of caring and positively acting on the complex, but beautiful world we are all part of today (see Figure 12).

Figure 12. Children drawing their pictures for the refugees

CHAPTER SUMMARY

Educators that impact children's lives at an early age, should have the commitment to improve every day the quality of children's experiences and learning environments by designing effective early learning opportunities and contexts where children can grow integrally and be prepared for the future and the uncertain world they will most likely be living in.

This chapter reveals and explains how natural language and literacy acquisition as early as infancy can thrive, when children are exposed to well prepared, purposefully designed, rich verbal, emotional and experiential environments. In Tatiana's class, we could see how invaluable lifelong learnings are built, where children are "Enculturized" in rich contexts full of life and worthy learning that matter. Pedagogical Impacts are powerful opportunities for building autonomy and deep learning, where thinking is valuable, visible and actively promoted as a vehicle of language and literacy acquisition.

When children are exposed to places where they can assertively communicate with caregivers and build trustful and strong relations, and live and learn the importance of language and literacy as a foundation for all their learning, they start to engage and become curious about why people read and write. Then all forms of communication thrive. The reader could witness effective ways to deepen those language and literacy foundations and their favorable outcomes when children are exposed to engaging conversations with empowered caregivers and parents that appreciate and promote deep and simple adult-child interactions every day with their children.

Through the project entitled amazing animals, the storybook, "Mr. Wiki, the Savior Frog" and the letters to children's refugees from Ukraine, the reader witnessed how very young children can think skillfully with what they know, attempt to read and write, and seek to comprehend rather than just know. These skills will prepare them for more complex subjects and learnings in their futures.

Educators in early childhood classrooms should aim to support the best possible opportunities for children to learn and grow safely and happily. Now we know what very young children can convey in terms of understanding and participation in their language and literacy awareness and development, their intellectual learning, and the beginning of their Global Competency, empathy and social responsibility. But most of all, we now know how all these early valuable experiences are shaping their brain architecture, their hearts and souls, and their character that will deeply influence later outcomes in their lives and who they will become as adults.

REFERENCES

Ballantyne, K. G., Sanderman, A. R., & McLaughlin, N. (2008). *Dual language learners in early years: Getting ready to succeed in school*. National Clearinghouse for English Language Acquisition.

Blythe, B., & Associates. (1998). The teaching for understanding guide. Jossey-Bass.

Boix Mansilla, V., & Jackson, A. (2013). Educating for global competence: Learning redefined for an interconnected world. *Mastering Global Literacy*, 1–24. Retrieved from www.pz.harvard.edu/ site/ default/ files/Educating% 20for% 20Global% 20Competence% 20Short% 20HHJ.pdf

Brown, C. S. (2014). Language and literacy development in the early years: Foundational Skills that Support Emergent Readers. *The Language and Literacy Spectrum,* (24), 35-48. Retrieved from https://files.eric.ed.gov/fulltext/EJ1034914.pdf

Chiu, M. M., McBride-Chang, C., & Lin, D. (2011). Ecological, Psychological, and Cognitive Components of Reading Difficulties: Testing the Component Model of Reading in Fourth Graders Across 38 Countries. *Journal of Learning Disabilities*, *45*(5), 391–405. doi:10.1177/0022219411431241 PMID:22183193

Costa, A. (2001). *Developing minds: A resource book for teaching thinking*. Association for Supervision and Curriculum Development.

Eslava, J. (2014). *Entre el Amor y los Límites: Ayudando a los hijos a alcanzar la autorregulación e la conducta*. Panamericana Editorial Ltda.

Foundation, The Hawn. (2011). *The MindUP Curriculum: Grades PreKh2: Brain-Focused Strategies for Learning and Living* (Illustrated ed.). Scholastic Teaching Resources.

Gallingane, C., & Sophia Han, H. (2015, September 11). Words can help manage emotions: Using based strategies for vocabulary instruction to teach emotional words to young children. *Childhood Education*, *91*, 351–362.

Goleman, D. (2008). *Emotional intelligence*. Retrieved from: https://danielgoleman.info/topics/emotional-intelligence

Immordino-Yang, M. H., & Damasio, A. R. (2007). We Feel therefore we learn: The relevance of affective and social neuroscience to education. *Mind, Brain and Education: The Official Journal of the International Mind, Brain, and Education Society*, *1*(1), 3–10. doi:10.1111/j.1751-228X.2007.00004.x

Krechevsky, M., Mardell, B., Rivard, M., & Wilson, D. (2013). *Visible learners: Promoting Reggio inspired approaches in all schools*. Jossey-Bass.

Li, J., Akiva, T., & Winters, D. (2018). *Simple Interactions tool*. Simple Interactions. https://www.simpleinteractions.org/the-sitool.html

Malaguzzi, L. (1987). *Reggio Emilia Approach*. Retrieved from https://www.reggiochildren.it/en/reggio-emilia-approach/100-linguaggi-en/

Moszkowski, A. (1921). *Conversations with Einstein*. Horizon Press.

National Institute of Child Health and Human Development. (2000). *Report of the National Reading Panel. Teaching children to read: An evidence-based reading instruction: Report of the subgroups* (NIH, Publication No.00-4754). Washington, DC: US. Government Printing Office.

National Reading Panel. (2000). *Teaching children to read: An evidence-based assessment of the scientific research literature on reading and its implications for reading instructions*. Rockville, MD: National Institutes of Child Health and Human Development. Retrieved from www. Nationalreadingpanel.org/publications/summary.htm

Perkings, D. N. (2014). *Future wise: Educating our children for a changing world*. Jossey-Bass.

Perkins, D. (2001). Thinking for understanding. In A. Costa (Ed.), *Developing minds: A resource book for teaching thinking* (pp. 446–450). Association for Supervision and Curriculum Development.

Perkins, D. (2009). *Making learning whole: How seven principles of teaching can transform education*. Jossey-Bass.

Perkins, D. N. (2016). Lifeworthy learning. *Educational Leadership, 73*(6), 12–17.

Project Zero. (2016). Retrieved December 12, 2016, from www.pz.harvard.edu/ projects/

Rinaldi, C., Reggio Children, & Project Zero. (2001). Documentation and assessment: What is the relationship? In Making learning visible: Children as individual and group learners. Reggio Children srl.

Ritchhart, R. (2015). *Creating cultures of thinking: The 8 forces we must master to truly trasform our schools*. Jossey-Bass.

Ritchhart, R. (2015). *Creating cultures of thinking: The 8 forces we must master to truly transform our schools*. Jossey-Bass.

Ritchhart, R., Church, M., & Morrison, K. (2011). *Making thinking visible: How to promote engagement, understanding, and independence for all learners*. Jossey-Bass.

Ritchhart, R., & Perkins, D. N. (2008). Making thinking visible. *Educational Leadership, 65*(5), 57–61.

Romeo, R. R., Leonard, J. A., Robinson, S. T., West, M. R., Mackey, A. P., Rowe, M. L., & Gabrieli, J. D. E. (2018). Beyond the 30-Million-Word Gap: Children's Conversational Exposure Is Associated with Language-Related Brain Function. *Psychological Science, 29*(5), 700–710. doi:10.1177/0956797617742725 PMID:29442613

Salmon, A. (2018). *Frameworks That Promote Authentic Learning. Authentic Teaching and Learning for PreK-Fifth Grade: Advice from Practitioners and Coaches*. Routledge. doi:10.4324/9781351211505

Strickland, D., & Schickedanz, J. A. (2009). *Learning about print in preschool: Working with letters, words and beginning links with phonemic awareness* (2nd ed.). International Reading Association.

Tishman, S., Jay, E., & Perkins, D. (1993). Teaching thinking dispositions: From transmission to enculturation. *Theory into Practice, 32*(3), 147–153. doi:10.1080/00405849309543590

Vygotsky, L. S. (1978). *Mind in society: The development of higher psychological processes*. Harvard University Press.

Wiske, M. S. (Ed.). (1998). *Teaching for understanding: Linking research with practice*. Jossey-Bass.

Zorfass, J., & Urbano, C. (2008). A description of foundation skills interventions for struggling middle-grade readers in four urban Northeast and Island Regions school district (Issues &Answers Repot, REL 2008-No.042). Washington, DC: U.S. Department of Education, Institute of Education Sciences, National Center for Education.

Zuk, J., Yu, X., Sanfilippo, J., Figuccio, M. J., Dunstan, J., Carruthers, C., Sideridis, G., Turesky, T. K., Gagoski, B., Grant, P. E., & Gaab, N. (2021). White matter in infancy is prospectively associated with language outcomes in kindergarten. *Developmental Cognitive Neuroscience, 50*, 100973. doi:10.1016/j.dcn.2021.100973 PMID:34119849

Chapter 2
The Didactic in Initial Literacy:
Between the Perception and Representation

Rosa Julia Guzmán
Universidad de La Sabana, Colombia

Johanna Chocontá
Universidad de La Sabana, Colombia

ABSTRACT

This chapter presents reflections derived from various investigations carried out with both children and teachers about the literacy process in school. There is a tendency to extrapolate results from different disciplines such as psychology and sociology, among others, to direct application in the classroom. Teachers follow different trends, without adapting to the teaching and learning needs of reading and writing. The great absence in these discussions is usually didactics, a discipline that deals with studying teaching practices. In advanced research, it has been found that teachers ignore pedagogy, put didactics as an adjective and the activity as a noun; however, although the proposed activities are very interesting, if they are not articulated around an objective that gives them meaning, they do not favor learning. Hence, it is necessary to understand the teachability of reading and writing, which implies didactic knowledge of the content and refers to what is teachable and how it can be taught.

INTRODUCTION

Literacy is a topic of global concern. Governments are worried about making all their citizens literate because they know that it is a condition for development. After all, it generates possibilities to reduce poverty; however, the results are not always as expected, sometimes because not everyone can attend school and other times because despite going to school, not everyone manages to become literate in the full sense of the word. It is to this second situation that allusion will be made in this chapter; hence the focus on didactics. The chapter aims to highlight the need to return to didactics, influenced by the beliefs

DOI: 10.4018/978-1-6684-5022-2.ch002

The Didactic in Initial Literacy

and conceptions that both teachers and students have, and the reasons why the didactics of initial reading and writing move between teaching practices based on auditory and visual perception.

We will begin by exposing what is meant here by literacy,

According to UNESCO (2021), 'literacy is understood today as a means of identification, understanding, interpretation, creation, and communication in an increasingly digitized, text-based, information-rich and rapidly changing world' (2021). This organization states in the same document:

Even in the 21st century, worldwide, at least 750 million young people and adults do not know how to read or write and another 250 million children are also unable to acquire basic math and literacy skills, leading to the exclusion of numerous social groups that are unable to fully integrate into their communities or environments (UNESCO, 2021, n.p).

The call of the UNESCO is also consistent with the Sustainable Development Goals (SDGs) proposed by the United Nations (UN), since, if this problem is addressed, not only SDG 4, *quality education*, but also SDG 1, *no poverty*, and because it is two of the most important objectives worldwide, the states have established commitments translated into generating policies and concrete actions to quickly close this gap (ONU, 2022). On the other hand, according to Economic Commission for Latin America and the Caribbean (ECLAC, in Spanish CEPAL), citing UNESCO – INNOVEMOS 2012 claim: 'Literacy is a social process, which is related to the distribution of knowledge within society. For this reason, it can be understood as a right of individuals and a duty of societies' (2014, p. 7) and adds that it is not possible to achieve effective democracy if a large part of the population has not become literate.

In the document cited above, it is also stated that the concept of literacy has been modified concerning the object because it is no longer considered only a process of handling basic skills, but rather a continuous process of development in reading, writing, and mathematics. There has also been a change in what for: there has been a move from a perspective strictly focused on what is productive, towards a perspective that relates it to work, social and personal development demands. Lastly, attention has been shifted from the subject to the context, seeking to 'ensure the conditions for people to read and write. It is about developing written culture by promoting literate societies that give social value to these skills and are committed to lifelong learning' (CEPAL 2014, pp. 7-8).

It is known that the school can produce functional illiterates when it does not train students as social users of reading and writing. The concepts of literacy - illiteracy have changed from the all-or-nothing classification: that is, there may be people who have some literacy, such as knowledge of letters and the ability to put together simple sentences, but are not fully literate, in both are not in a position to function with properly in society. This conception derives from the modifications that have been made to the concept of literacy, mentioned in the previous paragraph. These modifications demand more complex actions on the part of the school and the communities because they must promote the construction of literate and literacy environments that allow continuous learning and the development of people. This is stated in the UNESCO document – INNOVEMOS 2012, cited in an ECLAC document (2014): if you seek to decode letters, less effort is required than if you seek to enable people for lifelong learning.

Even though Comenius, considered by many to be the father of didactics, in his work The Great Didactic defined the Pampedia 'as an *artificium docendi* destined to imagine an education for all in everything' (González-Novoa & Perera-Méndez, 2021 p. 24). Today this ideal continues to be one of the greatest challenges in Latin America, in part because, as mentioned by the Inter-American Development Bank - IDB (2018): 'Several studies document that teachers in the region do not have good practices in the classroom' (p. 29). These gaps are due in part to the unfavorable economics of education in which some Latin American educational systems are found (Ibagón, 2015); the low salaries of educators where some must get more than one job, taking time away from preparation and planning (Murillo & Román, 2013); the learning levels of students in Latin America (IDB, 2018); and the lack of recognition of social uses of reading and writing from the knowledge of the population and in the context in which the students find themselves as a basis for planning and promoting the best ways to teach literacy from everyday life (Adarve, Santa Cruz & Fraga, 2016) are some of the educational tensions that affect initial literacy.

Due to the above, it is clear that the main problem with the lack of literacy is the condition of marginality, understood as a form of poverty, in which people remain, which sometimes coincides with deficient processes in their teaching. ECLAC (2014, p. 19) states that illiteracy 'increases the present and future socioeconomic vulnerability of adults' and even leads to this condition of vulnerability being maintained for several generations. Having said this, we can affirm that the importance of teaching reading and writing transcends the achievement of good academic results and is situated at the level of guaranteeing the inclusion of people in the literate world, which in turn is a guarantee of possibilities for life.

Didactic

We understand didactics in the same sense as Litwin (2008, p. 94) explains it: 'As a theory of teaching practices signified in the socio-historical contexts in which they are inscribed'. That is to say that didactics, although it is based on support disciplines such as psychology, anthropology, sociology, or neuroscience among others, requires reflection on practices, to understand how to adapt the proposals to each particular context.

On the other hand, Díaz V. (2016)

Didactics has an explanatory character, like all science, didactics explains the phenomena that are related to its object (the teaching-learning process in terms of laws and principles that are successively overcome). It describes the phenomena as they are, in what circumstances they occur, and explains their essence. This open nature of didactics translates into the provisional nature of its postulates, finding knowledge in continuous review by those who must apply it. (p73).

In turn, the reflection on the application of certain knowledge on how to teach, leads to the design of new teaching proposals, thus forming a circle of permanent review, design, implementation, and evaluation that contributes to enriching the theoretical and practical knowledge of teaching. teaching, and enriching the pedagogical knowledge of the teacher.

Figure 1. Didactic review circle
Source: Authors

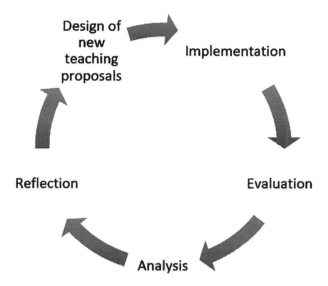

This process of permanent review and analysis of teaching is opposed to the uncritical application of teaching methods for reading and writing, which have been present in classrooms for many years, which, instead of being cyclical processes, tend to be linear and repetitive.

According to Litwin (2008), the method is a certain way of proceeding to articulate knowledge as an objective production and knowledge as a matter of (subjective) learning. 'Referring to the method implies recovering its classic definition, as the orderly and systematic way of teaching. To refer to the method, from its origin, is to refer to a construct of philosophy' (p. 68). Following this clarification, rather than the application of methods, it could be affirmed that techniques are used in classrooms, understood as 'procedures that seek to effectively obtain, through a determined sequence of steps or behaviors, one or several precise products' (Secretariat of Public Education of Mexico, 2014). In this same sense, Díaz-Barriga mentions that 'didactics is, necessarily, a central discipline in the teacher training process. It cannot be considered just an instrumental discipline (...)' (Díaz, 2009, p. 53).

Under the above, it is risky to speak of precise techniques and products, especially if one takes into account that learning as a process in the human being occurs uniquely, with individual rhythms, which, being unknown to the teachers, are it tends to dehumanize education and homogenize practices, expecting everyone to obtain the same results at the same time and in the same way (O. Baez & D'Ottavio, 2020). This practice has been maintained for a long time in the classroom and has been the object of defenders and detractors of both methods, without significant progress being made in the results, among other reasons, because literacy is still considered as the process of recognition of letters and their corresponding sounds.

Table 1 presents the relationships between the source that gives rise to the methods of teaching reading and writing, even though research has shown that these processes are much more complex than previously believed and are based on thought, teaching persists through traditional methods that, in reality, have resulted in techniques that are based on visual, auditory and motor perceptual processes.

Table 1. Relationships between the source that gives rise to the methods of teaching reading and writing

Source	Process	Method
Associationism	Analytical	Phonetic
		Alphabetical
		Syllabic
		Visual
Syncretism	Synthetic	Global
Mixed	Analytical - synthetic	Normal words
Behaviorism	Analytical - synthetic	Graduate vocabulary
Constructivism	Constructive	Not method. Creation of writing situations
Socioconstructivism	Social construction	Not method. Creation of shared construction situations

Source: Guzmán (2017)

It is worth analyzing what happens when didactics is abandoned and the teacher's action focuses on the use of a certain technique because this implies resorting to mechanical action, leaving aside the teacher's reflection on their practices. In this case, the teaching power is given to the technique and not to the teacher through didactic reflection. Perhaps to a great extent, this is the reason why many teachers continue to teach by relying on children's visual, auditory, and motor perceptions, through activities that they consider playful.

Another risk involved in abandoning didactics is that there is a tendency to substitute pedagogical concepts for those of other disciplines such as psychology, without even reflecting on this concerning their own students' needs. These speeches sometimes restrict the teacher's action on what he considers to be the best thing to teach. An example of the above occurs with the theory of learning channels such as the Visual Auditory and Kinesthetic (VAK). Many teachers consider that these are the only ways in which a student can learn and consider it an absolute truth, ignoring that there are many more possibilities in which our brain acquires knowledge. In this regard, Robson (2012) clarifies that, if a teacher considers that there is a preponderant channel in his students, his teaching practices may focus on that specific channel and lose other learning opportunities. The author mentions that:

The Learning and Skills Research Center- LSRC identify 71 different approaches (…). Nevertheless, the LSRC do suggest that there is considerable variability between the different learning styles approaches, and that is difficult to be clear about the impact of any of them (p. 5).

For this reason, teachers should consider that there are not just a few ways, but many, as Malaguzzi (Edwards, 2012) mentioned, children have many languages and ways to learn what interests them. During the analysis of the practice, the teacher's ability to perceive the differences, the changes, however simple they may be, and the recognition of these with the planned purposes, is essential to strengthening the reflection (Litwin 2016).

Likewise, it has been shown in previous research that teachers who are teaching children to read and write 'ignore pedagogy, put didactics as an adjective and the activity as a noun' (Guzmán and Ecima, 2011, p. 10). Making the activities the substantive in the work can lead teachers to lose the purpose of teaching and to consider themselves satisfied that the students are happy with the activities, forgetting

The Didactic in Initial Literacy

that teaching is different from entertaining. Likewise, putting didactics as an adjective implies delegating resources, materials, and activities, the condition of guarantee of learning in students, and forgetting the teacher's reflection. Additionally, ignoring pedagogy leads to ignoring the essential purposes of the education of human beings.

In short, there is a great difficulty in not putting didactics at the center of teaching. Without the reflection that didactics demands, the teacher depends on the techniques that he uses and on chance, without respect to responding to the learning needs of children, as Freire mentions (1998, in García, 2014).

Critical reflection of practice is a requirement of the relationship between theory and practice. Otherwise, theory becomes blah, blah, blah, and practice becomes pure activism... Teaching does not consist of transferring knowledge but creating the possibilities to produce or build knowledge... You cannot teach without learning at the same time (...) (Freire, 1998, p. 54, cited in García, 2014, p. 97).

Between the Perception and Representation

The techniques used by teachers to teach children to read and write focus on auditory, visual, and motor perception. This leads students to recognize the sounds (alphabetic, syllabic, or words) if they rely on phonetics; in visual perception, in case of using the recognition of the traces of the letters and in the motor, in case of focusing on the execution of the letters. In other words, the connection between the writing system thought and language is not promoted. Even writing is not understood as a system, but rather as the sum of sounds and isolated graphic forms and their possible combinations, forgetting that writing is a system of representation.

Representation is a very complex process. According to Cabrejo (2007) 'A representation is not a direct copy of the object but is the result of a construction process in which the subject performs actions and reads the effect of the action' (p. 133). For his part, Flórez (2007) affirms that if representations did not exist, 'each condition that reaches the system would be new, there would be neither previous experience nor anticipation nor recognition of phenomena that affect it' (p. 160). When children are learning to read and write, in addition to having been exposed to the strokes we call letters, they are trying to understand how the combination of those strokes can represent something that we do not see; this is a very complex mental process.

In this same line, Ferreiro (1998, p. 13) states: 'The construction of any representation system involves a process of differentiation of the elements and relationships recognized in the represented object and a selection of those elements and relationships that will be retained in the representation'. Additionally, it is necessary to point out that writing is a representation of language, which in itself is a mental representation. In this regard, Vygotsky (1979, p. 175) states: 'Written language is a very particular verbal function. It is the algebra of language. It allows the child to access the highest abstract plane of language'. This statement leads us to think of the need to transcend the teaching of reading and writing as essentially perceptive processes, to place them on the cognitive level.

In this attempt to recover the relationship between thought, language, and writing, there have been processes of teaching reading and writing with constructivism as a support, which highlights the action that the subject makes on the object of knowledge, which in this case it is the writing system. However, the decision to rely on constructivism to teach does not always manage to promote in children the relationship between writing, language, and thought, because in many cases there is mediation by the teacher, based on erroneous interpretations of what it means to bring constructivism to the classroom, due to difficulties in the ways of proposing writing situations (misunderstandings sourced of teachers and other professionals unrelated to the exercise of teaching). In practice, many teachers have found it sufficient to invite children to write; they are not taught or proposed a way to do it and above all, writing activities are wasted to promote cognitive progress concerning their understanding of a system; it is assumed that since the subject builds his learning, this will happen without the teacher's intervention. The consequence has been the delay in the literacy of the students and sometimes their absence.

The erroneous interpretations of constructivism have even led to affirm that the teacher should not teach, but should accompany the children in the construction of the written language, which has generated much confusion among teachers and has stripped them of their essential work, which is didactic reflection. What is reflected on, if not taught? How can they design and prepare classes if it is argued that the teacher should not teach?

This leads to specifying what is meant by teaching. We understand by teaching, the systematic, planned, and thoughtful action, of a person who knows something, to a person who intends to learn it. It is necessary to highlight the three terms of the concept of teaching: systematic, planned and reflected because all of them are opposed to the idea that the teacher does not teach, but accompanies. However; of course, it is possible to teach with a didactic strategy based on constructivism: it is necessary to plan situations in which children make social use of reading and writing, recognize their cognitive conflicts, and take advantage of the interactions between students and theirs with the teacher, to help them overcome cognitive conflicts and thus take them to another level. It is necessary to clarify that the preparation of these classes is usually more complex than that of a traditional class, because it requires the attention of each child, instead of planning massive teaching, but it has a great advantage that we make sure that the children are understanding how the writing system works.

Given the situation of lack of learning of reading and writing due to applications in the classroom derived from erroneous understandings of constructivism, neuroscience has recently been used and the studies advanced by Dehaene (2017) have been taken as a basis, who affirms that regardless of the language being learned to read and write, phonetic recognition occurs in the same area of the brain. This statement has led to hasty conclusions that the best way to teach reading and writing is by teaching the sound of letters. However, Dehaene clarifies that after this recognition there is a connection with the lexical route (p 135) and clarifies that there is a difference between the connection speed between the word and the lexical route, when the word makes sense to the person who sees it and when you don't have it. That is, what supports the recognition of sounds is what the brain stores in its lexical route. The other sounds also activate the brain, but they are not directly related to language.

Dehaene's contributions allow us to affirm that the connection that occurs between the sounds of words and the lexical route requires their mental representation. This leads us to state that successful literacy requires prior knowledge of words and sentences, in a process that is recognized as emergent literacy and that consists of bringing children closer to the social uses of the spoken and written language that is produced by being part of a literate community. 'Emerging literacy refers to how the skills of speaking, listening, reading and writing become more complex' (Flórez et al., 2007, p.17). These authors add that it is what the little ones: 'have learned about the function, content, form of written language and the attitude they have towards it, before entering the school grade in which formal instruction begins' (2007, p.17).

As can be seen following the previous statement, when children arrive at school they already have a path concerning reading and writing, which includes processes of an abstract order, such as those related to the function of reading and writing, and perceptual, which have to do with the knowledge of some letters that they have seen in advertisements and other text bearers in their environment, as long as they

The Didactic in Initial Literacy

are present in the context. This situation raises the differences that may exist between children regarding their knowledge and understanding of the written language, according to the context of origin. These differences must be known and taken into account by the teacher to organize his teaching proposal.

The Role of the Teacher and Didactics in Initial Literacy

What is it then, and what does the teacher do in this initial literacy process?

As already stated, didactics imply the teacher's reflection on their practices in the classroom. It is convenient to keep this requirement in mind because teaching is very sensitive to modifications based on fashion trends. This is how, despite some current trends based on reading the contributions of Dehaene (2017), who has worked in neuroscience and has studied the processes that are triggered in the brain when a person reads, it has been interpreted that should begin to teach reading and writing from the knowledge of the sound of the letters (phonetic method), this same author wonders if the knowledge about the reading process directly indicates a better way of teaching and affirms:

At this point, a lot of caution is needed. My impression is that neuroscience is still far from prescriptive. A wide gap separates the theoretical knowledge accumulated in the laboratory from the practice in the classroom. Its application poses problems that teachers are generally able to solve better than the expectations based on the theory of scientists (p, 263).

These theories produced by scientists in different areas need to be analyzed by the teacher but keeping in mind that, as Dehaene points out, their claim is not to be prescriptive in teaching. In this same sense, Ferreiro and Teberosky (2007) manifest themselves, who clarifies that the results of their research on the process of construction of the written language cannot be taken as the steps of a teaching method. This exercise of thinking about the relevance and use of research results in teaching support disciplines is part of the didactic reflection.

From a didactic perspective, it is worth analyzing that although, as Dehaene points out, the best predictor of learning to read is letter recognition, this is not a starting point. Dehaene states: 'Without the phonological decoding of written words, their opportunities are significantly reduced' (2017, p. 264). Later he adds: 'All teaching efforts should initially focus on one and only one goal, mastery of the alphabetic principle according to which each letter or graphene represents a phoneme' (2017, p. 274).

However, as already mentioned in this article, when children reach that point, which Ferreiro and Teberosky (2007), based on their research, call the alphabetic hypothesis, they have already traveled a long way that teachers cannot ignore and add: 'The school is addressed to those who already know, implicitly admitting that the method is designed for those who have already traveled, alone, a long previous journey' (2007, p. 356). It is the task of didactics to make this type of analysis of contributions from other disciplines because otherwise, there is a risk of generating difficulties in children's understanding of the writing system.

On the other hand, it is necessary to take into account the following statement by Dehaene: 'The regions that show the greatest response to words are considered part of the lexical route, while the regions that show the most activation for pseudowords are thought to be involved in the direct phonological route' (2017, p. 135) because it suggests different brain processes when the meaning of the word is known, than when it is not, which in turn indicates that reading requires processes other than phonological because it refers to the language and not to the recognition of spellings.

The importance of the relationship between writing and reading and their teaching must be recognized by teachers because from preschool the close relationship between writing and reading with thought should be maintained (Guzmán and Chocontá, 2018, p.12) and therefore, assume writing as a representation system and not as a transcription code (Ferreiro and Teberosky, 2007). These same authors affirm, referring to learning to read and write, that it is: '(…) a learning process that does not go through the acquisition of isolated elements that will later be progressively assembled, but through the constitution of systems where the value of the parts are redefined based on the changes in the total system' (2007, p. 23).

The contributions of neuroscience are very important for the teaching of reading and writing, as well as those of other disciplines such as linguistics, psychology, and sociology among others. However, the main source of knowledge about teaching is in the didactic reflection, which implies knowledge of all these contributions, but also their adaptation to the classroom and, above all, the permanent observation of what happens with the learning processes of the students. As Dehaene (2017) points out, teachers often know better how to solve problems that theories have not been able to answer.

Another very important aspect of didactic reflection is knowledge of the context in which it is taught. Teachers need to know where their students come from and what path they have traveled concerning their relationship with reading and writing, to propose teaching strategies that allow them all to advance. For this, it requires relating its students with the social uses of reading and writing, promoting the development of orality, promoting advances for the hypotheses that children are considering about how the writing system works, and also helping them to develop both phonological awareness and letter knowledge and letter's stroke.

This knowledge of the context allows us to know the experiences that children have had before entering school: how their orality has developed, what reading and writing practices they have been exposed to, what their representations are about what it is to read and what it is to write, their hypotheses about so that one reads and writes, why one reads and writes, among other aspects.

It is also necessary to know how they interpret those strokes that we call letters. Do they differ from numbers and other graphic signs? Have they had contact with different text bearers, such as storybooks, newspapers, and advertisements, among others? What do they do when they have one of these bearers within their reach? Although this question seems like an obvious answer, it is not. In investigations that we have carried out, it has been found that while a middle-class child is asked what a newspaper is for, he answers: to find information, to read the news…, lower-class children answer: to clean the glasses, to collect the garbage, to ripen the avocados…

As can be seen, the situation of children entering school in each of the conditions is very different concerning their knowledge of how writing works as a system for representing ideas, messages, and information, among other possibilities. Consequently, if the two children are directly related to the sound of the letters, for the first of them it will be clear that they are part of the representation system that we call writing, while for the second it will only be a transcription code, comparable to the situation of an adult Spanish speaker when exposed to Chinese writing signs.

The following figure shows the relationship between the context and the processes of reading and writing:

The Didactic in Initial Literacy

Figure 2. Relations between the context and the processes of reading and writing
Source: Authors

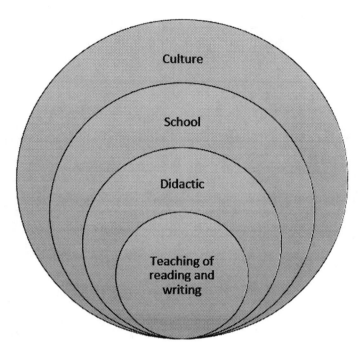

Reflection on teaching practices is a very complex process because it is not reduced to experimenting with different activities, to see which one works best. After all, while doing this exercise, many children may pass through the classroom and leave without having had the opportunity of learning to read and write. Didactic reflection presupposes theoretical knowledge about thought, language, reading, and writing as systems of representation, as well as about the development of children, the place of these processes in culture, and forms of teaching that have been validated in different contexts and situations.

On the other hand, it demands knowledge of the children's context of origin, to generate an initial teaching proposal that responds to their needs; but the teacher cannot wait for his action to finish to evaluate it: he needs to evaluate it before putting it into practice, during its putting into practice and after having done it. He also needs to know what aspects he should focus his reflection on and learn to think in an orderly and systematic way about his practices, objectify them through writing and dialogue with his colleagues, and make decisions about what he considers to be modified.

Didactic reflection is a very complex process, which demands a lot of effort from the teacher, but it is the main source of construction of teachers' knowledge; in this case, knowing how to teach reading and writing.

An example of an adequate didactic exercise for initial literacy is based on knowing the children's context of origin, which is usually done by filling out forms on sociodemographic aspects and is complemented with an initial evaluation to find out how they arrive in the classroom. Based on this knowledge, the teacher makes an initial proposal that responds to the needs of the students and is subjected to the first reflection process carried out by the teacher, who, when putting it into practice, will continue evaluating it to make the required adjustments on time. Lastly, he/ she will make a final reflection on what worked well and what needs to change.

As the groups of students are always heterogeneous, a meaningful didactic proposal, which we propose based on the results of research carried out in different classrooms of diverse contexts, should contemplate the following aspects, which should always lead to reflection by the teacher:

Table 2. Didactic proposal

Activity	Developing Process
Access to different reading materials: stories, magazines, manuals, newspapers, cookbooks, and other text bearers.	Knowledge about the uses and social functions of writing.
Reading aloud stories and other texts.	Relationship with different types of texts and recognition of the meaning of voice inflections.
The use of games to recognize the letters and their sounds, to identify their names, and other common elements.	Recognition of letter shapes, sounds, and names.
Writing spontaneous texts.	Statement of hypotheses about the functioning of the writing system.
Joint review of children's spontaneous writing to produce cognitive conflict and help them overcome it by comparing the child's writing with the conventional one.	Advance in the knowledge of the functioning of writing as a representation system.
Short writing repetition exercise, understanding that the function of good handwriting is to facilitate the reader's task.	Improvement of the stroke of the letters.

CONCLUSION

The interest in ensuring that the entire population is literate is undeniable as a condition for achieving human and social development, as well as for strengthening democracy and the full participation of people in society. In this process, the school takes on a special value, because it is the institution to which society has delegated the task of teaching all its members to read and write. To comply with it, the importance of didactic reflection is highlighted, as an essential process to support the proposals that are carried out in the classrooms, clarifying that it is quite complex and requires a lot of effort and dedication on the part of teachers.

A very important part of the didactic reflection consists of studying the contributions coming from other disciplines such as sociology, psychology, linguistics, anthropology, economics, and neuroscience, among others, to understand how the reading and teaching processes are carried out. writing in children, as well as the consequences of having a literate population, to design didactic strategies that allow adapting the findings of the disciplines to the needs of the students, according to their learning and development contexts. None of these disciplines has the mission of giving formulas to teachers; nor are they aimed at providing teaching methods that can be brought into the classroom. Nor is it valid to believe that it is taught without the need to resort to any basic theory and to believe that it is learned only through practice, because as Ferreiro affirms 'there is no practice without theory (implicit or explicit)' (1998, p.10); the important thing is to build a theory that serves the practice. It is the task of teachers to appropriate these contributions and from them create learning situations in their classrooms, through well-supported and organized teaching processes.

The Didactic in Initial Literacy

Throughout history, different disciplines, especially psychology, have permeated classroom work and have been taken up by teachers, ignoring that the results of experimental research do not constitute teaching proposals. Currently, there are two very marked trends in the way of approaching children's literacy, based on a false dichotomy in the teaching of reading and writing, between the convenience of beginning with the sound of the letters or avoiding intentional and systematic teaching of them. Underlying the first is the belief that learning is eminently perceptual, and the second is the idea that children learn to recognize letters and their sounds on their own. What is common to these two tendencies is the assumption that learning to read and write is something simple, that is carried out with the participation of a single process: either perceptual or cognitive.

The reality is that both processes are required. It is as important to promote cognitive advances in children so that they understand writing as a representation system, as it is to help them to know the elements that make up the system: the letters and other graphic signs. Reading and writing especially demand the participation of different levels of the nervous system. While the brain produces the ideas that it wants to express through language, the eye and the hand must serve as vehicles to capture them. In this exercise, several processes come into play simultaneously: mental representation, regulation by the linguistic system of what is being written, visual processing, phonological processing, and motor functions; between all of them they are regulated in permanent interaction.

All this makes sense within a cultural context, because reading and writing are very sophisticated ways of representing language and thought, which are interpreted according to the meanings and meanings that culture has endowed them with and with which children begin to be participants when they acquire mastery of writing and reading and not only when they know the letters.

Consequently, the didactic proposals for work in the classroom need to be developed based on representation, but without forgetting the elements of visual and auditory perception, in both ascending and descending processes. These didactic decisions must be very elaborate because the interaction between these two processes depends on the one hand, the motivation of children to make use of reading and writing as a way to participate in the literate culture, and on the other hand, the facility or difficulty that the overload of only one of these options can bring to children.

Ultimately, didactic reflection determines the quality of teaching and the quality of readers and writers that society aspires to have. For this reason, it is necessary to train teachers to teach reading and writing, with the understanding that it is a highly complex process that moves between perception and mental representation and that it has a great impact on society and people's quality of life.

REFERENCES

Adarve, M., Santa Cruz, S. N., & Fraga, S. C. (2016). *Tensión entre formación entre formación permanente y prácticas de enseñanza. Desafíos de alfabetización inicial en escenarios de primera infancia. Ponencia presentada en I Jornadas sobre las Prácticas de Enseñanza en la Formación Docente*. Universidad Nacional de Quilmes. https://ridaa.unq.edu.ar/handle/20.500.11807/757

Baez, M., & D' Ottavio, M. E. (2020). La diversidad en el aula: el desafío de interpretar la singularidad de los procesos de alfabetización inicial. *Ciencia y Educación, 3*(3), 31-40. doi:10.22206/cyed.2019.v3i3.pp31-40

Banco Interamericano de Desarrollo. (2018). *Profesión: profesor en América Latina ¿Por qué se perdió el prestigio docente y cómo recuperarlo?* Author.

Cabrejo, E. (2007). Representaciones mentales, acción y construcción. In Lenguaje y saberes infantiles. Universidad Francisco José de Caldas. Cátedra Unesco en Desarrollo del niño.

CEPAL. (2014). *El analfabetismo funcional en América Latina y el Caribe. Panorama y principales desafíos de política.* https://repositorio.cepal.org/bitstream/handle/11362/36781/S2014179_es.pdf?sequence=1&isAllowed=y

Dehaene, S. (2017). *El cerebro lector.* Siglo XXI.

Díaz, A. (2009). *Pensar la didáctica.* Amorrortu editores.

Edwards, C., Gandini, L., & Forman, G. (2012). *The hundred languages of children. The Reggio Emilia experience in transformation* (3rd ed.). Praeger.

Ferreiro, E. (1998). *Alfabetización. Teoría y práctica.* Siglo XXI Editores.

Ferreiro, E., & Teberosky, A. (2007). *Los sistemas de escritura del niño.* Siglo XXI México.

Flórez, R., Restrepo, M. & Schwanenflugel, P. (n.d.). *Alfabetismo emergente. Investigación, teoría y práctica. El caso de la lectura.* Universidad Nacional de Colombia.

García, M. (2014). Estrategias didácticas. Modos de enseñar y aprender. In I. Hurtado & F. García (Eds.), *Manual de didáctica: aprender a enseñar* (pp. 97–119). Pirámide.

González-Novoa, A. & Perera-Méndez, P. (2021). Panglotia, pampedia y pansofía: el realismo pedagógico en Comenio. *Pedagogía y Saberes*, (54), 23-36. doi:10.17227/pys.num54-11286

Guzmán, R. (2017). Aprendizaje de los profesores sobre alfabetización y métodos de enseñanza. *Revista Folios*, *46*(46), 105–116. doi:10.17227/01234870.46folios105.116

Guzmán, R., & Chocontá, J. (2018). *Desarrollo infantil y escritura. Vínculos entre infancia, cultura y pensamiento.* Universidad de La Sabana. doi:10.5294/978-958-12-0476-2

Guzmán, R., & Ecima, I. (2011). Conocimiento práctico y conocimiento académico en los profesores del nivel inicial. Seis preguntas. *Revista Folios*, *34*(34), 3–14. doi:10.17227/01234870.34folios3.13

Ibagón, N. (2015). La educación, un derecho que cuesta: Dimensión fiscal y su relación con la política educativa en América Latina. *Revista Educación y Humanismo.*, *17*(28), 29–37. doi:10.17081/eduhum.17.28.1164

Litwin, E. (2008). El campo de la didáctica: la búsqueda de una nueva agenda. In A. Camilloni, A. Davini, G. Edelstein, E. Litwin, M. Souto, & S. Barco (Eds.), *Corrientes didácticas contemporáneas* (pp. 91–115). Paidós.

Litwin, E. (2016). *El oficio de enseñar. Condiciones y contextos.* PAIDÓS.

Murillo, J., & Román, M. (2013). Docentes de Educación primaria en América Latina con más de una actividad laboral. Situación e implicaciones. *Revista Mexicana de Investigación Educativa – RMIE*, *18*(58), 893-924.

Robson, S. (2012). *Developing thinking and understanding in Young children; an introduction for students*. Routledge. doi:10.4324/9780203133354

Secretaría de Educación Pública de México. (2014). *Estrategias y técnicas didácticas*. Recuperado de http://iteatlaxcala.inea.gob.mx/SEducativos/Formacion/ESTRATEGIAS%20Y%20TECNICAS%20DIDACTICAS.pdf

UNESCO. (2021). *Alfabetización para el desarrollo Febrero 19 de 2021*. https://es.unesco.org/news/alfabetizacion-desarrollo

United Nations. (2022). *Sustainable Development Goals* https://www.un.org/sustainabledevelopment/

Vigotsky, L. (1979). El desarrollo de los procesos psicológicos superiores. *Critica*.

ADDITIONAL READING

Brailovsky, D. (2017). *Didáctica del nivel inicial en clave pedagógica*. Ediciones novedades educativas.

Comenio, J. (1991). Didáctica Magna (4th ed.). Editorial Porrúa, S.A.

Gómez, I., & García, F. J. (Eds.). (2014). Manual de didáctica: aprender a enseñar. Pirámide.

KEY TERMS AND DEFINITIONS

Activity: Unit of work that includes a teaching and learning purpose; it implies the articulation of a set of actions and the elaboration of a product.

Didactic: It is the theory of meaningful teaching practices adequate to the socio-historical contexts in which they are immersed.

Literacy: Process of interpretation and communication through different media.

Method: A determinate way of proceeding that articulates the knowledge as objective production and the knowledge as a learning issue (subjective).

Perception: The first knowledge of a thing is through the impressions communicated by the senses.

Reading: Process of construction of meaning from the interpretation of graphic and linguistic signs.

Reflection: It is the thought or consideration of something with attention and detail to study it or understand it well.

Representation: Result of a construction process in which the subject performs actions and reads the effect of the action.

Teaching: Systematic, planned, and thoughtful action, by a person who knows something to a person who intends to learn it.

Writing: Process of mental representation that allows the expression of thinking and communication.

Section 2
Critical Literacy and Media

Chapter 3
Critical Literacy:
Using This Framework in Early Childhood Classrooms

Paula Renata Castillo
https://orcid.org/0000-0003-1484-2076
Universidad San Francisco de Quito, Ecuador

ABSTRACT

This chapter reviews the definition of critical literacy education as well as the benefits of applying this approach. It analyzes the statement that literacy is not a technical skill, but in fact, it is always embedded in socially constructed epistemological notions and power relations in society. The author includes a reflection on how texts are not neutral and the need to encourage children to interrogate what they read and to use language as a way to question inequalities and oppression. The chapter analyzes why this approach has been rarely implemented in early childhood classroom. The author proposes the need for educators to reflect about how their beliefs regarding literacy influence their teaching practices. It argues that children's literature can be a resource to dialogue about identity, culture, diversity, and power relations in society. Finally, it analyzes the importance to build a curriculum based on children´s interests and needs as well as to create spaces for critical literacy in early childhood classrooms.

INTRODUCTION

Living in a globalized, unequal and conflicting society fosters the need for increased appreciation of diversity as well as the development of critical thinking and reflection skills in order to analyze social, political and power issues. Critical literacy focuses on people reading their world and the words for issues of literacy as an inquiry process deconstructing and reconstructing texts for aspects of power, position and privilege" (Kuby, 2013, p. 14). This framework supports students to question inequalities and oppression in their everyday life. Comber (2001) states that critical literacy stimulates students to use language in powerful ways in order to embrace changes in their communities and the world, as well as to question practices of privilege and injustice. Critical literacy is an approach that has been mostly applied in elementary and secondary classrooms and is rarely included in early childhood classrooms

DOI: 10.4018/978-1-6684-5022-2.ch003

(Comber, 2003; Vasquez, 2014). Kuby (2013) states that this absence is not because young children are not ready to engage in critical literacy practices, but because teachers still need to analyze the ingrained beliefs that they have regarding what is appropriate during the early years of education. It is essential for educators to reflect about their previous experiences as learners and how those have shaped their beliefs about what it means to be literate and how literacy should be taught.

BACKGROUND

Literacy teaching has been a controversial issue for as long as society has had a formal schooling system (Meier, 2009). Educators have not yet agree on what it means to be literate and the most appropriate method to teach young children to read and write. The different definitions of literacy and the teaching approach is influenced by educators previous experiences as well as their ideology as educators. It is also important to comprehend that texts are not neutral and why it is important to teach literacy as a skill that is not only technical. Literacy should encourage people to think critically, question texts, as well as transform themselves and the world around them. An approach that supports students to do this is critical literacy which is rooted in the principles of critical pedagogy, which enhances the need to work towards the pursuit of democracy and justice (Lewison, Leland & Harste, 2015).

Definition(s) of Literacy

Literacy is complex and its definition is influenced by time, contexts, cultures as well as the needs and practices of the people who use it. The definitions of what it means to be literate also reflect different theoretical, ideological and philosophical perspectives. "Early literacy development and instruction during both the preschool period and the first years of formal schooling is certainly the most studied and arguably the most theoretically and politically contentious area of literacy teaching and practice" (Teal et al., 2009, p. 77). There has also been controversy regarding what are the essential skills that children must develop in order to be considered literate. The different perspectives also establish what are the appropriate learning experiences and resources that educators should implement in order to support students in becoming literate. Luke and Freebody (1999) assert that "literacy is never neutral (…) it is always situated within a series of ideologies or beliefs that shape what we do" (p. 14). The approaches are based on diverse learning theories as well as ideologies about what being literate means (Cadiero-Kaplan, 2002).

There is no one definition or fixed concept of what literacy means. Rather, literacy can be defined depending on the context, goals of education in an specific society and ideology of the curriculum. A definition that is focused on a skills-based approach to literacy sees texts as an objective reality that should be decoded by the learner in order to comprehend the meaning written by the author. According to this approach, it is necessary to teach how to decode smaller pieces of language and when this has been mastered, children can then learn to decode words and later on phrases (Meier, 2009). However, reading is not only about decoding symbols in order to comprehend a message but actively reflecting on how the meaning of a text is connected to our lives (Fain & Horn, 2011).

According to Street (2003), literacy is not simply a technical and neutral skill, but is always embedded in socially constructed epistemological notions and power relations in society. According to Comber (2014) literacy encompasses operational, cultural and critical dimensions. Willinsky (2007) argues that, a critical approach to literacy encourages people to question what they read and to take actions that embrace changes in society. Luke and Freebody (1997) assume a sociological perspective of reading and writing in which literacy is influenced by cultural and political expectations as well as social actions and their consequences. Reading is about empowering students and deconstructing texts (Comber, 2003).

Literacy and Ideology

According to Cadiero-Kaplan (2002), any definition of what it means to be a literate person is based on an ideological perspective that is fundamentally political. Literacy practices are grounded in historical, social, economic and philosophical views that provide the lenses through which educators, and society in general, value what is necessary during the process of becoming literate. "What is read, how it is read, and how children are taught to interact with text is not neutral, it reflects an ideology" (Meier, 2009, p. 76). Literacy can be taught as a tool of critical inquiry or as the passive transmission of knowledge and ideologies. It can be a vehicle for posing and solving important social issues or for accepting official explanations and solutions (Lewison, Leland & Harste, 2015). There is a strong relationship between what is valued as knowledge, what skills should be developed and the ideology of people in charge of making education policies and creating the curriculum that will be implemented.

Not only the curriculum, and teaching approach is defined depending on what society values as literacy. The texts, books and other resources that young children are exposed to in order to support them to become literate is strongly influenced by the ideology of those who make the decisions in the education system. The resources that are used in the literacy teaching process reflect the principles that is intended to be transmitted by people who have power in society. According to Apple (1998), texts are chosen according to certain people's ideology as well as economic interests, and only some knowledge is selected and legitimized through their contents. It is necessary that educators analyze how the production of textbooks is related to the larger process of cultural reproduction.

Texts Are Not Neutral

According to Fairclough (2014), language is socially conditioned by components of society and the power relationships that exist within it. It is influenced by historical, political, economic and cultural issues in a community. Language is influenced by socio-cultural as well as political discourses and it can either support or disrupt the status quo in society. When we reflect about literacy learning and teaching, it is essential to analyze that texts are defined by the worldviews of the authors and the context were these are written. Because texts are not neutral, children need to become aware of how the identity, background, and interests of the author are represented in what he/she writes. "Texts are socially constructed and created from particular perspectives. As such, they work to have us think about and believe certain things in specific ways" (Vásquez, 2016, p. 9). Even though there may be no explicit intention by the author to influence the reader's perspective about an issue, when creating a text, the author will always include his worldview. Bias is an unavoidable part of expression; readers who analyze that texts have biases have a deeper and more critical understanding than readers who merely accept the author's statement and position about an issue. It is the reader's job to take an active role and to "question issues such as who wrote the text, what the author wanted us to believe, and what information the author chose to include or exclude in the text" (McLaughlin & DeVoogd, 2004, p. 6). Even young children who are developing literacy skills need to be conscious that the author may have the purpose of persuading them in some way.

Just as texts are never neutral, the ways we read texts are also never neutral. Each time we read, write, or create, we draw from our past experiences and understanding about how the world works. We therefore should also analyze our own readings of text and unpack the position(s) from which we engage in literacy work. (Vásquez, 2016, p. 9)

When we read our comprehension of the author´s message is influenced by our worldview, previous experiences and the context that surrounds us. Responses to reading are socio-culturally constructed, assembled from interwoven cultural histories and circles we inhabit (Enriquez, Johnson, Kontovourki & Mallozi, 2016). According to Rosenblatt (2005), from a transactional reading perspective, the role of the author and the reader shifts because the reader can go beyond the literal meaning of a text. Critical responses or attempted transformations of a text is another way the readers transact with it (Enriquez, Johnson, Kontovourki & Mallozi, 2016). Critical literacy supports the transaction process because readers become texts critics who comprehend a variety of information sources from a critical stance (McLaughlin & De Voogd, 2004).

Definition of Critical Literacy

Critical literacy derives from, and is indebted to a broader movement in social theory known as critical theory (Willinsky, 2007). Aligned with critical theory, critical literacy is committed to examining how structures of power stabilize existing representations and render them as perceivably objective and/or natural. Drawing on Freire´s (2000) theory of emancipatory education, critical literacy strives to reestablish how individuals relate to texts by considering the agency readers have to not only understand, but to use texts for greater socio-political awareness. In other words, critical literacy endeavors on using the process of literacy to encourage students to both reflect on their own position within a social order that is encoded by complex power structures and to consider their roles as potential agents of change. As Quintero (2008) notes, critical theory conceives of literacy as an instrument of expression, interpretation, and transformation. Luke and Freebody (1997) argue that teaching literacy has to involve a moral, political and cultural decision about the kind of literate practices that are needed to enhance people's agency over their life trajectories. Critical literacy involves "reading against the grain, asking harder and harder questions, seeing underneath, behind and beyond texts, trying to see and call how these texts establish and use power over us, over others, on whose behalf, in whose interests" (Luke & Freebody, 1997, p. 4). It seeks to go beyond conventional notions of reading and writing to a level of critiquing and challenging texts, recognizing connections between one's life and the social structure of the text, engaging in critical thinking, and moving towards transformation of one's self and one's world (Evans, 2010).

Critical literacy education departs from the assumption that literacy is not only a technical skill, but a process that is socially constructed and imbued and reflective of existing structures of power. The epistemological underpinnings of critical literacy create new questions and demands on educators regarding the purpose and processes of teaching literacy. "Critical literacies are not just orientations to teaching literacy but a way of being, living, learning, and teaching" (Vásquez, 2016, p. 4). Teaching literacy from a critical perspective is not focusing on specific issues but rather it involves practices that invite students to live critically (Vásquez, Tate & Harste, 2013). Educators should plan significant experiences that can serve as a medium in reflecting about injustice within children´s communities. According to Vásquez (2014), this literacy framework supports students and teachers to work towards disrupting the problematic inequality among members of a society. It encourages students "to question the everyday world,

Critical Literacy

to interrogate the relationship between language and power, to analyze popular culture and media, to understand how power relationships are socially constructed, and to consider actions that can be taken to promote social justice" (Lewison, Leland & Harste, 2015, p. 3). Vásquez (2014) states that critical literacy should be a frame through which students and teachers make meaning and actively participate in the world both inside and outside of formal education settings.

Critical literacy is not "a piece of knowledge to be fed to students but is rather a culture of thinking that engages students in observing their world in ways that move them toward considering issues of equity and access" (Stribling, 2014, p. 46). It provides a vehicle for educators to challenge children's thinking, support them in questioning the authority of texts, explore various viewpoints, and reflect about social and political issues that are part of their lives (Comber & Simpson, 2007). When children are exposed to read critically and to inquire about the world, they are encouraged to make connections between the messages and their lives. "Critical literacy is also about imagining thoughtful ways of thinking about reconstructing and redesigning texts and images to convey different, more socially just and equitable messages that have real life-effects in the world" (Vásquez, 2003, p. 2). It seeks to empower students to take actions that embrace changes in pursuit of equality among all members. This framework supports students in examining their social world and reflect upon the actions that they can take to transform it (Gregory & Cahill, 2009).

Dimensions of Critical Literacy

Lewison, Flint and Van Sluy (2002) propose a critical literacy framework that provides a method for learning to read between the lines and to form alternative explanations to the messages that texts present. Van Sluy, Flint and Lewison (2005) proposed the following four dimensions that are necessary to work with students within a critical literacy curriculum: (1) disruption of the commonplace; (2) interrogation of multiple perspectives; (3) focus on socio-political issues, and (4) the taking of action and promotion of social justice.

The disruption of the commonplace is the first dimension. Beliefs and worldviews influence how people interact with others around them, the decisions they make and the social groups they join. "Without a critical perspective, these beliefs and assumptions are seen as sensible and innocent, often just the way things are, and not in need of examination" (Lewison, Leland & Harste, 2015, p. 8). In order to have a critical viewpoint, it is necessary to take a step aside and question how we perceive the world and how we use these perceptions to make sense of our experiences. Another aspect is "to examine how cultural and historical influences have shaped all aspects of life, including the experience of schooling" (Lewison, Leland & Harste, 2015, p. 9). Finally, disrupting the common place requires students to examine how social norms are transmitted through a variety of cultural artifacts and how they shape our identity.

The second dimension is considering multiple viewpoints. When applying critical literacy as an educational framework, people use their current knowledge and previous experiences to change what happens in our classrooms (Comber, 2003). "We also strive to appreciate multiple realities as an attempt to stand in the shoes of others, to understand experience and text not only from a personal experience but also from others' viewpoints" (Lewison, Leland & Harste, 2015, p. 10). Part of this dimension is educators asking themselves and the students to consider other perspectives in order to gain a more complex and richer understanding of the issue or topic being studied (Lewison, Leland & Harste, 2015). When selecting materials, books and other resources, educators should choose texts that include the voices of diverse members in society, especially those who have often been marginalized.

The third dimension of critical literacy focuses on the socio-political. "Advocates of critical literacy suggest that although teaching is a non-neutral form of social practice, it often takes place with no conscious awareness of the sociopolitical systems and power relationships that are part of every teaching episode" (Lewison, Leland & Harste, 2015, p. 11). Students are asked to take a critical perspective by focusing on how language is not neutral and is often used to maintain the dominance of certain groups over others. The aim is to analyze the relationship between language and power, as well as to challenge the unequal power relationships in society. In order to do this, it is necessary to investigate how texts can have messages that appear to be neutral or part of the status quo but in fact aim to perpetuate oppression of some groups over others (Lewison, Leland & Harste, 2015).

Taking action to promote social justice is the fourth dimension of a critical literacy framework. According to Lewison, Leland and Harste (2015), "another aspect of enacting critical social practices in the classrooms means using language and other sign systems to get things done in the world" (p. 12). In order to take action students are asked to openly dialogue about issues of oppression and inequality, and the actions they can take to transform the system. It is important to acknowledge that in this framework there are no specific steps, methods or experiences about its application in the classroom (Lewison, Flint & Van Sluy, 2002; Van Sluy, Flint & Lewison, 2005; Lewison, Leland & Harste, 2015). Lewison, Leland and Harste (2015) argue that their goal of placing the model in a context is "to move away from romanticized notions about the implementation of critical practices" (p. xxxiii). They state that political, economic, cultural and social factors shape the school context where the model is applied so each experience with critical literacy is unique.

CRITICAL LITERACY IN EARLY CHILDHOOD

Early childhood is a crucial moment in life because during this period, children form their initial notions about relationships in society as well as the value of literacy in their lives (Comber, 2003). According to Comber (2003), critical literacy creates opportunities for young children to dialogue and examine issues of power, gender, social class, religion, culture and race, presented in the texts that they read or listen to during read alouds. Kim (2016) states that this framework is a medium for helping children to critically examine books and to find their own voices in order to rewrite the stories that they have been exposed to. Young children should deeply about issues regarding equity and oppression to become active participants in their community. This literacy approach supports early learners to become agents of change who take actions towards social justice in order to build an egalitarian society. However, it is still rarely applied in early childhood school settings. Even though there are many benefits in using this literacy framework to teach young children, it is still rarely applied in early childhood classrooms (Kuby, 2013; Vásquez, 2014). Comber (2003) notes that "critical literacy, with its focus on power and language, has not been a force in early childhood literacy education" (p. 588). Kuby (2013) states that this absence is not because young children cannot engage in critical literacy practices, but because educators still need to reflect about the embedded beliefs that they have about what is developmentally appropriate during the early years of education.

Arguments Against Using Critical Literacy in Early Childhood

There are educators who believe that using a critical literacy approach to teach reading and writing during early childhood is not appropriate. Educators and family members of young children may assume that they are not mature enough to understand and dialogue about complex issues in society. According to Kuby (2013), some argue that young children are not prepared to dialogue about social issues like oppression and injustice. "There is an assumption that kindergarten students are too young to discuss the "isms" that undergird social inequities, much less to take action toward creating a more just world" (Stribling, 2014, p. 46). However, children experience themselves or witness poverty, discrimination and injustice. "In some instances, engaging in critical literacies is seen as a subversive act that happens behind closed doors" (Vásquez, 2014, p. 19). Because of myths related to children's capability to dialogue about social justice and critically engage with literature, educators who use this teaching approach may face difficulties, resistance and even negative reactions from administrators, colleagues and parents. However, it is necessary to first analyze what are arguments that teachers have against critical literacy during the early years of education.

Several educational researchers have found different reasons why teachers believe that it is not appropriate to use critical literacy as a framework in early childhood classrooms. Some teachers state that children need to learn functional aspects of reading before being able to question what they read (Comber and Simpson, 2007). Chafel and Neitzel (2012) argue that teachers find that critical literacy is not developmentally appropriate for young children because they are not prepared to reflect about issues like oppression and social justice. Other teachers argue that using a critical literacy approach may be dogmatic because teachers may influence or even impose on children what they should say and think (O'Brian, 2007). Educators have argued that "sometimes children are left with guilt and fear in a critical curriculum as they deconstruct power relationships, especially if opportunities of reconstruction and social change are not provided" (Kuby, 2013, p. 44). According to Chafel and Neitzel (2012), many pre-service as well as in-service teachers find critical literacy texts troublesome and not developmentally appropriate for young children. People who critique this approach argue that teachers may impose their beliefs on students about social justice issues (Kuby, 2013). According to O'Brian (2007), educators question that teachers may be putting words in the mouth of their students or that students only say what teachers want to hear. But it is important to consider that these objections are based on a misleading idea claiming that a teacher is being neutral when she or he does not challenge the authority relationship constructed between texts and readers. Another misleading claim is that all texts will remain neutral unless a teacher intervenes (O'Brian, 2007).

Sahni (2007) suggests that children do not conceive reality in terms of social, political or power relations, except when these relations are embodied in people they know or interact with. Dyson (2007) states that some teachers who teach using a critical literacy approach sometimes ignore young children's social world and how they make sense of it. Sahni (2007) argues that educators should respect childhood and allow them to grow, instead of treating young children as miniature adults and challenging them to think critically about social structures that are part of their lives yet are still too distant or complex for them to comprehend. It is more useful to support children to write creative stories where their role in society is a more powerful one than helping children to acquire the ability to think and act critically about realities in their lives. Nevertheless, it is with stories that children construct their identities, negotiate relationships, and position themselves in the world (Sahni, 2007).

Besides the reason mentioned above, there are other situation in which early childhood teachers argue is not appropriate to apply critical literacy. Castillo (2018) found that all of the participants in her study believe that early childhood students should be supported in developing critical literacy skills. However, they had concerns about applying this literacy framework within their current teaching context. Among the reasons they mentioned are that children will be developmentally ready to develop critical literacy skills during the next school year, but not in the current grade she is teaching now. "Participants felt that during this stage of development children are still only interested in talking about themselves and because of this it would be difficult to stimulate them to think critically about the books they read" (Castillo, 2018, p.154). This claim is interesting because their current teaching level is early childhood. However, they do state that children will be ready next school year. Other participants narrated that because it is a full English immersion program, children in their classrooms need to develop language skills before being exposed to critical literacy (Castillo, 2018).

SOLUTIONS AND RECOMMENDATIONS

Even though there are arguments against using critical literacy in early childhood, these are due to misunderstandings of these approach. Vásquez (2014) posits that critical literacy is just taking root in early childhood classrooms and, because of this, it is necessary to share experiences with others who value and apply this literacy approach. Teachers need to consider the potential role of critical literacy in preparing children to meet the ever changing and unprecedented pace of transformation in the literate world (Harwood, 2008). "Young children are capable of challenging the everyday representations of culture, knowledge and power that exist within texts, while also advocating for social change and action" (Harwood, 2008, p. 2). Educators, parents policy makers and other actors involved in early childhood education should analyze the need to include a critical approach when teaching children how to read and write. Critical literacy needs to begin with the youngest learners in order to prepare them for the ever-changing literate world as well as the unequal and oppressive society where they live.

In order to questions misconceptions about children development and their capability to engage in critical literacy as a learning approach, educators need to reflect about their previous experiences as learners as well as their current teaching practices. It is essential that educators reflect about how their beliefs influence the teaching practices that they apply. Early childhood educators can foster critical literacy development by providing children opportunities to explore the relationships between language practices, power relations and identities within the texts that they read (Comber, 2003). A critical literacy curriculum should be built based on children's experiences regarding social justice issues. Children's literature is a powerful tool to encourage them to critically think about the messages in the texts and how they can become active participants in society.

Reflection About Teacher Beliefs

Educators should be aware of the idea that "our interests may be inextricably linked to our personal histories and therefore how these histories position us in our classroom" (Vásquez, Tate & Harste, 2013, p. 25). Teachers are highly influenced by their previous experiences as learners. Past events act as a filter through which they see the education process and shape their beliefs about what it means to be literate. Many educators' experiences developing literacy skills did not include analyzing what they were reading or questioning the perspectives that an author presented (McLaughlin & DeVoogd, 2004). This is one of the reason why teachers do not use critical literacy as the teaching framework during early childhood. Educators must analyze how their ideologies and beliefs become part of the work that they do when teaching literacy to young children (Vásquez, Tate & Harste, 2013).

According to Kuby (2013), in order to become aware of their ideologies, teachers must go through a process of unpacking; which means to closely examine and explore how and what makes up their experiences, conversations, memories and traditions that build their worldview. "From a critical literacy perspective examining one's assumptions, values and beliefs is part of understanding the position from which we speak, we teach and the discourses that shape those positionings" (Vásquez, Tate & Harste, 2013, p. 23). However, disrupting the commonplace is not easy or natural because it requires that teachers deeply analyze their beliefs and reflect on how they are related to their teaching practices. Educators should have spaces to dialogue about how their ideology influences the way they teach in order to first become aware and then take the appropriate actions in order to make the changes they consider appropriate and relevant.

Teacher education programs should support pre-service teachers to analyze how critical literacy can be implemented as a teaching framework from the first years of schooling. Vásquez, Tate and Harste (2013) argue that in order to develop the skills and knowledge to teach according to the aims of critical literacy, pre-service teachers should experience learning with this framework. Rather than lecturing pre-service teachers about critical literacy, they should have multiple opportunities to experience firsthand "what it is like to be a learner where the university teacher builds the curriculum around their inquiry questions, passions and interests from a critical literacy perspective" (Vásquez, Tate & Harste, 2013, p. 3). The experiences that future educators live should lead them to learn the elements of critical literacy proposed by Lewison, Leland and Harste (2015) which are to: disrupt the commonplace, interrogate multiple perspectives, unpack socio-political issues and take actions towards social justice.

Building a Critical Literacy Curriculum

Vásquez (2007) states that there is an essential need to construct a curriculum that is socially just and unbiased, where issues like race, class, gender, and fairness are constantly on the agenda. While working across the curriculum in the content areas, diverse students' cultural knowledge, including their funds of knowledge, multimodal and multilingual practices, should be used to build curriculum (Vásquez, 2016). "One of the hard things about creating a critical curriculum is that few of us have had the opportunity to actually live such a curriculum. For the most part, we have taught consumer literacy rather than critical literacy" (Lewison, Leland & Harste, 2015, p. 59). According to Vásquez (2014), many teachers who engage in critical literacy practices treat social issues as variables to be added to the existing curriculum. However, this is the wrong way of including critical literacy as part of the curriculum. The analytical and critical component is not add-on but an integral aspect of what counts as literacy for all learners (Haneda, 2006).

Lewison, Leland and Harste (2015) argue that the curriculum is a negotiation between what kids want to learn and the established goals. When educators value what kids know and the issues that they care about, they can build a powerful curriculum that has the potential to be transformative. According to Vásquez, Tate and Harste (2013), disrupting the commonplace and interrogating multiple perspectives are essential aims of a critical literacy curriculum that cannot be prepackaged or preplanned because it is built on children's cultural questions about everyday life. Pre-school children need to be given opportunities to examine the ideologies of everyday texts that they bring to the classroom (Vásquez, 2007).

A critical literacy curriculum arises as teachers and children tune into the issues of social justice that unfold through classroom conversations and pose critical questions that lead to dialogue and action. "Through engagement in a critical curriculum, students raise various social justice and equity issues, using them to interrogate, obstruct, contest and or change inequitable situations" (Vásquez, 2014, p. 122). According to Comber (2000), teachers should design a permeable curriculum where children are encouraged to contribute to its content with issues that are relevant to them. Students learn best when they are exploring topics and issues that are relevant for them, that connect to their lives, and that connect with real questions they have about the world. Educators should plan experiences for children to become aware of how inequality and oppression are not only present in stories that they read, but also part of their life. Curriculum should also be built with the everyday texts that surround children's lives and that they bring to school (Vásquez, 2014).

These texts can be so common that we do not carefully take notice of them. As a result, we can be less aware of the kinds of messages about our world which they convey. These texts can be interrogated, deconstructed, and analyzed to uncover different views of the world they could represent. (Vásquez, 2007, p. 7)

"The world as text, however, can be read from a critical literacy perspective" (Vásquez, 2014, p. 614). Children can raise questions about their everyday lives that could be used as a basis for conversations that would generate a critical curriculum. The curriculum must be participatory, and children should not be just consumers, rather, they must construct curriculum through their contributions to class discussion based on their experiences, knowledge and background. Furthermore, because a critical curriculum arises from a critical sociological analysis of the contemporary economic and political conditions, it cannot be traditionally taught; it needs to be lived (Vásquez, 2014).

Creating Spaces for Critical Literacy

Children need spaces in schools to reflect about topics like race, sexual identity, gender roles, and poverty. When teaching under the tenants of a critical literacy framework, educators need to create an environment where students are supported "to disrupt what is considered to be normal by asking new questions, seeing everyday issues though new lenses, demystifying naturalized views of the world and visualizing how things might be different" (Lewison, Leland & Harste, 2015, p. 7). According to Kim (2016), it is essential to build a supportive literacy environment where children can openly talk and include their own perspectives and beliefs in order to answer open questions. Fain and Horn (2011) also argue the need for creating spaces for dialogue and reflection that support children in developing critical literacy skills. According to Stribling (2014), teachers should create spaces that respect students' ideas, concerns and struggles, and to model ways of engaging in difficult conversations.

Children should be encouraged to reflect about socio-political issues that affect their community and the actions that they can take in order to embrace an egalitarian society. Whitmore, Martens, Goodman and Owocki (2005) contend that critical texts, addressing social justice issues such as culture, race, gender, sexuality, ability and socioeconomic status, lead children to search for answers to powerful questions about these issues. Whitmore, Martens, Goodman and Owocki (2005) found that by raising and

Critical Literacy

resolving questions with texts that narrate socio-political issues, children were supported to challenge the status quo in society and connect new perspectives to their personal understandings of the world.

Children's Literature

Storytelling is how people share their thoughts, feelings and experiences. Children enjoy listening to stories, retelling stories that they read, and creating their own narratives. Reading or listening to a story gives them the opportunity to acquire new knowledge and is also a source of pleasure and enlightenment (Galda, Sipe, Liang & Cullinan, 2013). Books are a source of inspiration to open up new worlds and develop new and divergent ways of thinking. "Literature can transform children´s ways of knowing which makes a book the greatest single resource for educating our children to become contributing members of society" (Galda et al., 2013, p. 8). Literature enables children to explore and understand their world, enrich their lives, and widen their horizons. Stories are a powerful tool that supports children to become reflective and critical thinkers as well as to develop fairness, respect and empathy. Stories portray experiences of joy, hope, loneliness, fear and belonging (Short, Lynch-Brown & Tomlinson, 2014). Children's literature provides an engaging opportunity for children to identify themselves in the stories and to learn how other people may think and feel (Galda, Sipe, Liang & Cullinan, 2013). Good stories challenge children to question their beliefs about people's culture and diversity.

Living someone else's life through a story can help children develop a sense of social justice and a greater capacity to empathize with others. All children benefit from stories that involve them in the lives of characters who struggle with disabilities, politics, or difficult circumstances or show lives differ because of culture or geography. (Short, Lynch-Brown & Tomlinson, 2014, p. 7)

Books present a microcosm of ideologies, values, beliefs and worldviews. The messages in children's literature have the potential to influence the way that young readers view themselves and what they consider to be appropriate behaviors in their culture (Chaudhri & Teale, 2013). Some children's books continue to be an instrument for the reproduction of the mainstream culture and the perpetuation of the status quo (O'Neil, 2010). Many books only present the ideologies, values, and beliefs of the dominant culture in a society. Some stories are interwoven so tightly into the experiences that people live that it can be easy to not notice its influence on how they think about themselves as well as the people and the world around them (Short, Lynch-Brown & Tomlinson, 2014). However, books can be a tool to stimulate children to value diverse perspectives about the world as well as to analyze the messages presented by the author (Taylor, 2003).

According to Bishop (1990), children should be exposed to books that are mirrors of their reality as well as windows that encourage them to learn about others. "Books present different kind of realities; providing spaces for readers to connect their own experiences and understanding for purposes of reaffirming those experiences and understandings, or for taking issue with the realities that are presented for them" (Vásquez, 2003, p. 11). When children cannot see themselves in the books that they read or when their identity is presented in a distorted or negative way, they learn a powerful negative lesson (Bishop, 1990). Educators must recognize "that particular students' experiences and understandings are marginalized when they do not find themselves in books or when the realities presented do not represent their experiences" (Vásquez, 2003, p. 11). Classrooms need to be places where all children, independently of their background, have books in which they can find their mirrors as well as books that are windows that present new perspectives about the world to them (Bishop, 1990).

Choosing the "Right Book"

Children need to be exposed to a variety of genres, formats and topics in order to learn about themselves and the world when they read. The messages that books give children influence in their worldviews. "The experiences we have during our lives shape and are shaped by the books that are important to us" (Galda, Sipe, Liang & Cullinan, 2014, p. 39). According to Collins and Safford (2008) teachers must make wise choices about the books that they suggest to children to read. However, there is no such thing as a critical literacy text. Rather, there are texts through which educators may better be able to create spaces for critical literacies (Vásquez, 2017). Short, Lynch-Brown and Tomlinson (2014) suggest that educators who aim to support children in thinking deeply and critically should choose books that have multiple layers of meaning and invite readers to linger longer. Vásquez (2014) argues the books that are an appropriate resource to encourage dialogue and reflection include content that invite children to interact with others and discuss diverse issues in society.

Compelling and interesting texts should be available, and teachers should encourage children to read them in order to discuss language, its functions, power and identity (Collins & Safford, 2008). When teachers engage children in critical literacy activities they expose them to a variety of formats, genres, authors and diverse worldviews presented in texts. Comber, Nixon and Reid (2007) state that teachers should extend the variety of literacy that children are exposed to by including issues and topics that capture their interests and are relevant to their lives. When children are engaged with the story and characters, they feel motivated to reflect about power relations in society and issues like discrimination, inequality and oppression. The analysis of a text is not limited to deconstructing it, but more importantly, should lead to the reconstruction of a new text that embraces the transformation of society (Vásquez, 2014).

Critical Literacy as Joyful

Questioning the message that an author is sending does not mean it has to be a boring experience for children. Vásquez (2014) states that "critical literacy does not involve taking a negative stance rather, it means looking at an issue or topic in different ways, analyzing it, asking questions…and hopefully being able to suggest possibilities for change or improvement" (Vasquez, 2014, p. 17). Using critical literacy in early childhood classrooms can be joyful and engaging. Reading can be joyful when children are supported in rewriting the texts and offering new perspectives, and to challenge what they read and to take action. Exposing young children to authentic literature is the first step in engaging them with reading as a joyful activity. Children also need to live significant experiences that bring them and books together for diverse purposes. "These experiences include reading widely for personal purposes, reading critically to inquire about the world, and reading strategically to learn about literacy" (Short, Lynch-Brown & Tomlinson, 2014, p. 276). Short, Lynch-Brown and Tomlinson (2014) suggest that literature responses and drama responses not only support children to become critical readers but are also engaging and joyful.

Whitmore and Meyer (2009) state that reading can be joyful and support children to become critical readers by implementing the following strategies: 1) Relying upon authentic reading materials that give children the opportunity to transact with texts that lead them to accomplish something in their lives, 2) Supporting children to view reading as a social process that requires them to interact, respond, and engage with others in order to co-construct meaning for the texts they read, 3) Celebrating the diversity of languages and cultures by exposing children to a variety of text and give them to opportunity to learn about themselves as well as other cultures and worldviews, 4) Creating democracy through critical literacy in order to support children in their reading of the world and how they can be caring and active citizens who embrace changes in society.

Implementing Critical Literacy in Early Childhood Classrooms

An essential part of schooling is to create spaces and devote time to encourage young children to question dominant and powerful discursive practices in order to support them to be active participants who seek change in society (Vásquez, 2007). However, because of children's developmental stage, teachers may struggle to find suitable pedagogical strategies that work to support and promote critical literacy in early childhood settings. Read-alouds are appropriate experiences to support children in relating to different issues in the story, to analyze how the story may be related to their own experiences, and to ask critical questions about the characters, the message(s) and the illustrations the books present.

Read Alouds

The shared experience of listening to a story together fosters a sense of community in the classroom where all members can dialogue about the story and how it relates to their lives. There are not specific books that can be used to foster the development of critical literacy. However, global literature can be used to explore and inquire about diverse voices and multiple perspectives in society (Short and Thomas, 2011). Before, during or after reading a book together, teachers can scaffold students and support them in developing the strategies needed to confront issues of racism, sexism, injustice and discrimination. Below are examples of activities that can support the development of the four dimensions of critical literacy proposed by Lewison, Leland & Harste (2015) during early childhood. However, it is essential to learn about children´s lives in and outside school and find ways to connect books, topics and strategies that best suit their interests and needs.

Disruption of the Commonplace

Educators should support children in questioning the unequal power relations in their community. This can be achieved by helping children reflect on their daily lives and how they have experienced themselves or have witnessed experiences of oppression (Vásquez, 2003). In order to help children disrupt the commonplace, educators can support children's reflection on how they make sense of the world around them is influenced by their cultural, social and linguistic background. Ideas about people and the world are learned by interacting with members of the community where children grow, as well as by being exposed to cultural artifacts such as literature (Lewison, Leland & Harste, 2015). A powerful strategy to disrupt the commonplace is being exposed to children's books that present diverse people's worldviews. An example of an activity is to read books about holidays around the world and reflect about what this holidays represent and what people celebrate.

Interrogation of Multiple Perspectives

Young children are aware of differences, inequalities and injustice and must be guided to appreciate diversity. Without proper guidance and support in valuing diversity they develop prejudices and stereotypes. Children around three years old begin to develop the ability to be aware and understand another person's perspective (McCloskey, 2012). Reading books that tell a story from another character´s perspective help children become aware of how people have diverse feeling and thoughts about the same event.

Focus on Socio-Political Issues

Critical literacy involves a commitment to justice and equity, and a critique of texts and the world as an important mechanism for social change. When reading a book that is meaningful for them, preschoolers can recognize characters who are acting unjustly or situations where the rights of another are not being respected. Becoming aware of biases in a text is also part of this dimension. Lewison, Leland and Harste (2015) argue that young children can analyze how texts are not neutral by being initially exposed to deliberate and noticeable examples of illustrations as well as narratives that are biased.

Taking Action to Promote Social Justice

An essential aspect of critical literacy is encouraging students to take action in order to embrace changes and build and egalitarian society. In order to take action students can be asked to openly dialogue about issues of oppression and inequality and the actions they can take to transform the system. Children can use diverse literacies to express their thoughts, feelings and propose solutions to real life problems. They can share their creations with other members of the community to encourage them to become part of the changes (Lewison, Leland & Harste, 2015).

FUTURE RESEARCH DIRECTIONS

The first suggestion for future research is to explore how critical literacy could be developed using other forms of literacy such as music, advertising, theater and visual arts. Comber, Nixon and Reid (2007) argue that in order to support children's developing literacy skills, it is necessary to include an ample repertoire of literacy and communication practices that are part of their communities. Literacy is not only about printed texts and because of this it is necessary to recognize that visual and performing arts are integral elements of literacy to be included in the curriculum and teaching practices (Lapp, Flood, Head & Langer, 2009). Another suggested study can explore how play, movement and art can be tools that support children expressing their ideas about the messages that they are questioning, and as instruments to rewrite texts and take actions that disrupt the commonplace. According to Vásquez (2017), new technologies can support children in creating new messages that not only critique the texts they are exposed to, but also to propose new ways to transform and build better communities. A study can be designed that analyzes how these diverse kinds of communication serve as a tool in supporting children's critical literacy development as well as reflecting upon how multiliteracies should be analyzed and questioned.

Finally, I study can examine how family members and other members of the community can support young children develop critical literacy skills. According to Terrel and Watson (2018), literacy development in young children is highly influenced by interactions with adults who read to and with them. Critical literacy should be part of living a critically literate life (Vásquez, Tate & Harste, 2014). According to McLaughlin and DeVoogd (2004), critical literacy extends beyond teaching and learning to everyday experiences outside of formal education settings. Children are surrounded by messages in the news, tv shows and the media. These everyday texts can be viewed through the lenses of critical literacy. Parents, siblings, librarians can engage in dialogues with children about the messages in the texts. They can also support children to take actions in order to disrupt the status quo and build a better society.

CONCLUSION

The epistemological underpinnings of critical literacy create new questions and demands on educators regarding the purpose and processes of teaching literacy.

There are different perspectives regarding what are the essential skills that children must develop to become literate. Educators have not yet reached a consensus and the issue of literacy teaching still generates controversy among the different actors of the education system. One of the frameworks to support children to become literate is critical literacy which "…focuses on people reading their world and the words for issues of literacy as an inquiry process deconstructing and reconstructing texts for aspects of power, position and privilege" (Kuby, 2013, p. 14). It involves the use of language to question inequalities and oppression that students experience in their everyday life within their schools and communities (Comber, 2001).

Early childhood classrooms would greatly benefit from a critical approach to children´s literature as it can serve as a point of departure for conversations about complex topics such as identity, culture, diversity and power relations within society. There are many benefits in implementing critical literacy beginning with the first years of formal schooling. However, this framework is still rarely applied in early childhood classrooms (Vásquez, 2014). Young children who are developing early literacy skills can become engaged in activities that invite them to question and reflect about the texts that they read and listen to (Comber, 2003; Kuby, 2013; Vásquez, 2007; 2014). The lack of implementation of this framework is often due to teachers beliefs regarding literacy. Educators must deeply reflect on the not so obvious literacy teaching practices that are determined by our ideology (Kuby, 2013). Teachers need to reflect on their own ideology and beliefs about literacy, and also on the aims of the curriculum, materials and methods that they use to support students in the process of developing literacy skills (Cadiero-Kaplan, 2002). Before using a critical literacy approach, educators need to become critical literate themselves. This means that they must go beyond the process of comprehending a text toward deeper levels of analyzing and critiquing the messages that we are exposed to.

In order to be critically literate, early childhood educators should analyze the decisions they make regarding the curriculum, the books they choose to read, and the topics that they dialogue with children about. Most importantly, they should analyze on whether they are seeing children in their classrooms as consumers of knowledge or as active participants who should be supported in becoming agents of change. Questioning what is often taken for granted and taking action towards building a better society are also essential in order to become a critical person who disrupts the status quo in society (McLaughlin & DeVoogd, 2004). Pre-service teachers should be supported to critically read the messages that they are exposed to, and who use literacy to build a better society (Tatto & Coupland, 2003; Stribling, 2014).

Teacher education programs have a very important role in preparing future early childhood educators to implement critical literacy and social justice as educational frameworks in their classrooms.

A meaningful engagement with critical literacy requires educators to be attuned to the lived experiences of their students, and mindful of creating a curriculum based on children´s interests and needs. Early childhood educators should connect the literacy curriculum with children's real interests and issues that they are living. Educators' responsibility is to nurture an engagement with literacy by encouraging children to read for authentic purposes, make personal connections, and not only focus on comprehension but to question what they read and propose meaningful changes (McLaughlin & DeVoogd, 2004). The books that children are exposed to should present diverse realities and worldviews in order to support readers in connecting and reaffirming their own experiences and how they understand reality (Vásquez, 2003). Children need to be exposed to stories, characters and illustrations that encourage them to acquire critical literacy skills as well as to value diverse worldviews in order to develop a sense of empathy, justice and fairness (O'Neil, 2010). According to Collins and Safford (2008), when children are engaged with the story and characters, they feel motivated to reflect on power relations in society and issues like discrimination, inequality and oppression. Education should aim to support children in becoming conscious of issues like oppression, injustice and inequality, as well as to question the stereotypes about members of their community and the world around them.

REFERENCES

Apple, M. (1998). The culture and commerce of the textbook. In L. E. Beyer & M. W. Apple (Eds.), *The curriculum: Problems, politics, and possibilities* (2nd ed., pp. 157–176). State University of New York Press.

Bishop, R. S. (1990). Mirrors, windows and sliding doors. *Choosing and Using Books for the Classroom, 6*(3).

Cadiero-Kaplan, K. (2002). Literacy ideologies: Critically engaging the language arts curriculum. *Language Arts, 79*(5), 372–381.

Castillo, R. (2018). *Teachers' beliefs about critical literacy in early childhood classrooms*. ProQuest Dissertations Publishing.

Chafel, J., & Neitzel, C. (2012). "I would like to see how they got poor and see what it's like to be poor": An analysis of young children's literacy responses to a critical literacy text about poverty. *Journal of Poverty, 16*(2), 147–170. doi:10.1080/10875549.2012.667058

Chaudhri, A., & Teale, W. H. (2013). Stories of multiracial experiences in literature for children, ages 9-14. *Children's Literature in Education, 44*(4), 359–376. doi:10.100710583-013-9196-5

Collins, F., & Safford, K. (2008). The right book to the right child at the right time: Primary teaching knowledge of children's literature. *Changing English, 15*(4), 415–422. doi:10.1080/13586840802493068

Comber, B. (2000). What really counts in early literacy lessons. *Language Arts, 78*(1), 39–49.

Comber, B. (2001). Critical inquiry or safe literacies: Who's allowed to ask which questions? In S. Boran & B. Comber (Eds.), *Critiquing whole language and classroom inquiry* (pp. 81–102). NCTE.

Comber, B. (2003). Critical literacy: Power and pleasure with language in the early years. *Australian Journal of Language and Literacy, 24*(3), 168–181.

Comber, B. (2014). Literacy, poverty and schooling: What matters in young people's education? *Literacy, 48*(3), 115–123. doi:10.1111/lit.12041

Comber, B., Nixon, H., & Reid, J. A. (2007). *Literacies in place: Teaching environmental communications*. Primary English Teaching Association.

Comber, B., & Simpson, A. (2007). *Negotiating critical literacies in the classroom*. Taylor and Francis.

Dyson, A. H. (2007). Relational sense and textual sense in a U.S. urban classroom: The contested case of Emily, girlfriend of a ninja. In B. Comber & A. Simpson (Eds.), *Negotiating critical literacies in the classroom* (pp. 3–18). Taylor and Francis.

Enriquez, G., Johnson, E., Kontovourki, S., & Mallozi, C. A. (2016). *Literacies, learning and the body: Putting theory and research into pedagogical practice*. Routledge.

Evans, S. (2010). The role of multicultural literature and interactive read-alouds on student perspectives toward diversity. *Journal of Research in Innovative Teaching, 3*(1), 92–104.

Fain, J. G., & Horn, R. (2011). Valuing home language to support young children's talk about books. In R. J. Meyer & K. F. Whitmore (Eds.), *Reclaiming literacy: Teachers, students and researchers regaining spaces for thinking and action* (pp. 209–218). Routledge.

Fairclough, N. (2014). *Power and language*. Routledge.

Freire, P. (2000). Pedagogy of the oppressed. *Continuum*.

Freire, P., & Macedo, D. (1987). *Literacy: Reading the word and the world*. Bergin & Garvey.

Galda, L., Sipe, L., Liang, L. & Cullinan, B. (2013). *Literature and the child*. Cengage Learning.

Gregory, A. E., & Cahill, M. A. (2009). Constructing critical literacy: Self-reflexive ways for curriculum and pedagogy. *Critical Literacy: Theories and Practices, 3*(2), 6–16.

Haneda, M. (2006). Becoming literate in a second language: Connecting home, community, and school literacy practices. *Theory into Practice, 45*(4), 337–345. doi:10.120715430421tip4504_7

Harwood, D. (2008). Deconstructing and reconstructing Cinderella: Theoretical defense of critical literacy for young children. *Language and Literature, 10*(2), 1–13.

Kim, S. J. (2016). Opening up spaces for early critical literacy: Korean kindergarteners exploring diversity through multicultural picture books. *Australian Journal of Language and Literacy, 39*(2), 176–187.

Kuby, C. R. (2013). *Critical literacy in the early childhood classroom: Unpacking histories, unlearning privilege*. Teachers College Press.

Lapp, D., Flood, J., Head, S. B., & Langer, J. (2009). The communicative, visual, and performative arts: Core components of literacy education. In J. V. Hoffman. & Y.M. Goodman (Eds.), Changing literacies for changing times: An historical perspective on the future of reading, public policy and classroom practices (pp. 3-16). Routledge.

Lewison, M., Flint, A., & Van Sluys, K. (2002). Taking on critical literacy: The journey of newcomers and novices. *Language Arts, 79*(5), 382–392.

Lewison, M., Leland, C., & Harste, J. C. (2015). *Creating critical literacy classrooms: Reading and writing with an edge* (2nd ed.). Routledge.

Luke, A., & Freebody, P. (1997). Shaping the social practices of reading. In S. Muspratt, A. Luke, & P. Freebody (Eds.), *Constructing critical literacies: Teaching and learning textual practice* (pp. 185–225). Hampton Press.

Luke, A., & Freebody, P. (1999). Further notes in the four resource model. *Practically Primary, 4*(2), 5–8.

McCloskey, E. (2012). Conversations about jail: Inclusive settings for critical literacy. *Early Childhood Education Journal, 40*(6), 369–377. doi:10.100710643-012-0528-7

McLaughlin, M., & DeVoogd, G. L. (2004). *Critical literacy: Enhancing students comprehension of text*. Scholastic.

Meier, N. (2009). Reading first? *Critical Literacy: Theories and Practices, 3*(2), 69–83.

Meyer, J. R., & Whitmore, K. F. (2011). Reclaiming joy: Spaces for thinking and action. In R. J. Meyer & K. F. Whitmore (Eds.), *Reclaiming literacy: Teachers, students and researchers regaining spaces for thinking and action* (pp. 279–288). Routledge.

O'Brian, J. (2007). Children reading critically: A local history. In B. Comber & A. Simpson (Eds.), *Negotiating critical literacies in the classroom* (pp. 37–54). Taylor and Francis.

O'Neil, K. (2010). Once upon today: Teaching for social justice with Postmodern picture books. *Children's Literature in Education, 41*(1), 40–51. doi:10.100710583-009-9097-9

Quintero, E. (2008). La pedagogía crítica y los mundos de niños y niñas. In P. McLaren & J. L. Kincheloe (Eds.), Pedagogía Crítica: De qué hablamos, dónde estamos (pp. 277-286). Graó.

Rosenblatt, L. M. (2005). *Making meaning with texts*. Heinemann.

Sahni, U. (2007). Children's appropriate literacy: Empowering pedagogy from young children's perspective. In B. Comber & A. Simpson (Eds.), *Negotiating critical literacies in the classroom* (pp. 19–37). Taylor and Francis.

Short, K. G., Lynch-Brown, C., & Tomlinson, C. M. (2014). *Essentials of children's literature*. Pearson.

Street, B. (2003). What's new in new literacies studies? Critical approaches to literacy in theory and practice. *Current Issues in Comparative Education, 5*(2), 77–91.

Stribling, S. M. (2014). Creating a critical literacy milieu in a kindergarten classroom. *Journal of Language & Literacy Education, 10*(1), 45–63.

Tatto, M. A., & Coupland, D. B. (2003). Teacher education and teachers' beliefs": Theoretical and measurement concerns. In J. Raths & A. McAninch (Eds.), *Teacher beliefs and classroom performance: The impact of teacher education* (pp. 123–182). Information Publishing Age.

Taylor, F. (2003). Content analysis and gender stereotypes in children's books. *Teaching Sociology, 31*(3), 300–311. doi:10.2307/3211327

Teale, W. H., Hoffman, J., Paciga, K., Garrete, L. J., Richardson, S., & Berkel, C. (2009). Early literacy: Then and now. In J. V. Hoffman & Y.M., Goodman (Eds.), Changing literacies for changing times: An historical perspective on the future of reading, public policy and classroom practices (pp. 76-97). Routledge.

Terrell, P., & Watson, M. (2018). Laying a firm foundation: Embedding evidence-based emergent literacy practices into early intervention and preschool environments. *Language, Speech, and Hearing Services in Schools, 49*(2), 148–164. doi:10.1044/2017_LSHSS-17-0053 PMID:29621796

Van Sluys, K., Flint, A. S., & Lewison, M. (2005). Researching critical literacy: A critical study of analysis of classroom discourse. *Journal of Literacy Research, 38*(2), 197–233. doi:10.120715548430jlr3802_4

Vásquez, V. M. (2007-a). Constructing a critical literacy curriculum with young children. In B. Comber & A. Simpson (Eds.), *Negotiating critical literacies in the classroom* (pp. 55–67). Taylor and Francis.

Vásquez, V. M. (2007-b). Using the everyday to engage in critical literacy with young children. *The NERA Journal, 43*(2), 6–11.

Vásquez, V. M. (2014). *Negotiating critical literacies with young children*. Routledge. doi:10.4324/9781315848624

Vásquez, V. M. (2016). *Critical literacy across the k-6 curriculum*. Routledge. doi:10.4324/9781315642277

Vásquez, V. M. (November 1, 2017). Critical literacy. *Oxford Research Encyclopedia of Education,* 1-17.

Vásquez, V. M., Muise, M. R., Adamson, S. C., Chiola-Nakai, D., & Shear, J. (2003). *Getting beyond "I like the book": Creating space for critical literacy in K-6 classrooms*. International Reading Association.

Vásquez, V. M., Tate, S. L., & Harste, J. C. (2013). *Negotiating critical literacies with teachers: Theoretical foundations and pedagogical resources for pre-service and in-service contexts*. Routledge. doi:10.4324/9780203081778

Whitmore, K. F., Martens, P., Goodman, Y., & Owocki, G. (2005). Remembering critical lessons in early literacy research: A transactional perspective. *Language Arts, 82*(4), 296–307.

Willinksy, K. (2008). Of critical theory and critical literacy: Connections to the legacy of critical theory. In K. Cooper & R. E. White (Eds.), *Critical literacies in action: Social perspectives and teaching practices* (pp. 3–20). Sense Publishers.

Chapter 4
Early Years Critical Literacies and Rights:
A Review

Myles Bittner
https://orcid.org/0000-0001-5718-2229
University of Massachusetts, Amherst, USA

ABSTRACT

Critical literacies as a field carries immense potential to provide students tools to build a better, more caring, and just world. This is especially true for students at the earliest years of education as they create the foundations for active citizenship in society. When these tools are connected to discourses that focus on equal treatment of all humans anywhere in the world, there is hope that future generations will actively resist long-standing systems of mistreatment. This literature review seeks to bring together two bodies of work and ponder at how they might work in relation to one another. This literature is then analyzed in relation to the physical location in which they take place to open understandings of how geopolitics, history, and culture impact what can and should be done. Critical literacies and discourses around human rights create complex intersections that share more in common than what might appear at surface level. Educators and educational policies should work to better understand these intersections to support the holistic development of any student.

INTRODUCTION

For anyone who has spent time with and listened to students in early years education settings it should be obvious that their ideas are almost always connected to broader issues in society. Yet oftentimes the structures embedded within educational systems do not provide supportive space for students and teachers to truly explore these ideas. On one hand there have been monumental and creative shifts by early years educators and how they approach challenging issues to support students' engagement with perspectives from around the globe. At the same time, there are continued efforts to implement top-down notions of "school-readiness" that take away from these critical thinking spaces (Bentley & Souto-Manning,

DOI: 10.4018/978-1-6684-5022-2.ch004

2019). Early years educators continue to find unique ways of incorporating issues that impact children worldwide and support them in developing critical tools for deep exploration in the classroom.

Without finding ways to continually support this essential work, young students will not have the skills, tools, or resources to actively reflect and act upon future injustices around the globe. Additionally, they will be at risk of inheriting siloed understandings of complex topics related to their own lived realities. Students should be given the opportunity to act in the best interests of their personal well-being. Doing so requires strong foundations built in the earliest years of education.

This paper seeks to expand upon the intersection of research within critical literacies in early years education and ideas centered around the rights of being human. In reviewing the relevant literature, this paper attempts to take a step back and view where such work has been or currently is taking place in hopes of showing where future efforts may be welcome and/or needed. The literature reviewed is then organized geographically, allowing for an analysis of themes based on historical, political, and cultural differences. Doing so, will generate questions around why specific educational efforts take place in relation to unique configurations of space and time dependent on location.

This review does not seek to provide a complete picture on all that has taken place within these bodies of literature but attempts to highlight a few examples of how it has been done. This organization and interpretation will inform future research that seeks to understand the complex nature of engaging in critical literacy practices that are connected to concepts around the rights of being human. The examples presented showcase how educators, researchers and students can work together to engage in educational practices that build foundations for active citizenship in the world while also seeking to challenge those who limit these abilities for others.

One aspect to keep in mind in the generation of this literature review is that the search process was conducted in English, through United States based infrastructure. This undoubtedly has an impact on the material one is exposed to and can draw upon. As this work moves forward it is important to remain vigilant on such limitations and work to support and uplift various and under-represented perspectives. Due to the nature of this work, finding ways to apply insights into classroom settings and talking about it in a conventional academic manner are two very different elements and should be seen as useful in their own capacity while also being able to support one another.

BACKGROUND

Critical literacies and direct links to discourses around rights within early years education are concepts that have many similarities, but often remain separate within the research literature or at least not explicitly connected. This section expands upon these two concepts and attempts to put them in conversation with one another. In doing so, this review hopes to create a line of thinking that generates new inquiry for what could be as our world engages with continual transformations within educational pedagogy and research while confronting the complex realties faced by humans everyday across the world.

Critical Literacies

Critical literacy in general is a broad term with various contextualized meanings. For the purposes of this review, Hilary Janks' definition from the 2013 article, "Critical Literacy in Teaching and Research" is used as a starting point:

Critical literacy is about enabling young people to read both the word and the world in relation to power, identity, difference and access to knowledge, skills, tools and resources. It is also about writing and rewriting the world: it is about design and re-design. (p.227)

This framing from Janks shares many similarities with other popular scholars within critical literacy studies. One shared aspect relates to the re-designing that such an approach to reading the world creates. This is an essential piece of critical literacy that allows those engaged in its practice to actively participate in uncovering and challenging power relations while considering those often left on the margins.

This work is never easily done and often is seen as too complex for young learners, however there are many scholars showing that this is not the case. These scholars argue that engaging even the youngest of audiences in critical literacy practices is very much possible and in fact, highly necessary (Bentley & Souto-Manning, 2019; Botelho et al., 2014; Dyson, 2013; Vasquez, 2014; Vasquez et al., 2019; Comber, 2011). At the same time, it is important to understand the dangers in creating a homogenous idea around what critical literacy is and does. While there are similarities across various interpretations, they each build from the unique contexts and relationships in which they originate. Ultimately, what these many interpretations of critical literacies do share is that any engagement should be rooted within the situated lives of individuals and their educational spaces (Comber, 2011).

Rights Discourses

Context not only plays a major role in critical literacies, but also in discourses around rights in education (Petersen, 2021). The environments in which students and teachers work from provides the content and material for reflective engagement. This aspect is central to any practice that seeks to contribute and fight for the protection of human rights. Learners need to see how the skills and knowledge they build within educational spaces play out within their own lived realities. Without seeing and participating in these direct connections, such work would fail to showcase its powerful impact at the level of individual.

The phrase "rights in education" is used intentionally to capture a broader notion containing ideas such as human rights education, peace education and civic education. While each of these are their own respective fields of inquiry with very particular origins, they share underlying components that seek to engage students in ideas around what it means to be an active, participating human in a globalized world. Much like the notion of critical literacies, it is important to acknowledge the range in definitions for these educational practices.

However, what they do share is their ability to challenge educators and students to think about the ways in which people are not always afforded equal opportunities and what can be done when those opportunities are not available. Discourses around rights in education draw upon international standards in which power and policy collide. Examples of this include the Universal Declaration of Human Rights (UDHR) and the UN Convention on the Rights of the Child (UNCRC).

These bodies of work carry tremendous weight (either through legal obligations or public discourse) within the international community and should be utilized as resources from which educators can draw upon. These major governing bodies do not come without important critique. Their shortfalls should be acknowledged and carried through any implementation be it in classrooms or political offices. One of these is the notion of rights as universal standards and how they have largely been based upon longstanding missions that carry colonial legacies (Williams & Bermeo, 2020).

The very notion of rights as described within documents like the UDHR or UNCRC is an idea captured by major world players at the time of their creation. While there may be similarities in other contexts, it should be known that what one sees as someone's right may not be a universal experience (Williams & Bermeo, 2020). This criticism is important to consider as educators continue to think about incorporating this line-of-work into education. Keeping this in mind, this review does not attempt to compress rights in education into a particular framework that carries a complex and destructive history. Rights in education in this sense is a floating construct that indexes particular ways of viewing and learning about oneself in relation to the world's ecosystem.

METHODS

Undertaking this review involved many different steps and decisions that require careful deconstruction. It is essential to acknowledge the importance choices play in what is being reviewed and analyzed. What is generated in this report is a reproduction of collective knowledge available for further engagement. This review provides a snapshot from one of infinite angles. Below, these decisions are further expanded upon in an effort to provide transparency and to show the thinking that went into what is ultimately presented.

To begin the research process the question primarily used as a guide was, *what research has been done around the intersection of critical literacies specifically focused on rights discourses situated in early years education settings*? This question contains a few aspects worth clarifying. The first being the concept of critical literacies which has been elaborated upon earlier in this review. In this question, the term critical literacies is used as an umbrella category to produce specific research around the interplay of classroom practices that address power relations and access to resources (Comber et al., 2001; Crafton et al., 2007; Janks, 2013).

The second concept is the phrase, "rights discourses". This is a concept that connects to various educational fields, but in particular to the Human Rights Education movement (Bajaj et al., 2017). As noted, the concept of rights discourses is used to cast a large net on topics of study that might take place within education settings. In general, these concepts pertain to ideas of participation, agency, freedom, voting rights and access to education. These concepts can be connected to international legal frameworks as discussed within documents such as the Universal Declaration of Human Rights or the United Nations Convention on the Rights of the Child. These resources provide foundations to protect individuals around the world in hopes of fostering compassion, equality, and care.

The final aspect of this question that is important to expand upon is the limitations of the term "early years education". This term is intended to capture a timeframe of education for students at pre-entry all the way to the first three years of primary school. Generally, these students range from 3-years-old to 7-years-old. Within this range are many complex developmental stages and to condense them into one concept such as early years does not afford them a complete representation. Yet, doing so for the purposes of this review is essential to create a platform from which to work. It should also be noted that the term early years is used cautiously as an idea like early childhood which is commonly used within the United States, does not always apply internationally.

Search Process

The initial stage in the actual search process stemmed directly from the research question. It was to identify multiple Boolean search phrases (Jesson et al., 2011). These search terms have been included in the table 1.

Table 1. Boolean search phrases used in literature review

Search # 1	Human Rights Education	Early Childhood Education	Literacy OR Literacies
Search #2	Rights	Early Childhood OR Early Years Education	Critical Literacies
Search #3	Rights	Early Education	Critical Literacies

To conduct the literature search, the online databases of ERIC and WorldCat were utilized through a public university libraries system. These results were then refined to a timeframe of 2010-2020. Empirical articles were primarily selected due to their systematic organization and ability to communicate relevant pedagogy taking place within educational settings. Again, these were decisions made by the reviewer in an effort to maintain consistency and organization. Overall, twenty articles were analyzed in fuller detail.

The selection of articles was based on two primary factors. The first being the relevancy of the Boolean search terms and how they were discussed by various authors. While the second was the clarity in which authors connected ideas around rights as discussed earlier in this review with that of critical literacies practices. This second factor was partially impacted by constraints around time in the review process. In order to account for that which may have been missed, this review attempts to provide a momentary snapshot which could be compiled alongside others to create a more complete picture.

Once the twenty resources were further explored, a system for thematic coding was developed for deep analysis (Braun & Clarke, 2006). The intent in this coding process was to surface thematic similarities across various geographical locations and how practitioners engage with implementation in similar and different ways. Microsoft Excel spreadsheets and online mapping applications were utilized to assist in the organization of these data.

Categorizing themes around geographical location became one of the most descriptive lenses to engage with this work. The more time spent with these data it became clear that certain locations seemed to be producing unique insights which required further investigation. The three main locations captured in this review are the United States, Australia, and Northern Europe. This of course is not representative of all work that would fit the inclusion criteria, but what in this review, was selected for further analysis. As stated before, it is important to stay vigilant that there very well could be major resources missing from this review in addition to the limited geographical representation. Resources that might have gone overlooked could include book chapters, oral histories, journals that look at these same ideas through different terminology or resources that go beyond the academic marketplace.

By narrowing the scope of reviewed research to the United States, Australia, and Northern Europe, this review admittedly neglects a wide range of potential work that could be helpful in addressing the original research question. There is a breadth of monumental scholars who have addressed issues around critical literacies and rights from locations around the world. For example, figures like Paulo Freire have

Early Years Critical Literacies and Rights

had tremendous impacts on critical literacy research, and the school of work he and others have continued to inspire cannot be overlooked. However, within this review it became helpful to think about the research from the United States, Northern Europe, and Australia in relation to how commonly accepted notions of rights play out or do not play out within early years education settings.

The primary reason for focusing on work from these three regions is due to the the bulk of the research being found through the methods indicated earlier and its availability for analysis. Additionally, these geographical locations are widely discussed in more accessible ways from the databases used for this review. This omittance of work from other settings from around the world is important to highlight and must be understand as a potential limitation to this review.

Thinking about how a country like the United States subscribes to widely accepted ideas of rights and then contrasting it with what played out in the research literature became an important thinking tool. So, while this review could incorporate a variety of additional insights from around the world, it decided to take a few explicit examples from the often thought of "leaders" in rights discourses as a starting point. This investigation again was not all encompassing and did not seek to be so from the beginning but aims to generate further questioning and analysis between what plays out in the earliest years of education.

In the following sections, a deeper dive into themes and their relation to geographical location will follow. These findings will then be connected to the implementation of critical literacies and discourses around the rights of being human. One must be careful to not draw lines of causality in this analysis process. This review intends to create spaces for inquiry around why specific topics gain more attention in certain places compared to others. It is in these spaces that more critical and reflective work can take place in hopes of addressing the needs of particular contexts while supporting the development of early years education students.

FINDINGS

The themes presented below showcase what stood out in empirical works through this research process. The goal was to better understand aspects of critical literacies around human rights concepts and how they emerge in response to the surrounding environments of a classroom. This space that surrounds an educational environment is an important feature to consider. From thinking about the material and non-material aspects that interact with teachers and students to the geopolitical pressures at a particular moment in time, there are endless ways to analyze what takes place at any given second. This review sticks with a more robust lens into the analysis process and looks at this work through the perspective of events in relation to their geographical location made up of political and environmental histories. Drawing this distinction allows for a clearer path into the research and simplifies the process of finding themes.

Understanding the work being done in classrooms through perspectives that take account of place-based ecologies has a long history in educational research (Comber, 2011). This review argues for its continued need as it relates to concepts around rights and critical literacies. Without taking into account the unique circumstances students and educators are surrounded by, this work cannot truly start from a place of relevance. The ideas inherent in rights discourses must be practiced in a way that impacts the individual lives of learners. It is only from such a foundation that the tools and resources learned within the process can be applied to other contexts. Critical literacies help learners bridge those divides and allow for more engaged, active, and just transformations.

In the following sections, specific contexts are used to illustrate how critical literacies around rights discourses can be applied to classroom practices. From these examples, future educators can build upon the essential ideas and reflect on how they might be translated into their own unique classrooms. These examples also invite reflection on what is missing as it relates to the situated realities of learners and teachers. Thinking about the challenges faced by educational environments alongside their geographical location provides insight into how rights discourses can be used to support future generations.

Race and Identity in the United States

For much of the literature that took place in the United States what remained common throughout was a keen focus on practices where students and teachers engaged with social issues around race and/or identity. This work often carried an additional component to push against or challenge current societal norms that came up in relation to context (Dyson, 2020; Kuby, 2011; Kuby, 2013; Kuby & Rucker, 2020; Vasquez & Felderman, 2012).

Anne Haas Dyson -a prolific figure within the field of critical literacies- provided one article that exemplifies the exploration of identity through critical literacy practices. Dyson's article, "'We're Playing Sisters, on Paper!': Children Composing on Graphic Playgrounds follows the many literacies taking place in a common U.S. classroom (2020). Dyson highlights various examples of critical literacy practices that not only show what children this young are capable of, but that if provided the space, tools, and support to harness them, can make wonderful things happen (2020). Dyson demonstrates this by providing a range of examples from the classroom. From an impromptu pretend play scenario of transforming a cardboard box into a vehicle, to the resourcefulness and ingenuity of a continually marginalized student who takes control of their identity through literacy skills (2020).

Dyson and the students in her piece challenge various demands placed on educational spaces that do not allow for such unorthodox exploration. Dyson takes this an additional step further and builds upon Maxine Greene and the idea around human freedom (2020, p.4). The freedom to explore and see things in one's own way is essential to early years education if not all years. These are elements relevant to international standards that protect this freedom for all human beings. Dyson reminds readers of this continual fight to recognize educational moments that carry meaningful learning opportunities against what are regularly thought to be measurable and codifiable moments of learning (2020).

Another United States based piece that also looks at this first theme of race and identity is Candace Kuby's 2011 article, "Humpty Dumpty and Rosa Parks: Making Space for Critical Dialogue with 5-and 6-Year-Olds". In this article, Kuby explores the student generated inquiries around being told to not sit on an outside bench (p. 37). The students alongside teacher support explore these fissures (p. 40) and look at what can be learned not only in tools to better understand one's own challenge but also historical injustices due to the color of one's skin. Facilitating inquiry into this theme of racial injustice, so rampant in United States history and society is an example of critical literacy activities that teach justice, rights, and equity.

As highlighted above, works that grapple with identity and race often pull from the lived realities of students and support them in critical reflection. There are also ways to connect with students around rights issues that may not be their exact lived experience, but something they have been a witness to. For example, in their article based in the suburbs of Chicago, Silvers and colleagues (2010) investigate environmental injustices after the destruction of Hurricane Katrina. One of the important elements in this article is that the educators clearly demonstrate how this work can create bridges between contexts.

Early Years Critical Literacies and Rights

By working from images and stories seen in media about Hurricane Katrina, the teachers in this situation build from the emotional responses of students to explore in-depth, various concepts around environmental impacts on the lives of individuals (Silvers et al., 2010).

Finding ways to support critical literacy skills that connect to contexts outside of students' immediate realities is a delicate, but important task. Silvers et al., show how this work can be done and remind readers of how it always builds from the personal and localized connections at the core (2010). The United States and the world more broadly need to recognize the potential in work that provides young learners opportunities to connect to those around them in a way that fights for basic human rights. Students are increasingly being bombarded with social media feeds and viral stories that show them the worst of humanity across the globe. While there are many who find this as a purely negative development of the modern world, it is also a reality that education systems need to work with. If educators can find ways to appropriately discuss and learn from these videos, images and stories, future students will be provided the tools to digest them and act upon them in meaningful ways. If students are left to ingest these complex emotions in isolation, who knows what their future holds.

The empirical work presented from the United States shows how relevant exploring issues related to race, identity (being young and in control of your freedom) and place are to critical literacies work and the implementation of rights discourses. Taking a step back and viewing this work from wider perspectives opens additional lines-of-inquiry. Thinking about what has been happening in the United States over the past ten years and the hostile political climate created by generations of inequality show the need for such context-based exploration and looking at ways to expand it to the world around. The historical foundations that the United States have been built upon directly influence the conversations and work being done in all classrooms and as these various examples show, when done well, it can be extremely impactful.

The earliest years of education should be seen as a time to engage with this work and to build the foundations for active participation in society. This important movement can only continue with the support of educators, community members, politicians and researchers and should be done in concert with constant reflection on theory and best practice. U.S. educators, researchers and policy makers should continually take into account contextual history and how it relates to critical literacy practices while also asking questions that push beyond immediate context.

Frameworks in Northern Europe and Australia

The second element to focus on that interplays with geographical location is how educators were able to connect critical literacy practices to broader frameworks of international rights and legal policies. These efforts within the literature reviewed were primarily based in Northern Europe and Australia. There were two notable exceptions within the United States (Montgomery et al., 2017; Wisneski, 2019).

The theme of connecting to broader frameworks was particularly clear in the work from Northern Europe and Australia because, generally the authors would draw identifiable connections to the critical literacy skills being incorporated into classrooms to specific elements either in the UDHR or UNCRC.

Linking classroom activities to broader frameworks is an important pedagogical step and as demonstrated from the research within Northern Europe and Australia it shows educators' commitment to ensuring global approaches to the protection of rights. Classrooms should be safe spaces for students to grapple with the very ideals societies are founded upon. Without such spaces, future generations will be less prepared to engage with the pressing issues of modern life. From environmental destruction to the

Early Years Critical Literacies and Rights

tragedies of war, current education systems need to be equipped to provide tools to all students so that they can meet the needs of their communities no matter where they live.

Two examples of these ideals that appeared in the literature from the Australian context were agency and participation. Both are essential aspects of the UNCRC and finding ways to connect early years students to these abstract notions can be a challenging task. Yet it is essential to find ways of providing students with tools to act upon their protected rights and to challenge when these are not being met for themselves or others. Huser (2019) provides a detailed roadmap to connecting these ideas. Through multiple levels of engagement with students, Huser demonstrates that it is possible to have critical conversations around notions of participation and agency and that in doing this, young children can become active players in advocating for individual rights (2019).

In the contexts Huser describes, students are invited into the process of determining their own levels of participation within the process of research. The students alongside Huser walk through what participation means and create definitions that both parties mutually agree upon. Students can then reflect on their interpretations and act in ways they believe to be in their best interest (2019). This investigation showcases the complex dynamics often overlooked in research with young children and in doing so opens spaces to link such ideas to broader frameworks like the Convention on the Rights of the Child.

Huser's work in Australia shares similarities to Ann Quennerstedt's exploration of early years education in Swedish primary schools (2019). Quennerstedt takes readers through a classroom in which the teacher investigates elements of human rights tied to frameworks like the Convention on the Rights of the Child. Quennerstedt not only demonstrates the high level of training this takes for teachers, but that teachers play an important role in exploring these concepts alongside their students (2019). The teachers in Quennerstedt's research act as "interaction leaders" (p. 72) to support students in identifying appropriate documents and scaffolding different levels of engagement with them. This work is important in that it shows how complex this field is and that the teachers play an important role in bridging the gap between international policy and providing children with enough knowledge (tools) so that they can understand what their rights as humans are.

The two resources discussed from Quennerstedt and Huser show how educators can appropriately connect the work being done in classrooms to larger international frameworks that provide legal authority upon the lives of children. In doing so, educators equip students with tools to critically identify, engage and act upon their own lives in ways that are protected by international standards and discourse. Doing this creates opportunities to spread knowledge in hopes that when such needs are not being met, others can step in and advocate for those without access to needed resources. This ground-level work is so essential to these educational movements and will continue to support longitudinal developments in various educational spheres (Tibbitts, 2017)

It is complex work, and the field continues to grapple with what needs to be done to address challenges around implementation (Quennerstedt, 2019). What remains clear from these research projects compared to the ones highlighted from the United States. context is that these educational moments connect to a more international notion of rights and living in a global community compared to one that is singular in the Unites States context.

This review does not seek to favor examples from either context but attempts to illuminate the educational work being done and generate questions around similarities and differences. Something of note to consider in these two regional contexts is that the United States has a complicated history regarding international bodies and their regulations such as the UDHR or UNCRC. Even though the United States

Early Years Critical Literacies and Rights

was involved in their creation and continue to be a key player in enforcement, they remain one of three countries in the world who have not ratified the UNCRC (Human Rights Watch, 2014).

Bringing this back to classroom practices and the examples presented throughout these pieces of literature there appears to be clear differences in the way critical literacy scholars in the United States discuss rights with those in Northern Europe or Australia. While there certainly needs to be more work to investigate if this idea holds true, it is worth surfacing in an effort to think critically upon and ask why this might be? Early years educators that seek to incorporate rights discourses into their teaching practices need to be aware of the complex realities of how this work manifests in different contexts. While many of the principal ideas remain similar, there are real challenges in moving from one geographic location to the next. Yet, this idea is core to thinking about how this work interacts in a global sphere. Future research needs to better understand the challenges in moving this educational work across the globe.

Needed in the United States

The final element important to highlight from the review of this literature is not something necessarily shared, but something urgently missing. This applies specifically to the United States context and was inspired by what was emerging particularly within the research based in Australia (Exley et al., 2014). Looking at what is missing, showed a major lapse in work within United States contexts that connect critical literacies to democratic elements such as voting rights. While there is work that looks at the way citizens participate and act within a democracy (Krechevsky et al., 2014; Montgomery et al., 2017) there was little that compared with the in-depth exploration offered by Exley and colleagues (2014).

These authors were able to demonstrate how classrooms can transform into spaces that prioritize democratic processes to support curriculum decisions and insights (Exley et al., 2014). The students in this classroom generate discussion around voting and how this process supports stories being read in class. The educators in this context show how these are essential aspects in maintaining harmony within the educational space (2014). The authors were then able to connect this organic idea to wider frameworks of how to support such models of critical literacy.

It is not that this work does not happen in other classrooms and research, but the authors of this article found a way to bring them together in a coherent and clear manner while demonstrating how crucial they were to the specific location. These educational scenarios could have easily played out in many early years classrooms around the world, but we must ask why this is not more common in the United States given its recent discourse around voting. Or if it is being done, why do these efforts not connect to larger frameworks that fight for the protection of all individuals' access to such fundamental processes.

The past few years in the United States have exacerbated the need for introducing ideas around voting at the earliest years of education. They have also shown that this work needs to move forward carefully in order to not put young children at the forefront of political games. Examples of work such as that presented by Exley et al. showcase how these educational practices can be done in a thoughtful, authentic, and compassionate manner. So many in the United States fear losing control of their children's education and what better way to demonstrate educators' confidence in future generations by providing them the tools to interact in democratic life at the most basic levels. This work does not need to be riddled with doubt, instead educators can approach such moments step-by-step while empowering all those who want to be a part of a better tomorrow.

DISCUSSION

At this point, this review has highlighted some of the work that has been done around critical literacies and rights discourses within early years education in relation to geography. Framing these works through this geographical lens allows for engagement with similarities and differences while keeping context in mind. A visual metaphor is helpful in providing another perspective from which educators and researchers can build. An image of a world map with each of the discussed examples detailing critical literacy practices and their connecting to rights discourses highlighted provides a good foundation. In thinking through this visual representation, the intersection of critical literacies and rights discourses within early years education will be able to illuminate where such engagements have made impacts and where future efforts might be most needed.

This visual representation acknowledges the simplification of the educational practices that takes place within each learning context. This metaphor does not serve as a singular way to think about critical literacy practices and their connection to rights discourses. However, it does provide another way to think about putting this knowledge into practice and how geography, history and politics play into their developments in a more digestible manner to some. The visual is another way to contextualize this work for future learners and practitioners.

The bodies of work reproduced in this review share a great deal in common and work towards similar goals, yet what has become evident is that there are differences based on the contexts the work takes place in. To create more robust frameworks for this line-of-inquiry, exploration needs to be done alongside an investigation of what works where and why. This is not in an attempt to copy exact models into other contexts, but to provide a roadmap to continually build upon.

The literature reviewed has shown that issues of race, identity and freedom can be explored within early years education and that engaging in these investigations is especially crucial to U.S. education systems if not all. When this work then connects to larger international frameworks around legal protections of human rights, there is much to be gained. Doing so requires high levels of quality teacher training and an understanding that educators need not transmit expert knowledge, but rather play the role of brokers in bridging the divides between classroom practices and legal protections (Mentha et al., 2015). Connecting to larger frameworks, be it the UDHR or UNCRC, is essential in not only continuing this educational practice, but to also show how this work relates to global protections on what it means to be human. If these efforts are introduced at the earliest years of education, there is hope that as students continue through various education systems, they will not only retain these foundational skills but continue to act upon them and defend efforts that attempt to dismantle them.

ACKNOWLEDGMENT

This research received no specific grant from any funding agency in the public, commercial, or not-for-profit sectors.

REFERENCES

Bajaj, M., Canlas, M., & Argenal, A. (2017). Between rights and realities: Human rights education for immigrant and refugee youth in an urban public high school: Human rights education for newcomer youth. *Anthropology & Education Quarterly, 48*(2), 124–140. doi:10.1111/aeq.12189

Bentley, D., & Souto-Manning, M. (2019). *Pre-k stories: Playing with authorship and integrating curriculum in early childhood.* Teachers College Press.

Botelho, M., Kerekes, J., Jang, E., & Peterson, Sh. (2014). Assessing multiliteracies: Mismatches and opportunities. *Language and Literature, 16*(1), 1–20.

Braun, V., & Clarke, V. (2006). Using thematic analysis in psychology. *Qualitative Research in Psychology, 3*(2), 77–101. doi:10.1191/1478088706qp063oa

Comber, B. (2011). Critical literacy in the early years: Emergence and sustenance in an age of accountability. In J. Larson & J. Marsh (Eds.), Handbook of research in early childhood literacy. Academic Press.

Comber, B., Thomson, P., & Wells, M. (2001). Critical literacy finds a "place": Writing and social action in a low-income Australian grade 2/3 classroom. *The Elementary School Journal, 101*(4), 451–464. doi:10.1086/499681

Crafton, L., Brennan, M., & Silvers, P. (2007). Critical inquiry and multiliteracies in a first-grade classroom. *Language Arts, 84*(6), 510–518.

Dyson, A. H. (2013). *Rewriting the basics: Literacy learning in children's cultures.* Teachers College Press.

Dyson, A. H. (2020). "We're Playing Sisters, on Paper!": Children composing on graphic playgrounds. *Literacy, 54*(2), 3–12. doi:10.1111/lit.12214

Exley, B., Woods, A., & Dooley, K. (2014) Thinking critically in the land of princesses and giants: The affordances and challenges of critical approaches in the early years. In J. Z. Pandya & J. Ávila (Eds.) Moving critical literacies forward: A new look at praxis across contexts (pp. 59-70). Routledge.

Human Rights Watch. (2014). *25th Anniversary of the Convention on the Rights of the Child.* Humanrightswatch.org.

Huser, C. (2019). 'I want to share this video with you today.' Children's participation rights in childhood research. *Human Rights Education Review., 2*(2), 45–63. doi:10.7577/hrer.3322

Janks, H. (2013). Critical literacy in teaching and research. *Education Inquiry, 4*(2), 225–242. doi:10.3402/edui.v4i2.22071

Jesson, J., Matheson, L., & Lacey, F. M. (2011). Doing your literature review: Traditional and systematic techniques. *Sage (Atlanta, Ga.).*

Krechevsky, M., Mardell, B., & Romans, A. N. (2014). Engaging city hall: Children as citizens. *New Educator, 10*(1), 10–20. doi:10.1080/1547688X.2014.868212

Kuby, C. (2011). Humpty Dumpty and Rosa Parks: Making space for critical dialogue with 5- and 6-year-olds. *YC Young Children, 66*(5), 36–40, 42–43.

Kuby, C. R. (2013). 'OK this is hard': Doing emotions in social justice dialogue. *Education, Citizenship and Social Justice*, *8*(1), 29–42. doi:10.1177/1746197912448714

Kuby, C. R., & Rucker, T. G. (2020). (Re)Thinking children as fully (in)human and literacies as otherwise through (re)etymologizing intervene and inequality. *Journal of Early Childhood Literacy*, *20*(1), 13–43. doi:10.1177/1468798420904774

Mentha, S., Church, A., & Page, J. (2015). Teachers as brokers: Perceptions of 'participation' and agency in early childhood education and care. *International Journal of Children's Rights*, *23*(3), 622–637. doi:10.1163/15718182-02303011

Montgomery, S. E., Miller, W., Foss, P., Tallakson, D. & Howard, M. (2017). *Banners for books: "Mighty-hearted" kindergartners take action through arts-based service learning*. Academic Press.

Petersen, M. J. (2021). *Human rights education what works?* The Danish Institute for Human Rights. https://www.humanrights.dk/publications/human-rights-education-what-works

Quennerstedt, A. (2019). Teaching about and through children's human rights in early school years. In A. Quennerstedt (Ed.), Teaching children's human rights in early childhood education and school: Educational aims, content and processes (pp. 56-73). Utgivare: Örebro University.

Silvers, P., Shorey, M., & Crafton, L. (2010). Critical literacy in a primary multiliteracies classroom: The Hurricane Group. *Journal of Early Childhood Literacy*, *10*(4), 379–409. doi:10.1177/1468798410382354

The United Nations. (1948). *Universal Declaration of Human Rights*. Author.

The United Nations. (1989). Convention on the Rights of the Child. *Treaty Series*, *1577*, 3.

Tibbitts, F. (2017). Evolution of human rights education models. In M. Bajaj (Ed.), *Human rights education: Theory, research, praxis* (pp. 69–95). University of Pennsylvania Press. doi:10.9783/9780812293890-005

Vasquez, V. M. (2004). *Negotiating critical literacies with young children*. L. Erlbaum Associates. doi:10.4324/9781410611109

Vasquez, V. M., & Felderman, C. B. (2012). *Technology and critical literacy in early childhood*. ProQuest Ebook Central. doi:10.4324/9780203108185

Vasquez, V. M., Janks, H., & Comber, B. (2019). Critical Literacy as a Way of Being and Doing. *Language Arts*, *96*(5), 13.

Wargo, J. (2019). Sounding the garden, voicing a problem: Mobilizing critical literacy through personal digital inquiry with young children. *Language Arts*, *96*(5), 275–285.

Williams, H. M. A., & Bermeo, M. J. (2020). *A Decolonial Imperative: Pluriversal Rights Education*. Academic Press.

Wisneski, D. (2019). Playing well with others: Collaborating on children's right to play. *Childhood Education*, *95*(6), 50–55. doi:10.1080/00094056.2019.1689060

Chapter 5
Teachers Taking the Lead to Help Children Cope With Stress Through the Use of Language and Cognitive Pedagogical Units

Carmen Adriana Medrano
https://orcid.org/0000-0003-0912-3851
Florida International University, USA

ABSTRACT

This chapter will discuss how teachers use and further develop strategies to help children expand their cognitive abilities, improve oral language, and express their emotions. The work presented was done with young English language learners children ages 2 to 3, within a family childcare home (FCCH) setting in Miami Dade County. During the initial stages of the COVID-19 pandemic, teachers from family childcare homes noticed children with stress created by the many difficult situations their families were going through. The author developed a pedagogical unit based on the storybook called Wimberly Worries written by Kevin Henkes. This pedagogical unit used the teaching for understanding framework and visible thinking routines. It is the author's goal to present this work to inspire teachers in the creation of similar pedagogical units.

INTRODUCTION

Early childhood educators have the precious responsibility of working with young children. While many of their daily tasks include caregiving, each one of these educators carries a responsibility to provide an environment where children flourish and grow, developing to their full potential. Each interaction offers the opportunity to shape children's futures. Yet when queried about what they do all day, teachers and caregivers create a list that includes feeding, caring, playing, singing, cleaning, wiping noses, picking up toys, planning, and teaching—often with little thought about how these small, meaningful interactions are shaping children's futures. Taking these individual activities, one by one, it is sometimes forgotten

DOI: 10.4018/978-1-6684-5022-2.ch005

that these individual interactions, when compiled on a day-to-day basis, lead to an understanding of how these children feel and how to guide them in expressing their feelings. This has become even more important in today's society where children are bombarded by technology, videos, music, news, politics, and other factors that affect them in both positive and negative ways.

In addition, during the past two years, we have been faced with the introduction of a new virus that has affected the entire world. The COVID-19 pandemic has been described as a "unique multidimensional and potentially toxic stress factor for mental health," which has had a particularly strong influence on children and adolescents due to its interruption of social contacts, which are of eminent importance for psychosocial development (Brakemeier et al., 2020).

The work presented in this chapter illustrates how teachers supported children in the classroom during the pandemic, using strategies that reinforced their socio-emotional, language, and cognitive development.

THEORETICAL FRAMEWORK

Between 2010 and 2020, the Hispanic/Latino population in the United States experienced explosive growth, increasing from 1.6 million in 2010 to 1.9 million in 2020 (Census Bureau, 2020). This growth in diverse populations has provided both increased opportunities as well as new challenges for the education system, tasked with the need to provide educational opportunities to young children who come to the classroom speaking little or no English and may be considered disadvantaged when compared to their English-speaking peers. To address this challenge, teachers are faced with finding new and innovative methods to meet the needs of these diverse populations of children. The educational barriers experienced by children who are non-English speaking and who also have not been exposed to literacy activities within their families in their home language present both a challenge and an opportunity to the educators providing for them in current-day classrooms.

The importance of language as a foundation for children's school success has been well-documented for later academic success, as well as later success in life. Vocabulary, conversational skills, and children's ability to think critically are required skills for later learning. Research in language learning also documents the use of children's native language as an important tool in helping children learn a new language and strengthening their acquisition of vocabulary, conversational skills, and other important skills in a new language.

According to work from Cummins and colleagues (2001), the use of children's native language strengthens children's abilities in their second language acquisition. Research conducted in Miami Dade County on Head Start children (Lopez & Greenfield, 2004) demonstrated that when young children learn a second language using their first language as a base, it helps them understand the important components of language development such as syntax, vocabulary, semantics, pragmatics, and phonological awareness in their second language.

The study discussed in this chapter provides a qualitative look at a program that makes use of current research and new practices to create a lesson plan for a group of Hispanic children with Spanish as a first language and English as a second language at a family childcare home. A large percentage of the children enrolled in family childcare homes located in Miami, Florida speak English as a second language and Spanish as their first and home language. Teachers were encouraged to speak children's native language (Spanish) while facilitating new vocabulary, scaffolding conversations, and encouraging children to think critically. Language plays an important role in the acquisition of vocabulary.

Teachers Taking the Lead

In this study, quality children's literature in Spanish was used as a venue to prompt children's thinking. According to Hillegass (2005), children need to be exposed to a variety of books that they can connect with and that contribute to class discussions and projects. Leland and colleagues (2018) reiterated that literature is very appropriate for linguistically and culturally diverse students because children can hear what other children are thinking and English Language Learners (ELLs) benefit from being included in these types of conversations.

While sharing literature with children, the dialogic reading approach was used as a strategy to help children develop language skills. Dialogic reading is an interactive activity conducted with narrative and expository texts. It includes questions and dialogues throughout the conversation that promote children's literacy and language skills. It also helps teachers develop meaningful conversations and encourage the children to actively participate in the story by prompting open-ended questions and inviting children to respond to these questions and explain their thinking. It also supports children's reflection and thinking about the story, which develops comprehension skills and oral language.

Another research-based strategy called Text Talk was also implemented in this study. This is a strategy studied by Beck and McKeown (2007). In their study about the acquisition of vocabulary, they argued that challenging content can be introduced using pictures from storybooks and constructing meaning from linguistic content. "This approach is designed to enhance young children's ability to construct meaning from decontextualized language, promoting comprehension and children's language development" (p.13). In their research, they encouraged children to learn sophisticated words from story books and use them as a source of explicit vocabulary activities. The teacher read the story text, and when a new word was encountered, explained it within the context of the story. Finally, the teacher asked the children to use that word within their familiar context.

This study also implemented thinking routines to facilitate the development of thinking skills. These routines operate as tools to promote thinking (Ritchhart, 2002). In her action research, Salmon (2010) encouraged teachers to engage in the use of thinking routines. Salmon's findings indicated that thinking routines helped children make thinking visible and facilitated teachers in the process of becoming more reflective about different venues to invite children's inquiries about the world.

All these strategies previously presented were used in the Peek-a-Book Language and Literacy program and were put together within a lesson plan based on the Teaching for Understanding framework. This framework is based on placing understanding first. Children learn to develop thoughtful tasks such as generalizing, explaining, comparing, classifying, and applying (Blythe,1998). According to Ritchhart (2015), "Understanding goes beyond merely possessing a set of skills or a collection of facts in isolation; rather, understanding requires that our knowledge be woven together in a way that connects one idea to another" (p. 47). The use of the Teaching for Understanding framework allows teachers to promote understanding.

The storybook "Wemberly Worries" (English version) or "Prudencia se Preocupa" (Spanish version) (Henkes, 2010), was chosen to create this pedagogical unit. Wemberly Worries is a story about a little mouse called Wemberly who worries about everything. It is a warm and comforting story that helps children cope with big worries and little worries. This story was chosen because its theme invites children to identify and connect Wemberly's daily worries like spilling juice, the first day of school, and finding new friends, with their worries and problems.

The pedagogical unit was created following the same outline as proposed by Blythe (1998). The components of the Teaching for the Understanding framework are:

- Throughlines: Refers to the concepts that the teacher wants her students to understand after the course
- Generative topics: Refers to themes that are interesting for children and connect to their previous experiences
- Understanding goals: Based on the generative topics proposed, the researcher creates understanding goals. These goals, also called throughlines, identify the concepts, processes, and skills that teachers want children to understand.
- Performances of understanding: These are the activities that give children the opportunity to apply their prior knowledge in a variety of situations. It requires that the student goes beyond the information presented to demonstrate an understanding of the topic. These performances of understanding are intended to help children think more deeply about the topic proposed.
- Ongoing assessment: As stated by Blythe (1998), "Ongoing assessment occurs in the context of the performance of understanding, which, in turn, are anchors to understanding goals" (p. 80).

METHODOLOGY

Research Design

The author used a qualitative design for the extension of the research study. This design consisted of collecting and analyzing qualitative data to understand the problem and generate new ideas. A local Family Child Care Home that implemented the Teaching for Understanding framework to plan lessons. The director was the owner and teacher at the Family Child Care Home. This is an early childhood education center that provides childcare and education to young children (birth to 5 years old).

Settings

The COVID-19 pandemic has caused millions of deaths around the world as well as lasting health problems in some who have survived the illness (Hopkins 2022). The years 2020 and 2021 have been particularly stressful for young children due to the many changes created by the COVID-19 pandemic. They may experience feelings of fear, anger, sadness, worrisome, numbness, or frustration. On February 3, 2020, the U.S. declared a public health emergency due to the coronavirus outbreak, and on March 13, 2020, the US government declared COVID-19 a national emergency, and a stay-at-home mandate was issued.

All these sudden changes had a direct impact on young children's socio-emotional state, bringing along a sense of fear, anxiety, and stress. Many factors played a role in this sense of insecurity, such as the global lockdown, families working from home, parents losing their jobs, social distancing, schools being closed, having online classes, and many other changes that directly impacted the lives of our children. For young children and adolescents, the pandemic and lockdown had a greater impact on emotional and social development compared to adults.

In a preliminary study during the ongoing pandemic, it was found that younger children (3-6 years old) were more likely to manifest symptoms of clinginess and the fear of family members being infected than older children (6-18 years old), although psychological conditions of increased irritability, inattention, and clinging behavior were observed in all children irrespective of their age groups (Viner, 2020). Based on a questionnaire completed by the parents, findings revealed that children felt uncertain, fearful, and isolated. It was also shown that children experienced disturbed sleep, nightmares, poor appetite, agitation, inattention, and separation-related anxiety (Jiao, et al, 2020). Furthermore, due to prolonged confinement at home, children's increased use of the internet and social media predisposed them to use the internet compulsively, access objectionable content, and also increased their vulnerability to getting bullied or abused (Cooper, 2020; UNICEF, 2020).

The Center on the Developing Child (2022), provided various ways to support children during the COVID-19 outbreak. Their main suggestions referred to providing quality interactions with children through the Serve and Return technique, which meant creating a back-and-forth interaction, so children could feel that the adult is responding to their needs for attention through listening and responding in a back-and-forth conversation. This study also suggested maintaining social connections to keep them actively involved with others. Other research recommended children be physically protected, in a safe, loving emotional environment, and actively doing creative and joyful activities (Bartlett Griffin,& Thomson, 2020).

Neuroscience research suggests that having young children under the same caregiver during their first years of life helps with the formation of secure attachments between the child and the caregiver (National Center on Child Care Professional Development Systems and Workforce Initiatives, 2019). Advances in neuroscience also indicate that the earliest years are critical for brain development, as these early experiences are crucial in the formation of stronger and more secure attachments to adult caregivers (Sorrels, 2017). Children with secure attachments are more likely to get along with other children, respond and interact positively with adults, and accept comfort from others when they are hurt or upset. These children have greater confidence in their abilities, and they can cope with changes and challenges. Family childcare homes are the perfect scenario for children to create these secure attachments. The fact that they have small groups and mixed ages allows them to respond quickly and warmly to the child's distress and basic needs with the appropriate degree of nurturing.

Research Participants

The participants in this study were 12 children of a family childcare home, the teacher, and the director. In this chapter, the author presents the interaction between the teacher and four children. Participants were Spanish-speaking with a balanced composition of boys and girls. The teachers were females, with an age range between 40-64 years old, and of Latin American background.

Research Problem

The effects that the COVID-19 pandemic has had on children's academic and socio-emotional states, particularly at the beginning stages, have been significant. When children experience stress, it is reflected in their inability to communicate their distress with words. Frequently, they communicate it through behaviors that are difficult to understand and redirect. These children may have a significant delay in language because of the stress they are experiencing and may demonstrate aggression or withdrawal as a way of coping with their feelings. This study aims to improve children's thinking skills, oral language, and socio-emotional development, which have been impacted by the COVID-19 pandemic. This addresses how the creation of pedagogical units may impact the oral language, thinking, and socio-emotional development of children aged 2-4 years

Observations

The researcher used an observational method to gather data. The observations were made through two videos made by the teacher in the classroom setting (Link to videos on the reference page). Thematic analysis was used to analyze data collected from the video documentation, such as concept maps and charts created by the teacher with the help of the children. These data were further connected to the children's performances of understanding in the Teaching for Understanding lesson plan.

Textual Analysis

The performances of understanding of the Teaching for Understanding lesson plan described below were used to analyze children's changes in their cognition, thinking, and socio-emotional state.

The Teaching for Understanding lesson plan from the Peek-a-Book Program described below (See Table 1), presents the contents of the lesson plan using the Teaching for Understanding format.

Table 1a. The teaching for understanding lesson plan from the Peek-a-Book program

Throughlines	Generative Topic
Things that worry me How do I feel when I am worried? Big and small things that worry me Things that my friends suggest I can do when I feel worried Things I can do when I feel worried	The way I feel
Understanding Goals	**Understanding Goals**
Children will understand the difference between big worries and small worries. Questions What are things that worry you the most? What are some small things that you worry about? What are some big things that you worry about?	Children will understand different options and perspectives to resolve a problem. Questions How can we help our friend solve her problem? What things would you do if you were in your friend's situation?

Teachers Taking the Lead

Table 1b. The teaching for understanding lesson plan from the Peek-a-Book program

	Performances of Understanding	Types of Performances of Understanding	Ongoing Assessment
1	The children will think of all the things that worry them. The children will brainstorm many things that worry them. The children will explore their major worries and explain why these worries worry them.	Exploration	Informal: The teacher will ask open ended questions about their fears. Criteria: Answers are connected to their own experiences. Answers are connected to the questions. Answers are in complete sentences. Documentation: The teacher will write down children's responses in a concept map format.
2	The children will explore other children's perspectives about their fears. The children will listen and compare their way of thinking with the way other children think about the same situation. The children will understand that there are many ways of looking at similar circumstances. The children will classify worries into big worries and small worries.	Guided Investigation	Informal: Through open-ended questions, the teacher will explore with children various options for the questions. Criteria: Answers are connected to the questions asked. Answers provide options for the situations given. Answers are in complete sentences. Documentation: The teacher will write children's big and small worries on a board. The children will make connections between all children's answers.
3	The children will share with their families what they discussed in this unit about feelings. They will describe their pictures. Children will explain to their parents the meaning of their pictures.	Final Project	Formal: The teacher will invite the parents to a special presentation of the projects about the way the children feel Criteria: Expressive vocabulary, explanation of ideas, concept connections. Relief of stress and anxiety Documentation: The children will draw pictures illustrating the ways they felt

Performance of Understanding #1

For this performance of understanding, the teacher used a routine called "Connect, Extend, and Challenge." This routine helps students connect new ideas to those they are already familiar with. It encourages children to reflect on what they know and extends their thinking as a result of what they are learning or experiencing (Ritchhart et al., 2011). Using the dialogic reading in which the teacher prompts a question to invite the children to start a conversation, the teacher shared with the children the storybook "Prudencia se Preocupa." She asked the children about their worries, what they do when they are worried, and how these worries make them feel.

Thinking Words:

Thinking words were linked from the Performance for Understanding 1 of the Teaching for Understanding lesson plan, to the children's responses and the teacher documentation as follows:

Think – brainstormed – explained – classified:

- The teacher encouraged the children to think of all the things that worry them
- Using a concept map, the children brainstormed many things that worry them
- The teacher wrote down what the children said about the things that worry them.
- Children explored their major worries and explained why these worries worried them
- The children classified these worries into big worries and small worries. The teacher documented these worries on a chart.

The following is a transcript of the conversation between the teacher (T) and the children during the activity:

T: Today we will do a brainstorming session on things that you worry about. What do you worry about?
Child #2: The chu chu train sound
T: The sound of the train? Okay, we will write here: The loud sound of the train. What do you do when you feel worried? How do you feel?
Child #2: Fear
T: You get afraid. What do you worry about?
Child #3: Being left all by myself, and a car hits me
T: How do you feel when you are left alone? What do you think?
Child #3: That a robber will come and get me.
T: Yes! That is very worrisome.
T: Child #4, what do you worry about?
Child #4: I worry about thunder.
T: Why?
Child #4: Because it sounds so loud! Sometimes, not so loud.
T: Tell me, what do you do when there is a storm?
Child #4: I get afraid.
T: And what do you do?
Child #4: I protect myself at home and I am safe.
T: So, just like Prudencia, we also have many worries.

Figure 1 below, shows the children when they were orally elaborating a concept map. The teacher wrote their responses on the paper as she created a concept map

Teachers Taking the Lead

Figure 1. Picture of children creating a concept map of the things that worried them

Performance of Understanding #2

For this performance of understanding the teacher used the "Circle of Viewpoints Routine," which is a routine used to help children explore perspectives. This routine helps children understand how other children view situations similar to the ones they are experiencing. It helps children listen to new ideas and understand that other people have different ways of looking at the same situation Project Zero's Thinking Routine Toolbox (2020).

Thinking Words:

Thinking words were linked from the Performance for Understanding 2 of the Teaching for Understanding lesson plan, to the children's responses, and the teacher's documentation as follows:

Explored – listened – compared – understood

- The children explored other children's perspectives about their fears.
- The children listened and compared their way of thinking with the way other children think about the same situation.
- The children understood that there are many ways and perspectives of looking at similar circumstances.
- The children expressed their big and small worries

Figure 2 shows the children orally expressing their big worries and small worries.
The teacher documented their responses on a board.

Figure 2. Children's chart about big and small worries

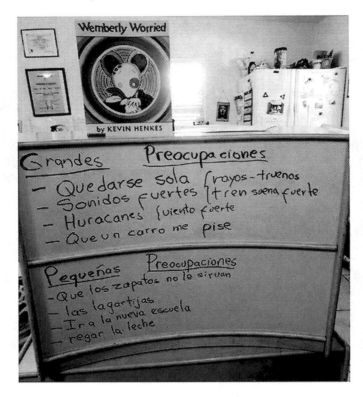

Translation of the big and small worries written on the board:
Big worries:

Staying by myself (Lightning, thunder)

Loud sounds (A train's loud sound)

Hurricanes (Strong winds)

That a car will hit me

Small worries:

That shoes won't fit me

Lizards

Go to a new school

Spilling milk

Teachers Taking the Lead

The following is a dialogue between the teacher (T) and the children while discussing the fear of thunder that one of the children had:

T: Today, we are going to talk about the different perspectives or ideas we have about the same situation. We will use the "Circle of Viewpoints Routine." Today, we will explore what [Name of Child #1] worries about which is: thunder. I have a question: How can we help her solve her problem of worrying about thunder? Who has an idea?

Child #1: Clouds sometimes collide, and thunder appears! And sometimes you don't have to be afraid, just go home so that they take care [of you], go into your house.

T: Aha! That is a good idea, to be at home. So, we're going to write it here: Be at home, stay at home. That is a good idea. What other idea do you have? What idea do you have for your friend?

Child #3: To hug your mom, and right there you are not afraid anymore.

T: Ok, so I am going to write here: Hug your mom, so that you are not afraid. That idea is great! What other idea do you have?

Child #4: If there is thunder, one day my mom told me: "If there is thunder when the clouds are this way, they collide, and water comes out. Then when water comes out, boys and girls need to go to their homes and hug their moms".

T: I will make a note of that, so boys and girls need to go to their homes and hug their moms.

Child #4: So that we are not afraid.

Child #3: But I already said that!

T: Yes, but she summarized it. Do you have another idea? Do you have an idea to help our friend cope with her fears of thunder?

Child #5: Stay home with your dad and hug him in bed.

Child #1: No. I stay with my mom.

T: Okay with mom and dad. What do you think? With mom and dad lying in bed. Why "lying in bed"?

Child #4: So that we can hug our dad.

T: Oh! To hug mom and dad. So, love and hugs help us to not be afraid, right? Very good!

Child 4: Or we can do a family hug!

T: Oh! I love that idea. I will write, in summary, that a family hug helps us to feel safe and not be worried.

Child #2: And with the doggy!

T: And with the doggy! Thank you, bye.

Performance of Understanding 3

For this performance of understanding the children worked on their final project of the pedagogical unit and shared their pictures with their families.

Thinking Words:

Thinking words were linked from the Performance for Understanding 3 of the Teaching for Understanding lesson plan to the children's responses and the children's documentation as follows:

Share – describe – explain

- The children shared what they discussed in this unit about feelings with their families.
- The children described their pictures to their families

Figure 3 and 4 show the children explaining to their families the meaning of their pictures

Figure 3. A girl sharing her picture with the family.

Figure 4. Another girl sharing her picture with the family

DISCUSSION

In the children's dialogue, it was evident that all children orally explored various ideas, based on their background knowledge about the topic. During the teacher-children interaction, the teacher accepted all answers as valid answers and wrote them on a concept map and on a board. She repeated the children's statements and wrote them. These facilitated children's understanding that their thinking could be made visible through writing. It also stimulated children to talk as it empowered them to continue brainstorming new ideas and making contributions to the conversation.

The teacher prompted the children to think about different situations and invited them to elicit their ideas to the group:

Child # 5: Stay home with your dad and hug him in bed
Child #1: No. I stay with my mom.
Child 4: Or we can do a family hug!

T: I will make a note of that, so boys and girls need to go to their homes and hug them moms.
Child # 4: So that we are not afraid.

The conversation continued, and the teacher repeated the statement to the child: "So that we are not afraid". At that moment, another child replies: "But I already said that." This is evidence that the children are carefully listening to everyone's responses and are eagerly giving different perspectives to a given situation.

Child #4 continued the conversation by saying: "Stay home with your dad and hug him in bed." To which child #1 responded: "No. I stay with my mom." In this short dialogue, children were comparing their behaviors in case of a hurricane. One child would stay with his mom, while the other with her dad. The teacher continued by saying:

T: Oh! To hug mom and dad. So, love and hugs help us to not be afraid, right? Very good!
To which child #4 replies: Or we can do a family hug!

The children continued brainstorming, elaborating, and expressing new ideas and points of view:
The teacher responded to child # 4:

T: Oh! I love that idea. I will write, in summary, that the family hug helps us to feel safe and not be worried.
Child #4 responded: And with the doggy!
T: And with the doggy! Thank you, bye"

FINDINGS

The conversations between the teacher and the children led to a comparison of the thinking skills that children manifested with the performances of understanding described in the Teaching for Understanding lesson plan. In the conversation, it is evident that the teacher asked questions that prompted students to think about possible answers to her questions, express their feelings, and find the right words to express their ideas.

Developing Thinking Skills

In Performance for Understanding #1, on various occasions the teacher asked children to brainstorm other worries they had, inviting them to deepen their thinking into other issues that may worry them. The teacher wrote their responses on a concept map. This allowed the students to see their thinking in writing, making their thinking visible. Each thought was placed inside a circle that identified every child's thinking. They were also encouraged to think about their thinking when the teacher asked the child to explain her thinking by asking: "What do you worry about?". She responded: "I worry about thunder", and the teacher followed up with another thinking question: "Why?". The child responded with a justification for her response: "Because they sound so loud! Sometimes, not so loud".

Finally, the children are invited to classify their worries into big worries and small worries. The teacher wrote their responses on the board to make their thinking visible. After the children had a brainstorming conversation, they also talked about other small worries. They brainstormed new ideas such as: "I am also worried about shoes not fitting me, I am afraid of lizards, of spilling milk, and going to a new school." This dialogue illustrates the many instances in which the teacher developed thinking skills with children using tools such as the thinking routine "Connect, Extend, and Challenge", in which the children connected their ideas with other ideas they already knew and extended their thinking in new directions.

The dialogue encouraged by the teacher also helped children think in different ways. She used the thinking routine "Circle of Viewpoints". This routine is used to help children explore perspectives.

T: How can we help her solve her problem of worrying about thunder? Who has an idea?
Child #1: Clouds sometimes collide, and thunder appears! And sometimes you don't have to be afraid, just go home so that they take care [of you], go into your house.
T: Aha! That is a good idea, to be at home. So, we're going to write it here: Be at home, stay at home. That is a good idea. What other idea do you have?
T: What idea do you have for your friend?
Child #3: To hug your mom, and right there you are not afraid anymore.
T: Ok, so I am going to write here: Hug your mom, so that you are not afraid. That idea is great! What other idea do you have?
Child #4: If there is thunder, one day my mom told me: 'If there is thunder when the clouds are this way, they collide, and water comes out. Then when water comes out, boys and girls need to go to their homes and hug their moms".

In this dialogue with the children, it is evident that they continue to explore new ideas elaborating on their thinking, bringing new words to the conversation, and sharing ideas they have heard from home.

Developing Socio-emotional Development

The teacher also asked open-ended questions to help children relieve some of their stress or worries, such as when she asked, "What do you do when you feel worried? How do you feel?" This helped children identify and name their emotions, which is an important component of socio-emotional development. The teacher was persistent with questions to help children talk about their emotions. For example, on another occasion, she asked: "How do you feel when you are left alone? What do you think?" These types of questions supported children's emotional state by allowing them to verbalize their feelings. The teacher also helped children find possible solutions to their fears. The teacher asked: "And what do you do?" The child replies: "I protect myself at home and I am safe". With this dialogue, the teacher is empowering the child to make proactive decisions, and to solve problems effectively.

Developing Oral Language Skills

In all conversations, the teacher was supporting the children's language development. She encouraged children to talk openly using complete sentences. The use of open-ended questions facilitated an extensive conversation about a topic of their interest. They were all invited to orally participate in the conversa-

Teachers Taking the Lead

tion providing their views and thoughts. It is important to note that these conversations were done in the children's first language. The use of home language made a special connection between children, their families, and their school. They were able to demonstrate their oral language capabilities and also felt appreciated and valued. The teacher built upon children's language, facilitating a conversation where all components of language were encouraged. While maintaining and building upon their home language skills and culture, children were able to organize and develop proficiency in English

IMPLICATIONS

The inclusion of oral language curricula in early childhood programs is needed. Teachers should focus on helping children develop receptive and expressive language in their native language (Spanish), to help them build their literacy foundation in the second language (English). Also, the implementation of strategies that help children develop thinking abilities, and perspective-taking skills are needed for future success. These types of programs also promote the development of socio-emotional skills and mental health.

Implications for Teachers

Teachers should recognize and value children's first language and expose them to literature in their native language. They should use quality storybooks to support the acquisition of oral language, thinking and socio-emotional skills, and most importantly the love and joy of reading. If the teacher does not speak the child's language, she should make all efforts to provide visible signs of the home language throughout the learning environment, through books and other relevant material in the child's first language (NAEYC, 1995).

Teachers must have access to professional development in which they learn to develop lesson plans that meet the needs of children and help them gain a deep understanding of the world around them. Pedagogical units should stress the importance of building on their oral language and thinking skills, and support children in their emotional and critical thinking development.

Implications for Parents

Parents should be encouraged to read to their children frequently and ask them meaningful questions about the story. Parents should also be encouraged to participate in programs where they learn to share storybooks with children daily. They should recognize that reading to their children in their native language is very beneficial to the acquisition of early literacy skills in their language and the new language. As a recommendation of the National Association for the Education of Young Children (1995), " Parents and families should be actively involved in the learning and development of their children. Teachers should actively seek parental involvement and pursue establishing a partnership with children and families" (p. 4)

Implications for Stakeholders

Stakeholders should recognize the change in demographics in Miami-Dade County and offer more opportunities to the community by providing access to programs that help children learn the language seamlessly. They should also offer language and literacy programs in early childhood settings that enhance the acquisition of oral language development. Stakeholders should provide professional development and coaching that assists teachers in the implementation of lessons that help children expand their knowledge, think critically about a topic, search for different solutions to a situation, and go beyond rote memorization. These lessons require thinking and should be based on children's needs. Finally, as argued by the National Association for the Education of Young Children (2019), it is important to increase financial support for early learning services, ensuring that resources are available for all children.

RECOMMENDATIONS

This chapter illustrates the need in our communities to offer children innovative and research-based strategies for learning. The findings show that children who are exposed to language and literacy opportunities in their native language made significant improvements in their receptive and expressive language. The implementation of intentional teaching strategies that support children in the use of specific thinking strategies, such as thinking routines, is important as they develop thoughtful conversations with their teachers and peers. Children as young as 2-3 years old who were exposed to quality literature gained new vocabulary that they were able to use in other contexts. By using children's literature that focuses on children's daily needs, including the needs of linguistically and culturally diverse children, teachers recognized and valued children's heritage and most importantly, utilized developmentally appropriate practices in their diverse classrooms. As stated by The National Association for the Education of Young Children Position Statement (2019), "All children have the right to equitable learning opportunities that help them achieve their full potential as engaged learners and valued members of society".

CONCLUSION

The work presented in this chapter highlights the importance of providing children with opportunities to develop skills they will need to succeed in a constantly changing world with diverse and new opportunities. The teacher's role should continue to move away from that of transmitting knowledge, to becoming a facilitator and mentor for children as they construct their knowledge based on their own experiences. Today, more than ever before, teachers are faced with children who come to the classrooms with stress produced by the many challenges that society, their families, and life in a new and changing world present. Within this context, early childhood programs should consider changing their teaching approach, and developing formats and lesson plans that are connected to the reality in which children live. Facilitating interactions in which children's thinking is recognized and valued, as well as paying close attention to non-academic needs, will continue to challenge educators who are charged with providing strong, social-emotional foundations for the children they serve. A curriculum that addresses all areas of development and that effectively responds to the 21st-century population presents new and continuing concerns for

Teachers Taking the Lead

those who must meet the needs of children to thrive and survive in an ever-changing world. To this task, educators must work to develop additional and innovative programs to prepare young children for coping with the challenges they will face in their future endeavors.

REFERENCES

Barlette, J. D., Griffin, J., & Thomson, D. (2020). *Resources for supporting children's emotional well-being during the COVID-19 pandemic*. Retrieved from https://www.childtrends.org/publications/resources-for-supporting-childrens-emotional-wellbeing-during-the-covid-19-pandemic

Beck, I. L., & McKeown, M. G. (2001, September). Text Talk: Capturing the benefits of read aloud experiences for young children. *The Reading Teacher*, *1*(55).

Beck, I. L., & McKeown, M. G. (2007). Increasing young low-income children's oral vocabulary repertoires through rich and focus instruction. *The Elementary School Journal*, *107*(3), 251–271. doi:10.1086/511706

Blythe, T. (1998). *The teaching for understanding guide*. Jossey Bass.

Brakermeier, E. L., Wirkner, J., Knaevelsrud, C., Wurns, S., Christiansen, H., & Lueken. (2020). Die Covid-19- Pandemie ais Herausdorderunf fur die pshyschische Gesundheit. Z. *Kiln. Psychol. Psychother. 49*(1).

Bzoch, R. K., League, R., & Brown, L. V. (2003). *Reel 3 receptive-expressive emergent languages test. Examiner's Manual*. Pro-Ed.

Bzoch, R. K., League, R., & Brown, L. V. (2003). *Reel-3 receptive-expressive emergent languages test*. Pro-Ed.

CDC Data and statistics on children's mental health. (2019). CDC. https://www.ncbi.nlm.nih.gov/pmc/articles/PMC7444649/#bib0006

Cooper, K. (2020). *Don't let children be the hidden victims of COVID-19 pandemic*. UNICEF. https://www.unicef.org/press-releases/dont-let-children-be-hidden-victims-covid-19-pandemic.

Cummins, J. (2001). *Bilingual children's mother tongue: Why is it important for education.* http://iteachilearn.org/cummins/mother.htm

Duncan, S. E., & Ávila, E. A. (2000). *PreLAS 2000 Assessment Kit*. CTM Mc Graw Hill.

Dunn, M. L., Padilla, R. L., Lugo, E. D., & Dunn, M. L. (1986). *TVIP: Test de Vocabulario en Imagenes Peabody. Adaptación Hispanoamericana*. Pearson.

Espinosa, M. (2015). *Getting it right: For children from diverse backgrounds*. Pearson Education.

Harvard Graduate School of Education. (2020). *Project Zero's Thinking Routines Toolbox*. http://www.pz.harvard.edu/thinking-routines

Harvard on The Developing Child. (n.d.). *How to support children (and yourself) during COVID-19 outbreaks.* https://developingchild.harvard.edu/resources/how-to-support-children-and-yourself-during-the-covid-19-outbreak/

Henkes, K. (2010). Prudencia se preocupa. Harper Collins Publishers.

Hillegass, M. M. (2005). Early childhood studies. In S. Frost & F. Sibberson (Eds.), School Talk (Vol. 10, pp. 1–3). Academic Press.

Jiao, W. Y., Wang, L. N., Liu, J., Fang, S. F., Jiao, F. Y., Pettoello-Mantovani, M., & Somekh, E. (2020, June). Behavioral and Emotional Disorders in Children during the COVID-19 Epidemic. *The Journal of Pediatrics, 221,* 264–266.e1. doi:10.1016/j.jpeds.2020.03.013 PMID:32248989

Johns Hopkins Medicine. (n.d.). *What is Coronavirus?* https://www.hopkinsmedicine.org/health/conditions-and-diseases/coronavirus

JUST. (2019). *Aligned Professional Development Systems Planning and Implementation Guide.* JUST.

Krechevsky, M., Mardell, B., & Wilson, D. (2013). *Visible learners: Promoting Reggio inspired approaches in all schools.* John Wiley and Sons Inc.

Leland, H. C., Lewison, M., & Harste, J. C. (2018). Teaching children's literature. Academic Press.

Lopez, L. M., & Greenfield, D. B. (2004). The cross-language transfer of phonological skills of Hispanic Head Start children. Early Childhood Science Education Research Trends in Learning and Teaching. *Bilingual Research Journal, 28.*

Medrano, C. A. (2015). *The effects of implementing a Spanish language program for young children of Hispanic Background* [Doctoral dissertation]. Nova Southeastern University.

National Association for the Education of Young Children. (1995). *Responding to Cultural diversity. Recommendations for effective early childhood education. A position statement of the National Association of Young Children.* Author.

National Association for the Education of Young Children. (2019). *A position statement of the National Association for the Education of Young Children: Advancing equity in early childhood education.* Author.

Peek-a-Book Language and Literacy Program. (2021a). *Prudencia se preocupa Círculos de puntos de vista.* https://youtu.be/AKnQwiZYKpE

Peek-a-Book Language and Literacy Program. (2021b). *Prudencia se preocupa: Generar, clasificar, conectar, elaborar mapas conceptuales.* https://youtu.be/_5lrvL9SOZ0

Perkins, D. (2009). *Making learning whole: How seven principles of teaching can transform education.* Jossey Bass.

Ritchhart, R. (2015). *Creating cultures of thinking: the 8 forces we must master to truly transform our schools.* Jossey Bass.

Rithchhart, R. (2019). *Intellectual character: What it is, why it matters and how to get it*. Jossey Bass.

Rithchhart, R., Church, M., & Morrison, K. (2011). *Making Thinking Visible*. Jossey Bass.

Salmon, A. K. (2010). *Tools to enhance young children's thinking*. Young Children's. NAEYC.

Sorrels, B. (2017). *Reaching and teaching children exposed to trauma*. Gryphon House Inc.

UNICEF. (2020). *UNews*. https://news.un.org/en/tags/unicef

US Census Bureau. (2020). Retrieved in July 2022. https://usafacts.org/data/topics/people-society/population-and-demographics/our-changing-population/state/florida/county/miami-dade-county?endDate=2020-01-01&startDate=2010-01-01

Viner, R. M., Russell, S. J., Croker, H., Packer, J., Ward, J., Stansfield, C., Mytton, O., Bonell, C., & Booy, R. (2020). School closure and management practices during coronavirus outbreaks including COVID-19: A rapid systematic review. *The Lancet. Child & Adolescent Health*, *4*(5), 397–404. doi:10.1016/S2352-4642(20)30095-X PMID:32272089

Vygotsky, L. S. (1978). *Mind in society: The development of higher psychological processes*. Harvard University Press.

Whitehurst, G. J., & Lonigan, C. J. (1998). Child development and emergent literacy. *Child Development*, *68*(3), 848–872. doi:10.1111/j.1467-8624.1998.tb06247.x PMID:9680688

KEY TERMS AND DEFINITIONS

Attachment: Attachment is the strong emotional bond that is present between the caregiver and the child over time (Sorrels, 2017).

Children's Literature: Refers to the selected high-quality children's books used to inspire children to love reading.

Dialogic Reading: This is an interactive technique in which the teacher actively interacts with the child as they both talk about the story. The teacher asks questions related to the story and repeats and expands based on the child's responses using open-ended questions (Whitehurst & Lonigan 1998).

Documentation: This is the practice of learners observing, recording, interpreting, and sharing the products of learning to deepen and extend learning (Krechevsky et al., 2013).

Dual Language Learners: Young children whose first language is not English, including those learning English for the first time in the preschool setting as well as children who have developed various levels of English proficiency.

Early Literacy: Refers to the skills and abilities learned by children before entering school.

Generative Topics: Refers to the concepts or ideas that are interesting for children and connect to their previous experiences.

Ongoing Assessment: Ongoing assessment occurs in the context of performances of understanding, which in turn are anchors to understanding goals.

Oral Language Development: The ability to express feelings and needs through words.

Overreaching Understanding Goals/Throughlines: The overreaching understanding goals or throughlines identify the concepts, processes, and skills that teachers want the students to understand.

Performances for Understanding: These are tasks that help children build and demonstrate their understanding.

Receptive Language: This term refers to the vocabulary that children acquire through interaction with people in the environment (Bzoch et al., 2003).

Visible Thinking: This term refers to a research-based program that encourages children to think critically and to make their thinking visible to other people (Ritchhart, 2011).

Visible Thinking Routines: These are tools for promoting thinking (Ritchhart, Church & Morrison, 2011).

Chapter 6
Encouraging Critical Literacy:
Justice and Equity With Children's Literature

Joyce C. Fine
https://orcid.org/0000-0002-1042-1461
Florida International University, USA

ABSTRACT

In this chapter, the author explains the difference between teaching critical thinking and critical literacy with children's literature. She suggests ways teachers may select current children's literature that touches upon social justice and equity instead of just reading aloud old favorites that do not stimulate students' thinking about their world. She shares the steps for analyzing student diversity in classrooms and creating classroom libraries that match students' backgrounds and interests. Also, she describes a practical way teachers may prepare to conduct critical literacy discussions using a Classroom Literacy Folio. The folio includes summaries, personal connections, possible ways diversity may be included in selected books, and lesson ideas for how to introduce students to current issues so even young children can think critically. Included is a sample format, a completed Classroom Literacy Folio page, and suggestions for some of the latest children's literacy books that emphasize social justice and equity.

INTRODUCTION

According to Cervetti et al. (2001), there is a difference between critical thinking and critical literacy. An example of teaching critical thinking with children's literature is when teachers ask students to analyze the plot in a fairy tale. They might ask students to identify the point of view of the narrator, if the characters are round or flat, or if the illustrations add to the quality. Critical literacy focuses on sociopolitical issues expressed in all forms of literacy in its broadest definition including movies, videos, advertisements, and books. It involves engaging students to understand power and inequities in the world (Labadie et al., 2012) and act on what they analyze (Behrman, 2006). If teachers are teaching critical literacy, they might ask students to think about the assumptions of power, social justice, and equity and

DOI: 10.4018/978-1-6684-5022-2.ch006

become agents of social change (Coffey,2010). As Miller and Sharp (2018) say, "If we want students to grow up believing in, and fighting for, equity for all, then it starts with the stories we read together."

BACKGROUND

Many teachers are aware of the potential of children's literature to expand children's horizons. Bishop (1990) suggested children's literature has the potential to mirror the world and open windows to appreciate the world of others, as well as sliding doors to experience the lives of others. In the increasingly shrinking world, this suggests a guiding principle for teachers. Yet, research (Lickteig & Russell, 1993) has shown that most teachers read aloud their old favorites, classics such as *Charlotte's Web*. Even though these are captivating books that deserve to be shared, they do not include issues some more current national and international books present which are conducive to critical literacy discussions. There are newer publications that bring a global perspective to students. Short (2018) has suggested ways for teachers to broaden the worldview of adolescents. While she recognizes the importance of including the classics in literature, she encourages teachers to pair classics with young adult global literature that reflects more current contexts with more relevance to the students' lives. Elementary school teachers can also create text sets for younger students to compare conditions around the world or from different time periods. The teachers in Comber & Simpson's (2001) edited book also explains how they have brought critical literacy into their reading instruction with socially disadvantaged students. Vasquez (2004) explains how expanding the curriculum to include global issues can still meet the mandated curricular competencies. Short (2018) advocates changing the curriculum, if possible, by replacing some of the required readings with global literature to facilitate students' world perspectives so differences are positive, not problematic. Moll (2017) advocates that teachers introduce transculturality, the concept of using one's language and funds of knowledge (Gonzalez et al., 2016) from their own culture to achieve one's goals. Students will become inspired by stories from diverse cultures, realizing how ingenious others can be.

From a Sociocultural perspective, newer books have the potential to stimulate critical literacy and may create a more welcoming classroom for diverse student populations who may be newcomers to our communities. This chapter suggests activities for teachers to prepare for meaningful critical discussions using examples of recently published children's books.

Why should teachers bring critical literacy discussions to the classroom? According to the Freedom to Teach statement by four professional teacher organizations

teachers are uniquely important leaders who, in educating current and new generations of students, bear responsibility for this country's future. They are trained professionals with one of the hardest and most demanding jobs, a job that requires deep commitment, but brings little financial reward (Strauss, 2022)

Yet, "in the recent culture wars, they are being treated as enemies" (Strauss, 2022) according to the statement, which is the first time these groups have joined together to demand the freedom to do their jobs. They feel they are being attacked if they bring in issues related to race, gender, sexual orientation, or other topics. The teachers want to "exercise their professional judgment to decide which materials best suit their students in meeting the curriculum" (Strauss, 2022).

MAIN FOCUS OF THE CHAPTER

The Freedom to Teach statement raises questions about what teachers should be doing to include critical literacy with discussions about equity and social justice. They should have a well-developed classroom library, be able to identify books that include elements of diversity, and be able to prepare lessons to facilitate classroom discussions on these topics. This chapter addresses ways to accomplish this goal based on research the author has employed in graduate classes with master's candidates. Children's literature books on the topic are suggested for different ages. Furthermore, rules for conducting discussions are shared along with suggestions for ways teachers may prepare for the discussions.

SOLUTIONS AND RECOMMENDATIONS

Creating a classroom library is a critical component of a quality teaching space. It is where teachers house literature that speaks to their students' lives, identities, and worlds. It is the means for students to learn how to deal with the personal, social, and political aspects of their lives. Creating a classroom library helps teachers screen books, match their students' interests in the curriculum, and keep books appropriate to students' developmental levels. Finding that information requires some qualitative inquiry by teachers. Once teachers become familiar with their students, they can begin to build customized libraries for their students.

What are the topics that stimulate discussion about social justice and equity in the classroom? Topics should relate to the curriculum. There is concern about what is included in the curriculum. Some recent laws, such as one in Florida (HB1557), have placed limits on what can be brought into the curriculum related to sexual orientation or gender identity in kindergarten through grade 3 or in a manner that is not age-appropriate (communications@eog.myflorida.com). In the upper grades, gender identity and sexual orientation are the topics that adolescents face in their lives (Ivey, 2014) and motivate them to read and participate in discussions. Adolescents read books that help them understand their own identities (Ivey & Broaddus, 2001). They like to read to vicariously live through experiences and consider the moral consequences of these actions (Ivey & Johnston, 2013). Adolescents read texts that help them think through situations in their own lives (Ivey & Broaddus, 2001; Moje et al., 2008). Many other topics are appropriate for both elementary and secondary classrooms that encourage students to discuss issues of equity and justice and that can impact students' social and emotional development (Ivey & Johnston, 2013).

How can teachers prepare lessons that will encourage critical literacy discussions? One of the most important steps is to know your student population. Teachers can meet students and their families to learn about their cultures. Posing questions on interest inventories also provides information for teachers to determine what students want to learn. Teachers can then make a diversity chart of their students. This would consist of a list of students, their names, their first language, the level of their English language proficiency, the language spoken at home, the student's cultural background, and the student's instructional reading level. Table 1 is an example of the diversity chart about classroom students.

Table 1. Diversity chart about classroom students

Child's Name (*First Name Only*)	Child's First Language	Child's Level of English Language Proficiency	Language(s) Spoken in the Home	Child's Cultural Background	Child's Instructional Reading Level
Student 1					
Student 2					
Student 3, etc.					

Next, teachers should survey their classroom library. They might list the categories of books, the number of each type of book they have, whether the books match the diverse backgrounds of their students, and how the books are displayed in the room. It is best to have the fronts of some of the books facing the children rather than only the spines, to invite students to read these books. The books should also be at eye-level for students to easily access them. The categories of books to aim to incorporate might include ones on different ethnicities, religions, nationalities, social classes, gender issues, exceptionalities, and ages, and books that are below grade level, on grade level, and above grade level. Other books might be the ones that are digital or online books that are accessible to students via available classroom technology.

By conducting this environmental literacy survey, teachers will be able to analyze if they have books that match students' cultural and linguistic backgrounds and interests. According to Francois (2013), this builds relationships between teachers and students and humanizes reading instruction. If they do not have any books in some of the categories, they can identify where they need to add them to their classroom library collections.

After considering the students and the classroom literacy environment, teachers might prepare a Children's Literature Folio (CLF) with a page for each book in their classroom. Creating questions will help the teacher prepare to teach using the CLF. Each page can be put in a binder or kept online for quick reference. The questions include (a) bibliographic information such as the title, author, illustrator, publisher, date of publication, type of book (picture, novel, chapter), and the number of pages; (b) the genre and format; (c) characteristics that put the book in the category; (d) the teacher's summary and theme; (e) the personal response of the teacher such as a Text-Self, Text-Text, or Text-World connection; (f) whether the book has a specific diversity connection, and, if so, how it addresses student diversity and equity, and how to create and advocate for an inclusive classroom by designing a discussion that is culturally responsive to this book; (g) what accommodations or modifications could be made to meet the diverse needs of the students considering their background knowledge, reading level, and the text complexity; and (h) how to instruct the students using an instructional approach or strategy to analyze the genre or format. These teaching points will allow the teacher to create thoughtful critical literacy discussions on topics of social justice and diversity. Table 2 is an example of a blank Children's Literature Folio page.

Encouraging Critical Literacy

Table 2. Children's literature folio page

Children's Literature Folio Page	
A. Bibliographic Information	
Author(s):	Title:
Publisher: Year:	X Picture Book ☐ Novel ☐ Chapter Book
Illustrator(s):	Number of Pages:
B. Genre/Format	
C. Identify three (3) characteristics that put this book in the genre/format	
1.	
2.	
3.	
D. Your summary of the book Theme:	
E. Personal response to the book (T-T, T-S, T-W)	
F. Does this book have a specific diversity focus? If yes, how does it address student diversity and equity? How would you create and advocate for an inclusive classroom by designing a discussion that is culturally responsive to this book?	
G. What <u>accommodations or modifications</u> would you make to meet the diverse needs of your students considering their background knowledge, reading level, and the text complexity?	
H. How would you teach your students using an instructional approach or strategy to analyze that <u>genre or format</u>?	

What are the characteristics used for evaluating and selecting books with diverse perspectives? Based on a chapter in *Children's Books in Children's Hands* (Temple, et al., 2019) there are aspects of books that set them apart as exemplary. The first is whether the author and illustrator present authentic perspectives. This means that the author and illustrator should present insider voices. Another is if the culture is presented multi-dimensionally. Characters should not be presented as stereotypes from cultures. Others are that the details are accurate, and the language is authentic.

What are some examples of current books that have topics that allow for discussions of diversity and equity? One favorite is *Esperanza Rising* by Pam Munoz Ryan. This book shares the experiences of a young Mexican girl whose well-to-do family endures hardships resulting in her immigration to California and becoming a farmworker. A book that addresses a question that children of mixed heritage are often asked is *Where Are You From?* by Yamile Saied Méndez. Other children may find themselves in *Not So Different* by Cyana Riley about being biracial and finding ways they are different and ways they are the same, but unique individuals. *We're Different, We're the Same*, a Sesame Street book by Bobby Kates addresses looking different on the outside but having feelings and needs the same on the inside. *Everyone Counts* by Judy Sierra discusses the inclusion of all. Feeling different is the topic of Jacqueline Woodson's *The Day You Begin* which is about walking into a room and seeing no one who looks like you. She also wrote *The Year We Learned to Fly* which is a tribute to Black History. Other books that focus on Black History or cultural pride are *Child of the Civil Rights Movement* by Paula Young Shelton, *I Am Enough* by Grace Byers, *All Because You Matter* by Tami Charles, *Happy in Our Skin* by Fran Manuskin or *The ABCs of Black History* by Rio Cortez.

Conversations may begin with young children. There are current books that address diversity and social justice for preschool and primary-aged children. The list has grown considerably in the last few years. This includes *All Different and Beautiful: A Children's Book about Diversity, Kindness, and Friendship* by Belle Belrose (2020), *I know the Secret of Diversity* by Aleks Harrison (2022), *No Body is the Same: A Book about Body Positivity* by Dr. Joh Layke and Donald Benedict (2022), *What If We Were All the Same: A Children's Book About Ethnic Diversity and Inclusion* by C. M. Harris (2021), *Preschool Book About Race: Every Shade of Smile: Kids Book About Race, Diversity, and Inclusion for Baby, Toddlers, and Preschooler* by Nicole M. Gray (2022). More books include *What If?: What Makes You Different Makes You Amazing!* By Sandra Magsamen (2019), *Celebrate Our Differences: A Dragon's Story About Different Abilities, Special Needs, and Inclusion* by Steven Herman (2021), *Family Means...* by Mathew Ralph, *The Big Umbrella* by Amy June Bates and Juniper Bates (2018), *The World Needs More Purple People* by Kisten Belle and Benjamin Hart (2020), *All People Are Beautiful* by Vincent Kelly and Cha Consul (2021), *You Are Enough: A Book About Inclusion* by Margaret O'Hair (2021), It's Ok to be Different: A Children's Picture Book About Diversity and Kindness by Sharon Purtill and Sujata Saha (2019), *We're Different, We're the Same* by Bobbi Kater and Joe Mathieu (1992), *What Makes a Family* by Hannah Bruner and Sandie Sonke (2021), *Our Diversity Makes Us Stronger: Social Emotional Book for Kids about Diversity and Kindness* by Elizabeth Cole and Julia Kamenshikova (2021), *Our Skin: A First Conversation About Race* by Megan Madison, Jessica Ralli and Isabel Roxas. These books allow even early childhood teachers to discuss equity and social justice, a topic new to the curriculum for this age.

A Native American book, *Indian No More* by Charlene Willing Mcmanis and Traci Sorell, is appropriate for students from 9-12 years old. This book is contemporary realistic fiction about a family that moves off the reservation, the prejudice they face, as well as their feelings of loss. Another book by Traci Sorell that is positive for younger children is *We Are Grateful: Otsalihega* about the Cherokee community gatherings to celebrate the changing of the seasons. It has the Cherokee syllabary, created by Sequoyah in the back. By the same author, *We Are Still Here! Native American Truths Everybody Should Know* is a brief history of how the United States has treated Native Americans. A popular book from the Native American perspective, winner of the 2021 Caldecott medal, is *We Are Water Protectors* by Carole Lindstrom. It encourages safeguarding the Earth's waters.

Three popular books about Asian cultural pride are *I Am Golden* by Eva Chen, *Eyes that Kiss in the Corners* by Joanna Ho, and *The Name Jar* by Yangsook Choi. Another book that teaches pride in one's culture, in this case, the Muslim religion, is *The Proudest Blue* by Ibtihaj Muhammad, about a young girl whose sister wear's her hijab to school for the first time. Two classic books about the Jewish religion are *Number the Stars* by Lois Lowry and *The Keeping Quilt* by Patricia Polacco. These books "open windows" to cultures. There are important books that provide sliding doors into the lives of people with disabilities. Patricia Polacco has written about her difficulties learning to read in *Thank You, Mr. Falker*, and *Junkyard Wonders*. Other popular books are *Wonder* by R. J. Palacio, *Fish in a Tree* by Lynda Mullaly Hunt, *All My Stripes* by Shaina Rudolph, and *Just Ask!: Be Different, Be Brave, Be You* by Sonia Sotomayer and Rafael López. These books raise understanding and acceptance for special needs students. Table 3 is an example of a completed Children's Literature Folio page.

Table 3. Sample children's literature folio page

Children's Literature Folio Page	
A. Bibliographic Information	
Author(s): Anna Kim	Title: Danbi Leads the School Parade
Publisher: Viking (Penguin Young Readers Group) Year: 2020	☐Picture Book ☐Novel ☐Chapter Book
Illustrator(s): Anna Kim	Number of Pages: 40
B. Genre/Format –	
Books with Diverse Perspectives	
C. Identify three (3) characteristics that put this book in the genre/format	
1. Language is used authentically, with Danbi writing her name using Korean characters on the classroom board.	
2. The author presents an authentic perspective, focusing on telling a story similar to her own experiences when she first started school in the U.S. as a young Korean girl who did not yet understand English.	
3. The details are accurate: Danbi's name is written correctly in the illustration showing her name in Korean characters.	
D. Your summary of the book Theme: community, friendship, and immigration	
Danbi is navigating her first day of school in the U.S., without understanding English. Her new friendship with her classmate Nelly helps her start to feel at home by the end of the book.	
E. Personal response to the book (T-T, T-S, T-W)	
(T-W) Especially in Miami, we often work with students who are new to the U.S. and/or new to the English language. (T-S) Several of my students have written about their experiences learning English and navigating starting school without knowing English.	
F. Does this book have a specific diversity focus? If yes, how does it address student diversity and equity? How would you create and advocate for an inclusive classroom by designing a discussion that is culturally responsive to this book?	
Yes, this book encourages students to be welcoming to new students and learn about their classmates and their cultures, which is a valuable attitude to have in an inclusive classroom.	
G. What accommodations or modifications would you make to meet the diverse needs of your students considering their background knowledge, reading level, and the text complexity?	
A discussion of the context for the story (Danbi being new to the U.S.) could be useful for students.	
H. How would you teach your students using an instructional approach or strategy to analyze that genre or format?	
I would ask students to write about their first time in an unfamiliar environment (school or otherwise), create a classroom map of the students' family backgrounds, and introduce an onomatopoeia lesson connected to the text.	

Source: Jennifer Peña, a Master of Science student at Florida International University

When teachers prepare CLF pages for these books, they have lesson plans that have thoughtful questions ready for discussions that give students a chance to learn more than good stories; the students have opportunities to learn to be accepting of the diversity in the world and work towards equity for all where people can thrive together.

However, sometimes there are situations that cause challenging moments in the classroom. There are suggestions for handling different situations. A book that gives insight into handling these is *Navigating Difficult Moment in Teaching Diversity and Social Justice* edited by Mary E. Kite, Kim A. Case, and Wendy R. Williams (2021). Although the book is geared for college classrooms, one of the excellent suggestions in the book for conducting culturally relevant discussions is to provide ground rules for the discussion. Susan B. Goldstein discusses these in Chapter 2, "Ground Rules for Discussing Diversity:

Complex Considerations." These ground rules may be applied to elementary and secondary classrooms. These might be developed with a class or could be shared as they are with an explanation of what each means. These suggestions are 1) Assume good intentions which means that questions may stem from a desire to understand a situation. 2) Allow people to make mistakes. Sometimes when one does not fully understand the situation or the science behind a situation, they may say something that is incorrect. 3) That brings us to the third rule which is to avoid personal attacks. A participant may criticize a comment, but not the student. The next rule 4) is to allow multiple perspectives. People come from diverse cultural backgrounds and bring those ideas to the classroom. Everyone does not have to agree with them, they only need to respect them. The 5th rule is to be respectful. There should only be one person speaking at one time and there should be no interruptions. The 6th rule is to use terms that do not offend. There are terms that are not appropriate for the classroom that need to be off-limit. The 7th is to be aware of non-verbal reactions such as rolling one's eyes or crossing one's arms to be defensive. The 8th is to acknowledge that different backgrounds and life experiences impact our views on issues. Sometimes when there is one person in the group who seems to represent a particular group, the 9th rule is to refrain from expecting that person to speak or represent everyone from that group. The 10th rule is to maintain the confidentiality of what is shared in the classroom. The saying that what happens in Vegas, stays in Vegas can be applied to the discussions in a classroom. That might be difficult to enforce, but it will help to create the 11th rule to create an environment in which people are willing to voice their opinions.

Once you have established discussion rules, and begin a discussion, we may find that students' comments are unexpected, and our own responses may not be what we want. What to do in these circumstances may be a matter of personal challenge. Sometimes, it might be best to allow another student to respond. That gives the teacher a moment to regroup. Then, the teacher might explain that the comment might have caused some pain to others, making them physically or psychologically uncomfortable. This might include the teacher as well as the students. This type of challenge should not suggest that we do not include discussions of equity and social justice. Instead, it suggests that we might participate in "anticipatory teaching" in which the teacher does extra preparation, focusing on word choice, for example, because what is said may be examined very closely. This type of teaching was described by Perry et al. (2009) regarding teachers of color whose authority may be questioned when discussing equity and social justice. I think that any teacher should work on anticipating questions and possible barriers when bringing these topics to the classroom.

Recently, the Florida Legislature brought up the issue of teachers trying to influence students' thinking on diverse topics. While teachers are trying to discuss equity and social justice, to help classrooms become more inclusive, the legislature realized that teachers have the power to influence students disproportionally. To minimize the power, a university's Faculty Senate where I work proposed that professors put a statement in their syllabi about the fact that professors are presenting information that is not meant to intimidate or influence students. The statement is the following:

"No lesson is intended to espouse, promote, advance, inculcate, or compel a particular feeling, perception, viewpoint, or belief."

FUTURE RESEARCH DIRECTIONS

Emerging trends in children's literature, in many different genres and formats, are to address diversity by including concepts related to social justice and equity. Teachers should keep abreast of the new books by subscribing to different publishers' websites and booksellers online. Researching the effects quality discussion has on students' interest and reading achievement would be a step for future inquiry. Are the students reading more books and better-quality books because of their reading relevant books and participating in quality discussions? Family literacy studies might be broadened by sharing books to read at home. What then would be the effect on parents? What would be their reaction? Would they feel more included or would there be pushback on some of the concepts?

DISCUSSION

The above literature selections make excellent contributions to classrooms for students at various stages of maturity and ability. Teachers should always consider those factors as well as several other considerations, not only about the students but also about the context and intersectionality of who the teacher is. The context includes descriptions of the community and the school where the school is located. Is it one in which there is diversity? Are there people of different ethnicities, religious beliefs, gender identities, and cultural backgrounds present? If so, a sensitivity to their experiences adds to the richness of the exchanges. Intersectionality is about the identity and group membership of the teacher because this can affect the success of the pedagogy. Are there points of congruency between the community and the teacher? As Ruddell and Unrau (2013) describe in their chapter, "Reading as a Motivated Meaning-Construction Process: The Reader, the Text, and the Teacher," all three aspects are crucial. The reader has prior beliefs and knowledge, involving affective conditions such as motivation to learn, attitude toward reading and the content, sociocultural values, and beliefs. The text, as suggested above, brings ideas of equity and social justice. The only way to nurture these ideas is for there to be a classroom that has a safe and secure learning environment as created and encouraged by the teacher. The teacher's own identity, motivation to engage the students, understanding of students' meaning-making processes, knowledge of strategies for teaching reading, and the teachers' personal and world knowledge all contribute to the ability to successfully present and lead discussions that will allow students to grow with complex ideas. When all these conditions come together, critical literacy can occur.

Many years ago, teachers had very didactic materials about morals for teaching reading, emphasizing how children should behave. As the concept of childhood evolved and the field of Children's Literature progressed, the texts became more entertaining and visually appealing. Perhaps, educators could be focused on cultivating students' behaviors again but with high-quality literature exposing them to ideas of equity and social justice.

CONCLUSION

Students at various stages of social development are more interested in books that have diverse perspectives and are relevant to what they are seeing in their world. They may participate in reading discussions that affect how they understand their lives and the lives of others when teachers encourage critical literacy related to social justice and equity with children's literature.

ACKNOWLEDGMENT

This research received no specific grant from any funding agency.

Thank you to Jennifer Peña, a master's student at Florida International University, for sharing a copy of one of her Children's Literature Folio pages.

REFERENCES

Behrman, E. H. (2006). Teaching about language, power, and text: A review of classroom practices that support critical literacy. *Journal of Adolescent & Adult Literacy*, *49*(6), 490–498. doi:10.1598/JAAL.49.6.4

Bishop, R. S. (1990). Walk tall in the world: African American literature for today's children. *The Journal of Negro Education*, *59*(4), 556. Advance online publication. doi:10.2307/2295312

Cervetti, G., Pardales, M. J., & Damico, J. S. (2001). A tale of differences: Comparing the traditions, perspectives, and educational goals of critical reading and political literacy. *Reading Online*, *4*(49). wwwreadingonline.org/articles/art_index.asp?HREF=/articles/cervetti/index.html

Coffey, H. (2010). *Critical literacy*. LEARN NC: University of North Carolina at Chapel Hill School of Education. Retrieved from www.learnc.org/lp/pages/4437

Comber, B., & Simpson, A. (Eds.). (2001). *Negotiating critical literacies in classrooms*. Erlbaum. doi:10.4324/9781410600288

Francois, C. (2013). Reading is about relating: Urban youths give voice to the possibility for school literacy. *Journal of Adolescent & Adult Literacy*, *57*(2), 141–149. doi:10.1002/JAAL.218

Goldstein, S. B. (2021). Ground rules for discussing diversity: Complex considerations. In M. E. Kite, K. A. Case, & W. R. Williams (Eds.), *Negotiating difficult moments in teaching diversity and social justice* (pp. 17–29). American Psychological Association. doi:10.1037/0000216-002

Gonzalez, N., Moll, L. C., & Amanti, C. (Eds.). (2005). *Funds of knowledge: Theorizing practices in households, communities, and classrooms*. Erlbaum.

Ivey, G. (2014). The social side of engaged reading for young adolescents. *The Reading Teacher*, *68*(3), 165–171. doi:10.1002/trtr.1268

Ivey, G., & Broaddus, K. (2001). "Just plain reading": A survey of what makes students want to read in middle school classrooms. *Reading Research Quarterly*, *36*(4), 36350–36377. doi:10.1598/RRQ.36.4.2

Ivey, G., & Johnston, P. H. (2013). Engagement with young adult literature: Outcomes and practices. *Journal of Literacy Research*, *47*, 297–327. doi:10.1177/1086296X15619731

Kite, M. A., Case, K. A., & Williams, W. R. (Eds.). (2021). *Navigating difficult moments in teaching diversity and social justice*. American Psychological Association. doi:10.1037/0000216-000

Labadie, M., Mosley Wetzel, M., & Rogers, R. (2012). Opening spaces for critical literacy: Introducing books to young readers. *The Reading Teacher*, *66*(2), 117–127. doi:10.1002/TRTR.01097

Lickteig, M. J., & Russell, J. F. (1993). Elementary teachers' read-aloud practices. *Reading Improvement*, *30*(4), 202–208.

Miller, D., & Sharp, C. (2018). *Game changer! Book access for all kids*. Scholastic.

Moje, E. B., Overby, M., Tysvaer, N., & Morris, K. (2008). The complex world of adolescent literacy: Myths, motivations, and mysteries. *Harvard Educational Review*, *78*(1), 107–154. doi:10.17763/haer.78.1.54468j6204x24157 PMID:19756223

Perry, G., Moore, H., Edwards, C., Acosta, K., & Frey, C. (2009). Maintaining credibility and authority as an instructor of color in diversity-education classrooms: A Qualitative inquiry. *The Journal of Higher Education*, *80*(1), 80–105. doi:10.1080/00221546.2009.11772131

Ruddell, R. B., & Unrau, N. J. (2013). Reading as a motivated meaning-construction process: The reader, the text, and the teacher. In D. A. Alvermann, N. J. Unrau, & R. B. Ruddell (Eds.), *Theoretical models and processes of reading* (6th ed., pp. 1015–1068). International Reading Association.

Short, K. G. (2018). Globalizing literature in the English Language Arts classroom. *English Journal*, *108*(2), 108–110.

Strauss, V. (2022, March 22). Teachers to cult warriors: Stop treating us as enemies. *The Washington Post*. https://www.washingtonpost.com/education/2022/03/22/teachers-demand-freedom-to-teach/?fbclid=IwAR1MfM78LuuDeARr3nZ-yPYDDzRotPYgwn84kP9DeMOz7O2ekmQDXJUfCdc

Temple, C., Martinez, M., & Yokota, J. (2019). *Children's books in children's hands: An introduction to their literature*. Pearson.

Vasquez, V. M. (2004). *Negotiating critical literacy with young children*. Erlbaum. doi:10.4324/9781410611109

ADDITIONAL READING

Miller, D., & Sharp, C. (2018). *Game changer!: Book access for all kids*. Scholastic.

Teaching for Change. (2022). http://socialjusticebooks.org

KEY TERMS AND DEFINITIONS

Analysis of Students' Cultural and Linguistic Background: Reflect on the match if students can find themselves in a book in the classroom.

Children's Literature Folio: A collection of individual plans, one for each literature book in a teacher's classroom, with guidelines for teaching with the books.

Classroom Diversity Chart: A chart on which the teacher lists students' ethnicity, first language, language spoken in the home, reading proficiency.

Classroom Library: Classroom selection of children's literature.

Classroom Library Survey: A means for evaluating the diversity in one's library.

Critical Literacy Discussions: Classroom discussions based on children's literature that allow students to explore current issues.

Cultural Pride: Delight in one's background.

Discussion: Verbal exchanges to deepen understanding.

Freedom to Teach: A statement from 4 literacy organizations requesting the public to respect teachers' ability to select books that address critical literacy topics and discuss them to promote social justice and equity.

Genre: Categories of literary compositions characterized by style and content.

Inclusion of Disabilities: Acceptance of differences.

Section 3
Storytelling and Multiliteracies

Chapter 7
Utilizing Digital Storytelling Tools and Thinking Routines for Cultivating Multiliteracies in Contemporary Classrooms

Tharrenos Bratitsis
https://orcid.org/0000-0003-4257-2755
University of Western Macedonia, Greece

Kiriaki Melliou
https://orcid.org/0000-0002-7297-7852
Greek Ministry of Education and Religious Affairs, Greece

ABSTRACT

Pedagogies that foster inclusion, diversity, and the celebration of difference are central in contemporary classrooms that are characterized by an ethnically diverse population with multiple learning styles and ranging abilities. A powerful and flexible venue for educators to address the complex literacy needs of all students is incorporating multimodalities into teaching that draw upon a variety of modes including visual, linguistic, gestural, oral, and spatial. The chapter offers theoretical foundations about the pedagogy of multiliteracy through digital storytelling and provides specific examples of tools and strategies such as thinking routines and story element creation tools that are framed within the Harvard's Project Zero's dispositional framework and the StoryLogicNet project. Using these frameworks and tools, the authors seek to contribute authentic examples on developing and advancing young students' multiliteracy skills for inside and outside the classroom.

DOI: 10.4018/978-1-6684-5022-2.ch007

Utilizing Digital Storytelling Tools and Thinking Routines

INTRODUCTION

The rapid advancement of Information and Communication Technologies (ICTs) over the past decades has significantly affected everyday life and, at extent, education. Several learning and teaching approaches arise in the literature (Grant & Bolin, 2016) for addressing the needs of children who are nowadays born in a multimodal, media-dominated society, mainly via digital technology. In this society, children begin interacting with such technologies and a huge variety of information from a very young age, even their early infancy. Prensky (2001) introduced the term "digital natives" for children who are born in a digital environment and find it very natural to interact with corresponding technologies, but also with information. On the other hand, he also claimed that despite that interaction the children do not possess digital competencies as an inborn skill.

Furthermore, pedagogies that foster inclusion, diversity and the celebration of difference are central in contemporary classrooms that are characterized by an ethnically diverse population with multiple learning styles and ranging abilities. At the same time the 21st century creates more persistent expectations for higher and wider levels of literacy from all students in order to communicate across differences and make meaningful contributions to their societies. A powerful and flexible venue for educators to address the complex literacy needs of all students is incorporating multimodalities into teaching that draw upon a variety of modes including visual, linguistic, gestural, oral, and spatial.

This chapter reflects upon three pillars which combined can address the aforementioned situation, namely Multiliteracies, Digital Storytelling and Thinking Dispositions. The element of convergence for all three is that of making meaning via multimodal communication channels in order to achieve successful communication, also being able to understand different perspectives of various elements (people, conditions, events, etc.).

The chapter is structured as follows: first a brief introduction is made to the theoretical framework regarding Digital Storytelling and Multiliteracies development. The utilization of the former in order to treat the latter is then discussed, under the scope of an EU funded project. Following, a dispositional view of multiliteracies and stories of migration in Early Childhood Education is discussed, before the concluding discussion.

BACKGROUND

The world is facing unprecedented challenges, and this time has underscored the importance of equiping young students with all of the competences that are needed to communicate successfully with others in culturally diverse classrooms. At the same time the 21st century creates more persistent expectations for higher and wider levels of literacy from all students in order to communicate across differences and make meaningful contributions to their societies. A powerful and flexible venue for educators to address the complex literacy needs of all students is incorporating multimodalities into teaching that draw upon a variety of modes including visual, linguistic, gestural, oral, and spatial.

Multiliteracy, the ability to identify, interpret, create, and communicate meaning across a variety of visual, oral, corporal, musical and alphabetical forms of communication involving an awareness of the social, economic and wider cultural factors that frame communication is strongly connected to multimodality. This interplay between different representational modes and the freedom to use any medium and tool to create meaning provide students with the opportunity to learn in an environment that is more engaging and relevant to their lifeworlds. Multiliteracy aims to make online and traditional classroom teaching more inclusive of cultural, linguistic, communicative, and technological diversity. In addition, the use of and access to a variety of literacies and modes of meaning making broaden the teaching landscape and create opportunities for students to take ownership of their own learning process and develop knowledge and skill sets relevant to the 21st century.

Putting multiliteracy into practice requires open-ended means for sharing and verbalizing thoughts and ideas. As such, the authors of this chapter propose Digital Storytelling. Digital Storytelling (DS) is the combination of traditional, oral narration with multimedia and communication tools combining different types of multimedia material, including images, text, video clips, audio narration and music to tell a short story on a particular topic or theme. Considering that today's students are not only targets of messages but also producers of communications, engaging them in digital storytelling activities can facilitate their participation in meaning-making networks where knowledge is being built up through various modalities and not just through written words. The chapter offers theoretical foundations about the pedagogy of multiliteracy through DS and provides specific examples of tools and strategies such as dispositions, thinking routines and story element creation tools that are framed within the Harvard's Project Zero's research-based conceptual framework and the StoryLogicNet project, an initiative from a group of European organizations - universities, schools and companies, co-funded by the Erasmus+ Programme. Using these frameworks and tools, the authors seek to contribute fresh perspectives on developing and advancing students' multiliteracy skills for inside and outside and classroom, in formal, non-formal and informal education settings, grounding their approach upon Vygotksy's learning theory and his interpretation of meaning-making for learning.

MULTILITERACY

Multiliteracy (The New London Group, 1996; Cope and Kalantzis, 2000) is the ability to identify, interpret, create, and communicate meaning across a variety of visual, oral, corporal, musical and alphabetical forms of communication. As a term, beyond a linguistic notion of literacy it also involves the awareness of the social, economic and wider cultural factors that frame communication itself around these different semiotic channels. Contemporary pedagogy which focuses on multiliteracies is to create the conditions for citizens and prepare them for being capable of facing today's challenges, being able of critical understanding the community context they live in (Cope & Kalantzis, 2006) or of collaborating and negotiating with others who are different to themselves in order to forge a common interest (Cope & Kalantzis, 2015). Specifically, Multiliteracy Pedagogy aims to develop the skills described by the 4Cs framework (Dede, 2010; NEA, 2012; NRC, 2013), namely communication, collaboration, co-creativity and critical thinking. According to this framework, these four skills should be considered in a holistic, interrelated way and not separately, as they are considered as significant for success on both an academic level and everyday life. These skills are increasingly being recognized as highly significant for students, as well as requirements for success in future work and life (Binkley et al., 2012). Overall, Multiliteracy Pedagogy facilitates the development of students' individual and collaborative interests and abilities through the use of new digital media, allowing them to interact and collaborate by engaging in a process of knowledge construction with a broader community of peers, also developing their critical thinking. Students are provided with opportunities to learn in a flexible environment, develop digital literacies and communication competences, as well as abilities to lead and work in teams. Values, attitudes and behaviors are also cultivated, through activities that encourage active participation and engagement in school and community environments (Drew, 2013; Tan & McWilliam, 2009).

Overall, Multiliteracy Pedagogy supports teachers and students as well as parents in negotiating complex and various discourses through multimodal texts constructed in the European contemporary multicultural and multilingual social context. A multiliteracy approach of creative language learning emerges from the cultural, linguistic, and technical experiences that learners bring into the classrooms and aims at the further development of a broad range and new forms of literacies. Students and their families can contribute to their community and to their future via the growing availability of new technologies, communication channels and increased access to cultural and linguistic diversity.

Multiliteracies are related to multimodality for diverse forms of expression making use of the available ICTs, as opposed to the monomodal typical classroom, deprived from the creativity brought by diversity. Multiliteracies offer variability of meaning making in different cultural, social or domain-specific contexts without the language to focus on the national language via utilising multimodal tools. As such, multiliteracies are directly related to citizenship education (e.g. EACEA, 2012; European Commission, 2013).

Consequently, young learners can identify and transfer the identified patterns of cross-cultural meaning exchange within countries. Multiliteracies are also connected to the multimodal ways of meaning exchange and making via written-linguistic modes of meaning interface with oral, visual, audio, gestural, tactile and spatial patterns of meaning.

Multiliteracy is connected to multimodality, the freedom to use any medium and tool to create meaning in the new technologies' world. As such, the oral and textual language format has lost its pivotal importance. Meaning is now shaped with more semiotic means, evident in the multimodal meaning expression using diverse media and tools.

Digital Storytelling

Storytelling has been evident since the appearance of humans. It has been utilized for communication, but also learning. According to McDonald (1998) storytelling was a fundamental way of teaching basic social principles. Egan (1989) highlights its value for teaching/preserving cultural capital, moral values and history, as also Bruner (1991) considers that storytelling preserves the values of a civilization. For McDury & Alterio (2003) stories are a means of conveying information and messages, but also cultivating motivation. Others consider that stories are used to provide meaning to experiences (Schank, 1990; Abrahamson, 1998). Specifically, Schank (1990) in his work of "Tell Me a Story". Narrative and Intelligence» reflects upon Vygotsky's (1978) view of stories as means of connecting with prior knowledge and improving memory differently. It is a fact that neuroscience nowadays highlights meaning as a key function for allowing information to pass from short-term to long-term memory, where, through encoding, it connects to existing neural "circuits" or creates new neural connections. These can be considered as corresponding to what Piaget (1952) referred to as mental models. They are abstract constructs in the human mind which categorize and characterize knowledge in a meaningful, easy to access way. Considering that good stories are easy to remember, as Rex et al. (2002) clearly state, it could be considered that this happens as they correspond to stronger neural connections, which in turn reflect knowledge; it is easier to remember or recall something you already know! Furthermore, Vygotsky (1978) described a process of knowledge externalization which takes place through social interaction, especially when a group of people shares an experience. In this case the existing mental models are triggered in order to provide meaning to the incoming information from that experience which can be expressed through a story during the interaction. Thus, also in this case storytelling provides foundation for learning interactions. The previous statement provides added value to Pedersen's (1995) work on storytelling as a didactic approach, useful or applicable to all subjects and educational levels.

DS is the result of the combination of traditional, oral narration with multimedia resources and communication tools in the contemporary era. Robin & McNeil (2012) describe it is a contemporary art form that combines different semiotic systems in order to create the narration of a short story on a specific subject or concept. Inheriting and further enhancing the educational attributes of traditional storytelling, DS can be utilized for cultivating additional skills and literacy types associated with modern society (Moutafidou & Bratitsis, 2013).

There are many ways for utilizing digital stories for educational purposes. One of them is as educational material when they can be used for presenting new material in a way that attracts students' attention more (Robin, 2008). In this case, mainly the teacher creates the digital story or selects an existing one. Furthermore, Burmark (2004) argues that digital stories make the teaching content more understandable and thus they facilitate the interaction of students with it. Contemporary technologies make it easy for them to express and exchange thoughts, ideas and opinions for and through digital stories, using various online tools and platforms, while sharing them with a wider audience. Not only by interacting through a story but also by creating and sharing one as means of expression, they have the opportunity to improve their writing skills (Gakhar & Tompson, 2007), while they become more engaged, active and productive in individual or collaborative communication activities (Bratitsis, Kotopoulos & Mandila, 2011). Thus, digital stories can also be created by students themselves within teaching interventions. Modern technologies, such as augmented reality and interactive multimedia, allow for digital stories to be utilized in various educational environments following very innovative approaches (Bratitsis & Ziannas, 2015; Bratitsis, Bardanika & Ioannou, 2017). Therefore, DS has a special educational potential even when students are asked to create their own digital stories, as recorded in the literature (Bratitsis, 2015).

Despite the type and context of a digital story, its creation usually follows a series of intermediate steps. There are many models of the digital story creation in the literature and many scholars hold storytelling workshops, worldwide. The schematic diagram in Figure 1 in one of the most accepted models, as described by Samantha Mora. It consists of 8 steps. Similar diagrams can be found in the literature, usually consisting of 7 or 8 steps. Lambert (2013) one of the founders of the DS area, described 7 steps in the digital story creation: 1) Owning your insights, 2) Owning your emotions, 3) Finding the moment, 4) Seeing your story, 5) Hearing your story, 6) Assembling your story, and 6) Sharing your story. Examining these two sequences, the similarities are apparent. One has to be inspired, think of and design a story. Sometimes this involves research for further information. Then the digital version of the story should be designed, digital material should be created and/or gathered in order to be structured (storyboard creation). Then the digital story is to be created and shared, leading to potential feedback collection and evaluation of whether the initial goal is met. In the case of Lambert's 7 steps, the first 3 steps are about creating the story, steps 4 and 5 are about designing the digital version, step 6 about creating it and step 7 about sharing it.

Utilizing Digital Storytelling Tools and Thinking Routines

Figure 1. The digital storytelling process
Source: Mora (n.d.)

Digital storytelling is a way to present new material and capture attention, facilitate interaction and increase a full complement of literacy skills, including, according to Robin (2006):

- Research Skills: Documenting the story, finding and analysing pertinent information;
- Writing Skills: Formulating a point of view and developing a text;
- Organizational Skills: Managing the scope of the story, the materials to be used and the time it takes to complete the task;
- Digital Skills: learning to use a variety of tools, such as digital cameras, scanners, microphones and multimedia authoring software;
- Presentation Skills: Deciding how to best present the story to an audience;
- Interview Skills: Finding sources to interview and determining questions to ask;
- Interpersonal Skills: Working within a group and determining individual roles for group members;
- Problem-Solving Skills: Learning to make decisions and overcome obstacles at all stages of the project, from inception to completion; and
- Assessment Skills: Gaining expertise by critically evaluating their own and others' work.

Overall, DS is a very creative process. The potential social interaction after publishing a story increases the possibility for releasing improved/modified versions of a story, depending on whether the goals initially set were met or not. This is a fundamental difference between traditional and DS. But the most important attribute is that DS provides means for communicating meaning in a multimodal manner, taking advantage of modern technologies such as interactive, internet-based tools.

Collaborative Story-Writing for Multiliteracy Development

The term 'collaborative writing' refers to written works created by more than one individuals in a collaborative way. This process has been proven particularly effective as a teaching method. Collaborative writing takes advantages of the 4Cs and the multiliteracy pedagogy, offering multimodal ways of self-expression and wider community impact.

Children can learn a lot from writing stories and by engaging in a writing process in cooperation with others. In fact, collaborative writing provides the means for teachers to engage in effective literacy instruction, not through isolated skills' lessons, but within the framework of constructing texts filled with personal and collective meaning (Button, Johnson, Furgerson, 1996).

Furthermore, this process stimulates the development of key transversal competences like creativity, communication, teamwork and even foreign languages. Collaborative writing is also flexible, as by appropriately selecting the writing (storytelling) topics it is possible to explore particular relevant subjects.

Storytelling and more specifically DS seems to be ideal means for multimodal communication, thus facilitating Multiliteracies. This multimodal expression of thoughts, ideas and opinions provides also the opportunity to children to share them with a larger audience (as described by DS) which easily accessible nowadays via ICTs. At the same time they have the opportunity to improve skills and competencies by creating their own stories. Children also become more active and productive in individual or collaborative communication activities.

In the case of DS, one has to show instead of tell. DS refers to a dynamic process which involves the teller, the audience/viewers and the story itself. At the very core of DS is meaning making and meaning communicating through the stories which are transmitted via digital technologies in a more unified world, the world of the 21st century. This provides children the opportunity to reach out and even interact of collaborate with peers from very diverse backgrounds (in matters of gender, ethnicity, etc.), further highlighting the last two steps of Samantha Mora's model (Figure 1). In the process, children learn to utilize contemporary ways of transmitting meaningful messages through their stories, in a way that complies with the digital era they live in. Thus, DS seems to be able to significantly facilitate Multiliteracy development in its totality.

Overall, the most important benefit of DS, is innovative and critical thinking, problem solving and decision making, collaboration, creativity, innovation and development of digital literacy. DS and Creative Writing (CW) are the two sides of the same coin (Bratitsis, 2015). CW techniques improve the stories which are the core constituents of DS. In fact, DS and CW are two distinct fields that share an important common point (Bratitsis Chesi, Godio, Barroca, Fruhmann, Broer, Szczygielska, Gonzalez, Martin, Toia, & Malita, 2014; Melliou, Moutafinou & Bratitsis, 2014; Bratitsis et al. 2011): the story and also the digital medium, selecting a meaningful topic and spending more time on the story creation is fundamental for an effective and successful digital story. A second common point is the wide range of the stories. Creative writing includes all kinds of writing.

CW and DS include creativity techniques, processes and frameworks for both idea generation and problem solving. They can both stimulate creativity and imagination for telling a story. Thus, they seem to perfectly serve the needs of Multiliteracy Pedagogy.

The StoryLogicNet Approach

Considering the issues discussed in the previous section, the EU funded project with the name "StoryLogicNet – Collaborative Writing for Children's Multiliteracy Skills Utilising Multimodal Tools" (Erasmus+ Programme, Keay Activity 2, Proj No 2018-1-PT01-KA201-047325) was designed and implemented from 2018 to 2021 (hereinafter SLN).

The first attempt within the project was to design a framework (Bratitsis, 2021) to support the following outcomes by identifying key competencies that the SLN tool would support cultivating. This framework is anchored in the central multiliteracies concept of design as an active and dynamic process applied to each semiotic activity, including language use, for the production and understanding of a text.

Figure 2 presents a schematic diagram of the framework, indicating that four areas were combined and examined: Multiliteracies, Collaborative Writing, Digital Storytellind and Digital Skills (as core constituents of all contemporary pedagogies). As SLN (http://www.storylogicnet.eu/) was an EU funded project, it focused in the EU context, but can be applicable on a wider level. The arrows depict the connections between the fields and one can easily identify that the connecting notion is that of meaning making and conveying.

Figure 2. StoryLogicNet competences framework
Source: Bratitsis (2021a)

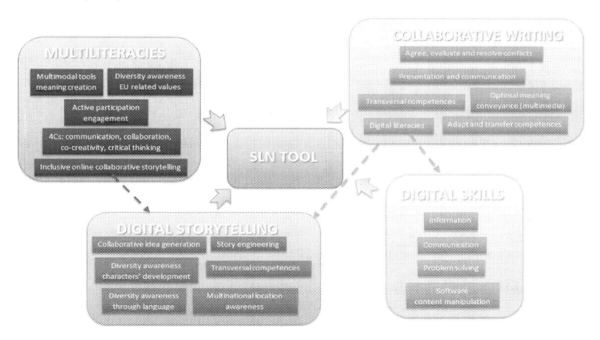

Following the framework, the SLN tool was designed and implemented, taking into account the key components which appear in Figure 2. The interconnection of the competences is highlighted in Figure 3, where the keywords are colored following the coding in Figure 2. For example, "Communication" appears half green and half orange, corresponding to the areas of DS and Collaborative Writing. As seen in Figure 3, the main core of the tool and the proposed approach in multimodal presentation for meaning conveyance, which is also the core of multiliteracy.

Figure 3. StoryLogicNet competences interconnection
Source: Bratitsis (2021a)

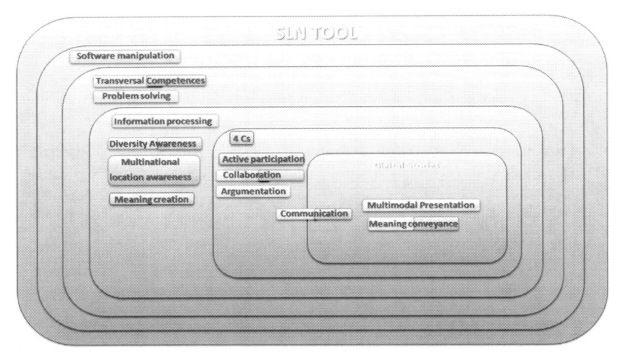

Nowadays the viewer discovers meaning via interpreting fragments of the story in order to build the story in his/her mind him/herself. Thus, he/she becomes an active participant in the story creation and the challenge for the storyteller is to provide as many fragments as appropriate and not more. The user actively participates in the story creation using different technical and storytelling tools including but not limited to: withholding, anticipation, discovery, the law of contradiction, location as allegory, visual metaphors, triggers and anchors as well as seeking visual expressions for time, tense and flow of location.

The SLN tool comprised in two constituents. The first was a community platform for collaborative writing of stories for preselected issues related to migration, diversity, citizenship and other modern topics. Both the available topics and the story-structure which was designed specifically for the tool were selected so as to support multiliteracy competences, mainly ones deriving from the 4Cs framework. Children (aged 6 to 15) worked on the platform and wrote and shared their stories. Three to six roles were incorporated in the writing of the stories, as the latter were divided in three distinct acts which included writing and illustration. Each individual or group attempted to interpret the previous story fragment (act) in order to continue the story towards its conclusion. At the end, an evaluation rubric was integrated in the tool in order to support the role of the critical reviewer, a role that was intendent to further support meaning argumentation and collaboration among children.

The second constituent of the SLN tool was a toolkit, comprising of a series of CW based templates and tools which also were adapted from the Design Thinking approach (Bratitsis, 2018) in order to facilitate meaningful story construction. The toolkit included 32 printable cards with detailed instruction on how to utilize them in educational settings and additional ideas for extending their usage. The connection of these tools with multiliteracy are discussed here through an example originating from the Design Thinking approach.

Design Thinking comes from the entrepreneurial world and concerns commercial product design and manufacturing. As a term it relates to understanding and applying the way a product designer thinks and acts in order to solve complex problems (Brown, 2009), thus constituting a problem-solving approach in essence. It is extremely useful for dealing with complex, poorly defined or unknown problems (such as societal ones which are tightly connected to education), as it strongly contains the element of search and testing from the perspective of a designer (Liu, 1996). It is analyzed into a sequence of steps with an iterative character, through which designers: a) perceive a problem through a representational form, b) studying ideas and relationships in order to find possible solutions, and c) reflect on these plans to enhance their design efforts (Do & Gross, 2001; Lloyd & Scott, 1995).

As mentioned by Cross (2011), design thinking relates generally to a systematic, but iterative problem-solving process. Usually a problem is also formulated as a starting point for exploration. Unlike analytical / scientific thinking, design thinking involves the introduction of ideas through a phase of brainstorming with little or no boundaries (Robson, 2002). The focus on design thinking is research, which clearly demonstrates that skills at the core of design thinking mentality are critical to students' overall development and success. There are several design thinking models in the literature, with the dominant one being dSchool, proposed by the Stanford University. It comprises 5 stages / steps (Figure 4): empathize, define, ideate, prototype and test.

Figure 4. The dSchool design thinking model
Source: https://medium.com/@makerwomen/design-thinking-process-1a599a5cdefe

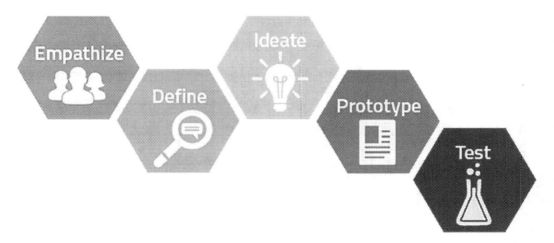

Figure 5 depicts an empathy map, a tool often used in the first step of Design Thinking in order to understand life aspects of a potential product user. This leads, in the second step of the process, to the definition of requirements and parameters for the product. There are several variations of the empathy map in the literature, comprising of 3 to 6 fields. The map in Figure 5 comprises in 6 fields and is considered a more advanced version of it. In short, the fields are used for reflecting upon and describing core aspects of a character, including: a) actions and speaking attributes (Say & Do), b) Thoughts & Feelinings, c) elements of the character's environment (SEE – HEAR), and d) inner thoughts, obstacles and motivations (PAINS – GAINS). This way, a spherical examination of a character can be made.

Figure 5. Empathy map example from the SLN toolkit
Source: Bratitsis (2021b)

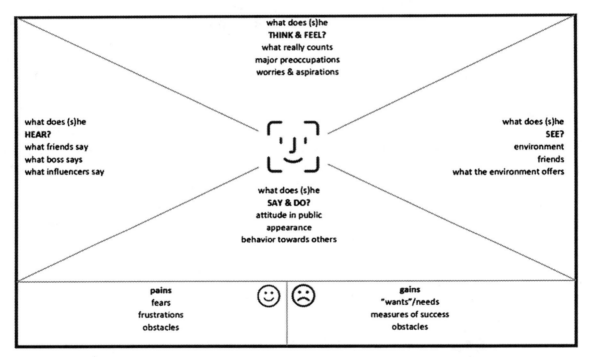

In the case of multiliteracy, the SLN approach proposed the utilization of an empathy map for developing a character of a story (usually the main character). This may allow for the child to study a character in multiple ways in order to gain a deeper understanding of various aspects of this character. The character can be one from an existing story, real or fictional, which is related to a specific issue (e.g. a migrant child, a person with deficiencies and/or diverse attributes, etc.). Of course a new character can be built with this tool for a new story that a child or a collaborating group of children are designing.

There are several levels of difficulty which are connected to the appearance of an empathy map, excluding the number of fields. Consequently, the map can be totally empty having only the main labels of the fields or it can include more or less descriptive prompts (such as the ones shown in figure 5) or provocative questions. For example in the THINK & FEEL field, a provocative question could be "what keeps the character awake at night" or "what makes the character wake up in the morning". These questions reflect upon the inner fears and motivations of the character, allowing for a multi-perspective and critical examination of that character.

Utilizing Digital Storytelling Tools and Thinking Routines

Concluding with a more specific example which has been tested by the authors in various workshops, the examined character is a migrant child facing specific circumstances (e.g. a financial or war migrant with both parents, or only one) that faces xenophobic behaviors in a new school environment. By reflecting upon such a situation, children can examine and eventually understand the inner thoughts of such a person (possibly of their age) and consequently empathize with him/her which would then allow them to connect with his/her inner world and start reflecting upon their behavioral patterns towards individuals with diversities of any kind. The key element in such an approach is making meaning out of the situation by connecting to one's own experiences, attitudes and beliefs.

The next section proposes extensions to those ideas by bringing into the discussion the notion of dispositions and corresponding strategies which can be combined with DS in order to equip diverse students with new ways to create and share meaning.

A Dispositional View of Multiliteracies and Stories of Migration in Early Childhood Education

A move toward a broader definition of literacy, away from a definition that focuses solely on skills and knowledge, has been fundamental in the shift towards multiliteracies. Adopting this concept the authors implemented the Visible Thinking (VT) and Re-Imagining Migration (RM) pedagogical frameworks to engage early childhood young students in a powerful learning experience to understand migration through DS. VT is a flexible and systematic, research-based conceptual framework that aims to integrate the development of students' thinking with content learning across subject matters (Ritchhart & Perkins, 2008). The RM framework (2022) is designed to prepare educators to respond to the demands of changing demographics associated with human migration flows and to ensure that young people grow up understanding migration as a shared condition of our past, present, and future in order to develop the knowledge, empathy and mindsets that sustain inclusive and welcoming communities. Both frameworks have been developed in partnership with Project Zero (PZ) research center at the Harvard Graduate School of Education and take a dispositional approach to the pedagogy of multiliteracies. The notion of dispositions is that people behave in a more or less informed and appropriate way guided not only by knowledge and skills but by predilections or tendencies (Tishman & Palmer, 2006). In other words the general idea of dispositions in the educational context concerns not so much a student's knowledge and skills as how the student invests those abilities (Perkins, Tishman, Ritchhart, Donis, & Andrade, 2000).

For the authors a major point of relevance between the pedagogy of multiliteracies and the key principles of VT and RM frameworks was the dispositional view of learning in a world on increasing diversity and complexity. The RM educational framework identifies five core dispositions necessary to navigate a world on the move. They propose a set of dispositions as the overarching learning goals of a curriculum for preparing children to face migration from their roles in society (see Figure 6).

Utilizing Digital Storytelling Tools and Thinking Routines

Figure 6. Five dispositions for a world on the move
Source: Reimagining Migration https://reimaginingmigration.org/

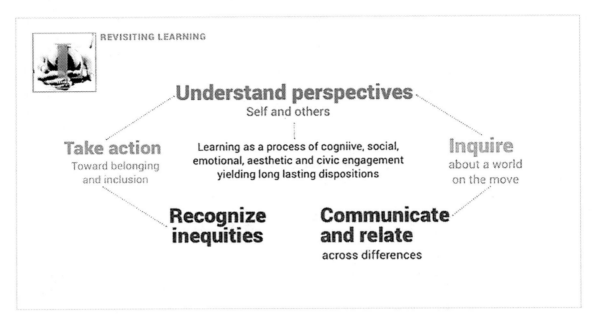

These dispositions highlight the cognitive, social, emotional, and ethical dimensions of learning and development.

- Understand one's own and others' perspectives, empathically.
- Inquire about human migration with care and nuance, be caring and curious about shared human experience.
- Communicate across difference, building relationships: Listening with understanding and empathy.
- Recognize inequities in human experiences and migration.
- Take action to foster inclusive and sustainable societies.

Developing dispositions – whether it is a disposition to strive for understanding, to listen empathetically and mindfully, or employ voice and action to foster inclusion– occurs within a cultural context. According to the VT framework (2009) it is within cultural contexts that students develop patterns of behavior that become their habits. Therefore, developing an understanding about migration needs an en-culturative approach where students experience school as a place of rich opportunities that help them to foster an inclination toward using multiple literacies to communicate across difference. This dispositional view of literacy includes the the capacity to listen and reason with understanding and empathy and the sensitivity to include marginalized voices (Boix-Mansilla, 2015) rather than understanding only how to decode. While educators, respond to the demands of more diverse and complex classrooms it is crucial to nurture the dispositions that will best prepare young students to create and share meanings in ways that integrate a range of modes of expression to convey their message. These forms of expression and meaning making go beyond traditional literacy learning that is limited in a skills-centered approach (Drewry, Cumming-Potvin, & Maor, 2019).

Dispositions are formed when people routinely engage in specific patterns of behavior (Tishman & Palmer, 2006). Accordingly, the authors used PZ's thinking routines to develop a disposition in children of embracing cultural diversity and seeing migration as an opportunity of turning the diverse perspectives that different students bring in class into multimodal stories that are effectively communicated through new multiliteracies. The thinking routines are research-based tools to promote thinking. Project Zero authors (Ritchhart, Church & Morrison, 2011) purposefully prefer to use the term "thinking routines" instead of "thinking strategies," because they want them to be understood within the notion of a culture, something that people do on a regular basis. The thinking routines are structures through which students both collectively and individually initiate, explore, discuss, document and manage their thinking.

These structures are (Salmon & Melliou, 2021)

- explicit: they have names to identify them, e.g., See-Think-Wonder,
- instrumental or goal-centered: they are goal directed and purposeful,
- they have a thinking goal and a few steps: they are easy to learn and easy to remember
- individual and group practices,
- useful across a variety of contexts, and
- able to reveal students' thinking and make it more visible.

Global Thinking Routines (GTRs) on the other hand are thinking structures or micro-teaching tools carefully designed to nurture global dispositions. Meant to be used frequently, across content, over time, and as an integral part of a learning environment, these routines are essential contributors to creating a classroom culture of global competence (Boix-Mansilla, 2016). The table below shows the Harvard PZ thinking routines and global thinking routines used for the creation of digital stories in the early childhood classroom (see Table 1).

Table 1. Project Zero thinking routines and global thinking routines

Thinking Routines	Dispositions	Steps
Step In - Step Out - Step Back	Understand perspectives own and others' empathetically	Identify a person or agent in the situation you are examining. • Given what you see and know at this time, what do you think this person might feel, believe, know, or experience? • What else would you like or need to learn to understand this person's perspective better? • Given your exploration of this perspective so far, what do you notice about your own perspective and what it takes to take somebody else's?
The Three Why's	Inquire about human migration with care and nuance	Identify or name the topic, question, issue you are examining. Then consider: • Why might this [topic, question, issue] matter to me? • Why might it matter to people around me [family, friends, community, city, nation]? • Why might it matter to the world?
How Else & Why?	Communicate across difference, building relationships	What I want to say is… student makes a statement and explains intention. • How else can I say this? & Why? Consider intention, audience and situation to reframe (language, tone, body language). • How else can I say this? & Why? Consider intention, audience and situation to reframe (language, tone, body language)
Unveiling Stories	Recognize inequities in human experiences and migration by revealing multiple layers of meaning	Educators select some – not all – of the routine's questions depending on their goals • What is the story? • What is the human story? • What is the world story? • What is the new story? • What is the untold story?
Does it fit? *(In the case of early childhood education the authors used only one of the four different "fits" to evaluate options for action)*	Take action to foster inclusion and sustainable societies	Fit your options to the Criteria. Identify the criteria or attributes that feel important for you to consider in this situation and then evaluate each option against those. Ask yourself: • How well does each option fit the criteria?

Filoxenos: Digital Stories of Reception

The influx of migrants and refugees to Piraeus Greece has put local authorities that work intensely with state organizations and NGOs under considerable pressure to provide protection and accommodation to asylum seekers and vulnerable children. Teachers need to identify meaningful ways to successfully integrate refugee boys and girls into the public schools alongside their Greek peers. They must manage the unique obstacles faced by refugee children who must deal with disrupted families, insecure housing and a rising discrimination under a politically polarized climate in the region (OECD, 2019). Against this backdrop the authors a university professor and the educational coordinator for early childhood education in Piraeus explored a digital storytelling-based approach to engage newly-arrived children of four public kindergartens and begin to integrate them with their local peers. To design a rigorous and ethical research for children the authors asked teachers to organize a meeting with the parents. Willing to address the linguistic issues of the families that didn't speak Greek, and to ensure that they can voice

Utilizing Digital Storytelling Tools and Thinking Routines

their concerns about their children's participation the teachers asked several bilingual parents to serve as interpreters in the meeting. The authors spoke with the parents explaining the voluntary nature of the research and informed them about their role in protecting children's anonymity and potential for pscyological harm and obtained written parental permission.

The study was geared towards understanding migration and empowering immigrant origin children who did not speak greek to be heard and to listen to each other stories. Both authors adopted the role of "critical friend" and worked intensively with the early childhood teachers on constructing opportunities for diverse learners to create and communicate meaning across a variety of visual, musical and digital forms of storytelling.

Aiming to integrate a dispositional view into the process of DS the authors designed an elaborate diagram (Figure 7) that consists of five (5) steps each one of them includes a number of story-making subtasks related to the development of the (5) dispositions for a world on the move included in the RM framework.

Figure 7. Five steps for the development of dispositions through storytelling

Empathize with others	Reason with carefully-treated sources of evidence	Express with purpose and audience in mind	Envisioning inclusion	Recognize, reflect and revise actions
Using: Opening images and provocations representing migration *To:* Identify the idea of the story by exploring different perspectives	*Using:* Multimedia sources of information (video, animation) *To:* Build the scenery and the characters	*Using:* Stop motion photography with plasticine figures in separate poses *To:* Develop photographed frames of the story	*Using:* Digital sound files, music and sound effects *To:* Convey the message of the story and build linguistic and cultural barriers	*Using:* Video creator and the schools' blogs *To:* Edit all digital files into a continuous movie, share the story and collect online feedback

Aiming to evaluate the dispositional approach of multiliteracies for making sense and constructing meaning of migration the authors focused on the indicators of children's "well-being" and "involvement" instead of solely assessing the learning outcome (the story). The assessment of "well-being" and "involvement" has been created by Ferre Laevers (2011) and his team at Leuven University. "Well-being" is defined as a state in which one feels at ease, shows spontaneity, is self-confident and enjoys its presence and interactions with others (Laevers et al., 2013). The levels of "Well-being" indicate that the basic needs of children are satisfied and refer to the degree to which they feel at ease, show vitality and self-confidence (Laevers, 2011). "Involvement" signals how children are concentrated, absorbed and fascinated, how they are engaged in activities and operating at the very limits of their capabilities (Laevers & Declercq, 2018). "Involvement" according to Laevers (2011) is evident when children are concentrated and focused, interested and fascinated and when they are operating at the very limits of their capabilities. According to Laevers (2011) high levels of "well-being" and "involvement" show meaningful learning, which is characterized by a number of dispositions such as engagement, fascination, curiosity and profound interest and are also considered as key components of the pedagogy of multiliteracies.

A five-point scale was used for both "well-being" and "involvement" observations checklists with one (1) being the lowest level and five (5) being the highest. Before embarking on the DS process, teachers were asked to use the checklists to assign scores for both indicators to all children of their class based on their observations and experience from the beginning of the school year. Teachers identified twelve (12) non speaking-greek students with scores below 3 in all five levels of the well-being and involvement variables.

In order to collect data about the impact of their approach, the authors asked teachers to repeat the assessment procedure only for the 12 immigrant origin children that needed more attention. The teachers observed the sessions and the scores assigned over this period indicated higher levels in both "well-being" and "involvement scales. The digital media used in the sub-tasks of the project were described as "stimulating inputs" that not only raised the levels of enjoyment and participation but also equips linguistically and culturally diverse children with new ways to create and share meaning.

DISCUSSION AND FUTURE RESEARCH DIRECTIONS

Preparing our youth to participate successfully in a world of increasing social, cultural, ethnic, and linguistic diversity requires the inclusion of multiple literacies and modes for making meaning. As already mentioned, students are now living in a digital era and are surrounded by huge amounts of information, transmitted through various, multimodal semiotic channels. Within such an environment, communication itself has been altered.

For effective communication, meaning making is essential. The role of education is to prepare children from their early years to become useful and competent citizens of society, as it is and as it will become. Despite children being born as native digital users (Prenksy, 2001), still the have increased learning needs deriving from the fact that they are born in a multimodal, media-dominated society, mainly via digital technology.

In this chapter, the concept of Multiliteracy has been discussed as being directly connected with the aforementioned situation. It has connected it with two other pillars, that of Digital Storytelling and Thinking Dispositions. The element of convergence for all three is that of making meaning via multimodal communication channels in order to achieve successful communication, also being able to understand different perspectives of various elements (people, conditions, events, etc.).

Through examples that the authors have tested in real settings with young children, the dynamics of utilizing digital storytelling and thinking dispositions has been highlighted. Although additional research is needed to verify and generalize the outcomes of the corresponding studies, the examples presented in this chapter verify two concrete outcomes: a) multiliteracies is a contemporary need and goal of education, and b) digital storytelling and thinking routines facilitate multiliteracy cultivation.

ACKNOWLEDGMENT

We are grateful for the help of the collaborating partners in this work—the teachers, students and the parents of the 4th public Kindergarten school of Piraeus and the Pedagogiki private primary school, Greece without whom the Filoxenos project would not have happened. We would like to especially thank the young children who participated in the activities and their parents/ caregivers for volunteering their consent. You have made your school a better place. Finally, we would like to express our gratitude to Dr. Angela Salmon for our long lasting collaboration and constant support in our efforts.

Part of this work was co-funded by the Erasmus+ Programme of the European Union, Action KA2 for School Education, Project No: 2018-1-PT01-KA201-047325 "StoryLogicNet".

REFERENCES

Binkley, M., Erstad, O., & Herman, J. (2012). Defining twenty-first century skills. In P. Griffin, B. McGaw, & E. Care (Eds.), *Assessment and Teaching of 21st Century Skills* (pp. 17–66). Springer. doi:10.1007/978-94-007-2324-5_2

Boix-Mansilla, V. (2015). *Finding our way into each other's worlds: Musings on cultural perspective taking*. Retrieved on April 9, 2022, from http://www.pz.harvard.edu/sites/default/files/FINDING%20OUR%20WAY%20INTO%20EACH%20OTHER%C2%B9S%20WORLDS.pdf

Boix-Mansilla, V. (2016). How to be a global thinker: Using global thinking routines to create classroom cultures that nurture global competence. *Educational Leadership*, 74(4), 10–16.

Bratitsis, T. (2015). Digital Storytelling, Creative Writing and 21st Century Literacy. *Bulletin of Educational Reflection and Communication*, 55.

Bratitsis, T. (2018). Storytelling digitalization as a Design Thinking process in educational context. In A. Moutsios-Rentzos, A. Giannakoulopoulos, M. Meimaris (Eds.), *Proceedings of the International Digital Storytelling Conference - "Current Trends in Digital Storytelling: Research & Practices"* (pp. 309-320). Academic Press.

Bratitsis, T. (2021a). Multiliteracy education competences framework. Deliverable O1A1, StoryLogicNet – Collaborative Writing for Children's Multiliteracy Skills Utilising Multimodal Tools, EU PROJECT No. 2018-1-PT01-KA201-047325

Bratitsis, T. (2021b). StoryLogicNet Toolkit. Deliverable O1A4, StoryLogicNet – Collaborative Writing for Children's Multiliteracy Skills Utilising Multimodal Tools, EU PROJECT No. 2018-1-PT01-KA201-047325

Bratitsis, T., Bardanika, P., & Ioannou, M. (2017). Science education and augmented reality content: The case of the water circle. In M. Kinshuk, D. Chang, D. Sampson, NS. Chen, R. Vasiu, & R. Huang (Eds.), *Proceedings of the 17th IEEE International Conference on Advanced Learning Technologies - ICALT 2017* (pp. 485-489). IEEE. 10.1109/ICALT.2017.64

Bratitsis, T., Chesi, P., Godio, C., Barroca, A., Fruhmann, P., Broer, Y., Szczygielska, E., Gonzalez, R., Martin, M., Toia, M., & Malita, L. (2014). European educators' training needs for applying digital storytelling in their teaching practice. In *International Conference on Information Communication Technologies in Education - ICICTE 2014* (pp 194-204). Academic Press.

Bratitsis, T., Kotopoulos, T., & Mandila, K. (2011) Kindergarten children as story Makers: The effect of the digital medium. In F. Xhafa, L. Barolli, & M. Köppen (Eds.), *Proceedings of the IEEE 3rd International Conference On Intelligent Networking and Collaborative Systems - INCoS 2011* (pp. 84-91). 10.1109/INCoS.2011.108

Bratitsis, T., & Ziannas, P. (2015). From early childhood to special education: Interactive digital storytelling as a coaching approach for fostering social empathy. *Computer Science Procedure*, 67, 231–240. doi:10.1016/j.procs.2015.09.267

Brown, T. (2009). *Change by design. How Design Thinking Transforms Organizations and Inspires Innovation*. HarperBusiness.

Bruner, J. (1990). *Acts of meaning*. Harvard University Press.

Burmark, L. (2004). Visual presentations that prompt, flash & transform. *Media and Methods*, 40(6), 4–5.

Button, K., Johnson, M., & Furgerson, P. (1996). Interactive Writing in the Primary Classroom. *The Reading Teacher*, 49(6), 446–454.

Cope, B., & Kalantzis, M. (2000). *Multiliteracies: Literacy learning and the design of social futures*. Psychology Press.

Cope, B., & Kalantzis, M. (2006). *The Learning by Design Guide*. Common Ground.

Cope, B., & Kalantzis, M. (2015). The Things You Do to Know: An Introduction to the Pedagogy of Multiliteracies. In B. Cope & M. Kalantzis (Eds.), *A Pedagogy of Multiliteracies: Learning By Design* (pp. 1–36). Palgrave. doi:10.1057/9781137539724_1

Cross, N. (2011). *Design Thinking: Understanding How Designers Think and Work*. Berg Publishers. doi:10.5040/9781474293884

Dede, C. (2010). Comparing frameworks for 21st century skills. In J. Bellanca & R. Brandt (Eds.), 21st Century Skills: Rethinking How Students Learn (pp. 51-76). Solution Tree Press.

Do, E. Y.-L., & Gross, M. D. (2001). Thinking with diagrams in architectural design. *Artificial Intelligence Review*, 15(1/2), 135–149. doi:10.1023/A:1006661524497

Drew, S. V. (2013). Open up the ceiling on the common core state standards: Preparing students for 21st-century literacy---now. *Journal of Adolescent & Adult Literacy*, 56(4), 321–330. doi:10.1002/JAAL.00145

Drewry, R. J., Cumming-Potvin, W. M., & Maor, D. (2019). New Approaches to Literacy Problems: Multiliteracies and Inclusive Pedagogies. *The Australian Journal of Teacher Education*, 44(11), 61–78. doi:10.14221/ajte.2019v44.n11.4

EACEA. (2012). *Citizenship Education in Europe*. Education, Audiovisual and Culture Executive Agency P9 Eurydice. Retrieved on April 15, 2022, from https://eacea.ec.europa.eu/education/eurydice

Egan, K. (1989, Spring). Memory, imagination, and learning: connected by the story. *The Docket: Journal of the New Jersey Council for the Social Studies*, 9-13.

European Commission. (2013). Co-creating European citizenship. Policy review. Publications Office of the European Union, EUR 25948.

Gakhar, S., & Thompson, A. (2007). Digital storytelling: Engaging, communicating, and collaborating. In R. Carlsen, & DA. Willis (Eds.), *Proceedings of the Society for Information Technology and Teacher Education International Conference 2007* (pp. 607-612). Chesapeake, VA: AACE.

Grant, N. S., & Bolin, B. L. (2016). Digital Storytelling: A Method for Engaging Students and Increasing Cultural Competency. *The Journal of Effective Teaching*, *16*, 44–61.

Laevers, F. (2011). *Experiential Education: Making Care and Education More Effective Through Well-Being and Involvement*. Leuven University / Centre for Experiential Education, Belgium. Retrieved March 1, 2022 from https://www.child-encyclopedia.com/sites/default/files/textes-experts/en/857/experiential-education-making-care-and-education-more-effective-through-well-being-and-involvement.pdf

Laevers, F., & Declercq, B. (2018). How well-being and involvement fit into the commitment to children's rights. *European Journal of Education Research Development and Policy, Special Issue: Learner agency at the confluence between rights-based approaches and well-being, 53*(3), 325-335.

Laevers, F., Moons, J., & Declercq, B. (2013). *A process-oriented monitoring system for the arly years* [POMS]. CEGO Publishers.

Lambert, J. (2013). *Digital Storytelling. Capturing lives, creating community*. Routhledge. doi:10.4324/9780203102329

Liu, Y.-T. (1996). Is designing one search or two? A model of design thinking involving symbolism and connectionism. *Design Studies*, *17*(4), 435–449. doi:10.1016/S0142-694X(96)00018-X

Lloyd, P., & Scott, P. (1995). Difference in similarity: Interpreting the architectural design process. *Planning and Design*, *22*(4), 383–406. doi:10.1068/b220383

McDonald, M. (1998). Traditional storytelling today: An international sourcebook. Fitzroy Dearborn.

McDrury, J., & Alterio, M. (2003). *Learning through storytelling in higher education: using reflection and experience to improve learning*. Kogan Page.

Melliou, K., Moutafidou, A., & Bratitsis, T. (2014). Children's Rights: A narrative video using Digital Storytelling and Visible Thinking approach created by kindergarteners. *International Digital Storytelling Conference Digital Storytelling in Times of Crisis*.

Morra, S. (n.d.). *8 steps to great digital storytelling*. Retrieved August 15, 2018 https://edtechteacher.org/8-steps-to-great-digital-storytelling-from-samantha-on-edudemic/

Moutafidou, A., & Bratitsis, T. (2013). Digital Storytelling and Creative Writing: Two Parallel Worlds with a Common Place. *Proceedings of the 1st International Conference on Creative Writing*.

NEA. (2012). *Preparing 21st century students for a global society*. National Education Association.

NRC. (2013). *Education for life and work: Developing transferable knowledge and skills in the 21st century*. National Academies Press. National Research Council.

OECD. (2019). *OECD Future of Education and Skills 2030: OECD Learning Compass 2030*. OECD Publishing. Retrieved on April 12, 2022, from https://www.oecd.org/education/2030-project/teaching-and-learning/learning/learning-compass-2030/OECD_Learning_Compass_2030_concept_note.pdf

Pedersen, E. (1995). Storytelling and the art of teaching. *English Teaching Forum, 33*(1), 2-5.

Perkins, D. N., Tishman, S., Ritchhart, R., Donis, K., & Andrade, A. (2000). Intelligence in the wild: A dispositional view of intellectual traits. *Educational Psychology Review, 12*(3), 269–293. doi:10.1023/A:1009031605464

Piaget, J. (1952). *The origins of intelligence in children*. International University Press.

Prensky, M. (2001). Digital Natives, Digital Immigrants Part 2: Do They Really Think Differently? *On the Horizon, 9*(6), 1–6. doi:10.1108/10748120110424843

Reimagining Migration. (2022). Retrieved on March 26, 2022, from http://www.pz.harvard.edu/projects/re-imagining-migration

Rex, L., Murnen, T., Hobbs, J., & McEachen, D. (2002). Teachers' Pedagogical Stories and the Shaping of Classroom Participation: "The Dancer" and "Graveyard Shift at the 7-11". *American Educational Research Journal, 39*(3), 765–796. doi:10.3102/00028312039003765

Ritchhart, R., Church, M., & Morrison, K. (2011). *Making Thinking Visible: How to Promote Engagement, Understanding, and Independence for All Learners*. Jossey-Bass.

Ritchhart, R., & Perkins, D. N. (2008). Making Thinking Visible. *Educational Leadership, 65*(5), 57–61.

Robin, B. (2006). The educational uses of digital storytelling. In *Proceedings of Society for Information Technology & Teacher Education International Conference*. Chesapeake, VA: AACE.

Robin, B. (2006). The educational uses of digital storytelling. In *Proceedings of Society for Information Technology & Teacher Education International Conference* (pp.709-716). Chesapeake, VA: AACE.

Robin, B. R., & McNeil, S. G. (2012). What educators should know about teaching digital storytelling. *Digital Education Review, 22*, 37–51.

Robson, M. (2002). "Brainstorming". Problem-solving in groups. Gower.

Salmon, A., & Melliou, K. (2021). Understanding and Facing Migration Through Stories for Influence. In I. M. Gómez Barreto (Ed.), *Handbook of Research on Promoting Social Justice for Immigrants and Refugees Through Active Citizenship and Intercultural Education* (pp. 205–231). IGI Global. doi:10.4018/978-1-7998-7283-2.ch011

Schank, R. (1990). *Tell me a story: Narrative and intelligence*. Northwestern University Press.

Schank, R. C. (1999). *Dynamic memory revisited*. Cambridge University Press. doi:10.1017/CBO9780511527920

Tan, P. L., & McWilliam, E. (2009). From literacy to multiliteracies: Diverse learners and pedagogical practice. *Pedagogies, 4*(3), 213–225. doi:10.1080/15544800903076119

The New London Group. (1996). A pedagogy of multiliteracies: Designing social futures. *Harvard Educational Review, 66*(1), 60–93. doi:10.17763/haer.66.1.17370n67v22j160u

Tishman, S., & Palmer, P. (2006). *Artful Thinking. Stronger Thinking and Learning through the power of Art. Final Report.* Project Zero-Harvard Graduate School of Education.

Visible Thinking. (2009). Visible Thinking Resource Book for Making Thinking Visible. Cambridge MA: Harvard University Press.

Vygotsky, LS (1978). *Mind in society: The development of higher psychological processes.* Academic Press.

ADDITIONAL READING

Bratitsis, T. (2017). Contextualized educators' training: the case of Digital Storytelling. In P. Anastasiades & N. Zaranis (Eds.), *Research on e-Learning and ICT in Education: Technological, Pedagogical and Instructional Perspectives* (pp. 31–43). Springer International Publishing.

Bratitsis, T., & Lampropoulou, N. (2019). StoryLogicNet: a proposal for Multiliteracy Education through Collaborative Writing. *4th International Conference on Creative Writing*.

Korosidou, E., & Bratitsis, T. (2019). Infusing Multimodal Tools and Digital Storytelling in Developing Vocabulary and Intercultural Communicative Awareness of Young EFL Learners. In A. Liapis, G. Yannakakis, M. Gentile, & M. Ninaus (Eds.), *Games and Learning Alliance. GALA 2019* (pp. 191–200). Springer.

Melliou, K., Bratitsis, T., & Salmon, A. (2018). "Out of Eden Learn": An online community for an inclusive world created by Harvard's Project Zero research center. In *International Conference Software Development and Technologies for Enhancing Accessibility and Fighting Info-exclusion*. Aristotle University of Thessaloniki.

Melliou, K., Moutafidou, A., & Bratitsis, T. (2014). Digital Comics Use to develop Thinking Dispositions in Early Childhood Education. In *The 14th IEEE International Conference on Advanced Learning Technologies – ICALT2014 Advanced Technologies for Supporting Open Access to Formal and Informal Learning* (pp 502-504). IEEE.

Melliou, K., Moutafidou, A., & Bratitsis, T. (2018). The "journey" of the Piraeus low-income schools in Out of Eden Learn. In *International Conference on Thinking – ICOT18* (pp. 84-92). Florida International University.

Moutafidou, A., & Bratitsis, T. (2018). Digital storytelling: giving voice to socially excluded people in various contexts. In *International Conference Software Development and Technologies for Enhancing Accessibility and Fighting Info-exclusion*. Aristotle University of Thessaloniki. 10.1145/3218585.3218684

KEY TERMS AND DEFINITIONS

Design Thinking: Relates to understanding and applying the way a product designer thinks and acts in order to solve complex or ill-defined through an iterative process.

Digital Storytelling: Is the combination of traditional, oral narration with multimedia and communication tools combining different types of multimedia material, including images, text, video clips, audio narration and music to tell a short story on a particular topic or theme.

Dispositions for a World on the Move: One way to think about the dispositions is as the overarching learning goals of curriculum preparing young people for a world on the move. They are highlighting cognitive as well as social, emotional, and ethical dimensions of learning and development.

Multiliteracy: Is the ability to identify, interpret, create, and communicate meaning across a variety of visual, oral, corporal, musical and alphabetical forms of communication.

Reimagining Migration: Is a learning framework that presents migration as an opportunity. RM is catalyzing a community of educational leaders and social organizations around making migration a part of their curriculum and culture so that all students can feel supported in their social, emotional, academic, and civic growth.

Thinking Routines: Harvard Project Zero research-based tools to promote thinking.

Visible Thinking: It is a flexible and systematic research-based conceptual framework, which aims to integrate the development of students' thinking with content learning across subject matters. Visible Thinking began as an initiative to develop a research-based approach to teaching thinking dispositions.

Chapter 8
Crafting Stories of Voice and Influence:
Children's Cognitive and Emotional Engagement in Listening and Telling Stories

Angela K. Salmon
https://orcid.org/0000-0002-3411-9398
Florida International University, USA

ABSTRACT

The interplay between language, cognition, and the effects of emotions promote language and literacy development. Children have a natural inclination to build on other children's stories, which is the origin of the collective stories of voice and influence discussion. Stories are empowering venues that give children a voice and simultaneously open windows for them to step inside someone else's shoes, make connections, take perspective, and construct meaning. Stories make us human; children become aware of the world around them by listening and sharing stories. This action research project reports the process of children listening to stories and tailoring the telling of a story to a specific audience. Children were cognitively and emotionally engaged in interpreting stories and transmitting their messages through dialogic thinking and boundary objects. The children made their stories visible using a pedagogy of multiliteracies to tell stories in a natural, playful, safe, and engaging way.

INTRODUCTION

Tell me and I forget, teach me and I may remember, involve me and I learn. (Benjamin Franklin)

My childhood memories are filled with warm storytelling experiences that emerged from Uncle Victor's (my aunt's husband) oral traditions. Uncle Victor was born and raised in a small agricultural village in Ecuador where the activities end at sunset and the families gather for dinner and storytelling at the light

DOI: 10.4018/978-1-6684-5022-2.ch008

of a candle because there was no electricity. Families had no access to children's books in those days but had a rich oral tradition. Heath (1982) refers to oral traditions as ways of making meaning from stories and contents about the real world. My big family, which consisted of my mother, siblings, grandmother, uncle, aunt, and cousins, shared a house at the beach near Uncle Victor's village during the summers. There was still limited electricity access and no distracting electronic devices, of course. We gathered in an open terrace after dinner to hear Uncle Victor, who was a natural bedtime storyteller. He captivated our attention with "The Adventures of Juan De Oso." Every summer marked a new season, and each season had several episodes. We were always eager to hear about Juan de Oso; Uncle Victor had the ability to create suspense. He triggered our imagination with invitations to predict the end of each episode. Uncle Victor gave us ownership and agency by giving us a protagonist role and inviting us to tell the endings. Every episode was so real for us; our contributions to the story were a mix of fantasy and reality. Brown (2018) says that when we have the courage to walk into our story and own it, we get to write the ending, but they own us when we don't own our stories of failure, setbacks, and hurt. Juan de Oso became a family icon. Uncle Victor passed away many years ago, but the Adventures of Juan de Oso are still alive in all of us. We always bring up episodes that caused an impact in our lives at our family gatherings. This story is a testament to the power of oral traditions in fostering language and literacy development. Heath's (1982) ethnographic research found that literacy events, such as "The Adventures of Juan de Oso," reflect the culture that children learn as they grow up.

Stories are powerful tools to cognitively and emotionally engage children in understanding issues of global significance. Children need to develop a strong, solid sense of who they are to develop resilience in a complex and changing world. Listening and telling stories are powerful venues to help children develop self-awareness, which is an important point of reference for interacting with the world. At the same time, children learn to see other perspectives. Stories help teachers listen to children's voices and understand their worlds.

As a literate society, we expect children to become literate to succeed in life. Unfortunately, many programs easily forget the natural conditions that foster language learning, turning literacy programs in artificial, meaningless, and disengaging experiences. This study aims to prove how natural approaches to language and literacy development that cognitively and emotionally engage children are efficient and lifelong lasting. This happens through stories and activities that are meaningful for the lives of the children.

The chapter gives the reader a bird's eye view into storytelling for voice and influence, as a means not only to promote language and literacy development but also to embrace children's right to participate with a voice. It amplifies the roles of nature and nurture, the interplay between language, cognition, and the effects of emotions to promote language and literacy development through storytelling. It discusses the benefits of listening to stories and the multiple sign symbols that children can use to have a voice. Finally, it approaches the uses of multiliteracies including play.

Not all emergent literacy experiences are the same. The National Council of Teachers of English's (NCTE) (2013) definition of 21st century literacies is aligned with the premise that literacy has always been a collection of cultural and communicative practices shared among members of groups. Schools should take account of social factors outside of school in helping pupils acquire the reading and writing skills required by schooling. Studies (Heath, 1982, Street, 2012) show that both oral and written traditions are important to promote readers and writers. What matters is how children make sense of the world from books and stories; this happens when children relate stories to their real world. Both oral and written traditions contribute to children's language and literacy development, especially when

Crafting Stories of Voice and Influence

the adults promote children's active participation. Children will become literate if adults offer them the opportunity to listen, talk, read and write (Resnick & Snow, 2009).

Stories have a powerful influence on children; the environment determines the level of involvement and interaction with stories. Parents talk to their newborn babies with the expectation that they will eventually talk the same way. In Vygotsky's (1978) words, children grow into the intellectual life of those around them. Parents who read to their children model reading behaviors; they do this because they believe their children will read like the other club members. Heath (1982) discovered that children growing up in mainstream communities are expected to develop habits and values that attest to their membership in a "literate society." Likewise, Smith (1987) uses the metaphor "The Literacy Club" to describe the social nature of literacy learning. *Digital collective stories for voice and influence (DCSVI)*, a concept that my colleagues and I developed to refer to children's cognitive and emotional engagement in tailoring the telling of a story to a specific audience (Salmon & Melliou, 2021), is another way of communicating.

THEORETICAL BACKGROUND

Human beings are social by nature, which means that communication is an essential and prevalent characteristic in people. People communicate in different ways: The early signs of human evolution were captured in cave drawings or sculptures that communicate stories, rituals, and other messages that transcend in history. Children think in stories; this chapter aims to capture the power of children's stories and their capacity to communicate their own stories to influence others. There is a huge body of research that suggests that children learn to read by reading and to write by writing (Cazden, 2004; Resnick & Snow, 2009; & Smith, 1987). Language and literacy acquisition occur when children find a meaning and a purpose for communicating. We foster children's emergent literacy when we create opportunities to cognitively and emotionally engage children as readers and authors. Children will find a sign system or language to do it (talking, drawing, writing, acting, digitizing, and more) when they are intrinsically motivated and feel the need to communicate what is relevant in their lives.

Early childhood experiences and emotions have a big impact on brain development, which determines children's learning. My research and experience working with children clearly reflect the strong relationship between nature and nurture and the implications on children's language and literacy development with implications in second language learners.

Nature vs. Nurture in Storytelling

Language as an innate condition of human beings, although the environment plays a critical role in helping children understand their world. For Vygotsky (1978), language arises as a means of communication between children and the people around them. Children's oral and written language acquisition depends on the quality of adult-child interactions. Language acquisition for Krashen (2016) is a natural phenomenon in which children acquire the language as a result of interactions with others and the need to communicate.

The nurturing aspect of language and literacy development refers to opportunities that adults create to emotionally engage children in talking about topics that are relevant to their lives. Furthermore, children's books serve as mediators to expand children's horizons and see the world from different perspectives and help them develop a theory of mind. *Theory of mind* is the capacity to understand what other people know, think or feel (Premack y Woodruff, 1978).

Storytelling is a valuable approach to promote empathy in children. For Boix-Mansilla (2014), stories make us human. Learning to tell stories matters because doing so helps us to make sense of the world and our experiences. Emotions are a nurturing aspect in children's learning. For neuroscientist Immordino-Yang (2016), children's emotional and social relationships shape their learning and shape the brain development that determines their learning.

With a good selection of children's books teachers can create multiple possibilities to engage children in meaningful conversations and extend those conversations to actions. Children's books transform human experience. Rudine Sims Bishop (1990) uses the mirrors, windows, and sliding glass doors metaphor to explain the impact of children's literature on children's lives. Children's books, for her, are like mirrors when a story reflects who they are; stories validate children's stories, identities, and culture. Books also work as windows when children can take perspective and see other people's stories and like sliding glass doors when we can step inside another person's story and interact. Bishop's metaphor is aligned with neuroscience: When we hear a story, a mirroring effect produces similar brain activity as the speaker (Hasson, et al, 2012). It also builds neural coupling, which means that stories activate parts of the brain that make listeners turn the story into their own ideas and experiences. In other words, stories produce similar brain activity as the speaker (storyteller). Emotionally charged stories liberate dopamine making the event easier to remember.

Literacy is a tool for learning, because stories in any form constitute a sliding glass door to step inside another person's story, develop empathy, and engage. We need to educate for peace more than ever in this complex world. Maria Montessori (1949, p. 27) said that education is a means, perhaps the only genuine means, of eliminating war once and for all. For her, children need real choices as they grow. Taking an author's role or a digital storytelling role offers children the opportunity to step in someone else's story, empathize, and decide the direction of the story. Bratitsis and Ziannas' (2015) study revealed that any type of storytelling, including digital storytelling, help children connect the emotions of the story-characters and the interchange between them with the story's plot and the narration's evolvement to formulate hypotheses about the characters' actions and the possible causes for their emotional state.

Critical Literacy

Stories are a language that children understand, which is an excellent approach to give them a message or help them understand concepts. Stories have the potential to cognitively and emotionally engage children. Through stories, children make connections to past knowledge and experiences, recreate or invent stories, and elevate their voice. The use of critical literacy to extend a children's book mediates children's construction of knowledge and helps them identify problems, develop empathy, and collectively find solutions.

The interplay between language and cognition challenges teachers to design learning experiences that cognitively engage children in understanding concepts in depth and create in them the need to communicate. Resnik and Snow (2009) say that speaking and listening make children smarter. Thus, the adults' role is to offer children opportunities to explore the world and create spaces where children can talk about it. Children's books certainly bring the world to children's hands and help children construct meaning.

There is no consensus on the definition of critical literacy, but for Leland, Lewison, and Harste (2018), critical literacy practices encourage students to explore the depth of prior knowledge that they have and to explore their understandings and misunderstandings of a topic, to question their everyday world and to consider actions that can be taken to promote social justice. Children are capable of critically analyzing stories and taking perspective when engaged in a story.

Children learn about the world when they) ask questions, listen to others, discuss topics and collaborate in solving problems. Children's expressive use of oral and written language is aligned with cognitive activities and the functions of the language (Halliday, 1975. Adults play an important role in creating conditions that challenge children's curiosity and establish what Vygotsky (1978) defines as the Zone of Proximal Development (ZPD). The ZPD refers to the distance between what learners can do without help and what they can achieve with guidance and encouragement from an adult or skilled partner.

Children love to tell stories and listen to each other's stories because they think in stories. Children's stories uncover children's funds of knowledge. Moll (2019) defines *funds of knowledge* as a socio-cultural approach that values the knowledge that children bring from home; this approach reveals experiences that families have to construct knowledge. The funds of knowledge reveal what is relevant in the lives of the children. Language and literacy are part of everyday life experience. Hart and Risley's (1995) study on toddlers and preschoolers in professional, working-class, and very low-income families found huge differences in children's language development over time that established a word gap. Those differences were marked by opportunity setting a research agenda that places emphasis on children's early experiences in life as a foundation for language and literacy.

Educators with social responsibility use children's literature to promote the awareness and engagement required to work on global issues of significance. Stories can promote social and moral development in young children (Edwards, 1986). Children's books are empowering tools when children are active participants and have a voice. Lesaux and Harris' (2015) research recommends a knowledge-building approach to literacy instruction that brings the world to students in a meaningful way. Storytelling opens the world to the children. Adults who formulate questions that spark children's curiosity and connections to the children's lives are promoting critical literacy. A good question establishes ZPD and gives children ownership (Salmon & Barrera, 2021). Children's experiences with the world give them the opportunity to talk about things that matter to them. For that reason, the quality of adult-child conversations is the foundation of language development (Cazden, 2004). Children learn to talk because they want to talk about the world, not because they want to talk about language.

Critical literacy allows children's participation. Children have the right to participate in all matters affecting them and freely expressing their views. Young children's participation is key to developing a culture of listening, human rights, and democracy. Participation increases children's self-esteem, self-efficacy, communication, negotiation, conflict resolution, and decision-making skills. Teachers, conversely, learn more about the children, and gain respect for children's ideas, interests, and needs. Conversations that invite children to take perspective, compare, contrast, see the cause and consequence of actions, and so forth, help the children visualize problems and understand themselves. For Freire (1972), what an educator does in teaching is to make it possible for the students to become themselves.

Functions and Conditions of Language and Literacy Learning

Language is an essential social and cognitive human attribute. Both oral and written language develop when children find a meaning and a function. Young children communicate even before talking. Care givers can distinguish if a child's cry is because he is hungry, in pain, or tired; these are all functions of language. For the linguist Michael Halliday (1975), social interaction is a necessary condition for language learning. For him, children not only learn the language but also learn the culture through that language through their interactions with parents and caregivers. Halliday (1975) proposes 7 functions in categories that are a good reference for identifying children's communicative intentions.

- **Instrumental:** Obtain things. For example, I want to play.
- **Personal**: Communicate personal feelings, thoughts. For example: "I love you"
- **Regulatory:** Regulate other people's actions, it is used to tell others what to do. For example: Tell me more.
- **Imaginative**: Create, imagine. For example: "There was upon a time a…"
- **Interactive**: Interaction with other people, this language is used to connect with others. For example: Let's do it!
- **Heuristic**: Discovery. When language is used to gain knowledge. For example: Why is the sky blue?
- **Informative**: Inform ideas, knowledge. The use of language to convey information. For example: The bananas are sweet.

Having a back-and-forth conversation with a child may seem like a small thing, but it turns out that it is everything when it comes to helping them learn language. Turn-taking is a basic and natural condition to engage children in a conversation. Turn-taking applies not only to oral interactions but also to other symbol systems such as writing and drawing. Children need an audience and a response when they tell a story. It is like any conversation: When people talk to each other, the conversation continues when there is a two-way communication pattern. Involving children in high-quality interactions when their peers share their stories by inviting them to ask questions, share their thoughts, and complement each other creates a safe environment for authors. Research (Hirsh-Pasek, et al. 2015) found that the quality of interactions between parents and children matters more than the number of words children hear. Children establish a connection with their audience when they share their stories. This motivates children to stay in the interaction longer and, therefore, provides them with more opportunities to learn.

Another important framework to understand language learning is Brian Cambourne's (Crouch & Cambourne, 2020, p. 27) 8 conditions of learning, which are aligned with young children's natural language learning. The conditions of learning that support young children's natural language development:

- **Immersion:** When children are immersed in an environment where oral and written language are used to communicate. Where children can see oral and written language at work.
- **Demonstration:** When adults demonstrate how language works. The goal of demonstration is for learners to witness and engage in the processes of what is being learned.
- **Engagement:** This is a participatory stance taken by a learner about what is being demonstrated. For learning to occur, a learner must engage in any demonstration in which they are immersed.
- **Expectation:** This condition is related to the image of the child or the beliefs about the learners' capabilities. With high expectations, the adult gives more, and vice versa.
- **Responsibility:** This is a self-regulated response. Children take the responsibility of talking, reading, and writing because they feel the need to use the language to communicate.
- **Employment:** Children need time and opportunity to practice. Adults should create those spaces where children can learn to talk, read, and write.

Crafting Stories of Voice and Influence

- **Approximation:** Just like children's initial attempts to communicate are celebrated, so are children's approximations to communicate through scribbles or drawings..
- **Response:** Communication is a two-way process. When an adult responds to children's approximations (language sounds), they find a reason to continue making attempts to communicate.

Author's Chair and Beyond

The Author's chair is a designated only for children who volunteer to share their stories. In this space children can have a turn-taking experience when they share their stories. It allows teachers to help children be heard and seen. It is a crucial element to foster children's participation; it gives them the opportunity to use the language for authentic purposes and lets them take responsibility to use the language for authentic purposes, employ the language skills that they know, and make approximations (Figure 1). Furthermore, the Author's Chair is an opportunity to respond to each other; children take turns to tell and listen to stories. In this exchange, children put the different functions of the language to work. As a conversation progresses, the listener and speaker roles are exchanged back and forth.

Figure 1. The author's chair, a place where children share their stories using puppets

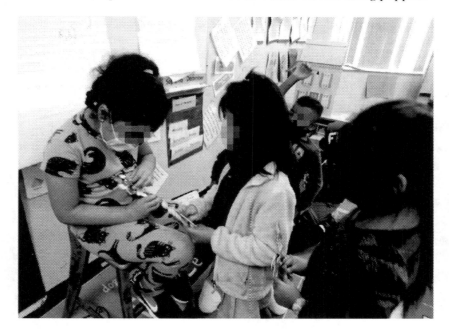

Discussing authors and how they were inspired to tell a story is a good motivation for children to see themselves as authors. The Author's Chair creates a culture of sharing; it gives children the message that they can be authors. Children have a voice through the Author's Chair. When children tell a story, they need an audience who can provide feedback, or the belief that someone might be influenced by their stories. The Author's Chair is a special time and place where writers who wish to share their final products can do it.

There are rules to make the Author's Chair work: The teachers should create a risk-free space where children feel safe to share and empowered to do it. Adults and children should agree on important rules to make this happen:

- Voluntary (children have the right to share their stories or not)
- Sign up if you want to share
- Listen with understanding and empathy to your peers' stories
- Ask clarification questions
- Respect perspectives
- Don't judge
- Complement something that you like
- Share your thoughts
- Make suggestions

The Author's Chair is the last step in the writer's process; it helps children develop skills to express their perspectives and their right to participate and have a voice. Krashen (2016) says that language acquisition requires meaningful interaction in the target language, during which the acquirer is focused on meaning rather than form. The use of good children's literature and discussions about the stories are a good starting point. The use of good children's books along with critical literacy is a child-friendly approach to spark children's curiosity and imagination that enables children to communicate their thoughts and feelings.

Multiliteracies

Stories are a part of human history. People "read" the world and make sense of it using multiple channels of communication other than traditional reading and writing. People communicated orally or through drawings before printing was invented. Nowadays, there are multiple ways of telling stories and sharing them on small or big scales. Dyson's (1988) research found that as children mature and gain experience, they learn new and more complex ways of manipulating paints, clay, language and other symbolic material. For her, children engage in the thinking processes of organizing and abstracting as they work to portray their messages.

Children learn to make sense of the world when they are involved and motivated. Children externalize their thoughts through different sign systems (Gardner, 1980). Language, as we see it, is more than just the words being used; it includes any set of symbols used to construct share meanings. Children are natural symbol makers (Dyson, 1990). Adults should facilitate multiple forms to express their perspectives, ideas, and interests to enable children's participation. As Malaguzzi's (Edwards, Gandini & Forman, 1998) "The Hundred Languages of Children" poem says, there are infinite ways that children can express, explore, and connect their thoughts, feelings and imaginings. He highlights the importance of providing children with one hundred ways to share their thinking about the world around them. Ferris Jabr (2019) says that we give life to the stories we tell, imagining entire worlds and preserving them on rock, paper and silicon. Children naturally use multiliteracies to tell their stories.

The use of multileracy, such as pretend play, drawing, modeling, and digitizing, are some of the multiple languages or symbol systems (Gardner, 1980) that children use to inquire, investigate, and make sense of their world. These languages are symbolic and are open to the endless potentials in children.

They believe in the potential of a child's ability to wonder. It is the belief that there are "multiple ways of seeing and multiple ways of being" (Reggio Children, 2022).

Our brains are developed to tell stories. Everyday human communication revolves around stories of one's experiences. Children tell what happens to them, but they also create stories that they imagine. Stories that children tell inform adults about their thoughts. A day after the terrorist attack on the Twin Towers on September 11, 2001, in New York City, the 3-year-old children in a preschool where I was working were enacting the story. They were building towers, some of them were wearing firefighters dress-up uniforms pretending to fight the fire. Other children created aircrafts with Lego blocks and pretended crashing towards the tall Lego buildings. I am sure that those children's parents were unaware that the children were capturing the scenes of the tragedy on TV. Shank (1990) says that explaining the world is a critical aspect of intelligence. Comprehending events around you depend upon having a memory of prior events available for help in interpreting events.

For children, play is a cognitive activity; in many instances, it is enacting a story. In previous research (Salmon & Lucas, 2011), when preschool children were asked: *what is thinking?* many children's responses were stories. For example, a five-year-old said: Well, it was dark, and we were cold, so we got some blankets. When children are involved in pretend play, drawing, and acting, they are naturally thinking. Ritchhart and Perkins (2008) say that when learners speak, write, or draw their ideas, they deepen their cognition. Crouch and Cambourne (2020, p. 108) say that learners' brains construct meaning using whatever stimulus, or medium, is available --printed, graphic, oral, etc. -- while thinking and interacting alongside other learners. Children are constantly making connections to their experiences.

Literacy changes as society and technology change. In their position and guidelines (2013), the NCTE states that 21st century students require literacies that are "multiple, dynamic, and malleable" in nature. Among NCTE literacies (2013) this chapter highlights: Digital storytelling as an opportunity to meet 21st century literacies; design and share information for global communities to meet a variety of purposes; and build intentional cross-cultural connections and relationships with others so to pose and solve problems collaboratively and strengthen independent thought.

Digital Collective Stories for Influence and Play

Digital storytelling combines stories with technology and allows children to tell stories using different sign systems such as voice, play, text, drawings, audio, and video from software such as Stop Motion or other. Digital storytelling is inclusive, it functions as an Author's Chair. Children develop their language from the back and forth of conversations, even when they are on the receiving, or listening. They learn by observing how other people react to what they say (Resnick & Snow, 2009).

In response to NCTE's 21st Century Literacies recommendations my colleagues Kiriaki Melliou, Veronica Boix-Mansilla, and I conceptualized *Digital Collective Stories of Voice and Influence* (DCSVI) (Salmon & Melliou, 2021) to the process of cognitive and emotionally engaging children to create a story together. This definition arose from our observations on our multi-site research (in the United States and Greece) where children were immersed in reading, drawing, writing, and digitizing their stories. In the digitizing process, children were engaged in collective dialogic thinking to craft their stories. Davis and Arend (2013) define dialogical thinking as role playing by people in which they can enter empathetically into opposing arguments and viewpoints, thereby examining their own thinking and recognizing its strengths and weaknesses (p. 109). Children influenced each other through their individual stories. When children immerse in symbolic play, while they manipulate and control their environment, they are constantly exchanging viewpoints. Digital stories give children more ownership and agency when they contribute with their characters to tell their stories.

When children share their stories, they learn to think interdependently, collaborate and take perspectives, especially in the process of bringing a story alive through digital technology. They use multiliteracy to bring their story alive during the creative process. During the digitizing process of their stories, we noticed that the children's collective efforts came up with a story with different viewpoints. There was a dynamic combination of symbolic play and boundary objects. For Star and Griesemer (1989), boundary objects are a way of looking at complex situations through different perspectives. The Twin Towers story is a good example to explain this concept. When the children were enacting the event, they were taking different roles to recreate the story that each of them understood. The lens of boundary objects can help us to understand how the various actors involved can cooperate on a project. Their creations with the Lego blocks reflected a symbolic play activity. For Bratitsis (2018), the center of attention in storytelling is not the story as a literature-related product, but the collaborative design process with the digital story functioning as a medium which additionally involves emotional understanding and literacy.

The presence of play was evident in the digitizing stage. According to Piaget (1951), the different types of play the children engage in reflect their cognitive development. Children aged 5 and 6 years old are in the preoperational stage of Piaget's cognitive development. During this stage, children begin to engage in symbolic play and learn to manipulate symbols. Children develop symbolic thinking, which is the ability to use symbols to represent things. This type of play allows children to manipulate and control their environment and gives them a sense of accomplishment. They become more focused on the social aspects of play, develop the ability to reason, and their constructive play transitions from functional to symbolic play at this stage. Children's play can become a serious cognitive engagement; it gives them the opportunity to externalize their thinking, especially if they can reflect on their play (Salmon, 2015).

The act of digitizing a story involves children in a slow-motion microsphere type of play followed by continuous reflection. Through make-believe play using objects to recreate a story the children have a voice to externalize their thoughts, reveal their concerns, and express their interests.

METHODOLOGY

Background and Setting

The data presented in this chapter were drawn from multisite action research in South Florida in the United States for three years. The study was also conducted in refugee camps in Greece. This chapter only includes data from the kindergartens in South Florida as follows:

- **Kindergarten A** afterschool program from a Title I school
    - Participants: 27 children (12 girls & 15 boys)
    - Most of the children (97%) come from Latin American immigrant families
    - 23 children were bilingual
    - 2 children spoke only Spanish
    - 2 children spoke only English
    - We collected data once a week during ten weeks in the afterschool program for one hour. The children had to complete their worksheet homework before participating in the program

Crafting Stories of Voice and Influence

- **Kindergarten B** from a Title I school
    - Participants: 17 children (8 boys & 9 girls)
    - Due to the Pandemic, the attendance was irregular. Some children participated via Zoom (13 children in person, 4 children virtual)
    - Around 50% of the children come from Latin American Immigrant families, 47% were African American and 3% mixed races.
    - The Latin American children were bilingual, except for three children who only spoke Spanish
    - The African American children spoke only English

*** Title I schools serve low-income students. Title I funds aim to bridge the gap between low-income students and other students. The U.S. Department of Education provides supplemental funding to local school districts to meet the needs of at-risk and low-income students.

- **Kindergarten C** afterschool program from a community-based center

    - Participants: 7 girls and 11 boys
    - Immigrant Central American indigenous descendent
    - All children were bilingual (English and Spanish) except for two Hattian who spoke only English, and one recently arrived girl who only spoke Spanish.

Research Goals

- Examine how children's literature embodies perspectives on the types of stories that children talk about, draw, write or tell
- Investigate in what ways stories help children understand and value their identities, emotions, thoughts, and respect for diversity
- Discover how the exchange of stories and perspectives help children make connections between their own lives and their peers
- Explore how literature opens a window to the world and help them learn from the many visible and invisible stories around them
- Explore how children use multiple literacies to create boundary objects and agency

Project Design

The project was designed with Cambourne conditions for learning (Crouch & Cambourne, 2020) and Halliday's (1975) functions of language in mind. The research team and teachers used these frameworks to plan authentic learning experiences followed by child-centered discussions that helped the children make sense. The activities engaged children in learning language through how it is used to communicate meaning.

The project aimed to help children develop a strong self-identity and agency through storytelling while they gain language and literacy skills in their first and second language. The project consisted of reading stories to the children and promoting critical literacy through developmentally appropriate book extensions.

The books were intentionally selected to approach migration, identity, second language issues, empathy, community, and diversity. Although we had a set of preselected books, since this is an action research project, we used data to select books that meet the needs of the children.

We used dialogic reading, a read aloud modality that engages adults and children in a conversation about the story. We use thinking routines (Ritchhart & Perkins, 2008) to leverage children's thinking and learning and global thinking routines (Boix-Mansilla 2016) to cognitively and emotionally engage the children before, during and after reading stories. For example: we use the See-Feel-Think-Wonder thinking routine to introduce a book. The children are invited to see the cover of a book, share what they feel about the image, then share what they think about the image, and finally, share what they wonder. Another example is the Step Inside thinking routine to take perspective.

The book extensions varied depending on the story's theme. For the book extensions, we used a variety of materials to help children respond to stories using multiple literacies. A research team member usually modeled the use of resources to extend the story.

Data Collection and Analysis Procedures

The study used action research. Action research is about evaluating your practice to check whether it is as good as you would like it to be, identifying any areas that you feel need improving and finding ways to improve them (McNiff, 2016, p. 9). I organized research teams consisting of graduate assistants and a volunteer in the afterschool programs (Kindergartens A & C). The school program's research team consisted of a graduate assistant and the teacher whose role was participant researcher. The study involved researchers and participants working together to understand the problems and find solutions.

The children had opportunities to listen and tell their stories using different strategies and media, including technology. Important elements of the experience are that they can:

- slow down to observe the world carefully and listen attentively to others
- exchange stories and perspectives with one another; and
- make connections between their own lives and bigger human stories.

The study collected qualitative data that consisted of field notes, videos, audio-recordings, and children's artifacts.

Upon collecting the data, the research team met to analyze, categorize, and the data and search for patterns in it. After analyzing the data, the research team set goals and activities for the next session and discussed a focus. During the analysis we revisited the research questions to be clear about what we were looking at.

FINDINGS AND DISCUSSION

The settings where the study occurred show certain communication patterns. In the three settings we used similar children's books and follow-up activities that included the use of thinking routines (Ritchhart & Perkins, 2008) to cognitively engage children. Crouch and Cambourne (2020) said that effective teaching

Crafting Stories of Voice and Influence

requires us be the thinkers we want our learners to be: curious, aware, considerate, industrious, interpretive, affirmative, and, yes, inventive. The study's limitations did not allow us to learn more about the children's experiences at home, but we were able to learn about the children's lives through their stories.

We were respectful with the children's right to dignity and privacy. We protected their identities by using fake names.

Use of Children's Books

Children's books were powerful catalysts to open conversations and help children process concepts and misconceptions.

Identity

Young children need a strong, solid sense of who they are and what their place is in today's rapidly changing world. Knowing themselves, being self-aware, provides children with a point of reference to understand and interact with their families, communities, and society.

We read Robert and Saoussan Askar's "From Far Away" story. This is an empowering story, because Saoussan is the story's co-author. Robert Munsch received a letter from a Kindergarten child name Saoussan; the letter was about her story of migration that turned into a book. The story is about a Lebanese family who emigrated to Canada due to war. Saoussan's first cultural shock was the language and Halloween. We considered this story a good resource to create mirrors and windows, since most of the children are immigrants who in their majority are English Language Learners (ELL).

The children had different responses in each setting.

Kindergarten A: Many children were newcomers from Venezuela and Colombia. In most of their stories, these children talked about the difficulties that their families were experiencing before emigrating to the USA. On several occasions, the children's stories were about family separation. Here is an example of one child's story:

Daniel: I come from Colombia. I packed my Teddy, and I came from Colombia. My sisters couldn't come.
Teacher: Tell me more
Daniel: In Colombia it was bad. There were broken things, so we had to go to Miami.
Teacher: What type of broken things are you talking about?
Daniel: The houses... my brother and sister's house and some buildings

Kindergarten B: The teacher had more opportunities to interact with the children and have them work together. The children's stories were more related to identity issues. Here is an example.

Clara 1: In pre-K I did not know English. I was sad I was very shy and scared because I didn't speak
    English, but when you talked to me, I felt happy. Now I speak two languages!!
Rita 2: I didn't know that you were sad
Clara 1: Because nobody talked to me. I was very sad
Rita 2: Sorry that I didn't talk to you
Clara 1: Now I know English, I also Speak Spanish (with pride)

Kindergarten C: Only a few children responded to the story with stories about their journey of coming to the United States. However, four children said that they will not tell their secrets. We were surprised to hear them in four different tables, so they were not influencing among themselves. Another child described her life in Colombia where she lived with her grandmother, then she had to come to the United States only with her mother.

Educators underestimate the wealth of knowledge that students bring to the classroom, especially when teaching in diverse and marginalized settings. By listening to stories, children can mirror personal experiences that can mirror their own stories. Research (Leland, et al., 2018) says that social issues, multicultural, and international children's literature shatters images of "the other" by presenting characters who are both like ourselves and those who are very different from us. In stories that capture children's attention, the children identify with the main characters; thus, reading creates an opportunity to develop empathy.

In Kindergarten C, there were three Hondurean cousins (two boys and one girl) who lived in the same house. These children became one of our research focus to explore literature as windows to the world and perspective taking. Their stories and drawings were similar in some aspects but different in others. Most of all, they allowed us to see the children's perspectives on each other's story.

Empathy Building

We read "What if…?" by Berger & Curato (2018), a story about a girl who is determined to express herself, no matter what! She drew, sculpted, built, carved or collaged to express herself. The story was a provocation for Juan to draw a family. He was the first child signing in to share with the class. Juan drew a family. As part of the Author's Chair, the children were invited to give Javier feedback and ask questions.

David 1: Who is this person? (Pointing to the drawing)
Juan: My mother
Carla 2: What's your mother's name
Juan: I don't know. She is in Honduras (Juan's eyes are in tears)
Vilma (Juan's cousin): He doesn't have a mother hugging him to make him feel better.

One of our goals was to examine the effect of children's books on the types of stories that children draw, write or tell. I came to the conclusion that some children had a need to tell their stories even if they were unrelated to the book's theme. Although "What if…?" had nothing to do with Juan's story of migration or his family, the Author's Chair offered him a space to express himself. There were several instances like this, in the three schools, when children told emotional stories that were unrelated to the book.

Good stories do more than create a sense of connection: They build familiarity and trust and allow the listener to enter the story where they are, making them more open to learning (Boris, 2017). Children are intrinsically motivated to tell their stories when they are cognitively and emotionally engaged through a variety of authentic experiences and stories that are relevant to children's lives. Listening to stories that children can relate to helps them establish connection and a sense of belonging. Children's identities and emotional experiences and the learning environment that they are exposed to are influencing what they can do (Immordino-*Yang*, 2016).

Crafting Stories of Voice and Influence

We selected "This is Me: A Story of Who we Are & Where we Came From" by Curtis & Cornell. Using a child-friendly approach, the story portrays stories of different people who must emigrate suddenly. They must leave everything behind and they can only pack something meaningful. After listening to the story, the children were invited to draw an object that is meaningful for them. In response to this book extension, a child who just joined Kindergarten A grabbed a marker and drew a story of leaving his father behind. He said that he was sad because his father was left behind.

Emotions

We made some changes in Kindergarten C in response to some children's reactions and Juan's story. Another child who was eager to share his story forgot to sign in, so he couldn't share his story when he wanted to. He destroyed his drawing and said, "I hate my life." We thought that in the next session it was important to help children identify and talk about feelings, so we selected the Color Monster book by Llenas (2012.) We invited the children to use some puppets to tell what makes them feel happy, sad, angry, and calm; then, we invited them to share what makes them feel any of those feelings.

When the children shared their stories, some of the children brought up that some of them are bullied. When children experience violence at school, such as bullying, there are negative consequences that can follow them for years. To talk about feelings, the children created puppet characters with wooden sticks (see figure 2). This was a powerful venue to engage children in conversations about their stories. The use of storytelling as an early intervention is a key resource in preventing aggressive behaviors from occurring in the first place, and it helps to build a positive school climate for all students.

Figure 2. Story characters that worked as puppets

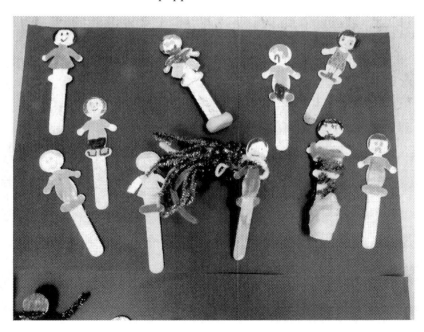

Diversity

In Kindergarten C, after reading "Rosalia: The Honduran American" by Osoria (2020), a story of a girl from Honduras who shares with her American classmates about her culture, the children were invited to share some traditions from their countries. Juan and his cousins, Vilma and Eric, who were seated at different tables, came up with similar drawings of their houses. The three of them were invited to share what they drew. We learned that the three children lived in the same house. What caught our attention is when Vilma said, "This is not his house (pointing at Eric). He is not part of the family. His skin is darker, and he doesn't have a mom." Then Juan said, "His mother was expecting a baby when she was crossing the river." Eric didn't say anything, but Juan got a little bit distressed. This conversation opened many questions about children's vulnerability, self-identity, sense of belonging, and racism. Vilma is a kind girl, we knew that she didn't want to hurt her cousin, but it was important to talk about the respect for diversity and human beings. We decided to share the book "Brown: The many Shades of Love" by Johnson James & Moore (2020) in our next session.

In the next session, after reading "Brown: The many shades of love," the children are invited to find out their skin tone looking at the book's skin colors. Here is the interaction between a child and one of the research team members:

Adult: Do you and your father share the same skin color?
Keith: No, he is less dark than me. But I'm darker than him.
Adult: What is your mum's skin color?
Keith: Light. So, your mum is light, and your father is darker.
Adult: You are mix from your mom and your father's skin color.
Keith: I am a mix my sister's skin color. She is older than me.
Adult: What is your sister's skin color? Same as you?
Keith: Yeah."

Digital Storytelling

The process of digitizing a story creates a social play setting where children communicate with each other as they play with small toys to create a story. When children are involved in play to solve a problem, they use objects that represent different things, but collectively they reconcile meanings (see Figure 3).

Crafting Stories of Voice and Influence

Figure 3. Symbolic play: Children using the characters that they designed to digitize their story

Children immerse themselves in symbolic play when they manipulate and control their environment, which gives them a sense of accomplishment Digital stories give children more ownership when they contribute with their drawings, puppets, and other elements to tell their stories.

CONCLUSION

This project brought benefits to the children and many lessons to the research team. The children developed language and literacy with a purpose in a risk-free playful environment. Stories help children develop a theory of mind. The learning experiences were meaningful, inclusive, engaging, collaborative, empowering, and sustainable. They helped to bridge the gap between the classroom and the children's homes. As Mikkelsen (1990) says, Heath's work has helped us to see that we must change classrooms to help non-mainstream children adapt to a society that prizes the paradigmatic mode above dramatic play and personalized narrative. Digital storytelling involved children in play and gave them a sense of agency and voice.

Language and Literacy Experiences

Children develop strong language and literacy skills through everyday interactions and by reading and writing to learn and communicate. Reading high-quality children's books and engaging children in critical literacy help them become good thinkers. Reading and writing to learn carries a strong message: We read and write to learn and connect with the world. Children learn to read by reading and to write by writing (Resnick & Snow, 2009). Thus, any literacy program should create opportunities for children to speak and listen as the foundation skills for reading and writing.

Not all children have the same language and literacy experiences. Both oral and written storytelling traditions are important (Heath, 1982, Street, 2012). Language, cognition, and emotional aspects of human beings carry an important weight in both types of storytelling traditions. Everyday human communication revolves around personal stories. Shank (1990) says that when people talk, they talk about the knowledge they have about the world around them. The children's stories that are shared here are all a testament of their knowledge and experiences.

Multiliteracy

Traditionally, literacy has referred to the ability to read and write. Multiliteracy is the ability to identify, interpret, create, and communicate meaning across a variety of visual, oral, corporal, musical and alphabetical forms of communication. However, in today's technology-driven world, the word literacy has expanded to encompass an ability to communicate through a variety of mediums. In real life contexts, children have a hundred ways to communicate. Children as social meaning makers create boundary objects to collectively reconcile meanings.

Critical Literacy and Thinking

Children's books are great resources to create intentional connections by creating mirrors, windows and glass sliding doors (Bishop, 1990). Books are provocations to involve children in deep conversations. Most of the time they uncover their live events, conceptions and misconceptions, such as the skin color episode.

Critical literacy and children's participation in crafting and sharing their stories were a good invitation for dialogic thinking, which offers opportunities to think interdependently, share different points of view, and use frames of reference. In the case of the three cousins, they share a house and similar family experiences, but each of them told a different story. They tried to make sense of the story by presenting their perspectives.

Cambourne's conditions of learning play an important role in designing learning experiences. Having high expectations of children as thinkers and communicators opens space for critical literacy. The use of thinking routines in the process of reading and discussing about books fosters higher levels of understanding and create a ZPD. Crouch and Cambourne (2020) sustain that a critical understanding that learners must develop about reading is how a reader purposefully constructs, deconstructs, and reconstructs meanings from symbols. The children took responsibility to make decisions as they shared their thinking.

Participation

Giving children an opportunity to participate and to have a voice through their stories is a right. Markowska-Manista (2018, p 57) highlights article 12 from the Convention on the Rights of the Child that says, "States Parties shall assure to the child who is capable of forming his or her own views the right to express those views freely in all matters affecting the child, the views of the child being given due weight in accordance with the age and maturity of the child." The Author's Chair and Digital Storytelling are powerful and inviting venues to promote children's participation. Children see this as an opportunity to be seen, heard and listened to. Children were eager to share in the three settings, However, in Kinder C, some children considered the Author's Chair as a place to tell secrets, and some of them said that they did not want to tell their secrets. This affirms that children's stories carry social and emotional baggage that needs to be respected. Brown (2012) says that children find ways to protect themselves from vulnerability,

Crafting Stories of Voice and Influence

from being hurt, diminished, and disappointed; they put an armor on using their thoughts, emotions, and behaviors as weapons. Children take their armor off by telling stories. Teachers should be prepared to create a safe environment to help children share their stories and handle vulnerability. A participatory approach allows children to recognize that their actions and voices are crucial and can become effective tools to implement change that would benefit them and their communities (Markowska-Manista, 2018).

Sense of Belonging

Stories create a sense of belonging: When children listen or share a story, they feel they are not alone. They establish connections with others. Neuroscientists Immordino Yang (2016) and Hasson, et al. (2012) have shown evidence of brain activity and hormones that show a connection between the speaker and the listener. Boix-Mansilla and Rivard (2014) say that when a student feels security and support, they get the sense that they are accepted for who they are. The students feel that everyone belongs in the classroom or school when there is inclusion. They are bringing their authentic selves when they can bring their own unique attributes and strengths to the environment. The opportunity to share gave children a voice and empowered them to make their thinking visible. In Kindergarten C, their secrets raised many questions when some children said that they did not want to share. Perhaps the environment was not safe enough for some of them. Remember that in one of the conversations a child made her cousin vulnerable by saying that he is not part of the family because he was poor, his skin color was darker, and he doesn't have parents. To create a safer environment, we used broad prompts to support the children's thinking to help them change this misconception and be more empathetic.

Digital Storytelling and Boundary Objects

People who solve problems together build a community of thinkers who can contribute to the solution with pride. DSCVI promote dialogic thinking to create boundary objects towards creating a story. The process of digitizing a story creates a social play setting in which children communicate with each other as they play with small toys to create a story. Children who are involved in play to solve a problem create contexts and use symbolic play to create stories that they want the world to hear.

DSCVI is an empowering, inclusive and developmentally appropriate approach to fostering storytelling and developing language and literacy, including second language. In the study, the children were excited each time we introduced a new way to communicate. Digital storytelling allows children to use several sign symbols such as drawings, modeling, puppetry, writing, talking, and music. Digitizing their stories was a great opportunity to bring them together. Crouch and Camborne (2020) said that language is more than just words: It includes any set of symbols used to construct and share meanings.

Developmentally Appropriate Practices

Digital storytelling and engaging activities to extend children's books are critical to support meaning making in children. Digital storytelling is a slow-motion microsphere type of play. Research on play (Salmon, 2016) confirms its benefits: It contributes to the child's cognitive, socio-emotional, ethical, and physical development.

LIMITATIONS

We had a time limitation in kindergartens A & C. We were able to work with the children once a week for 1.5 hours during the afterschool program. The children's attendance is irregular in this type of program. Conducting research on Friday afternoons is also not the ideal time because the children are tired.

Digital storytelling is not complicated and is easy to implement. However, this is possible when children have a culture of listening and telling stories and use critical literacy to process stories.

Kindergarten B was a better setting to implement these ideas because the teacher created a culture of listening and sharing at all times during class.

FUTURE RESEARCH DIRECTIONS

It was hard to triangulate the data drawn from the children's stories and their personal experiences due to time limitations and a lack of parental involvement. Parental involvement would play an important role for future research. Parental involvement can also inform researchers about the family's storytelling traditions, beliefs and other funds of knowledge. The children's response about not being able to tell their secrets is important information to explore. Is this part of the children's culture? Are there any socio-political issues that inhibit children from telling their stories? Studying the development of language use in relation to written materials in the home and community requires a broad framework of sociocultural analysis (Heath,1982, Street, 2012). In the three school settings, the children shared stories that make them vulnerable; there is a need for interdisciplinary research to inform teachers how to have conversations about trauma from the teacher's role.

ACKNOWLEDGMENT

Some ideas and research reported here were developed with much appreciated support from Florida International University Humanities Grant and Visible Thinking South Florida. The positions taken are of course not necessarily those of these organizations. I also thank the schools for opening their doors. I am eternally thankful to my colleagues Kiraki Melliou and Veronica Boix-Mansilla for their unconditional support and inspiration. I also want to acknowledge my research assistants Kenia Najera, Maria Ximena Barrera, and Jiamin Xu, teacher researcher Sharon Smith and teacher Hafsa Haider, and volunteers Anais Vela and Muriel Summers for their generous disposition and thoughts to make this study a strong learning experience.

REFERENCES

Berger, S., & Curato, M. (2018). *What if…?* Little, Brown and Company.

Bishop, R. S. (1990). Mirrors, windows, and sliding glass doors. *Perspectives - Gerontological Nursing Association, 1*(3), ix–xi.

Boix-Mansilla, V. (2016). How to be a Global Thinker: Using global thinking Routines to create classroom cultures that nurture global competence. *Education Leadership, 74*(4), 10-16.

Boix-Mansilla, V., Rivard, M., & The ID Global Group. (2014). *The many stories library. Milestone learning experiences: A guide for teachers.* ID-Global, Project Zero. Retrieved April, 2022 from https://pz.harvard.edu/sites/default/files/The%20Many%20Stories%20Library%20Project.pdf

Boris, B. (2017). *What makes storytelling so effective for learning? Learning the way.* Harvard Business Publishing. Retrieved March 2022 from https://www.harvardbusiness.org/what-makes-storytelling-so-effective-for-learning/#:~:text=Connecting%20learners,them%20more%20open%20to%20learning

Bratitsis, T. (2018). Storytelling digitalization as a Design Thinking process in educational context. In A. Moutsios-Rentzos, A. Giannakoulopoulos, M. Meimaris (Eds.), *Proceedings of the International Digital Storytelling Conference - "Current trends in digital storytelling: Research & practices"* (pp. 309-320). Academic Press.

Bratitsis, T., & Ziannas, P. (2015). From early childhood to special education: Interactive digital storytelling as a coaching approach for fostering social empathy. *Procedia Computer Science, 67*, 231–240. doi:10.1016/j.procs.2015.09.267

Brown, B. (2012). *Daring greatly: How the courage to be vulnerable transforms the way we live, love, parent, and lead.* Avery Publishing Group.

Cazden, C. (2000). *Classroom discourse: The language of teaching and learning.* Heinemann.

Cazden, C. (2004). The value of conversations for language development and reading comprehension. *Literacy, Teaching and Learning, 9*(1), 1–6.

Children, R. (2022). *100 languages: No way, the hundred is there.* Retrieved March 19, 2022 from https://www.reggiochildren.it/en/reggio-emilia-approach/100-linguaggi-en/

Crouch, D., & Cambourne, B. (2020). *Made for learning: How the conditions of learning guide teacher decisions.* Richard C. Owen Publishers, Inc.

Curtis, J., & Cornell, L. (2016). *This Is Me: A Story of Who We Are & Where We Came From.* Workman Publishing.

Davis, J. R., & Arend, B. (2013). Seven ways of learning: A resource for more purposeful, effective, and enjoyable college teaching. Sterling, VA: Stylus Publishing.

Edwards, C. (1986). *Promoting social and moral development in young children: Creative approaches for the classroom.* Teachers College Press.

Edwards, C., Gandini, L., & Forman, G. (1998). *The hundred languages of children: The Reggio Emilia approach, advanced reflections.* Ablex Publishing Corporation.

Gardner, H. (1980). *Artful scribbles: The significance of children's drawings.* Basic Books, Inc.

Halliday, M. A. K. (1975). *Learning how to mean: Explorations in the development of language.* Edward Arnold. doi:10.1016/B978-0-12-443701-2.50025-1

Hart, B., & Risley, T. R. (1995). *Meaningful differences in the everyday experience of young American children*. Paul H Brookes Publishing.

Hasson, B., & Risley, T. R. (1995). *Meaningful differences in the everyday experience of young American children*. Paul H Brookes Publishing.

Hasson, U., Ghazanfar, A. A., Galantucci, B., Garrod, S., & Keysers, Ch. (2012). Brain-to-brain coupling: A mechanism for creating and sharing a social world. *Trends in Cognitive Sciences*, *16*(2), 114–121. doi:10.1016/j.tics.2011.12.007 PMID:22221820

Heath, S. B. (1982). What no bedtime story means: Narrative skills at home and school. *Language in Society*, *11*, 49-76. https://www.jstor.org/stable/4167291

Hirsh-Pasek, K., Adamson, L. B., Bakerman, R., Tresch Owen, M., Michnick Golinkoff, R., Pace, A., Yust, P. K. S., & Suma, K. (2015). The contribution of early communication quality to low-income children's language success. *Psychological Science*, *26*(7), 1071–1083. doi:10.1177/0956797615581493 PMID:26048887

Immordino-Yang, M. H. (2016). *Emotions, learning, and the brain: Exploring the educational implications for affective neuroscience*. W.W. Norton & Company.

Jabr, F. (2019). The story of storytelling. *Harper's Magazine*. Retrieved March 2022. https://harpers.org/archive/2019/03/the-story-of-storytelling/

Krashen, S. (2016). The purpose of education, free voluntary reading, and dealing with the impact of poverty. *School Libraries Worldwide*, *22*(1), 1–7. doi:10.29173lw6901

Leland, C., Lewison, M., & Harste, J. (2018). *Teaching Children's Literature: It's critical*. Routledge.

Lesaux, N., & Harris, J. (2015). *Cultivating knowledge, building language: Literacy instruction for English Learners in Elementary School*. Heinemann.

Llenas, A. (2012). *The Color Monster: A Story About Emotions*. Little, Brown and Company.

Markowska-Manista, U. (2018). The ethical dilemmas of research with children from the countries of the Global South. Whose participation? *Polish Journal of Educational Studies*, *71*(1), 51–65. doi:10.2478/poljes-2018-0005

McNiff, J. (2016). *You and your action research project*. Routledge Taylor & Francis Group. doi:10.4324/9781315693620

Mikkelsen, N. (1990). Toward greater equity in literacy education: Storymaking and non-mainstream students. *Language Arts*, *67*(6), 556–566.

Moll, L. (2019). Elaborating funds of knowledge: Community-oriented practices in international contexts. *Literacy Research: Theory, Method, and Practice*, *68*(1), 130–138. doi:10.1177/2381336919870805

Montessori, M. (1949). *Education and peace* (H. R. Lane, Trans.). Henry Regnery.

Munsch, R., & Martchenko, M. (1995). *From Far Away*. Annick Press.

NCTE. (2013). *NCTE framework for 21st century curriculum and assessment*. Retrieved March 22, 2022 from https://cdn.ncte.org/nctefiles/resources/positions/framework_21stcent_curr_assessment.pdf

Osoria, C. (2020). *Rosalia - The Honduran American*. Christine Osoria.

Piaget, J. (1951). *Play, dreams, and imitation in childhood* (C. Gattegno & F. M. Hodgson, Trans.). Routledge and Kegen Paul, Ltd.

Premack, D., & Woodruff, G. (1978). Does the chimpanzee have a theory of mind? *Behavioral and Brain Sciences*, *1*(4), 515–526. doi:10.1017/S0140525X00076512

Resnick, L., & Snow, C. (2009). *Speaking and listening for preschool through third grade*. University of Pittsburg and The National Center on Education and the Economy.

Ritchhart, R., & Perkins, D. N. (2008). Making thinking visible. *Educational Leadership*, *65*(5), 57–61.

Salmon, A. (2016). Learning by thinking during play: The power of reflection to aid performance. *Early Child Development and Care*, *186*(3), 480–496. doi:10.1080/03004430.2015.1032956

Salmon, A., & Lucas, T. (2011). Exploring young children's conceptions about thinking. *Journal of Research in Childhood Education*, *25*(4), 364–375. doi:10.1080/02568543.2011.605206

Salmon, A., & Melliou, K. (2021). Understanding and facing migration through stories for influence. In *Handbook of research on promoting social justice for immigrants and refugees through active citizenship and intercultural education*. IGI Global. https://www.igi-global.com/chapter/understanding-and-facing-migration-through-stories-for-influence/282314

Salmon, A. K., & Barrera, M. X. (2021). Intentional questioning to promote thinking and learning thinking skills and creativity. *Thinking Skills and Creativity*, *40*, 1–10. doi:10.1016/j.tsc.2021.100822

Schank, R. (1990). *Tell me a story: Narrative and intelligence*. Northwestern University Press.

Smith, F. (1987). *Joining the literacy club: Further essays in education*. Heineman.

Star, S., & Griesemer, J. (1989). Institutional ecology, translations and boundary objects: Amateurs and professionals in Berkeley's Museum of Vertebrate Zoology, 1907-39. *Social Studies of Science*, *3*(19), 387–420. doi:10.1177/030631289019003001

Street, B. (2012). Society Reschooling. *Reading Research Quarterly*, *2*(47), 216–227. doi:10.1002/RRQ.017

Vygotsky, L. (1978). *Mind in Society: The Development of Higher Psychological Processes*. Harvard University Press.

ADDITIONAL READING

Carlile, P. (2002). A pragmatic view of knowledge and boundaries: Boundary objects in new product development. *Organization Science*, *13*(4), 442–455. doi:10.1287/orsc.13.4.442.2953

Gregory, A. E., & Cahill, M. A. (2009). Constructing critical literacy: Self-reflexive ways for curriculum and pedagogy. *Critical Literacy: Theories and Practices*, *3*(2), 6–16.

Immordino-Yang, M. H. (2008). The smoke around mirror neurons: Goals as sociocultural and emotional organizers of perception and action in learning. *Mind, Brain and Education: the Official Journal of the International Mind, Brain, and Education Society*, *2*(2), 67–73. doi:10.1111/j.1751-228X.2008.00034.x

Mead, G. H. (1967). *Mind, self, and society*. University of Chicago Press. doi:10.7208/chicago/9780226516608.001.0001

Nguyen, M., Vanderwal, T., & Hasson, U. (2019). Shared understanding of narratives is correlated with shared neural responses. *NeuroImage*, *184*, 161–170. doi:10.1016/j.neuroimage.2018.09.010 PMID:30217543

Paul, R. W. (1987). Dialogical thinking: Critical thought essential to the acquisition of rational knowledge and passions. In J. B. Baron & R. J. Sternberg (Eds.), Teaching thinking skills: Theory and practice (pp. 127–148). W H Freeman/Times Books/Henry Holt & Co.

Perry, B., & Winfrey, O. (2021). *What happened to you? Conversations on trauma, resilience, and healing*. Bluebird/Macmillan Ltd.

Piaget, J. (1972). *To Understand Is To Invent*. The Viking Press, Inc.

KEY TERMS AND DEFINITIONS

Author's Chair: This is the final step in the writing process. A special time and place where writers can share their stories.

Boundary Objects: A way of looking at complex situations through different perspectives.

Collective Stories for Influence: Inclusive approach to involve children in dialogic thinking as a starting point to craft their stories.

Critical Literacy: These are practices that encourage students to explore the depth and understanding of a topic to promote critical discussions about power, gender, social class, religion, culture, and race.

Dialogic Thinking: Understand the thinking process and its many elements to provide students opportunities to practice thinking through meaningful discussions and provide well- targeted facilitation.

Digital Storytelling: It is a multimedia presentation combining a variety of digital elements within a narrative structure (a story).

Multiliteracy: The ability to identify, interpret, create, and communicate meaning across a variety of visual, oral, corporal, musical and alphabetical forms of communication.

Chapter 9
Integration of Media and New Literacies in Teacher Education Programs:
Preparing Teachers to Adapt to New Literacies

Maria Dolores Lasso
https://orcid.org/0000-0001-5241-1037
Universidad San Francisco de Quito, Ecuador

ABSTRACT

Preparing teachers to meet the challenges of an ever changing and growing multicultural and diverse population of students must become a focus of attention when thinking about the 21st century teacher education. The purpose of this study is to explore how three different teacher education programs are facing the challenge of preparing teachers to incorporate visual texts and diverse forms of literacy as they prepare to become educators. Literature about teacher identity development, teacher education, and teacher literacy education was reviewed to provide an understanding of the notions around the new of incorporation of new literacies as a way to engage future education professionals in the current challenges of the professional practice.

INTRODUCTION

Despite the constant claims about the relevance of the teachers' role to change educational paradigms, there are very few efforts being conducted to revise the teacher education curriculum programs around the world (Cochran-Smith, 2021). Preparing teachers to meet the challenges of an ever changing and growing multicultural and diverse population of students must become a focus of attention when thinking about the 21st century education. In order for today's teachers to comply with these expectations it becomes essential to find interventions within the teacher education programs that provide opportunities

DOI: 10.4018/978-1-6684-5022-2.ch009

for future teachers to develop understandings and skills that will enable them to engage in professional practices that address the diverse individual and collective needs of students and their families. According to Dotger (2013), "teacher preparation institutions fall short of helping teachers acquires and develop the necessary interpersonal skill sets to engage and communicate…" (p.805). Teacher education programs typically include a Literacy Education class in their curriculum program. This classes tend to focus on teaching reading and writing and rarely incorporate other ways of communication and information interpretation into their teaching. The purpose of this chapter is to explore how three different teacher education programs are facing the challenge of preparing teachers to incorporate visual texts and diverse forms of literacy as they prepare to become educators. This is a qualitative narrative study in which three teacher undergraduate programs will be studied using public information about their courses in order to determine if new literacies have been incorporated in the teacher preparation process. As teachers learn about education and teaching as a profession their own professional identity is influenced by their new understandings of literacy education. This chapter aims to determine if teacher education programs are integrating new literacies as part of their curriculum or what are they doing to provide future teachers with the skills and attitude required to face the challenges of today's literacy education.

BACKGROUND

Teacher education faces the challenge of preparing professionals using the past experiences to confront the future challenges that new generations of an ever evolving society must confront. Teachers are required to adapt and adjust the way they think and the way they teach as a way to respond to their students' needs, in many cases teacher education programs fail to adjust fast enough to provide future teachers with enough strategies and tools for them to become flexible and adaptable learners as their students' needs continuously change (Cochran-Smith & Zeichner, 2005). As teachers adopt new literacies as part of their professional identity development their understandings about literacy education evolve as well as their teacher identity. In order for future teachers to be able to construct their professional identity, adapt and adjust their perceptions, knowledge and skills to meet their students' needs they need to start by learning about themselves, reflecting about their positionalities and beliefs in order to be able to understand others and the culturally diverse environment that today's educational settings embrace (Beijaard, Meijer & Verloop, 2004). The first part of this literature review explains the relevance of providing future teachers with opportunities to explore their teacher identity during their professional education process as means to identify their individual strengths and weaknesses before confronting the complex and demanding social environments that house educational settings. In the second section, the literature review focuses on teacher education by presenting several viewpoints of what is currently taking place and the challenges of teacher education to effectively respond to the society demands. Finally it explains what teacher education should consider when focusing on incorporating new literacies as way for preparing teachers for the current and future needs of Literacy Education.

Development of Teacher Identity and Positionality

Literature indicates that one of the most relevant elements in teacher preparation to meet today's diverse student population needs is to provide future teachers with opportunities to explore their identities and develop their own voice based on their individual positionality (Korthagen, 2003). According to Blommaert (2005), "Identity is who we are" (p. 203), he explains how each individual actions are based on how each person understands, interprets the world involving a variety of situating processes (positionalities) in relation and in reaction to the context in which they are in. Reflecting about what we have lived and who we are allows us to identify those aspects of our past that have provided us opportunities and detriments to achieve our potential. Being aware and analyzing the influence of our positionality in the process of constructing knowledge (epistemology) has an evident relationship with the way we communicate and use language when we teach, therefor it is intrinsically related in the process of what Blommaert (2005) describes as critical discourse analysis. Many times we are not aware of the stereotypes we carry within us and through our unconscious actions we might be reproducing behaviors or ideas that we consciously believe to be wrong. The recognition of this hidden biases help us negotiate our positionality as oppressors or oppressed within our multiple identities, allowing us to consciously reconstruct our knowledge through the process of self-awareness about our views and understandings allowing us to construct a unifying path between our beliefs and our own voice acquisition as we evolve as individuals and adapt to an ever changing world. "Teachers need to be careful about making assumptions, and should talk the time to get to know their students, students' communities, and their actual lived experiences" (Sleeter, 2005, p.107). The infinite process of construction of knowledge through awareness and reflection has a direct impact in the way we develop our discourse, the way we approach our students and the way we teach.

In the past years emphasis has been given to reflective teaching a valued component of effective teaching practices within the context of multicultural education. According to Sleeter & Grant (2009) teachers need to become reflective practitioners in order to prepare students to become citizens who embrace diversity and feel compromised with the need to reconstruct an every changing society by addressing social inequality and the needs of the oppressed. Part of becoming educators is being aware of the influence of the process of reflection about how we teach and why we teach and how teacher discourse affects the way students learn and develop as individuals (Walsh, 2013). Teachers professional identity evolves as teachers embrace new learnings during their formal education. Reflective practice should begin during teacher education programs in which future teachers are expected to reflect about one self's and the systematic study of family and culture beliefs teachers so they can begin to understand how their own experiences are different from others (Sleeter & Carmona, 2017). Only through this type of reflective analysis of their own beliefs and systematic inquiry into diverse cultures can pre-service teachers and teacher educators begin to construct a pedagogy that makes diversity an explicit part of the curriculum and prepare to incorporate into their teaching the different elements that emerge from the social context where education takes place (Swennen & White,2021).

Teacher Education

Consensus about what constitutes good teaching remains unestablished (Darling-Hammond & Oakes, 2019). While in other professions the essential elements that characterize their professionals have been identified in the teaching profession those elements are still being discussed (Korthagen, Loughran & Russel, 2006). As the discussion continues to take place millions of children are undergoing educational experiences that will impair their potential as adults. Having an effective teacher continues to be lottery, but research consistently shows that better prepared teachers are more likely to overcome challenges and continue to pursue their career in education (Beijaard, Meijer & Verloop, 2004). Determining what makes teachers effective in an ever changing context should become a priority if education aims to break the vicious cycles of oppression (Harro, 2000). Achinstein & Ogawa (2006) study shows how teacher education programs are currently not providing enough time to prepare their students to constructively confront the challenges of institutional culture and social interactions within the educational settings.

According to Linda Darling-Hammond (2006), effective teacher education programs have been identified as those, "…whose graduates are sought out by principals and superintendents because they prove consistently capable of creating successful classrooms and helping to lead successful schools" (p.5). Cochran-Smith (2021) identifies the following as essential outcomes of any teacher education program, future teachers should be able to: understand the social and historical context in which the educational systems developed in order to be advocates for change; learn and experience the relationships between culture and schooling; appreciate how their beliefs and expectations about children influence who they are and how they teach; recognize the value of the use of scholarship on learning, pedagogy, and language in their teaching practice.

Teacher Literacy Education

Lapp, Flood, Brice Heath & Langer (2009) in their chapter about communicative, visual and performative arts explain the evolution of the integral components of literacy instruction in time. They specifically stress the need for stretching teacher education in order to prepare school teachers to confront the challenges that arise due to the arrival of the information economy as one of the elements that affect the evolution of literacy education. Future teachers need to be ready to adapt their strategies to the rapid change manifested in the use of audience made texts as they continuously need to reconstruct their beliefs about what teaching should look like in a world where communication does not rely exclusively on printed text, but on a myriad of unceasingly changing symbols. "Teacher education must accept the challenge of enabling instructors to feel at ease with a multitude of symbol systems. This is done most effectively when students and teachers are full partners in learning" (Lapp, Flood, Brice Heath & Langer, 2009, p. 9). Today more than ever teachers need to understand the crucial role of partnership with their students in the teaching and learning process to be able to keep up with the literacy education demands and to foster significant connections between school and everyday life (Gore, 2021; Darling-Hammond & Oakes, 2019). Formal education systems are now responsible for providing their student with opportunities to become lifelong learners. This paradigmatic shift in education pushes the need to rethink the way teachers teach, the resources teachers use and especially the way students and teachers are being assessed (Cochran-Smith, 2021; Flores, 2016).

Educational systems need to catch up with the students' literacy needs, schools need to jump out of the traditional paradigms about the meaning of being literate and began to adopt all the possible signs, symbols and texts that will foster students to develop new understandings. The recognition of multiliteracies as essential resources for learning, urges teacher education programs to radically change in order to incorporate ways in which students learn to cope with change and gain skills to become lifelong learners in a more effective way. The effectiveness in the partnership of teachers and students in the learning process should be considered when assessing teacher's effectiveness due to its importance in providing the students to actively participate in the learning process to make it more meaningful for themselves and more contextualized to the current realities that surround the students' lives and needs (Gore, 2021).

Fostering collaboration and interactions in the learning process and the need to provide teachers with skills and tools that will enable them to create different types of learning environments in which the students can use social networking to represent their ideas. Online learning environments are becoming more and more sophisticated in order to provide students with opportunities to access experts, share

Integration of Media and New Literacies in Teacher Education Programs

previous knowledge and understandings in the most effective ways recognizing the relevance of social interactions in the knowledge construction process.

MAIN FOCUS OF THE CHAPTER

This content analysis study was limited to programs ranked by Quacquarelli Symonds (QS). This independent internationally recognized higher education ranking that uses consistently several indicators to evaluate the quality of academic programs in all fields. The QS ranking was used to identify teacher education programs that were considered to excel in different aspects as representative cases to conduct this study. The ranking included several renown teacher education programs, but only the first 10 programs that offered undergraduate degrees in teacher education where preselected, from those only three cases where chosen to be studied based on their geographical location in the US: University 1 representing the northeast, University 2 representing the midwest and University 3 representing the south of the United States. The universities in the ranking located in the US west coast did not have enough public documents about the literacy education initiaves within their teacher education under graduate programs. In some of the universities selected as cases for this study more than one type of Education major was offered. For comparative purposes of this study the focus was on Elementary Education majors only. The research was conducted using a content analysis approach in which the researcher might selected public documents from each different institution about their approach to literacy education as part of their undergraduate major in Elementary Education. This approach allows to explore how the integration of new literacies takes place in different teacher education programs in the selected universities. These methodology allows the researched to collect data from official public documents to conduct the analysis using maximum variation sampling by establishing set of criteria through specific characteristics. Data gathering was conducted using an embedded analysis, in order to understand each case individually in order to be able to identify issues within each case and then look for common themes among the cases studied.

The study was conducted using an independent case analysis approach followed by a cross case analysis through content analysis method based on public documents attainable through the institutional web page.

Individual case analysis was conducted by taking notes that will enable the researcher to create a case description for each of the selected teacher education programs. Based on the individual analysis of each case, direct interpretation of the data produced patterns enabling themes for analysis to develop generalizations based on what was learned.

Different Ways of Approaching Literacy Education

The way in which Teached Education programs approach new literacies varies according to the public access documents and information collected for this study. In some documents the information allowed to find similar practices among each case, but also the documents allow to differentiate their individual approach to literacy education. Profiles where created for each university based on the public access documentation found on their institutional web page in order to describe the context of their program and the way literacy education was approached at the time the study was conducted.

Teacher Education Program Profiles

For each one of the cases selected for study a profile was developed in order to stablish basic commonalities and also to identify the distinctive elements that characterize each of them. A general description of the program and its mission is provided, accompanied with a brief description the program's curriculum structure, followed by the specific information about the possible scenarios in which the integration of new literacies might occur within each teacher education program.

Independent Case Analysis

Case 1: University 1 - Northeast

- General description: The School of Education is divided into four departments from which the Teacher Education, Special Education, Curriculum and Instruction (TESPECI) offers two teacher education majors: Elementary and Secondary. For the purpose of this study only the Elementary Education major will be analyzed. According to its mission the programs aim to improve human conditions through education to serve diverse populations to make the world more just. The emphasis of this program is preparing teachers to work with children without disabilities or mild disabilities from grades one to six. All Education majors are required to complete a second major All Elementary and Secondary Education programs lead to endorsement for Initial Licensure in their state. All Education majors graduate must complete 120 credits that include Core curriculum, the education major and a second major.
- Curriculum structure: The curriculum is structured in two areas: foundational area and professional courses. The foundational area involves themes such as child development and learning in diverse contexts; while the professional courses provided an integrated approach of learning theories, instructional strategies and models, curriculum and school organizational practices, educational technology, effective assessment procedures and instruments through the disciplinary contents of reading, language, literature, mathematics, science and social studies. Practicum courses begin during sophomore year and finish with a full time practicum in senior year.
- Core curriculum: University 1 requires a set of 12 required core courses to all their students.
- Major Curriculum: The major is composed by 20 courses from which two are psychology requirements, a mandatory Math class and all education majors complete three pre-practicum experiences (1 day/week for 10 weeks) and one full practicum experience (5 days/ week for 14 weeks)
- Subjects related to the integration of new literacies: The Elementary Education program requires 20 classes, from which based on their title Teaching Reading (Class1), Teaching Language Arts (Class 2), and Teaching Bilingual Students (Class 3) are related to Literacy Education. Based on the course descriptions obtained from a public domain the integration of new literacies in teacher literacy education is not evident. In the Teaching Reading class according to the course description the emphasis will be on the formal aspects of the literacy development process, phrases such as, *"Emphasis will be placed on the social, political, and cultural context of reading instruction"* (Course Description, Case 1, Class 1), lead us to believe that there is no explicit inclusion of alternative texts in the Teaching Reading course; but the description does mention *"Students will gain understanding of major theoretical perspectives on literacy development and the myriad*

strategies for teaching reading in a variety of contexts" (Course Description, Case 1, Class 1), which could be interpreted as the inclusion of new texts as part of the teaching reading process. In the Teaching Language Arts class the description declares "*Students will be exposed to theoretical approaches to both oral and written language development in addition to a wide variety of teaching methods*" (Course Description, Case 1, Class 2) pointing out the emphasis to literacy learning utilizing different methods but focusing on oral and written language. In the Teaching Bilingual Students according to its description students will learn about legislation and history of English Language learning, it states, "*Reviews and applies literacy and content area instructional approaches*" (Course Description, Case 1, Class 3). Neither one of the course descriptions show any evident attempt to integrate new literacies in the teacher education process.

- Other literacy education related initiatives: There is no information in public domains about special programs or initiatives promoted or sponsored by University 1 to integrate new literacies into the undergraduate teacher education process. Nevertheless, several advanced courses and a specialized practicum site for a Reading Specialists program where found.

Case 2: University - Midwest

- General description: The School of Education at University 2 offers a Bachelor of Arts and a Bachelor of Science in Elementary and Secondary Education. For the purpose of this study only the Elementary Teaching major will be studied. According to its mission the program focuses on the study and improvement of teaching and learning through promoting respect to individuals regardless of any specific conditions or circumstances. This program is designed for students that want to become K-8 grade teachers. It is a practice based program in which students are expected to engage with high leverage teaching practices to meet the needs of all types of students. It is a four semester program in which the students are exposed to courses as they work in an elementary classroom setting. In order to obtain a major in Education, students are admitted on their junior year or as soon they have completed the University 2 General Studies Requirements. Upon completion of the degree, qualified students are recommended to the State Department of Education for provisional teacher certification.
- Curriculum structure: In order to obtain a Bachelor in Arts of Bachelor in Science in Education all students must complete all the courses required by University of 2 General Studies Curriculum and 48 credits from the Undergraduate Elementary Teacher Education Program and other specific program requirements such as First Aid Training and other.
- Core Curriculum: The General Studies is composed by 45 credits in Humanities, Natural Science, Social Science, Mathematics and three methods classes recommended to students depending on their major.
- Major Curriculum: The Undergraduate Elementary Teacher Education Program is composed by 48 credits that must be completed through the successful completion of 22 specific courses to obtain the major. Courses cover foundations of education, teaching methodologies for the different disciplines, inclusion and the practicum classes.
- Subjects related to the integration of new literacies: From the Undergraduate Elementary Teacher Education Program, two courses, according to their nomenclature, specifically empha-

size on Literacy Education: Literacy I: Developmental Reading and Writing Instruction in the Elementary School (Class 1), and Literacy II: Individualizing Reading and Writing Instruction in the Elementary Classroom(Class 2). From the nomenclature it can be assumed that other classes might incorporate new literacies as part of their contents, information about the following classes was also explored: Culturally Responsive Pedagogy: Education in a Multicultural Society (Class 3), Children as Sensemakers (Class 4), and two classes that focus on digital technologies, Digital Technologies K-8 (Class 5). Full versions of the Literacy I and II classes' syllabus where available in the institutional webpage which help to collect data about of the courses.

While conducting the data analysis to determine the integration of new literacies in the teacher education program the documents analyzed report that in Class 1 the syllabus description mentions that the focus of the course will be to, *"develop a foundational understanding for how to teach and support diverse children in becoming strategic and capable readers, writers, listeners and speakers"* (Syllabus, Case 2, Class 1), no explicit texts about the integration of new literacies is recorded, but could be inferred. In the same document the course goals specifically state, *"general trends of literacy development including emergent literacy"* and *"provide students with opportunities to integrate their use of reading, writing, listening, speaking, viewing, and constructing"* (Syllabus, Case 2, Class 1) showing that the integration of new literacies as part of the teacher education program is evident through the recognition of emergent literacies and showing students to appreciate opportunities to integrate their individual perceptions into the language arts curriculum. Class 2 on the other hand, showed that the focus of this course is specifically in the reading development, but the description mentions, *"Dispositions to construct meaning through reading, writing, viewing, and speaking"* (Syllabus, Case 2, Class 2), showing that future teachers must understand that the meaning construction process relies not solely in reading and writing but also in what students observe and say. In the course goals the future teachers are expected to learn about the relationship between their prospective students and the text in general, it is not clearly stated they types of 'text' to be considered, it could be used in a broader sense than the notion of text being considered only as the reading material assigned to prospective students in class is inferred by the researcher based on the use of the word text throughout the syllabus. The documents do not provide evidence of the program having an intention to develop student awareness about different types of texts or the need for them to become responsive to the new literacies their students are and will be exposed to as society evolves. It seems that both literacy classes are focused on the instruction of reading and writing based on current official demands. As the class about Education in a Multicultural Society is analyzed data shows that the course embraces teachers' adaptability, *"This course is focused foremost on cultivating an understanding of how teachers can act and think in ways that maximize the learning opportunities for all students; in essence, what it means to be an effective, culturally responsive educator.* (Syllabus, Case 2, Class 3). This teacher education program shows that the incorporation of the students' context in the process of meaning construction is very relevant for teacher education, in the Children as Sensemakers course's description it is showed as it explains, *"Studies elementary students as individuals who construct understanding of the world around them as they interact with others as well as the physical objects around them"* (Syllabus, Case 2, Class 4) and in the Digital Technologies course the incorporation of the rapid changes in the students environment is also taken into consideration as an important element in teacher preparation for the classroom practice, *"Given the speed of change in technology, we will emphasize the affordance of new and developing educational media, online and blended learning, mobile learning, social networking, as well as more traditional classroom tools"* (Syllabus, Case 2,

Integration of Media and New Literacies in Teacher Education Programs

Class 5). Showing a balance between the discipline oriented courses focus on current standards (Class 1 & 2) and the other classes focus on inclusiveness and responsiveness as a key element to integrate new literacies and incorporate flexibility and adaptability in the teacher education curriculum is evident (Class 3, Class 4 & Class 5).

- Other literacy education related initiatives: The School of Education of this program has several groups and centers to support research and development in the field of Education, from which the following show to have interests related to the integration of new literacies in the process of teacher education among others.

    ○ Clinical Rounds is a project that seeks to incorporate disciplinary literacy education to avoid fragmentation in teaching.
    ○ Interactive Communications and Simulations a center that works in the integration of technology in the learning process that understands that the internet is not passive, but an active space where learning takes place.

Case 3: University 3 - South

- General description: The College of Education at the University 3 is divided into five departments from within two undergraduate degrees are offered. For the purpose of this study the Bachelor of Science in Applied Learning and Development through the Early Childhood-6th grade Early Childhood-6th grade Generalist program will be analyzed. According to its mission the program seeks to contribute to the advancement of knowledge and the professional practice of teaching and learning to promote social justice and democracy in a rapidly changing social context. The emphasis of the undergraduate programs is to understand child development, learning theory and methods and disciplinary elementary school content; students are expected to have field experience in public schools. All University 3 students must complete 42 credits from the statewide core curriculum. All students seeking teacher certification must complete a Professional Development Sequence of coursework. To obtain their degree students expected to complete 124 hours of coursework.
- Curriculum structure: In order to complete the required coursework for the Early Childhood-6th grade Early Childhood-6th grade Generalist program students must complete the University-wide core curriculum (42 coursework hours); the prescribed work for the Bachelor of Science in Applied Learning and Development (24 coursework hours plus foreign language requirements); the major requirements (51 coursework hours) which includes the professional development sequence and elective courses.
- Core curriculum: All students must complete the University's Core Curriculum. University 3 has a statewide core curriculum it is composed by 14 courses that include writing, qualitative reasoning, global cultures, cultural diversity in the United States, ethics and leadership and independent inquiry.
- Major Curriculum: The major curriculum in this program is composed by two main elements: prescribed work and major requirements. Prescribed work includes mandatory courses for all

undergraduate programs in Education offered at University 3; it includes a course in children's literature, basic psychology, four courses on science education, two courses on mathematics education and the opportunity of students to gain or demonstrate proficiency in a foreign language. Major requirements include a set of seven courses in applied learning and development; a set of four courses for curriculum specialization that focus on reading, language arts, teaching English as a second language and reading difficulties; the Professional Development Sequence a set of six courses restricted by admission criteria that focus on the professional practicum focusing on teaching methods, educational administration and classroom interactions.

- Subjects related to the integration of new literacies: The amount of information about the courses of this programs was limited to the very short course descriptions found in the institutional webpage, therefor the analysis will be based on the few accessible elements of the program.

The curricular component described as prescribed courses the class on Children's Literature (Class 1) can be considered for the purpose of this study. The Major requirements curriculum component focuses on literacy education, within this curricular component the following classes emerge according to their nomenclature: Digital Literacy for Teaching and Learning (Class 2), Acquisition of Language and Literacies (Class 3), Language Acquisition (Class 4) and Sociocultural Influences on Learning (Class 5). Access to class syllabus was restricted so the only consulted documents for analysis was the course descriptions found in the university catalogue.

In Children's Literature's (Class 1) course description it is stated that the class will focus on *"Evaluation, selection, and proper and creative use of books and other media with children"* (Course description, Case 3, Class 1), the description does not explicitly mention new literacies but the fact that the description incorporates "other media" might show that alterative texts would be included in the course. The catalogue describes a class for the undergraduate program in education that is not mentioned as a mandatory course in the major requirements: Digital Literacy for Teaching and Learning (Class 2). According to this class' description *"Emphasis on the development of critical perspectives (including pedagogical, social, technical, cultural, ethical, economic, legal, and political) to help youth fully participate in digital learning"* (Course description, Case 3, Class 2), no explicit texts about the integration of new literacies is recorded, but could be inferred, it also mentions the fact that the class will be learner centered showing the program's efforts to integrate the students' needs and their context as an important element to be considered when understanding how to teach and how students learn. The class entitled Acquisition of Language and Literacies (Class 3) allows an explicit acknowledgement of the existence of different types of literacies, the course description mentions the incorporation of home and the learners' perspectives and context into the process of language acquisition and literacy development. The course description of Language Acquisition (Class 4) states that social aspects of language are relevant during its acquisition process, while Literacy Acquisition focuses on the transition between language acquisition and literacy growth, in both classes the relationship with new literacies is not evident the topic could certainly be part of either course. The course entitle Sociocultural Influences on Learning (Class 5) presents a very interesting approach to the influence that the social context might have in the learning process, the connection with new literacies is not evident in the course description but the fact that human learning is approached from multiple perspectives allows potential for the integration of evolving literacies and their role in the learning process. The documents provide evidence that the program has an intention to develop student awareness about different types of texts or the need for them to become responsive to the new literacies their students are and will be exposed to as society evolves.

It seems that the selected classes for the analysis implicitly mention the existence and incorporation of new literacies as part of the class contents.

- Other literacy education related initiatives: The catalogue includes the course of Adolescent Literacy that could be an elective for the Early Childhood-6th grade Early Childhood-6th grade Generalist program students. In the course description of this class it is evident the integration of new literacies as a relevant part of the teacher education curriculum at University 3, through the study of Adolescent Literacy (Class 6), practices inside and outside of school and how it might influence the identity development process in adolescents and their community involvement.

Cross Case Analysis

Three teacher education programs' course where analyzed to determine if new literacies where integrated into their curriculum. To conduct the analysis the number of courses that shared similar characteristics was identified in each of the programs. The categories for analysis where: courses with evident emphasis in Literacy Education, courses with non-evident emphasis on Literacy Education that might include new literacies in their contents and courses that evidently incorporate new literacies based on their course descriptions or syllabus. The table below show how only two courses out of the three teacher education programs analyzed evidently showed the integration of new literacies in their curriculum. While eight courses showed to have evident relationship with literacy education and five other courses might have included literacy related topics. The integration of new literacies into the teacher education programs is apparent in the description of some of the educational technology courses of two of the teacher education programs.

Table 1. Cross case analysis

Descriptions	Case 1	Case 2	Case 3
Literacy Education			
Number of courses with evident emphasis in Literacy Education	3	2	3
Number of courses with non-evident emphasis on Literacy Education that might include new literacies in their contents	0	3	2
Number of courses that evidently incorporate new literacies based on their course descriptions or syllabus	0	1	1
Technology – New Literacies			
Technology related courses that mention new literacies	0	1	1
Non - technology related courses that mention new literacies	3	5	5
Other Initiatives That Promote Integration of New Literacies in Teacher Education			
Master in Education programs with emphasis in Literacy Education are offered	Yes	Yes	Yes
Institutional projects or centers that promote literacy education	No	Yes	No

While conducting the data analysis to determine the integration of new literacies in the teacher education program the documents analyzed in their majority did not have an explicit description of the integration of new literacies, but the Early Childhood-6th grade Early Childhood-6th grade Generalist program at the College of Education of the University 3 showed to have more classes than the other cases, showing that they have recognized the existence of new literacies and technologies as part of the language acquisition and development process. University 2 has several independent projects and centers that support different aspects of education from which many revolve about improving literacy education and incorporation of technology in the language development process.

It is relevant to mention that while the undergraduate teacher education programs that were studied for this investigation barely evidenced through their public documentation the integration of new literacies into their teacher education programs, the master level courses offered by this institutions had a more evident focus on exploring the social context and student needs as part of their programs.

SOLUTIONS AND RECOMMENDATIONS

As the study began to emerge several options where consulted in order to determine which teacher education programs where to be considered for this study. In order to determine how are the best teacher education programs integrating new literacies into their curriculum, the first task was to determine which where the best teacher education programs. Most of the best known Education programs where consulted but very few offered undergraduate education degrees, most of them focus on offering a very ample range of graduate degrees in Education.

From the undergraduate programs selected for this study all had an institutional core curricular component derived from the institutional philosophy and a professional component mostly designed using standards and guidelines from professional organizations such as the International Reading Association (IRA), among others. In most cases this core curriculum had very similar components common to all the academic areas offered for undergraduate degrees at each institution. While the professional component of the different education undergraduate programs consulted had some identifiable differences. Case 2 professional curriculum design was perfectly aligned with the International Reading Association standards, showing an absolute compliance to their postulates, their emphasis in Literacy Education was clearly aligned with language teaching focusing on phonemic awareness and phonics, language and running records (to measure language development using standards) and other strategies and methods that according to Goodman (2014) & Cranbourne (2009) are artificial classroom practices that disregard the natural language acquisition process that takes place during childhood. In most of the undergraduate programs considered for this study, the public documents consulted show that Literacy Education that is conceived as fostering students opportunities to meet current discipline based standards and existing curriculum demands; the documents lack of information to support that future teachers where given opportunities to learn to become critical in order to be able to adapt and adjust to future needs and demands through opportunities to learn about the way children today uses different types of texts to construct meaning.

As a general conclusion, the curriculum elements of the three programs studied did not have an evident recognition of new forms of literacy and the need for teachers to incorporate them into their professional practice consistently with Cochran-Smith (2021) when they explain the lack of adaptability of teacher education programs with the reality of the professional demands.

Cambourne (2009) explained about, the need of integrating the real world into curriculum development, then the natural world must inform what goes on in teacher education programs as a way to ensure natural learning to occur. Contrary to what the author claims the literacy education courses in the programs studied continue to have a traditional approach to Literacy Education focusing on the formal acquisition of conventional skills based on text as print far from what reality needs and claims about what means to be literate in this day and age. Case 3 showed a consistent effort to incorporate elements that could lead for the incorporation of new literacies as part of their teacher preparation, for example, their course descriptions constantly mention the need to produce student centered education initiatives, the integration of technologies and new ways of communication as part of the literacy education elements. Duffy, Webb & Davis (2009) explain, "… we have a responsibility to study our own teachers and their ability to be professional in the reality of the world in which they will work" (p.195).

Teacher education programs should openly embrace and acknowledge new literacies to provide future teachers with the knowledge, skills and tools they need to adapt and change as the students continue to evolve. Coinciding with Darling-Hammond, Hyler & Gardner (2017) effective teacher education needs to be revisited through research evidence that will allow programs to understand the future teacher needs based on what teachers are unable to confront today. As educators we often complain about the lack of action in promoting change to meet the practical and real needs of teacher education. Pretending to approach literacy education using the same approach from a decade ago is taking away opportunities for future teachers to overcome the real challenges of today. Duffy, Webb & Davis (2009) suggest, "… we have not generate enough research data convince policy makers that education teachers is essential and that training is inadequate" (p.190).

Due to time constraints the main limitation of this study was that all the data gathered was obtained through internet searches of the teacher education institutional webpage's public domain. Future studies should contact the teacher education programs, conduct interviews and/or surveys in order to gain a more in-depth understanding of the way each teacher education program structure and the way they function. Through this study it was evident that the higher education institutions analyzed had other initiatives, aside from their undergraduate Elementary Education programs, to foster literacy education. It is necessary to conduct further research to explore other initiatives related to literacy education that are taking place through research centers, special projects and specially graduate studies. Incorporating the understanding and interpretation of new literacies and critical digital learning should become indispensable elements withing any literacy educaion program as way to recognize they limitless adoption of technologies as means for communication, language use and an essential part of our daily life.

FUTURE RESEARCH DIRECTIONS

There is a vast amount of research about the effect, use and integration of technology in education, but not enough research about educators learning how to embrace and incorporate media and new literacies as part of the language arts curriculum. The adaptability of teacher education is mandatory if future teachers are expected to actively embrace change as society continues to change the way in which we communicate, use language and exchange ideas. Further research about what teachers need to learn in order to be able to adapt their practice to their students needs is much needed. Teachers' ability to learn, to become flexible learners and their ability to adopt new technologies and languages should become a priority in an effort to equip teachers with much needed skills.

CONCLUSION

Teacher education programs must review their curriculum in order to prepare their students to embrace successfully the ever-changing challeges of the teacher profession. The different means and skills used by new generations as communication tools are integrated in schools in an effort to provide youth with relevant and applicable learning experiences. The meaning of being literate depends on the social context where is utilized, people who are literate in the 21st century need to be able to read, interpret and create a vast variety of information. Meanwhile, as Flores (2016) explains the teacher education curriculum in colleges of education remains focusing on preparing teachers with knowledge and skills applicable to previous generations. Loughran & Hamilton (2016) describe how technological tools, new literacies and learning media are an integral part of everyday life, teachers no longer have the choice to integrate technology in their classes, technology is an intentional and unintentional part of the educational process; and so is the use of new literacies as part of the language curriculum. The acknowledgement and acceptance of this new reality will allow teacher educators around the world to understand that preparing teachers goes beyond providing them with specific knowledge and skills, rather equipping them with abilities to observe the world and adapt these new occurences to the learning context (Lasso, 2018). Swennen & White (2021) emphasize on the need of teachers being to become adaptable, to develop the muscle required to adopt new technologies as an intrinsic part of their profession, and to learn how to read the world, the way people communicate and provide their students with the tools to communicate effectively, to read critically and to actively participate using new literacies effectively (Gore, 2021). Status quo is always a comfortable choice, teacher educators must promote a more horizontal relationship with their students, foster opportunities for them to read critically to evaluate information, assess the current and future challenges of education and enable them to learn how to use technology to find trustworthy information. The time has come for teacher educators to start becoming an example of flexibility, adaptability and willingness to embrace change (Lasso, 2018); preparing teachers by reproducing previous practices can no longer be admisible. In order to recruit more talented young future teachers, prepare future educators to avoid teacher burn out teacher educators need to step out of our comfort zone and learning about the way new generations communicate, adopt new technologies as part of our pedagogy in teacher education programs and critically observe the world around as as a way of learning about how people learn today.

REFERENCES

Achinstein, B., & Ogawa, R. (2006). (In) Fidelity: What the Resistance of New Teachers Reveals about Professional Principles and Prescriptive Educational Policies. *Harvard Educational Review*, 76(1), 30–63. doi:10.17763/haer.76.1.e14543458r811864

Beijaard, D., Meijer, P., & Verloop, N. (2004). Reconsidering research on teachers' professional identity. *Teaching and Teacher Education*, 20(2), 107–128. doi:10.1016/j.tate.2003.07.001

Blommaert, J. (2005). *Discourse: Key topics in sociolinguistics*. Cambridge University Press. doi:10.1017/CBO9780511610295

Cambourne, B. (2009). Revisiting the Concept of "Natural Learning". In J. V. Hoffman & Y. M. Goodman (Eds.), *Changing literacies for changing times* (pp. 125–145). Taylor & Francis.

Cochran-Smith, M. (2021). Rethinking teacher education: The trouble with accountability. *Oxford Review of Education, 1*(47), 8–24. doi:10.1080/03054985.2020.1842181

Cochran-Smith, M., & Zeichner, K. M. (2005). *Studying Teacher Education: The Report of the AERA Panel on Research and Teacher Education*. Retrieved from: https://mjcoonkitt.wordpress.com/2013/01/17/cochran-smith-zeichner-2005/

Crehan, L. (2016). *Exploring the impact of career models on teacher motivation*. International Institute of Educational Planning. http://repositorio.minedu.gob.pe/bitstream/handle/123456789/4889/Exploring%20the%20impact%20of%20career%20models%20on%20teacher%20motivation.pdf?sequence=1&isAllowed=y

Creswell, J. W., & Poth, C. N. (2018). Qualitative Inquiry & Research Design. *Sage (Atlanta, Ga.)*.

Darling-Hammond, L. (2006). *Powerful Teacher Education: Lessons from Exemplary Programs*. Jossey Bass.

Darling-Hammond, L., Hyler, M. E., & Gardner, M. (2017). *Effective Teacher Professional Development*. Learning Policy Institute. https://files.eric.ed.gov/fulltext/ED606743.pdf

Darling-Hammond, L., & Oakes, J. (2019). *Preparing Teachers for Deeper Learning*. Harvard Education Press.

Dotger, B. H. (2013). *"I had no idea!" Clinical Simulations for Teacher Development*. Information Age Publishers.

Duffy, G. G., Webb, S. M., & Davis, S. (2009). Literacy Education at Crossroads. In J. V. Hoffman & Y. M. Goodman (Eds.), *Changing literacies for changing times* (pp. 189–197). Routledge.

Flores, M. A. (2016). Teacher Education Curriculum. In J. Loughran & M. L. Hamilton (Eds.), *International Handbook of Teacher Education* (pp. 187–230). Springer. doi:10.1007/978-981-10-0366-0_5

Goodman, K. S. (2014). *What's whole in Whole Language in the 21st century?* Garn Press.

Gore, J. M. (2021). The Quest for Better teachers. *Oxford Review of Education, 1*(47), 45–60. doi:10.1080/03054985.2020.1842182

Harro, B. (2000). The Cycle of Socialization. In M. Adams (Ed.), *Readings for diversity and social justice* (pp. 15–20). Routledge.

Korthagen, F., Loughran, J., & Russel, T. (2006). Developing fundamental principles for teacher education programs and practices. *Teaching and Teacher Education, 22*(8), 1020–1041. doi:10.1016/j.tate.2006.04.022

Korthagen, F. A. (2003). In search of the essence of a good teacher: Towards a more holistic approach in teacher education. *Teaching and Teacher Education, 20*(1), 77–97. doi:10.1016/j.tate.2003.10.002

Lapp, D., Flood, J., Brice Heath, S., & Langer, J. (2009). The Communicative, Visual and Performative Arts: Core Components of Literacy Education. In J. V. Hoffman & Y. M. Goodman (Eds.), *Changing literacies for changing times* (pp. 3–16). Taylor & Francis.

Lasso, M. D. (2018). Letting Go of Teacher Power: Innovative Democratic Assessment. In E. Jean Francois (Ed.), *Transnational Perspectives on Innovation in Teaching and Learning Technologies* (pp. 200–224). Brill Sense.

Loughran, J., & Hamilton, M. L. (2016). Developing an Understanding of Teacher Education. In J. Loughran & M. L. Hamilton (Eds.), *International Handbook of Teacher Education* (pp. 3–22). Springer. doi:10.1007/978-981-10-0366-0_1

Sleeter, C., & Flores Carmona, J. (2017). *Un-standardizing Curriculum. Multicultural Teaching in the Standards Based-Classroom*. Teachers College Press.

Sleeter, C. E. (2005). *Un-standardizing curriculum: Multicultural teaching in the standards based classroom*. Teachers College Press.

Sleeter, C. E., & Grant, C. A. (2009). *Making Choices for Multicultural Education: Five Approaches to Race, Class and Gender* (6th ed.). Wiley & Sons, Inc. (Original work published 1999)

Swennen, A., & White, E. (Eds.). (2021). *Being a Teacher Educator*. Routledge.

Walsh, S. (2013). *Classroom Discourse and Teacher Development*. Edinburg University Press. doi:10.1515/9780748645190

ADDITIONAL READING

Cochran-Smith, M., Grudnoff, L., & Orland-Barak, L. (2019). Educating Teacher Educators: International Perspectives. *New Educator*, *1*(16), 5–24.

Hulburt, K. J., Blake, A. C., & Roeser, R. W. (2020). The Calm, Clear, and Kind Educator: A Contemplative Educational Approach to Teacher Professional Identity Development. In O. Ergas & J. K. Ritter (Eds.), *Exploring Self Toward Expanding Teaching, Teacher Education and Practitioner Research* (pp. 17–36). Emerald Publishing Limited. doi:10.1108/S1479-368720200000034001

Ladson-Billings, G. (2021). *Culturally Relevant Pedagogy: Asking Different Questions*. Teachers College Press.

Lasso, M. D. (2018). *Chosen Life Paths among Educational Leaders That Inform Teacher Preparation Programs Regarding Teacher Leadership Development* (Accession No. 10983822) [Doctoral Dissertation, New Mexico State University, Las Cruces]. ProQuest Dissertations Publishing.

Livingston, K. (2016). Teacher education's role in educational change. *European Journal of Teacher Education*, *39*(1), 1–4. doi:10.1080/02619768.2016.1135531

Loughran, J. (2014). Professionally Developing as a Teacher Educator. *Journal of Teacher Education*, *65*(4), 271–282. doi:10.1177/0022487114533386

Ruohotie-Lyhty, M. (2018) Identity-Agency in Progress: Teachers Authoring Their Identities. In Research on Teacher Identity: Mapping Challenges and Innovations (pp.13-23). Springer.

Zeichner, K. M., Payne, K. A., & Brayko, K. (2018) Democratizing Teacher Education. In The Struggle for the Soul of Teacher Education (pp. 171-196). Routledge.

Section 4
Multi-Languages

Chapter 10
Maximizing the Impact of Language and Early Intervention on Literacy Among Deaf and Hard of Hearing Students:
A Critical Assessment and Recommendation

Leanna Hodges
https://orcid.org/0000-0001-5304-9412
Baylor University, USA

ABSTRACT

Deaf and hard of hearing (DHH) children struggle to develop reading success and proficient language. The journey to reading success begins when a child is diagnosed with a hearing difference and receives early intervention services. Access to early intervention services sets the foundation for DHH students' language and reading achievement. If a child cannot achieve fluent language, their reading will follow suit. This chapter explains how DHH children's language impacts their reading development. First, the chapter describes the research related to early intervention, communication modes, and reading in the DHH population. Second, the chapter explains how language affects reading development in DHH children. Lastly, the chapter includes resources and recommendations for DHH children's parents and teachers. The resources and recommendations focus on practical strategies to grow DHH children's language and, therefore, their reading.

INTRODUCTION

Deaf and Hard of Hearing (DHH) children lack age-appropriate language and reading skills. This chapter summarizes the background and explains the need for skilled reading among DHH children. Throughout the chapter, the author elucidates the unique set of challenges in DHH children's reading and language development to connect DHH children's language delays to their reading achievement. Second, the author explicates the prerequisites for successful reading development according to Scarborough's Reading Rope (2001). Scarborough's Reading Rope serves as the theoretical foundation for this chapter. In the last section, the author provides resources and recommendations for parents and teachers of DHH children. The resources and recommendations aim to provide strategies to grow DHH children's language and, therefore, their reading.

BACKGROUND: COMMUNICATION AND READING AMONG DHH CHILDREN

Deaf and Hard of Hearing children encounter challenges in their reading and language development. In this section, the researcher argues that DHH children face a unique set of obstacles to developing skilled reading due to the lack of language access. To make this argument, the author explores three topics. First, the author provides background information on the DHH population. Second, the author explores the breadth of possible communication options for DHH children, recognizing the depth and context each faces barriers to full implementation. Third, the author explains Scarborough's Reading Rope (2001) as the theoretical foundation for this chapter and within the context of DHH learners.

A hearing difference diagnosis is a low-incidence disability but still affects a considerable part of the population. The World Health Organization (WHO) reports that there are 430 million people who are DHH or are diagnosed with a hearing difference (2021). The DHH population in the WHO's report includes adults and children with hearing differences. To narrow the scope, the Universal Newborn Hearing Screening (UNHS) tests all infants after birth to screen for possible hearing differences. The UNHS identified 61,475 babies with a hearing difference out of the 3,545,388 screened (CDC, 2021). Once the DHH child receives the official diagnosis, families begin to proceed to the next step in the process.

After a child receives a diagnosis, the family has to decide which interventions fit their family's needs. For example, audiologists can fit their child for hearing aid/s, cochlear implant/s, or a Bone Anchored Hearing Aid (Cohen, 2003; Eisenberg et al., 2004). A Teacher of the Deaf and hard of hearing (TOD) can connect the family to Deaf individuals and help the family communicate with their DHH child (Luft, 2008). In addition, there are different avenues the family of DHH children may utilize for *through the air* communication.

The DHH Population and the Possible Communication Options

The DHH population uses a variety of communication modes (Tomaszewski et al., 2019). The three main communication options are oral communication, Total Communication, and American Sign Language. The first communication mode is oral communication. Oral communication, or spoken language, is when a family decides to use verbal speech as their child's primary mode of communication. When a family selects oral communication, the family must rely on hearing with assistive technology. Some examples of hearing assistance are cochlear implants, hearing aids, and the BAHA. DHH students who use oral

Maximizing the Impact of Language and Early Intervention

communication do not reach the average academic level as their hearing peers (Bat-Chava et al., 2013; Hayes et al., 2009; Nicholas & Geers, 1997). Alternatively, Bell and Houston (2014) explain that oral communication is possible with high parent involvement, hearing technology, and oral communication. Bell and Houston (2014) indicate that speech and spoken language are possible with high parent involvement, hearing technology, and careful monitoring. The data on the success of oral communication are conflicting as some studies show that oral communication is beneficial (Bell & Houston, 2014), helpful with particular supports (Bergeson-Dana, 2014), or not helpful (Bat-Chava et al., 2013).

The next communication mode is Total Communication. Total Communication provides an avenue for the professionals working with the DHH student to use whatever communication tools the student needs (Hands and Voices, 2020). The tools encompassed in Total Communication are sign language, spoken language, fingerspelling, gestures, or even standing on their head if it gets the job done—students who utilize Total Communication sign and talk, often simultaneously. The DHH students and families need individualizes Total Communication because each child has unique strengths and struggles. Donald Conner et al.'s (2000) empirical study compared students' expressive language using Total Communication to oral communication for students with a cochlear implant. The authors concluded that the students who used oral communication had higher consonant production accuracy, but Total Communication students had significantly higher expressive language. For this reason, McDonald Connor et al. (2000) explained the benefits of cochlear implants in oral and Total Communication that cochlear implants.

American Sign Language (ASL) is the language the American Deaf community uses to communicate. There are many different sign languages worldwide, as ASL is not a universal language but a significant mode of communication in the United States. As a scholar and educator in the United States, of course, most of my engagement and research on this mode of communication has been on ASL. Language experts consider American Sign Language an actual language (National Institute on Deafness and Other Communication Disorders, 2019). An argument for ASL comes from a participant in Rosen's (2000) study on perceptions of early intervention in the Deaf community. The participant states:

"The best bet, even with amplification, is early exposure to ASL. This way, if implantation fails, then ASL is a viable backup. Even if amplification or oral skills are a success, ASL will allow the deaf child to accept their identity, deaf culture, and deaf history. Being able to hear or not is often a red herring. Language is the key." (p. 335)

Most of the research related to ASL is not against hearing, listening, or oral language but emphasizes the fundamental right of DHH children to have access to language (National Association of the Deaf, 2016). Holcomb et al. (2022) state that ASL phonology can positively impact reading in DHH children. Hoffmeister et al. (2022) study results showed that knowledge of ASL syntax had a significant positive correlation with English literacy.

There are many communication modes available for families of DHH children. Each family unit, as well as circumstances outside of the family, are different, so the final decision on communication mode lies with the family. In addition, there are strengths and weaknesses to each of the three main communication modes, and each family must compare the available options to determine which early interventions are the best fit for their family. While selecting a communication mode is vital, understanding the background information on reading in DHH children is also essential to creating successful reading experiences.

Scarborough's Reading Rope Applied to DHH

Scarborough (2001) explains that word recognition and language comprehension are necessary to achieve skilled reading. Skilled reading is more than fluency, accuracy, or word reading. Understanding that skilled reading is comprised of word recognition and language comprehension serves as the theoretical background for this chapter. For example, "Skilled readers derive meaning from printed text accurately and efficiently" (Scarborough, 2001, p. 1). Deaf and hard of hearing children have difficulty with word recognition skills such as phonological awareness and decoding (Syverud et al., 2009). Having a hearing difference naturally creates a barrier to accessing the phonological component of skilled reading (Deng & Tong, 2021). This chapter focuses specifically on the language comprehension aspect of SRR but not the word recognition piece.

Language comprehension in the DHH population is multifaceted. Language development provides the foundation for learning and comprehending the written word on a page (Antia et al., 2020; Deng & Tong, 2021; M. L. Hall et al., 2019; Pizzo & Chilvers, 2019; Scarborough, 2001; Sehyr & Emmorey, 2022; Zhao et al., 2021). Mayer (2007) states through the air language refers to conversational language in whatever mode the student uses, such as oral communication, Total Communication, and ASL. Unfortunately, DHH students are behind their hearing peers in language comprehension (Allen et al., 2014; Coppens et al., 2012; Duncan & Lederberg, 2018; Goberis et al., 2012; Mayer, 2007), and the implication of language difficulty impacts DHH children's reading.

Deaf and hard of hearing students struggle to achieve skilled reading (Deng & Tong, 2021; Easterbrooks & Lederberg, 2021; Harris, 2015; Traxler, 2000). Wang et al. (2013) concluded that DHH students read lower than a typical sixth-grader when graduating high school. Similarly, Traxler (2000) reported a fourth-grade reading level for DHH students upon high school graduation (Goberis et al., 2012; Kirk Thagard et al., 2011). Fourth and lower than sixth-grade reading levels still determine that DHH children do not achieve typical reading and writing skills like their hearing peers (Mayer, 2007).

Achieving fluency in a language is essential for reading success in DHH children. Early intervention opens the door for a DHH child to acquire language. Oral communication, Total Communication, and ASL are the three main communication options the family can choose depending upon their DHH child and family's needs. In this section, the author explains that language is essential for skilled reading in DHH children (Scarborough, 2001). However, due to circumstances and family experiences, DHH children do not continually develop language at the same rate as their hearing counterparts. As a result of the lack of language access, DHH struggles to achieve skilled reading.

THE PREREQUISITES FOR SUCCESSFUL DHH READING DEVELOPMENT

There are two main tributaries discussed in this chapter that feed into the river of reading success. First, early intervention provides a variety of supports for families of DHH children. Second, language comprehension lays the foundation for reading success. Early intervention and language are necessary for a DHH child to have successful reading development.

Maximizing the Impact of Language and Early Intervention

Early Intervention: The Key to Success

The first tributary in this chapter is early intervention. Imagine early intervention as a small tributary that feeds into the river known as literacy. The CDC (2018) defines early intervention as the list of supports that a family or a child can receive if they have developmental delays or disabilities. Intervention options for families with a DHH child begin once the child is diagnosed with a hearing difference. According to the Bill of Rights for DHH children (National Association of the Deaf, 2016), parents of DHH children have a right to access early intervention services. Families have multiple options for services, such as audiological services, speech therapy, assistance from a TOD, and many more (National Association of the Deaf, 2021; Subbiah et al., 2018).

At the onset of the diagnosis, a family has access to a wealth of resources available to support, guide, and encourage the families and DHH students to succeed in all areas of their lives. The families have access to multiple professionals and interventions as their family forges their path, as 96% of DHH children are born to hearing families (Goldin-Meadow & Mayberry, 2001; Moroe, 2018). These families must make decisions such as hearing assistive technology, communication mode, and goals for their DHH child. While other families worry about breastfeeding, which onesie to put on their child, and adjusting to life with a newborn, these parents worry about navigating life with a child with a hearing difference. Early intervention and professional assistance provide families with tools for their children to achieve language and reading success.

The journey to literacy begins when a family discovers that their child has a hearing difference (Chang, 2017; Gascon-Ramos et al., 2010; Moeller, 2000; Subbiah et al., 2018; Yoshinaga-Itano et al., 1998). Ideally, a child should receive a diagnosis with early intervention or at birth, so the family can immediately access professionals and supports. The Joint Committee on Infant Hearing (2007) indicated that the early detection timeline is to have a Universal Newborn Hearing Screening (UNHS) within one month. If the newborn does not pass the UNHS, the baby will take another hearing test. The baby receives a diagnosis of a hearing difference if the baby fails the additional hearing test. Unfortunately, the UNHS does not catch every child with a hearing difference, as a DHH child may develop a hearing difference progressively or result from sickness. Ultimately, reading development hinges on a prompt diagnosis of a hearing difference so families can access the appropriate supports.

Early intervention is helpful as it provides the families with the support needed for their child to be as successful as possible (Clark et al., 2020; Gascon-Ramos et al., 2010; Nickbakht et al., 2021; Pimperton et al., 2017; Rosen, 2000). Parents guide the intervention supports based on the DHH child and family's needs, goals, and desires (Nickbakht et al., 2021; Pimperton et al., 2017). For example, families may experience help from an audiologist to gain their child access to hearing sounds through a hearing aid, cochlear implant, or a BAHA (Cohen, 2003; Eisenberg et al., 2004). Additionally, a family may elect for their child to attend speech therapy to practice spoken language and articulation(Yoshinaga-Itano, 2014). A family may also utilize a TOD to navigate this new process by connecting them with Deaf professionals, families with DHH children, and teaching them sign language (Luft, 2008).

Families have the right to decide the communication path for their DHH child. For example, some families may decide against hearing devices and utilize American Sign Language (ASL) instead of spoken language. Byrd et al. (2011) describe two students whose parents selected ASL only as their form of communication. The parent wanted to forgo cochlear implants and utilize ASL, but someone reported the family to Child Protective Services. The committee favored the side of the mom, stating that deciding against a cochlear implant is permissible. Ultimately, each family has a right to determine the appropriate communication route for their DHH child. Families of DHH children desire their child to have some speech therapy with a Speech-Language Pathologist (SLP). Some families choose for their child to speak and use oral communication as their primary mode of communication.

In contrast, others want their children to communicate basic wants and needs if they encounter a position where speech is necessary. Also, some parents may even forgo speech therapy if they do not want their child to speak, as each situation is complex and context-dependent (Byrd et al., 2011; Yoshinaga-Itano, 2014). Intervention depends on the family's Individualized Family Service Plan (IFSP) to determine the services that meet their DHH child's needs.

A TOD is a certified professional who supports a DHH child's language and communication needs. After a child is diagnosed with having a hearing difference, a TOD begins to meet with the family at the child's home. After identification, the TOD becomes a confidant, expert, and resource provider for families of DHH children. In addition, the TOD serves as the case manager for parents and consults with the rest of the IFSP team to provide services and reach the goals the family creates. For example, a TOD can help a family learn to sign language, work with hearing equipment, understand their child's hearing difference, and adjust to their child's hearing difference (Storbeck & Calvert-Evans, 2008). In addition, assistance from the TOD during early intervention to identify a communication mode is imperative to focus on language and communication to prevent language delays (Yoshinaga-Itano, 2014). A TOD assists a family by asking the parents what they envision for their child (Storbeck & Calvert-Evans, 2008). If a child has profound hearing loss, a family may learn sign language, but others may not. The TOD's job is to provide information and support for families but not demand or require families to choose a particular communication mode because each child and family have different needs and desires (Storbeck & Calvert-Evans, 2008).

Early intervention services provide resources and tools for families, and these tools correlate to higher language and literacy levels in DHH children (Geers et al., 2019; Moeller, 2000; Yoshinaga-Itano et al., 1998). However, there is limited research on how early intervention impacts reading in DHH children, but research is available on the impact of early intervention on language acquisition (Moeller, 2000; Yoshinaga-Itano, 2003). Moeller (2000) and Yoshinaga-Itano's (2003) research state that earlier intervention was a significant factor in language acquisition for DHH children. The earlier a DHH child received early intervention services, the higher the students scored on the language level assessment. For example, Yoshinaga-Itano's (2003) participants scored higher on language assessments when identified with a hearing difference before six months of age. Also, Moeller (2000) indicated that family involvement also played a critical role in language levels. A family's involvement had a strong positive correlation, whereas limited involvement was associated with language delays. According to Geers et al. (2019), early intervention and intensity helped DHH children's language, literacy, and outcomes in other academic areas.

Early intervention is the key to successful language development. In this section, the author argues that early intervention allows DHH students to begin learning a language. A child needs to have a diagnosis of a hearing difference to start receiving support from professionals. Ultimately, early intervention and diagnosis open the door for learning.

Language Comprehension as a Prerequisite for Skilled Reading

The purpose of this section is to show research-based evidence to educate about the struggle DHH encounter with language comprehension. Researchers state that DHH students' language and vocabulary acquisition lags behind their hearing counterparts (Allen et al., 2014; Coppens et al., 2012; Goberis et al., 2012; Mayer, 2007). Language is a vital tributary and essential for a thriving river of literacy (Deng & Tong, 2021).

Goberis et al. (2012) indicate that the pragmatic and social language of DHH children is behind their hearing peers. DHH students mastered 6.6% of the complex language targets at six, while 100% of the hearing children mastered the challenging language targets (Goberis et al., 2012). Coppens et al. (2012) and Allen et al. (2014) indicate that longitudinally 67.7% of DHH children are behind their hearing peers linguistically in school (Texas Education Association, 2021). A longitudinal study conducted by Coppens et al. (2012) indicated that DHH students stayed behind their hearing peers in language over time and did not "close the gap" (p. 126). Deng and Tons (2021) studied 336 Chinese kindergarten-second grade DHH students and discovered that language weaknesses may lead to difficulties with comprehension.

Exposure to language and building vocabulary is an essential tributary to achieving healthy, flowing literacy. Unfortunately, the DHH population commonly struggles to acquire language as 96% of DHH children are born to hearing parents and often have never met a DHH person (Marshall et al., 2018; Young, 2018; Young & Tattersall, 2007). This section of the chapter proposes to describe language in DHH children compared to their hearing peers. For example, (Goberis et al., 2012) conducted a study comparing the pragmatic language of DHH children to that of their hearing counterparts. These results were shocking as only 6% of DHH children mastered the pragmatic target language compared to 100% of their hearing peers!

Approximately 80% of children born with a hearing difference get a cochlear implant (Humphries et al., 2012, 2016). Unfortunately, the implant itself does not guarantee language comprehension (Hall et al., 2019; Humphries et al., 2016). Often, those individuals are encouraged to pursue oral communication (Humphries et al., 2012). Therefore, there is a possibility that these DHH people with cochlear implants may never have language comprehension in spoken language. If a child can hear but cannot comprehend what they hear, they will not be able to replicate the language they are hearing.

There is a consensus on this topic and a plethora of research stating that DHH children have difficulty acquiring a language (Allen et al., 2014; Antia et al., 2020; Coppens et al., 2012; Goberis et al., 2012; Mayer, 2007).

The Implications for Skilled Reading Development

While many hearing students struggle with reading, DHH students experience unique adversity as DHH students learn differently than their hearing counterparts (Harris, 2015; Marschark et al., 2009; Syverud et al., 2009; Wang & Williams, 2014; Webb et al., 2018). Harris (2015) explains that each DHH child also learns differently because of their family experiences, the unique language of communication, the degree of hearing difference, and hearing technology. A family may use Spanish as a primary mode of communication at home. The DHH child may have to navigate Spanish, English, and signed language. Navigating three languages can impact the vocabulary of the DHH student as they hear Spanish words at home and English words at school. Another student may have a family who uses spoken and signed languages to communicate. The second family learns to sign and uses both spoken and signed language. The second child has more exposure to English and signed language. Consequently, the second student in this scenario has a higher language score and academic level than the student from a trilingual family. Family experiences, outside influences, and life have an impact on DHH children's language, which impacts a DHH child's tributary that flows into literacy.

Most researchers agree that language comprehension is a contributing factor to DHH children's struggles with reading (Allen et al., 2014; Andrews & Baker, 2019; Antia et al., 2020; Brown & Watson, 2017; Deng & Tong, 2021; Goberis et al., 2012; W. C. Hall, 2017; Kirk Thagard et al., 2011; Lederberg et al., 2013; Marschark et al., 2009; Mayer, 2007; Sehyr & Emmorey, 2022; Zhao et al., 2021). Imagine a student who wears hearing amplification and is reading about various activities at the beach. The student cannot wear their hearing equipment while at the beach because the water will destroy the hearing equipment. Instead of the child picking up the vocabulary of the objects around them at the beach, they miss many conversations and incidental language because they cannot participate in the conversations around them (Tomaszewski et al., 2019). While the child can read the words on the page, the child does not have the background language for what a shovel or sandcastle is. The child can not know what the words in the story mean because they lack the appropriate background knowledge.

Scarborough (2001) determines that historically, students with a language impairment often struggle to read. The empirical studies are also overwhelmingly consistent, as Goldin-Meadow and Mayberry (2001), Izzo (2002), Silvestri and Wang (2018), Wauters et al. (2021), Falk et al. (2020), and Deng and Tong (2021) unanimously indicate that language development and language skills contribute to reading development.

Understanding Scarborough's Reading Rope explains why DHH students struggle with literacy; they still struggle with language comprehension. Tuckwiller et al. (2010) state that "If the ultimate goal of reading is to comprehend, then vocabulary is an integral component of reading comprehension, as an unknown word cannot be comprehended" (p. 1). A child who can decode words fluently cannot always read fluently. For example, a DHH child can read a book about a new subject, such as dinosaurs, including Tyrannosaurus, Brachiosaurus, and Velociraptor. In this scenario, the book has no pictures and contains complex vocabulary. As the child does not have the vocabulary to understand the different types of dinosaurs, the child will be unable to comprehend the text or even fill out a Venn diagram comparing the three different types of dinosaurs. In this scenario, literacy is lacking due to the absence of vocabulary.

A child can achieve reading success when a DHH child has access to early intervention and language from the onset of the hearing difference. Meanwhile, a DHH cannot develop skilled reading if they do not have a language. However, a child cannot comprehend a story if they do not have a way to communicate their understanding. Ultimately, a DHH student's low language development reflects directly on the low skilled reading levels of DHH students. The river also struggles when the tributaries trickle into a river instead of flowing.

RESOURCES AND RECOMMENDATIONS FOR PARENTS AND TEACHERS

This section provides some solutions and recommendations for parents, TODs, and general education teachers of DHH children to increase their language level. While the author is a teacher speaking to parents to parents and teachers, of course, these solutions and recommendations are by no means limited to this audience. Parents of DHH, TOD, and general education teachers have unique roles in the language and literacy of the DHH population, so the recommendations are organized accordingly.

Parents of Deaf and Hard of Hearing Children

First, the author will provide recommendations, resources, and solutions for parents of DHH children. The first recommendation is for parents to contact the DHH child's school or provider. Depending upon the location of the family, the resources may be different. For example, some fantastic organizations for parents in Texas are Hands and Voices, Statewide Outreach Center (SOC), Deaf mentors, and other families with DHH children. Texas Hands and Voices is a fantastic organization that connects parents and families of DHH children. Individuals interested can reach them at their website (https://www.handsandvoices.org/). Statewide Outreach Center is managed by Texas School for the Deaf. "Family Signs" is a free program provided by the SOC that teaches sign language to families! The SOC also hosts many camps and summer programs for families and students. There are also scholarships and grants for admission if families cannot financially afford the summer camps. Individuals interested can find the resources from the SOC (https://www.texasdeafed.org/).

Honestly, parents acquiring sign language alongside a DHH child will improve a DHH child's language. The first words the author recommends for families to focus on are household and frequently used items. Parents of DHH children can print off the word and sign and attach them to objects around the house. For example, print the sign for the microwave and then attach the label to the microwave. As the parent, or child, uses the microwave, utilize the sign, say the word, and then fingerspell the word. Allowing them the opportunity to see, hear, sign, and spell the word builds their language comprehension. If a parent needs help learning sign language, the family can reach out to the DHH child's TOD. Parents of DHH children can also access free resources such as Family Signs through SOC, Deaf individuals on every social media platform, or accessing the Deaf community in our area. Being involved with the Deaf community is a fantastic way to build sign language vocabulary because this allows an opportunity for individuals to learn from experts. Deaf individuals are very patient with new signers, especially as a parent of a DHH child. Even if a DHH child mainly communicates with spoken language, hearing devices and batteries may die or malfunction. If a DHH child's hearing device(s) malfunction, the DHH child will always have sign language to reinforce their spoken language. Parents of DHH children are encouraged to make learning sign language a priority, as language acquisition is the foundation for successful academics.

Since the author of this chapter is not a parent of a DHH child, she relied on the information from parents of DHH children and the DHH individuals to brainstorm recommendations. As stated in the chapter, higher language skills correlate to more proficient reading (Allen et al., 2014; Andrews & Baker, 2019; Antia et al., 2020; Brown & Watson, 2017; Goberis et al., 2012; Hall, 2017; Kirk Thagard et al., 2011; Lederberg et al., 2013; Marschark et al., 2009). What barriers are parents of DHH children encountering? Parents do not have to become fluent overnight, but just take it one day at a time, one sign at a time. No one who learns signed language regrets it; only those who do not understand sign language have regret.

Teachers of the Deaf and Hard of Hearing

Second, the author will provide recommendations, resources, and solutions for TODs. In this section, the author offers realistic and practical examples and activities for TODs. As a TOD, the author understands the responsibility and weight upon TOD's shoulders as DHH children fall behind their hearing peers in language and academics (M. L. Hall et al., 2019; Traxler, 2000). Since TOD cannot control what happens in the home, TOD must spend time with DHH children wisely. The time the author spends with

Maximizing the Impact of Language and Early Intervention

her DHH students never feels like enough to tackle their language, auditory, advocacy skills, academics, and whatever other IEP goals students have. The author shares a few crucial tips that directly apply in the classroom setting.

Provide Access to a Tablet With Sign Dictionaries

The first recommendation for teachers is to get a tablet. On the tablet, the author recommends that teachers download sign language dictionaries. There are many different sign language dictionaries to download based on the tablet purchased. Some examples of apps are ASL Core, Signing Exact English (SEE) app, and Sign ASL. The author's next step is for teachers to instruct students to look up unfamiliar words while independently reading. This skill helped the author's students to take the initiative in their learning. Texas also allows DHH students to use tablets (on guided access) on state tests, so this skill is practical and generalizable.

When introducing the sign language apps to the students, teachers need to model appropriate use of the app while reading stories aloud. Next, teachers should read normally until the teacher arrives at a word that their students do not know. Pause and ask the students to read the selected word. If the student cannot read the word, bring the tablet to the student and show the student how to type the word into the app and look up the sign. Then, have the students go through the passage and highlight or write down the words that the students do not know. After that, show the students how to look up the word in the sign language dictionary app. Once the students understand how to use the dictionary app, create opportunities to use the dictionary during reading, so the students begin to automatically use the app when they do not know a word.

Create Meaningful Vocabulary Experiences

The primary responsibility in a TOD career is teaching DHH children deep and specific vocabulary. TOD can build deep and specific vocabulary by selecting a few key vocabulary words from the guided reading book. Before a teacher reads the actual book, it is vital to pre-teach the key vocabulary. Teachers can pre-teach the vocabulary by having the students spell the word, write the word, look the word up in the sign language dictionary, and find a picture of the word. Then, the students can draw pictures of the selected words. Next, the students can interact with the key vocabulary to aid in comprehending the new vocabulary. Once the students know the vocabulary, TOD can focus on word accuracy in the passage. When the word first comes up in the passage, teachers can stop the students and make a big deal about it being one of the "new words"! Taking the time to focus on a deep understanding of the words in the guided reading books each week increased the author's students' comprehension exponentially!

Provide Opportunities for Vocabulary Development

The author recommends that TODs find time to encourage vocabulary development outside of the typical school day. Encouraging vocabulary outside of the school day is not possible for everyone, but this strategy significantly impacted the vocabulary growth of the author's DHH students. For example, the author's school district allowed students to attend summer school due to regression from COVID-19 on the students' yearly language goals.

Maximizing the Impact of Language and Early Intervention

During summer school, the author focused on language for four hours. The students started the day with a scavenger hunt that led the students to a small prize. The lessons focused on teaching directions and names for objects during this time. For example, the author focused on directional vocabulary, sequencing, names of familiar objects outside, including stop sign, street, sidewalk, etc. After the scavenger hunt, the summer school attendees had a morning meeting where the author asked the students about what had happened during class. The author focused on retention and recalling events during this time. The students often have an unclear understanding of time, so the author additionally focused on discussing what happened yesterday, last week, and last month. The author also focused on what even will happen in the future to increase the concept of time. For example, one of the students went to a restaurant but did not know the word restaurant but instead called it *eat*. The morning meeting provided an intentional time to focus on the DHH students' practical vocabulary.

The summer school attendees walked off campus every Friday for a field trip. The students and teachers walked downtown and worked on vocabulary for objects the students see in daily life. The group went into a dentist's office and learned about the experience of getting teeth cleaned; the students and teachers discussed the names of familiar objects such as a bench, light pole, stop sign, traffic light, road, and safety for crossing the streets, and much more. The author describes that it was equally fantastic and heartbreaking to their DHH students through their hometown and provides names for items the students saw and experienced their entire lives.

Creating the time for intentional language opportunities is essential for DHH students who struggle to achieve the same language and reading levels as their hearing counterparts. Some other examples for TOD to implement are providing a pizza social, going on field trips, planning a zoo meet-up, or going to the park. Any extra opportunity benefits DHH students as TODs strive to increase language and reading development.

General Education Teachers

First, if a general education teacher is even reading this chapter, the author offers commendations! Thanks for taking the time to learn more about educating the DHH children in the classroom. The author wanted to take the time to provide a few pieces of advice for working with a DHH child in the classroom. Teaching itself is a difficult job, and teaching grows in difficulty as additional duties are added to a teacher's already-over-filled plate.

The first piece of advice is to ask and plead for patience with DHH children. The DHH students in the class may struggle to reach classroom expectations because of the student's lack of language exposure and not due to their cognition or capabilities. Deaf children can accomplish the same as their hearing peers when provided the proper support! DHH students need a safe environment so that DHH students will take learning risks!

The second piece of advice is to provide the interpreters and TOD with the lesson plan. Taking the time to plan the lesson is not always possible, but it truly impacts the children's ability to present the information. For example, if an interpreter has time to prepare the correct vocabulary, an interpreter can research different ways to sign it, look up what the word means, or ask for advice from other interpreters. Providing lesson plans and material in advance to the TODs provides time for the TOD to modify assignments, print out visuals, make graphic organizers, or pre-teach the vocabulary before the class learns it, so the DHH students have a foundation to learn at the same level as their hearing peers.

CONCLUSION

This chapter guided readers on the journey DHH children go through as they struggle to achieve literacy. Tributaries such as early intervention and language impact the flow of the river, known as literacy. The struggle with literacy in DHH students is well-researched (Goberis et al., 2012; Kirk Thagard et al., 2011; Marschark et al., 2009; Traxler, 2000). To create authentic, long, and lasting change, the professionals and parents who work with DHH children must strive toward proficient language and literacy together! However, information is lacking on how professionals and parents can assist in striving for literacy in DHH children. The author provided research, information, and practical tips for parents and professionals to combat this struggle to achieve thriving and fluent literacy. In this chapter, the author discusses factors that may impact a DHH child's language and then, finally, on how their language affects literacy (Allen et al., 2014; Andrews & Baker, 2019; Antia et al., 2020; Brown & Watson, 2017; Goberis et al., 2012; W. C. Hall, 2017; Kirk Thagard et al., 2011; Lederberg et al., 2013; Marschark et al., 2009). Striving for change in a community with a historical struggle is difficult.

ACKNOWLEDGMENT

First, I want to acknowledge my amazing husband. I want to recognize Dr. Kaul, Dr. Werse, and Dr. Franz for taking the time to support me, help me see the greatness I have inside of me, and encourage me to share it with the world. Thank you for being patient with me as I wrote this chapter on top of my job and doctoral work. Thank you for believing in me and supporting me. I also want to acknowledge my son, Travis. I want this world to be a better place for you, son. You deserve the world at its best, and I hope to fight to make this world worthy of you. Last but not least, I want to acknowledge my friends, family, and colleagues. Thank you for your unyielding support through these past few months. I honestly could not have completed this chapter without the support from my community! Thank you!

REFERENCES

Allen, T., Letteri, A., Hoa Choi, S., & Dang, D. (2014). Early visual language exposure and emergent literacy in preschool Deaf children: Findings from a national longitudinal study. *American Annals of the Deaf*, *159*(4), 346–358. Advance online publication. doi:10.1353/aad.2014.0030 PMID:25669017

Andrews, J., & Baker, S. (2019). ASL nursery rhymes: Exploring a support for early language and emergent literacy skills for signing Deaf children. *Sign Language Studies*, *20*(1), 5–40. doi:10.1353ls.2019.0007

Antia, S., Lederberg, A., Easterbrooks, S., Schick, B., Branum-Martin, L., Connor, C., & Webb, M.-Y. (2020). Language and reading progress of young Deaf and hard-of-hearing children. *Journal of Deaf Studies and Deaf Education*, *25*(3), 334–350. doi:10.1093/deafed/enz050 PMID:32052022

Bat-Chava, Y., Martin, D., & Imperatore, L. (2013). Long-term improvements in oral communication skills and quality of peer relations in children with cochlear implants: Parental testimony. *Child: Care, Health and Development*, *40*(6), 870–881. doi:10.1111/cch.12102 PMID:24028465

Bell, A., & Houston, K. (2014). Red flags: Barriers to listening and spoken language in children with hearing loss. *Perspectives on Hearing and Hearing Disorders in Childhood, 24*(1), 11–18. doi:10.1044/hhdc24.1.11

Bergeson-Dana, T. (2014). Spoken language development in infants who are deaf or hard of hearing: The role of maternal infant-directed speech. *The Volta Review, 112*(2), 171–180.

Brown, P., & Watson, L. (2017). Language, play and early literacy for deaf children: The role of parent input. *Deafness & Education International, 19*(3/4), 108–114. doi:10.1080/14643154.2018.1435444

Byrd, S. A., Kileny, S., & Kileny, P. (2011). *The right not to hear: The ethics of parental refusal of hearing rehabilitation.* Academic Press.

CDC. (2018, April 11). *What is "Early Intervention" and is my child eligible?* Centers for Disease Control and Prevention. https://www.cdc.gov/ncbddd/actearly/parents/states.html

CDC. (2021, June 16). *Summary of diagnostics among infants not passing hearing screening.* Centers for Disease Control and Prevention. https://www.cdc.gov/ncbddd/hearingloss/2019-data/06-diagnostics.html

Chang, P. (2017). Breaking the sound barrier: Exploring parents' decision-making process of cochlear implants for their children. *Patient Education and Counseling, 100*(8), 1544–1551. doi:10.1016/j.pec.2017.03.005 PMID:28291575

Clark, M., Cue, K., Delgado, N., Greene-Woods, A., & Wolsey, J.-L. (2020). Early intervention protocols: Proposing a default bimodal bilingual approach for deaf children. *Maternal and Child Health Journal, 24*(11), 1339–1344. doi:10.100710995-020-03005-2 PMID:32897446

Cohen, N. (2003). Cochlear implant candidacy and surgical considerations. *Audiology & Neurotology, 9*(4), 197–202. doi:10.1159/000078389 PMID:15205547

Coppens, K., Tellings, A., Van der Veld, W., Schreuder, R., & Verhoeven, L. (2012). Vocabulary development in children with hearing loss: The role of child, family, and educational variables. *Research in Developmental Disabilities, 33*(1), 119–128. doi:10.1016/j.ridd.2011.08.030 PMID:22093656

Deng, Q., & Tong, S. (2021). Linguistic but not cognitive weaknesses in Deaf or hard-of-hearing poor comprehenders. *Journal of Deaf Studies and Deaf Education, 26*(3), 351–362. doi:10.1093/deafed/enab006 PMID:33824969

Duncan, M., & Lederberg, A. (2018). Relations between teacher talk characteristics and child language in spoken-language Deaf and hard-of-hearing classrooms. *Journal of Speech, Language, and Hearing Research: JSLHR, 61*(12), 2977–2995. doi:10.1044/2018_JSLHR-L-17-0475 PMID:30458501

Easterbrooks, S., & Lederberg, A. (2021). Reading fluency in young elementary school age deaf and hard-of-hearing children. *Journal of Deaf Studies and Deaf Education, 26*(1), 99–111. doi:10.1093/deafed/enaa024 PMID:32909026

Eisenberg, L., Iler Kirk, K., Schaefer Martinez, A., Ying, E., & Miyamoto, R. (2004). Communication abilities of children with aided residual hearing. *Archives of Otolaryngology—Head & Neck Surgery, 130*(5), 563–569. doi:10.1001/archotol.130.5.563 PMID:15148177

Falk, J., Anderson Di Perri, K., Howerton-Fox, A., & Jezik, C. (2020). Implications of a sight word intervention for Deaf students. *American Annals of the Deaf, 164*(5), 592–607. doi:10.1353/aad.2020.0005 PMID:32089538

Gascon-Ramos, M., Campbell, M., Bamford, J., & Young, A. (2010). Influences on parental evaluation of the content of early intervention following early identification of deafness: A study about parents' preferences and satisfaction. *Child: Care, Health and Development, 36*(6), 868–877. doi:10.1111/j.1365-2214.2010.01092.x PMID:20666784

Geers, A., Moog, J., & Rudge, A. (2019). Effects of frequency of early intervention on spoken language and literacy levels of children who are deaf or hard of hearing in preschool and elementary school. *Journal of Early Hearing Detection and Intervention, 4*(1), 15–27.

Goberis, D., Beams, D., Dalpes, M., Abrisch, A., Baca, R., & Yoshinaga-Itano, C. (2012). The missing link in language development of Deaf and hard of hearing children: Pragmatic language development. *Seminars in Speech and Language, 33*(04), 297–309. doi:10.1055-0032-1326916 PMID:23081790

Goldin-Meadow, S., & Mayberry, R. (2001). How do profoundly deaf children learn to read? *Learning Disabilities Research & Practice, 16*(4), 222. doi:10.1111/0938-8982.00022

Hall, M., Hall, W., & Caselli, N. (2019). Deaf children need language, not (just) speech. *First Language, 39*(4), 367–395. doi:10.1177/0142723719834102

Hall, M. L., Hall, W. C., & Caselli, N. K. (2019). Deaf children need language, not (just) speech. *First Language, 39*(4), 367–395. doi:10.1177/0142723719834102

Hall, W. C. (2017). What you don't know can hurt you: The risk of language deprivation by impairing sign language development in deaf children. *Maternal and Child Health Journal, 21*(5), 961–965. doi:10.100710995-017-2287-y PMID:28185206

Hands and Voices. (2020). *Communication considerations: Total Communication.* Hands and Voices. https://www.handsandvoices.org/comcon/articles/totalcom.htm

Harris, M. (2015). The impact of new technologies on the literacy attainment of deaf children. *Topics in Language Disorders, 35*(2), 120–132. doi:10.1097/TLD.0000000000000052

Hayes, H., Geers, A., Treiman, R., & Moog, J. (2009). Receptive vocabulary development in deaf children with cochlear implants: Achievement in an intensive auditory-oral educational setting. *Ear and Hearing, 30*(1), 128–135. doi:10.1097/AUD.0b013e3181926524 PMID:19125035

Hoffmeister, R., Henner, J., Caldwell-Harris, C., & Novogrodsky, R. (2022). Deaf children's ASL vocabulary and asl syntax knowledge supports English knowledge. *Journal of Deaf Studies and Deaf Education, 27*(1), 37–47. doi:10.1093/deafed/enab032 PMID:34788799

Holcomb, L., Golos, D., Moses, A., & Broadrick, A. (2022). Enriching Deaf children's American Sign Language phonological awareness: A quasi-experimental study. *Journal of Deaf Studies and Deaf Education, 27*(1), 26–36. doi:10.1093/deafed/enab028 PMID:34392343

Humphries, T., Kushalnagar, P., Mathur, G., Napoli, D., Padden, C., Rathmann, C., & Smith, S. (2012). Language acquisition for deaf children: Reducing the harms of zero tolerance to the use of alternative approaches. *Harm Reduction Journal*, *9*(1), 16. doi:10.1186/1477-7517-9-16 PMID:22472091

Humphries, T., Kushalnagar, P., Mathur, G., Napoli, D. J., Padden, C., Rathmann, C., & Smith, S. (2016). Avoiding linguistic neglect of deaf children. *The Social Service Review*, *90*(4), 589–619. doi:10.1086/689543

Joint Committee on Infant Hearing. (2007). Year 2007 position statement: Principles and guidelines for early hearing detection and intervention programs. *Pediatrics*, *120*(4), 898–921. doi:10.1542/peds.2007-2333 PMID:17908777

Kirk Thagard, E., Strong Hilsmier, A., & Easterbrooks, S. (2011). Pragmatic language in Deaf and hard of hearing students: Correlation with success in general education. *American Annals of the Deaf*, *155*(5), 526–534. doi:10.1353/aad.2011.0008 PMID:21449250

Lederberg, A. R., Schick, B., & Spencer, P. E. (2013). Language and literacy development of deaf and hard-of-hearing children: Successes and challenges. *Developmental Psychology*, *49*(1), 15–30. doi:10.1037/a0029558 PMID:22845829

Luft, P. (2008). Examining educators of the Deaf as "Highly Qualified" teachers: Roles and responsibilities under IDEA and NCLB. *American Annals of the Deaf*, *152*(5), 429–440. doi:10.1353/aad.2008.0014 PMID:18488531

Marschark, M., Sapere, P., Convertino, C., Mayer, C., Wauters, L., & Sarchet, T. (2009). Are Deaf students' reading challenges really about reading? *American Annals of the Deaf*, *154*(4), 357–370. doi:10.1353/aad.0.0111 PMID:20066918

Marshall, C., Jones, A., Fastelli, A., Atkinson, J., Botting, N., & Morgan, G. (2018). Semantic fluency in deaf children who use spoken and signed language in comparison with hearing peers. *International Journal of Language & Communication Disorders*, *53*(1), 157–170. doi:10.1111/1460-6984.12333 PMID:28691260

Mayer, C. (2007). What really matters in the early literacy development of Deaf children. *Journal of Deaf Studies and Deaf Education*, *12*(4), 411–431. doi:10.1093/deafed/enm020 PMID:17566067

Moeller, M. (2000). Early intervention and language development in children who are Deaf and hard of hearing. *Pediatrics*, *106*(3), e43–e43. doi:10.1542/peds.106.3.e43 PMID:10969127

Moroe, N. (2018). Why fix it if it's not broken! The role of audiologists in families of hearing children born to deaf parents. *Hearing, Balance and Communication*, *16*(3), 173–181. doi:10.1080/21695717.2018.1499990

National Association of the Deaf. (2016). *Bill of rights for Deaf and hard of hearing children*. National Association of the Deaf. https://www.nad.org/resources/education/bill-of-rights-for-deaf-and-hard-of-hearing-children/

National Association of the Deaf. (2021). *Early intervention services*. National Association of the Deaf. https://www.nad.org/resources/early-intervention-for-infants-and-toddlers/information-for-parents/early-intervention-services/

National Association of the Deaf—NAD. (n.d.). Retrieved October 10, 2021, from https://www.nad.org/resources/american-sign-language/community-and-culture-frequently-asked-questions/

National Institute on Deafness and Other Communication Disorders. (2019). *American Sign Language*. NIDCD. https://www.nidcd.nih.gov/health/american-sign-language

Nicholas, J., & Geers, A. (1997). Communication of oral deaf and normally hearing children at 36 months of age. *Journal of Speech, Language, and Hearing Research: JSLHR*, *40*(6), 1314–1327. doi:10.1044/jslhr.4006.1314 PMID:9430751

Nickbakht, M., Meyer, C., Scarinci, N., & Beswick, R. (2021). Family-centered care in the transition to early hearing intervention. *Journal of Deaf Studies and Deaf Education*, *26*(1), 21–45. doi:10.1093/deafed/enaa026 PMID:32783059

Padden, C., & Humphries, T. (1990). *Deaf in America: Voices from a Culture*. Harvard University Press.

Pimperton, H., Kreppner, J., Mahon, M., Stevenson, J., Terlektsi, E., Worsfold, S., Yuen, H. M., & Kennedy, C. R. (2017). Language outcomes in Deaf or hard of hearing teenagers who are spoken language users: Effects of Universal Newborn Hearing Screening and early confirmation. *Ear and Hearing*, *38*(5), 598–610. doi:10.1097/AUD.0000000000000434 PMID:28399063

Pizzo, L., & Chilvers, A. (2019). Assessment of language and literacy in children who are d/deaf and hard of hearing. *Education Sciences*, *9*(3), 223. doi:10.3390/educsci9030223

Rosen, R. (2000). Perspectives of the Deaf community on early identification and intervention: A case for diversity and partnerships. *Seminars in Hearing*, *21*(04), 327–342. doi:10.1055-2000-13468

Scarborough, H. (2001). *Connecting early language and literacy to later reading (dis)abilities: Evidence, theory, and practice*. Guilford Press, Handbook for research in early literacy.

Sehyr, Z., & Emmorey, K. (2022). Contribution of lexical quality and sign language variables to reading comprehension. *Journal of Deaf Studies and Deaf Education*, *27*(4), 1–18. doi:10.1093/deafed/enac018 PMID:35775152

Silvestri, J., & Wang, Y. (2018). A grounded theory of effective reading by profoundly Deaf adults. *American Annals of the Deaf*, *162*(5), 419–444. doi:10.1353/aad.2018.0002 PMID:29478997

Storbeck, C., & Calvert-Evans, J. (2008). Towards integrated practices in early detection of and intervention for Deaf and hard of hearing children. *American Annals of the Deaf*, *153*(3), 314–321. doi:10.1353/aad.0.0047 PMID:18807406

Subbiah, K., Mason, C., Gaffney, M., & Grosse, S. (2018). Progress in documented early identification and intervention for deaf and hard of hearing infants: CDC's hearing screening and follow-up survey, united states, 2006–2016. *Journal of Early Hearing Detection and Intervention*, *3*(2), 1–7. PMID:31745502

Syverud, S., Guardino, C., & Selznick, D. (2009). Teaching phonological skills to a Deaf first graders: A promising strategy. *American Annals of the Deaf, 154*(4), 382–388. doi:10.1353/aad.0.0113 PMID:20066920

Texas Education Association. (2021). *Annual Statewide Report on Language Acquisition for Deaf and Hard of Hearing and Deafblind Students 0-8 Years of Age.* https://tea.texas.gov/reports-and-data/legislative-reports

Tomaszewski, P., Krzysztofiak, P., & Moron, E. (2019). From sign language to spoken language? A new discourse of language development in Deaf children. *Psychology of Language and Communication, 23*(1), 48–84. doi:10.2478/plc-2019-0004

Traxler, C. (2000). The Stanford Achievement Test, 9th Edition: National norming and performance standards for Deaf and hard-of-hearing students. Journal of Deaf Studies & Deaf Education, 5(4), 337. doi:10.1093/deafed/5.4.337

Tuckwiller, E., Pullen, P., & Coyne, M. (2010). The use of regression discontinuity design in tiered intervention research: A pilot study exploring vocabulary instruction for at-risk kindergartners. *Learning Disabilities Research & Practice, 25*(3), 137–150. doi:10.1111/j.1540-5826.2010.00311.x

Wang, Y., Spychala, H., Harris, R., & Oetting, T. (2013). The effectiveness of phonics-based early intervention for deaf and hard of hearing preschool children and its possible impact on reading skills in elementary school: A case study. *American Annals of the Deaf, 158*(2), 107–120. doi:10.1353/aad.2013.0021 PMID:23967767

Wang, Y., & Williams, C. (2014). Are we hammering square pegs into round holes?: An investigation of the meta-analyses of reading research with students who are D/deaf or hard of hearing and students who are hearing. *American Annals of the Deaf, 159*(4), 323–345. doi:10.1353/aad.2014.0029 PMID:25669016

Webb, M., Patton-Terry, N., Bingham, G., Puranik, C., & Lederberg, A. (2018). Factorial validity and measurement invariance of the Test of Preschool Early Literacy-Phonological Awareness Test among Deaf and hard-of-Hearing children and hearing children. *Ear and Hearing, 39*(2), 278–292. doi:10.1097/AUD.0000000000000485 PMID:28837426

World Health Organization. (2021). *Deafness and hearing loss.* World Health Organization. https://www.who.int/news-room/fact-sheets/detail/deafness-and-hearing-loss

Yoshinaga-Itano, C. (2003). From screening to early identification and intervention: Discovering predictors to successful outcomes for children with significant hearing loss. *Journal of Deaf Studies and Deaf Education, 8*(1), 11–30. doi:10.1093/deafed/8.1.11 PMID:15448044

Yoshinaga-Itano, C. (2014). Principles and guidelines for early intervention after confirmation that a child is deaf or hard of hearing. *Journal of Deaf Studies and Deaf Education, 19*(2), 143–175. doi:10.1093/deafed/ent043 PMID:24131505

Yoshinaga-Itano, C., Sedey, A., Coulter, D., & Mehl, A. (1998). Language of early- and later-identified children with hearing loss. *Pediatrics, 102*(5), 1161–1171. doi:10.1542/peds.102.5.1161 PMID:9794949

Young, A. (2018). Deaf children and their families: Sustainability, sign language, and equality. *American Annals of the Deaf*, *1631*(1), 61–69. doi:10.1353/aad.2018.0011 PMID:29731473

Young, A., & Tattersall, H. (2007). Universal newborn hearing screening and early identification of deafness: Parents' responses to knowing early and their expectations of child communication development. *Journal of Deaf Studies and Deaf Education*, *12*(2), 209–220. doi:10.1093/deafed/enl033 PMID:17277310

Zhao, Y., Wu, X., Sun, P., & Chen, H. (2021). Relationship between vocabulary knowledge and reading comprehension in Deaf and hard of hearing students. *Journal of Deaf Studies and Deaf Education*, *26*(4), 546–555. doi:10.1093/deafed/enab023 PMID:34265846

ADDITIONAL READING

Antia, S. D., Lederberg, A., Easterbrooks, S., Schick, B., Branum-Martin, L., Connor, C. M., & Webb, M.-Y. (2020). Language and reading progress of young Deaf and hard-of-hearing children. *Journal of Deaf Studies and Deaf Education*, *25*(3), 334–350. doi:10.1093/deafed/enz050 PMID:32052022

Coppens, K., Tellings, A., Van der Veld, W., Schreuder, R., & Verhoeven, L. (2012). Vocabulary development in children with hearing loss: The role of child, family, and educational variables. *Research in Developmental Disabilities*, *33*(1), 119–128. doi:10.1016/j.ridd.2011.08.030 PMID:22093656

Goberis, D., Beams, D., Dalpes, M., Abrisch, A., Baca, R., & Yoshinaga-Itano, C. (2012). The missing link in language development of Deaf and hard of hearing children: Pragmatic language development. *Seminars in Speech and Language*, *33*(04), 297–309. doi:10.1055-0032-1326916 PMID:23081790

Hall, M. L., Hall, W., & Caselli, N. (2019). Deaf children need language, not (just) speech. *First Language*, *39*(4), 367–395. doi:10.1177/0142723719834102

Hall, W. (2017). What you don't know can hurt you: The risk of language deprivation by impairing sign language development in deaf children. *Maternal and Child Health Journal*, *21*(5), 961–965. doi:10.100710995-017-2287-y PMID:28185206

Humphries, T., Kushalnagar, P., Mathur, G., Napoli, D., Padden, C., Rathmann, C., & Smith, S. (2016). Avoiding linguistic neglect of deaf children. *The Social Service Review*, *90*(4), 589–619. doi:10.1086/689543

Lederberg, A., Schick, B., & Spencer, P. (2013). Language and literacy development of deaf and hard-of-hearing children: Successes and challenges. *Developmental Psychology*, *49*(1), 15–30. doi:10.1037/a0029558 PMID:22845829

Marschark, M., Sapere, P., Convertino, C., Mayer, C., Wauters, L., & Sarchet, T. (2009). Are Deaf students' reading challenges really about reading? *American Annals of the Deaf*, *154*(4), 357–370. doi:10.1353/aad.0.0111 PMID:20066918

Mayer, C. (2007). What really matters in the early literacy development of Deaf children. *Journal of Deaf Studies and Deaf Education*, *12*(4), 411–431. doi:10.1093/deafed/enm020 PMID:17566067

Young, A. (2018). Deaf children and their families: Sustainability, sign language, and equality. *American Annals of the Deaf, 1631*(1), 61–69. doi:10.1353/aad.2018.0011 PMID:29731473

KEY TERMS AND DEFINITIONS

Deaf: The term Deaf does not refer to a medical diagnosis. The term Deaf refers to the individuals in the Deaf community (*National Association of the Deaf - NAD*, n.d.). The Deaf community is a rich group and culture of individuals utilizing a shared language, American Sign Language. The individuals in the Deaf community may have a hearing difference but do not have to have a hearing difference to be a part of the community (Padden & Humphries, 1990).

Deaf and Hard of Hearing (DHH): Deaf and hard of hearing was chosen because of the individuals reviewed in this study. Deaf individuals (as defined above) and hard of hearing individuals who medically have a hearing difference. These individuals may use sign language, spoken language, or a combination but do not consider themselves part of the Deaf community (Padden & Humphries, 1990).

Chapter 11
Developing an Inventory to Evaluate Communication Skills of Children With Normal Hearing and Hearing Loss

Esra Genc

https://orcid.org/0000-0002-9229-1452

Tokat Gaziosmanpasa University, Turkey

Yildiz Uzuner

Anadolu University, Turkey

ABSTRACT

Researchers state that communication skills, which are developed before language acquisition and have very important place in language development, are 1) directing attention, 2) turn-taking, 3) imitation, 4) communicative purposes, and 5) conversation. As in all children, communication skills in children with hearing loss are very important. It is very important to identify children who have problems with their communication skills and to provide appropriate education. Standardized tests are generally used to assess children's language and communication skills in Turkey, but there are no informal tools that allow the assessment of early communication skills. Therefore, in this chapter, firstly, communication skills will be briefly defined and the disadvantages and advantages of formal and informal assessment and evaluation approaches will be discussed. Afterwards, the scope and development process of the informal communication skills inventory (ICSI) based on natural data collection in various contexts will be presented with sample items from the inventory.

DOI: 10.4018/978-1-6684-5022-2.ch011

Developing an Inventory

INTRODUCTION

Hearing loss refers to deficits in children's hearing that arise for a variety of reasons and to varying degrees. Thanks to newborn hearing screening, children diagnosed shortly after birth start using hearing aid technologies according to the degree and type of loss. Developing oral language skills are possible by accessing early auditory stimuli and providing appropriate educational conditions. Today, children with severe and profound sensorineural hearing loss who cannot access sound with hearing aids can hear acoustic stimuli thanks to the cochlear implant. It is very important to note that cochlear implant applications can contribute to oral language acquisition when combined with early and effective educational interventions (Paul, 2001). Regardless of hearing status, communication skills are very important in language proficiency, interpersonal interaction, and living in a community.

Moreover; language and literacy development mutually affect each other. While literacy supports language development, interactive language skills also support literacy development. Most children with hearing loss start school with insufficient language development. They also have difficulties in literacy skills built on inadequate language structure (Albertini & Schely, 2003). For this reason, it is very important to identify children who have problems with their communication skills as early as possible and to provide the necessary training. Formal (standardized tests), and informal such as observations, interviews, inventories assessment, and evaluation methods are utilized to evaluate communication skills in children.

Standardized tests are mainly used in Turkey to assess children's language and communication skills. Formal assessments are inadequate when they are used to interfere with and support children's communication skills. In the evaluations to be made when it comes to language and communication development, the product and the process in which the product is obtained gains importance. Dealing with the process is a guide for an expert or teacher on the curriculum that will be planned later. However, no informal tools in Turkey allow the assessment of early communication skills. For this reason, in this chapter after giving a brief definition of communication skills in children, we will discuss the disadvantages and advantages of both formal and informal assessment and evaluation approaches. It is important and necessary to develop informal language and communication skills inventories that allow children to evaluate their functional language in natural contexts and interactions. Therefore, it necessary to develop a valid, reliable, and convenient inventories. We have developed the Informal Communication Skills Inventory (ICSI). So, we will present its developing process, collecting natural data and the representative items derived from the content of our inventory.

COMMUNICATION AND LANGUAGE

Communication is everywhere in our lives and is an integral part of dail living. In its general meaning, it can be explained as the process of information exchange, in which various messages are sent and received between living things. Interpersonal communication, on the other hand, is the transfer of individuals' feelings, thoughts, wishes to other people. Language is the tool used in interpersonal communication. Language is used as a tool in interpersonal communication in almost all known societies (Sanders, 1982). Thanks to the language that symbolizes thoughts, people can perform many tasks required by social life, such as giving and receiving information and establishing social interaction.

It is known that children acquire their communication skills and language through various interaction experiences with the individuals around them in their culture, even though there is no systematic teaching

(McLean & Snyder-McLean, 1999). The development of communication skills predates the acquisition of oral language. Communication skills are very important in the acquisition and development of oral language. Language and communication are concepts that complement each other. Because of this, it is known that their development is influenced by each other, and that the development of one affects the development of the other.

Language and communication skills are very important for people to belong to a society and to establish social interaction. Schirmer (2000) states that language is also very important for the development of literacy. The fact that the language acquisition processes of children with hearing loss are similar to their hearing peers suggests that the literacy processes of children with hearing loss may also be similar in environments where meaningful, purposeful and functional literacy experiences are provided. The ability of people, who are social beings, to communicate correctly and effectively is closely related to their knowledge of the language of that society and the system of rules regarding language (Keenan, 1974). All languages consist of a system of the rules that compose them. These systems of the rules can be called as components of language.

COMPONENTS OF LANGUAGE

The whole system of the rules that determine the structure and content of words, sentences and discourses belonging to a language is called the components of the language. These rules, which enable the organization of the language, are divided into sections within themselves to correspond to certain areas. Individuals can become competent in a language thanks to the development in all the components of this language. Language acquisition and development is also possible with the development of all these language components (Capone, 2010; Owens, 2008; Pence & Justice, 2008).

It is stated that difficulties in language components cause many problems such as analyzing and synthesizing text structure rules in reading comprehension (de Villiers & Pomerantz, 1992). Language components are phonology, morphology, syntax, semantic and pragmatic. Phonology includes the rules for vocalizing syllables and words by determining the sequence and distribution of phonemes, the smallest units that allow meaning change in language. The sequence and order of morphemes, which is the smallest meaningful unit in that language, is within the scope of morphology. On the other hand, syntax is the rules that determine the order in which the words that make up the sentences will come together and which word combinations can be considered in relation to the meaning they express. Semantic is the rules that govern the meaning of words and sentences in a language. Pragmatic is the use of language for various purposes in various contexts (Capone, 2010; Owens, 2008; Pence & Justice, 2008). It is known that these components, which are mutually related to each other, support each other's development. In other words, no component is developed completely independently of the others (McLean & Snyder-McLean, 1999; Otto, 2006). In addition, pragmatism determines other components' characteristics (Bates, 1976; Capone, 2010; Pence & Justice, 2008). Considering the explanations about the components of the language, it is evident that the form and structure of the language should be determined according to the context in which the language is used and the purpose of its use. Accordingly, the context in which the pragmatic is used determines which semantic and syntactic rules will be used according to the communication purpose. It can be said that communication skills are that refer to the pragmatic component and aim to improve language use in various social contexts. These skills, which began to develop long

Developing an Inventory

before the development of spoken(oral/sign) oral language, are also the basis for the development of the late phases of any language.

COMMUNICATION SKILLS

Children who have not yet acquired the spoken language use their communication skills to convey their wishes and needs. It is important to note that communication skills, each of which is considered to be very important in the development of oral language, are intertwined with each other and make significant contributions to the development of each other (Pieterse et al., 1989). Generally, researchers identify the communication skills as; 1) directing attention, 2) imitation, 3) turn-taking, 4) communicative purposes, 5) conversation (Cole, 1992; McLean & Snyder-McLean, 1999; Pieterse et al., 1989).

Directing Attention Skills

Social interaction between adults and children in early childhood begins with directing attention skills. The ability to direct attention can be considered as the basic step of communicating. It includes skills such as directing a glance, mutual gaze, topical gaze, and gaze shifting. The development of these skills, which are also closely related to cognitive development, are related both to each other and oral language development (Pieterse et al., 1989). In the literature, studies with various names, such as joint attention and eye contact, are used interchangeably with the skills examined under the heading of directing attention in this section and/or as an umbrella term for these skills.For this reason, although they are named differently, they are basically all attention-related skills that serve language development.

It is seen that the studies on attention-direction skills in children with hearing loss are mostly comparative studies based on mother-child pairings. In studies comparing hearing mother-hearing-impaired children and hearing mother-child spouses, joint attention skills of hearing-impaired children are lower than their hearing peers (Bortfeld & Oghalai, 2018; MacGowan et al., 2021). A study comparing hearing and hearing-impaired children and hearing mothers' spouses observed that children with cochlear implants exhibited joint attention skills similar to hearing-impaired children and more than hearing-impaired children (Tasker et al., 2010).

Imitation

Children who base their expressions on the behaviors of others with imitation behavior learn many skills and behavior patterns related to their own culture. Thus, the transmission of many cultural characteristics between generations is ensured (Meltzoff & Moore, 1997). When imitation skills are examined based on language development, it is known that children first imitate their mothers' gestures and facial expressions about four weeks after birth.

Imitation skills have been classified in various ways according to the body region in which they are exhibited, the time in which they are exhibited, and the learning function they serve. Imitations according to the body area exhibited; Object imitation is motor imitation and vocal-verbal imitation (Rogers et al., 2008). In addition, Zaghlawan (2010), according to the use of the object by its function in real life, stated that they were divided into functional and non-functional. The types of imitation classified as temporal are; it is delayed and immediate imitation (Rogers et al., 2008). Another type of imitation is generalized imitation. Generalized imitation can be explained as the child who is reinforced for an imitation behavior imitates other behaviors. Such imitation behaviors are very important when examining the effect of imitation on learning (Meltzoff & Moore, 1989). According to another classification, imitation is divided into two as spontaneous and directed. It is called spontaneous imitation, when the imitated behavior is performed voluntarily by the imitator without any direction. Encouraging a child to imitate in modeling or mutual imitation by another person is called directed imitation (Zaghlawan, 2010). Finally, imitation in the context of communication skills is divided into three categories: imitating actions, gestures and sounds (Pieterse et al., 1989).

In imitation studies conducted on children with hearing loss, it is seen that verbal instant imitation skills (Kondaurova et al., 2020; Wang et al., 2013) and non-verbal instantaneous imitation skills (Orr, 1998; Wang, 2020) are examined based on structured or semi-structured interactions. The studies were generally conducted as a comparison study with children with normal hearing and hearing loss. In their findings, it was observed that both children with hearing loss and cochlear implants performed lower than their hearing peers in instant verbal and non-verbal imitations (Kondurova et al., 2020; Wang et al., 2013; Wang et al., 2020).

Turn-Taking

Interpersonal communication, beyond the proficiency of individuals in oral language, during conversations; The fluency of their speech is affected by many important variables such as order of speech, consistency of expressions, and gap times during transitions. These components, which ensure the fluency of conversations and synchronization in interpersonal communication, fall within the scope of turn-taking from communication skills.

The basis of turn-taking is based on early parent-child interaction. During these periods, it is observed that adults who accept children as conversation partners speak to children as if they were in a conversation, match the acoustic qualities of babies' vocalizations, and produce short and repetitive speeches directed at the baby in an effort to encourage the baby's greater participation (Gratier & Devouche, 2011). During these interactions, it is seen that adults expect babies after their own statements. Adults who accept babies' glances, gestures, mimics, and pronunciations as answers, turn-taking, and continuation of the discussion, regardless of their significance.Such interactions prepare children to turn-taking in conversation (Cole, 1992; McLean & Snyder-McLean, 1999). In a study on turn-taking skills in the early period, it was seen that 32- and 36-week-old babies increased their vocalization frequency with the presence of their parents and produced mutual sounds with their parents (Caskey et al., 2011).

In studies examining turn-taking skills in children with hearing loss, it is seen that comparison studies are conducted according to their hearing peers. When comparing children with cochlear implants and children with normal hearing according to mother-child interaction, it was observed that children with cochlear implants showed less sequential participation and more overlapping participation than children with normal hearing (Kondaurova et al, 2020; Tait et al., 2007). However, although their verbal sequence and skills are less compared to their hearing peers, it is seen that their development within themselves is higher than that of hearing children (Tait et al., 2007).

Communicative Purposes

Communicative purposes can be briefly defined as intending to convey and express a request (Coggins & Carpenter, 1981). Communicative purposes, which are very important in developing language skills, are the prerequisite of verbal language. At the same time, it is one of the most important factors that ensure continuity in the transition from the beginning of language development to the word level (Dore, 1974; Cole, 1992; Roth & Spekman, 1984; Pieterse et al., 1989). Wetherby and Rodriguez (1992), who studied the development of communicative goals in children over time, looked at 15 typically developing children's communicative goals in both structured and unstructured settings for one year. They found that the number of requests and explanations increased as the children moved from the preverbal to the multi-word stage. The research results show that the frequency of displayed communicative goals increases in direct proportion to language development. It was also stated that the context influenced the communicative aims displayed. Yont et al. (2003) investigated the communicative purposes of 12-month-old infants in their interactions with their mothers. Researchers have discovered that labeling occurs more frequently during book reading activities. The research results revealed that the communicative goals displayed by children vary according to the context.

It is seen that various classifications have been made regarding the types of communicative purposes. However, it is seen that researchers use different terms to mean the same meaning. Dore (1974), Pieterse et al. (1989), and Roth and Spekman (1984) used the term communicative intent in their classifications. Halliday (1975) and Tough (1981) used the term communicative function in their classifications. In addition to the classifications made, it is evident that "communicative behavior" and "communicative act" are used interchangeably to refer to the same concept (Curtis et al., 1979; Day, 1986; Whetherby & Rodriquez, 1992; Beattie & Kysela, 1995; Yont et al., 2003).

It is seen that the communicative purposes studies conducted with children with hearing loss were taken from the interactions in various contexts and the conversations with the teacher during the lesson at school via video recording. Curtis et al. (1979), Day (1986), and Genc et al. (2017) found that children exhibit a variety of communicative purposes in different contexts (Curtis et al. (1979), Day (1986), and Genc et al. (2017)), whereas studies that collected data from a single environment, such as the classroom, found that children use certain communicative purposes more frequently (Beattie & Kysela, 1995). Based on this information, we can say that children's communicative goals are related to the situation and that collecting natural interaction data from different situations will help us get a better idea of what those goals are.

Conversation

Conversation; It is a communication skill that includes initiating communication, giving appropriate responses in ongoing interaction, maintaining communication and ending it appropriately. Children who invite adults around them to a conversation with behaviors such as gazing, smiling, and crying in the early stages initiate communication on a subject, situation, or event. The communication initiated by the adults responding to these communications initiated by the children turns into a mutual conversation. A mutual conversation is entered into when the interaction partners adapt to answering them appropriately within the framework of turn-taking. (Cole, 1992; Stone, 1988). Conversation skills can be examined in two parts as the form and function of the conversation. The form of the conversation; includes starting, maintaining, and ending a conversation. The function of the conversation includes a topic introduction, topic maintenance, topic ending, repair communication breakdown, topical cohesion, and discourse types. In Foster's (1986) study, five children and their families took part in a longitudinal examination of the conversation initiation skill. This examination revealed that the ability to initiate a conversation developed with age, such as the ability to take turns speaking. Foster has observed that older children tend to initiate more conversations. The researcher explained the reason for the development in children with the development in both language and cognitive skills.

According to the findings of research on communication disorders related to conversation skills in children with hearing loss, there is no difference between the groups of children with hearing loss and children with normal hearing in terms of the number of communication breakdowns (Fitzpatrick et al., 2020). However, the type of strategy used differs between the groups, and children with normal hearing can use different strategies than children with hearing loss (Most, 2002). Children with hearing loss are at the same level as their hearing peers with regard to topic start and maintenance, according to studies (Most et al., 2010), while children with cochlear implants initiate more subjects than their hearing peers (Toe & Patsch, 2013). When the studies are examined in terms of how the data are collected, it is seen that the data of a group of studies were collected through conversations, interactions, or games between children and adults in semi-structured environments (Fitzpatrick et al., 2020; Most, 2002; Most et al., Meilijson, 2010). In another group of studies, it is seen that data were collected through conversations held in semi-structured environments (Church et al., 2017; Toe & Patsch, 2013) between spouses of children with hearing loss-normal hearing or children with cochlear implants-normal hearing.

ASSESSMENT AND EVALUATION IN LANGUAGE AND COMMUNICATION DEVELOPMENT

Problems experienced in language and communication development also negatively affect other areas of development (Bishop & Adams, 1990). Depending on the relationship between literacy and language skills, problems experienced in language skills also negatively affect literacy development (Erickson, 1987). Children who have problems in the development of language and communication skills must be identified and educated as early as possible (Bishop & Adams, 1990). The preparation of appropriate education programs for children's needs can be revealed as a result of a comprehensive evaluation (Pieterse et al., 1989). The information obtained as a result of an evaluation and the methods used to collect this information are two of the criteria that are considered when classifying measurements and evaluations. Measurements and evaluations can be divided into two categories: formal measurement and evaluation and informal measurement and evaluation. Both of these approaches have their advantages and disadvantages (Otto, 2006).

Formal Measurement and Evaluation

Standardized tests are used in formal assessment and evaluation (Notari-Syverson & Losardo, 1996; Otto, 2006). Standardized tests are ways to measure something. They are made, scored, and interpreted by experts based on standards that have already been set, and the results are compared to certain norms. In standardized tests, the application and evaluation of tests are applied in the same way for everyone within the framework of predetermined rules with standard steps. The data are collected simultaneously and the results obtained are evaluated according to the norm group data by following the rules of the test

Developing an Inventory

(Notari-Syverson & Losardo, 1996; Oosterhof, 2003). Special training is required to apply and evaluate the tests according to certain standards (McLoughlin & Lewis, 2005).

The validity and reliability of formal assessments and evaluations are high. They are designed to provide a valid measurement of the behavior that is intended to be measured. Formal methods used in language assessments generally contain stimuli designed specifically to reveal various linguistic expressions. These assessments create a general framework to reveal the desired linguistic response (Otto, 2006). It can be said that these tests allow the evaluation of the resulting product because of the evaluation of the linguistic expressions that emerge as a result of the stimuli, and they do not take the process into account (Oosterhof, 2003). Therefore, they cannot provide comprehensive examples of children's language. However, it is not a correct method to make a decision based on the obtained score since it is a matter of planning and making a decision about linguistic skills (Owens, 2008). In formal methods, language data is taken from an isolated environment. Since the environments in which the tests are made are different from the real environments, a few or more stimuli affect the answers given compared to the real world (Otto, 2006; Owens, 2008).

Another important point about standardized tests is whether the child can understand the test items correctly. If the items are not understood correctly, the lack or inaccuracy of the answers does not show the lack of language skill that is tried to be measured in real terms. Especially for preschool children, lack of attention and interest may cause negative test results. In light of this information, it is emphasized that evaluating a language using formal methods is accurate but has its limitations, and as a result, it needs to be supplemented by methods that are less formal (Owens, 2008).

Standardized Tests Frequently Used in Language Assessments in Turkey

When we take a look at the standardized tests that are used on a regular basis in Turkey, we can see that they can be separated into two categories: those that have been adapted to Turkish and those that have been developed in Turkish. Concurrently, there are language examinations included within the general development examinations. For the purposes of receptive and expressive language evaluations in general, the norm group for linguistic tests was comprised of children whose cognitive development was typical. The following is a list of standardized language examinations that are utilized quite frequently in Turkey:

Table 1. Standardized relative tests frequently used in Turkey

	Tests Developed in Turkish	**Tests Adapted to Turkish**
Language Tests	• TIFALDI: Turkish Expressive and Receptive Language Test (Kazak-Berument & Guven, 2013) • AAT: Ankara Articulation Test (Ege et al., 2004) • SST: Turkish Pronunciation and Phonetics Test (Topbas, 2004)	• TEDIL: Turkish Early Language Development Test (Topbas & Guven, 2011) • TODIL: Turkish School Age Language Development Test (Topbas et al., 2013) • PLS-5: Preschool Language Scale (Sahli & Belgin, 2017) • PPWT: Peabody Picture Word Test (Katz et al., 1974)
Language Subtests Under General Developmental	• GECDA: Gazi Early Childhood Assessment Tool (Temel et al., 2006) • AGTE: Ankara Developmental Screening Inventory (Savasir et al., 1994)	• DENVER II: Developmental Screening Test II (Anlar et al., 2009)

Informal Measurement and Evaluation

In informal assessments and evaluations, their performance is evaluated within themselves, not according to the group. In these evaluations, the product that emerges as a result of the evaluation and the process in which the product emerges gain importance. Informal measurement tools; criterion-dependent: observation, interview, self-assessment, informal language inventories, oral and written language analyses, and others. In criterion-dependent assessments, children's performances are evaluated according to their previous performances (McLoughlin & Lewis, 2005).

Informal methods for evaluating language and communication skills are also taken from the natural environments in which language data occur. Due to the fact that the data was collected from children's natural contexts and interactions, it exemplifies both the verbal and nonverbal communicative behaviors of children. Due to the fact that assessments and evaluations are tailored specifically to children, education planning can be made that is both more appropriate and more effective. In the same vein, evaluating how well children perform provides us with a clearer picture of how successfully the applied education program operates. There are positive and negative aspects in informal measurement and evaluation. Accordingly, compared to the formal measurement and evaluation method; preparation, recording, and evaluation of data requires more time (Otto, 2006). It is also stated that the examples of conversation are insufficient to reflect all of the child's communication skills. People who will make the evaluations in informal assessments and evaluations should be competent in the subject area. Despite all of these problems, informal measurement and evaluation methods can be used to test children's everyday language and communication skills (Owens, 2008).Informal language/communication inventories, which are informal measurement tools, provide comprehensive and accurate examples of language skills in children, as they enable the evaluation of the process. In these inventories, which allow the evaluation of the functional languages used by children in natural contexts and natural interactions, children's verbal and non-verbal communication skills can be exemplified by obtaining language data from natural social contexts. However, in some communication skills inventories, it is seen that the data are obtained through questions directed to families about the child's communication skills (Dewart & Summers, 1995). Some of the inventories examined in this sense are given below.

The Pragmatics Profile of Everyday Communication Skills in Children Revised Edition was developed by Dewart and Summers (1995). Based on interviews with the child's primary caregiver or caregivers, the inventory aims to provide a general perspective on children's communication skills. It has been developed for children aged 0-10. Inventory of children; it contains various questions aimed at obtaining information about the communicative function, communication participation, and response skills. It is stated that the inventory, which can be used for children with typical development, language development delay, specific language disability, hearing impairment, visual impairment, physical difficulties, and learning difficulties, can be used by speech-language therapists, educational psychologists, clinical psychologists, and teachers. As a result of the interviews, the strengths and weaknesses of the children are determined.

The Guide to Analysis of Language Transcripts-Second Edition (Retherford, 1993) has been developed in order to describe various aspects of language production and to analyze the development level of the determined structures, to be suitable for children aged 1-6 with normally developing, language disorders or delayed language. The content of the inventory includes semantics, syntax, and usage, which are components of the language. In the inventory, data is collected by teachers or experts by recording natural language examples used by children in various contexts with a video camera. In the data analy-

Developing an Inventory

sis, the interactions recorded with the video camera are transcribed to show the context elements. The language samples translated into the text are placed in the analysis tables, and the frequency, number, and form of the child's use of the determined actions are exemplified.

Bader Reading and Language Inventory-Seventh Edition, although the inventory developed by Bader and Pearce (2012) is basically about reading, it includes sections related to language. The target population is preschool, primary, secondary, and high school students and adults with typical development, reading problems, hearing and vision difficulties, and adults in the inventory collect data from the target population. By showing the picture that is suitable for the person's level, the instruction "look at the picture and tell me as much as you can about the picture" is given. The answers are recorded and translated into text. The expressive verbal language checklist is filled according to the written answers. Thus, the strengths and weaknesses of the participants are determined.

In assessing language and communication skills in Turkey, although there are studies in which researchers examine language data from interactions with natural or general boundaries according to checklists they create themselves or according to existing checklists, the informal language and/or communication skills inventory that has been developed or translated into Turkish has not been achieved. For this reason, it is aimed to develop a valid, reliable, and useful informal communication skills inventory that aims to reveal children's strengths and weaknesses by providing comprehensive and accurate examples of children's functional communication skills.

DEVELOPMENT OF INFORMAL COMMUNICATION SKILLS INVENTORY

Language and communication inventories developed in the international arena and language and communication measurement tools developed in Turkey or adapted to Turkish were examined in the development of the Informal Communication Skills Inventory (ICSI) (Aksu-Koc et al., 2019; Dewart & Summers, 1995; Retherford, 1993; Savasir et al., 1994). Content analyses were performed on inventories of informal language and communication skills (Bader & Pearce, 2012; Dewart & Summers, 1995; Retherford, 1993). In the content analysis; the answers to the questions of what is the purpose of the inventories, what their contents are, who the target populations are, who can use them, how the data are collected, how they are analyzed and reported, how the validity and reliability studies are carried out were sought. In the inventory that will be developed in line with the analysis results obtained, it has been decided how the answers to the related questions will be. Accordingly, it was decided that ICSI should include directing attention skills, imitation, turn-taking, structure of conversation, communicative purposes, and function of conversation, and communication skills, suitable for children aged 0 5;11. Within the scope of ICSI; an information form, interview form, 6 checklists, and an implementation procedure were prepared.

After deciding on the scope of the ICSI, checklists were first developed. For each communication skill, books and studies in the literature were examined, previously made checklists and classifications were reviewed, and the items to be placed under each communication skill checklist were determined. Functional definitions were made for each of these items, and examples were prepared. Analysis forms of the checklists to be used in the analysis process were created in line with the prepared checklists. The interview form, information form and the implementation procedure of the ICSI were prepared. While developing the checklists, various researches were designed, their operability was examined, and applications were made. These studies have been presented at national or international congresses. After the final forms of the developed checklists were given, expert opinions were taken, and arrangements were made according to expert opinions.

Validity, Reliability, and Usability Studies

Content validity; It can be defined as the items in the measurement tool adequately cover and represent the subject and behavior area, which is the tool's purpose (Mills & Gay, 2019). Content validity in ICSI was obtained with the opinions of three experts working in areas such as language and communication skills, assessment and evaluation, and family education in children with hearing loss. Experts were asked to evaluate the clarity, comprehensibility, and relevance of definitions and examples for each item on the checklists, to determine if they met the relevant communication skill correctly and completely, taking into account the degree of suitability, and to provide any suggestions.In line with the feedback from the experts, the checklists were finalized with 100% consensus.

Within the scope of the reliability study, a reliability study between encoders was carried out in ICSI. Inter-coder reliability is the degree of consistency between coding different coders using the same tool on the same data (Mills & Gay, 2019). Inter-coder reliability study was conducted with the first and second authors. Inter-coder reliability study was conducted on 35% of the data collected within the study's scope after the SSI's development. Before the reliability studies, the authors conducted coding learning sessions to analyse the checklists for 3 different participants. The authors independently analyzed the video observation recordings determined after the learning sessions. Afterward, the coding was compared, and the reliability formula between the coders (Consensus / Consensus + Disagreement X 100) was applied (Toe et al., 2007). Intercoder reliability; 92% for attention-directing skills, 99% for imitation, 97% for turn taking, 95% for conversation structure, 99% for communicative functions, and 99% for conversation structure.

The most important limitation of informal language and communication skills inventories is that collecting natural language and communication data requires a lot of time due to observing natural interactions in various contexts. In order to ensure usefulness during the collection of natural communication skills data within the scope of ICSI, preliminary interviews are conducted with the families to learn the context information of the children and their daily routines for a week. Natural interactions occurring in various contexts, which are thought to answer the checklists the most among the learned routines, are recorded with a video camera. Since the videotape analysis method requires a lot of time during the examination and analysis of the records, the checklists are filled by watching the camera recordings with detailed checklists. In addition, a Remote Data Collection guide was created to enable data collection in different situations (online, offline, and face-to-face) to increase the utility of the ICSI.

Scope of Informal Communication Skills Inventory

Checklists: The informal communication skills inventory consists of six checklists. It has been observed in the literature that researchers typically consider five sub-dimensions of communication skills. These include directing attention, imitation, turn-taking, communicative functions, and conversation skills (Cole, 1992; McLean & Snyder-McLean, 1999; Pieterse et al., 1989).Conversation skill was divided into two as structure and function within the scope of ICSI, and 6 checklists were prepared. Figures 1-6 show sample items of the checklists within the scope of the ICSI.

Developing an Inventory

Figure 1. Representative item from directing attention skills checklist

DIRECTING ATTENTION SKILLS		
Participant's Name and Surname:		Observation/Video No:
Evaluator's Name and Surname:		Analysis Date:
The ability to directing attention is different from the child's casual look at his environment. The child is aware of and is interested in the people, objects and events to which he or she directs his attention. When s/he looks at an object with his communication partner or shifts his gaze between the communication partner and the object, he is aware of the presence of both the communication partner and the object. Start the video. Watch the child's behavior carefully. When you see a behavior of the child that corresponds to one of the items in the checklist, put a tick in the frequency column of the relevant item in the checklist.		
DIRECTING ATTENTION SKILLS	DESCRIPTION / EXAMPLE	
Directing gaze	Description: The child directs his/her attention to the people, objects * and events around him/her. Examples: Child; • He/she directs his attention to the people around him in order to ask for something or to report something. • When he is called, he looks at the caller by rolling his eyes or turning his head. • When he hears a sound (e.g. when he hears a car, animal or music), he looks in the direction of the sound by squinting or turning his head. • When there is an event around (e.g. a running child falls to the ground), he looks at the event. • When spoken to, he looks at the face of the person speaking for a while. He watches the face and speech of the person speaking for a while. • When approached to give him a favorite object (e.g. pacifier, toy) or food, he looks at the person and/or what he is holding.	

Figure 2. Representative item from imitation checklist

IMITATION			
Participant's Name and Surname:			Observation/Video No:
Evaluator's Name and Surname:			Analysis Date:
Start the video. Carefully monitor the expressions and behaviors of the child and the communication partner. When you see an expression or behavior of the child that corresponds to one of the items in the checklist, put a tick in the frequency column of the relevant item in the checklist. In observed behaviors, two different types of imitation can be observed at the same time, which are on the checklist on the same behavior. When you think that a type of imitation exhibited by the child is suitable for two different items, do not hesitate to mark both items. The gestures, mimics and actions that are meant to be described by the expression "Non-Verbal Expressions" in the items. "Verbal Expressions" are sounds, words, clauses and sentences.			
IMITATION TYPES		DESCRIPTION / EXAMPLE	
SPONTANEOUS IMITATION	Spontaneous Verbal Imitation	Description: The child spontaneously imitates the sounds he hears in his environment, trying to reproduce them as much as possible immediately after the adult. Examples: After a person does any of the following examples, the child spontaneously imitates it. • Vowel sounds: aaaa, ooooo. • Syllables containing a consonant + a vowel: bu, me. • Patterns containing a consonant + a vowel: mamama, dadada. • Syllables containing a single vowel + consonant: Düt düt. • Two-syllable patterns: Dadi-dadi. • Phrases: Mama is over. Dad is gone. • Sentences: Let's collect the toys.	
DEFFERED IMITATION			

Figure 3. Representative item from turn-taking checklist

TURN-TAKING		
Participant's Name and Surname:		Observation/Video No:
Evaluator's Name and Surname:		Analysis Date:
Start the video. Carefully monitor the behavior of the child and the communication partner when they are interacting with each other. When you see the sequential or overlapping participation of the child corresponding to one of the items in the checklist, put a tick in the frequency column of the relevant item in the checklist.		
TURN-TAKING		DESCRIPTION / EXAMPLE

VERBAL TURN-TAKING	In order participation	Description: While the child is in conversation/interaction with the communication partner, he/she listens to the communication partner. When the communication partner takes a turn, she realizes that it is her turn and takes her turn. After speaking in words, phrases or sentences by making sounds in his own turn, he gives the communication partner an aural, visual, tactile turn.
		Examples:
		Adult and child looking at a book together:
		    Child: Meow meow. (She shows the picture of the cat in the book. Then she stops and looks at the adult.)
		    Adult: Yes, the cat came and said meow. What does she want? (He speaks by looking at the cat that the child showed him. Then he keeps silent and looks at the child.)
		    Child: He's hungry.
		    Adult: Ah! Let's give him some milk then. (Conversation continues as a sequential conversation.)
		
		Adult and child take turns singing a children's song together:
		    Adult: A tiny little bird was frozen. (She waits, staring at the child.)
		    Child: It was put on my window. (She waits, looking at the adult.)
		    Adult: I took him in… continues sequentially.

NON-VERBAL TURN-TAKING		

Figure 4. Representative item from form of conversation checklist

FORM OF CONVERSATION	
Participant's Name and Surname:	Observation/Video No:
Evaluator's Name and Surname:	Analysis Date:
Start the video. Carefully monitor the behavior of the child and the communication partner while they are in conversation. When you see a child's statement or behavior in the chat that corresponds to one of the items in the checklist, stop the video and write the minute and second of the video in which the behavior was seen in the time column of the relevant item in the checklist. While examining the structure of the conversation, it should be examined within the framework of the question of what he did. The question of why initiation, continuation and termination is done should be considered in the function of the conversation section.	
FORM OF CONVERSATION	DESCRIPTION / EXAMPLE
Initiation	Definition: The child initiates the conversation by communicating his interest or what he wants to achieve with verbal (word, phrase, sentence, etc.) and/or non-verbal (smiling, eye contact, crying, touching, showing, etc.) expressions to the communication partner. Examples: • The child communicates that he is ready to chat by touching his communication partner and starts the conversation. • The child approaches the adult and says "mom!" She starts the conversation. • Ask a child friend, "Shall we play house?" He starts the conversation by asking. • The child starts a conversation with the adult by first making eye contact and then looking at the storybook (the book conveys the desire to look).

Developing an Inventory

Figure 5. Representative items from communicative purposes checklist

COMMUNICATIVE PURPOSES

Participant's Name and Surname:	Observation/Video No:
Evaluator's Name and Surname:	Analysis Date:

Start the video. Carefully monitor the expressions and behaviors of the child and the communication partner. When you see an expression or behavior of the child that corresponds to one of the items in the checklist, put a tick in the frequency column of the relevant item in the checklist.
In observed behaviors, two different types of communicative functions can be observed at the same time, which are in the checklist on the same behavior. When you think that a behavior or expression exhibited by the child is suitable for two different items, do not hesitate to mark both items.
The gestures, mimics and actions that are meant to be described by the expression "Non-Verbal Expressions" in the items. "Verbal Expressions" are sounds, words, clauses and sentences.

COMMUNICATIVE PURPOSES	DESCRIPTION / EXAMPLE
Greeting	**Description:** When the child sees a familiar person, he/she greets him/her with gestures, facial expressions and/or verbal expressions. Examples: • The child says "brother" when he sees his older brother. • When he sees his friend coming towards him in the park, he looks at him and smiles. • When he wakes up in the morning, he says "good morning" to his mother who enters his room.
Giving information	**Definition:** The child tells something about a situation, event or object with gestures, facial expressions, body movements and/or verbal expressions. Examples: • When the child takes the glass with hot milk in his hand to drink, he quickly puts the glass back and opens his fingers, looks at his mother and makes sounds. The child informs his mother that the milk is hot. • The child gives information about the name of the animal in the picture by touching the picture of the rabbit they are talking about with the adult and saying "rabbit". • When the child hears the sound of a car, he says "my father is here". He informs that his father is coming.

Developing an Inventory

Figure 6. Representative item from function of conversation checklist

FUNCTION OF CONVERSATION		
Participant's Name and Surname:		Observation/Video No:
Evaluator's Name and Surname:		Analysis Date:

Start the video. Carefully monitor the behavior of the child and the communication partner while they are in conversation. When you see an expression or behavior of the child in the chat that corresponds to one of the items in the checklist, put a tick in the frequency column of the relevant item in the checklist.
The function of the conversation should be examined within the framework of the question of why the topic is started, maintained and ended.

FUNCTION OF CONVERSATION		DESCRIPTION / EXAMPLE
TOPIC INTRODUCTION	Giving information	**Description**: The child initiates a conversation by giving information about the subject, situation, event with strategies such as describing, explaining, commenting, and reporting about a subject, situation, event with gestures, facial expressions and/or verbal expressions. It should be noted that here the child is the initiator. Examples: • The child starts a conversation by showing the adult the cat coming towards them with his finger. (The adult can continue the conversation by saying "Oh the cat has come".) • The child starts a conversation by touching the airplane picture in the storybook and saying "airplane". (The adult can continue the conversation by answering.) • The child starts a conversation by saying "I am playing with Legos" to his father who enters the room. (The adult can continue the conversation by answering.)
TOPIC MAINTENANCE		
REPAIR COMMUNICATION BREAKDOWN		
TOPIC ENDING		
TOPICAL COHESION		
EXTENDED TURNS		

Analysis forms: The analysis forms created under the same headings as the checklists are in the form of a table consisting of two columns after the instruction on how to use them, and there is one row for each item. The first column contains the names of the items, while the second column is left blank. The second column is left blank, marking can be done when a behavior or expression regarding the items is

Developing an Inventory

seen. Analysis forms were created in the same format for each checklist included in the inventory. At the bottom of each form, there is a small version of the same table format to summarize the data.

Information form and interview form: The information form includes questions about demographic, educational and audiological variables that aim to obtain various information about the child and his/her family. Appropriate spaces are left under the questions so that answers can be written in the form. The interview form was prepared in a semi-structured interview format. There are questions on the form regarding daily routines, such as what the child's daily routines are, what he/she does during the day, what days and times his routines change, who he/she is with during these routines, what his/her favorite games and toys are, and what times and interactions are more enjoyable and participatory. In addition, spaces have been left under each question on the form for taking notes.

Preliminary report and final report: Two different reports are prepared as a preliminary report and a final report within the scope of the ICSI. The preliminary report has been developed to be used if you want to get quick results and plan quickly. The preliminary report is the form that contains the items in all the checklists and that the practitioner will mark as yes or no after watching the video in general. The presence or absence of communication skills is considered in the preliminary report. On the other hand, the final report form has been prepared in more detail to reflect the frequency of display of each item in the checklists. In addition, there is a section where the implementer can report their opinions and suggestions. Both forms were developed in parallel with the developed checklists.

Implementation Procedure: The implementation procedure is a guideline on how the SPO is applied and how the data collection and analysis process will be carried out. The steps to be followed in data collection and analysis in the application procedure and the points to be considered are explained in detail.

Implementation of Informal Communication Skills Inventory

The implementation of the ICSI consists of nine steps under the headings of data collection and analysis in line with the developed procedure. The application procedure is given in Figure 7.

Figure 7. Implementation procedure

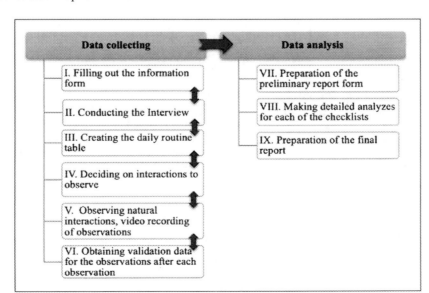

As it can be seen in Figure 7, data collection and analysis in ICSI sequentially takes place. Each step in implementing the ICSI is a preparation for the next step. In other words, each step uses the information obtained from the previous step. For this reason, if there is missing information at any stage of ICSI, it is important to go back, complete the deficiencies, and proceed to the next step.

1. **Filling out the information form:** The information form can be filled in with the parent(s) face-to-face or remotely (video call, phone call). Or, the form can be delivered to the parents, and they can be asked to read the form carefully and fill it in completely. The prepared form may be supplemented with questions by the researchers depending on the special needs of the child and the special situation of the family, depending on the intended use of ICSI. It is important to get answers to all questions while filling out the form.

2. **Conducting the Interview:** The main purpose of the interview is to determine the children's one-week routine programs. For this reason, it is important to learn the details about the context information (with whom, where, when, how) and to ensure that there is no lack of information while getting the answers to the questions in these interviews, which are prepared in semi-structured interview format. During the interview, the answers are written in a short and fast way, using the interview form, in the blank spaces for each question in the form. In order for the conversation to be listened to again, when necessary, it should be recorded with audio or video recording. Interviews can be conducted face-to-face or remotely (online, offline) with the participating parent(s).

3. **Creating the daily routine table:** In line with the information obtained from the interviews, the child's weekly daily routines are created exactly. This table includes information such as activities done during daily routines, people participating in these activities, and the time of activities. The purpose of creating the whole diary table is to decide on the observations to be made. While creating the daily routine table, the interview with the parent is recorded. The interview form, which is quickly noted during the interview, is reviewed by listening to the audio recording, and the missing parts are quickly completed. It is not necessary to make a detailed and literal breakdown here. It is important to get the answers to the questions asked and put them in writing. Then, based on this breakdown, one-week routine interactions are tabulated by specifying the average hour.

4. **Deciding on interactions to observe:** Daily routine interactions are familiar activities that children participate in, that occur all the time in their lives. For this reason, the functional communication skills of family children emerge during their daily routines in the most natural way. For this reason, observations of communication skills in ICSI are based on observation of daily routine interactions. Based on the information in the daily routine table, it is decided together with the families which activities will be observed. In selecting observation activities, attention should be paid to the variety of contexts to accommodate the diversity of discourse, the variety of activities to allow for the display of different communicative skills, and the appropriateness of families. It is thought that the interactions that enable the evaluation of the items of the communicative objectives' checklist within the scope of the ICSI will also allow exemplary behaviors to be exhibited in turn-taking, imitation, directing attention, and conversation skills to a large extent. From this perspective, it is important to choose the activities to be observed. Therefore, it is important to know the contents of the checklists before deciding on the activities to be observed.

5. **Observing natural interactions, video recording of observations:** The interactions that are decided to be observed with the family based on the daily routine tables are recorded with a video camera. At the same time, they take place in natural environments at specified days and hours.

Developing an Inventory

They are video recorded so that interactions can be of repetitive interest. After determining the activities that are decided to be observed, it should be decided how the observations will be made. Video surveillance recordings can be scheduled offline, online or face-to-face. In offline shootings, families can record the activities determined by themselves and send them to the researcher/expert. In the online method, however, the researcher and parent can record the observations by connecting online on the specified dates and times using one of the appropriate online video calling methods, or the researcher can record the observations himself. The method of observation must be determined based on the circumstances of the families.. If an online or offline collection method is decided, the "Remote Data Collection Guide" developed within the scope of ICSI should be shared with the participating families. Families should be informed in detail about taking various measures to ensure the validity and reliability of the data described in the guide.

It was decided to consider the natural process of interactions in which data are collected over observation periods in ICSI. In other words, it was decided to make observations until the end of the interaction. Observations should be terminated at the points where interactions are blocked, discontinued, and the child or parent is bored. When deciding how many different interactions to observe, the child's routine activities and the scope of the activities should be considered. However, the main purpose of the ICSI is to move forward in various contexts. Therefore, obtaining data from at least two different contexts is important. Activities or interactions decided to be observed in line with all this information are recorded on video without deteriorating their nature and affecting their naturalness.

6. **Obtaining validation data for the observations after each observation:** The naturalness of the data obtained in the ICSI depends on the naturalness of the participants during the interaction. For this reason, it is important to check the naturalness of the data after the shooting. After the video recording is finished, it is necessary to ask the parents some questions and record them to understand the naturalness of the recorded activities and people and for the situations that attract the researcher's attention during the observation or that he does not understand. There is no standard form of questions in conversation-style interviews where the naturalness of the observations is questioned. These questions develop spontaneously according to the observed interaction. Below are some sample questions. The questions can be varied according to the context.
    a. Was your child's behavior the same as usual? Were there any differences? If so, what do you think?How were you, were you as usual?
    b. Do you always interact or play like this?
    c. Why did you perform this activity or play the game?
    d. Why did you use these objects or toys?
    e. When do you switch from game to game?
7. **VII. Preparation of the preliminary report form:** Before the detailed analysis of the checklists, the preliminary report is prepared. The preliminary report form is prepared by watching the observation videos of the items in all checklists and then marking them as yes or no. Before completing the preliminary report, the evaluator should know what all of the items on the checklists mean and how to explain them. This is an important step that affects the process's validity, reliability and usefulness. While performing the analysis, the video is started and the video is watched until any communication skills in the preliminary report are seen. When a child demonstrates any communication skills, the video is paused and the checkbox next to the skill is marked.The video

continues to be watched by playing from where it left off. When another communication skill is seen, the video stops and the relevant item is marked. Since the number of communication skills is not considered in the preliminary report, the video continues if another example of the marked skills is seen again.

8. **Making detailed analyzes for each of the checklists:** Recorded video camera images are monitored and analyzed in line with each communication skill checklist included in the inventory. Video recordings for each of the checklists are replayed. Particularly for researchers and practitioners who are new to ICSI, it is necessary to watch the relevant video more than once in the analysis of some checklists. These checklists are divided into sections as suggested within themselves, and it is important to watch the videos for each section in a section-oriented manner. Accordingly, the turn-taking checklist is divided into 2 parts and the chat function checklist is divided into 3 parts and analyzed by watching it repeatedly. Checklists that are part of the inventory are listed in the order that should be used to do the analysis. When it comes to analyzing all skills, go in the order given. However, when an analysis is required for only one checklist, analysis can also be performed starting from the relevant checklist. The points to be considered in the analysis in general are as follows briefly.
    a. The instruction that is located at the very top of the form is read, and the information section is filled out in accordance with the appropriate video recording. The video is started and watched until any items in the analyzed checklist are seen.
    b. When a child shows any of the communication skills on the checklist, the video is stopped and the frequency column of the item in question is filled in. .
    c. The video is resumed from where it left off and watched until the next communication skill is seen. The next communication skill may be related to the same item as the previous skill or to a different item.
    d. Each communication skill seen is marked in the frequency column on the right of the relevant item. This process is continued until the whole video recording is finished and the whole video is finished.
9. **Preparation of the final report:** The final report form is based on the checklists for which detailed analyses were made. The results report form is designed to indicate the frequency for each item on the checklist.

CONCLUSION

Informal inventories in the assessment of communication skills allow a comprehensive assessment of children's functional language and communication skills. In this section, the development process, scope and application of ICSI are described, and children's communication skills are evaluated with detailed checklists on communication skills based on natural language data from various natural contexts. It allows the evaluation of functional communication skills and the revealing of their strengths and weaknesses, depending on data collection from examples of the language used in daily life and the communication skills exhibited. Evaluation of communication skills with detailed checklists allows for a comprehensive evaluation. It is known that developmental delays in language and communication skills in children negatively affect all areas.

For this reason, it is crucial that children with deficits in these areas receive a comprehensive evaluation and training tailored to their individual needs. As with all children who have difficulties in the development of language and communication skills, ICSI is a valid, reliable, and useful measurement tool that can be used in the planning of education programs and in examining the effectiveness of the education applied. In addition, the information it provides to teachers, families, and experts regarding children's communication skills is regarded as a guide in the education of children with hearing loss. In addition, it is thought that researchers working on communication skills in children will make scientific contributions to the field by providing a valid, reliable, and useful measurement tool that allows comprehensive evaluation of children's functional communication skills.

REFERENCES

Aksu-Koc, A., Acarlar, F., Kuntay, A., Mavis, I., Sofu, H., Topbas, S., Turan, F., & Akturk-Ari, B. (2019). *Türkçe İletişim Gelişimi Envanteri (TİGE)* [Turkish Communicative Development Inventory manual]. Detay Publishing.

Albertini, J. A., & Schley, S. (2003). Writing, characteristics, instruction and assessment. In M. Marschark & E. P. Spencer (Eds.), *Oxford handbook of deaf studies, language and education* (pp. 97–109). Oxford University Press, Inc.

Bader, L. A., & Pearce, D. L. (2012). *Bader Reading and Language Inventory* (7th ed.). Pearson Education.

Bates, E. (1976). *Language and context the acquisition of pragmatics*. Academic Press.

Beattie, R. G., & Kysela, G. M. (1995). A descriptive study of communicative intensions used by hearing teachers and preschool children with hearing loses. *Journal of Childhood Communication Disorders*, *17*(1), 32–41. doi:10.1177/152574019501700106

Bishop, D. V., & Adams, C. (1990). A prospective study of the relationship between specific language impairment, phonological disorders and reading retardation. *Journal of Child Psychology and Psychiatry, and Allied Disciplines*, *31*(7), 1027–1050. doi:10.1111/j.1469-7610.1990.tb00844.x PMID:2289942

Bortfeld, H., & Oghalai, J. S. (2018). Joint attention in hearing parent-deaf child and hearing parent-hearing child dyads. *IEEE Transactions on Cognitive and Developmental Systems*, *12*(2), 243–249. doi:10.1109/TCDS.2018.2877658 PMID:33748419

Capone, N. C. (2010). Language assessment and intervention: A developmental approach. In B. B. Schulman & N. C. Capone (Eds.), *Language development foundations, processes and clinical applications* (pp. 1–33). Jones and Barlett Publishers.

Capone, N. C. (2010). Language assessment and intervention: A developmental approach. In B. B. Schulman & N. C. Capone (Eds.), *Language development foundations, processes and clinical applications* (pp. 1–33). Jones and Barlett Publishers.

Caskey, M., Stephens, B., Tucker, R., & Vohr, B. (2011). Importance of parent talk on the development of preterm infant vocalizations. *Pediatrics*, *128*(5), 910–916. doi:10.1542/peds.2011-0609 PMID:22007020

Church, A., Paatsch, L., & Toe, D. (2017). Some trouble with repair: Conversations between children with cochlear implants and hearing peers. *Discourse Studies*, *19*(1), 49–68. doi:10.1177/1461445616683592

Coggins, T. E., & Carpenter, R. L. (1981). The communicative intention inventory: A system for observing and coding children's early intentional communication. *Applied Psycholinguistics*, *2*(3), 235–251. doi:10.1017/S0142716400006536

Cole, E. B. (1992). *Listening and talking a guide to promoting spoken language in young hearing-impaired children*. Alexander Graham Bell Association for the Deaf.

Curtiss, S., Prutting, C. A., & Lowell, E. L. (1979). Pragmatic and semantic development in young children with impaired hearing. *Journal of Speech and Hearing Research*, *22*(3), 534–552. doi:10.1044/jshr.2203.534 PMID:502512

Day, P. S. (1986). Deaf children's expression of communicative intentions. *Journal of Communication Disorders*, *19*(5), 367–385. doi:10.1016/0021-9924(86)90027-4 PMID:3771827

de Villiers, P., & Pomerantz, S. (1992). Hearing impaired students learning new words from written context. *Applied Psycholinguistics*, *13*(4), 409–431. doi:10.1017/S0142716400005749

Dewart, H., & Summers, S. (1995). *The pragmatics profile of everyday communication skills in children*. Nfer-Nelson.

Dore, J. (1974). A pragmatic description of early language development. *Journal of Psycholinguistic Research*, *3*(4), 343–351. doi:10.1007/BF01068169

Ege, P., Acarlar, F., & Turan, F. (2004). *Ankara Artikülasyon Testi (AAT)* [Ankara Articulation Test]. Ankara University, Scientific Research Project Publication.

Erickson, M. (1987). Deaf readers reading beyond literal. *American Annals of the Deaf*, *132*(4), 291–294. doi:10.1353/aad.2012.0711 PMID:3442290

Fitzpatrick, E., Squires, B., & Kay-Raining Bird, E. (2020). What's that you say? Communication breakdowns and their repairs in children who are deaf or hard of hearing. *Journal of Deaf Studies and Deaf Education*, *25*(4), 490–504. doi:10.1093/deafed/enaa010 PMID:32463866

Foster, S. H. (1986). Learning discourse topic management in the preschool years. *Journal of Child Language*, *13*(2), 231–250. doi:10.1017/S0305000900008035 PMID:3745330

Genc, E., Uzuner, Y., & Genc, T. (2017). A study on the communicative functions used in various contexts by a child with hearing loss. Ankara University Faculty of Educational Sciences Journal of Special Education, 18(3), 355-381.

Gratier, M., & Devouche, E. (2011). Imitation and repetition of prosodic contour in vocal interaction at 3 months. *Developmental Psychology*, *47*(1), 67–76. doi:10.1037/a0020722 PMID:21244150

Halliday, M. A. K. (1975). Learning how to mean. In *Foundations of language development* (pp. 239–265). Academic Press. doi:10.1016/B978-0-12-443701-2.50025-1

Katz, J., Onen, F., Demir, N., Uzlukaya, A., & Uludağ, P. (1974). Peabody Picture Vocabulary Test Form B. *Hacettepe Bulletin of Social Sciences and Humanities*, *6*, 129–140.

Kazak-Berument, S., & Güven, A. G. (2013). Turkish expressive and receptive language test: I. Standardization, reliability and validity study of the receptive vocabulary sub-scale. *Turkish Journal of Psychiatry*, *24*(3), 192–201. PMID:24049009

Keenan, E. O. (1974). Conversational competence in children. *Journal of Child Language*, *1*(2), 163–183. doi:10.1017/S0305000900000623

Kondaurova, M. V., Fagan, M. K., & Zheng, Q. (2020). Vocal imitation between mothers and their children with cochlear implants. *Infancy*, *25*(6), 827–850. doi:10.1111/infa.12363 PMID:32799404

Kondaurova, M. V., Smith, N. A., Zheng, Q., Reed, J., & Fagan, M. K. (2020). Vocal turn-taking between mothers and their children with cochlear implants. *Ear and Hearing*, *41*(2), 362–373. doi:10.1097/AUD.0000000000000769 PMID:31436755

MacGowan, T. L., Tasker, S. L., & Schmidt, L. A. (2021). Differences in established joint attention in hearing-hearing and hearing-deaf mother-child dyads: Associations with social competence, settings, and tasks. *Child Development*, *92*(4), 1388–1402. doi:10.1111/cdev.13474 PMID:33325060

McLean, J., & Snyder-McLean, L. (1999). *How children learn language*. Singular Publishing.

McLoughlin, J. A., & Lewis, R. B. (2005). *Assessing students with special needs* (6th ed.). Prentice Hall.

Meltzoff, A. N., & Moore, M. K. (1989). Imitation in newborn infants: Exploring the range of gestures imitated and the underlying mechanisms. *Developmental Psychology*, *25*(6), 954–962. doi:10.1037/0012-1649.25.6.954 PMID:25147405

Meltzoff, A. N., & Moore, M. K. (1997). Explaining facial imitation: A theoretical model. *Infant and Child Development*, *6*(3-4), 179–192. PMID:24634574

Mills, G. E., & Gay, L. R. (2019). *Educational research: Competencies for analysis and application* (12th ed.). Pearson.

Most, T. (2002). The use of repair strategies by children with and without hearing impairment. *Language, Speech, and Hearing Services in Schools*, *33*(2), 112–123. doi:10.1044/0161-1461(2002/009) PMID:27764464

Most, T., Shina-August, E., & Meilijson, S. (2010). Pragmatic abilities of children with hearing loss using cochlear implants or hearing aids compared to hearing children. *Journal of Deaf Studies and Deaf Education*, *15*(4), 422–437. doi:10.1093/deafed/enq032 PMID:20624757

Notari-Syverson, A., & Losardo, A. (1996). Assessing children's language in meaningful contexts. In K. N. Cole, P. S. Dale, & D. J. Thal (Eds.), *Assessment of communication and language* (pp. 257–280). Brookes.

Oosterhof, A. (2003). *Developing and using classroom assessments* (3rd ed.). Prentice Hall.

Orr, C. (1998). Improving oral imitation in preschool children with and without hearing impairment. *Physical & Occupational Therapy in Pediatrics*, *18*(3-4), 97–107. doi:10.1300/J006v18n03_07

Otto, B. (2006). *Language development in early childhood* (2nd ed.). Pearson Prentice Hall.

Owens, R. E. (2008). *Language development an introduction* (7th ed.). Pearson.

Paul, P. V. (2001). *Language and deafness* (3rd ed.). Singular Thomson Learning.

Pence, K., & Justice, L. M. (2008). *Language development from theory to practice.* Pearson Prentice Hall.

Pieterse, M., Treloar, R., & Cairns, S. (1989). *Small steps: An early intervention program for children with developmental delays.* Macquire University Press.

Retherford, K. S. (1993). *Guide to analysis of language transcripts* (2nd ed.). Thinking Publication.

Rogers, S. J., Young, G. S., Cook, I., Giolzetti, A., & Ozonoff, S. (2008). Deferred and immediate imitation in regressive and early onset autism. *Journal of Child Psychology and Psychiatry, and Allied Disciplines, 49*(4), 449–457. doi:10.1111/j.1469-7610.2007.01866.x PMID:18221343

Roth, F. P., & Spekman, N. J. (1984). Assessing the pragmatic abilities of children: Part 1. Organizational framework and assessment parameters. *The Journal of Speech and Hearing Disorders, 49*(1), 2–11. doi:10.1044/jshd.4901.02 PMID:6700199

Sacks, H., Schegloff, E. A., & Jefferson, G. (1974). A simplest systematics for the organization of turn taking for conversation. *Language, 50*(4), 696–735. doi:10.1353/lan.1974.0010

Sahli, A. S., & Belgin, E. (2017). Adaptation, validity, and reliability of the Preschool Language Scale-Fifth Edition (PLS-5) in the Turkish context: The Turkish Preschool Language Scale-5 (TPLS-5). *International Journal of Pediatric Otorhinolaryngology, 98,* 143–149. doi:10.1016/j.ijporl.2017.05.003 PMID:28583491

Sanders, D. A. (1982). *Aural rehabilitation: A management model* (2nd ed.). Prentice-Hall.

Savasir, I., Sezgin, N., & Erol, N. (1994). *Ankara Gelişim Tarama Envanteri (AGTE)* [Ankara Developmental Screening Inventory]. Turkish Psychological Association.

Schirmer, R. B. (2000). *Language and literacy development in children who are deaf.* Allyn and Bacon, Inc.

Stone, P. (1988). *Blueprint for developing Conversational competence: A planning / instruction model with detailed scenarios.* Alexander Graham Bell Association for the Deaf.

Tait, M., De Raeve, L., & Nikolopoulos, T. P. (2007). Deaf children with cochlear implants before the age of 1 year: Comparison of preverbal communication with normally hearing children. *International Journal of Pediatric Otorhinolaryngology, 71*(10), 1605–1611. doi:10.1016/j.ijporl.2007.07.003 PMID:17692931

Tasker, S. L., Nowakowski, M. E., & Schmidt, L. A. (2010). Joint attention and social competence in deaf children with cochlear implants. *Journal of Developmental and Physical Disabilities, 22*(5), 509–532. doi:10.100710882-010-9189-x

Temel, Z. F., Ersoy, O., Avcı, N., & Turla, A. (2004). *Gazi Erken Çocukluk Değerlendirme Aracı (GEÇDA)* [Gazi early childhood assessment tool]. Matsa.

Toe, D., Beattie, R., & Barr, M. (2007). The development of pragmatic skills in children who are severely and profoundly deaf. *Deafness & Education International, 9*(2), 101–117. doi:10.1179/146431507790560011

Toe, D. M., & Paatsch, L. E. (2013). The conversational skills of school-aged children with cochlear implants. *Cochlear Implants International*, *14*(2), 67–79. doi:10.1179/1754762812Y.0000000002 PMID:23453220

Topbaş, S. (2006). Turkish articulation and phonology test (SST): Validity, reliability and standardization. *Turkish Journal of Psychology*, *21*(58), 39–58.

Topbaş, S., & Güven, S. (2011). *Türkçe Erken Dil Gelişimi Testi (TEDİL)* [Test of Early Language Development-Third Edition: Turkish]. Detay Publishing.

Topbaş, S., & Güven, S. (2013). *Türkçe Okul Çağı Dil Gelişimi Testi (TODİL)* [Test of Language Development-Fourth Edition: Turkish]. Detay Publishing.

Tough, J. (1981). *Talk for teaching and learning* (2nd ed.). Ward Lock Educational.

Wang, D. J., Trehub, S. E., Volkova, A., & Van Lieshout, P. (2013). Child implant users' imitation of happy-and sad-sounding speech. *Frontiers in Psychology*, *4*, 351. doi:10.3389/fpsyg.2013.00351 PMID:23801976

Wang, Z., Zhu, X., Fong, F. T., Meng, J., & Wang, H. (2020). Overimitation of children with cochlear implants or hearing aids in comparison with children with normal hearing. *Infants and Young Children*, *33*(1), 84–92. doi:10.1097/IYC.0000000000000157

Wetherby, A. M., & Rodriguez, G. P. (1992). Measurement of communicative intentions in normally developing children during structured and unstructured contexts. *Journal of Speech and Hearing Research*, *35*(1), 130–138. doi:10.1044/jshr.3501.130 PMID:1735961

Yalaz, K., Anlar, B., & Bayoğlu, B. (2009). *Denver II Developmental Screening Test, standardization for Turkish children*. Developmental Child Neurology Association.

Yont, K. M., Snow, C. E., & Vernon-Feagans, L. (2003). The role of context in mother-child interactions: An analysis of communicative intents expressed during toy play and book reading with 12-month-olds. *Journal of Pragmatics*, *35*(3), 435–454. doi:10.1016/S0378-2166(02)00144-3

Zaghlawan, H. (2011). *A parent-implemented intervention to improve spontaneous imitation by young children with autism* [Unpublished doctoral dissertation]. University of Illinois, Urbana, IL, United States.

KEY TERMS AND DEFINITIONS

Communication Skills: It is the skills of directing attention, imitation, turn-taking, communicative purposes and conversation that individuals display in order to express their wishes and needs.

Communicative Purposes: It is the intention and expression of a request by individuals with looks, smiles, gestures, facial expressions, vocalizations and/or verbal expressions.

Conversation: It is a communication skill that includes initiating communication, giving appropriate responses in ongoing interaction, maintaining communication and ending communication appropriately.

Directing Attention Skills: It is the fact that people consciously and consciously directing glance the entities and events around them with the intention of communication, mutual gaze, topical gaze, and gaze shifting between people and objects.

Hearing Loss: Hearing loss is damage to the senses that occurs for various reasons and to varying degrees.

Imitation: Imitation is an attempt by children to exhibit the behavior or expressions of others as similarly as possible, either immediately after them or after a certain period of time.

Informal Communication Skills Inventory: It is a measurement tool that examines communication skills in children with comprehensive and accurate examples based on natural routine interactions, and aims to reveal children's strengths and weaknesses.

Language: Language is a system of various codes and symbols used as a tool in interpersonal communication for different and various purposes such as exchanging information and interacting.

Standardized Test: Standardized test are measurement tools whose implementation, scoring and interpretation processes are carried out by experts according to predetermined standards, and the results are compared according to certain norms.

Turn-Taking: Turn-taking is mutual interaction, verbal and/or non-verbal expressions are displayed in a certain order or at the same time while in communication.

ENDNOTE

This chapter was produced from the first author's doctoral dissertation under the supervision of the second author.

Section 5
Language, Cultural Awareness, and Perspective

Chapter 12
Trans[cultura]linguación:
An Intercultural Approach to the Revitalization of Indigenous Languages

Yecid Ortega
https://orcid.org/0000-0002-4039-074X
Queen's University Belfast, UK

ABSTRACT

Learning languages with the intention to understand cultures is the central premise of trans[cultura]linguación. The purpose of this chapter is to describe and reflect on the teaching and learning process of the Quechua language for students in Toronto (Canada) and other participants in the diaspora who wanted to learn more about the Quechua culture or revitalize their heritage language. Deploying a hybrid ethnographic approach to collect data from public online and in-person classes, this research project evidenced a cultural-oriented approach to assert Quechua speakers' identity and to spark curiosity for learning Indigenous languages in international contexts. A Quechua Collective, along with language teachers, used a synergic pedagogical approach to engage students in language learning and appreciation through various online and in-person interactive activities. This chapter sheds light on promising practices that seek to foster a sense of community, well-being, and the promotion of social cohesion and human coexistence.

INTRODUCTION

Culture is a vague and sometimes unclear concept yet it refers to the individual and collective ways of thinking, believing and knowing a specific group (Bhabha, 2004; Spencer-Oatey, 2008). Interculturality and interculturalism respectively refer to the processes of communication and interaction between people or groups with identities of different specific cultures, allowing for the integration and enrichment of coexistence among peoples (Dervin & Jacobsson, 2021). Similarly, an intercultural approach to education means moving beyond mere passive acceptance of multiple cultures and instead promoting dialogue and interaction between cultures (López Sáenz & Penas Ibáñez, 2006).

DOI: 10.4018/978-1-6684-5022-2.ch012

In light of these concepts, this chapter adds to the body of literature on intercultural education and expands on the term Trans[cultura]linguación (Ortega, 2019), which is a purposeful pedagogical transaction between languages and/or variations of the same language with a focus on comparing other languages. In this process, students learn about their own culture as they engage in language learning activities to intentionally learn about other cultures.

I utilized the Ontoepistemological Oneness for Teaching and Research framework - OTR - (Ortega, 2021a, 2021c) that succinctly elucidates how research and pedagogical approaches can work for humanization in relation to not only participants' sociocultural contexts, but their emotions in connections with their communities. Using a hybrid ethnographic coupled with a reflective research approach, I documented my observations of Quechua language teachers' pedagogical approaches during public in-person and online lessons for Latin Americans in the diaspora (in Canada) and others who were seeking to learn or revitalize their home and heritage language.

During these observations, I noticed how teachers and students reinforced their own cultural identities and they learned to respect and understand other peoples' differences. As an example of this, in the in-person class, a Quechua teacher (in Canada) explained cultural concepts while comparing them with Peruvian Spanish and English while students compare with other Latinamerican variations of Spanish and variations of English. In the meantime, online Quechua teachers in Perú were able to help students to connect back to their roots while (re)learning their ancestral language or simply sparking curiosity to learn the Andean language and culture. Most importantly, my reflections on the observations of the pedagogical exercises accounted for an intercultural approach to learning about power relations to critically observe what cultures hold more power than others (Walsh, 2012). Students and teachers realized not only that their (heritage/mother) language is an important part of their identity but as a way to interrogate and problematize Western colonial imposed forms of culture and language.

I argue that these experiences in language teaching promote critical intercultural education (Ferrão Candau, 2019) towards 1) a holistic approach in which teachers and students learn to respect other cultures, 2) a process of becoming aware of other cultures, 3) an understanding that there is not only truth, 4) the democratization of language teaching and learning, and 5) collaboration among peers. I propose that critical inter/pluriculturality can potentially engage the presence and equitable interaction of diverse cultures and the possibility of generating shared cultural expressions, through dialogue and mutual respect with the main goal of promoting global citizenship and human coexistence.

This book chapter is divided into the following sections, the first part provides an overview of the context and background of the inquiry process, framework, and methodology. The next part describes pedagogical practices considering the guiding concepts and the last part presents possible solutions, recommendations, and future directions for the revitalization of Indigenous languages.

CONTEXT AND BACKGROUND

Since I was young, I have always been interested in learning languages to understand other cultures. I became a language educator and researcher to promote language learning as a tool for intercultural understanding. As such, my role has been as an advocate for teaching and learning methodologies that seek to support the revitalization of endangered languages with a focus on interculturality. In the past few years, the centre of my research has been about exploring how languages can help us connect as humans, I learned to understand that languages are systems not only for communication but instruments of social cohesion. This interest has grown as I connected to various communities and learned the responsibility of language in their daily practices for self-determination and celebration of cultural identities.

This section describes the context for my reflective research approach. Before the pandemic, in 2019, I met a Quechua speaker (henceforward the Quechua teacher), a native of Apurimac, Cuzco in Perú through mutual friends in Toronto, Canada. She was beginning her doctoral studies at the University of Toronto in political science while I was finishing my doctoral work on Language and Literacies education at the same university. We connected right away as we disused different topics related to culture and language revitalization. I was glad to know that she was teaching the Quechua language to university students.

As a doctoral student in her first year, she shared with me how difficult was to connect with other Latin American students living in Toronto. I proposed to get together with other graduate students who might be interested in learning the Quechua language. Soon after, I spoke to the director of the Centre for Educational Research in Language and Literacies (CERLL) at the Ontario Institute for Studies in Education (OISE) about the possibility to sponsor a series of Quechua lessons. The director was glad for this initiative and provided us with the administrative and academic resources to pursue our goals. The Quechua teacher was grateful and asked me to organize all the programming, marketing, and communications of the invitations to the community for in-person classes and subsequent lesson planning (see figure 1). Since then, I worked hand in hand with the Quechua teacher to design a syllabus that would focus on the learning process in culture with a plurilingual approach.

Figure 1. Poster to call for in-person Quechua classes

We used our social media platforms and our contacts to distribute the poster. We had an overwhelming response of over fifty emails asking for more details about the content, location, and time. We responded to the emails and set up our first meeting in person. In the subsequent meetings, we had between 10 and 15 attendees fluctuating each follow-up Friday.

After the first semestre, the year of the pandemic started, and the Quechua teacher suggested creating a collective (Henceforward the Quechua Collective[1]) with me and other fellow attendees to connect with those interested in the Quechua language who are living in the diaspora. The Quechua lessons were later moved to online and details comparing the difference to teaching in person will be explained later in this chapter.

Framing the Project

This project was guided by an Ontoepistemological Oneness for Teaching and Research – OTR framework (Ortega, 2021a, 2021c) that conceptualized the ways of being and doing of individuals as human beings in connection to themselves, their communities, their languages, their identities and how they promote living well with each other in relation with other humans and non-human beings, mother earth and the universe.

This theoretical framework serves as a model to understand how practices promote shifting paradigms in language research and teaching connected to society and beyond (Macedo, 2019). This framework serves as a guide to describe how teachers and students embrace their emotions, feelings, and reasoning as humans with their hunger for teaching and learning. It also illustrates how their actions are geared towards making changes in society by promoting critical beings for decolonial praxis (Dei & Lordan, 2016). For Freire (1970), this praxis is enacted as a "reflection and action upon the world to transform it"(p.52). He argued that it is not enough for people to study the world, humans have a responsibility to create a more just world. This form of action problematizes and questions the inequalities that teachers, students, parents, and community members continuously experience, but also attempts to propose changes.

With this in mind, OTR poses as an analytical tool to help focus the experiences and pedagogical actions that foster social justice. OTR is represented through the image of a living and ever-evolving being in a profound relationship with others (See figure 2). OTR is fundamentally rooted in three constructs: Be[ing], Be[longing] and Be[coming].

Be[ing]: a person in a state of constant change and transformation. A verb ending in "ing" is the gerund in the English language and reflects an individual at the present moment. Be[ing], as a first construct, refers to that person (teacher, student, researcher) who is in continuous transformation and change. A person who puts humanity at the heart of their actions in an ever-evolving world.

Be[longing]: a person concerning community and places. This second construct refers to the idea of belonging not only to an affinity for a place but also to longing, a yearning desire to participate in changes that affect individuals and their communities positively. It is the very human emotional need to be an accepted member of a group with an inherent desire to belong and be an important part of something greater than themselves. In education, it refers to teachers' efforts to belong to a better school, city, country and world and how students eagerly seek to find and solidify their own identities as they attempt to pave the roads to their social and economic future.

Be[coming]: a person in the creation of their future. The third construct refers to who we are and who we want to be in a non-distant future. It implies how individuals create and plan their personal and professional futures. It is about the human being who goes from one idea to the next, but always looking toward more democratic, sustainable social and economically prosperous opportunities for all.

These three concepts are intrinsically embedded in actions and connections to communities, the contexts (the schools, the city, the country), others (teachers, students, parents etc.), and the universe and their future possibilities. The subject characterized by OTR urges actions to seek mutual benefits to live beyond the Western conceptualization of development (Acosta, 2013; Araujo Frías, 2013; Fals-Borda, 2015; Galeano, 1992; Gudynas & Acosta, 2011; León, 2008; Oviedo Freire, 2020; Rendon, 2008). In other words, this subject is an individual who exhorts educators and researchers to work tirelessly toward peaceful coexistence. OTR is a model proposed as a socially constructed subject embodying a cosmovision situated in a diverse, dynamic, and ever-changing historical time and social space (Oviedo Freire, 2020).

Figure 2. Onto-epistemological oneness for teaching and research - OTR (Artwork by Claudio Jaramillo)

OTR reveals the holistic connection between who we are, where we come from and our relations with others while engaging in research and teaching practice. This model promotes reflections on how colonial discourses of research and language teaching have separated us from our being, our connections with others and our cultural roots (Rivera Cusicanqui, 2010, 2010; Walsh, 2010). This framework is intended to be an inspiration for teachers and researchers to re-imagine and create a possible future rather than a utopian future (Brown & McCowan, 2018; Gudynas, 2011). In this way, actions lead to social transformation, with our eyes and hands-on social justice, especially while working for/with marginalized communities in diverse contexts (Dei, 2019; Dei & Lordan, 2016).

This project guided under OTR sought, in the words of Araujo Frías (2013), and paraphrasing Freire (1970), to interrogate obsolete educational systems that consider students as empty vessels waiting to be filled with knowledge. It suggests making space for a new paradigm in which students feel the desire to learn in a close relationship, with their emotions, intellect, and reason at the service of humanity (Galeano, 1992; Oviedo Freire, 2017; Rendon, 2008). Certainly, the Quechua Collective's actions have been geared towards embodying the tenets of this framework.

Methodology

The exploratory methodological approach utilized in this project was not collaborative in nature but a hybrid combination of ethnographic approaches in-person (offline), virtual (online) and in between (Kozinets, 2010; Przybylski, 2020) coupled with principles of reflective inquiry practice (Farrell, 2015) in an attempt to discover something new and interesting (Swedberg, 2020).

One particular reason I was attracted to this methodology was that "ethnography conducted on the Internet; a qualitative, interpretive research methodology that adapts the traditional, in-person ethnographic research techniques of anthropology to the study of online cultures and communities formed through computer-mediated communications."(Kozinets, 2006, p. 135). As such, the Quechua Collective as a cultural group allowed me to explore their social interactions that took place not only in person but overall in virtual environments (Given, 2008), by observing the Facebook group interactions, exchanging WhatsApp messages and participating in the Facebook/YouTube live interactive lessons. To know more about these and what pedagogical approaches were used to promote the revitalization of the Quechua language, I deployed the following overarching research question that guided my work and reflections: *What are the educational possibilities of a language revitalization program and how important are these for teachers and students?*

I documented the public in-person and the online sessions of the Quechua lessons through personal reflection notes and memos. I took notes on interactions between the students and teachers for a total of 134 notes that were sorted and coded by date, time, and topic on a Word document. Computer audio-visual screenshots were added for further content and theme analysis (Elo & Kyngäs, 2008; Krippendorff, 2004).

From the very beginning of the Quechua lessons, the collective gave me the role of a researcher to disseminate the collective's work, they gave me their consent to document my reflections on their public practices. This allowed me to consciously reflect on the Quechua Collective's experiences and actions to engage in the process of my continuous learning (Mortari, 2015). As a researcher, I not only saw myself lurking in the realms of the online public forums but felt a sense of responsibility to share, connect and participate because it was the interaction and the learning processes and not the people themselves, I was interested in. The collective itself held me accountable for my actions and requested full participation during the Quechua lessons and my constant technological support with Facebook live and Zoom chat moderation.

Using this hybrid methodology of observing and reflecting on the in-person and online sessions, allowed me to reflect on my responsibility while collecting data. My role in the process was the one of an observer with participation in which my purpose was to gain a deep understanding and familiarity with the Quechua Collective and their values, beliefs, and teaching practices. Although the Quechua teacher and other teachers gave me their consent to document their public practices, I was aware of my positionality. I was careful of my participation not to affect the decision-making processes of the collective to how they teach but was consciously documenting my participation in the classes. I was constantly reflecting and reevaluating my role as I tried not to create any harm to any of the collective's members or the online attendees.

After collecting the data and managing it through the NVivo 12 software, several rounds of coding were done to find common themes. I observed that an approach to teaching the language through cultural materials was central to learning and fostering cultural understandings of being, belonging and becoming humans. Through this hybrid methodology, I found that learning in-person or online asserted cultural identity while motivating participants to be proud of their own Abya Yala[2] heritage. In the next sections of the chapter, I thread in what I found in the form of these themes: 1) how a synergic, evolving, and ever-changing approach to teaching Quechua was utilized 2) the importance of revitalizing the Indigenous languages and 3) what it means to learn in-person and online.

A SYNERGIC PEDAGOGICAL APPROACH

Language is a type of social-cultural construction and interaction within a society (Mujiono & Herawati, 2021) and this evidences the link between language and the speaking community, as well as the purpose and function of the language itself (Bayyurt, 2016). Some of the evidence from the data collected in this project showed that monolingual ideologies have gradually given way to plurilingual communities, plurilingual persons, and plurilingual environments (Blommaert, 2010). My observations and documentation of the in-person and online sessions accounted for a synergic teaching practice striding between a plurilingual and translaguaging approach to teaching through culture.

Plurilingualism

From the beginning of in-person meetings to the online lessons, there was a paramount understanding and awareness of other cultures and languages and how this would help to learn and promote cultural and language diversity that develops a plurilingual competence (Coste et al., 2009; Galante, 2020). Plurilingual competence, defined as the ability to use multiple languages and cultural resources to fulfill communication needs was evidenced as participants were able to communicate with people from other backgrounds and enrich their repertoire in the process (Piccardo, 2020). Certainly, the participants in the Quechua language lessons demonstrated how these plurilingual approaches may stimulate students' curiosities about languages and cultures, improve their abilities to realize the connections between languages and between language and culture and contribute to openness and flexibility (Piccardo, 2020).

Plurilingualism also promotes the awareness of linguistic diversity, the functional use of various linguistic means, the similarities and differences between languages, the connection between languages and cultures, and the specific characteristics of each language, including the native language (Piccardo, 2013). It was observed how the Quechua teacher and others used this approach in their pedagogical approach to promoting the use of Spanish, English and Quechua to explain definitions of some words and phrases. This helped learners to gain intercultural competence and cultural awareness. Intercultural competence is about understanding others, cultural awareness is about understanding oneself. As one of the teachers put it "*Debemos entendernos a nosotros mismos primero y luego intentar entender a los demás. Solo de esta forma, nos volvemos conscientes de quienes somos en relación los demás*" [we should understand ourselves first and then try to understand others. Only this way we become aware of who we are and our relation to others.] (One Quechua teacher, January 28, 2022).

Additionally, Seelye (1998) explains that, within education, the objective of cultural awareness is to help students to pay attention to words, phrases and other things that contain cultural meanings that may distract them from communicating with others. This was evident during the classes when the Quechua teacher constantly provided support to scaffold students' development of abilities to handle different cultural encounters in distinct contexts. She gave examples of how to use the Quechua language when speaking to elders and to pay attention to who to talk to as different forms of language are used to respect those who have more knowledge.

In the end, understanding plurilingualism can also help learners to develop their intercultural competence. Byram (1997) suggests that intercultural competence includes the knowledge of others, self, skills to clarify, relate, interconnect, and discover, and it is the ability to respect other people's opinions, attitudes, beliefs, behaviours, and values from other cultures. This competence was substantiated when various online learners on the chat box commented on how similar, yet different Spanish is in different parts of latinamerica, and this stimulated their curiosity to learn more about each other.

Translanguaging

One interesting phenomenon that happened during both the in-person and online sessions relates to how students and teachers incorporated the language learned into their own lives as expressed by one of the online participants: "*Me agrada que ya he podido decir algunas palabras en Quechua a mi abuela y ya he podido ver como se pone feliz que al menos estoy tratando*" [I like it that I have already been able to say some Quechua words to my grandmother and I can see how happy she is that I am at least trying]. This act of "*Lenguajear*" (Maturana, 1978) demonstrated how language learners integrated what they learn in their modes of living as continuous interactions with other human beings. Maturana helps us to understand languaging as an approach to expressing our thoughts, emotions, and feelings as processes to make meaning. Similarly, other participants declared how they used Quechua and Spanish as they attempted to code switch while explaining and making clarifications, the Quechua teacher also used this switching of languages while teaching. This evidenced the meaning-making practices at the core of the lessons, here translanguaging was used to "deliberately changing the language of input and the language of output" (García & Wei, 2015, p. 224). For example, in most of the classes, after a teacher gave instructions or explained meanings in Quechua, they would change into their Spanish or English to answer questions or make any clarifications if some concepts were misunderstood, especially while explaining the linguistic structure of the Quechua language. By contrast, during communicative activities in breakout rooms during the Zoom sessions, some students flip languages for different purposes, such as backchannelling, asking for help, equivalents, and metalanguage (Aoyama, 2020). In a sense, the students became liaisons of linguistic resources leveraging communicative competence in two languages which implied that a translanguaging approach helped the class promote plurilingualism in sociolinguistic ways (Aoyama, 2020, p. 14).

Evidence from the collected data observed that promoting translanguaging in these classes had several positive impacts on the language learning process. It (a) enhanced learners' investment in target language learning (Cutrim Schmid, 2021, 2022), (b) improved the culturally related competencies and intercultural communications (Santos Alves & Mendes, 2006), and (c) developed metacognitive skills common to all languages (Bijeikienė & Meškauskienė, 2020), and (d) helped learners raise positive attitudes towards cultural and language diversity (Boeckmann, 2012).

Additionally, the Quechua teacher commented to me that is critical to educate all learners to be part of an increasingly multilingual society to encourage plurilingualism and allow all learners to develop their full range of languages (Boeckmann et al., 2012). Plurilingualism coupled with translaguaging would be a desire for every language learner, with a greater drive to learn more about languages in general and study additional languages and for revitalizing Indigenous languages. One aspect of teaching the Quechua language while acknowledging the variations of the Spanish language and explaining it in English to the Anglo[3] audience showed a supportive atmosphere that encouraged plurilingualism and translanguaging. This constant reassurance to create a safe space for students to swap, switch and mix languages, according to the Quechua teacher, boosted learners' confidence, pleasure, and understanding of several languages, while also allowing them to build a strong and positive sense of their own identities (Beockmann et al., 2011).

Trans[cultura]linguación

A translaguaging and plurilingual approach during the sessions showed how these challenged the monolingual and traditional forms of teaching languages. For example, translanguaging and plurilingualism focus on the learner using their full linguistic repertoire to make sense of and interact with the world around them. Furthermore, the data collected for this project revealed that the teachers' pedagogical approach was explicitly centred on the cultural aspects of learning the language. This purposeful focus on culture through language comparison has been conceptualized as Trans[cultura]linguación (Ortega, 2019). This notion describes the purposeful and direct approach to promoting languages in which cultures are the center of the teaching and learning process. Below, I present a couple of examples from my observations to illustrate this idea.

From the very beginning of the in-person lessons, the Quechua teacher used a cultural approach to help students understand core concepts that sometimes are not easy to translate into Spanish or English language. For example, figure 3 shows the different domestic animals in indifferent languages. Using this image, the Quechua teacher went beyond the basic meaning of the words and explained the importance of animals to her community. She mentioned that animals are part of the family, their community, and their daily life - *Ellos pertenecen a nuestra tierra*" [they belong to the land] she mentioned. According to Trans[cultural]linguación, the cultural aspect of the language was highlighted, the Quechua teacher described how, culturally, animals are sacred and part of the natural ecosystem to live well with each other, which is very important for her Indigenous cosmovision. Some of the students in this lesson also exchanged stories about how their pets are also important as they consider them part of their families. The Quechua teacher provided a few sentences in Quechua translated into English and Spanish on how to say my cat is part of the family = *Misiyqa Ayllum*. Through this exercise, I learned that the Quechua lesson did not focus on language structure, translations, or literal meanings, but on how central it is to

Trans[cultura]linguación

their culture by exchanging stories, anecdotes, and experiences. In a sense, I learned that languages are alive and embedded in the Quechua teacher's cultural practices and relations to her community.

Figure 3. Domestic animals presented in three languages

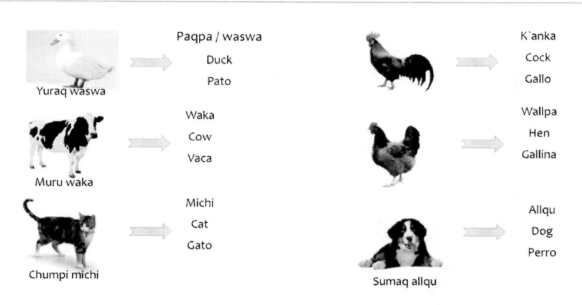

In another activity from one online session, Quechua teacher Fernando[4] explains some useful phrases to the audience using the three languages – English, Spanish and Quechua (figure 4). In this example, he provides some basic language to use in real life should anyone wants to visit Perú. He invited the audience to practice, repeat and say some of the phrases. Most importantly, he brought the idea that culturally, it is important to listen and listen carefully, he provided the example of listening to the sounds of the land, the rivers, the wind, and the animals but also *"Mirar con los ojos del alma"* [looking through the eyes of the soul], to look at what is not evident to the naked eye and listen to your emotions and feelings. He finished his ideas by mentioning that the most important to remember when learning Indigenous languages is who we are, and our connections with our communities and to do so, we need to hear, listen, feel, and see beyond our bodies. He invited us to close our eyes for a moment and listen to what is around us and feel with our hearts.

Figure 4. Useful phrases in Quechua with translations in Spanish and English

Allin Rimanakuypaq	Frases útiles	Useful phrases
Uyariy!	Escucha	Listens
Qhaway!	Mira	Look
Rimay!	Habla	Speaks
Ñawinchay!	Lee	Read
Qillqay!	Escribe	Writes
Yuyariy!	Recuerda	Remember
Kutipuy!	Regresa / de nuevo	Come back / again

Ultimately, what I experienced both during the in-person and online Quechua lessons was that students and teachers participated not only in a language exchange of ideas but a deep understanding of the relationship between languages and cultures, especially as a process of nurturance and socialization (Kramsch, 1998). In the two examples above, Trans[cultural]linguación was evidenced by how aspects of deep culture were embedded in the teaching practice and took center stage by providing personal experiences and promoting a more humanizing connection during the process. According to the Quechua teacher, learning a language is not about words, but how you relate to those words, how you can use them in real life to connect to others in your community, and overall, how you connect with the world around.

In the end, synergic teaching through the lens of plurilingualism, translanguaging and trans[cultura]linguación (figure 5) might help push back traditional boundaries of self and others while questioning, challenging, and shaping what it means to be human and maintain and convey culture and cultural ties to Indigenous and non-Indigenous communities while attempting to revitalize languages that are at the verge of extinction.

Figure 5. A synergic approach to revitalizing Indigenous languages

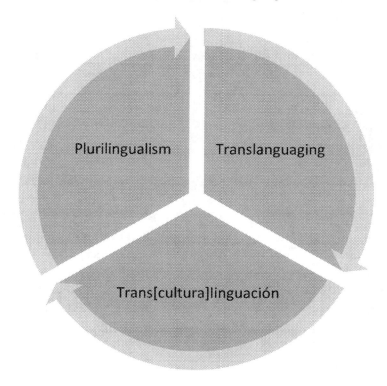

REVITALIZATION OF INDIGENOUS LANGUAGES

Although more than 40 million Indigenous people inhabit the continent named the Americas, not much has been done in the past decades to revive the historical legacy of these peoples' cultural and linguistic heritage(Coronel-Molina & McCarty, 2016). However, more recently, there has been a push for the revitalization of Indigenous languages across the continent from grassroots organizations to device some language policy and planning in various countries in the American Continent (Coronel-Molina & McCarty, 2016; McCarty et al., 2019).

The Quechua Collective as a cultural group has taken the revitalization of the Quechua language passionately. As an emerging organization dedicated to the revitalization of the native languages of South America (such as Runasimi-Quechua), it has committed to putting up personal and collective efforts to accomplish this mission in the past few years (2019 – 2022). One of their main goals has been to work tirelessly towards self-determination and sovereignty by building bridges of respect and solidarity with the brothers and sisters of the Abya Yala continent.

After the earlier in-person gatherings and lessons held in Toronto, the members of the Quechua Collective got together to put up a more serious agenda through a committed organization. They have been working hard to become a non-profit organization and official grassroots community. They pursued the delivery of lessons about Andean cultural celebrations and provided in-person and virtual Quechua language classes in 2020 and 2022 during the pandemic. Their materials were based on culturally appropriate methods and practices rooted in respect and reciprocity. They continuously attempt to promote development and academic research projects related to Indigenous Andean politics, Indigenous environmentalism, and land, food, and water sovereignty. Their ultimate hope is to support projects on educational programs through revitalization, specifically of language, while building national and international Indigenous communities and solidarity across Abya Yala and elsewhere.

In spring 2022, a panel presentation was led by the Quechua Collective, other organizations in the USA and CERLL. A highlight of this session was that a famous Quecha educator and artist, Literato Kani, spoke about his concerns related to the long imposition of the Spanish language for hundreds of years and most recently the English language in the current curriculum in Perú. He seemed very upset because he argued that *"No hay mucho que hacer a pesar de la educación que el trae a su comunidad, y me preocupa que el lenguaje se desaparezca en algún momento"* [there is little to be done despite the education I bring to his community, and I am extremely worried that the language at some point disappears]. He mentions how this has been a practice since colonization when the Spaniards came and imposed the Spanish language and other cultural practices such as Catholicism and tried to eliminate his culture and his languages, similarly to what has been called Epistemicide (de Sousa Santos, 2014).

In this panel presentation, he agreed with other presenters that despite the ongoing challenges and threats to his native language, it is paramount to continue the revitalization of languages. To this, he asserts that the only way to accomplish true revitalization is to *"re-vitalizar nuevamente"* (to provide energy again) languages by connecting with their communities from different angles such as the arts, education, and policy but overall strengthening their already acquired language skills and empowering the new generations to appreciate their own culture as he fears they only want to speak Spanish, go to the city and live an urban life.

For the Quechua Collective as a grassroots organization, engaging in the revitalization of their language has had the potential to assert Indigenous identity and strengthen family or community relationships. For non-Indigenous people, revitalization means to learn and understand the history of colonization but also to help make visible a language and culture that has often been excluded, overlooked, or ignored. In the end, revitalization continuously means to re-establish, to re-take, and re-vivir (to enliven) the language not only for communication but for self-determination, liberation, identity, and pride. In one of our communications, this was something clear for the Quechua teacher who says:

Mi rol desde acá en Canada es de poder brindar los espacios, medios y conexiones para revitalizar el Quechua, ya sea acá, o en Estados Unidos, o en Perú, o en Latinamerica, y quiero que todos ustedes nos ayudemos a cumplir esas metas desde sus diferentes posiciones. [My role, from here in Canada, is to be able to provide the space, the means and connection to revitalize the Quechua language, from here, the USA, Perú or latinamerica and I want that we all help each other to achieve those goals from our different positions]. (Personal communication, January 18, 2022)

The Quechua teacher in collaboration with others hopes to bring full use of the language to all walks of life (Hinton & Hale, 2013), those interested in Canada or elsewhere through online lessons, seminars or webinars. According to the members of the Quechua Collective in one online session and suggestions from some of the students, this goal can be accomplished by taking the necessary steps into action. These can be in the form of actual programs that encourage language practice with their communities in real life or seeking private and public funding from Canada or other international organizations. The next section briefly describes details of how the collective attempted to fulfill these goals to revitalize the language and culture by delivering in-person and online sessions.

Trans[cultura]linguación

LEARNING QUECHUA (IN-PERSON /ONLINE)

This section describes my experiences during the Quechua language lessons in-person and how these had to move online because of the pandemic. As a language educator with more than 20 years of teaching experience, I know that typically, second language education or foreign language education tends to focus on learning the structure of the language (grammar, pronunciation etc.) through a communicative approach. However, the Quechua teacher wanted to teach because she wanted to respond to what the attendees of the workshops wanted to learn.

During the first meeting, some people mentioned that the reason for learning Quechua was because they wanted to learn their grandparents' language while some others were just curious to learn an Indigenous language. I remember that in this first class, there were around ten people in the room and one of the attendees raised her hand and said.

I am Canadian, but my parents are from Perú and immigrated here to have a better life and never forced me to learn Quechua because they thought Spanish and English were better, so I am here to reclaim my roots. So, I thank the Quechua teacher for providing this opportunity to all of us. (From a memo note, November 22, 2019)

Conversely, the Quechua teacher said that the reason she wanted to teach the Quechua language and share her culture with all of them was precisely that a lot of people in the diaspora do not have access to this knowledge. She felt she had a responsibility and needed to dedicate time to preparing materials and resources for her classes.

For the next class, the Quechua teacher prepared PowerPoint slides with photos to explain some Quechua expressions and greetings in Spanish and English, she also explained these with stories from her own experiences. I remember vividly when she was describing the importance of the mountains, rivers, and trees to her community. She labelled the photos with vocabulary in the three languages so all the students would understand. At some point, she explained that some words cannot be translated into English or even Spanish and that she had to flip between languages to make meaning.

Typically, in second language teaching, lesson planning and preparation are done by organizing activities based on linguistic aspects of the language (grammar, vocabulary) or communications skills (listening, speaking, reading, and writing). Based on my experience as a language educator, the Quechua teacher asked me to help her prepare lessons focused on learning the cultural aspects of the Quechua language. Together, we devised a plan to teach through themes, this would allow students not only to learn the language but to promote language identity and cultural awareness among the attendees (See table 1).

Table 1. Weekly themes for the Quechua lessons

Intro Lesson	Abya Yala: Introducción y saludos
Lesson 1-2	Identidad Andina
Lesson 3-4	Relación con la tierra y el agua (animales, alimentación y vivienda)
Lesson 5-6	Familia y comunidad
Lesson 7-8	La Pacha Mama: Cosmovisión Andina
Lesson 9-10	Festividades y celebraciones
Week 11-12	Indigenous struggles: Western extractivism

A total of twelve classes were taught and the Quechua Collective met for the last time on lesson 12, the group did not meet again in person because of the COVID-19 Pandemic in 2020. At this point, at least six months passed since the last time we met. This was something that hit the collective hard because we relied on in-person conversations and exchange of ideas face-to-face. The solution was to meet online. After several meetings of deliberation, we decided to do the lessons via Zoom and then stream them via Facebook. Contrary to my expectations, the online lessons were more engaging. First, the Quechua teacher was not the only teacher, but we had wonderful teachers who were from across the continent - from the USA to local teachers from Perú. Also, a radio station joined the collective to broadcast the lessons via radio waves, so the lessons could reach remote rural areas with no internet coverage.

One of the key elements of learning the Quechua language in person was the real-life connection with a closer group of people. To this, in one of our meetings, one of the members of the collective says: *"Esto se siente como una familia, aprendemos de los unos a los otros y nos ayudamos en las buenas y las malas"* [We felt like a family, we learned from each other, and we supported each other in times of happiness and struggle]. Throughout the course, the lessons took us beyond the learning process and helped us connect as human beings. To this date, we still connect and meet each other in Toronto or online to share our experiences and knowledeges. Although learning in person has its advantages to connect at the human level as we could see each other's facial expressions and feel the emotions, we learned that online lessons brought more people and more international engagement. One day we had over two hundred people viewing the Facebook live session and the collective vigorously attempted to respond to comments on the chat both on Zoom and Facebook messenger. One of the many participants of the online session mentioned: *"No puede creer que somos más de 200 personas de toda Latinoamérica, se nota que queremos aprender, ¿verdad?"* [I cannot believe that we are almost more than 200 people across latinamerica, it looks like we all want to learn, right?].

We envisioned that a hybrid model of teaching might benefit all communities both in-person in Toronto and online for the international community of Quechua speakers in the diaspora and all the curious minds seeking to learn other languages. In the end, a balance between online and in-person presented an ideal teaching approach as it reached out to more people, especially those who have little access and live in remote areas. In session 2 of the online class, one of the participants commented on the advantages of this hybridity: *"Mira, yo acá estoy en Toronto y tengo la oportunidad de aprender en persona con la maestra, pero también he podido conectar con mis paisanos en Perú y otros de la región. Esto me permite aprender más de cómo se vive el lenguaje en la vida real"* [Look, I am here in Toronto, and I have had the opportunity to learn from the Quechua teacher, but I have also been able to connect with fellow Peruvian and others in the region]. This statement speaks to how the Quechua Collective continuously seeks to foster that connection between their practices and their communities while fostering a sense of belonging.

Based on these in-person and online experiences with the collective, the teachers and participants, I present, in the next section, possible solutions and recommendations to revitalize Indigenous languages and how to reach out and have more impact on communities in international contexts.

SOLUTIONS AND RECOMMENDATIONS

Observing the interactions and participating in the Quechua lessons taught me how important it is to promote the revitalization of languages no matter the challenges and difficulties this might bring. I learned how human relations are key during in-person teaching and the power of connecting across international boundaries during the online sessions.

Some participants of the Quechua lessons noted their concern about the vast influence of languages such as English, Spanish, Portuguese, French and others in education (especially in Perú, Ecuador, and Bolivia) and how these have been a thread to revitalization. These hegemonic languages have taken the leadership on a global scale, including now Chinese Mandarin and how at a societal level these languages have been used as commodities to acquire knowledge and move socially (Duchêne & Heller, 2012; Heller, 2003, 2011). Certainly, some of the teachers I have been working with within the past few years continue mentioning that they need to learn English because this allows them to secure jobs (Ortega, 2021b). This was not different for the Quechua teachers who mentioned that if they do not speak Spanish, they might not secure jobs once they are pushed into urban cities. Being aware of these concerns, I advocate for a shift in how education can approach the teaching of languages.

First, one remarkable difference between learning online and in-person was the possibility of connecting transnationally. In a sense, virtual learning connected learners, teachers, community members, and families from across Abya Yala and Turtle Island to learn or revitalize the Quecha language. This resonates with the tenets of intercultural education towards a plurality of understanding of other knowledges and blurring the ontoepistemological North/South borders (de Sousa Santos, 2008, 2018). It is recommended to continue the promotion of hybrid forms of learning and teaching. Certainly, the Quechua Collective demonstrated that it was possible to connect with others that never had the chance before (parents, families, and children) to engage in Quechua lessons as some of the audiences joined via cellphones, tablets or tuning on their radios from remote rural areas.

Second, community organizers and teachers can organize themselves to create their language revitalization groups to set up events, design lessons and propose projects to involve their communities in culturally relevant and appropriate practices. To this, I propose language teaching approaches that critically question the power relations by looking at how counter-narratives of oppression vis a vis language teaching and learning can emerge. I also suggest fostering critical pluricultural and intercultural education that would not only interrogate the colonial history of language teaching but purposely use culture as the centre of the pedagogical approach. The next section details how such a vision can be accomplished.

Critical Inter/Pluriculturality

Learning and teaching from societal margins have become a form of resisting hegemonic, monolithic and colonial forms of education, especially for Indigenous communities and their descendants (Hinton et al., 2018). Critical intercultural education has been fundamental as a project against epistemicide and other imposed attempts to eradicate the knowledge born from the struggles of the most marginalized communities (de Sousa Santos, 2010; Grosfoguel, 2019). According to Ferrão Candau (2019) and Walsh (2019, 2012), critical interculturality looks at challenging the status quo and addressing the power relations that have been put in place with marginalized peoples. Therefore, education with a critical intercultural education must purposely push the boundaries of normalized actions that continue affecting those who have been at the bottom. For example, some teachers, activists, and artists who gathered in the Quechua lessons have actively worked towards revitalizing the Quechua language as a way to counterattack the commodification of the Spanish and English languages. In spring 2022, I attended a public panel presentation sponsored by the Quechua collective and attended by Dr. Serafin Coronel Medina, Dr. Theresa McCarthy and well-known Peruvian Indigenous artists and educator Liberato Kani. In this presentation, all the presenters addressed the issues of language power from academic perspectives and the problems of English and Spanish as hegemonic languages in the education system for Indigenous communities.

Molina and McCarthy argued for more academic spaces not only in higher education programs but also in K-12 to welcome Indigenous Languages as part of the curriculum. Soon after, Liberato Kani advocated for more artistic forms to engage youth in using the languages to assert their cultural and linguistic identities with hip hop, poetry, and dance to resist the continuous imposition of the Spanish language in Indigenous schools.

The three presenters engaged with the audience at the end of the panel and discussed how they envision Indigenous language education at different educational and literacy levels in which projects and activities integrate artistic, linguistic, and cultural lessons to celebrate everyone's identities. Most of the suggestions were about how all languages and cultures from the different corners of the world need to be acknowledged and used not only for the purposes of communication but determination, liberation and questioning systems of oppression. To this, Liberato Kani asserted vigorously that there cannot be a true revitalization of languages when there is no true interrogation of the colonial past *"yo le digo a todos que es necesario interrogar el pasado colonial y tratarlo de cambiar con una pedagógica intercultural y critica a través de las artes, especialmente con los jóvenes"* [I would say to everyone that it is necessary to interrogate the colonial past and try to change it with an arts-based critical and intercultural pedagogy, especially for the youth].

Critical and inter/pluricultural education must be at the centre of any educational project at the grassroots level to push language policies and practices that respond to the community's needs. For example, in my work with other English teachers in Colombia, I witnessed how they created projects to address issues of homelessness, unemployment, and teenage pregnancy by using English and Spanish to raise awareness of the inequalities in Colombian society and foster a sense of cultural understanding (Ortega, 2021b). Similarly, the Quechua Collective responded to local and international needs to revitalize the Quechua language whether it is in person or online. The remaining question that must be asked is about what to do in the near future, especially in a post-pandemic world that has precisely affected the most marginalized, remote Indigenous communities. In the next section, I will shed some light on what research might do and what is expected from teachers and community members to commit to the revitalization of Indigenous languages in a longer and more sustainable way.

FUTURE RESEARCH DIRECTIONS

This chapter explored the possibilities of researching to understand the teaching and learning processes of a language different from English. Traditionally, the teaching of a second language or a foreign language has been done through a content-based approach, a communicative approach, a task-based approach, or an action-oriented focus. Unfortunately, these approaches do not necessarily recognize or include the myriad of possibilities incorporating the diversity of languages and cultures as the centre of pedagogical practices. However, plurilingual approaches have already started the discussions of including different linguistic repertoires in teaching and learning (Lau & Viegen, 2020).

Certainly, the in-person and online Quechua classes set a precedent as an example for educators to explore and appreciate the value of hybridity in teaching languages. Such an approach allows for learning from other cultures and languages and understanding diverse forms of producing knowledge. There is an increasingly broad consensus on the need to profoundly transform how languages are taught to democratize the pedagogical arena in which not only one language is taught but how many languages can interact ecologically (Piccardo & North, 2019; Taylor & Mohanty, 2020). Ultimately, this horizontalization approach to teaching languages has the potential to achieve linguistic revitalization to satisfy the need to seek synergies with other revitalization initiatives not only across the American continent but elsewhere (Coronel-Molina & McCarty, 2016; McCarty et al., 2019; Santamaría, 2017)

Additionally, researching the revitalization of Indigenous languages requires constant consultation with their communities. I was glad to participate in some of the Quechua collective online and in-person lessons. The members of the collective were pleased to know that as a researcher I have the role and responsibility to disseminate their work. This could not have been always possible without their consent and support. Based on my experiences within the Quechua Collective, I advocate for qualitative research to amplify the work of communities, in collaboration, consultation and in respect of the communities we work for/with (Bucholtz, 2021; Paris & Winn, 2014).

This exploratory hybrid ethnographic research demonstrated that there is much more to be done to support communities in the revitalization of Indigenous languages. For me, this project revealed that it is hard to maintain distance when working closely as a participant and observer of the teaching and learning practices. I learned that ethnography is about working with and for the communities to celebrate the knowledges produced at the centre of their cultural practices. Pedagogy and research must work in tandem not only to connect theory and practice but to seek transformation, and liberation and pursue culture-specific ways of being and living in relation to communities and their languages.

CONCLUSION

The main ideas described in this chapter resonate with the sentiments of promoting the well-being of others by celebrating the diversity of identities and cultures during the teaching and learning processes. Revitalizing Indigenous languages such as the Quechua language presented challenges but also the opportunity to reach out to audiences not only in Toronto where the Quechua Collective is based but beyond the Canadian borders. Reaching out afar one's context allowed one to learn from other ways of being and knowing the world.

I posit that the experiences with the Quechua Collective and the online and in-person lessons are in line with the current social justice and decolonial turn in foreign language education (Macedo, 2019). As such, approaches practiced in the Quechua classes provided by the Quechua Collective, their members and their communities are an attempt to understand the synergic forms of learning that challenge monolithic worldviews. I hope this experience sheds some light on how languages are taught but overall to spark more work for the revitalization of Indigenous languages worldwide, much necessary in a world that needs more convergences than divergences.

The experiences at the heart of the Quechua language teaching and learning reflect the constructs of the Ontoepistemological Oneness for Teaching and Research – OTR presented earlier in this chapter. First, the Quechua Collective, their members, and their teaching approaches to revitalize the Quechua language described connections to members' heritage and other communities – Be[longing]. Secondly, each one of the teachers but also the online and in-person participants asserted their own identities and acknowledged their role within their communities - Be[ing]. Third, according to the Quechua teacher and other invited facilitators, they saw their work to pave the road for future generations who are proud of their traditions, languages, and cultures. They felt the Quechua language can potentially be used in formal academic spaces or informal community spaces with their peers - Be[coming]. In the words of Liberato Kani, *"Uno debe forjar un future de sueños en relación con nuestro Pacha (Mother Earth). Solo amándonos a nosotros, nuestra Pacha y otros, Podemos salir adelante como Sociedad"* [one must forge a future with dreams in relation with our Pacha. Only by loving ourselves, our Pacha and others, we can move forward as society]. (Public Speech, March 25, 2022).

Liberato's words and the Quechua Collective's philosophy strengthen the idea of teaching and learning the Quechua language and other Indigenous languages for the purposes of self-determination, identity affirmation and liberation. In the end, I learned that language education should be about connections with the self and others to pursue social cohesion and humanization for all.

ACKNOWLEDGMENT

I would like to thank the many Indigenous communities I have worked with in the past few years. I am especially thankful to the Quechua Collective and the leadership of the Quechua teacher and their team for putting efforts to provide the resources to revitalize the Quechua language in the diaspora.

REFERENCES

Bhabha, H. K. (2004). *The Location of Culture* (2nd ed.). Routledge.

Bijeikienė, V., & Meškauskienė, A. (2020). The Value of Plurilingualism or What Factors affect the development of plurilingual competences. *Sustainable Multilingualism*, *16*(1), 131–144. doi:10.2478m-2020-0007

Boeckmann, K.-B. (2012). Promoting plurilingualism in the majority language classroom. *Innovation in Language Learning and Teaching*, *6*(3), 259–274. doi:10.1080/17501229.2012.725253

Boeckmann, K.-B., Aalto, E., Abel, A., Atanasoska, T., & Lamb, T. (2012). *Promoting plurilingualism: Majority language in multilingual settings*. Council of Europe.

Bucholtz, M. (2021). Community-centred collaboration in applied linguistics. *Applied Linguistics*, *42*(6), 1153–1161. doi:10.1093/applin/amab064

Coronel-Molina, S. M., & McCarty, T. L. (2016). *Indigenous Language Revitalization in the Americas*. Routledge. doi:10.4324/9780203070673

Coste, D., Moore, D., & Zarate, G. (2009). *Plurilingual and pluricultural competence. Language Policy Division*. Council of Europe. https://www.coe.int/t/dg4/linguistic/Source/SourcePublications/CompetencePlurilingue09web_en.pdf

Cutrim Schmid, E. (2021). A classroom-based investigation into pre-service EFL teachers' evolving understandings of a plurilingual pedagogy to foreign language education. *Landscape Journal*, *4*. Advance online publication. doi:10.18452/23383

Cutrim Schmid, E. (2022). 'I think it's boring if you now only speak English': Enhancing learner investment in EFL learning through the use of plurilingual tasks. *Innovation in Language Learning and Teaching*, *16*(1), 67–81. doi:10.1080/17501229.2020.1868476 de Sousa Santos, B. (2008). *Another knowledge is possible: Beyond northern epistemologies*. Verso.

de Sousa Santos, B. (2010). *Descolonizar el saber, reinventar el poder*. Ediciones Trilce.

de Sousa Santos, B. (2014). *Epistemologies of the south: Justice against epistemicide* (1st ed.). Paradigm Publishers.

de Sousa Santos, B. (2018). *The end of the cognitive empire: The coming of age of epistemologies of the south*. Duke University Press. doi:10.1215/9781478002000

Dervin, F., & Jacobsson, A. (2021). What is interculturality? In F. Dervin & A. Jacobsson (Eds.), *Teacher Education for Critical and Reflexive Interculturality* (pp. 11–21). Springer International Publishing. doi:10.1007/978-3-030-66337-7_2

Duchêne, A., & Heller, M. (2012). *Language in late capitalism: Pride and profit*. Routledge. doi:10.4324/9780203155868

Elo, S., & Kyngäs, H. (2008). The qualitative content analysis process. *Journal of Advanced Nursing*, 62(1), 107–115. doi:10.1111/j.1365-2648.2007.04569.x PMID:18352969

Farrell, T. S. C. (2015). *Reflective language teaching: From research to practice*. Bloomsbury Publishing.

Ferrão Candau, V. M. (2019). Educación intercultural crítica: Construyendo caminos. In C. Walsh (Ed.), *Pedagogías decoloniales: Prácticas insurgentes de resistir, (re)existir y (re)vivir (Pensamiento decolonial)- Tomo I* (1st ed., pp. 145–164). Editorial Abya-Yala.

Freire, P. (1970). *Pedagogy of the oppressed*. Seabury Press.

Galante, A. (2020). Plurilingual and pluricultural competence (PPC) scale: The inseparability of language and culture. *International Journal of Multilingualism*, 0(0), 1–22. doi:10.1080/14790718.2020.1753747

Given, L. (2008). Virtual Ethnography. In *The SAGE encyclopedia of qualitative research methods*. SAGE Publications, Inc. doi:10.4135/9781412963909.n484

Grosfoguel, R. (2019). Knowledges born in the struggle: Constructing the epistemologies of the Global South. In B. de Sousa Santos & M. P. Meneses (Eds.), *Epistemic Extractivism: A Dialogue with Alberto Acosta, Leanne Betasamosake Simpson, and Silvia Rivera Cusicanqui* (pp. 203–218). Routledge. doi:10.4324/9780429344596-12

Heller, M. (2003). Globalization, the new economy, and the commodification of language and identity. *Journal of Sociolinguistics*, 7(4), 473–492. doi:10.1111/j.1467-9841.2003.00238.x

Heller, M. (2011). Language as resource in the globalized new economy. In N. Coupland (Ed.), *Handbook of language and globalization*. Blackwell Publishing.

Hinton, L., & Hale, K. (2013). *The Green Book of Language Revitalization in Practice*. BRILL.

Hinton, L., Huss, L., & Roche, G. (Eds.). (2018). *The routledge handbook of language revitalization* (1st ed.). Routledge. doi:10.4324/9781315561271

Kozinets, R. V. (2006). Netnography. In V. Jupp (Ed.), *The SAGE Dictionary of Social Research Methods* (p. 193). SAGE Publications, Ltd. doi:10.4135/9780857020116.n127

Kozinets, R. V. (2010). *Netnography: Doing Ethnographic Research Online*. SAGE Publications.

Kramsch, C. (1998). *Language and Culture* (H. G. Widdowson, Ed.). OUP Oxford.

Krippendorff, K. (2004). Content Analysis: An introduction to its methodology. *Sage (Atlanta, Ga.)*.

Lau, S. M. C., & Viegen, S. V. (2020). *Plurilingual pedagogies: Critical and creative endeavors for equitable language in education*. Springer International Publishing. doi:10.1007/978-3-030-36983-5

López Sáenz, M. C., & Penas Ibáñez, B. (2006). *Interculturalism: Between identity and diversity*. Lang.

Macedo, D. (2019). *Decolonizing foreign language education: The misteaching of English and other colonial languages*. Routledge.

Maturana, H. R. (1978). Biology of language: The epistemology of reality. In G. Miller & E. Lenneberg (Eds.), *Psychology and Biology of Language and Thought*. Academic Press.

McCarty, T. L., Nicholas, S. E., & Wigglesworth, G. (Eds.). (2019). *A world of Indigenous languages: Politics, pedagogies and prospects for language reclamation*. Multilingual Matters., doi:10.21832/MCCART3064

Mortari, L. (2015). Reflectivity in research practice: An overview of different perspectives. *International Journal of Qualitative Methods*, *14*(5). doi:10.1177/1609406915618045

Ortega, Y. (2019). "Teacher, ¿Puedo hablar en Español?" A reflection on plurilingualism and translanguaging practices in EFL. *Profile: Issues in Teachers' Professional Development*, *21*(2), 155–170.

Ortega, Y. (2021a). *Pedagogies of be[ing], be[longing] and be[coming]: Social justice and peacebuilding in the English curriculum of a marginalized Colombian public high school* [Thesis]. https://tspace.library.utoronto.ca/handle/1807/109308

Ortega, Y. (2021b). Transformative Pedagogies for English teaching: Teachers and students building social justice together. *Applied Linguistics*, *42*(6), 1144–1152. doi:10.1093/applin/amab033

Ortega, Y. (Director). (2021c, December 14). *Onto epistemological oneness for teaching and research*. https://youtu.be/SJ-B6JemzkU

Paris, D., & Winn, M. T. (2014). Humanizing research: Decolonizing qualitative inquiry with youth and communities. *Sage (Atlanta, Ga.)*. Advance online publication. doi:10.4135/9781544329611

Piccardo, E., & North, B. (2019). *The Action-Oriented Approach: A Dynamic Vision of Language Education*. Multilingual Matters.

Przybylski, L. (2020). *Hybrid ethnography: Online, offline, and in between*. SAGE Publications.

Santamaría, J. I. (2017). Red de escuelas Ruk'u'x Qatinamït y revitalización del idioma kaqchikel. *Onomázein, NE*, *3*(3), 115–136. doi:10.7764/onomazein.amerindias.07

Santos Alves, S., & Mendes, L. (2006). Awareness and Practice of Plurilingualism and Intercomprehension in europe. *Language and Intercultural Communication*, *6*(3–4), 211–218. doi:10.2167/laic248.0

Spencer-Oatey, H. (2008). *Culturally Speaking: Culture, communication and politeness theory*. Bloomsbury Publishing.

Swedberg, R. (2020). Exploratory research. In C. Elman, J. Mahoney, & J. Gerring (Eds.), *The production of knowledge: Enhancing progress in social science* (pp. 17–41). Cambridge University Press. doi:10.1017/9781108762519.002

Taylor, S. K., & Mohanty, A. K. (2020). A multi-perspective tour of best practices: Challenges to implementing best practices in complex plurilingual contexts—The case of South Asia. In E. Piccardo, A. Germain-Rutherford, & G. Lawrence (Eds.), Routledge Handbook of Plurilingual Language Education. Routledge.

Walsh, C. (2019). *Pedagogías decoloniales: Prácticas insurgentes de resistir, (re)existir y (re)vivir (Pensamiento decolonial)- - Tomo II* (1st ed.). Editorial Abya-Yala.

Walsh, C. E. (2012). *Interculturalidad crítica y (de)colonialidad: Ensayos desde Abya Yala*. Abya-Yala.

KEY TERMS AND DEFINITIONS

Abya Yala: A term that means land in full maturity, and it is the term designated by Indigenous peoples in latinamerica to the land. I use this term instead of Latin America to bring importance to knowledges rooted in Indigenous heritage.

Anglo: In this chapter, this concept refers to those who speak English since they were born. I do not use the term native speaker of English.

Interculturality: It refers to the existence, equal interaction, and potential for the creation of shared cultural expressions via communication and respect for one another.

Pachamama: Also known as Pacha, is the name given by Andean Indigenous people to Mother Earth.

Plurilingualism: It describes the ability of a person with multiple language proficiency and the capacity to switch between them as needed for conversation.

Revitalization: The idea of invigorating, restoring, or providing new life or fresh conditions.

Runasimi: Also written as Runa Simi, it is the Quechua language´s original denomination.

Trans[cultura]linguación: The pedagogical intention to highlight culture at the centre of language teaching practices to compare, learn, and understand other cultures.

Translanguaging: The process whereby multi/bilingual speakers or learners use their linguistic resources to make sense of and interact with the world around them.

Turtle Island: It is the name given to the land (in North America) by some Indigenous peoples, as well as by some Indigenous rights activists.

ENDNOTES

[1] This is pseudonym.

2. Abya Yala means land in full maturity, and it is the term designated by Indigenous peoples in Latin America to the land. I use this term instead of Latin America to bring importance to knowledges rooted in Indigenous heritage.
3. Anglo refers to those who speak English since they were born. I do not use the term native speaker of English.
4. Pseudonym.

Chapter 13
Raising Awareness of the City as a Text:
Multimodal, Multicultural, and Multilingual Resources for Education

Amparo Clavijo Olarte
Universidad Distrital Francisco José de Caldas, Colombia

Rosa Alejandra Medina
University of Massachusetts, Amherst, USA

Daniel Calderon-Aponte
Universidad Distrital Francisco José de Caldas, Colombia

Alejandra Rodríguez
Universidad Distrital Francisco José de Caldas, Colombia

Kewin Prieto
Universidad Distrital Francisco José de Caldas, Colombia

María Clara Náder
Universidad Distrital Francisco José de Caldas, Colombia

ABSTRACT

In this chapter, the authors explore the semiotic landscape of the city to analyze multimodal, multicultural, and multilingual resources for language and literacy education. In this ethnographic study, teacher-researchers explore urban literacies as social, artistic, political, cultural, and pedagogical practices that connect different community actors, diverse texts, and local realities. Data were collected through community tours, photographs (a corpus of 387 photographs), and semi-structured interviews with graffiti artists and community inhabitants. The findings reveal that semiotic and linguistic landscapes that surround schools can be harnessed to develop critical place awareness and to recognize the audiences and purposes of multimodal texts embedded in the environments. It also leads to the recognition of multicultural and linguistic diversity that is rarely reflected in school-centered curriculum and decontextualized textbooks.

DOI: 10.4018/978-1-6684-5022-2.ch013

INTRODUCTION

This chapter reports the partial findings of a two-year ethnographic study on literacy and local pedagogies for social transformation. The main purpose of this study was to investigate the social and cultural aspects of multiculturalism and multilingualism that are present in the historic district of Bogota, the capital city of Colombia. This chapter reports on the experiences of five novice teacher-researchers (language teachers and students in a master's in Applied Linguistics program) and two university-based researchers.

Drawing on our commitment to collaboratively develop ethnographies of place (Pink, 2008) in two communities in the historical district of Bogotá (La Candelaria and Santafé), we visited places, interacted with community inhabitants, and took pictures as samples of semiotic elements that reflected multiculturalism and multilingualism in the community.

This collaborative ethnography was a learning space for novice teacher- researchers. Weekly working sessions were held throughout the project as in a graduate seminar where all members could dialogue and exchange their experiences, knowledge and insights regarding the places we studied during collaborative ethnography. We found ourselves discussing and (re)thinking theoretical, methodological, and analytical aspects. In other words, the development of this research was not a straightforward path. For example, during the data collection phase, we adapted methodological elements; during the analysis phase as a group, we explored and deepened theoretical elements that were relevant. As for the phases of the ethnography, we began by identifying the research question. As teachers and researchers in the field of local and world language literacy education, we noticed that in our city very few studies inquire about the community and linguistic resources of the historic district of Bogotá and their pedagogical potential for multicultural and multilingual education. With this study we aimed at identifying connections between languages and literacies in the city, its multilingual and multicultural resources and their potential for critical and decolonial language and literacy education.

In the beginning of the study, we drew on three main constructs: Community-Based Pedagogies (Sharkey, Clavijo & Ramírez, 2016), linguistic landscape (Landry & Bourhis, 1997), and ethnography of place (Pink, 2008). As we engaged in dialogue, data collection, and analysis we refined our conceptual framing by delving into *urban literacies, semiotic landscapes, multiculturalism and multilingualism*. In the analysis of findings, we also made connections to decolonial epistemologies as we found that multiple samples centered on indigeneity, Afro-Colombian culture, and subaltern ideologies.

While previous studies suggest that cities are linguistically configured through diverse texts (Cenoz & Gorter, 2008; Landry & Bourhis, 1997) and that these can be used as elements for inquiry and teaching of languages -English more specifically- (Sayer, 2010), in our study we were able to encounter elements that can potentially engage students and teachers in critical multilingual and multicultural literacies. Other studies explore other cities and how they bring multilingual and multicultural richness (Mora et al., 2018), for the case of Bogotá, it becomes necessary to document the multicultural and multilingual diversity from its semiotic, textual and discursive configuration. Bogota, and particularly the historic district, has features that make it a hub for diverse Colombian and international cultures and languages.

Our interest in inquiring about multicultural and multilingual diversity in Bogotá led us to notice literacy practices and multimodal texts present in the city; all of these practices and texts configure the city as a multicultural and multilingual space. Likewise, beyond identifying these linguistic and semiotic resources, we also paid attention to possible curricular applications that teachers can develop when they become aware of these semiotic resources and their sociocultural meanings. We hope that this chapter inspires citizens, teachers, and students to appreciate, interact and read the city as a vibrant text.

Raising Awareness of the City as a Text

The exploration of the historic district (see map of places visited in figure 1) allowed us to recognize the importance of semiotic landscape (graffiti, and multicultural, multilingual texts) as it can generate opportunities for multimodal and critical literacies.

Figure 1. Map of La Candelaria neighborhood located in the historical center of Bogotá
Retrieved from Google Maps on May 5, 2022

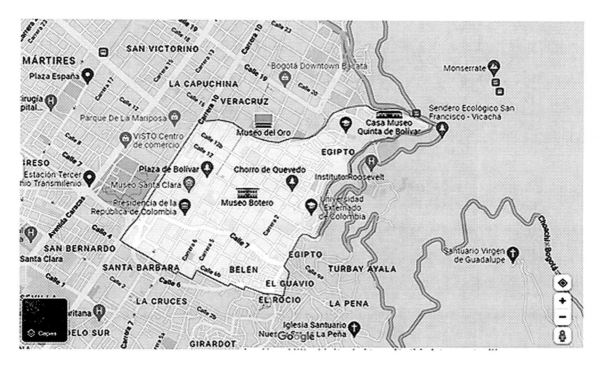

Considering all aspects above, we posed these research questions:

1. How is multiculturalism and multilingualism conveyed in the semiotic landscape of the historical district of Bogotá?

2. What are the implications of recognizing the semiotic and multicultural resources of Bogota historic district for literacy education across the curriculum?

In the section below, we present the theoretical framework that supports our study.

BACKGROUND/THEORETICAL FRAMEWORK

Our study is grounded in *urban literacies, semiotic landscape, multiculturalism and multilingualism*. We understand urban literacies as social, artistic, political, cultural and pedagogical practices that connect different community actors, diverse texts, and local realities expressed by individuals and collectives

(Clavijo-Olarte et al., 2021). We deem the semiotic landscape as consistent with the proposals of Jaworski and Thurlow (2010) who define it as "any public space with a visible inscription made by means of a deliberate human intervention for the construction of meaning" (p. 2).

Urban Literacies

Urban literacies are framed within the social and spatial turn in language education. We understand urban literacies as social, artistic, political, cultural and pedagogical manifestations and practices that connect different community actors with diverse texts. In this sense, Lozano et al. (2020) argue that studying urban literacies contributes to connecting students' cultural and linguistic resources with those of communities. The spatial turn in language and literacy education emphasizes critical reading of texts and other semiotic resources within and across different spaces (classrooms, homes, schools, communities, online spaces). These spaces are materialized, interactive, multimodal, and multisensory and evolve over time (Kramsch, 2018; Mills, 2015). Such practices are influenced by global and local contexts of learning (Steffensen & Kramsch, 2017).

Semiotic Landscape, Multiculturalism, and Multilingualism

In this study, we examined the semiotic landscape of the historic district of Bogotá to trace how the city is a multicultural and multilingual space. We initially wanted to focus on the linguistic landscape that informed multiculturalism and multilingualism in the city. However, while we engaged in ethnographic tours, we expanded our focus to include nonlinguistic signs as well. Shohamy and Gorter (2009) have studied the semiotic signs of communities in Israel using the concept of *linguistic landscape* which is defined as the "linguistic objects that mark the public space" (as cited by Ben-Rafael et al., 2006, p. 14).

Thus, we adopted a view on semiotic landscape (SL) which includes both linguistic signs as well as other multimodal resources (images, color, location, spatial organization). Thurlow's & Jaworski (2011) define SL as "any public space with a visible inscription made through deliberate human intervention for the construction of meaning" (p. 2). In our context, the semiotic landscape includes murals, graffiti, street plaques, advertisements, posters, and other artistic and linguistic inscriptions, and spoken languages that are available for residents and passers-by.

Towards Critical Multiculturalism in the City

Bogota is the largest and most populated city in Colombia. As political and economic powers are concentrated in the city, and due to the internal displacement from the armed conflict, and opportunities for employment and education, the city is home to people from all over the country, including people from mestizo, Afro-colombian, and indigenous backgrounds. In recent years, due to globalization, tourism from North America and Europe has increased in the historic district. Multiple ethnic, racial, and linguistic groups are represented here. We used the term multiculturalism to address the diversity we observed in the semiotic landscape of the city. We understand multiculturalism as an "ideal in which members of minority groups can maintain their distinctive collective identities and practices" (Song, 2020). Another scholar, Villodre (2012) describes its origin in Canada through the Multiculturalism Act issued in 1988. This policy advocates for respecting the presence of different cultures in a territory. In our study, we were able to identify distinctive collective identities of different groups. We recognize that multiculturalism does not necessarily imply an exchange between cultures - interculturalism- but we identified it as an initial stage in the recognition of diversity (Villodre, 2012).

In Colombia, Jonkman (2020) reviews the legal adoption of multiculturalism in the context of early 1990s ethno-cultural reforms in Latin American states. This time has been called "the multicultural awakening". In 1991, Colombia adopted a constitution that recognized its nation as multicultural and multiethnic (Jonkman, 2020). As a response to nationalist and mestizo ideologies present in previous legislation, and influenced by neoliberalism, these states granted particular rights for minority populations including "linguistic rights to provisions of collective land tenure and substantive access to national political arenas" (Jonkman, 2020, p. 13). Some scholars have criticized this form of liberal multiculturalism as it erases race, history and current, racial and ethnic conflict. Multiculturalism seems then to reinforce instead of undoing structures of domination.

As a response to liberal multiculturalism May (2009) proposes critical multiculturalism which

combines both structural and culturalist concerns – linking culture to power, and multiculturalism to antiracism – in its advocacy of a greater politics of recognition and representation within education and the wider public sphere (May, 2009, p. 45).

For May (2009), critical multiculturalism engages actively with postmodernist conceptions and analyses of the contingent nature of identity, while still holding onto the possibility of an emancipatory, group-based politics – that we can actually change things for the better. He stresses that "[...] critical multiculturalism provides a defensible, credible, and critical paradigm that can still act as a template for the possibilities of a more plural, inclusive, and democratic approach to both education and wider nation-state organization in this new century" (May, 2009, p. 45).

The definition above, as adapted in our study, appears to be an ideal as not all semiotic landscape that represents ethnic and linguistic diversity is emancipatory, antiracist or political; however, we still recognize that there is semiotic landscape that conveys antiracist, and emancipatory messages. In our study, we claim that both liberal and critical multiculturalism are manifested through the semiotic landscape and the different social and cultural practices of the inhabitants of the historic district.

Multilingualism in the Study

For this study, we observed multilingualism in the semiotic landscape of the historic district. As we explained above, the Colombian context is diverse both ethnically and linguistically. The linguistic diversity of Colombia as a multilingual state is the product of a history of ancient migrations brought about by the Amerindian peoples as well as movement from people from other latitudes (Trillos & Etxebarria, 2002, p. 1).

Our view of multilingualism in the study is informed by different sociocultural and post-structural approaches to diverse language practices. Firstly, we take Blackledge and Creese's (2010) multilingualism as a lens to understand multiple "language practices in interrelationships'' (p. 66). This view of multilingualism is critical as it connects language practice to identity and acknowledges tensions and struggles for ethnic groups to maintain their affiliation to their cultures and linguistic varieties in contexts of linguistic and cultural hegemony. Secondly, we take elements from Otsuji & Pennycook (2010) metrolingualism. Our view of multilingualism in the study allowed us to observe both fixed and fluid language practices in the city. As we explain in the findings, we found the coexistence of monolingual and translingual practices in the historic district. Therefore our notion of multilingualism in the study also follows metrolingualism, "where fixity ... fluidity ... hybridity ... coexist and co-constitute each other" (Otsuji & Pennycook, 2010, p. 252). Finally, we take up Ortega's (2017) take on equitable multilingualism. This implies understanding language as an open space in which linguistic plurality is neither romanticized nor punished but becomes an essential component for the construction of social justice. We find multilingualism as an essential component in the larger ideal of attaining social justice. We argue that in the context of our study, it is relevant to take the elements above as we understand multilingualism without romanticizing language practices and looking at tensions but also fluid practices with the ideal of attaining social and linguistic justice.

Our collaborative ethnography of the historic district of Bogotá implied observation and analysis of the semiotic, multicultural and multilingual resources offered by the city to study the urban literacies and semiotic landscapes. With these perspectives we understand literacies in a situated and sociocultural way that includes social, artistic, political, cultural and pedagogical practices. We report below some studies around the world that contributed to our theoretical and methodological approaches.

Previous Studies on the Semiotic Linguistic Landscape and Multilingual Literacies in Communities

There is an array of studies that have shaped the cornerstone for our own interest regarding the semiotic linguistic landscape and multilingual literacies among the communities. Herein, we present some previous research that has addressed ethnography and teacher practices in diverse communities drawing on local semiotic landscapes and sociocultural diversity.

From the outset, our study draws on the seminal work of Landry and Bourhis (1997) who coined and introduced the concept of the linguistic landscape. As they both suggest, the linguistic landscape refers to "the visibility and salience of languages on public and commercial signs in a given territory or region" (Landry & Bourhis, 1997, p. 23). Nonetheless, the language on public and commercial signs cannot be deemed as neither an isolated nor neutral affair whatsoever. In this regard, it was pivotal for us to comprehend that the linguistic landscape of the city center of Bogotá comprises, as suggested by Landry and Bourhis (1997) an informational and symbolic function. The former one refers to the distinctive marker which delineates the territorial limits of a language group in a given geographical space, and the latter one serves as the feeling of social status, value and identity in relation to the language(s) displayed in the linguistic landscape of a community and place (Landry & Bourhis, 1997).

The previous pivotal understanding on the city linguistic landscape afforded us more opportunities to expand on research regarding literacies and education aspects. For example, in their article on transnational literacies and community literacies for teachers, Jiménez, Smith and Teague (2009) show how linguistic landscape, photographs, and instructional sequences based on a traditional immigrant community in Texas have the potential to serve for multilingual literacy development. Students' diverse socio-cultural backgrounds and heterogeneous communities with transnational ties have the potential to serve as language and literacy resources.

In the European context, Cenoz & Gorter (2008), engaged in photographic analysis of the linguistic landscape regarding minority languages, official languages and English in the written symbols of two cities in Spain and the Netherlands. They highlighted bilingualism and multilingualism as the main discoveries within the signs among the cities.

Similarly, in the US context, Garvin (2010) studied the individuals' cognitive and emotional responses to the linguistic landscape (LL) of Memphis in the U.S. The study revolves around these questions. How is the LL read by the public? How do individuals interact with the LL?. In what ways do individual residents understand, interpret and interact with the LL in their communities? What are their thoughts and feelings about multilingualism or changes in the linguistic landscape? The researcher used walking tours as a methodology and interviewed some residents of Memphis. The results showed that the LL served as a catalyst or stimulus text mediating understandings of public space while eliciting emotional and psychological statements of belonging and identity in time and place. The author claimed that the linguistic landscape is never neutral.

In Colombia, inspired by teachers' local knowledge (Canagarajah, 2002), teacher education as research (Cochran-Smith, 2005), and community- based pedagogies (Marshall & Toohey, 2010; Murrell, 2001); Sharkey, Clavijo-Olarte, and Ramírez (2016) examined the cases of four public high school teachers in Bogota, Colombia. The teachers participated in community-based pedagogy workshops and infused community explorations and literacies in the social science, language arts, and science curricula. The findings report that linking teacher development with communities and families increases teacher appreciation of their students' diverse socio-cultural backgrounds, student engagement, and develops community, and academic literacies. In the same city but at a different location, In the same vein, Medina et al. (2015), studied the semiotic landscape of a public University in Bogotá and considered that the graffiti, posters, cartoons, bulletin boards, flyers and notices, represent a wealth of texts to read in the university community.

In another Colombian city, Medellin, Mora et al. (2018) reported initial findings on a collaborative study created by pre-service EFL teachers in a Colombian university. Drawing on city literacies, and metrolingualism, the participants were mostly in-service elementary and middle school teachers, but one study involved pre-service teachers. Field notes, photographs, videos and teacher interviews and questionnaires were the most common data sources for the studies. In most of the contexts the linguistic data was multilingual. Digital spaces were also employed to portray micro papers, and small ethnographic trajectories in two studies.

Similarly, in Brazil Iddings et al, (2011), inquired about the nature and processes of "conscientização" (critical awareness) for adult street dwellers in a popular neighborhood in Sao Paulo, Brazil. The authors used an ecosocial semiotic theoretical framework to analyze the graffiti literacies. For them, "an ecosocial semiotic framework suggests that people shape their environment through the use of signs, and these signs in turn shape them as part of the complex, dynamic, and nonlinear process in which the environment and its meanings are actively co-produced" (Iddings et al., 2011, p. 5). They interviewed five adults in the neighborhood community regarding their thoughts about and experience of graffiti. The results revealed that graffiti literacy in Sao Paulo has become an important resource in the community helping people engage in critical perspectives of the world around them.

A study developed by Mexican researchers, Córdova Hernández et al. (2017) revealed the relevance of the linguistic and semiotic landscape to the process of indigenous language revitalization and literacy. They claim that the relationship between linguistic landscape and indigenous concepts can be mediated by the interconnection of language and remembering as well as the retrieval of the endangered language through strategies of recalling experiences mediated through that particular language. They argue that the semiotic landscape allows written language (discourse) to interact with other discourses (visual images, spatial practices, and cultural dimensions), to aid the emergence of indigenous self-representation and cultural values toward language revitalization.

In a highly multilingual context in Oceania, Schneider (2016) examined the role of literacy as practiced in communities presented with an 8-month ethnography in Papua New Guinea. Through photographs and field notes the researcher portrays the multilingual (Tok Pisin, English, and local languages) practices in the streets, home, school, church, and community services. The multilingual practices of the community revolve around multilingual hybrid texts. The author advocates for local literacy as highly multilingual, and for shared practices.

Franco´s (2013) study on the presence of languages in the linguistic landscape of Almeria, Spain explored texts to evidence how cultural practices and beliefs and the historical circumstances of the moment, become an inherent part of the linguistic landscape. His analysis evidenced the status of Spanish in the commercial streets of Almeria and assesses the local status of other languages with a focus on English.

Poveda (2012) carried out an ethnographic study on immigrant students' socio academic trajectories in Spanish secondary education. He explored the literacy artifacts placed by students in different locations of a public secondary school and the semiotic landscape of Spanish in Madrid, Spain. He reported two broad types of literacy artifacts that configured the school's semiotic landscape: political texts and graffiti. The artifacts were tied to the two youth expressive styles, social groups and ethnic background present in the school: Spanish (left-wing anarkas) and Latinamerican (reggaetoneros) students. Poveda´s (2012) analysis revealed that anarka texts occupied official spaces in the school and were construed as "in place" while reggaetonero artifacts occupied unofficial spaces and were construed as "out of place."

In conclusion, all the studies above-mentioned have have explored the possibilities for using local, transnational, and socio-cultural resources for language and literacy development. These have afforded us a significant understanding of multimodal, multicultural and multilingual aspects that are embedded in urban settings.

Raising Awareness of Urban Multimodal, Multicultural, and Multilingual Resources for Language and Literacy Education

This ethnography includes perspectives of teacher- researchers as collaborative ethnographers, while exploring the multimodal and multicultural nature of the texts and discourses of two neighborhoods in the historic district of Bogotá. In this collaborative ethnography, we posed the following questions:

1. How is multiculturalism and multilingualism conveyed in the semiotic landscape of the historical district of Bogotá?
2. What are the implications of recognizing the semiotic and multicultural resources of Bogota historic district for literacy education across the curriculum?

We analyzed how local people engage with multimodal texts, and linguistic landscapes to inform instructional literacy practices in teacher education programs.

We engaged in a detailed analysis of the semiotic and linguistic landscape of the historic center. In the photographic corpus collected we find three dimensions that describe the messages we observed: political and ideological, multicultural and multilingual, and socioeconomic dimensions. These dimensions can overlap and occur simultaneously in the same message.

Raising Awareness of the City as a Text

Research Design

In this study, we engaged in *Collaborative and participatory ethnography of place*. There was an ongoing negotiation of interpretations of the meaning of places, texts and art through the photographs, marked in the social context of the field experiences. For Clavijo-Olarte and Austin (2022), the collaborative perspective of the study addresses the epistemological negotiations within the group that were mediated by the horizontal relationships established among the researchers. We adopt Lassiter´s (2005) understanding of collaborative ethnography as an approach that "explicitly emphasizes collaboration at every point in the ethnographic process" (p. 16). We believe that the epistemological and methodological decisions made as a group, which are essential elements of the transformative research paradigm (Guba & Lincoln, 2005) provided an equal status and created a positive and inclusive research environment for this collaborative ethnography to be the consolidation of the learning experience of two years of work.

The participatory perspective of this research process also allowed us to value the knowledge gathered through the interactions with the participants (artists, teachers, and residents) as we learned to be open to learning and understanding other ways of knowing and being in the institutions. Mertens' (2017) contribution helps us to illustrate the participatory dimension of ethnography. The participatory nature of our methodological approach recognizes both the value of the researchers' knowledge and that of the participating communities. Mertens (2017) invites researchers to recognize their own power and cultural lenses and how they influence their relationships with research participants in order to enter communities respectfully and build relationships that recognize the knowledge that community members bring to the studies.

The place-based perspective of the study allowed us to understand the complexities of texts within places. It also provides insights into the socio-economic changes of this place to adopt new social practices derived from tourism, social mobility and gentrification. We gained insight into art as a political stance expressed multimodally and sharpened our understanding of how public schools are responding to the needs of students and their families who come to this part of the city to make a living. Touring this geographic space of the city implied walking its streets with other views that undoubtedly allowed us to redefine our conception of the Historic District. Equipped with the cameras of our cell phones, in each tour we were able to explore and discover how the historic district is configured in a textual and linguistic plurality. We were able to find, for example, that in this space of the city converge texts such as historical plaques, advertisements, commercials, murals, pamphlets, graffiti, stickers and stencils, among others. The photographic records were taken on different dates and different routes. Each co-investigator was documenting his or her routes photographically and capturing images that not only served to identify the semiotic and linguistic landscapes of the historic district, but also responded to our subjectivities and interests as individual researchers.

After compiling a photographic corpus of 387 photographs of the semiotic and linguistic landscapes, as co-researchers we discussed and analyzed the different texts that we were able to find in our ethnographic tours. The sessions are enriched with convergent and divergent points of view and interpretations of the varied textual configuration of the historic district. Likewise, we created an analysis format for the photographic records where we were able to establish the date of the photographs, the typology, the elements present in the texts and our interpretations of them (See annex #3).

Approaching ethnography from collaborative, participatory and place based dimensions helped us connect places, semiotic landscapes, social issues and diverse perspectives beyond the school context.

Based on semiotic landscapes and places, teachers and literacy scholars can create new pedagogical possibilities.

Data Collection

As researchers, we took 387 photographs of the different texts (graffiti, street signs, commercial advertisements) that we were able to find and discover in our ethnographic walks. The criteria we used was based on documenting the semiotic resources in the historic district of Bogotá through the visual and linguistic texts that could serve as pedagogical content to learn about the social, cultural, political and historical reality of the city. We discussed and analyzed the social and political content of the texts and the place where the texts were found. We also met to share convergent and divergent points interpretations of both visual and linguistic signs regarding its multicultural and multilingual content. We documented each photographic record according to date, typology, discursive content, and our interpretations of them (See annex #3).

Findings

In this section we present the findings that aim at responding to the questions posed.

1. How is multiculturalism and multilingualism conveyed in the semiotic landscape of the historical district of Bogotá?

2. What are the implications of recognizing the semiotic and multicultural resources of Bogota historic district for literacy education across the curriculum?

Political, Multicultural, and Multilingual Dimensions of Urban Semiotic Landscapes and Its Implications for Literacy Education

Below we present the three dimensions of the semiotic and linguistic landscape that we found in the Historic District of Bogota. The photographs we collected reflected one or more of the following dimensions.

Table 1. Dimensions of the semiotic landscapes

	Dimensions of the Semiotic Landscape in the Historic Center
1.	The semiotic landscape as a political, ideological text
2.	The semiotic landscape as a multicultural and decolonizing space
3.	The semiotic landscape as a multilingual and translanguaging space

These dimensions of the semiotic and linguistic landscape have the potential to foster critical literacy, and the appreciation of the multicultural and multilingual elements that urban spaces offer. Connecting students' identities with authentic cultural and linguistic experiences of the places they inhabit trans-

Raising Awareness of the City as a Text

forms teachers' pedagogical work and makes learning more meaningful (Lozano, Jiménez-Caicedo, & Abraham, 2020).

1. Political and Ideological Dimensions of Semiotic Landscapes

Through our explorations in the historic district, we encountered different signs that conveyed subaltern political and ideological messages. These signs included murals, graffiti, stickers, stencils and posters that work as counternarratives to dominant ideologies such as capitalism, mestizo-whiteness, and patriarchy. This goes in line with sociological research that has studied the connection between urban art and political imaginaries. In a former sociological study from the same city, Uribe Mendoza (2016) claims that political imaginaries can be studied through their semiotic materialization. In our study, it was common to see messages that represented social movements, indigenous and Afro-Colombian communities, feminism, and resistance to police brutality. Next, we present two examples that portray subaltern political and ideological messages.

Figure 2. Graffiti and police violence
Photo taken by the authors in Santafé

In the mural above the use of English has ideological and political purposes as it is used to denounce police violence, especially against graffiti artists. Using English in this case may have symbolic motivations since it would imply that the graffiti artists know the language and possess a certain level of education. They want to communicate with similar audiences, bilingual or English- understanding audiences.

In the bubble message on the top right corner "You" refers to the police, as an antagonistic group, the others in the discourse; while "the tribe" indexes the graffiti artists represented by a human figure with African features opposing a reptile with helmet, gun and boots representing the police. The nonhuman figure is an allegory of policy inhumanity. This mural denounces the assassination of street art artists by police officers. On the night of August 19th, 2011, 16 year old graffiti artist Diego Becerra was shot by a police officer while he and two friends were making graffiti in a middle class neighborhood in Bogotá. Police terror is a transnational phenomenon that has been resisted and studied in Colombia, Brazil, and the U.S. This phenomenon has been linked to racism and has historic roots in coloniality (Alves, 2019). Reading these signs on the street requires taking a critical stance towards discourse and image to raise awareness of social phenomena that oppress marginalized communities, in this case to understand police brutality and racism in Colombia.

The image below illustrates subaltern ideological and political imaginaries of semiotic landscapes.

Figure 3. Miner at Carrera Septima Avenue in Bogotá
Photo taken by the authors

The image depicts the face of a worker wearing a miner's helmet with light, the worker is looking into the distance. The colors of the poster are red and yellow which are political colors associated with the leftist thinking. The workers body uses a red filter with a gray scale star. Here, there is a reference to the red star. This has been traditionally a symbol of revolution. From the socialist perspective, its five points represent the five fingers of the worker's hand. On the picture's left side there is a legend "We build the world, let's change history". Just above there are some small yellow letters, but it is not clear what they mean, it could be the tag or brand of the artist. The image evokes the power of the working class.

There are two important elements which make us think in some new ideological aspects joined into he leftist and revolutionary thinking. The first is a small light blue symbol that represents the transgender or gender inclusive movement, this contrasts with the traditional strong masculine figure of the worker. The second element is the representation of richness on the worker's head, it shows how being rich is not any longer exclusively a matter of gold but also a matter of knowledge and wisdom.

It is also important to point out that this text is located on the Carrera 7 which is one of the most important avenues in the city. This avenue is particularly relevant due to its length, economic activities and even as a scenario for social demonstrations. It is thus possible to assert that this text also reflects the city as a political place.

2. The Semiotic Landscape as a Multicultural and Decolonizing Space

In this section, we analyze the multicultural and multilingual texts in the semiotic landscape of the historic district in Bogotá. The multicultural analysis draws attention to signs that represent the richness of the ethnic, historic, linguistic, and cultural realities of Colombian peoples, especially racialized groups such as indigenous and Afro-descendent communities.

Within our discussions and analysis, we identified the preponderance of natural elements related to indigenous peoples, such as crops, mountains, weavings and rivers. Artistic murals in La Candelaria recognize the ancestry and current presence of the indigenous peoples in the territory and are visible in one of the most visited squares of the historic district. These signs encourage homage and recognition of the multicultural identity fabric that weaves our country.

Figure 4. Semiotic landscape and multiculturalism
Photo taken by the authors in La Candelaria

    This mural is located near jewelry shops that sell emeralds in the historic district. The mural depicts a foundational myth of the The Muzo people, the myth of Fura (on the left) and Tena (on the right). The image shows emeralds, butterflies, snakes, and water, and two mountain peaks in the background. The Muzo people were a Caribbean people in conflict with the Chibcha peoples who resided in the eastern Colombian Andes. The myth tells the story of beautiful Fura and her partner Tena. Fura was unfaithful to Tena and in revenge Tena killed her lover before committing suicide. Fura's tears turned into emeralds and butterflies. The Muzo people considered that Fura and Tena were turned into mountain peaks; there is a river running between these two (Ocampo, 2013). These mountains became special places for adoration of their deities (Caldera, 2008, p.167). Nowadays, the lands that were inhabited by the Muzo people in Boyacá continue being a source for emeralds. Analyzing this mural within the more recent socio-historical context, can lead to conversations on transnational exploitation and the precarious lives of emerald miners in the country (Ramírez, 2021). A critical reading of this image can be conducted through making connections with other texts related to emerald mining like news articles and books.

Raising Awareness of the City as a Text

Black Feminine Presence

This photo taken by the teacher researchers was found within a set of pictures displaying female looking, ethnic portrayals nearby the local public school. These images created by urban artist @japu811 are full of African and feminine symbols. The image below points at Black intersectional feminism (Crenshaw, 2017) by centering the symbolic power of racialized and gendered bodies. These bodies are not common in mainstream media, which is dominated by mestizo- white representations and Western aesthetic ideals.

Figure 5. Semiotic landscape and multiculturalism
Photo taken by the authors in La Candelaria

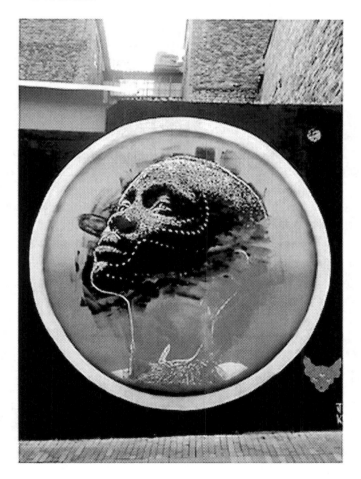

This image shows the face of a Black woman looking at the sky, constructing a visual image by gazing left upside and far away that may indicate hope and futurity. The white dots that run across her face are reminiscent of traditional African tribal makeup. White makeup represents purity, hope, and light (Afroculture.net). The pink, pastel, and light blue colors are typically associated with femininity. The facial expression, chin up no smile indicates some superiority and dignity. The composition in both its nonverbal and visual element is a tribute to Black Colombian women. Historically, Afro-Colombian territories have been marginalized, and discriminated against by white- mestizo supremacy, capitalist forces and political and war dynamics.

Although graffiti Colombian artists center on racialized communities in the historic district, to symbolically counteract histories of white-mestizo dominance, the concrete process of decolonizing resources and territories is still a pending task in Latin American societies (Mignolo & Escobar, 2013). From a critical literacy perspective, reading semiotic landscapes in the larger historic, and sociological contexts teachers, and students can contribute to decolonization beyond taking it merely as a metaphor (Tuck & Yang, 2012).

3. Semiotic Landscape Highlighting Multilingualism and Translanguaging

In our ethnographic walks around the historic district, besides Colombian Spanish which is the most common language in the city, we observed the written presence of colonial and global languages: English, French, and Arabic. Other languages that were less represented were Hebrew, Russian, and Chinese in hospitality businesses. The prevalence of global languages in this area visited by tourists indicates how multilingualism is linked to dialogical cosmopolitanism (Canagarajah, 2013) and globalization (Hua, Otsuji, & Pennycook, 2017). Canagarajah (2013) defines dialogic cosmopolitanism as "mutual collaboration, with an acceptance of everyone's difference" (Canagarajah, 2013, p. 196). The coexistence of different historically named languages in this area depicts how the city adapts to global and cosmopolitan flows.

Interestingly, indigenous languages were not available in written forms. However, they were available in auditory modalities. For example, Embera, Arhuaco or Ika and Quichua were spoken by some street vendors of crafts and clothing. The indigenous presence is strong in this area as indigenous organizations are based there. One of these is The National Indigenous Organization of Colombia (ONIC) which is an organization representing the indigenous peoples of Colombia, that comprise some 800,000 people, 2% of the Colombian population (https://www.onic.org.co/). This organization has led national strikes to defend the rights of indigenous peoples of Colombia.

The following images showcase global languages on wall art and small business signs. They evidence the multilingual construction of the historic district.

Raising Awareness of the City as a Text

Figure 6. Poem written in French language
Photo taken by the authors in La Candelaria

The image illustrates a text in poetic style that indexes romantic meaning, using French as the language of love. The verbal message about love is reinforced by using visual modes. The text appears to be handwritten. It mixes upper and lower case letters. The text starts and ends with ellipsis to indicate an unfinished text. The small pink hearts are integrated as punctuation marks, elements of calligraphy, and in replacement of the "o". The text is written on a white scroll which resembles a letter. It was the only example of graffiti that emulated a different genre, in this case the epistolary. The text reads "I don't know if I am ready or even capable to do what I am preparing for but I am going to try because I feel that I need to and because you inspire it in me". The use of contractions, circumflex marks, and compound sentences in French indicates that the writer is a fluent French speaker. The lack of punctuation which makes this text read as a run-on sentence, emphasizes the sense of urgency of the message.

The signs below are located at a coffee shop in the historic center of Bogotá. Compared to the example above, these signs use multilingual and visual resources in a more integrated manner. We can evidence translanguaging in the pictures as diverse linguistic resources are used fluidly. For Lin (2018), "translanguaging emphasizes a fluid, dynamic view of language and de-center the analytic focus from the language(s) being used in the interaction to the speakers who are making meaning and constructing original and complex discursive practices" (p. 5).

Figure 7. Billboards from a local coffee shop in La Candelaria
Photo taken by the authors

These two billboards invite passers-by to enter the coffeeshop to taste some typical food and beverages from Colombia. Using drawings to attract people, illustrates the products that the coffee shop offers, making these contents available even for people who cannot decode the words on the boards. The pictures depict coffee plants, coffee grains, coca leaves, teacups, and the colors of the Colombian flag.

Raising Awareness of the City as a Text

Tourists who may not have access to Spanish can learn about Colombian beverages and foods, through interpreting the visual components and the words conveyed on the boards.

The left billboard uses translanguaging. Lexical resources from English and Spanish are used here as components of one single message. Most words are left without translation: for example, Colombian traditional beverages like *agua de panela* (brown sugar tea), *aromática* (herbal tea), *tinto* (black coffee), and *té de coca* (coca tea). By using the word *tinto* the add indexes Colombian Spanish, as this word may mean wine in different Spanish speaking countries.

These words are complemented by cognates or loan words that mean the same and are spelled similarly in English and Spanish, for example: *Expresso, Americano, Capuccino, Sandwich, Brownie, Chocolate*. These words are accessible for Spanish or English monolingual passersby as well as for bilingual audiences. The creator of this text displayed high crosslinguistic awareness of English and Spanish cognates to achieve their communicative goal.

The sign to the right offers a literal translation from Spanish "Venta en grano y molido". This literal translation "Sale *in grain* and ground" is not clear to a monolingual English reader who would use "Sale in *whole bean* or ground". It is evidence that the author of the message is a Spanish speaker who wanted to communicate their message to English readers.

We selected the signs below as they represent non-Latin alphabets from non-colonial languages. These signs are located at a Israeli restaurant.

Figure 8. Billboard and menu from an Israeli restaurant in La Candelaria
Photos taken by the authors

The restaurant sign uses the colors of the Israeli flag. The first sign is written using the Hebrew alphabet, then includes a Spanish phonetic transliteration l'jaim, which is transliterated as L'Chaim in English. There is also a literal word by word translation to Spanish "Por la vida". This is a toast expression in Hebrew used with friends and family to celebrate before drinking. The most context-appropriate expression in Spanish would be "*Salud*" which translates to cheers..

The food menu is written in Hebrew only. This reinforces the idea of authenticity and identity. Heller and McElhinny (2017) indicate how multilingualism indexes authenticity, which is commodified here. This menu assumes that the reader is either a member of the Hebrew reading community or is willing to interact with the servers to find out and learn about Israeli food.

The semiotic landscape revealed the multilingual practices of this part of the city. These include the use of global languages by local commerce in response to tourism and transnational flows. These signs allowed us to understand how Bogotá's urban texts show separate (monolingual) and integrated language ideologies (translanguaging) for different purposes such as expressing feelings, attracting customers, and displaying heritage.

To summarize, the semiotic landscape of the historic district of Bogota offered us three main dimensions to explore: 1) The semiotic landscape as a political, ideological text; 2) the semiotic landscape as a multicultural and decolonizing space; 3) the semiotic landscape as a multilingual and translanguaging space. These dimensions can contribute to developing critical literacy as teachers and students who engage in reading these signs. These can transcend shallow interpretations and look deeper for ideological, political, multicultural, and linguistic meanings as they connect them to larger histories, and other texts.

In the following section we address the solutions and recommendations of the ethnographic study recognizing the semiotic and multicultural resources of Bogotá´s historic district to answer the question: What are the implications of recognizing the semiotic and multicultural resources of the Historic Center of Bogota for researchers and school teachers?

IMPLICATIONS AND RECOMMENDATIONS

For teacher-researchers, this study led to developing awareness of the place, languages and literacies by promoting practices of reflection and inquiry in the face of the linguistic landscape offered by these urban spaces. Analyzing and reading the semiotic and linguistic landscape that surrounds schools offers opportunities to develop critical awareness and to recognize the purposes, audiences, and semiotic resources that students can interpret and create. It also leads to the recognition of multicultural and linguistic diversity that is rarely reflected in traditional curricular content and materials. This study brings potential implications for preparation of teachers; and integration of local knowledge for the education of new teacher-researchers.

IMPLICATIONS FOR RESEARCH AND TEACHER EDUCATION

This ethnography involved conducting collective and dialogic fieldwork to experience cultures, people´s social discourses, activities, literacies, and struggles firsthand. We visited small businesses, tasted the local food, had conversations with residents, street vendors, and explored historic sites. Both experienced and novice teacher researchers negotiated, debated, and co-constructed interpretations sharing different visions, trajectories, and professional and academic stages. We recommend that researchers and teacher researchers use collaborative ethnographies of place to foster critical literacy.

We understand that teaching from a social justice and critical literacy perspective implies a critical reading of places and semiotic landscapes around schools. After exploring the semiotic, multicultural and multilingual resources that places offer, teachers and students can transform the school curriculum. In teacher preparation programs, places and semiotic landscapes constitute curricular resources that respond to the needs of students. Teachers and students can develop a critical posture from embracing semiotic, linguistic and multicultural resources. We recommend that teachers use semiotic landscapes and place explorations to decolonize their curriculum, especially by centering linguistic diversity, multiculturalism, and social struggles that are materialized on the walls of the city.

CONCLUSION

In this chapter, we addressed the potential of semiotic landscapes to enrich the pedagogical practices of teacher and teacher- researchers. We contextualize this project from the theoretical perspectives of urban literacies, pedagogies of place, multilingualism, multiculturalism, and semiotic landscapes. We framed this project in an ethnographic, participatory and collaborative epistemology in which researchers dialogued with participants and were immersed in the places that teachers and students inhabit. We used discourse and multimodal analysis to interpret the semiotic landscape. Below we summarize our main findings.

To address the first research question: How does the urban semiotic landscape contribute to understanding urban literacies for language education? We took a poststructural and relational perspective of literacies (Leander & Boldt, 2013). We found that different actors were part of assemblages or networks of literacies in which different individuals in the community interact with passersby, places, social discourses, and multimodal texts that constitute urban literacy practices of their own. We identified literacy practices that are not traditionally recognized in school environments; for example, graffiti which can be a critical literacy resource to analyze artistic, political and multicultural elements,

In the photographic corpus collected we found three dimensions which describe the most salient features of the signs we collected: political and ideological, multicultural and decolonizing, and multilingual dimensions. These features can overlap and occur simultaneously in the same message. For example, we noticed how multilingual advertisements can have commercial or ideological connotations. Analyzing and reading the semiotic and linguistic landscape surrounding schools offers opportunities to develop critical awareness in students. Students can analyze the purposes, audiences, and semiotic configurations. Teachers and students can interpret and create or re-create some of these later on. Using semiotic landscapes as critical literacy resources leads to the recognition of multicultural and linguistic diversity that is rarely reflected in traditional curricular content.

To elaborate the second research question: What are the implications of recognizing the semiotic and multicultural resources of the Historic Center of Bogota for researchers and school teachers?, some of the implications worth highlighting were the collective and dialogic construction of knowledge through an ethnographic and participatory approach that benefited the different actors. For the researchers, it was an opportunity to exchange ideas in a more horizontal manner and contribute to the construction of interpretations. The researchers also learned that ethnographic research is fluid and adapts to contexts and circumstances. For teachers and university students, it implied the development of awareness of place, languages and literacies by fostering practices of reflection and inquiry in the semiotic landscape offered by the urban spaces.

FUTURE RESEARCH DIRECTIONS

For future research, we suggest delving into the following aspects: interculturality, the multilingual and multicultural nature of literacies, and the inclusion of multimodality. We believe that future research can go beyond multiculturalism and move towards interculturality. In this research, we evidenced multiculturalism, that is, the diversity of cultures that were present in the same place; however, we believe that for future research may focus on interculturality which Villodre (2012) defines as "'between cultures' that inhabit the same territory. Interculturality promotes communication between different cultures, the cultural meeting to contrast and learn from each other, awareness of the difference to resolve conflicts" (p. 70). We saw multiple cultures, but not addressing their interactions and tensions between different cultural groups.

One last aspect to be incorporated is the participatory nature of research in education beyond school buildings. We interacted with street vendors, artists, and small business owners. For future research, we believe that families, tourists, local authorities, and other actors can contribute valuable insights into urban literacies that go beyond school environments. We hope that future research addresses the pedagogical applications of place based and semiotic resources for critical literacy. This will benefit preservice and in-service teachers and involve education administrators.

ACKNOWLEDGMENT

We would like to specially thank the participation and collaboration of teachers from the two public schools, La Candelaria and Policarpa Salavarrieta for providing valuable insights about the uses of resources of the historic district of Bogotá; the graffiti artists that we interviewed, and the local resident, *doña* Maria, who kindly received us in her restaurant at La Concordia farmers 'market.

This study was funded by The Center for Research and Scientific Development at Universidad Distrital Francisco José de Caldas during 2019-2022. [Grant number 4-62-587-19].

REFERENCES

Alves, J. (2019). Setting the Tone: Micro/Macro Racial Aggression, Antiblackness and the Outlining of a Trans-National Research Agenda on Community Responses to State Terror. *Currents*, *1*(1), 79–94. doi:10.3998/currents.17387731.0001.107

Ben-Rafael, E., Shohamy, E., Amara, M. H., & Trumper-Hecht, N. (2006). Linguistic Landscape as Symbolic Construction of the Public Space: The Case of Israel. In D. Gorter (Ed.), *Linguistic landscape: A new approach to multilingualism* (pp. 7–30). Multilingual Matters. doi:10.21832/9781853599170-002

Blackledge, A., & Creese, A. (2010). *Multilingualism: A critical perspective*. Bloomsbury Publishing.

Caldera, L. A. B. (2008). Concepción sagrada de la naturaleza en la mítica muisca. *Franciscanum. Revista de las ciencias del espíritu*, *50*(149), 151-176.

Canagarajah, S. (2002). Reconstructing Local Knowledge. *Journal of Language, Identity, and Education*, *1*(4), 243–259. doi:10.1207/S15327701JLIE0104_1

Canagarajah, S. (2013). *Translingual Practice: Global Englishes and Cosmopolitan Relations*. Routledge. doi:10.4324/9780203120293

Cenoz, J., & Gorter, D. (2008). The linguistic landscape as an additional source of input in second language acquisition. *IRAL -. International Review of Applied Linguistics in Language Teaching*, 46(3), 257–276. doi:10.1515/IRAL.2008.012

Clavijo-Olarte, A., & Austin, T. (2022). Crossing linguistic boundaries with community literacies: A collaborative, place-based ethnography in two urban localities in Bogotá. In Language Education in Multilingual Colombia. Critical Perspectives and Voices from the Field. Multilingual Matters.

Clavijo-Olarte, A., Medina, R. A., Calderón, D., Rodríguez, A., Prieto, K., & Nader, M. C. (2021). *Investigating the social, cultural, linguistic and literacy practices to construct Bogotá as a multicultural place: Final Research Report*. Universidad Distrital Francisco José de Caldas.

Cochran-Smith, M. (2005). Teacher Educators as Researchers: Multiple Perspectives. *Teaching and Teacher Education*, 21(2), 219–225. doi:10.1016/j.tate.2004.12.003

Córdova Hernández, L., López-Gopar, M. E., & Sughrua, W. M. (2017). From linguistic landscape to semiotic landscape: indigenous language revitalization and literacy. *Studie z aplikované lingvistiky- Studies in Applied Linguistics*, 8(2), 7-21.

Crenshaw, K. W. (2017). *On intersectionality: Essential writings*. The New Press.

Franco Rodríguez, J. M. (2013). An alternative reading of the linguistic landscape: The case of Almería. *Revista Internacional de Lingüística Iberoamericana*, 21(1), 109–134.

Garvin, R. (2010). Responses to the Linguistic Landscape in Memphis, Tennessee: An Urban Space in Transition. In Linguistic Landscape in the City (pp. 252-272). Blue Ridge Summit: Multilingual Matters.

Guba, E. G., & Lincoln, Y. S. (2005). Paradigmatic Controversies, Contradictions, and Emerging Confluences. In N. K. Denzin & Y. S. Lincoln (Eds.), *The Sage handbook of qualitative research* (pp. 191–215). Sage Publications Ltd.

Heller, M., & McElhinny, B. (2017). *Language, capitalism, colonialism: Toward a critical history*. University of Toronto Press.

Hua, Z., Otsuji, E., & Pennycook, A. (2017). Multilingual, multisensory and multimodal repertoires in corner shops, streets and markets: Introduction. *Social Semiotics*, 27(4), 383–393. doi:10.1080/10350 330.2017.1334383

Iddings, A. C. D., McCafferty, S. G., & Da Silva, M. L. T. (2011). Conscientização through graffiti literacies in the streets of a São Paulo neighborhood: An ecosocial semiotic perspective. *Reading Research Quarterly*, 46(1), 5–21. doi:10.1598/RRQ.46.1.1

Jaworski, A., & Thurlow, C. (Eds.). (2010). *Semiotic landscapes: Language, image, space*. A&C Black.

Jiménez, R., Smith, P., & Teague, B. (2009). Transnational and Community Literacies for Teachers. *Journal of Adolescent & Adult Literacy*, 53(1), 1–16. doi:10.1598/JAAL.53.1.2

Jonkman, J. (2020). Underground multiculturalism: Contentious cultural politics in gold-mining regions in Chocó, Colombia. *Journal of Latin American Studies*, *53*(1), 1–28. doi:10.1017/S0022216X2000098X

Kramsch, C. (2018). Is there still a place for culture in a multilingual FL education? Language Education and Multilingualism. *Landscape Journal*, *1*, 16–33. doi:10.18452/19039

Landry, R., & Bourhis, R. Y. (1997). Linguistic Landscape and Ethnolinguistic Vitality: An Empirical Study. *Journal of Language and Social Psychology*, *16*(1), 23–49. doi:10.1177/0261927X970161002

Lassiter, L. (2005). Collaborative Ethnography and Public Anthropology. *Current Anthropology*, *46*(1), 83–106. doi:10.1086/425658

Lassiter, L. (2005). *The Chicago guide to collaborative ethnography*. University of Chicago Press. doi:10.7208/chicago/9780226467016.001.0001

Leander, K., & Boldt, G. (2013). Rereading "A pedagogy of multiliteracies" bodies, texts, and emergence. *Journal of Literacy Research*, *45*(1), 22–46. doi:10.1177/1086296X12468587

Lin, A. M. (2018). Theories of trans/languaging and trans-semiotizing: Implications for content-based education classrooms. *International Journal of Bilingual Education and Bilingualism*, *22*(1), 5–16. doi:10.1080/13670050.2018.1515175

Lozano, M. E., Jiménez-Caicedo, J. P., & Abraham, L. B. (2020). Linguistic Landscape Projects in Language Teaching: Opportunities for Critical Language Learning Beyond the Classroom. In *Language Teaching in the Linguistic Landscape* (pp. 17–42). Springer. doi:10.1007/978-3-030-55761-4_2

Marshall, E., & Toohey, K. (2010). Representing family: Community funds of knowledge, bilingualism, and multimodality. *Harvard Educational Review*, *80*(2), 221–241. doi:10.17763/haer.80.2.h3446j54n608q442

May, S. (2009). Critical Multiculturalism and Education. In J. A. Banks (Ed.), *The Routledge International Companion to Multiculutural Education* (pp. 33–48). Routledge.

Mertens, D. (2017). Transformative Research: Personal and Societal. *International Journal for Transformative Research*, *4*(1), 18–24. doi:10.1515/ijtr-2017-0001

Mignolo, W. D., & Escobar, A. (Eds.). (2013). *Globalization and the decolonial option*. Routledge. doi:10.4324/9781315868448

Mills, K. A. (2015). Doing digital composition on the social web: Knowledge processes in literacy learning. In *A Pedagogy of Multiliteracies* (pp. 172–185). Palgrave Macmillan. doi:10.1057/9781137539724_10

Mora, R. A., Pulgarín, C., Ramírez, N., & Mejía-Vélez, M. C. (2018). English literacies in Medellin: The city as literacy. In *Learning Cities* (pp. 37–60). Springer. doi:10.1007/978-981-10-8100-2_4

Morgan, B. D. (2002). Critical practice in community-based ESL programs: A Canadian perspective. *Journal of Language, Identity, and Education*, *1*(2), 141–162. doi:10.1207/S15327701JLIE0102_03

Murrell, P. (2001). *The community teacher: A new framework for effective urban teaching*. Teachers College Press.

Ocampo, J. (2013). *Mitos y Leyendas Indígenas de Colombia – Indigenous Myths and Legends of Colombia*. Plaza & Janes Editores.

Ortega, L. (2017). New CALL-SLA Research Interfaces for the 21st Century: Towards Equitable Multilingualism. *CALICO Journal*, *34*(3), 283–316. doi:10.1558/cj.33855

Otsuji, E., & Pennycook, A. (2010). Metrolingualism: Fixity, fluidity and language in flux. *International Journal of Multilingualism*, *7*(3), 240–254. doi:10.1080/14790710903414331

Pink, S. (2008). An urban tour: The sensory sociality of ethnographic place-making. *Ethnography*, *9*(2), 175–196. doi:10.1177/1466138108089467

Poveda, D. (2012). Literacy artifacts and the semiotic landscape of a Spanish secondary school. *Reading Research Quarterly*, *47*(1), 61–88. doi:10.1002/RRQ.010

Ramírez, J. P. (2021, January 4). Playing the 'Green Lottery': Life Inside Colombia's Emerald Mines. *The New York Times*. https://www.nytimes.com/2021/01/04/travel/colombia-emerald-mines.html

Sayer, P. (2010). Using the Linguistic Landscape as a pedagogical resource. *ELT Journal*, *64*(2), 143–154. doi:10.1093/elt/ccp051

Schneider, C. (2016). Talking around the texts: Literacy in a multilingual Papua New Guinean community. *Written Language and Literacy*, *19*(1), 1–34. doi:10.1075/wll.19.1.01sch

Sharkey, J., Clavijo Olarte, A., & Ramírez, L. M. (2016). Developing a Deeper Understanding of Community-Based Pedagogies with Teachers: Learning with and From Teachers in Colombia. *Journal of Teacher Education*, *67*(4), 306–319. doi:10.1177/0022487116654005

Shohamy, E., & Gorter, D. (Eds.). (2009). *Linguistic Landscape: Expanding the Scenery*. Routledge.

Song, S. (2020). Multiculturalism. *The Stanford Encyclopedia of Philosophy*. Available at https://plato.stanford.edu/archives/fall2020/entries/multiculturalism

Steffensen, S. V., & Kramsch, C. (2017). The ecology of second language acquisition and socialization. In P. Duff & S. May (Eds.), *Language Socialization* (3rd ed., pp. 17–32). Springer., doi:10.1007/978-3-319-02255-0_2

Thurlow, C., & Jaworski, A. (2011). Tourism discourse: Languages and banal globalization. *Applied Linguistics Review*, *2*(2011), 285–312. doi:10.1515/9783110239331.285

Trillos, M., & Etxebarria, M. (2002). Legislación, política lingüística y multilingüismo en Colombia. In Ponencia presentada en el Congreso Mundial sobre Políticas Lingüísticas Linguapax IX, celebrado en Barcelona, España, del (Vol. 16). Academic Press.

Tuck, E., & Yang, K. W. (2012). Decolonization is not a metaphor. *Decolonization*, *1*(1), 1–40.

Uribe Mendoza, C. (2016). *El arte urbano y la producción de sentidos políticos juveniles. In Democracia y Participación Política*. Ibañez.

ADDITIONAL READING

Comber, B. (2016). *Literacy, place, and pedagogies of possibility*. Routledge.

Demarest, A. B. (2015). *Place-based curriculum design: Exceeding standards through local investigations*. Routledge.

Gee, J. P. (2015). *Literacy and education*. Routledge.

Jank, H., Dixon, K., Ferreira, A., Granville, S., & Newfield, D. (2014). *Doing critical literacy: Texts and activities for students and teachers*. Routledge.

Medina, R. A., Galindo, L. M., & Olarte, A. (2015). Reading the community critically inthe digital age: A multiliteracies approach. In P. Chamness, M. Mantero, & H. Hindeibro (Eds.), *Readings in Language Studies (5)* (pp. 45–66). ISLS.

Serafini, F. (2014). *Reading the visual: An introduction to teaching multimodal literacy*. Teachers College Press.

Villodre, M. M. (2012). Pluriculturalidad, multiculturalidad e interculturalidad, conocimientos necesarios para la labor docente. *Hekademos. Revista Educativa Digital, 11*, 67–76.

KEY TERMS AND DEFINITIONS

Collaborative Ethnography: A critical collaborative ethnographic for us refers to a way of knowing that allows for multiple perspectives on creating knowledge and for understanding the complexity of particular contexts of teachers and their learners.

Linguistic Landscape: Texts and discourses composed mainly by linguistic signs that make part of community environments.

Literacy: Is viewed as a social practice that involves individuals in making sense of the world through their interaction with printed, visual, or multimodal texts.

Multimodal Texts: Text that mix more than two semiotic resources for example visual, linguistic, spatial, and gestural modes.

Place-Based Pedagogies: Pedagogies that promote authentic engagement with people, places and things outside the classroom while addressing curriculum contents and responding to students' sociocultural backgrounds and needs.

Semiotic Landscapes: Any public space with a visible inscription made through deliberate human intervention for the construction of meaning.

Translanguaging: The fluid use of multiple linguistic and semiotic resources as a single repertoire.

Urban Literacies: Are understood as the social, artistic, political, cultural and pedagogical manifestations that are represented through various texts such as murals, graffiti, posters, historical plaques, advertisements, and city spaces such as religious and historical buildings, government institutions and schools, and social and economic phenomena expressed by individuals and collectives.

Chapter 14
"Twenty-Six Letters of the Forest Alphabet" or Community Social Learning Among the Ba'Aka in the Central African Republic

Urszula Markowska-Manista
https://orcid.org/0000-0003-0667-4164
University of Warsaw, Poland

ABSTRACT

The chapter discusses three areas of education for indigenous children from the Ba'Aka hunter-gatherer community in the CAR: public, formal education; private, missionary-run institutions; their traditional, collective education, metaphorically called "the forest alphabet." Children used to be socialized into engaging with the forest-based on the relationship of reciprocal cooperation, protection, and justice. However, this relationship has become incongruent and undesirable in a reality dominated by developmental projects, deforestation, missionary activities, and environmental conservation initiatives. Each undermines indigenous epistemic rights and relationships with and claims to the land. Missionary and state education are shown as posing challenges to indigenous children, while particular attention is paid to forest education in terms of the social learning and engagement of Ba'Aka children in the environment in which they grow up, and in terms of their resistance and adaptation strategies in the face of these developments.

DOI: 10.4018/978-1-6684-5022-2.ch014

"Twenty-Six Letters of the Forest Alphabet" or Community Social Learning Among the Ba'Aka

INTRODUCTION

This paper discusses the struggles of indigenous children from the Ba'Aka hunter-gatherer community inhabiting the Sangha-Mbaéré rainforest region in the Central African Republic in the face of changing ecological and sociopolitical climates. Ba'Aka children find themselves standing at a crossroads (Markowska-Manista 2019), confronted by a choice between three educational pathways: (1) their traditional, collective education, metaphorically called "the forest alphabet" (2) private, missionary-run ORA method schools, and (3) in the public, formal educational system, dating back to the colonial era. The Ba'Aka refer to the forest as a "Father" and "Mother" with whom they have an inextricable bond. Children used to be socialized into engaging with the forest based on this relationship of reciprocal co-operation, protection, and justice (Ichikawa, 1996). However, this relationship has become incongruent and undesirable in a reality dominated by developmental projects and deforestation, missionary activities working to transform their indigenous culture, as well as environmental conservation initiatives designed in the Global North. Each in their own way undermines indigenous epistemic living rights, and relationships with and claims to the land. I discuss these 3 areas of education for Ba'Aka children indicating (in the case of missionary education and state education) the challenges of being students. I outline forest education as resistance and adaptation strategies of Ba'Aka children in the face of these developments as they grapple with being silenced and made invisible. It is a paradox that the voices of those, whose polyphonic singing was included on the *Representative List of the Intangible Cultural Heritage of Humanity* in 2008, remain unheard.

In this text, based on desk research and my own fieldwork (ethnographic) materials, I pay particular attention to the social learning (Salali et al., 2019) and engagement of Ba'Aka children in education in the environment in which they grow up. The perspective and experiences of children as active participants (Munn, 2010) who shape their own and their communities' futures are important aspects for understanding the complexity of this environment and the process of multidimensional, holistic education.

In order to better acquaint the reader with the sensitive context of Ba'Aka life in which it is currently impossible to fully pursue traditional community social learning, I have analyzed academic literature and reports from the period of my research (2002-2022). The article is written in a decolonial approach (Datta, 2018) and based on a humanizing research methodology (Reyes et al. 2021). Decolonial approach refers here to breaking down the established patterns of thinking about the Other and showing the complexity and persistence of the factors of colonial entanglement of minority groups in the "production of knowledge" and (globally) transmitted knowledge about them, which usually does not include their voices and their own representations of their everyday life. Humanizing research is a methodological stance turned toward a research effort in which inquiry involves "dialogic consciousness-raising and the building of relationships of dignity and care for both researchers and participants" (Paris 2011: 137). This makes it possible to highlight the contribution of the non-dominant community to the research. At the same time, it highlights the importance of this community in explaining the meanings of the Ba'Aka everyday world to the researcher, allowing us to understand the non-Eurocentric ways of knowing others and the 'non-human', that is the multidimensional ecology of human relations and relationships with the surrounding material and immaterial world (Magnat 2020).

By discussing the metaphorical 26 letters of the forest alphabet - that is, the process of forest education - I point out how children acquire different knowledge resources, how they develop diverse abilities and skills to survive in the traditional environment, and the challenges of passing on ancestral knowledge based on oral stories in the 21st century.

"Twenty-Six Letters of the Forest Alphabet" or Community Social Learning Among the Ba'Aka

Indigenous groups around the world, through diverse and unique methods, employ diverse strategies to resist the colonization of their ways of life, education, beliefs, and activities in symbiosis with nature. Being a traditional hunter-gatherer society on the move, today the Ba'aka face great difficulties in cultivating and expressing their knowledge of the world and the protection of nature. These difficulties arise, among other things, from the approach of educational and social institutions as well as organizations, including developmental non-governmental organizations, which, despite their best intentions, still fail to understand and incorporate the perspective of indigenous communities' thinking and acting. Because they operate in a non-own socio-political context, but within Western initiatives and orders, these organizations are often caught up "in the complexities and power relations configured by post-colonial conditions that continue to prevail in such contexts" (Khan et al., 2010: 1418). Critical reflexivity in a humanizing approach requires intentional listening (Paris, 2011). How, then, can the Ba'Aka decolonize their own process of socially useful indigenous education to provide their children with an education that meets their needs, ensures survival in harmony with nature, tells their story, and shows us the possibilities for survival in the age of climate change?

The Fragile Context of Ba'Aka's Everyday Life

In order to understand the situation of the educational crossroads at which Ba'Aka children and adolescents have been in for several decades, it is first necessary to analyze the context in which their daily lives take place, that is, the colonial and postcolonial entanglement that this indigenous community experienced and continues to experience. This entanglement relates to three key dimensions: systemic, interactional (inter-ethnic relations during the settlement phase and semi-settled life in villages and settlements) and the dimension of transmission. The systemic dimension is related to the centuries-long oppression of indigenous communities, their social exclusion and the perpetuation of their poverty, poverty here being both a factor and an effect of exclusion and marginalization processes. Marginality here means limited participation in a top-down defined social order and limited access to the privileges, goods and basic social institutions of that order and the social practices characteristic of the majority society. In turn, lack of access and non-participation and thus limited contact (interaction) with the majority society intensify the process of deepening marginalization and social exclusion of minorities. Marginalization influences interactions because people, groups that are perceived as inferior, without social status, appear as if outside the social structure (Szarfenberg 2006).

The second type of entanglement refers to the complex relationship between the forest population and the settled population (in villages and towns) as well as cultural diffusion. In the past, the latter consisted, as Collin Turnbull (1974) writes, in a mutual provision of various services between Pygmies and Bantu (Grinker 2011) and did not constitute a slave-master relationship of the kind we can observe today. However, researchers are divided on this issue. They refer to historical contexts and studies of social and cultural configurations in mutual interactions and relationships (hunter-gatherers and farmers), contextualized ecological and economic knowledge of both groups, as well as practices that uncover distinctions between local living patterns and the complexity of Ba'Aka - hunter-gatherers and farmers behavior (see Kohler 2005; Köhler and Lewis 2002).

The third type of entanglement relates to discourse that stereotypes the 'Pygmies' (a commonly used term for Ba'Aka hunter-gatherers, but in fact pejorative for the Ba'Aka themselves), portraying them through idealized images and infantile formulations as "the most childlike of all races", "children of the forest", "simple creatures", or "forest people" leading romantic and harmonious lives free from violence and the influence of Western civilization. The latter dimension refers to representations in words and images about the 'other', the distant and even the 'exotic', and the lack of the participation of the voices of the community in matters concerning its members (lack of opportunities for participation, absence from research, literary and media discourses).

Today, we look at the era and legacy of colonialism through the lens of critical theory, decoding European systems of knowledge about the so-called 'colonized' Other and attempting to reinterpret the simplistic narratives in the languages of nineteenth- and twentieth-century Western writers and scholars (Saunders 2019) in which indigenous Central Africans were implicated. Examples of colonial images (Mayer 2002) and imperial perceptions of the Other, including the hunter-gatherers of the former French colony of Ubangui and Shari (now the Central African Republic), can still be found in many contemporary popular science publications, guidebooks and travel books or travel agency offers. Also, the practices of globalized tourism to slums or the last unspoiled places of planet Earth (national parks, nature reserves), described and advertised in the media, although referring in some ways to the ethnographic idea of learning about the Other in their natural habitats of everyday life, are reminiscent in the dimension of perception of 19th and 20th-century observations of 'objects' on display - human zoos (Blanchard et al., 2008). At the same time, they resemble trading in tradition, for which, as a relic of times past, a demand is created by the international tourism of the rich who post video and photo accounts of their "journeys to the past" on social media.

The awareness of centuries-old colonial and post-colonial forms of entanglement and dependence of this group on imposed rules and activities, helps to explain the contemporary problems of disregarding the voices and consequently the lack of voice of indigenous communities and the disappearance of their identity in the globalizing world of Central African states. At the same time, it reveals a series of 'civilizing', developmental practices involving the territorial and mental dispossession of indigenous peoples from their traditional lands and the deprivation of natural resources and cultural heritage based on the oral transmission of knowledge - the key to survival in harmony with nature. Moreover, the continuation of these practices deprives the Ba'Aka of initiative. They are the ones who continue to be the recipients of externally designed development support programs, the silent participants in top-down imposed activities, and finally the peeped-at participants in 'forest expeditions', 'traditional dances and polyphonic chants' organized for tourists.

The space of confrontation and interpretation and the deconstruction of the relationship between the spectators and those being looked at creates the tangible difference between: "the past and today". Unlike a hundred years ago when living exhibits ("Pygmies"[1]) were transported to Western countries and displayed in cages (Bradford, 1992; Pittas, 2011), in the 21st century, it is the spectators (tourists) who travel to the dwelling places of "ethnological exhibits" with the rainforest or savannah in the background. And the interactions that occur as a result of cross-cultural contact, sometimes redefine the knowledge and meanings of the relationships of the viewers and the viewed (Mowforth, Munt 2009). Today, colonial practices have their soft forms reflected for instance in power relations. They can refer to entering the world of the Ba'aka without knocking and peering into almost every corner of their daily lives, or handing out candy and plastic gadgets. These practices apply double standards and involve, for example, photographing and filming (without often asking for permission) an individual or community against the background (a household, a place where food is cooked, a place where children play, a place where sick people are treated). Being aware that such practices transgress ethical boundaries and established norms of respecting privacy, why do we not carry them out in our contexts, but do not hesitate to perform them in the living environments of communities outside Europe?

"Twenty-Six Letters of the Forest Alphabet" or Community Social Learning Among the Ba'Aka

Colonial ideology entangling colonized societies systemically, interactively and in the dimension of representation about the Other, became rooted in aid culture and mass culture. It is worth adding that "(…) without examining Orientalism as a discourse one cannot possibly understand the enormous systematic discipline by which European culture was able to manage—and even produce—the Orient politically, sociologically, militarily, ideologically, scientifically, and imaginatively" (Said, 1995: 3). According to researchers from the Association pour la Connaissance de l'Histoire de l'Afrique Contemporaine, colonial ideology and the orientalization of Others have not been reworked in postcolonial societies of former colonizers and societies that have experienced colonization (Markowska-Manista, 2014). In his book 'Decolonizing the Mind' published in 1986, Kenyan writer Ngungi Wa Thiongo advances the thesis that colonialism had deeper effects than imposing control over land and resources on a population through military conquest and political dictatorship. Colonial violence also dominated the mental space of the colonized, even after independence, and its effects are still felt and noticeable in many countries. Nigerian writer Chimamanda Ngozi Adichie (2009) also points to these aspects in her presentation 'The danger of a single story'.

Hence, the colonial and post-colonial entanglements of hunter-gatherers need to be considered in terms of systemic dimensions and inter-ethnic relations, and in terms of the word and image present in research, literary and media discourses. The systemic entanglements lie in the legacy of political chaos handed down by the colonizers and the instruments of state governance. They refer to the linguicide, culture- and ethnocide, which kill oral histories, music and hunter-gatherers' memories of their cultural heritage and erode the indigenous knowledge conditioning their ability to survive in their traditional habitats and their ability to protect the rainforest.

"26 Letters of the Forest Alphabet": A Relic Essential to Our Times

The traditional community social learning of the Ba'Aka egalitarian society (Lewis, 2017) is based on four pillars of collective coexistence. The first two involve learning the methods and strategies of obtaining food: hunting and gathering. The others refer to: education preparing an individual to entering into a partnership or marriage; assimilation of moral and cultural rules specific to the group to which the individual belongs; dependence on and obedience to "teachers" and dependence on the way of life of the particular ethnic group, clan or family to which the individual belongs, which involves contributing to its maintenance and ensuring its continuance (Koulaninga 2009).

Significantly, 'forest education' has been conditioned by respect for and knowledge of the philosophy of living in symbiosis with nature, knowledge of tradition and practical knowledge of the equatorial forest as the primary habitat of hunter-gatherers. Forest education teaches children the language of the forest, that is, how to listen to the sounds the forest makes and how to read them. It also teaches how to move silently in the forest in order to become an integral part of it. Moreover, forest education teaches a balanced language for communicating with nature. Such communication based on direct contact with nature is key to maintaining a balance between man and the forest and is essential for union with nature.

This learning was traditionally based on oral transmission and storytelling contained in the metaphorical letters of the forest alphabet. In the process of collective social learning, the community - each member and so parents, other adults, and other children (Lew-Levy 2017), transmit simple, practical laws of life to the child (Hewlett 2021) and tell stories addressing everyday collective life, weather, activities, diseases, violation of social norms and social practice (Scalise Sugiyama 2017). These are related to the appropriate behavior towards other people (as group members, as human beings) and nature, as well as fulfillment of duties towards God, the spirit of the forest, parents, family members, neighbors and the community as a whole, and the forest as a living environment, referred to as 'Father and Mother'. The traditional upbringing of children in indigenous communities is thus intended to impart to children the skills and customs that are necessary for survival in the group, shaping certain patterns of emotional response (Olszewska-Dyonizak 2001).

The basis of customary forest social learning passed on orally and through the activities of parents and individual community members is a decalogue specific to the traditional hunter-gatherer way of life described as the 26 letters of the metaphorical 'Forest Alphabet'. Forest education is one organized and carried out intentionally by adults belonging to a particular group. It deals not only with traditional ways of survival and customs, but also teaches awareness and skills for transitioning from the world of the rainforest and its associated cosmology to the world outside the forest. It introduces also by music (Rouget, Buckner, 2011) the principles of ecological balance, self-defense in threatening situations and methods of how to act in a sustainable way in a rainforest environment that changes with the seasons (Markowska-Manista 2010). Among other things, it teaches how to recognize if a forest path has been walked by a human or animal, how to find wild yam based on the observation of dry leaves, how to extract termites from a termite mound, how to treat illnesses with leaves and bark, how to store fire and start fire with metal and stones, how to weave a raffia mat, how to climb trees, or how to recognize a liana containing clean and cool potable water.

The main goal of traditional Ba'Aka education is therefore to support the child to become an independent adult, a partner in a relationship and a person responsible for his or her family. When children grow up, they will have to interact with their environment, hence the need to acquire skills that will enable them to meet their own needs and those of their families. Initially, during childhood, it is the child's responsibility to learn basic indigenous values. This is an essential requirement in the process of best identifying with the group to which the individual belongs (Hewlett, Lamb, 2009). It is also a requirement to keep the secrets (including taboos) of the group and to be obedient to the 'teachers' and therefore to all adults in matters of group wellbeing.

Traditional Ba'aka upbringing, being the totality of influences and interactions of the social environment (clan, group), has so far met the criteria of an upbringing shaping the development and personality of the child. It was an upbringing that prepared the child for a life in a hunter-gatherer community, a clan in an encampment, grounded in the ideology of a particular upbringing group.

Living for centuries in small groups in the rainforest space, the Ba'Aka were mainly engaged in hunting, gathering and fishing. Their activities changed with the rhythm of the seasons and were based on an unwritten biennial calendar marking the time of gathering and hunting. Traditional education enabled them to prepare medicines for various ailments, read the signs of passing time, the changing seasons (rainy and dry) and decipher the speech of animals, birds, insects and plants. Even today, going into the forest with the Ba'Aka to hunt, forage for fruit or catch fish, one can observe their symbiosis with the environment and the ease with which they read the letters of the forest alphabet and dialogue with nature expressed through singing, especially polyphony (Sarno, 1993).

Ba'aka activities are mostly communal, although different activities (ways of fishing, ways of hunting) are divided according to gender, age and experience gained (Lewis 2017). The children, accompanying their parents on their daily treks to the forest and savannah, learn – depending on the season - to search for and collect edible caterpillars, beetles living in the trunks of dead trees and termites. The boys learn techniques for collecting honey from forest bees, hunting small rodents (e.g. forest rats using self-made traps), and fishing. These treks can be metaphorically compared to shopping expeditions. The forest, like a granary, provides them with the food they needed to satisfy their hunger and the products from which they make their basic tools. The men hunt birds, antelopes, wild pigs, and armadillos, while the women collect edible roots, leaves, insects, snails, fruit and bark. They also used to hunt bongo antelopes and elephants (now under strict protection). Hunting large animals was often linked to an initiation process. The man who hunted the animal became a respected hunter. During the rainy season, the men track and hunt large animals. They are accompanied in these activities by adolescent boys. The Ba'Aka hunt collectively, using self-made nets, spears and arrows. The prey is subject to a traditional division between the hunters who participated in the hunting and killing of the animal and the owners of the nets into which the animal fell.

Today, with the change in Ba'Aka lifestyles and the synergy of many new factors both internal and external, linked to global transformations, also this traditional upbringing and education cannot and does not fulfill its objectives:

The young today can't make nets. There are elders who can pass on this knowledge and skill to them, the problem is that the young are not interested. It is arduous work, a lot of work. It is a long, arduous process to prepare such nets. Maybe that's why, too, these young people don't want to learn, sometimes out of laziness, sometimes they prefer to go through life lightly, or they're more interested in doing casual jobs for Gbay or Mbororo. This is a loss for tradition and a loss for the Ba'Aka themselves. Some parents do not make the effort to teach their children, even though the fathers have the knowledge, they know how it is done. (Father, hunter from Ngeyngey, Ba'Aka, 2012, Central African Republic).

Mission, NGOs Schools, and the ORA Method

The second pathway is an educational proposal of private pre-schools and schools, provided in the form of temporary projects to support the education and access to formal education of marginalized children - the Ba'Aka, as an indigenous population living in the CAR. It is an offer of support in the development of a group most vulnerable to marginalization, discrimination and exploitation in their daily social functioning. Undertaken with the support of NGOs, aid institutions and missions funded by grants and private sponsorship from abroad, it is implemented as grassroots teaching using the ORA method designed to teach children of forest populations who are pre-school and early school age.

The acronym ORA - the name of the teaching method - is derived from French and means: Observer - 'to observe, to reflect', Réfléchir - 'to reflect', Agir - 'to act, to decide' (Markowska-Manista 2020). It was developed by Antoine Huysman, a Dutch monk from the congregation of the School Brothers living in Cameroon based on his observations of the development of traditional teaching. According to its principles, children learn to perceive and understand the world around them, acquire basic reading, writing and counting skills in the decimal system (Huysmans 2014). Education takes place in preparatory schools in several languages (in CAR: the children's familiar dialect, the inter-ethnic official language Sango language and the official language, which is French), where the child learns to count, write, read and speak French at a basic level. This preparation is intended to help children acclimatize to a state school where French is the only language of instruction. This type of supportive education is one of the major objectives of the international project: *Project d'accompagement a l'autopromotion des Pygmees Bayaka en connvivialite avec les populations de la Sangha-Mbaere en Republique Centrafricaine*, CAR implemented since the 1990s among Hunter-gatherers in the Sangha-Mbaéré prefecture in the Central

African Republic. Part of the project's activities targeting children and adolescents is based on a two-year preparation of children in a process of pre-school education utilizing the ORA method.

Similar early childhood education projects are implemented among indigenous populations in South American and Central African countries. In the context of the African continent, ORA-method schools (classes) operate sporadically also in Cameroon and the Democratic Republic of Congo.

ORA is a type of grassroots education, an example of the method of radical emancipatory pedagogy, known in Latin American countries as the educational program of the *Pedagogy of the Oppressed*. Created by Paulo Freire, the concept of education as an instrument of liberation (Freire 2006), has been targeted in practice at groups of poor people living on the margins of society. The method is based on teaching the alphabet and numeracy simultaneously and making people aware of the conditions of poverty and exploitation in which they live. It takes into account the learner and the specificity of his or her socio-cultural environment, carrying the unequivocal message that education is the necessary tool for improvement. In its initial version, implemented in Cameroon and the Central African Republic, it was aimed exclusively at the needs of marginalized Pygmy children. For several decades now, due to the increase in ethnic diversity caused by population movement, it has been used not only by children from forest populations. An important objective pursued through the ORA method is the promotion of indigenous groups, who are treated as inferior in an ethnically heterogeneous environment due to historical backgrounds and strong social inequalities among hunter-gatherers and farmers (Markowska-Manista, 2012; Grinker, 1994). Nowadays, due to increasing internal and external (inter-state) migration, children belonging to different ethnic groups living near and in Ba'Aka villages are taught using this method. This situation places new demands on teachers. It used to be that the teacher taught in a particular in the dialect of a particular hunter-gatherer group, in Sango and in French. Today, as a result of ethnic diversification, there is an increasing need to communicate in the dialects and languages of children belonging to other ethnic groups and to include their cultural specificities in the curriculum. The key of this method today is to bring about changes in social organization through mutual contact, the interactions of all ethnically diverse children who come to ORA schools with a baggage of prejudices and stereotypes about their neighbors. What is important, therefore, is their daily school relationships, learning together, understanding similarities and respecting differences (food, dress, appearance), experiencing (games at break) and being motivated to continue their education. Nevertheless, due to the lack of evaluation and investment in staff preparation and staff support, this approach has also problematic aspects.

In its objectives, ORA is an attempt to implement elementary education based on integrated activities in the preschool area. The results of participatory observation I conducted in the CAR indicate that it is the only integral educational method in this area that incorporates elements of traditional Ba'Aka life and culture into school activities:

- physical activities to introduce the techniques of traditional hunting of various animals;
- theoretical introductory lessons conducted in dialect and in two languages, and practical complementary activities in the form of excursions to the forest, which familiarize children with their traditional habitat, teach them to recognize edible plants and where to find insects, birds and rodents;
- manual activities preceded by theory and analysis of drawings (drawings on the blackboard and in the ORA manuals published by UNESCO) which introduce the methods of traditional basket making, building rodent traps, mongulu huts, etc.

ORA education also addresses the issue of recognizing the Ba'Aka's human rights and self-promotion: showing them the value of their transient culture, which they very often fail to recognize. The human promotion of the Ba'Aka among neighboring ethnic groups is an important element of this education. The hunter-gatherer for centuries bound to other tribes by relations of servitude, are convinced of the need to continue (inherit) this dependence. This conviction makes them pass it on to their own children in intergenerational transmission. Observing daily Ba'Aka –farmer's relations and listening to statements about inter-ethnic relations, one gets the impression that the Ba'Aka are unable to modify these relations, which subordinate their lives to other ethnic groups. The Bantu, on the other hand, do not intend to change this state of affairs and 'free' the Ba'Aka from historical dependencies (Markowska-Manista, 2012). The 'Pygmies', pushed to the margins of social life in Central African societies of poverty and strife, have to some extent internalized the inferiority of their unique culture, intangible heritage and the imperfection of their biological structure (see Fanon 1985). This is another paradox, which highlights the power relations of dominant groups and makes one notice the gaps in the ORA method, which, after all, was also designed to promote the values of indigenous community culture among dominant communities and thus to dialogue and counteract inequality and social stratification.

School Education: The Official Curriculum and Its Challenges

Schools in the official system do not give proper attention to the values of cultural heritage of minorities but instead erode indigenous knowledge. The lack of connectivity between indigenous knowledge, forest social learning and education in official curricula further reinforces the educational and social exclusion of the Ba'Aka. Increasing inequalities, lack of future prospects and the inability to return to traditional lifestyles are denying the young Ba'Aka, Aka, Baka generation the chance to develop and participate in the multi-ethnic societies of central African countries. Successively, through decades of denial of their identity and cultural existence, they were excluded from the benefits of postmodernist development (Pemunta, 2013). As a vital factor of the rainforest ecosystem, these indigenous communities need protection (taking into account their indigene solutions of social justice, balance in the area of use of goods and riches of nature and knowledge of its needs) and support in their daily lives and the conditions necessary for the survival of their own community. However, daily life is changing faster than their adaptive capacity.

In the changing conditions of daily socio-cultural and economic functioning, Ba'Aka youth need an education that enables them to acquire literacy and numeracy skills as well as practical knowledge related to providing food and shelter - a roof over their heads - for themselves and their future families, thus education based on the letters of the forest alphabet. However, the Ba'Aka themselves as well as the organizations and missions supporting them do not quite know how to motivate and convince children and young people to go to school, which no longer participates as strongly as it once did in the process of traditional forest education. Statements from Ba'Aka parents (people around 40 years old who attended state schools in the late 1970s), already brought up in village structures rather than in forest settlements, indicate that there is a great need for schooling among indigenous community and a need for practical preparation for boys and girls based on traditional Ba'Aka education. Parents whose children have completed pre-school education using the ORA method point to its advantages and disadvantages, including its value for adult life and its facilitation in navigating a socially, ethnically and socially diverse environment

Thanks to that [Researcher: that, I was at school] I saw that I could become a person among others, it improved my self-esteem. Today, I pass on the same to my children. (Ba'Aka's father, 2012, Monasao, Central African Republic).

Ba'Aka parents see the opportunities that education provides: *School is a good thing. If you can read and count, it's easier for you later in life (Ba'Aka's mother, 2012, Monasao, Central African Republic).* They recognize the significant changes that schooling brings to their lives and the lives of their neighbors: *I can read the news; I can translate information from French into Mbendzele; I can count myself how much someone owes me for work done. If I find some diamonds I try to estimate their value myself; I can cultivate a field because I know how it should be done.*

Parents who use today what they learned at school as children are also aware of how the rapid changes in their living environment are preventing them from continuing their nomadic lifestyle and preparing their children for a life based on traditional education. They also face difficulties finding their way in the changes taking place (unemployment, increasing social disparities) and maintaining their Ba'Aka identity (their own and their children's). Still, despite the progressive changes, the dominant Ba'Aka group living in the Sangha Mbaere region lives on less than half a dollar a day. The barriers to the development of adults and children, as well as their limited opportunities to participate in state education, are not only due to individual difficulties in adapting to the realities of life in the 21st century and to political and legal constraints introducing stricter environmental regulations in which they could live until recently. Cultural, historical and socio-economic conditions also influence their perception of their needs and quality of life as citizens. For they are citizens of one of the paradoxically richest - poorest countries on the African continent. Despite its rich deposits of gold, diamonds and uranium, the Central African Republic has ranked penultimate among the world's poorest countries in the Human Development Index over the last decade (Human Development Report 2020). It is noteworthy that between 1990 and 2019 "mean years of schooling increased by 2.2 years and expected years of schooling increased by 2.3 years" (Human Development Report 2020: 2).

CONCLUSION

F. Fanon (1961) wrote that the colonized man will lose if he does not make a detailed analysis of his colonial situation in the context of being colonized. In the situation in which the Ba'Aka now find themselves, the tentacles of colonization make us all losers, as the indigeneous, useful knowledge of human survival in symbiosis with nature is being forgotten.

The systemic and non-systemic dimensions of entanglement and the prejudices passed down from generation to generation relating to the Ba'Aka seem to be so deeply ingrained in Central African communities that many do not even question the social stratification they face. The era of colonialism in Central Africa contributed to further (post-colonial) relations based on coercive conditions, related to the inequalities and intractable ties that have been constituted between hunter-gatherer and their neighbors. Its product is also Western stereotypical perceptions of 'Pygmies', which have been formed on the basis of colonial relations (from a European perspective) rather than on the basis of attempts to understand or accept information from representatives of hunter-gatherer culture.

In the 21st century, this indigenous community is confronted with a whole set of phenomena resulting from the globalization process: the transition from the hunting, gathering and agricultural stage to the hitherto little-known era of trade, information transmission and services (until now, they exchanged forest products). In the case of the difficulties piling up for the Ba'Aka of the equatorial forest, the transformation associated with forest exploitation and/or the creation and expansion of protected forest areas is an additional factor that excludes them from social participation. Ancient forest dwellers are confronted with these phenomena unexpectedly and without preparation. They do not know how to live outside the forest in an environment of dominant and more powerful 'Others'. This results not only in a process of social exclusion, but also in adaptation to living in extremely marginal conditions and sometimes conditions that are beneath human dignity. Customary laws and state legislations regarding the rights of possession and access to the forest of hunter-gatherers are in conflict.

The unequal distribution of income, the growing disparities, the lack of development prospects and the impossibility of returning to traditional lifestyles are damaging the chances of the young generation, including the Ba'Aka youth, to develop and participate in the multi-ethnic societies of central African countries. The 'Pygmies', perceived in the world of mass culture as a relic of old times, are an essential part of the rainforest ecosystem, hence they need support in their daily lives and the conditions necessary for the survival of their traditions and opportunities for participation in society and education. The scarcity of information available on the situation and opportunities for children's development, limited mainly to fragmentary reports from international organizations, contributes to the invisibility and scant presence in international discourse of the challenges faced by children from indigenous communities. The problems of children and adolescents also stem from a lack of perspectives and social malaise, hence they require a broader perspective and positioning in the current situation of the lives of the people of the Central African Republic. In the CAR, the vast majority of young people from the regions (outside the capital city) who complete primary or secondary education have no chance of obtaining a well-paid job.

The educational pathways described above, as a result of the rapidly and unevenly progressing processes of deforestation, resettlement, displacement, migration, as well as the strong, deepening global dependencies and the occurrence of ethnic conflicts in the region and the historical burden of feudal relations between 'Pygmies' and Bantu – hunter-gatherers and farmers (Bahuchet, Guillaume1982), often present a dissonance for the contemporary Ba'Aka family. The 'Pygmies' would like to continue living a traditional life with the opportunity to participate in education and civilizational development in the 21st century taking into account their history and knowledge. Therefore, they stand at a crossroads, looking for the optimal solution for a better future for their children in ethical symmetry with nature. Often, the choice falls on taking up a parallel position in the types of education described in the text. This causes dilemmas: do you take your child into the forest, to hunt and impart a traditional forest education based on respect for the material and immaterial worlds? Or send them to school at the same time for numeracy, reading and writing lessons in a system that colonizes their identity and cultural heritage?

Who the Ba'Aka will soon become - whether they remain faithful to forest education or fit into a universally applicable system - depends at the same time on how much they are able to decide for themselves, their places and spaces of everyday life, and on what - and to what extent - other participants in the socio-political system will allow them to define and participate in.

ACKNOWLEDGMENT

The text would not have been possible without the opportunity to conduct field research among the Ba'Aka in the Central African Republic, for which I, as a researcher, offer my sincere thanks. I would also like to thank Aleksandra Borzecka for her unfailing and irreplaceable support regarding language correction in the important topic of education.

REFERENCES

Adichie, C. N. (2009). *The danger of a single story*. Retrieved June, 2022 from https://www.ted.com/talks/chimamanda_ngozi_adichie_the_danger_of_a_single_story?language=pl

Ahluwalia, P. (2000). Towards (re)conciliation: The post-colonial economy of giving. *Social Identities*, 6(1), 29–48. doi:10.1080/13504630051345

Bahuchet, S., & Guillaume, H. (1982). Aka-farmer Relations in the Northwest Congo Basin. In E. Leacock & R. B. Lee (Eds.), *Politics and History in Band Societies* (pp. 189–211). Cambridge University Press.

Blanchard, P., Bancel, N., Boëtsch, G., Deroo, É., Lemaire, S., & Forsdick, C. (Eds.). (2008). *Human Zoos: Science and Spectacle in the Age of Colonial Empires*. Liverpool University Press.

Boyette, A. H., Lew-Levy, S., Jang, H., & Kandza, V. (2022). Social ties in the Congo Basin: insights into tropical forest adaptation from BaYaka and their neighbours. *Philosophical Transactions of the Royal Society B, 377*(1849), 20200490.

Bradford, P. V., & Blume, H. (1992). *Ota Benga: The Pygmy in the Zoo*. St Martin's Press.

Datta, R. (2018). Decolonizing both researcher and research and its effectiveness in Indigenous research. *Research Ethics Review*, 14(2), 1–24. doi:10.1177/1747016117733296

Fanon, F. (2004). *The Wretched of the Earth. 1961* (R. Philcox, Trans.). Grove Press.

Freire, P. (2006). Pedagogy of the Oppressed (30th ann. ed.). Continuum International Publishing Group.

Grinker, R. R. (1994). *Houses in the Rainforest: Ethnicity and Inequality among Farmers and Foragers in Central Africa*. University of California Press. doi:10.1525/9780520915664

Grinker, R. R. (2001). *In the Arms of Africa: The Life of Colin M*. Turnbull.

Hewlett, B. (2021). Social learning and innovation in adolescence: A comparative study of Aka and Chabu hunter-gatherers of Central and Eastern Africa. *Human Nature (Hawthorne, N.Y.)*, 32(1), 239–278. doi:10.100712110-021-09391-y PMID:33881734

Hewlett, B. S., & Lamb, M. E. (2009). *Hunter-Gatherer Childhoods. Evolutionary, Developmental & Cultural Perspectives*. Transaction.

Hewlett, S. B. (2000). Central African Government's and International NGOs' perceptions of Baka Pygmy development. In Hunter-Gatherers in the modern world (pp. 381–390). New York: Berghahn.

Human Development Report. (2020). Retrieved June, 2022 from https://hdr.undp.org/sites/default/files/Country-Profiles/CAF.pdf

Huysmans, A. J. (2014). *Guide Lecture ORA* [copies of materials from SMA's Monasao mission library]. Central African Republic.

Ichikawa, M. (1996). The co-existence of man and nature in the African rain forest. In R. Ellen & K. Fukui (Eds.), *Redefining Nature. Ecology, Culture and Domestication* (pp. 467–492). Berg.

Khan, F. R., Westwood, R., & Boje, D. M. (2010). 'I feel like a foreign agent': NGOs and corporate social responsibility interventions into Third World child labor. *Human Relations, 63*(9), 1417–1438. doi:10.1177/0018726709359330

Kohler, A. (2005). Of Apes and men: Baka and Bantu attitudes to wildlife and the making of eco-goodies and baddies. *Conservation & Society, 3*(2), 407–435.

Köhler, A., & Lewis, J. (2002). Putting Hunter-Gatherer and Farmer Relations in Perspective. A Commentary from Central Africa. In S. Kent (Ed.), *Ethnicity, Huntergatherers, and the "Other": Association or Assimilation in Southern Africa?* (pp. 276–305). Smithsonian Institute.

Koulaninga, A. (2009). *L'Education chez les pygmées de Centrafrique*. L'Harmattan.

Lew-Levy, S., Reckin, R., Lavi, N., Cristóbal-Azkarate, J., & Ellis-Davies, K. (2017/28). How Do Hunter-Gatherer Children Learn Subsistence Skills? *Human Nature (Hawthorne, N.Y.), 28*(4), 367–394. doi:10.100712110-017-9302-2 PMID:28994008

Lewis, J. (2017). Egalitarian social organization: The case of the Mbendjele BaYaka. In B. S. Hewlett (Ed.), *Hunter-Gathers of the Congo Basin* (pp. 219–244). Routledge. doi:10.4324/9780203789438-8

Magnat, V. (2020). Towards a Performative Ethics of Reciprocity. In N. K. Denzin & M. D. Giardina (Eds.), *Qualitative Inquiry and the Politics of Resistance Possibilities, Performances, and Praxis* (pp. 115–129). Routledge. doi:10.4324/9780429316982-8

Markowska-Manista, U. (2012). Obszary dyskryminacji i marginalizacji Pigmejów w Afryce Środkowej. In K. Jarecka-Stępień & J. Kościółek (Eds.), *Problemy współczesnej Afryki. Szanse i wyzwania na przyszłość* (pp. 83–97). Wyd. Księgarnia Akademicka.

Markowska-Manista, U. (2014). Kolonialne i postkolonialne uwikłania łowców-zbieraczy w Afryce Środkowej. *Przegląd Humanistyczny, 446*(05), 33–45.

Markowska-Manista, U. (2016). "Invisible" and "unheard" children in fragile contexts–reflections from field research among the Ba'Aka in the Central African Republic. *Problemy Wczesnej Edukacji, 35*(4), 39–50. doi:10.5604/01.3001.0009.7629

Markowska-Manista, U. (2017). The Written and Unwritten Rights of Indigenous Children in Central Africa – Between the Freedom of "Tradition" and Enslavement for "Development". In A. Odrowąż-Coates & S. Goswami (Eds.), *Symbolic Violence in Socio-educational Contexts* (pp. 127–142). Wydawnictwo Akademii Pedagogiki Specjalnej.

Markowska-Manista, U. (2019). Postcolonial dimensions of social work in the Central African Republic and its impact on the life of hunter-gatherer children and youth–a critical perspective. In T. Kleibl, R. Lutz, N. Noyoo, B. Bunk, A. Dittmann, & B. Seepamore (Eds.), *The Routledge Handbook of Postcolonial Social Work* (pp. 286–301). Routledge.

Markowska-Manista, U. (2020). The life of Ba'Aka children and their rights: Between the processes of poverty and deprivation. In D. Lawson, D. Angemi, & I. Kasirye (Eds.), *What Works for Africa's Poorest Children: From measurement to action* (pp. 287–301). Practical Action Publishing.

Mayer, R. (2002). *Artificial Africa's: Colonial Images in the Times of Globalization*. University Press of New England.

Mowforth, M., & Munt, I. (2009). *Tourism and Sustainability. Development, globalisation and new tourism in the Third World*. Routledge.

Munn, P. (2010). Children as active participants in their own development and ECE professionals as conscious actors. *International Journal of Early Years Education, 18*(4), 281–282. doi:10.1080/09669 760.2010.535325

Okoth, A. A. (2006). *History of Africa: African societies and the establishment of colonial rule, 1800-1915* (Vol. 1). East African Publishers Ltd.

Paris, D. (2011). "A friend who understand fully:" Notes on humanizing research on a multiethnic youth community. *International Journal of Qualitative Studies in Education: QSE, 24*(2), 137–149. doi:10.1 080/09518398.2010.495091

Pemunta, N. V. (2013). The governance of nature as development and the erasure of the Pygmies of Cameroon. *GeoJournal, 78*(2), 353–371. doi:10.100710708-011-9441-7

Pittas, P. (2011). Questioning Who We Are While Reading Ota Benga, The Pygmy in the Zoo and Joseph Conrad's Heart of Darkness. *Ágora, 20*, 1–2.

Reyes, C. C., Haines, S. J., & Clark, K. (2021). *Humanizing methodologies in educational research: Centering non-dominant communities*. Teachers College Press.

Rouget, G., & Buckner, M. (2011). Musical efficacy: Musicking to survive — The case of the pygmies. *Yearbook for Traditional Music, 43*, 89-121.

Said, E. W. (1995). *Orientalism*. Penguin.

Salali, G. D., Chaudhary, N., Bouer, J., Thompson, J., Vinicius, L., & Migliano, A. B. (2019). Development of social learning and play in BaYaka hunter-gatherers of Congo. *Scientific Reports, 9*(1), 1–10. doi:10.103841598-019-47515-8 PMID:31367002

Sarno, L. (1993). *Song from the forest. My life among the Ba-Benjellé Pygmies*. Bantam Press.

Saunders, R. A. (2019). Reimagining the colonial wildersness: 'Africa', imperialism and the geographical legerdemain of the Vorrh. *Cultural Geographies, 26*(2), 177–194. doi:10.1177/1474474018811669

Scalise Sugiyama, M. (2017). Oral storytelling as evidence of pedagogy in forager societies. *Frontiers in Psychology, 8*, 1–11. doi:10.3389/fpsyg.2017.00471 PMID:28424643

Szarfenberg, R. (2006). *Marginalizacja i wykluczenie społeczne. Wykłady*. Retrieved June, 2022 from http://www.owes.info.pl/biblioteka/wyklad_wykluczenie_spoleczne.pdf

Turnbull, M. C. (1974). *The Forest People*. Book Club Associates.

KEY TERMS AND DEFINITIONS

Forest Alphabet: the Ba'Aka traditional social learning, collective education traditionally based on oral transmission and storytelling.

Fragile Context of Everyday Life: Living conditions which have become difficult, and precarious due to climate change, deforestation, increasing marginalisation and discrimination against indigenous communities, as opposed to the past when the conditions were secure and enabled survival on the basis of traditional knowledge and established daily living strategies.

Indigenous Community Social Learning: Based on four pillars of collective coexistence. It involves learning the methods and strategies of obtaining food, learning the principles of cooperation and assimilating a common social life, understanding cosmology and the philosophy of living in harmony with nature and the natural rights of man as part of the natural world.

ORA Method: (Observer - 'to observe, to reflect', Réfléchir - 'to reflect', Agir - 'to act, to decide') designed to teach Ba'Aka indigenous children who are pre-school and early school age, integrating the indigeneous knowledge they know with new knowledge (basics of writing, counting, speaking in the official language – here in French).

Twenty-Six Letters of the Forest Alphabet: The process of transforming the knowledge and developing diverse abilities and skills in the area of forest education, concentrated on crucial steps for the survival of the indigenous community with its cultural heritage.

ENDNOTE

[1] "The colonial time neologism of 'Pygmy', although derogatory, is a collective identity for several linguistically diverse ethnic groups characterized by their small stature. The 'pygmies' are hunter-gatherer societies living in the equatorial rainforests across Central Africa" (Pemunta 2013: 334).

Section 6
Language, Literacy, and Culture

Chapter 15
Developing Intercultural Awareness Through a Pedadogy of Multiliteracies

Angela Yicely Castro Garces
Universidad del Cauca, Colombia

ABSTRACT

The language classroom as a space for reflection, interaction, and enactment calls for language teaching and learning that makes meaning and prepares intercultural communicators who value local knowledge, are sensitive to diversity, and are aware of their global community. This work aims to examine the role of a pedagogy of multiliteracies in the development of pre-service teachers' intercultural awareness. This study was conducted with a group of 12 pre-service teachers at a state university in Colombia. It was based on a pedagogy of multiliteracies, through the knowledge processes, approached from a qualitative interpretive case study perspective. The findings indicate that connecting personal experiences to those of others through global literacies and multimodal tasks helped develop intercultural awareness in relation to issues of ethnicity, gender, physical ability, and social class, thus expanding participants' limited nationalist perspective and taking them to embrace a more intersectional view of others.

INTRODUCTION

Intercultural communication and the emergence of new literacy practices have permeated all aspects of our lives. This is why preparing ourselves to understand, tolerate, and coexist in a friendly manner is urgent in this shrinking world where differences are to be seen as opportunities for sharing and complementing each other. Accordingly, "the globalization of the world community inevitably leads to cultural diversity" (Chen & Starosta, 1998, p. 29). Thus, the integration of teaching practices that foster intercultural awareness through strategic pedagogical practices that consider context and learners' realities is deemed necessary.

In view of that, in foreign language classrooms, it is essential to increase intercultural awareness (Baker, 2011; Chen & Starosta, 1998) to go beyond verbocentric views of language (Álvarez Valencia, 2016a;

DOI: 10.4018/978-1-6684-5022-2.ch015

Kress, 2000) and to include diverse literacy practices (Cope & Kalantzis, 2009; The New London Group, 1996) that favor intercultural understandings. A pedagogy of multiliteracies fosters the understanding of the multimodal nature of texts (Álvarez Valencia, 2016b) and global literature as identity cultural markers (Short et al., 2016). This work adds to the multiliteracies engagement to gain intercultural awareness for current and future teaching practices, thus contributing to teacher education that is more context-bound (Kumaravadivelu, 2001) and that values local knowledge (Canagarajah, 2005).

Additionally, the inclusion of multiple forms of reading and writing that favor "alternative and multicultural texts" (Mora, 2011, p. 3), expands our notion of literacy to an inclusive practice derived from the learners' needs, which can only be possible by considering their own realities, contexts, and life experiences, or what Freire (1987) would name reading the world. Equally, Freire (1987) maintains that "reading does not consist merely of decoding the written word or language; rather, it is preceded by and intertwined with knowledge of the world" (p. 29).

The goal of this chapter is to examine role of a pedagogy of multiliteracies in the development of pre-service teachers' intercultural awareness. It is based on a pedagogy of multiliteracies, through the knowledge processes, approached from a qualitative interpretive case study perspective.

BACKGROUND

The Intercultural Dimension and Intercultural Awareness

The study of intercultural communication has contributed to the development of interlinguistic and intercultural understanding, helping break social and geographic boundaries and build relationships among peoples of diverse origins. It has also brought about research agendas developed by advocates from different disciplines to advance the foreign language teaching (FLT) field. The terms vary according to the focus that diverse authors give to intercultural studies, including intercultural communication (Coulby, 2006; Hua, 2016), intercultural understanding (Kramsch, 2013), intercultural competence (Bennett, 1993; Bennet & Bennet, 2004; Deardorff, 2006; Liddicoat & Scarino, 2013), intercultural communicative competence (Byram, 1997; Byram et al., 2002), intercultural awareness, sensitivity and adroitness (Chen & Starosta, 1998), and cross-cultural communication (Bennett & Bennett, 2004; Woodin, 2016). Specifically, Chen and Starosta (1998) define intercultural awareness as the "cognitive aspect of intercultural communication competence that refers to the understanding of cultural conventions that affect how we think and behave" (Chen & Starosta, 1998, p. 28).

Additionally, Kramsch (2009) examines the intercultural dimension as central to the constitution of the subjective dimensions of language users. She maintains that "the subject is a symbolic entity that is constituted and maintained through symbolic systems such as language" (p. 13). Kramsch remarks that these subjective dimensions require particular sensitivity on the part of the language teacher and states that "pedagogies that reduce language to its informational value, be it grammatical, social, or cultural information, miss an important dimension of the language learning experience" (2009, p. 11). That means that language teachers are to create spaces in which the language can be meaningful so that it does not play a mere instrumental role, but becomes an important and intrinsic element of the language learner, with which they can solve real-life situations and live significant experiences.

Literacy and Multiliteracies

Literacy, defined by Street (2013) as social practices of reading and writing, has undergone shifts with the advance of technology, the different sociocultural changes of a globalized and globalizing world, and the recognition of the role of different modes of communication in the construction of meaning. Nevertheless, its early development was situated between the cognitive (text-level reading comprehension and its linguistic components) and social practices (what readers can do with the texts they approach). Street (2013), as an advocate for reading and writing that has a purpose on people's lives, contrasted autonomous and ideological models of literacy. His work discusses the oral and written traditions in non-schooled and schooled communities and how each influences their cognitive and social development.

Aligned to this, Cope and Kalantzis (2000) question that "literacy pedagogy has traditionally meant teaching and learning to read and write in page-bound, official, standard forms of the national language" (p. 9). They "attempt to broaden this understanding of literacy and literacy teaching and learning to include negotiating a multiplicity of discourses" (p. 9). Their approach to literacy provides a broader perspective that includes multiple modes of communication for a multisensory experience while considering globalism and diversity. They argue that "we are agents of meaning-making. Thus, it is essential to use a didactic literacy pedagogy that proposes a deeper approach to reading and interpreting meaning that considers the design of a variety of texts and ways of communicating" (p. 12).

Although initially developed for L1 contexts, a pedagogy of ML has been widely adapted to foreign language learning (Boche, 2014; Hepple et al., 2014; Kim & Omerbašić, 2017; Losada & Suaza, 2018; Luke, 2000; Medina et al., 2015; Meng, 2016; Michelson & Dupuy, 2014; Michelson, 2018), thanks to the wealth of possibilities it brings for interaction, real-life communication, and meaning-making in the language classroom. Through a pedagogy of ML, I encouraged PSTs to experience, conceptualize, analyze, and apply, following the Knowledge Processes proposed by Cope and Kalantzis (2006). The knowledge processes are the materialization of a pedagogy of ML in terms of being a practical guide to welcome reflection and action in a language class.

As foreign language teachers, we ought to engage our students with the language they are learning by exposing them to alternative pedagogies that are inclusive of diversity to expand their horizons and connect language with communities and different forms of life. As stated by Kramsch (2009), "the most important gift we can give our students is to explore with them (not for them) the immense wealth of meanings opened up by the language we teach" (p. 207).

Studies in the foreign language university classroom highlight it as a context for developing intercultural awareness. Some authors have developed models and processes for introducing cultural awareness (Baker, 2011; Boghian, 2016; Rappel, 2009), and others have explored the conditions, beliefs, and understandings for intercultural awareness to be developed (Liu, 2016; Wang, 2014). In fact, Liu (2016) endorses the language and culture liaison and inter-dependability through the development of a study in the Chinese context with university EFL students who have been mostly exposed to language grammar in their classes. She explores students' condition and attitudes towards intercultural communication and the sources from where knowledge and awareness are constructed.

Additionally, Clavijo (2000, 2007) has inquired into the role of literacy at different levels of education, reflecting upon primary school students, pre-service, and in-service teachers' understandings of literacy practices and the need to integrate school subjects to nurture more meaningful literacy practices. Alternatively, Rincón and Clavijo (2016) implemented community-based pedagogies to bring literacies closer to students' local realities. They affirm that "the inquiry that students did in their communities unfolded a wide variety of multimodal ways to represent their findings" (p. 77), which allowed for meaningful learning and more context-based language learning.

Alternatively, Kramsch (2013) reflects on subjectivity, otherness, a third place, and the integration of literature and communication in language teaching, which is in line with Pavlenko (2014), who, from a view of language and cognition, has also scrutinized the discursive world of individuals interacting in more than one language. These discourses are interpreted based on their stories and "narrative worlds" (p. 207), thus delving into communication practices that move between more than one language and are deemed intercultural. Additionally, Liddicoat and Scarino (2013) indicate that awareness emerges from the interrelation between language and culture in intercultural communication and meaning-making. They highlight the role of learners as interpreters of meaning who make connections, reflect, and interact socially.

MAIN FOCUS OF THE CHAPTER

This study is grounded in a social constructivist paradigm, which understands that meaning is constructed subjectively and that "intercultural differences and cultural memberships are socially constructed" (Hua, 2016, p. 12). This view aligns with the idea of learning for life and the construction of knowledge through experience (Honebein, 1996). Social constructivism, as an epistemological perspective, informs this study by providing participants with opportunities for knowledge construction and the development of intercultural awareness.

A social constructivist epistemology also connects with some of the principles of a pedagogy of Multiliteracies (ML). In particular, ML draws from constructivism in that it understands learning as the negotiation and construction of meanings that are also tied to identities. It acknowledges the multiple sources of knowledge construction and representation and their mediatory role in human development. This is why ML takes a broader view of the human representational process and considers a broad range of semiotic resources or modes of meaning-making people deploy in contemporary communications environments (Cope & Kalantzis 2009; The New London Group, 1996). In this regard, this study is carried out based on a pedagogy of ML that focuses on "modes of representation much broader than language alone, which differ according to culture, and context, and have specific cognitive, cultural, and social effects" (Cope & Kalantzis, 2009, p. 4).

This study was carried out during an academic semester at Universidad del Cauca, a State-funded University in Colombia, located in Popayán, the capital city of the Department of Cauca. The Department of Cauca has a very diverse population with people coming from Indigenous, Afrocolombian, and Mestizo backgrounds. The participants were a group of twelve pre-service teachers (PSTs) who came from this diverse background and thus curriculum was planned to be inclusive of that diversity.

This section exemplifies how a pedagogy of ML contributed to the development of PSTs' intercultural awareness. This was done by approaching global literature (Short et al., 2016) with an ML perspective (Cope & Kalantzis, 2000) through reading global stories and watching global documentaries. Additionally, I completed a journal to document my observations of all instances in which PSTs engaged with a pedagogy of multiliteracies and to analyze how these practices were likely to be connected to the development of intercultural awareness. Engaging with a pedagogy of ML brought possibilities for exploring new knowledge and gaining language and cultural insights; that is, the three Ms—multilingual, multicultural, and multimodal—view of literacy (Cope & Kalantzis, 2000).

Books with a multicultural and global perspective were chosen in order to provide rich opportunities for PSTs to discuss topics of concern to specific cultural groups around the globe and, in this way, open the doors for activating intercultural awareness. A careful selection of fictional and non-fictional books was possible thanks to a large list of global books previously gathered by Worlds of Words. This is an academic organization made up of a community of scholars and chaired by Dr. Kathy Short that examines "the potential of global literature for building intercultural understanding" (2016, p. vii). They evaluate books for cultural authenticity of the specific cultural groups the books portray, under the premise that "there is never one image of life within a group" (Short et al., 2016, p. 327). They raise awareness that books should have identity markers from cultures without falling under prejudices and stereotypes.

Through these books, PSTs developed global to global and global to local intercultural awareness. Short et al. (2016) propose that in global-to-global connections, "readers connect one culture to another," and in global to local connections, "readers connect global events to their own context" (p. 302). As part of reading and making sense of the books read, I developed a series of multimodal tasks to engage PSTs with a pedagogy of ML, mediated by and analyzed through the knowledge processes (Kalantzis & Cope, 2016).

To document and analyze PSTs' work on multimodal tasks, I grouped their answers and provided vignettes from individual voices by giving them pseudonyms, as an example, I present excerpts from Isabella, Dario, Paula, Ana, Manuel, and Andrea. Then the following categories, which show their engagement with a pedagogy of ML resulted. Table 1 presents the books and documentary approached, the author and origin, as well as the categories that came out after grouping and analyzing information.

Table 1. Global books read

Book / Documentary	Author and Origin	Multimodal Task Description	Categories of Analysis
Guji Guji	Chen (2004) Taiwan	Engaging students with diversity through a pedagogy of ML	Diversifying students' view
Sosu's Call	Asare (2002) Ghana		
The Danger of a Single Story	Adichie (2009)		Challenging stereotypes

Source: Author

Engaging Students With Diversity Through a Pedagogy of ML

In this section, I present how I engaged PSTs with diversity through multimodal texts and the pedagogy of ML. Afterwards, I introduce the types of engagement they underwent in the process. By reading *Guji Guji, Sosu's Call*, and by watching *The Danger of a Single Story*, I engaged PSTs with a pedagogy of ML. I encouraged them to Experience, Conceptualize, Analyze, and Apply, following the Knowledge Processes (Kalantzis & Cope, 2016).

The story of Guji Guji portrays a crocodile growing up amidst ducks. Although he might look physically different, what matters for him is the closeness they have developed and how they have learned to live in the difference. Despite being invited by a group of crocodiles to betray the ducks, through his actions, he demonstrates that family ties are beyond blood.

Multimodal task: PSTs experienced an intercultural situation by reading the story in groups. They identified the roles and moral values of the characters in the story by writing phrases that described the feelings they had while reading. These phrases opened a discussion, which they continued by conceptualizing and analyzing with specific excerpts from the story. They reasoned around these phrases relating them to intercultural groups. As a class, they were one intercultural group because of their affiliations to different groups. Every PST had the opportunity to mention group affiliations (social class, ethnic, gender, sex) they had and to share anecdotes as members of one or more groups. They also analyzed how the roles of each character in the story and their behavior had an impact on others.

In the end, students recreated the situation lived by the story's characters by applying the knowledge co-constructed. To meet this purpose, they had to write and perform a story based on their own life experiences, coming up with alternative solutions to include people who, in their opinion, were treated differently on the basis of any social marker (class, gender, ethnicity, etc.). Each group talked about different situations they had experienced and finally agreed to represent the one they found more appealing. They were excited and entertained preparing their performances and negotiating as a group to provide ideas that resembled the situation lived by Guji Guji, but now from their own perspective.

The story of Guji Guji raised identity awareness in them. PSTs were excited and touched by their partners' performances and messages. Sensitivity, inclusion, group work, belonging, identity construction, and tolerance were part of their discourse, which raised more intercultural awareness on them.

Sosu's call: He is just one of the boys of the small village, somewhere between the sea and the lagoon! Sosu lives with his family on a small island between the sea and a lagoon, and all he wants is to feel like a normal boy. "What use is a boy without a pair of good strong legs?" His dad does all he can to include Sosu in the routines of the village, but the elders worry that his presence will displease the Lagoon Spirit. Sosu cannot walk to school and so stays home and plays with Fusa, the family dog, while his family goes off to work or school. When a storm threatens to destroy the village, Sosu finds the strength and courage to drag himself to the shed where the village drums were kept. He beats out a loud warning that brings the village running back to rescue those left behind. Sosu's stature rises as media attention puts him and Fusa in the spotlight, and with the attention comes a wheelchair that allows Sosu to attend school (Asare, 2002, reviewed by Miller, 2002 -Worlds of Words).

Multimodal task: Analyzing Sosu's story woke up PSTs' feelings and reactions because they could compare this story to that of people they knew and provide alternatives for including Sosu in the school and in the community. They went through the steps of the knowledge processes randomly, experiencing, conceptualizing, analyzing, applying, experiencing, and analyzing again. This time they went back and forth while developing the activities I proposed. To start, they experienced and conceptualized Sosu's story by working around Sosu's image.

PSTs' described what they observed in the image. These descriptions showed how their views of the characters were informed by the image they analyzed. Next, they watched a video about people who had struggled and finally succeeded in life despite their disabilities. They wrote their takes on the video based on the following instructions:

Watch the video: *Top 10 Most Successful People with Disabilities*. Have you heard about any of these people before? Watching about these people made them continue their experiencing and conceptualizing process. In this way, the next statement was to write the words or phrases that came to their mind while they were watching the video. PSTs remarked positive aspects they became aware of by watching this video or related it to their background experience. It was good to see them touched by the stories presented, which related to the next question: Which story touched you the most? Explain. Afterwards, they analyzed and applied by answering the following questions: Do you know people with a special condition? How are their lives similar or different from the cases just seen?

Later, we went back to experience by reading Sosu's story. I asked PSTs to write a list of the words or expressions that referred to inclusion, exclusion, or caring, identified in the video of people with disabilities, Sosu's story, or from their own lexicon. After that, we analyzed specific parts of Sosu's story that they felt touched by. Finally, PSTs applied knowledge by proposing strategies to include people like Sosu in a school classroom.

The Danger of a Single Story: The problem with stereotypes is not that they are untrue, but that they are incomplete (Adichie, 2009).

Chimamanda Adichie, a Nigerian storyteller, invites us to reflect upon our understanding of others as people who have a voice and to read the world critically, welcoming different views and diverse stories. This TED Talk encourages people to hear the stories of others told in first person –not read from biased standpoints.

After developing a series of multimodal tasks around these three stories, PSTs' interactions and key phrases that marked their discussions and unveiled their gains in terms of diversifying their views of others were documented. The multimodal approach favored engagement with a pedagogy of ML through a variety of modes that encouraged the intercultural approach of texts to bring possibilities for reflecting about other realities and other views of the world. This plethora of possibilities exposed PSTs to multiple semiotic resources, taking advantage of the technological possibilities they had at hand. It was inclusive of all areas of design -linguistic, audio, spatial, gestural, visual, and multimodal (The New London Group, 1996), which derived in making semiotic and symbolic meaning (Pantaleo, 2005).

Diversifying Students' Views

PSTs engaged and connected with the stories read and watched because of their diverse and intercultural nature. Reflecting upon the sources of information of the stories and analyzing moments lived by the characters allowed them to experience, conceptualize, analyze, and apply. We started conceptualizing and building a critical framework by critically engaging in the analysis of phrases such as: "A rather odd-looking duckling hatched", which not only generated knowledge but were mainly a way to trigger discussion and analysis of group belonging and identity. In this line, they engaged with a pedagogy of ML that encouraged the discussion of complex and multiple identities, taking language learning beyond its informational value to live a meaningful experience (Kramsch, 2009).

To put it another way, knowledge served to transform limiting concepts of family, friendship, and other relationships by analyzing phrases such as: "No matter what they looked like, mother duck loved all her ducklings the same." This analysis engaged PSTs in understanding and discussing the experiences lived and the reactions and roles of each character in the story. They also compared and critically analyzed how they would react if they were in a similar situation by sharing anecdotes and group affiliations. The recreation of real-life episodes is supported by Michelson and Dupuy's (2014) work on global simulations in a language class, which was done to have students feel what life was like while embracing someone else's identity and cultural practices living multilingual and ML experiences.

To better illustrate this point, here figure 1 portrays a picture of PSTS' design of a multimodal task, in which they worked in groups to draw and perform stories that depicted inclusion and diversity.

Figure 1. The rose and the tomato
Source: Group 1

Group 1 recreated the life of a rose that was growing up amidst tomatoes, thinking she was a tomato. Many told her that she would never be a tomato because she was long and tasteless, while they were round and juicy. This group awoke sensitivity in their partners by teaching them the importance of tolerating others in the difference (Researcher's journal, February 10, 2020).

Figure 2. Tools in a carpentry
Source: Group 4

Group 4 performed a puppets show about tools in a carpentry (See Figure 2 above). They highlighted the role of each tool and how important each one felt, but at the end concluded how they were meant to be together, appreciate each other, and share in the difference (Researcher's journal, February 10, 2020).

In a similar fashion, by analyzing Sosu's life, PSTs engaged in meaning-making, which was triggered from their understanding of the book and based on how they analyzed the images within. Additional sources of information, including a video of successful people with disabilities and talking about specific cases of people they knew, brought more input to our discussion. In this way, we went beyond having a single story of people with disabilities (Adichie, 2009), which diversified our thoughts and views of them.

One of the journal entries read: "I observed PSTs reacting to the situations lived by the main characters of the story, which projected a critical framing (The New London Group, 1996). They referred to inclusion as a must in education and talked about the importance of recognizing diversity" (Researcher's journal, January 29, 2020). For instance, Isabella referred to knowledge of diversity when she affirmed: "The lack of information that people have about physical and cognitive disabilities makes them reject others. People in town rejected Sosu because of his condition, but they did not know of his capabilities" (Global literacies, Sosu's call, Excerpt, January 29, 2020). This critical framing, supported by a pedagogy of ML, led PSTs to reason about inclusive education and to propose terms and attitudes that they perceived as appropriate in these cases. This is a sign of engagement, which is not always communicated, but which could be enacted in the way students react or behave when facing specific situations. As stated by Bezemer and Kress (2016) "learning takes place both in communication and in engagement" (p. 62), or as stated by Palpacuer Lee (2018) "in teacher education classes, language teachers should be encouraged to collectively engage with multimodal texts, and to make interdisciplinary, embodied, and intercultural connections" (p. 135). This proves why engaging with multimodal texts helped PSTs build a critical framework by analyzing situations that raised their intercultural awareness.

It was commonplace to hear PSTs Conceptualize around Sosu's skills, Guji Guji's values, and Adichie's bravery. "Their experiencing new knowledge became meaningful as they compared and contrasted their own life experiences and decision-making to those of the people they were reading about" (Researcher's journal, February 10, 2020). As follows, Manuel's statement is a good example of qualities they highlighted in Sosu, "Sosu was skillful playing the drums" (Personal narrative, January 29, 2020). Manuel placed Sosu's skills higher than his disabilities, which was evidence of the transformed practice he was undergoing, based on his learnings from such stories.

"What PSTs were able to express, based on what was learned in the story and on their teaching knowledge, provoked lively discussions in which they compared cases of people in similar situations or the moment they had judged someone because of their origin, while listening to Adichie's story" (Researcher's journal, February 13, 2020). This is aligned to the study of teachers' knowledge, which according to Hammerness (2005), is a key component in teachers' careers that acknowledges how we cannot be detached from our sociocultural realities. The author asserted that gaining intercultural awareness expands specific cultural knowledge for practice, in practice, and of practice and allows individuals to realize that multiple identity dimensions play out during interaction.

Comparing these stories with those that some PSTs shared, mostly what was learned from Sosu, gave them the chance to analyze the gaps between those people who have economic resources or who find support in others and those who do not. "This was a good moment for PSTs to reflect and raise awareness on their society in terms of inclusion and equal opportunities in the difference. This topic touched them and showed their sensitivity towards diversity and towards people in need" (Researcher's journal, January 29, 2020).

Challenging Stereotypes

Watching Adichie's TED Talk the danger of a single story and comparing it to Guji Guji and Sosu's stories made PSTs challenge stereotypes and welcome diverse stories. We discussed how stereotypes are mostly beliefs and assumptions we have of other people, which we commonly learn from our peers, our family, or the media. Stereotypes create overgeneralized views of people that are seen as a collective rather than as individuals who might have specificities within a group. Yasir (2019) precisely refers to the need of challenging ethnocentrism and stereotypes in order to be inclusive of individual differences and able to gain intercultural communication skills.

Multimodal task: To begin, the word stereotypes was written on the board and PSTs discussed what it meant to them. Following, they were asked to think about the regional variation that exists in Colombia and to talk about their impression of people from specific places.

The next challenge given was to complete the following phrase:

People think I am... because...

This phrase made them think about themselves based on how other people saw them. Admittedly, people commonly think of stereotypes they have of others, but rarely do they think of the view others have of them. To analyze how others perceived them, they developed an introspection activity that uncovered diverse feelings and emotions. Following, PSTs watched the video, "The danger of a single story," and reflected upon its content, based on the questions below:

1. Mention any aspects that surprised you about the story.
2. Do you remember stereotypes you have held of other people?
3. Try to remember a Fidi in your life (Fidi was a houseboy in Adichie's family house, and the single story she had of him was that his family was very poor. This is what her mother had told her. She changed her single story of him when she went to visit his house and saw his family making baskets; then, she learned that they had skills beyond being poor).
4. How did your single story of that person change after you talked to her/him? PSTs were given the challenge to go talk to those "Fidis" in their lives, if they had not done so in the past, and to come and share their findings, explaining how the single story they had imposed on them had changed after their encounter.

It was rewarding to disclose PSTs' development of understanding through the activities derived from this video. Sharing their own stories of stereotypes towards others was not easy at the beginning, but little by little, they opened themselves to telling some shocking and at the same time beautiful stories while becoming actively engaged in the task. Their positionality shift regarding people they had come across was evident too, which marked a new beginning, as they mentioned. Many assured how important it was to know diverse stories of people to avoid judging others. In this way, they gained diversity and awareness beyond stereotypes (Researcher's journal, February 13, 2020).

As an illustration, Mariana reported: "people think I am friendly because I am always happy" (Global literacies, Danger of a single story, Excerpt, February 10, 2020). In this way, everyone expressed how they thought other people represented them and how the image that we portray is partially true and not always fair, based on how much others come to know us. Manuel complained, "People think I am mad because I am always serious" (Global literacies, Danger of a single story, Excerpt, February 10, 2020). "I understood this phrase as his cry for fairness and for selling a different image of himself to his partners, and also to indicate how little people knew him, which portrayed his emotional engagement with the activity proposed" (Researcher's journal, February 12, 2020). This perception is aligned with the following phrase they discussed from Guji Guji's story "I am not walking like a duck; I am a duck." This is an illustration of how people perceive others at first sight, and at some point, expect them to fit within a specific cultural group, one that holds the characteristics we expect –one single cultural view.

That means that knowing just one facet is not enough to understand and establish good communication with others. Here, Cope and Kalantzis' (2000) view of literacy, reconceptualizes literacy practices and finds alternatives for literacies pedagogy to fit the changing contexts and realities of today's learners through empowerment and critical decision-making. Such openness to several possibilities is inclusive of cultural diversity.

Thus, building a critical framework aids in the development of intercultural awareness that is informed by diversity of thought and action (Freire, 1970), or the development of what Freire called *conscientização* to explore and understand realities as moving and ongoing, so that those involved in education "may perceive through their relations with reality that reality is a process undergoing constant transformation" (p. 109). That is, understanding others' reality should surpass discourse and become action.

As a possibility to challenge stereotypes, besides providing alternatives for inclusion, after having read Sosu, Ana highlighted, "although there are many negative phrases that have historically been used for kids who have learning challenges, fortunately, I have learned about words that imply inclusion and opportunities, such as gifted, special education needs, normal, support, solidarity, equity, understanding and acceptance" (Global literacies, Sosu's call, Excerpt, February 4, 2020). These lines provide evidence of awareness of diversity gained by PSTs, while they critically engaged with the topic, which was expressed and discovered while they gave themselves the chance to know multiple stories.

PSTs told many different stories of people they had come across and remarked that giving themselves the opportunity to talk to these people was enough to know some of their stories and to change the way they perceived them" (Researcher's journal, February 13, 2020). To take a case in point, Dario argued, "a single story can make us underestimate a person or a place. (Global literacies, Danger of a single story, Excerpt, February 10, 2020)

Thus, coming to a deep understanding of others requires going beyond basic knowledge of them, or as remarked by Gómez-Rodríguez (2015), it is beyond essentializing a surface cultural view.

As an example of the biased and limited view that Paula had of Africa, she declared, "it really surprised me how African people are seen by people from other countries, by people like me" (Global literacies, Danger of a single story, Excerpt, February 10, 2020). She recognized how her view was changed by knowing all Adichie had gone through and by comparing this view to the experience of people from diverse origins.

To further discuss this point, here is an analysis of the role of stories in building critical engagement. Adichie (2009) suggested, "Stories matter. Stories have been used to dispossess, but stories can also be used to empower and humanize. Show a people as one thing, as only one thing, over and over again, and that is what they become" (00:17:36). The single story that Paula had of Africa was the one that had been repeated to her by the media. Now, having had the chance to know an additional story expanded her limited perception. Another example of how a single story narrows our view was presented by Andrea's take of the video "Her roommate thought she was poor just because she was African" (Global literacies, Danger of a single story, Excerpt, February 10, 2020).

As a matter of fact, it is not easy for us to recognize the biased views we have of others, and it is not common for us to accept the stereotypes we hold of other people because, in the end, this is all we know about them; thus, we take it as the whole truth. Along the same lines, some PSTs started to talk about past events, which they disconnected from their present selves when referring to stereotypes. Consider Isabella's comment, "When I was younger, I was scared of people with tattoos because I associated them with evil people; now I know it is not true" (Global literacies, Danger of a single story, Excerpt, February 12, 2020).

The recognition of a limited and stereotyped view of others placed in the past would relieve PSTs from the burden of being judgmental in the present. Accordingly, Kramsch (2009) asserted, "they cannot understand the Other if they don't understand the historical and subjective experiences that have made them who they are. But they cannot understand these experiences if they do not view them through the eyes of the Other" (p. 61). To gain these subjective views, otherness, and a third place, as introduced by Kramsch, are integral to the intercultural awareness learners need to be better intercultural communicators.

Indeed, the transformed practice was essential for their positionality shift regarding people they had come across. Many assured how knowing diverse stories helped them build a framework of tolerance of diversity and avoid being judgmental towards others. In this way, they gained diversity awareness by being actively involved in the task, which allowed overcoming stereotypes and engaging in the pedagogy of ML while diversifying their views of others.

Challenging Origin Preconceptions

The diverse economic, racial, and geographic backgrounds of the stories' characters provoked an intersectional analysis of their realities. Intersectionality, a term originally coined by Crenshaw (1989) as a critique to the disconnection between race and gender, and in an attempt to find justice for black women, is presented by Block and Corona (2017) to account for the many dimensions (e.g. racial, gender-based, sexual, social, ethnic) that we can engage with while exploring a person's experience. Analyzing the diverse backgrounds that come together makes a person's experience richer and varied, thus adding to the fact that no single cultural descriptor is enough to reach a deep intercultural understanding.

It is essential to note that exposing PSTs to global literature and global documentaries encouraged multimodal tasks from a global to global and global to local perspective. Such perspectives were proposed by Short et al. (2016) to approach stories that are inclusive of cultural identity markers that go beyond stereotypes and prejudices. This was possible by reading stories "set in a global context outside the reader's own global location" (p. 5), which brought informative knowledge of global cultural practices and promoted the valuing and connection to local knowledge. In this line, "PSTs could learn about other cultural practices, open themselves to diversity, and value local knowledge. They connected personal experiences to those of others, which encouraged going beyond othering, and raised awareness on social diversity" (Researcher's journal, February 13, 2020).

In point of fact, PSTs' development of intercultural awareness in relation to issues of gender, social class, physical ability, social practices, among others, which was documented in PSTs' artifacts, in their gaining of specific information about the contexts we were exploring and using this information to project a critical view, suggests that it is important to expand the typical transnational view of intercultural communication that implies that interculturality only takes place in the interaction between people from different nationalities and languages. As Álvarez Valencia (2021) pinpoints, interculturality materializes at the interstice of meaning-making encounters between members of distinct social groups and their identity affiliations which are determined by environmental, linguistic, national, racial, ethnic, sexual, gender, religious, institutional, political, physical, and social differences. This broader view of intercultural encounters allowed students to be aware of the intercultural nature of their encounters with texts from foreign communities and with other social actors such as their classmates. This broader perspective to interculturality opens a higher potential for developing intercultural awareness.

SOLUTIONS AND RECOMMENDATIONS

The new communication landscape and the multiplicity of discourses available in this globalized community have brought possibilities for coming together and developing understandings beyond geographical distance. Classroom experiences thus need to nurture inclusive practices that welcome diversity and approach language as a means for communication to build relationships, and make meaning in a space that welcomes reflection and interaction.

This study established a more explicit connection between intercultural awareness and ML practices by gaining better knowledge and understanding of diversity, going beyond print literacy, and provoking a meaning-making experience for participants. The main contribution was to articulate the principles of a pedagogy of ML with the development of intercultural awareness. It is pivotal to remark that although many studies have addressed the two areas separately (Baker, 2011; Cope & Kalantzis, 2000; Liddicoat & Scarino, 2013; The New London Group, 1996), this articulation had not been made, even less in the field of foreign language education.

The sociocultural view of literacy studies that focuses on events and practices of reading and writing (Barton & Hamilton, 2000; Street, 2013) has transformed the educational milieu and become part of educational research (Mora, 2011); hence, transforming the traditional view of reading and writing that was considered a monolingual, monomodal and monocultural activity (Cope & Kalantzis, 2000). Technology and the new communication landscape have opened avenues for New Literacies (NL) (Gee, 1996; Knobel & Lankshear, 2007; Perry, 2012). These new ways of acting in the world and with the world have reconceptualized what literacy practices are, how they interact and intersect in social events, requiring a different type of engagement with text or, as The New London Group (1996) posits it, a ML practice. A ML perspective thus implies a pedagogical approach to literacy (The New London Group, 1996) that brings possibilities for more inclusive, cultural, linguistic, communicative, and technological diversity in the classroom.

Gaining intercultural awareness expanded specific cultural knowledge and allowed PSTs to realize that multiple identity dimensions play out during interaction, including gender, ethnicity, social class, and physical ability. Texts and tasks did not intend to foster culture itself as a concept, but cultural knowledge and awareness of cultural differences. A pedagogy of ML fostered the understanding of the multimodal nature of texts (Álvarez Valencia, 2016b) and global literature as identity cultural markers (Short et al., 2016). This was done by identifying multiple texts in multiple modes and, through them, delving into others' cultural practices and life experiences.

The cultural knowledge embedded in attaining intercultural awareness was a possibility to engage in meaning-making while attempting to understand how cultural patterns support, deny and change structures and uses of language and multimodal literacies (Brice-Heath & Street, 2008). In this specific case, we leaned toward a more subjective view of culture (Berger & Luckman, 1996) in which static cultural descriptors that shape how we come to see others, based on the information provided to us, were challenged for a more subjective view by analyzing the social, economic and multi-faceted realities of the characters of the stories read as experienced by PSTs when analyzing Sosu's story. This is why Kramsch (2013) raises awareness on subjectivity and the impossibilities of considering specific cultural practices as the only descriptors needed to understand someone else's cultural experiences.

Furthermore, the development of intercultural awareness helped break social and geographic boundaries while experiencing the multiple layers of culture that went beyond a nationalist perspective (Dervin, 2006) to embrace a cross-sectional one (Block & Corona, 2017), which contributed to challenging PSTs' thoughts and behaviors towards difference (Chen & Starosta, 1998), thus adding to their intercultural awareness.

Putting thoughts and concepts into practice is part of Baker's (2011) notion of intercultural awareness, which is essential for real and successful communication to occur. Applying knowledge in real instances of communication took place through the knowledge processes in which PSTs experienced, conceptualized and analyzed a variety of situations that put those concepts and thoughts into action (Freire, 1970).

A mere focus on print literacies, posed as limiting by Kress (2000), would not bring possibilities for social practices of reading and writing (Street, 2013), and thus for a view of literacy that surpasses text decoding and welcomes the understanding of realities, the negotiation of meaning, and diverse communicative practices. Conversely, to experience a situated social practice (Perry, 2012), we engaged in an ideological model of literacy (Street, 2013) which recognized contexts, realities, and backgrounds and which introduced literacy events and practices (Barton & Hamilton, 2000) as the possibility to analyze the observable episodes and intangible literacy practices, which, beyond being dichotomous entities, could inform the whys behind literacy processes.

Expanding PSTs' view of literacy was possible when multiple forms of expression came into play (Mora, 2011), when literacy involved reading the world (Freire, 1987), and when they got engaged with a multiplicity of discourses; that is, a three Ms —multilingual, multicultural, and multimodal— view of literacy (Cope & Kalantzis, 2000).

FUTURE RESEARCH DIRECTIONS

Future research can focus on developing a longitudinal study that explores the application of a Pedagogy of ML in a similar population. The study can continue once PSTs graduate in order to analyze their intake and perceptions of this pedagogical strategy when they are practitioners. This is proposed because a study that can analyze participants in different moments of their careers will facilitate a comparison of their development as students and teachers. It will also give insights into how much they take with them once they graduate and how reality might provoke a change in perceptions. This is supported by what Farrell (2015) calls *a reality check vs a reality shock*, which would provide further evidence of participants' long enactment of this pedagogical strategy once they face their teaching contexts. Furthermore, a more extensive data collection process will also generate an in-depth analysis of specific cases with more time dedicated to examining individual participants' gains.

It is essential to understand that not all educators have the chance to adapt their curriculum to include this type of pedagogical strategy the way it was done in this study. For this reason, future projects can address alternatives for adapting a pedagogy of ML to fixed curricular plans by applying the concept of design, which conceives teachers as tailors of their own pedagogical practices, through the redesigning of the material they have at hand (The New London Group, 1996). It will bring possibilities for developing intercultural awareness through the design of multimodal tasks based on a standardized curriculum.

Additionally, in contexts in which the development of mere linguistic competence is favored, a pedagogy of ML can be implemented to promote language learning with a purpose. This draws on the idea that students should make meaning of the language they are learning to solve real-life issues. Another research endeavor is the possibility to continue developing classroom projects that explore ML in diverse settings, including but not limited to elementary and secondary rural schools to visibilize marginalized literacies (Kiramba, 2017). This proposal makes sense based on evidence collected in this project in which PSTs coming from rural settings had the most diverse stories, which are often not told unless given the possibilities through alternative pedagogical practices.

CONCLUSION

Attempting to examine the role that a pedagogy of ML plays in the development of PSTs' intercultural awareness made the language classroom a more inclusive place to better help prepare language teachers that are aware of the symbolic and explicit meanings that are uttered with the language they are learning.

The tasks allowed PSTs to gain local and global knowledge, challenge stereotypes and diversify their views by undergoing diverse types of engagement (Bezemer & Kress, 2016). They completed the knowledge processes components of a pedagogy of ML by experiencing, conceptualizing, analyzing, and applying the learnings gained from stories and which they confronted in the tasks that motivated discussion of multiple identities, taking new knowledge beyond its informational value (Kramsch, 2009) and avoiding essentialization of cultural practices. A pedagogy of ML fostered critical decision-making while opening the way to diversity education that surpasses thought and becomes action (Freire, 1970).

Going beyond a nationalist perspective that recognizes the intersectional (Block & Corona, 2017) categories that make up individuals and that part-take in their cultural encounters was pivotal for learning about specific people, and by scrutinizing the multiple layers of culture, without letting our subjective experiences (Kramsch, 1993) impose stereotyped stories on others. This motivated global to global and global to local connections (Short et al., 2016) within a critical framework that raised awareness of diverse cultural practices.

All in all, a pedagogy of ML presented an alternative for PSTs to gain intercultural awareness through varied modes of communication and language and cultural practices that started in the classroom and merged to other real-life settings. It was possible to go beyond the acquisition of mere linguistic resources to developing intercultural awareness. Additionally, the inclusion of multiple modes of communication favored meaning-making and intercultural practices for PSTs to go beyond literal meanings and start building understandings, recreating others' realities, and becoming more aware of diversity.

REFERENCES

Adichie, C. (2009). *The danger of a single story* [Video]. https://www.ted.com/talks/chimamandangoziadichiethedangerofasinglestory

Álvarez Valencia, J. A. (2016a). Social networking sites for language learning: Examining learning theories in nested semiotic spaces. *Signo y Pensamiento, 68*(68), 66–84. doi:10.11144/Javeriana.syp35-68.snsl

Álvarez Valencia, J. A. (2016b). Meaning making and communication in the multimodal age: Ideas for language teachers. *Colombian Applied Linguistics Journal, 18*(1), 98–115. doi:10.14483/calj.v18n1.8403

Álvarez Valencia, J. A. (2021). Practical and theoretical articulations between multimodal pedagogy and an intercultural orientation to second/foreign language education. In J. A. Álvarez Valencia, A. Ramírez, & O. Vergara (Eds.), *Interculturality in Teacher Education: Theoretical and practical considerations*. Programa Editorial Univalle.

Asare, M. (1992). *Sosu's call*. Sub-Saharan Publishers.

Baker, W. (2011). Intercultural awareness: Modelling an understanding of cultures in intercultural communication through English as a lingua franca. *Language and Intercultural Communication, 11*(3), 197–214. doi:10.1080/14708477.2011.577779

Barton, D., & Hamilton, M. (2000). Literacy practices. In D. Barton, M. Hamilton & R. Ivanic (Eds.), Situated literacies: Reading and writing in context (pp. 7-15). Routledge.

Bennett, J. M., & Bennett, M. J. (2004). Developing intercultural sensitivity: An integrative approach to global and domestic diversity. In D. Landis, J. Bennett, & M. Bennett (Eds.), *Handbook of intercultural training* (3rd ed., pp. 147–165). Sage. doi:10.4135/9781452231129.n6

Bennett, M. J. (1993). Towards a developmental model of intercultural sensitivity. In R. M. Paige (Ed.), *Education for the intercultural experience*. Intercultural Press.

Berger, P. L., & Luckman, T. (1996). *The social construction of reality: A treatise in the sociology of knowledge*. Penguin Books.

Bezemer, J., & Kress, G. (2016). *Multimodality, learning and communication: A social semiotic frame*. Routledge.

Block, D., & Corona, V. (2017). Intersectionality in language and identity research. In K. Rajagopalan (Ed.), *The Routledge handbook of language and identity* (pp. 507–519). Routledge.

Boche, B. (2014). ML in the classroom: Emerging conceptions of first-year teachers. *Journal of Language & Literacy Education, 10*(1), 114–135.

Boghian, I. (2016). A model for teaching cultural awareness in foreign language classes. In I. Boldea (Ed.), *Globalization and national identity. Studies on the strategies of intercultural dialogue* (pp. 967–981). Archipelag XXI Press.

Byram, M. (1997). *Teaching and assessing intercultural communicative competence*. Multilingual Matters.

Byram, M., Gribkova, B., & Starkey, H. (2002). *Developing the intercultural dimension in language teaching: A practical introduction for teachers*. Council of Europe.

Canagarajah, S. (Ed.). (2005). *Reclaiming the local in language policy and practice*. Lawrence Erlbaum. doi:10.4324/9781410611840

Chen, Ch.-Y. (2004). *Guji Guji*. Kane/Miller Book Publishers, Inc.

Chen, G. M., & Starosta, W. J. (1998). A review of the concept of intercultural awareness. *Human Communication*, *2*, 27–54.

Clavijo, A. (2000). *Una mirada a la lectura y la escritura desde la práctica de los docentes en la escuela. Revista Científica. No. 2*. Universidad Distrital.

Clavijo, A. (2007). *Prácticas innovadoras en lectura y escritura* [Innovative practices in reading and writing]. Universidad Distrital.

Clavijo, A., & Ramírez-Galindo, L. (2019). *Las pedagogías de la comunidad a través de investigaciones locales en el contexto urbano de Bogotá* [Community pedagogies through local research in the urban context of Bogotá]. Editorial UD.

Cope, B., & Kalantzis, M. (2000). Multiliteracies: The beginnings of an idea. In B. Cope & M. Kalantzis (Eds.), *Multiliteracies: Literacy learning and the design of social futures* (pp. 3–8). Routledge.

Cope, B., & Kalantzis, M. (2009). Multiliteracies: New literacies, new learning. *Pedagogies*, *4*(3), 164–195. doi:10.1080/15544800903076044

Coulby, D. (2006). Intercultural education: Theory and Practice. *Intercultural Education*, *17*(3), 245–257. doi:10.1080/14675980600840274

Crenshaw, K. (1989). Demarginalizing the intersection of race and sex: A black feminist critique of antidiscrimination doctrine, feminist theory, and antiracist politics. *University of Chicago Legal Forum*, *1*, 139–167.

Deardorff, D. K. (2006). Intercultural competence model. *Journal of Science in International Education*, *10*, 241–266.

Dervin, F. (2006). *Quality in intercultural education: The development of proteophilic competence*. University of Turku.

Farrell, T. (2015). Second language teacher education: A reality check. In *International perspectives of English language teacher education* (pp. 1–15). Palgrave Macmillan. doi:10.1057/9781137440068_1

Freire, P. (1970). Pedagogy of the oppressed. *Continuum*.

Freire, P. (1987). The importance of the act of reading. In P. Freire & D. Macedo (Eds.), *Literacy: Reading the word and the world* (pp. 29–36). Bergin & Garvey.

Fukunaga, N. (2006). "Those anime students": Foreign language literacy development through Japanese popular culture. *Journal of Adolescent & Adult Literacy*, *50*(3), 206–222. doi:10.1598/JAAL.50.3.5

Gee, J. (1996). *Social linguistics and literacies: Ideology in discourses*. Routledge Falmer.

Gómez-Rodríguez, L. F. (2015). Critical intercultural learning through topics of deep culture in an EFL Classroom. *Ikala*, *20*(1), 43–59.

Hammerness, K., Darling-Hammond, L., & Bransford, J. (2005). How teachers learn and develop. In L. Darling-Hammond & J. Bransford (Eds.), *Preparing teachers for a changing world* (pp. 359–389). Josey Bass.

Heath, S. B., & Street, B. (2008). *On ethnography: Approaches to language and literature*. Teachers College Press.

Hepple, E., Sockhill, M., Tan, A., & Alford, J. (2014). ML pedagogy: Creating claymations with adolescent, post-beginner English language learners. *Journal of Adolescent & Adult Literacy, 58*(3), 219–229. doi:10.1002/jaal.339

Honebein, P. C. (1996). Seven goals for the design of constructivist learning environments. In B. G. Wilson (Ed.), *Constructivist learning environments: Case studies in instructional design*. Educational Technology Publications.

Hua, Z. (2016). Identifying research paradigms. In Z. Hua (Ed.), *Research methods in intercultural communication* (pp. 3–22). Wiley-Blackwell.

Kalantzis, M., & Cope, B. (2016). New media and productive diversity in learning. In S. Barch & N. Glutsch (Eds.), *Diversity in der LehrerInnenbildung* (pp. 310–325). Waxmann.

Kim, G. M., & Omerbašić, D. (2017). Multimodal literacies: Imagining lives through Korean dramas. *Journal of Adolescent & Adult Literacy, 60*(5), 557–566. doi:10.1002/jaal.609

Kiramba, L. K. (2017). Multilingual literacies: Invisible representation of literacy in a rural classroom. *Journal of Adolescent & Adult Literacy, 61*(3), 267–277. doi:10.1002/jaal.690

Knobel, M., & Lankshear, C. (2007). *The new literacies sampler*. Peter Lang.

Kramsch, C. (1993). *Context and culture in language teaching*. Oxford University Press.

Kramsch, C. (2009). *The multilingual subject: What foreign language learners say about their experience and why it matters*. Oxford University Press.

Kramsch, C. (2013). Culture in foreign language teaching. *Iranian Journal of Language Teaching Research., 1*(1), 57–78.

Kress, G. (2000). Multimodality. In B. Cope & M. Kalantzis (Eds.), *ML: Literacy learning and the design of social futures* (pp. 182–202). Routledge.

Kumaravadivelu, B. (2001). Towards a postmethods pedagogy. *TESOL Quarterly, 35*(4), 537–560. doi:10.2307/3588427

Liddicoat, A., & Scarino, A. (2013). *Intercultural language teaching and learning*. Wiley-Blackwell. doi:10.1002/9781118482070

Liu, C. (2016). Cultivation of intercultural awareness in EFL teaching. *Journal of Language Teaching and Research, 7*(1), 226–232. doi:10.17507/jltr.0701.26

Losada, J., & Suaza, D. (2018). Video-mediated listening and Multiliteraces. *Colombian Applied Linguistics Journal, 20*(1), 11–24. doi:10.14483/22487085.12349

Luke, C. (2000). Cyber-schooling and technological change: ML for new times. In B. Cope & M. Kalantzis (Eds.), *ML: Literacy learning and the design of social futures* (pp. 3–8). Routledge.

Medina, R., Ramírez, M., & Clavijo, A. (2015). Reading the community critically in the digital age: A ML approach. In P. Chamness Miller, M. Mantero, & H. Hendo (Eds.), *ISLS Readings in Language Studies* (Vol. 5, pp. 45–66). International Society for Language Studies.

Meng, X. (2016). *A pedagogy of ML into practice: A case study in one grade one literacy classroom* [Doctoral thesis, University of West Ontario, Canada]. https://ir.lib.uwo.ca/cgi/viewcontent.cgi?article=5409&context=etd

Michelson, K. (2018). Teaching culture as a relational process through a ML-based global simulation. *Language, Culture and Curriculum*, *31*(1), 1–20. doi:10.1080/07908318.2017.1338295

Michelson, K., & Dupuy, B. (2014). Multi-storied lives: Global simulation as an approach to developing ML in an intermediate French course. *Journal of Linguistics and Language Teaching*, *6*(1), 21–49. doi:10.5070/L26119613

Mora, R. A. (2011). Tres retos para la investigación y formación de docentes en inglés: Reflexividad sobre las creencias y prácticas en literacidad. *Revista Q*, *5*(10), 1–20.

Palpacuer, L., & Christelle, J. L. (2018). Multiliteracies in action at the Art Museum. *Journal of Linguistics and Language Teaching*, *10*(2), 134–157. doi:10.5070/L210235237

Pantaleo, S. (2005). Young children engage with the metafictive in pictures books. *Australian Journal of Language and Literacy*, *28*(1), 19–37.

Pavlenko, A. (2014). *The bilingual mind and what it tells us about language and thought*. Cambridge University Press. doi:10.1017/CBO9781139021456

Perry, K. (2012). What is literacy? A critical overview of sociocultural perspectives. *Journal of Language & Literacy Education*, *8*(1), 50–71.

Rappel, L. J. (2009). *International awareness in second language education: Reflecting on my practice of ELT* [Unpublished master thesis]. Athabasca University, Canada.

Rincón, J., & Clavijo, A. (2016). Fostering EFL learners' literacies through local inquiry in a multimodal experience. *Colombian Applied Linguistics Journal*, *18*(2), 67–82. doi:10.14483/calj.v18n2.10610

Short, K., Day, D., & Schroeder, J. (Eds.). (2016). *Teaching globally: Reading the world through literature*. Stenhouse Publishers.

Street, B. (1984). *Literacy in theory and practice*. Cambridge University Press.

Street, B. (2013, September 27). *Multimodality and new literacy studies: What does it mean to talk about 'texts' today?* [Conference session]. Online Talk for Universidad Pontificia Bolivariana: Medellín-Colombia, King's College London.

The New London Group. (1996). A pedagogy of ML: Designing social futures. *Harvard Educational Review*, *66*(1), 60–92. doi:10.17763/haer.66.1.17370n67v22j160u

Wang, Y. (2014). *Views and attitudes of staff and students towards the significance of intercultural awareness in foreign language teaching and learning in an Australian university context.* [Doctoral thesis, University of Tasmania]. https://eprints.utas.edu.au/18238/1/front-wang-2014-thesis.pdf

Woodin, J. (2016). How to research interculturally and ethically. In Z. Hua (Ed.), *Research methods in intercultural communication: A practical guide* (pp. 103–119). Wiley Blackwell.

Yasir, M. (2019). *Intercultural communication in a world of diversity.* [Doctoral thesis, Cape Breton University]. https://www.researchgate.net/publication/336769181_Intercultural_Communication_in_a_World_of_Diversity

ADDITIONAL READING

Álvarez Valencia, J. A. (2014). Developing the intercultural perspective in foreign language teaching in Colombia: A review of six journals. *Language and Intercultural Communication, 14*(2), 1–19. doi:10.1080/14708477.2014.896922

Baker, W. (2015). *Culture and identity through English as a lingua franca: Rethinking concepts and goals in intercultural communication.* De Gruyter Mouton. doi:10.1515/9781501502149

Bautista, N. (2017). Constructing sociocultural awareness from the EFL classroom. *Gist: Education and Learning Research Journal, 15,* 149–172.

Bonilla, S. X., & Cruz-Arcila, F. (2014). Critical socio-cultural elements of the intercultural endeavor of English teaching in Colombian rural areas. *Profile Issues in Teachers'. Professional Development, 16*(2), 117–133.

Castañeda-Usaquén, M. (2012). Adolescent students' intercultural awareness when using culture-based materials in the English class. *Profile Issues in Teachers' Professional Development, 14*(1), 29–48.

Kalantzis, M., & Cope, B. (2008). Language education and Multiliteracies. In S. May & N. H. Hornberger (Eds.), Encyclopedia of Language and Education (2nd ed., pp. 195-211). Springer. doi:10.1007/978-0-387-30424-3_15

Llanes-Sánchez, J. P. (2018). Encounters with peripheral individuals and rural communities for cultural competence development: A case study of learners of Spanish in Colombia. *Colombian Applied Linguistics Journal, 20*(2), 230–247. doi:10.14483/22487085.13102

KEY TERMS AND DEFINITIONS

Global Literacies: Stories developed in a specific setting to make global to local connections (Short et al., 2016).

Intercultural Adroitness: Behavioral aspect of intercultural communication that displays our thoughts and feelings toward others.

Intercultural Awareness: Cognitive aspect of intercultural communication that projects our knowledge of diversity.

Intercultural Communication: Developing understanding of people from diverse origins to negotiate a multiplicity of meanings and enact them at specific situations.

Intercultural Sensitivity: Psychological aspect of intercultural communication that determines how we behave in face of a specific situation.

Knowledge Processes: Experiencing, conceptualizing, analyzing, and applying new knowledge (Cope and Kalantzis, 2006). It is the materialization of a pedagogy of multiliteracies.

Literacies: Reading and writing beyond the decoding and drafting of alphabetical texts to develop an understanding of the world around us.

Multiliteracies: Exploring new knowledge and gaining language and cultural insights; that is, the three Ms—multilingual, multicultural, and multimodal—view of literacy (Cope & Kalantzis, 2000).

Pedagogy of Multiliteracies: It is a practical guide to welcome reflection and action in a language class. It portrays modes of representation much broader than language alone, and adapts to specific cultural contexts (Cope & Kalantzis, 2009).

Verbocentricity: Focuses on language alone without taking into account diverse literacy practices that favor intercultural understandings.

Chapter 16
Development of Language and Identity Through Author's Chair and Draw and Tell in the Context of Storytelling in Early Childhood Classrooms

Jiamin Xu
https://orcid.org/0000-0003-1983-872X
Florida International University, USA

Kenia Najera
Florida International University, USA

ABSTRACT

Storytelling is powerful. Young children use stories to share experiences, cultural beliefs, and thoughts in their early years. This chapter aims to examine the impact of traditional and digital storytelling on language development and identity among young immigrant children. In a study conducted with young children, they were encouraged to tell and share their personal stories with their classmates in a comfortable and engaging environment created by the author's chair and the draw and tell technique. The authors observed and analyzed the children's work in the after-school program over time and saw that they developed social skills and became confident communicating in their newly acquired language by sharing their own stories. The power of language and culture immersion intertwines with stories that encourage young children to freely communicate and share in a safe space, which fosters children's identity and language development.

DOI: 10.4018/978-1-6684-5022-2.ch016

INTRODUCTION

This study's authors are doctoral students with different cultural backgrounds. The authors share the same passion for young children and are curious to explore children's abilities to acquire language and develop their identity. Both authors were part of a team participating in a qualitative study of an after-school program located in South Florida in the United States of America (USA). The program serves Central American immigrant children who have emigrated to the USA in the last three years.

One author is from China, a country that has 129 dialects, making every region unique and special. Nevertheless, some languages are considered nonstandard since they do not follow the same rules as the standard, thus such languages put those speakers at a social disadvantage (Agar, 1996). This author speaks the Sichuan dialect. She did not realize that language possesses such great power until she went to Canton with her parents when she was 9 years old. The Sichuan and Cantonese dialects differ in accents, pronunciation, and spelling, which posed a huge challenge for her to learn and comprehend Cantonese. Therefore, she instead spoke Mandarin with a Sichuan accent when communicating with her classmates. Language differences unfortunately created an invisible wall between her and her classmates. It became worse when they talked to her with an air of superiority. As a result, the superiority they perceived of one language and culture over another hindered their communication and ability to connect. She has avoided speaking the Sichuan dialect in public since then, despite once being very proud of it. She felt the need to hide her dialect and where she was from, but language is supposed to bring people closer through sounds and humanized culture (Agar, 1996).

We can lose our identity and even develop hostility toward our own language when adapting to other cultures and languages. The other author is a native of Tegucigalpa, Honduras, who emigrated to the USA in her early twenties. She studied and worked in a new society where the language and the culture were different from her own. She had a hard transition immersing herself into a new culture, values, costumes, and language. The fact of being a cultural outsider made her feel uncomfortable at times, especially when interacting socially with others. At school, she preferred to work in small groups where she felt more comfortable sharing ideas. However, it has taken longer than expected for her to feel comfortable speaking the new language freely. One factor she feels slowed down her transition to adapting to the new language was the fact that she speaks her native language at home with her family and friends. She believes her family could marginalize her for speaking English, her second language. With time she understood the value of being bilingual in a city where crossing from English to Spanish is the norm.

Having experienced the process of adapting to a new language to fit in socially, both authors decided to investigate how young children process leaving their home and family to embrace a new language, customs, and values. The authors would invite the children to tell their own stories through storytelling using Draw and Tell and Author's Chair techniques.

Educators and students encounter challenges regarding immigration issues related to diverse cultures and languages. The high number of families fleeing oppressive countries around the world and technological developments in the education field have led to the development of global competencies. Global competence refers to the dispositions and abilities children must develop that will prepare them to embrace a global society in a changing economy and multicultural linguistic society (Boix-Mansilla et al., 2013).

Different major educational public systems show how children who emigrate to the United States acquire English as a second or even third language. Students should be respected and valued for their background and the rich experiences they may add to a classroom. The curriculum should include social-emotional competencies through which children can develop empathy for others. It should introduce them to social and world issues at an early age with the idea of provoking their critical thinking, problem-solving, and awareness of inequality in the world (Boix-Mansilla et al., 2013), and in this way children will come to understand the cause and effect of global issues.

Educators in multicultural settings should consider multicultural literature and have a positive attitude toward the new language and new culture, the actual practice of introducing children's literature, and the literary support surrounding the children (Collins et al., 2014; Suarez-Orozco et al., 2018). We read a variety of books the children could relate to during our study, and we read some books to the children about ethnicity and race.

Immigrant students showed difficulties making this transition of coming to a new environment due to a lack of their family's involvement, their classmates' acceptance, and their own learning motivation. However, prior studies have shown that second-generation immigrant children are at less risk of academic failure compared to first-generation immigrants due to their cultural immersion in language and culture and their values (Suarez-Orozco, 2018; Suarez-Orozco & Suarez-Orozco, 2013).

The research study was conducted in a multicultural classroom with multiethnic children who were transitioning to an unfamiliar environment and a new language. It seems that pedagogy in today's classrooms is lagging behind societal changes, creating challenges for both educators and learners. Classrooms become more multicultural and multilingual at a fast pace, and we need to be aware of these challenges and be flexible to accommodate the newer learners. Thus, "it is crucial to engage children in conversations of global significance by adjusting themes such as conflict resolution [and] social justice […] to their level" (Salmon, 2010). We should encourage understanding and ownership of their own stories to facilitate such open conversations with young children in school.

The authors conducted research in a kindergarten after-school program during spring of 2022, inviting the children to listen to a variety of children's literature about ethnic, racial, and immigrant stories. We then invited them to express themselves orally, using the Draw and Tell Technique that encourages children to make their thinking visible. The participants were mostly Central American immigrants from kindergarten to first grade. They were primarily Spanish speakers or spoke their native mother tongue and were learning English as a second language. The authors focused on language learning and identity development for this qualitative study through collecting stories and analyzing how children respond to the new environment. The combination of the Author's Chair and the Draw and Tell Technique engaged children to work collaboratively and socially. Additionally, the participants had the opportunity to voice their personal life stories and listen to others to find space for both independence and cooperation.

CONCEPTUAL FRAMEWORK

Four essential components contributing to the foundation for this framework are the Author's Chair, the Draw and Tell Technique, identity, and language learning. The Author's Chair is designed for students to read aloud their writings in front of their peers (Graves & Hansen, 1983). It is possible, however, for young children who are just beginning to develop a language skill to lack writing skills. Young children benefit greatly from the Draw and Tell technique when it comes to expressing themselves through drawing. In this study, it combines the Author's Chair and the Draw and Tell Technique (Salmon & Lucas, 2011) in the context of storytelling, which creates a comfortable learning environment for young children to develop their identity and language.

Identity

Identity in early childhood is important because it impacts all areas of development—namely, cognitive, social, language, and physical (Vygotsky, 1962). Thus, much attention should be paid to children who immigrate under particular conditions, leaving their parents, grandparents, and extended family members behind to start a new life in a culture different from theirs and trying to understand a new language, going to new schools and making new friends. Integrating into a new community whose education, values, and language differ from those of their parents could be a difficult and traumatic transition. We humanize young children as storytellers by empowering them to tell their stories (Bratitsis et al., 2011).

Children start interacting with their peers and the adults in their communities as they grow up, so these social interactions shape their sense of belonging and self-acceptance as they interact with their environment. Both authors' stories, mentioned earlier, described their own experiences learning a new language and the interactions with a new community that shaped their thinking; those experiences, in combination with their families' support, enabled them to embrace the new challenges. According to Bronfenbrenner's (1977) human ecological theory, the multi-layered interactions in which the child develops socially affect the child's identity. This is similar to Vygotsky's (1978) social learning theory, which emphasizes the social context and the construction of learning and knowledge through social interaction. Vygotsky argued that children learn from more skilled peers and interactions with their primary educators. Therefore, it is in the early years that young children develop self-identity through play and other social interactions with others. They become aware of their environment and the social context, culture, values, and language in which they are growing up. Piaget's (1956) cognitive theory highlights cognitive development, although it also recognizes that social learning facilitates the acquisition of thinking processes. Another important viewpoint in the social domain is the recognition of our emotions and how to deal with them as part of our identity.

Immordino-Yang highlighted that

Emotions, like cognition, develop with maturity and experience, in this sense, emotions are skills-organized patterns of thoughts and behaviors that we actively construct in the moment and across our lifespan to adaptively accommodate to various kinds of circumstances, including academic demands. (2016, p. 20)

Young migrant children must have meaningful relationships with others who value and recognize their home language, culture, and values to build a positive self-concept and identities. In this way, they can develop healthy self-concepts and understand that they belong to a different culture than their parents or grandparents.

Language and Environment

Many linguists and psychologists stress the importance of providing a comfortable environment where students can learn new languages without anxiety. Chomsky (2002), a proponent of nativism, argued that behaviorism cannot explain the fact that infants learn about how language works and how it functions beyond what they are exposed to. Instead, nativists suggest that infants are born able to learn languages. For Chomsky (2002), children acquire new languages as they age because their brains contain the language acquisition device (LAD). When young children take the lead and engage in a language-rich environment through storytelling, their brains retain certain universal principles of language, comparable to a template, that allow them to acquire the language naturally. The natural ways that individuals acquire and maintain behavior are examined by social cognitivism. According to social cognitive theory, the social environment is also essential for acquiring a language (Bandura, 1977). In other words, language can be learned by observing and modeling what happens around them while utilizing their mental abilities.

Social interaction, like language exposure to the environment, plays an important role in language learning. Vygotsky (1962) asserted that there is an inextricable link between language development and social and cultural contexts. He concluded that early childhood language development relies on the formation of the zone of proximal development (ZPD) between a child and an adult with greater knowledge as well as involvement in social interaction. Young children who are engaged in storytelling can learn from their peers and researchers in the ZPD who are much more capable. In this case, language acquisition is aided by social interaction. Furthermore, Piaget and Cook (1952) and Bruner (1983) put more emphasis on how language learners construct their own learning through self-exploration and self-discovery in the environment. In fact, storytelling provides a great opportunity for young children to engage in meaningful interaction to facilitate their learning and construction of the new language.

Most importantly, code-switching is a common phenomenon that occurs while language learners who can speak more than one language interact with each other in a language-rich environment. In code-switching, a person changes languages or dialects back and forth during a single conversation, sometimes within the same sentence. Children choose code-switching to fill the language gap by using their first language (Nicoladis & Secco, 2000). As a language strategy, code-switching helps to improve communication and facilitate conversation among language learners (Shafi et al., 2020). However, according to Probyn (2015), there is not often a switch from the target language to another language in language classes, with the target language dominating the lessons. The opportunity to employ languages other than the dominant one is of the utmost importance for children.

All these theories of language learning consider an interactive environment an essential component. In the 1980s, Cambourne (1988) defined eight conditions of learning to facilitate children's literary development based on his 3 years of observations of young children's language development. The main idea of his conditions for language learning are that children must learn through immersion in the appropriate texts that are appropriately modelled by the teachers, by using all their senses, by taking an active role in their learning process, by interacting with and learning from their peers, and by taking risks (Cambourne, 1988). These conditions are of great significance to take into account while inviting young children to acquire the language. Rushton et al. (2003) supported Cambourne's (1988) conditions of learning with brain research showing that students are able to build and test their language knowledge in the social contexts of the classroom. Thus, an interactive language learning environment allows children to learn on their own. According to Perez-Prado (2021), a language-acquisition-friendly learning environment should be collaborative, meaningful, interactive, engaging, and mistake tolerant; it should also reflect diverse cultures and use visual tools and higher-order thinking skills. These definitions of what constitutes a good language learning environment essentially overlap to demonstrate that an interactive and engaging environment motivates young language learners from diverse backgrounds to develop their linguistic skills.

The Author's Chair and Draw and Tell Technique

The Author's Chair is one of the powerful tools to start with in the beginning phase of language learning, especially for developing reading and writing skills. Graves and Hansen (1983) found that authorship, which demonstrates students' high agency in English writing, is generated by students through the Author's Chair. Students are invited to share their stories in public as authors. Not only does it offer students the opportunity to publish, but it also fosters an atmosphere for sharing, gaining confidence, and practicing the language (Hall, 2014). Furthermore, it fosters childrens' compassion and respect while supporting their interactive social competency and taking the audience's needs into account (McCallister, 2008). Therefore, it is also a reading exercise. This creates a community of writers and readers in which the teachers stay back, but the students take on an active role in their language learning.

What's more, children who lack the vocabulary to develop their writing would benefit from the Draw and Tell Technique at the beginning of their language learning process. Vygotsky (1978) considered drawing graphic speech, and Newkirk (1989) viewed drawing as a kind of writing ability. Some might argue that drawing is a burden for children who are not talented or that it might distract students from the linguistic process. The teachers' focus and how they negotiate meaning from the children's work matter in this situation.

According to Salmon and Lucas (2011), the Draw and Tell Technique provides children with a means to communicate their thoughts by combining drawing with storytelling. Children can visualize their thoughts and operate at a metacognitive level through drawing, and through telling, children can express and explore increasingly complex ideas by revisiting, revising, and dialoguing through their drawings (Brooks, 2009).

The combination of the Author's Chair and the Draw and Tell technique highlights the significance of putting students in the roles of both authors and writers.

METHODOLOGY

This is a qualitative research study in nature, was conducted during an after-school kindergarten program within a mixed class that included 16 kindergarteners and first graders who had emigrated from Central America. Two of the children speak only English, three only Spanish or their native mother tongue, and the rest are bilingual. This program offers local families access to community resources aimed at improving children's health, preparing children for kindergarten, and increasing after-school and summer program quality.

The five people on the research team include two volunteers, one university professor whose expertise is in early childhood education, and two doctoral students. The research team visited the after-school classroom once a week for ninety minutes for 10 weeks, and during that time the team shared stories and books with the children to inspire them to tell their own stories. After each week's visit, the research team discussed and defined topics that interested those children for the next week, such as emotions, skin colors, imagination, and so on.

The Author's Chair and the Draw and Tell Technique were integrated into the context of traditional and digital storytelling to develop the children's literacy skills and identity. The children were first invited to create their stories by drawing them; they then shared their stories in the Author's Chair.

Observation and interview were the main methods of data collection. The researchers made video recordings over the course of ten weeks. The children's teacher was interviewed for ninety minutes after the research was completed. Additionally, the researchers collected the children's artifacts, noted the children's performance each week, and discussed changes with the research team. Through data analysis the authors also reflected on how children related to the stories the researchers shared and how language and cultural identity interacted when the children told their stories. Most importantly, the researchers used a triangulation method for verifying the collected data. The study's authors compared and contrasted their notes. Riessman (2008) argued that "the researcher does not find narratives but instead participates in their creation" (p. 21). At least two methods were used to verify the findings and results (Carter et al., 2014). The authors interviewed the teacher to verify their findings and also discussed them with the whole team.

Overall, two research questions were investigated in this research:

1. How does the implementation of storytelling in the classroom influence identity development among young immigrant children?
2. How does the combination of Author's Chair and Draw and Tell Technique in the context of storytelling influence the language development of young immigrant children?

FINDINGS

The findings of this study aim to answer the two research questions posed at the beginning regarding how the combination of author's chair and the Draw and Tell Technique in the context of storytelling influences young children's identity and language development. During the 10-week period the authors witnessed the children's increasing motivation to create comprehensive self-images in their stories and their willingness to explore diverse cultures through peer collaboration. In terms of children's language development, the results showed that they were able to learn a new language through natural interactions with their peers and adults in a comfortable learning environment created by the author's chair and Draw and Tell Technique, in which their confidence in speaking the new language and their imagination were enhanced as well. The findings of this study are detailed in this section.

Identity

My Choice

The interpretation of the data collected and of the analysis proved that storytelling intrinsically motivated the children to be part of the group and knew their experiences differed from their peers. For example, the author from Honduras read the children a book about a little girl who has emigrated from Honduras. The book talks about the typical food of Honduras and also mentions the feelings of shyness felt by the little girl encountering a new culture. The Honduran children in the after-school program told that they felt related to the story and started a conversation about other typical food their grandmothers cook at home and how sometimes they feel as shy and scared as the main character in the story.

The research team helped the children work on their personal stories during the Draw and Tell process and then later on sharing them with their peers. The research team and the rest of the children then became the audience. The story books used for this study focused on diversity, family structures, immigration, etc., with the hope that these readings would help the children understand other perspectives, inquire, communicate, recognize inequities, and act. According to Le Guin (2004), children experience this association by producing a story, sharing it, and being heard. In this sense, the experience promoted

Development of Language and Identity

each child's feeling of being part of a learning community and feeling proud of themselves while also allowing them to hear others' stories.

After working independently on their own stories, the children were invited to share them with the group. They first signed up and took turns to share accordingly. As shown in Figure 1 and Figure 2, during the process of creating and explaining their stories, the children made these stick puppets in which they highlighted their physical appearances. In Figure 1, the child mirrored himself with the clothes he was wearing that day. In Figure 2, the child represented her and her mother getting ready to go out.

Figure 1. 3D self-portrait

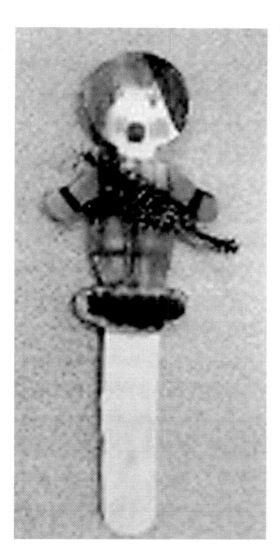

Figure 2. This is my mom and I going to the mall

The instances of sharing offered children a sense of self-efficacy throughout the process. Children had the opportunity to select the colors and materials to use. They created a "self-imagine" of the story, by being its main character. One child recreated the moment he and his parents had shared. He was able to explain to the audience why he had chosen the specific moment and why it was important to him. Figure 3 shows his story. The researcher had a conversation with him about his story, showing that he had the right to make a choice about his audience and what to share.

Jack: "I have a secret."
Researcher: "Could you share with me?"
Jack: "No! That's my secret."
Researcher: "Okay, I can keep your secret. Then could you share with me?"
Jack: "Yes, this is just you and me."
Researcher: "Sure, I wouldn't tell others."
Jack (pointed at his picture): "This is me. I took my father's phone and played it on my bed. My dad thought I was sleeping."

Development of Language and Identity

Figure 3. My secret. This child drew in different steps what his secret was.

Children opened their hearts to share particular stories through Draw and Tell. They spoke their insecurities about speaking the second language were fading as they were working in collaboration with others. They were able to ask how to spell words and communicate with their peers in both languages. The children's parents also stated in a parental meeting how the children were talkative at home about their experiences sitting on the Author's Chair. Parents said that the children were proud of telling others their stories and hearing others, as well.

Peer Collaboration

The authors could observe as time passed how eager these young children were to tell and share their personal and family stories in a collaborative manner. They seemed to feel safe sharing their stories. They learned to listen and also to be heard as they became storytellers. While one child was sitting on the author's chair and sharing, the other children were able to ask clarifying questions in order to know more about the story being told. The children also had the opportunity to share family stories to talk about their favorite dish, their favorite holiday celebration, and their personal preferences for toys and movies. They verbally described their ideas through drawings that were their representation of culture.

Powerful conversations happened among them during the drawing process at the table. They asked and answered questions, but at other times, some questions could not be expressed. As shown in Figure 3, when the child repeatedly said, "This is my secret" and could not share it with the other children. He was willing to share it with the research team.

The children became listeners and tellers. The fact that the children had a voice to decide what they wanted to share that day helped them to develop self-efficacy, self-control, and negotiation, which made them feel they were an important part of the class community. Moreover, they showed characteristics of their preferences, culture, and values.

Haas Dyson and Genishi have explained:

311

The storytelling self is a social self, who declares and shapes important relationships through the mediating power of words. Thus, in sharing stories, we have the potential for forging new relationships, including local, classroom "cultures" in which individuals are interconnected and new "we's" formed. [...] At the same time, those very images and rhythms reverberate in the memories of audience members, who reconstruct the story with the stuff of their own thoughts and feelings. In such ways, individual lives are woven together through the stuff of stories. (1994, p. 5)

According to the interview with the teacher, she also observed how the children were more inclined to tell tales among themselves during playtime. The children organized themselves on the playground, and she heard them bargaining in Spanish. Such observations suggest that, during leisure time, the students preferred to use Spanish rather than English. Empowering children to speak freely in the language of preference will enhance their identity and language development. They reserved English for completing their schoolwork. The authors witnessed that storytelling motivated the children to communicate with others. It offers the opportunity to mirror our experiences with others and to find identity in shared values, language, and culture.

The after-school teacher also mentioned that some of the monolingual Spanish children performed poorly on the language arts assessment that the program conducted to determine who required free tutoring services.

The children explored each other's physical features, such as skin and hair colors, during the construction of storytelling. They selected materials such as yarn, markers, and googly eyes to mirror themselves in their art creation. The authors found that from the variety of books read to the children during the time of this study, the children communicated among themselves despite their language differences. Most importantly, multiple literacies enabled them to recognize themselves in the stories, which helped them to find similarities among each other. The children found they had food preferences in common; they loved to eat tacos.

Figure 4 shows how children socially cooperated with each other while making the taco together. Children who like tacos for lunch worked in groups and verbally were telling the taco preparation steps and how their mothers served them for lunch.

Development of Language and Identity

Figure 4. Digital storytelling of taco making

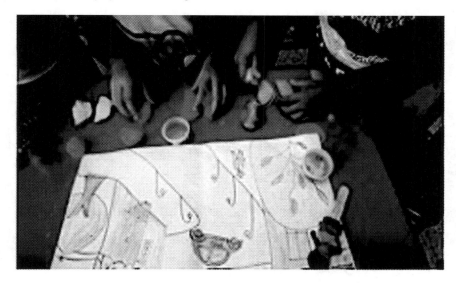

Language Development

Language Development Through Interaction

The combination of the Author's Chair and the Draw and Tell Technique in the context of storytelling creates an educational setting that fosters an atmosphere in which language learners can freely interact with one another. Children who can speak Spanish are able to learn from their peers who are bilingual in English and Spanish. Sophia can only speak Spanish. One of the authors pointed at the creature she was drawing and asked, "What's this?" Sophia stuttered and answered in Spanish, "ángel." The children next to her explained in English, "That's an angel." Peer learning is much more likely to happen when such interaction involves meaningful negotiation and modified input from young children in an environment where they are surrounded by supportive and encouraging individuals.

The process of putting one's thoughts down on paper can be very stressful for writers, especially learners in the process of acquiring a new language. Drawing is considered graphic speech (Vygotsky, 1978) or a kind of writing ability (Newkirk, 1989). Children who lack the vocabulary to develop their writing could benefit from the Draw and Tell Technique. They can visualize their thoughts and operate at a metacognitive level.

Figure 5. How I went to America

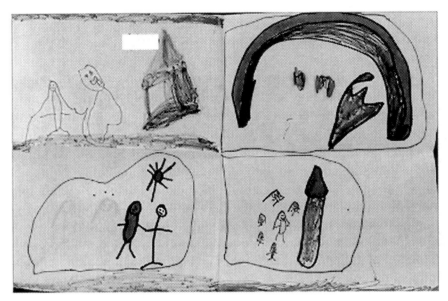

The children were invited to share their stories about how they came to America. The Figure 5 is the representation of one child's story, including four parts that are organized by different timelines. According to this child, there was a monster in her home country, so she and her family went to Miami. There was a rainbow in Miami and clouds in the sky. Later she went to a school located in Miami. Her family had a happy life there. Her drawing is her writing in her mind. Again, through sharing, children can express and explore ideas by revisiting, revising, and dialoguing through their drawings (Brooks, 2009). Once children have blueprints in their drawings, they will also be capable of having blueprints in their minds (Cahill & Gregory, 2016).

Some have asserted that the Author's Chair only serves as a way for students to demonstrate that they have learned writing skills, but it actually provides an open forum for all "authors" to share their insights into each other's work (McCallister, 2008). Therefore, it is also a reading exercise. The researchers observed through this study that this group of children openly and slowly participated actively in the draw and tell experience, and all the participants wished to be a part of the Author's Chair towards the end of our study. They had a space to talk about their family's interactions, pets, and even vacation experiences and showed their interest in exploring their peer's experiences.

Confidence

The Author's Chair is a powerful tool to develop young children's authorship in the beginning phases of language learning. Authorship, which demonstrates students' high agency in English writing, is generated by students through the Author's Chair, which not only offers all students the opportunity to publish but also creates a conducive atmosphere for them to share, gain confidence, and practice the language (Graves and Hansen, 1983; Hall, 2014).

The children were shy about sharing their stories on the first day when the research team introduced the Author's Chair. However, it gradually turned out that, for example, Ada, whose first language is

Spanish, pulled down her mask as she sat still on the chair. She held her picture up to tell us her story and spoke slowly in Spanish, "Esta es mi Familia" (This is my family). She seemed eager but somewhat uneasy to share her story. The following Friday, when sharing time rolled around, the kids were much more ready to share their stories. Ada was first in line. She sat on a chair, took off her mask, and wore a beaming smile, looking at the classmates who were playing around her. She showed the drawing to her classmates and, speaking in a louder voice than last time, said, "This is me, y mi mama" (This is me and my mother). In the fifth week of the study program, Ada approached one of the researchers before sharing on the Author's Chair, and said, "I've finished." She stood beside her table and pointed at her picture, saying, "This is my house, my mum, y my sisters, y my, my…" She stuttered as she tried to find the right word. The researcher asked, "Do you mean your brother or your friends?" She shouted out, "Yes, my friends!" Ada explained in both English and Spanish, yet her delivery back and forth in both languages showed that she was learning the language step by step through iterating with others by code-switching, thus becoming increasingly confident to share her writing in her newly learned language.

Ada's case is just one example of how authorship boosted the children's confidence and motivation. Language learning simultaneously occurred through interactions. It creates a community of writers and readers in which teachers stand back so students can take on an active role in their language development. Furthermore, the children's drawings increased in detail, and they used a greater variety of words in their drawings.

Figure 6 and Figure 7 are examples of drawings by children as responses to the children's book reading. Children who were engaged in the session shared what they had put in their suitcases when they left their home countries. Their drawings show that they wrote some words besides those items they drew. The children spelled out words by sound during this stage of language learning. They played around with the phonics and structures of words. They wrote at their own pace and made choices about what they wanted to write in this stress-free environment where they had rapt audiences. Furthermore, the same elements from the drawings are repeated several times in different ways. Drawing enhances children's ability to retain knowledge through all their senses while also engaging them in an enjoyable activity (Brooks, 2009). After children draw an object, they may also see it in their friends' pictures and hear it described again, which allows them to retain their memory of the language in a natural way.

Development of Language and Identity

Figure 6. What's in my suitcase by Elsa

Figure 7. What's in my suitcase by Vivian

Imagination

Using the Draw and Tell Technique, the children were able to express themselves through their drawings and stories in a way that allowed them to let their imaginations fly. The adults did not tell the children how or what to draw; rather, they facilitated the children's efforts to ensure they were free to envision their thoughts. Snow and rainbows existed simultaneously in their little worlds.

When the students were invited to tell their stories about their families, they drew different living environment, like the Figure 8, Tom was showing that his families lived on a rainbow, and outer space was black and blue. The following exchange took place with Tom while he was drawing:

Researcher: "What are you drawing?"
Tom: "This is a rocket ship."
Researcher: "Why are you drawing a rocket ship?"
Tom: "I am going to the clouds."

Figure 8. My family

Most importantly, the children's imaginative stories were meaningful to them. The stories they acted out were mostly based on their daily experiences. The Figure 9 shows a scene from Ada and Elsa's digital

Development of Language and Identity

story. Elsa is bilingual in English and Spanish, while Ada can only speak Spanish. Elsa shared with one author that she and Ada lived in different neighborhoods and one day they met each other on the street. Their mothers were very busy with work. They eventually became friends and visited each other's homes. They had never been to each other's house before, but they tried to make sense of the two characters in the collaborative story by making up their relationship. Digital storytelling can serve as a bridge between children's imaged world and the real world.

Figure 9. Digital storytelling by Ada and Elsa

Overall, the meaningful, deliberate, and compelling learning experiences employed in this study benefited the young children's language development and the development of their self-identity. This group of preschoolers and kindergarteners demonstrated growth in these two aspects during the study's 10 weeks of observations and discourse.

CONCLUSION

Traditional and digital storytelling provides a powerful opportunity for young children to develop their language skills and identity. Working through these kinds of experiences within storytelling, young immigrant children had the space to learn vocabulary and applied it when telling their stories to their peers. This opportunity helped the children to feel appreciated and valued for who they are and what they bring with them. They also collaborated in small groups to create digital stories. In this way, they used the acquired language to communicate their ideas to each other. Authors observed the children speaking comfortably in both English and Spanish. In fact, this language learning process is part of their new identity development. The students in this afterschool classroom developed self-awareness by presenting themselves in the story they created. Once they told their stories they reflected upon their natural thoughts and feelings during those special moments. They were proud to talk about their parents, grandparents and other topics that indistinctly reinforce their identities and personal preferences at early age in the new environment. Their self-esteem was also built through social interactions with their peers and adults by actively listening and responding. Storytelling offers young children a space to express themselves, be creative, and use their imagination to create stories together through which children show pride in their representations and demonstrate self-efficacy when working on their individual stories.

The combination of the author's chair and the draw and tell technique in the context of storytelling in this research created an engaging and interactive language learning environment in which students were empowered as authors and readers, especially in the context of social interactions. Therefore, if we expect them to be writers and readers, they should also be treated as writers and readers. By making words vividly through drawing, they are more likely to develop their creative thinking skills and imagination, further empowering them as writers and readers. Most importantly, they learned to appreciate others' work, which sent a message that every story was valued—in other words, every kid was valued. More confidence was gained to express themselves by using that language as they got the sense they were valued. While providing them with an interactive and engaging learning environment where they have their own pace to develop their language skills, teachers are supposed to stand back and let the children take control. A student-centered learning environment can help young children develop their language skills in a natural way. Also, they felt part of the community. They found each of them came from different places but now they are sharing the same value with each other.

This study found that traditional and digital storytelling is a powerful tool that can be integrated into the class to develop students' language skills and identity. However, there is still much to research regarding how these young immigrant children can successfully emerge into the new culture.

REFERENCES

Agar, M. (1996). *Language Shock: Understanding the Culture of Conversation*. Quill.

Bandura, A. (1977). *Social learning theory*. Prentice Hall.

Boix-Mansilla, V. B., Jackson, A., & Jacobs, I. H. (2013). Educating for global competence: Learning redefined for an interconnected world. *Mastering Global Literacy*, 5–27.

Bratitsis, T., Kotopoulos, T., & Mandila, K. (2011, November). Kindergarten children as story makers: The effect of the digital medium. In *2011 Third International Conference on Intelligent Networking and Collaborative Systems* (pp. 84–91). IEEE. 10.1109/INCoS.2011.108

Bronfenbrenner, U. (1977). Toward an experimental ecology of human development. *The American Psychologist*, *32*(7), 513–531. doi:10.1037/0003-066X.32.7.513

Brooks, M. (2009). Drawing, visualisation and young children's exploration of "big ideas.". *International Journal of Science Education*, *31*(3), 319–341. doi:10.1080/09500690802595771

Bruner, J. (1983). *Children's talk: Learning to use language*. Norton & Company.

Cahill, M. A., & Gregory, A. E. (2016). "Please let us write!" Sharing writing in the early childhood classroom. *YC Young Children*, *71*(2), 64–69. https://www.proquest.com/scholarly-journals/please-let-us-write-sharing-writing-early/docview/1818310134/se-2?accountid=10901

Cambourne, B. (1988). *The whole story: Natural learning and the acquisition of literacy in the classroom*. Ashton Scholastic.

Carter, N., Bryant-Lukosius, D., DiCenso, A., Blythe, J., & Neville, A. J. (2014). The use of triangulation in qualitative research. *Oncology Nursing Forum, 41*(5), 545–547. doi:10.1188/14.ONF.545-547 PMID:25158659

Chomsky, N. (2002). *Syntactic structures* (2nd ed.). Mouton de Gruyter. doi:10.1515/9783110218329

Collins, B. A., O'Connor, E. E., Suárez-Orozco, C., Nieto-Castañon, A., & Toppelberg, C. O. (2014). Dual language profiles of Latino children of immigrants: Stability and change over the early school years. *Applied Psycholinguistics, 35*(3), 581–620. doi:10.1017/S0142716412000513 PMID:24825925

Erikson, E. H. (1980). *Identity and the life cycle*. Norton.

Graves, D., & Hansen, J. (1983). The author's chair. *Language Arts, 60*(2), 176–183. https://www.jstor.org/stable/41961448

Haas Dyson, A., & Genishi, C. (Eds.). (1994). *The need for story: Cultural diversity in classroom and community*. Teachers College Press.

Hall, A. H. (2014). Beyond the author's chair. *The Reading Teacher, 68*(1), 27–31. doi:10.1002/trtr.1297

Immordino-Yang, M. H. (2016). *Emotions, learning, and the brain: Exploring the educational implications of affective neuroscience*. W.W. Norton.

Kim, J. H. (2015). *Understanding narrative inquiry: The crafting and analysis of stories as research*. Sage Publications.

Krashen, S. D. (1985). *The input hypothesis: Issues and implications*. Longman.

Lazar, A. M., Edwards, P. A., & Thompson McMillon, G. (2012). *Bridging literacy and equity: The essential guide to social equity teaching*. Teachers College Press.

Le Guin, U. K. (2004). *The wave in the mind: Talks and essays of the writer, the reader, and the imagination*. Shambhala.

McCallister, C. A. (2008). "The author's chair" revisited. *Curriculum Inquiry, 38*(4), 455–471. doi:10.1111/j.1467-873X.2008.00424.x

Newkirk, T. (1989). *More than stories—The range of children's writing*. Heinemann.

Nicoladis, & Secco, G. (2000). The role of a child's productive vocabulary in the language choice of a bilingual family. *First Language, 20*(58), 3–28. doi:10.1177/014272370002005801

Perez-Prado, A. (2021). *LAF with the habits of mind: Strategies and activities for teaching diverse language learners*. Institute for Habits of Mind.

Piaget, J. (1956). *The child's conception of space*. Routledge & K. Paul.

Piaget, J., & Cook, M. T. (1952). *The origins of intelligence in children*. International University Press. doi:10.1037/11494-000

Probyn, M. (2015). Pedagogical Translanguaging: Bridging discourses in South African science classrooms. *Language and Education, 29*(3), 218–234. doi:10.1080/09500782.2014.994525

Riessman, C. K. (2008). Narrative methods for the human sciences. Sage Publishing.

Rushton, S. P., Eitelgeorge, J., & Zickafoose, R. (2003). Connecting Brian Cambourne's conditions of learning theory to brain/mind principles: Implications for early childhood educators. *Early Childhood Education Journal, 31*(1), 11–21. doi:10.1023/A:1025128600850

Salmon, A. K. (2010). Making thinking visible through action research. *Early Childhood Education, 39*(1), 15-21.

Salmon, A. K., & Lucas, T. (2011). Exploring young children's conceptions about thinking. *Journal of Research in Childhood Education, 25*(4), 364–375. doi:10.1080/02568543.2011.605206

Shafi, S., Kazmi, S. H., & Asif, R. (2020). Benefits of code-switching in language learning classroom at University of Education Lahore. *International Research Journal of Management. IT and Social Sciences, 7*(1), 227–234. doi:10.21744/irjmis.v7n1.842

Skinner, B. F. (1957). *Verbal behavior.* Copley Publishing Group. doi:10.1037/11256-000

Suárez-Orozco, C., Motti-Stefanidi, F., Marks, A., & Katsiaficas, D. (2018). An integrative risk and resilience model for understanding the adaptation of immigrant-origin children and youth. *The American Psychologist, 73*(6), 781–796. doi:10.1037/amp0000265 PMID:30188166

Suárez-Orozco, M., & Suárez-Orozco, C. (2013, Fall). Taking perspective: Context, culture, and history. In M. G. Hernández, J. Nguyen, C. L. Saetermoe, & C. Suárez-Orozco (Eds.), *Frameworks and ethics for research with immigrants: New directions for child and adolescent development* (Vol. 141, pp. 9–23). Jossey-Bass.

Vygotsky, L. (1962). *Thought and language* (E. Hanf-Mann & G. Vakar, Trans.). MIT Press. doi:10.1037/11193-000

Vygotsky, L. (1978). *Mind in society: The development of higher psychological processes.* Cambridge University Press.

KEY TERMS AND DEFINITIONS

Affective Filter: Krashen (1985) defined the affective filter to illustrate how a student's attitudes or emotional factors might influence the effectiveness of language acquisition. Language learners who are negatively emotional block language input. Thus, it is necessary to stimulate learners' positive feelings while teaching language.

Author's Chair: The Author's Chair is a writing method used in the classroom that allows students to actively share their own works with their classmates as the audience. This unique opportunity to share their work encourages them to feel as though their particular writing output is recognized by their classmates.

Authoring: Authoring refers to the process of an author presenting an original manuscript to an audience.

Community of Learners: A community of learners is a group of people who support each other in their collective and individual learning.

Conditions of Learning: Cambourne (1988) highlights the importance of a rich language learning environment where teachers are facilitators and students take the lead to employ the language naturally.

Identity: Identity refers to an individual's distinguishing character or personality.

Language Acquisition: Language acquisition refers to how humans can develop the ability to understand and use language.

Language Acquisition Device (LAD): Chomsky (2002) developed the LAD in the 1960s. It refers to an alleged mental ability that enables a child to acquire language. It is a part of the nativist linguistic philosophy.

Narrative Approach: A narrative approach is cross-disciplinary in nature. It is a many-layered expression of human thought and imagination.

Self-Efficacy: Self-efficacy reflects confidence in the ability to exert control over one's own motivation, behavior, and social environment.

Zone of Proximal Development (ZPD): The ZPD, a central concept in Vygotsky's (1962) learning and development theory, refers to the area between what learners can achieve on their own and what they can do with adult supervision or in partnership with more capable classmates.

Chapter 17
Cultivating Cultural and Global Competence Through Collaboration With Diverse Groups of People

Sarah Evans
North Broward Preparatory School, USA

ABSTRACT

Can cultural and global competence be cultivated through experiential collaborations with diverse groups of people? There has been a great deal of attention placed on the importance of developing students' cultural competence; however, primary grade teachers often lack the resources and training necessary for thoroughly investigating diversity with young children. To build cultural competence, it is imperative to create meaningful opportunities in which students collaborate on common goals so that children can have positive experiences with people of different cultures. This chapter will explore a research-based method being used effectively in classrooms in the United States, Mexico, and Ecuador to develop students' cultural and global competence through project-based experiences that meet existing curricular needs. In addition to the methodology used to engage students in cross-cultural project-based collaborations, this chapter also includes practical strategies for the evaluation of participants' cultural competence as well as qualitative data that supports the findings.

INTRODUCTION

All too often in schools around the world, a dominant narrative is told about groups of people and the places from which they come. Nigerian writer Chimamanda Adichie (2009) explains in her TED talk, "The single story creates stereotypes, and the problem with stereotypes is not that they are untrue, but that they are incomplete. They make one story become the only story." When students have a limited perspective of a culture or place, they unintentionally form misleading stereotypes and biases which can have a negative impact on their interactions with others. This can reduce the opportunity for the

DOI: 10.4018/978-1-6684-5022-2.ch017

discovery and appreciation of similarities and differences. Therefore, Adichie (2009) argues that it is with a balance of stories and experiences that the single story can be overcome.

How do we create opportunities in schools for a balance of stories? As communities within our world become increasingly diverse, it is imperative for educators to become more intentional about building their own cultural competence as well as that of their students (Boix-Mansilla and Jackson, 2011). Cultural competence is defined by psychologists, healthcare professionals, and educators as the ability to understand and effectively interact with people from cultures different from our own to accomplish practical goals. The four components of cultural competence are *awareness, attitude, knowledge, and skills* (DeAngelis, 2015).

Researchers continue to agree that in a diverse world, one's cultural competence is the greatest predictor of success because of the way it equips us with tools for handling challenges presented by life and work (Livermore, 2011, p. xiii). However, in elementary classrooms throughout the United States, a vast number of teachers question the need for discussions about race in the classroom. Teachers report that this is because the topics can be difficult, uncomfortable, and controversial. Researcher, Demoiny (2017), suggests the real problem is that many elementary educators lack strategies and resources for addressing these issues.

Knowing that we have a responsibility to build students' cultural competence, it is no longer acceptable to turn a blind eye to a curriculum that does not intentionally develop an appreciation for diversity. Fernandez (2014) emphasizes that "the implicit and null curricula are as important as the explicit curriculum." Fernandez (2014) explains that it is easy to overlook that which is not taught such as the exclusion of people, voices, and events. However, a more complete understanding of history, events, and culture is an integral part of one's theological formation. The National Education Association (NEA) suggests cultural and global competence be cultivated through an innovative integration of international exchanges and diverse experiences. Global competence which encompasses the capacities of cultural competence is defined by the Asia Society as the capacity and disposition to understand and act on issues of global significance. Globally competent students are able to *investigate the world beyond their immediate environment, recognize perspectives, communicate ideas effectively with diverse audiences*, and *take action to improve conditions* (Boix Mansilla & Jackson, 2011). NEA recommends schools pivot away from solely studying culture through celebrations and events. Rather, it is recommended that schools teach culture through experiences in an effort to develop cultural competence in students and teachers.

With that came the driving question for this study, *Can cultural competence be cultivated through experiential collaborations with diverse groups of people?* This study was inspired by the need to dispel the single story inadvertently told in schools and the fears teachers have of "doing something wrong." It explores ways to provide an authentic understanding of cultural knowledge, beliefs, and values through hands-on experiences with diverse groups of people.

In an interview with Dr. Bena Kallick, co-founder of the Institute for Habits of Mind, she explained that she would cultivate cultural competence in children by building "equity consciousness," a term she defined as "the ability to pay attention to how much individuals have in common in order to know what makes their differences so special." To accomplish this, she suggested creating opportunities for people of different cultures to collaborate on meaningful projects that work toward a common goal. Likewise, when interviewing author, researcher, and educational consultant Dr. Angela Salmon, she also encouraged the concept of designing collaborative projects but added that these projects would be most beneficial if they were designed to solve real-world problems. Although Dr. Kallick suggested working with local children who have diverse backgrounds, Dr. Salmon identified the advantages of geographic diversity.

Cultivating Cultural and Global Competence

Ultimately, the recommendations of both experts align with NEA's recommendation to build cultural and global competence through innovative international exchanges.

Establishing a partnership with another school, particularly one that is located abroad, has its challenges. However, the schools participating in this collaboration are part of an international family of schools that connects more than 75 schools in over 30 countries. Tapping into this network allowed for collaboration with schools that are geographically and culturally unique. This combination made it possible to bring educators and students together to work toward common goals while building cultural competence.

Three schools and one orphanage participated in this collaboration. At a school located in South Florida, United States of America, students in kindergarten, third grade, and fifth grade collaborated with students of their same age at a school in Samborondón, Ecuador. Fifth-grade students learning to speak Spanish at the same school in the United States also collaborated with fourth-grade students at a school in San Roberto, Mexico. Finally, fourth-grade students from the American school worked on a collaborative project with children of various ages living at an orphanage in Haiti.

At the heart of this study, administrators and teachers collaborated virtually to design engaging interdisciplinary projects that encouraged students to learn about each other while working toward common goals. Working toward common goals, as advised by Dr. Kallick and Dr. Salmon, was intended to create authentic purposeful opportunities that organically challenged stereotypes and cultivated relationships among diverse groups.

The initial collaboration connected fifth-grade homeroom classes in the United States of America with sixth-grade STEAM (*science, technology, engineering, arts, math*) classes in Ecuador. Students met on the video platform Zoom with their partner class weekly for six weeks. In breakout rooms, collaborative groups created a home using Minecraft Education, a game-based learning platform, that incorporated representations of cultural features found in the contributing members' real homes. The provocation of cultural features from students' homes created an authentic purpose for looking closely at and appreciating one's own culture as well as listening with understanding and empathy to gain insight into the culture of others. After successfully piloting this project, the cross-cultural collaboration was expanded to include students in additional grade levels from the same three schools as well as children living at an orphanage in Haiti. New collaborations were tailored to meet the curricular needs of each grade level but continued to hold at its core, the development of cultural competence through collaborative projects.

Because of the way this cultural competence collaboration was established to invite stakeholders to co-create units, it has by design, already grown, and will continue to grow and change according to the needs of students and educators. To build cultural competence, it is imperative to create meaningful opportunities, such as those offered by this project, so children can have positive experiences with people of cultures different from their own. Due to the unique way in which teachers and students invested in common goals throughout these collaborations, participants organically became aware of their similarities, which aided their development of an appreciation for differences and thus, successfully impacted participants' equity consciousness.

PARTICIPANTS

Three independent schools participated in this collaborative project, North Broward Preparatory School in Florida, United States of America; Colegio Menor, in Samborondón, Ecuador; and San Roberto International School in Monterey, Mexico. All three schools are part of the Nord Anglia Education family of international schools. This was a multi-age project that engaged children from kindergarten through fifth grade.

BACKGROUND

Over the course of just two years, the world changed in unexpected and unprecedented ways leading to a greater need for interconnectedness. Boix Mansilla and Jackson (2011) support this notion and explain that rapid economic, technological, and social changes are what have led to an increase in global interdependence. With the globalization of economies, the digital revolution, mass migration, and the prospect of climate instability triggering new concerns, Boix Mansilla and Jackson (2011) are calling for a new kind of graduate, one who is not only culturally competent but also globally competent. In growing as globally competent students, children must also learn to be culturally competent. Therefore it is the responsibility of educators all over the world to create opportunities for children to practice and reflect upon their experiences with the capacities of both the cultural and global competencies.

For this reason, the United States Department of Education's International Affairs Office (2000) made a commitment to preparing students to positively contribute to a globalized world and engage with international communities to improve education. The department's primary objective is to increase the global and cultural competencies of all U.S. students because these competencies encompass the knowledge and skills necessary for successfully engaging in and acting on globally significant issues. This department also expresses the need to develop students' social and emotional skills as well as their ability to think critically and communicate with clarity and precision so they can more effectively work with others both locally and globally. This department emphasizes that "understanding and appreciating our diverse country and other parts of the world, including different religions, cultures, and points of view, are essential elements of global and cultural competence."

As part of the development of cultural competence, the Learning for Justice: Teaching Hard History Framework (2019, p 6) examines the importance of teaching about historical events that have led to prejudice and bias. Unfortunately, the organization notes that neither state departments of education nor the publishing industry provide effective guidance for teaching such difficult topics to young people. This is particularly true in elementary school. With a lack of guidance and resources for teachers to develop the competencies necessary for engaging in diverse societies, how can schools prepare our students to be both culturally and globally competent?

To begin with, according to the United States Department of Education's Framework for Cultural Competence (Appendix 1), developing a foundation for cultural competence, like the foundation for global competence, begins with the development of empathy and the ability to understand perspectives. This requires individuals to reflect deeply on what makes them who they are, investigating themselves in an effort to better understand others. Salmon (2017) recommends creating opportunities that invite students to explore their own identities, contexts, and realities. This, she says, cultivates opportunities for students to define themselves in a broader, global context, which in turn enables them to make important connections to all that is different. Boix Mansilla and Jackson (2011) however suggest students practice the disposition of perspective-taking and build their capacity for empathy when they collaborate with diverse groups of students. Given opportunities to be reflective about the way they view the world, students who possess the ability to take perspectives have an understanding of multiple contexts and traditions

Cultivating Cultural and Global Competence

and therefore are less likely to respond to differences in defensive or violent ways. Thus, they are better equipped to embrace differences as opportunities that enhance collaborations. Boix Mansilla and Jackson (2011) state the way in which our youth understand and react to diversity is dependent upon the quality of their preparation for living in diverse societies. Therefore, to develop students' perspective-taking dispositions, this cultural competence project began with students reflectively investigating their own biases, collaboratively interviewing each other, and exploring the cultural aspects that have influenced the designs of each other's homes.

In order to truly offer students a high-quality educational experience while creating an environment conducive to learning about how to positively contribute to our diverse society, researcher Ron Berger (2003) insists learning opportunities be intrinsically motivating. To accomplish this in a way that builds the capacity to be globally and culturally competent, Berger suggests engaging students in what he refers to as meaningful work. He defines this as work in which the outcome is useful to others. Berger (2014) explains that a school's primary purpose is the work its students produce. While a great deal of research suggests the emphasis in education should be placed on the process rather than the product, Berger argues that when students are intrinsically motivated by a process leading to an authentic and necessary impact, the product will represent the rigorous and deep learning that went into it. However, Berger (2003, p 78) notes that the challenge with this type of teaching and learning is that it will require a cultural shift in the way educators view a school's purpose. Fortunately, with mounting pressure on schools to develop cultural competence, schools have an opportunity to rethink the ways in which the most important content is taught or in this case, experienced in school.

This suggests that to create opportunities for students to develop the capacities outlined by the cultural and global competence frameworks, educators should develop curricula that invite students of diverse cultures to collaborate on meaningful work. This is additionally supported by the research of Boix Mansilla and Jackson (2011) who demonstrates that cultural and global competence can be cultivated in classrooms when teachers create project based learning experiences that provide students with multiple opportunities to examine what happens when cultures meet. She explains that students who are able to create and carry out an impactful plan for taking action, such as the type of meaningful work that can become a part of project based learning experiences, will believe in themselves as active contributors to our diverse world. This requires teachers to create opportunities that move beyond literary studies. Therefore, the work of these researchers proves that the type of deep meaningful learning necessary to build cultural competence occurs when students are emotionally engaged in the learning which is the foundation of the cultural competence collaboration examined in this chapter. Additionally, the work of neuroscientist, Mary Helen Immordino-Yang (2015) demonstrates that emotional engagement and personal relevance are the tools needed for students to learn. She argues that it is neurobiologically impossible to think deeply about something unless one cares about it. Thus, it can be concluded that in order for our students to truly develop cultural competence in school, educators must find ways to provide meaningful work to which students form emotional connections.

METHODOLOGY

The design of this collaboration was inspired by Mansilla and Chua's research (2017) which explains that in our increasingly diverse world, it is the schools' fundamental responsibility to prepare students for diversity and complexity. To accomplish this, she urges educators to create experiences through which children learn to pose questions and investigate cultural interactions. Therefore, teachers and leaders from the schools that collaborated on these cultural competence building projects, began to cocreate synchronous and asynchronous experiences to guide collaborative virtual learning for students. Inviting educators to co-create goals and learning opportunities was an important element in increasing teachers' investment and developing the emotional connections emphasized by Immordino-Yang and Berger. In the initial meeting, a framework for the first collaborative project was developed. After that, leaders worked synchronously and asynchronously to further develop the framework into a detailed plan. Then, teachers who would implement the project were invited to offer feedback and further tailor the project to their students' needs, interests, and skill sets. This open-ended design served as a platform for teachers and leaders to collaborate on common goals similar to the way their students would. In this way, giving teachers a voice and inviting them to co-create projects further developed their cultural competence as they too had an authentic reason to build relationships while developing impactful projects. While reflecting on the impact this collaboration has had on her school, the instructional facilitator at the participating school in Ecuador stated, "The cultural competence collaboration was an enriching experience not just for the students but also for the teachers and me."

Because the development of the dispositions necessary to build cultural competence can not be measured quantitatively, qualitative data was gathered through the use of the thinking routine, *Step In, Step out, Step Back* (Appendix 2), developed at the Harvard Graduate School of Education's Project Zero (2016). This routine has been recognized by Mansilla and Chua (2017) as "useful for researchers as pre-and post- measures of students developing targeted capacities." This thinking routine was designed to guide students in recognizing and analyzing their own biases while practicing the disposition of perspective-taking, the foundational competency of the cultural and global competence frameworks. Therefore, this routine was used at the beginning and end of each project to gather data because the routine not only evaluates potential growth but also enhances learning, an assessment quality identified by Tina Blythe (2019), project director at Harvard Graduate School of Education's Project Zero. Blythe argues that an accurate and fair assessment of understanding contains elements that further contribute to learning. Thus, assessment for understanding is not an end product but a process designed to inform students and teachers about what students understand and guide future steps for teaching and learning.

To pre-assess students' cultural competence, before being introduced to the cross-cultural collaboration project or to the students with whom they would soon collaborate, students used the *Step in* and *Step out* stages of the thinking routine to examine a photograph of the class of children with whom they would be meeting and working. The *Step in* section invited students to identify and document their own biases and perceptions about the group of students in the photo and encouraged discussion about how biases are formed. Students "stepped out" and raised questions about what they would like to know about the people in the photograph so they could better understand their perspectives. This brought awareness to students about their own biases and perceptions. Making students' thinking visible in this way intentionally highlighted biases so they could be addressed before and throughout the collaboration period. Noticing and understanding bias is an important step in the development of cultural competence. The Anti-Defamation League (2020, pg 11) warns that while attempting to minimize the development of prejudice, adults teach children to ignore differences, focusing only on similarities or being "color blind". To avoid this common mistake, at the end of the project, to evaluate growth and raise students' awareness of how their thinking changed from positively interacting with people they initially perceived as different, students completed the *Step back* section of the thinking routine by reflecting on their initial thinking, ability to effectively interact with others, and acceptance and respect for others' differences.

Cultivating Cultural and Global Competence

After completing the collaborative project, students and teachers were able to evaluate the development of cultural competence and used the information to influence future collaborations, discussions, and supplemental literature.

Once pre-assessments were completed and project plans were developed, classes began to meet on Zoom weekly. At all grade levels, the initial meeting had the same goals; to help students feel safe and comfortable and encourage students to ask questions to learn more about each other. These first sessions began with students being invited to contribute to the creation of group norms or expectations. This empowered students because their thinking was heard and valued by the group. From this whole group activity, students moved into breakout rooms with at least two students from each school. In their breakout rooms, students completed a getting to know you interview which encouraged students to ask questions, write for purpose, and begin talking about themselves. This practice helped build students' capacity for understanding perspectives, a foundational step toward becoming culturally and globally competent (Salmon, Gangotena, & Melliou, 2017). Students were observed making connections to each other's interests and talents which helped to develop emotional engagement in the partnership. After the first meeting, projects took a variety of forms depending on the needs of the grade level.

The first project, the pilot project, was designed for fifth-grade students in the United States who were nearing the end of their school year and middle school students enrolled in a STEAM course in Ecuador who were just beginning their school year. To meet the needs of both groups, an engaging project was developed to intentionally introduce students to new technology platforms while integrating the popular gaming platform, Minecraft Education. Because the National Council for Social Studies (NCSS) recommends a curriculum that encompasses what children already know about the world that surrounds them (Salmon, 2017), after interviewing and getting to know each other, students were invited to look thoughtfully at their own homes and create a list of elements in their home that have influenced who they are as a person. Teachers shared with students that they would be using their list to collaboratively build a home using Minecraft Education. The homes students designed were expected to incorporate students' cultural elements or influences as well as the contributions of their new partners. Minecraft Education was selected as the platform for the end product because of the potential this gaming platform had for connecting students to the project emotionally as well as encouraging dialogue due to its open-ended nature. Through authentic dialogue, children and teachers were frequently observed asking culture-based questions to deepen understanding and add detail to their project content. Students genuinely wanted to understand commonalities between themselves and others and were illuminated with curiosity and wonder when learning about each other's differences.

With the NCSS recommending a curriculum that develops concepts that are meaningful and relevant to students' lives, at the second meeting, each group member shared and discussed their list of influences found within their homes. Using the collaborative platform, Google Jamboard, participants worked together to illustrate a prototype of the home they planned to build in Minecraft. This provided students with an authentic purpose for sharing meaningful information about themselves and their culture, appreciating similarities and differences, learning about each other on a deeper level, and solving problems.

After finalizing their prototype, students met several times to complete their collaborative builds in Minecraft. In the end, group members presented to their classmates the homes they created in Minecraft. These presentations continued to build students' equity consciousness, as they deepened their understanding of how much they have in common and grew to appreciate each others' differences. It was evident students were emotionally engaged in learning more about each other as they were observed asking clarifying questions to gain a deeper understanding as well as to better contribute to the Minecraft home design. The learning permeated the walls of the classroom as students often worked outside of school on their projects as well. Each time students engaged in collaborative work, they added details to their schema about cultures and geography which helped to dispel single stories and stereotypes. As an unexpected benefit, teachers also further developed their own cultural competence as they collaborated on common goals and experienced positive interactions with educators from other schools.

Because of the impact this cultural competence collaboration pilot project had on teachers and students from all three schools, participants were eager to continue the partnership. Additionally, teachers working with other elementary-aged students were interested in participating in a similar collaboration. With that, teachers of additional grade levels partnered and began to co-create engaging and meaningful projects on which their students would collaborate. The following are examples of the ways grade-level teachers enhanced their existing curriculum through this collaboration.

The kindergarten teachers from the schools in the United States of America and Ecuador collaboratively designed a program that developed the early stages of cultural competence. Through this project, students were invited by their teachers to ask the students at their partner school about their own curiosities and wonders in relation to similarities and differences in each culture. For example, students were interested in learning about what each others' schools and playgrounds looked like so each class gave the other a virtual tour of their school. In another virtual session, students asked each other to share their favorite books. This gave students the opportunity to read for a purpose and also encouraged students to practice reading with fluency and expression. When students shared books about holidays, there were many questions related to culture and the ways in which students celebrate. In a final meeting, students brought to the screen a toy with which they enjoy playing. Students from both countries were surprised by the number of toys that could be found in both countries. Inviting children to pose and answer questions developed empathy and developed a greater appreciation for diversity.

At the school in Ecuador, third-grade students were engaged in a unit through which they applied their understanding of communities by creating a civilization. Meanwhile, in the United States, third-grade students were learning about how their family's culture contributed to the way they celebrate winter holidays. To integrate the themes and apply the learning from both projects, students at each school used their understanding of the holidays celebrated by their families to create a new holiday for the civilizations that were being designed by third-grade students in Ecuador. For this project, the students' common goals were to develop a holiday name, identify the holiday's purpose, and define how the holiday is celebrated. Students then had the opportunity to choose to create recipes, dances, songs, symbols, and traditions for the civilization's new holiday. This not only created opportunities for students to work together and learn about each other but also provided an authentic purpose for learning about the way different cultures celebrate holidays. Additionally, students developed their writing skills as they documented their thinking and communicated in written form. Figure 1 and figure 2 demonstrate the ways in which students collaborated with Google Slides using Thinking Maps to make their thinking visible.

Cultivating Cultural and Global Competence

Figure 1. Students added to this thinking map as they discussed their favorite holidays and their family traditions

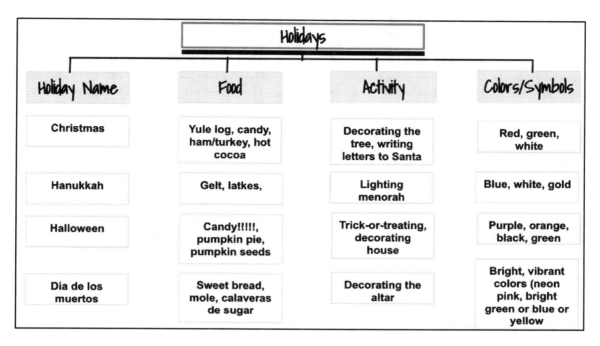

Figure 2. Students used this thinking map to identify the purpose of the new holiday they created as well as how they thought it should be celebrated

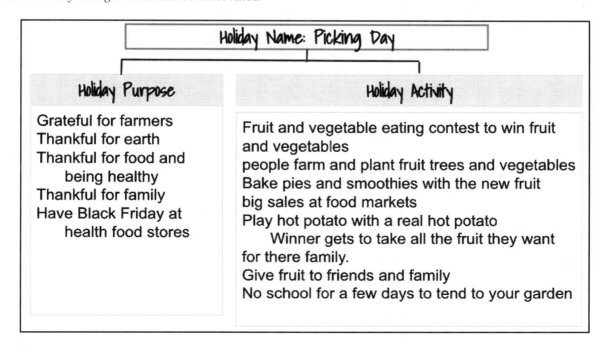

The United Nations (UN) identified and agreed on 17 Sustainable Development Goals (SDG), which all UN members agreed to work toward to end poverty, hunger, and disease throughout the world. In another cultural collaboration, the fourth-grade students at the school in America collaborated with children at an orphanage in Haiti to work toward ending hunger, one of the 17 SDGs. The children in both locations began a collaborative investigation about how to best grow tropical perennial plants for food in Florida and Haiti since both locations have similar plant hardiness growing zones. Through this project, students learned about the benefits of growing the types of plants that have the potential to offer an endless supply of food, even in the harsh growing conditions of both environments.

At the orphanage in Haiti and in the school garden in Florida, students grew the same plants for food. Due to unstable internet conditions in Haiti and a significant language barrier, the children contributed to a collaborative newsletter in which they wrote about plant progress, successes, and failures. Students also shared photographs of their plants and harvests. This type of meaningful work gave students in both countries an authentic purpose for reading and writing and provided them with authentic audiences.

Fifth-grade students in the United States of America and the international school in Ecuador took action toward the United Nations' Sustainable Development Goals as well. Collaborating teachers decided to use an existing unit from the American school in which students worked interdependently to invent a product that eradicates issues presented by the SDGs. Students at collaborating schools were grouped based on the SDG about which they were most passionate. They then used the Design Thinking Process developed at the Hasso-Plattner Institute of Design at Stanford to collaboratively create and promote a prototype of their invention.

At the start of this project, students met on Zoom with an expert from the international relief organization, Food for the Poor Inc., to learn and ask questions about the needs of the destitute people who live in developing nations. From this expert, they also learned about unique and inspiring ways organizations such as Food for the Poor are already providing aid to the materially poor. Additionally, students learned about the importance of understanding the types of resources that are and are not available in developing nations. This information aided students in designing creative inventions that have the potential to positively impact others.

After developing background knowledge and empathy, students met in breakout rooms to brainstorm ideas for useful inventions. Students then used the collaborative whiteboard, Jamboard, to illustrate and label iterations of their invention ideas. In their next session, students worked together to narrow their focus and develop their product design. This step created the opportunity for students to further develop their ability to be active listeners, remain open to continuous learning, and consider the perspectives of others. Additionally, students developed their research and writing skills as they investigated the science behind how to make their product work as well as have an impact. For example the group of students who created a backpack water filter first read about the devastating effects of contaminated water sources on the health of children and then researched various ways to filter water using natural resources.

A fifth-grade teacher from the school in the United States reflected on the experience stating, "Our cultural connection with our sister school in Ecuador was a wonderful experience for my students. With the common language of the United Nations Sustainable Development Goals, my students were allowed to have meaningful conversations about world problems that affect us all. To quote one student, 'The kids in Ecuador weren't so different from kids in Florida. We did a lot of the same things for fun and we cared about the same things, especially world hunger and climate change.' This gives me hope that my students will make a difference in the future!"

Cultivating Cultural and Global Competence

Figure 3 shows the ideations of three collaborative groups that designed inventions that would help with meeting the United Nations' Sustainable Development Goals.

Figure 3.

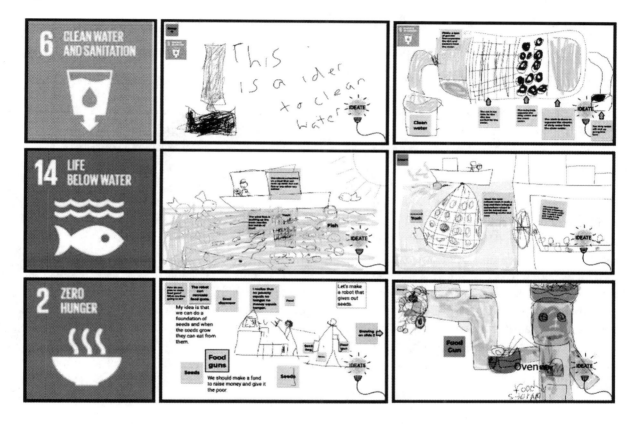

Once groups decided on the design of their invention, students met through Zoom with a panel of experts from Food for the Poor Inc. During this session, students presented to an expert their plans for their invention, its purpose, and their goals. Experts from Food for the Poor Inc. offered constructive feedback based on the experiences they had while working with people in developing nations and in some cases, suggested organizations students could connect with to further develop their idea. Students used the feedback to further refine their plans before building a prototype.

Designing prototypes collaboratively with culturally diverse group members offered many opportunities due to the unique perspectives and experiences of each student. Through this collaborative process, students were able to give each other advice based on the experiences they had with the resources they chose to use. For example, the group of students that worked toward SDG 14, *Life Below Water*, invented a product designed to float on water. However, they built the prototype using cardboard. They then advised their partners in the United States to avoid using cardboard as it disintegrated upon getting wet.

In another collaborative project, students learning Spanish through a World Language program in the United States collaborated with students learning English in Mexico to learn more about each other's daily lives and deepen their understanding of cultural holidays such as Dia de Los Muertos. In this collaboration, students used the platform Book Creator to ask and answer questions about each other using video, voice recordings, written language, art, and photographs. A Spanish teacher in America reflected on her students' experience stating, "This was a special opportunity to communicate with native Spanish speakers while creating together. Through written and oral language, students compared and contrasted their pets, cultural holidays, daily schedules, and favorite sports and colors. This was an incredible learning experience for students in both countries!"

FINDINGS AND DISCUSSION

Cultural competence collaborations through which students work toward common and meaningful goals, such as the ones discussed in this chapter, help children discover there is much they have in common with diverse groups of people while gaining an appreciation for the benefits of being unique. Through positive interactions with people of different cultures, children learn to recognize differences as characteristics that have the potential to enhance project outcomes while similarities have the potential to sow the seeds for creating connections. With that, collaborating on common goals helps build cultural and global competence in students. After her second year of participating with her students in the cultural competence collaborations, a teacher in Mexico noted, "The cross-cultural exchange is the project that has had the most lasting impression on my students!"

The growth in the way students thought about diverse populations is primarily evidenced in the *Step Back* section of the *Step in, Step out, Step back* thinking routine. Careful analysis of this data revealed three important themes: Participants increased their awareness of cultural biases, gained an understanding that they shared interests with people of diverse groups, and despite their initial concerns, language was not a barrier to communication, collaboration, and friendship.

Evidence from the qualitative data has been organized below according to the four major components of cultural competence; *awareness, attitude, knowledge, and skills*.

- **Awareness** - an acknowledgment of bias and prejudice

Student A

Based on the photograph in the thinking routine, Student A thought she would not be able to collaborate because the students looked like they were not able to speak English.
Step in:

"I think that they speak Spanish because of their names and that they go to a Hispanic school."

After collaborating with students from Ecuador, this student demonstrated an awareness that communication was not challenging and they had common interests. This also displays the development of an emotional connection to students in the group.
Step back:

"I used to think they only spoke Spanish but they did not. I used to think that we would not be similar but we were because we played tennis and watched the same shows. At first, I did not think they were going

Cultivating Cultural and Global Competence

to talk but they were very social and we talked a lot. My view changed like a landslide by knowing their personalities and how they are very similar to me. I think I had the best group."

Student B

This student's thinking about diverse groups and their potential to contribute changed from the beginning of the project to the end. After working with her partners in Ecuador, she reflectively remarked; Step back:

From now on, when I meet new people, I will not use names or the way their faces look to make judgments. Instead, I will talk to them and understand them.

Although it was uncommon for students to express biases in writing, students C and D shared their initial concerns based on their first impressions.

Student C

Step back:

"I first thought they would be talkative, loud, annoying people who did not pay any attention to anything I said. Who always had their camera off. Now I realize I can have conversations with them and talk about things we like, like sports, roller coasters, tv shows, and little brothers and sisters. Now I think it was really cool that they speak English almost fluently. I understand that my first impression was totally wrong and my thinking changed when I actually met these people and got to know them.

Student D

Step back:

"When we first saw the photo I thought a lot of the people were mean or other personalities. Now that I have met them I realize they are not. When we got put in our breakout rooms they started to talk. We got to know them and they started to get more comfortable and we started talking more and I realized they were kind."

While most students demonstrated open-mindedness and acceptance of others, students E and F expressed caution despite the positive experiences they had with these students. This demonstrates that these students are still in the early phases of becoming culturally and globally competent with some understanding of their own culture and ethnicity but are still working on learning about and embracing others.

Student E

Step back:

"Next time I meet someone I might still have a bias because I don't always trust new people but if I actually got to know them and find that they are a good person then I won't have a bias. I liked the people I worked with a lot. They liked anime like I do. I expected them to not like anime. We sometimes spoke in Spanish with each other too since it's easier for them."

Student F

Step back:

"In the future, when I meet someone, I will still have a bias. I say this because I could be talking to a bad guy without even knowing it. I am also really shy so I don't always want to start talking to someone to get to know them."

- **Attitude** - an openness to varying ideas and opinions

Student G

Student G shared that the next time she meets someone, despite her biases, she will look for commonalities and ask questions, demonstrating her interest in understanding perspectives and a willingness to learn about the cultural practices and worldviews of others.
Step back:

"The next time I meet somebody like this, I would probably have more wonders and go talk to them and figure out what we have in common because you always have at least one thing in common and one thing that is different. I will still probably have some biases but I will wonder a lot too."

Evidence also shows students learned skills they believe will help with cultivating friendships with others. This demonstrates an ability to understand perspectives as well as an interest in taking action to improve conditions in the world, one of the capacities for global competence.

Student H

Step Back:

"The next time I meet someone I am going to have more wonderment because I thought they would be boring but they were completely different. I am not going to make guesses about them. Instead, I will just go say hi and see what happens next.``

- **Knowledge** - being informed about other cultures

Students I and J demonstrate how this project helped to dispel bias and increase the likelihood of students reserving judgment.

Cultivating Cultural and Global Competence

Student I

Step Back:

"My experiences with them were that they are very cool, that they are nice and that they are really friendly. I learned that you should never judge a book by its cover. I also learned people don't like specific things just because of where they live."

Student J

Step Back:

"The next time I meet or see someone that is different I will think about what they might like. Also, I will think about what they might have in common with me. I will say hello and try my best to get to know them."

Student K demonstrated this project's potential for developing three of the four cultural competencies; *a willingness to learn about the cultural practices and worldview of others, a positive attitude toward cultural differences, and a willingness to accept and respect these differences.*

Student K

Step Back:

"I learned some new things about their cultures and realized they aren't as different as I thought."

- **Skills-** The ability to manage differences effectively.

Another common theme that surfaced from student reflections was an increase in the students' understanding of the importance of reserving judgment when they first meet someone. This demonstrates a positive attitude toward cultural differences and the benefits of collaborating with those who bring a unique perspective, a willingness to accept and respect these differences, and the foundation for developing the skills to work with others. Students L, M, and N demonstrated these foundational skills in their reflections.

Student L

Step back:

"My experience was wonderful. All of the kids were very open to everyone's ideas and listened to each other. We all added to each other's ideas and made our project even better. Overall I thought it was pretty cool meeting kids from another country. The next time I meet somebody I will think back to this time and will treat them with kindness as the kids and teachers in Ecuador treated us. The best but the experience was great!"

Student M

Step back:

"Next time I meet someone that looks like them, my perspective will change because now I know they can have the same interests as me and that they might be someone fun to hang out with. When I see someone new, next time I will talk to them and find out more about their personality and then I will make interesting conversations."

Student N

Step back:

"I think that next year if I see new kids in my class, I might still judge based on how they look but I won't let that stop me from meeting them and getting to know them. I'll go up to them, make them comfortable and talk to them more."

While most students expressed surprise when they learned the students spoke English despite their initial thoughts, student O, who recently moved to America from Costa Rica, was surprised to learn her partner spoke Spanish just as fluently as English. Because student O also spoke Spanish fluently, this became a similarity that the two students embraced. Her reflection highlights the enthusiasm the majority of students expressed toward meeting online with their "new friends." In the classroom, students frequently asked to meet with their cooperative groups and often engaged outside of school using social media and email, demonstrating the level of emotional engagement that leads to deep and meaningful learning emphasized by the work of Dr. Immordino-Yang. It is this type of emotional connection to learning that educators seek to develop in their classrooms.

Student O

Step back:

"It was really nice meeting this group. I enjoyed partnering with a girl who was shy at first but as we got deeper into the project became more confident. When I found out she spoke Spanish, I immediately admitted that I did too! From then on we got on as if we had known each other for years. I fully recommend doing this project again, as I think it was really fun for everyone! In this class, I found that these kinds of projects are so much fun that the time I spend with my partner passed too quickly!

CONCLUSION

The development of cultural and global competence in elementary-aged children is a vital part of preparing children to actively contribute in positive ways to a diverse society and interconnected world. Therefore, it is critical that educators commit to engaging students in meaningful opportunities to cultivate these competencies.

The evidence from each of these cross-cultural collaborations demonstrated a significant improvement in students' capacities for cultural and global competence. Additionally, these collaborations offered students authentic purposes for reading and writing and organically created meaningful work through which students were able to develop language and literacy. The cross-cultural group projects were successful largely in part due to the emotional connections students made to the work in which they engaged as well as the people with whom they worked, the intrinsic motivation developed from working toward common and meaningful goals, and the intentional integration of subjects and themes. Inviting students to work together on projects such as the ones investigated throughout this chapter created experiences for educators and students that fostered positive interactions with diverse groups of people. This led to the development of students' appreciation for not only their similarities but also that which they found unique. Therefore, it can be concluded that cross-cultural collaborations develop students' capacities to better understand, communicate with, and effectively interact with people who are different from themselves. This is the kind of work necessary to develop culturally and globally competent children who are prepared and motivated to have a positive impact on their immediate environment and the diverse world in which we live.

REFERENCES

Anti-defamation League. (2020). *Anti-Bias Building Blocks*. Anti-Defamation League.

Berger, R. (2003). *An Ethic of Excellence: Building a Culture of Craftsmanship with Students* (1st ed.). Heinemann.

Berger, R., Rugen, L., Woodfin, L., & Education, E. L. (2014). *Leaders of Their Own Learning: Transforming Schools Through Student-Engaged Assessment* (1st ed.). Jossey-Bass.

Blythe, T. (2019). *Teaching for Understanding: Ongoing Assessment.* Annenberg Learner. Retrieved August 20, 2021, from https://www.learner.org/wp-content/uploads/2019/02/7.OngoingAssessment.pdf

Boix Mansilla, V., & Jackson, A. (2011). *Educating for global competence: Preparing our youth to engage in the world*. The Asia Society.

Chimamanda Ngozi Adichie: The danger of a single story | TED. (2009, October 7). [Video]. YouTube. https://www.youtube.com/watch?v=D9Ihs241zeg&t=743s

DeAngelis, T. (2015). *In Search of Cultural Competence*. Monitor on Psychology. Retrieved August 20, 2021, from http://www.apa.org/monitor/2015/03/cultural-competence

Demoiny, S. B. (2016, November 30). *ERIC - EJ1150569 - Are You Ready? Elementary*. Academic Press.

Fernandez, E. S. (2014). *Teaching for a Culturally Diverse and Racially Just World*. Cascade Books.

Global competence is a 21st century imperative. (n.d.). National Education Association. Retrieved June 20, 2021, from https://citeseerx.ist.psu.edu/viewdoc/download?doi=10.1.1.184.8517&rep=rep1&t

Harvard Graduate School of Education. (2016). *Project Zero*. Retrieved March 7, 2021, from http://www.pz.harvard.edu/

Hilton, A. (2011). *Educating for Global Competence*. Asia Society. Retrieved March 10, 2021, from https://asiasociety.org/education/educating-global-competence

Immordino-Yang, M. (2015). *Emotions, Learning, and the Brain: Exploring the Educational Implications of Affective Neuroscience*. W.W. Norton and Company.

Livermore, D. (2011). *The Cultural Intelligence Difference*. American Management Association.

Mansilla, V. B., & Chua, F. S. (2017). Signature Pedagogies in Global Competence Education: Understanding Quality Teaching Practice. In S. Choo, D. Sawch, A. Villanueva, & R. Vinz (Eds.), *Educating for the 21st Century*. Springer., doi:10.1007/978-981-10-1673-8_5

Objective 1: Increase Global and Cultural Competencies of All U.S. Students. (2000). International Affairs Office. Retrieved March 15, 2021, from https://sites.ed.gov/international/objective-1-increase-global-and-cultural-competencies-of-all-u-s-students/

Pre-Service Teachers' Perceptions about Discussing Race in Social Studies, Multicultural Education. (2017). Retrieved February 12, 2021, from https://eric.ed.gov/?id=EJ1150569

Salmon, A. K., Gangotena, M. V., & Melliou, K. (2017). Becoming Globally Competent Citizens: A Learning Journey of Two Classrooms in an Interconnected World. *Early Childhood Education Journal*, 46(3), 301–312. https://doi.org/10.1007/s10643-017-0860-z

Strom, A. (2021, October 15). *Thinking Routines for a World on the Move. Re-Imagining Migration*. Retrieved January 4, 2021, from https://reimaginingmigration.org/thinking-routines-for-learning-to-live-in-a-world-on-the-move/

Teaching hard history: A framework for teaching American slavery. (n.d.). Learning for Justice. Retrieved March 10, 2021, from https://www.learningforjustice.org/sites/default/files/2021-11/LFJ-2111-Teaching-Hard-History-K-5-Framework-November-2021-11172021.pdf

KEY TERMS AND DEFINITIONS

Cultural Competence: The ability to understand, communicate, and effectively interact with people from diverse cultures.

Culture: The way in which racial, religious, or social groups live, believe, and practice customs.

Global Competence: The ability to understand and take action toward global issues.

Project-Based Learning: A teaching method in which students engage in meaningful projects.

Sustainable Development Goals: Seventeen goals with 169 targets agreed on by the United Nations to end poverty, hunger, and disease by the year 2030.

Thinking Map: A set of visual tools used for making the user's fundamental thought processes visible.

Thinking Routine: A set of questions, steps, or provocations used to scaffold and support deep thinking.

APPENDIX

Figure 4. United States Department of Education Framework for Developing Global and Cultural Competencies to Advance Equity, Excellence, and Economic Competitiveness

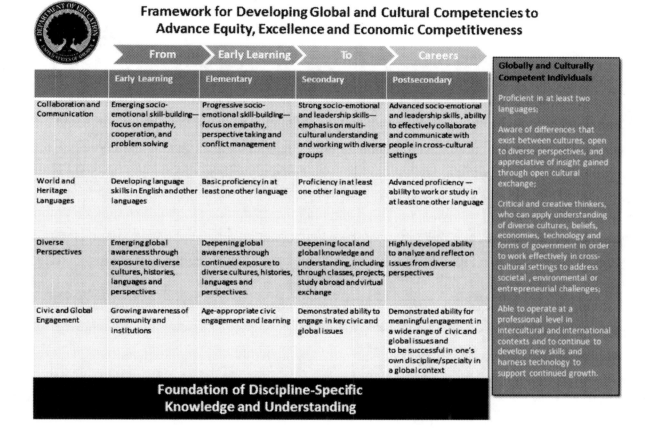

Figure 5. Step In, Step Out, Step Back thinking routine instructions

A THINKING ROUTINE FROM PROJECT ZERO, HARVARD GRADUATE SCHOOL OF EDUCATION

Step In - Step Out - Step Back

A routine for nurturing a disposition to take social/cultural perspective responsibly.

Step-in step-out step-back	
Choose:	Identify a person or agent in the situation you are examining.
Step In:	Given what you see and know at this time, what do you think this person might feel, believe, know, or experience?
Step out:	What else would you like or need to learn to understand this person's perspective better?
Step back:	Given your exploration of this perspective so far, what do you notice about your own perspective and what it takes to take somebody else's?

Purpose: What kind of thinking does this routine encourage?
While as human beings we are typically curious about the experiences and views of others, taking social perspective is a challenging cognitive and emotional task. A respectful approach to perspective taking requires that we avoid building stereotypes of others or projecting our own values and beliefs onto others. Understanding another person's world can be exciting and revealing. Yet perspective taking is also challenging and calls for practice over time.

This routine invites learners to take other people's perspectives e.g. religious, linguistic, cultural, class, generational; recognize that understanding others is an ongoing, often uncertain process; and understand that our efforts to take perspective can reveal as much about ourselves as they can about the people we are seeking to understand. The routine helps learners to identify individuals with various perspectives in a given situation; provide evidence for thoughts, values and feelings these individuals may hold; and explain how societal or more macro-forces—particularly roles and relationships—shape their perspectives. Scaffolding for healthy skepticism and reflection invites learners to take note of the biases and preferences that shape their understanding of others.

Application: When and where can I use it?
This routine can be adapted to a broad range of topics, from examining the perspectives of agents in a story, a historical event or a contemporary news article, to considering non-human perspectives such as species in an ecosystem, or collective perspectives such as interest groups in a given conflict. The routine can also be used to examine students' own perspectives in classroom situations or as they seek, for example, to create a math expression for a given problem. You may choose an image, a video, a story, or a classroom incident as provocation on which to ground students' thinking.

Launch: What are some tips for starting and using this routine?
It is important for students to have enough basic information about the perspectives they will examine to support an informed initial guess. It is important to help students avoid creating a "fictional character" that may confirm rather than challenge cultural stereotypes. When setting up the routine for students, you may want to highlight that understanding how others view the world can be exciting and sometimes challenging, setting expectations for complex reasoning. You may also mark a distinction between a more imaginative "step-in" and a more inquiry driven "step-out."

Continued on the next page.

Share your experience with this thinking routine on social media using the hashtags #PZThinkingRoutines and #StepInStepOutStepBack

PROJECT ZERO | PZ CONNECT

This thinking routine was developed as part of the PZ Connect project at Project Zero, Harvard Graduate School of Education.

Explore more Thinking Routines at pz.harvard.edu/thinking-routines

Step In - Step Out - Step Back, cont'd

In "step-in" make sure learners understand that they are reasoning with the information that they have, which is always limited. You may point to the speculative nature of their interpretations. In "step out," invite learners to see that there is more to understanding another person than the first impression they construct. As they share their views, students may detect stereotypes in their own initial thinking and feel uneasy about "having been wrong" in their guess. It is important to normalize the fact that we all have first impressions of others and others have them of us, and point to the importance of committing to understanding other persons' perspectives beyond initial assumptions. Under "step back," learners may explore how prior knowledge, cultural or linguistic perspectives inform or obscure their interpretation. Like other routines, this one lends itself well to small groups. Indeed, the different perspectives learners hold might become more visible through dialog. You may invite students to write their responses to each question individually on separate Post-its first and then share.

What is Global Competence?
Global competence can be defined as the capacity and disposition to understand and act on issues of global significance (Boix Mansilla & Jackson 2011). Globally competent students prepare for complex societies and a global economy by learning how to investigate the world beyond their immediate environment, framing and making sense of significant issues. How do migrant populations adapt to their new places of work and living? What tools do governments have to promote economic development and eradicate extreme poverty? What is an ecosystem and how do different ecosystems around the world work? Globally competent students also learn to recognize their own and others' perspectives, articulating and explaining such perspectives thoughtfully, empathically and respectfully. Globally competent students can communicate across differences, bridging cultural, linguistic, economic and religious divides – two additional capacities that are especially important to today's fragmented and interconnected societies. Most importantly, in order to be prepared to participate and work in today's world students, must learn to take responsible action. They need to learn to identify opportunities for productive action to develop and carry out informed plans. Prepared students, this framework suggests, view themselves as informed, thoughtful, compassionate and effective citizens and workers in changing times (Boix Mansilla & Jackson 2011).

Global competence is cast as a capacity to understand – meaning, broadly speaking, to use disciplinary concepts, theories, ideas, methods or findings in novel situations, to solve problems, produce explanations, create products or interpret phenomena in novel ways (Boix Mansilla & Gardner 1999). It focuses on issues of global significance and action to improve conditions; learning must be visibly relevant to students and the world. When significance is considered, global competence curricula becomes a call for authenticity, for carefully looking to the contemporary world for topics that matter most to examine (Perkins 2015).

Finally, "global competence" as a disposition speaks of student ownership and long-lasting transformation. Thinking dispositions, Project Zero researchers have proposed, involve the ability to think with information, the sensitivity to opportunities in the real world to do that, and the inclination to do so over time (Perkins et al 1993, Tishman et al 1993). Dispositions are about the "residuals" of learning beyond formal contexts (Ritchhart 2014); they are about the "kind of person" a student will become (Boix Mansilla & Gardner 2000). Broadly considered, global competence dispositions include:

- A disposition to inquire about the world (for example, engaging with questions of significance, exploring local-global connections, and seeking information beyond familiar environments, describing, explaining and developing a position about the world).
- A disposition to understand multiple perspectives--others' and their own (for example, considering cultural contexts, resisting stereotypes, and valuing our shared human dignity-- especially as students interact with others whose paths differ greatly from their own).
- A disposition toward respectful dialog (communicating across differences listening generously, sharing courageously, openly and appropriately given their audience and context).
- A disposition toward taking responsible action (being inclined to see and frame opportunities to improve conditions, and collaborating with others, and mobilize themselves to act).

Share your experience with this thinking routine on social media using the hashtags #PZThinkingRoutines and #StepInStepOutStepBack

PROJECT ZERO | PZ CONNECT

This thinking routine was developed as part of the PZ Connect project at Project Zero, Harvard Graduate School of Education.

Explore more Thinking Routines at pz.harvard.edu/thinking-routines

Chapter 18
Sociocultural and Linguistic Assets of a High School Student Named Maria:
Amigos y Anime

Michelle L. Ploetz
Atlanta Public Schools, USA

Kelly A. Hernandez
Miami Dade College, USA

ABSTRACT

This chapter tells the story of the language learning aspirations and educational experiences of Maria, a high school student from an immigrant family living in a large metropolitan area of the southeastern United States. Her story documents her quest to acquire literacy in a heritage language, Spanish, and to learn other foreign languages, French and Japanese. Her experiences have been shaped by the languages spoken in her home, the respective educational levels of family members and friends who provide academic support to her, the larger multilingual community in which she lives, interpersonal interactions with teachers, and popular culture. Vygotsky's sociocultural theory and other theories derived from this theory were used to analyze her experiences. Stories like hers can serve as a powerful resource for scholars and practitioners of language teaching and learning who seek to inform their practice through greater understanding of many sociocultural factors and linguistic assets that influence the success of language learners at the individual level.

DOI: 10.4018/978-1-6684-5022-2.ch018

INTRODUCTION

This chapter chronicles the story of the language learning aspirations and educational experiences of a 17-year-old high school student from an immigrant family, Maria (a pseudonym). Maria has studied four languages, English, Spanish, French and Japanese, and lives in a large metropolitan area in the southeastern United States (U.S.). Like 90% of American children from immigrant families (Annie E. Casey Foundation, 2021), she was born in the United States (U.S.). The research literature refers to these children as "second-generation immigrants." Second-generation immigrants bring considerable linguistic and cultural capital into the nation's schools. Indeed, 10% of the children in the U.S. speak a language other than English at home (National Center for Education Statistics, 2022). Furthermore, more than 400 languages are spoken by families whose children are enrolled in public schools (U.S. Department of Education, 2016).

However, these statistics shed little light on the language learning and literacy development experiences of second-generation immigrants, like Maria. These numbers do not tell educators how to leverage the rich linguistic backgrounds of their students in the classroom, nor provide insight into the quality of instruction these students receive or how it might be improved. Numbers do not put a student face to a demographic trend.

Using case study research, this chapter introduces the reader to Maria, a young woman who has studied four languages, English, Spanish, French, and Japanese. Her language learning experiences are examined to answer the following research questions:

1. What are the language learning and literacy development experiences of a second-generation immigrant pursuing studies in Spanish, French, and Japanese?
2. How do sociocultural theories of language learning account for Maria's experiences?
3. How can her experiences inform teaching practice and program design?

LITERATURE REVIEW

Two influential ways of thinking about case study research are introduced here. First, Stake (1995) classified case study research as being intrinsic, collective, or instrumental. An intrinsic case study involves the investigation of a single case, whereas a collective case study looks at multiple cases to explore similarities and differences among them. An instrumental case study, such as the one discussed in the present study, focuses on a single case for the purpose of explaining a theory. Flyvbjerg (2006) indicated that despite the conventional view that instrumental case studies "cannot contribute to scientific development," they produce context-dependent knowledge that enable "people to develop from rule-based beginners to virtuoso experts" (p. 221). Second, Yin (2009) asserted that even though case studies, especially those of a single sample, are not generalizable to a population, they may be generalizable to theories.

Thus, with the goal of building upon theory, this paper begins with a cursory review of sociocultural theories of learning and pedagogy (including Vygotskian sociocultural theory), funds of knowledge, heritage language education, and languaging. It was hypothesized that each of these could explain different dimensions of the learner experience and be used to answer the research questions above. Each theory is briefly described in this section with a statement of the author's assumptions of the value of each in analyzing Maria's story.

This present study utilizes Vygotsky's (1978) theory that language acquisition is socially motivated and mediated; it is a tool developed by humans for humans. Vygotsky argued that humans use tools, both physical and symbolic, to interact with the world around them (Lantolf & Thorne, 2007). Physical tools include such everyday items and objects such as tables, computers, and cars, whereas symbolic tools include human-designed systems (such as art, music, math or language) that facilitate human interactions with each other and the larger world. In Vygotsky's view, emotions (positive and negative) not only help student learning, but they also play an important role in language production (Vygotsky, 1978). When people communicate, they construct dialogues socially, and the emotions that are involved mediate learning outcomes. Like Vygotsky, Gredler (2001) observed that the way we process information and execute higher order thinking is through social interactions and within our cultural environments.

Vygotsky's sociocultural theory is fundamental to and ubiquitous in language education (Fahim & Haghani, 2012). It is germane to this study of the language learning experiences of Maria since she had early exposure to the sociocultural interplay of learning two languages. Compared to her monolingual peers, Maria had a head start in thinking about the sociocultural contexts in which languages are used. These early experiences certainly would have shaped her understanding of the world, her future learning, and her identity. The multifaceted social contexts in which Maria lives motivated the author to examine additional sociocultural theories of learning to understand Maria's story and glean insight into the design of language and literacy education.

Funds of Knowledge

The history of the conceptual framework that undergirds funds of knowledge (FoK) is essential to understand its implications for education in general and language education in particular. A synopsis of that history taken from Hogg (2011) is provided here to explain its evolution from the social sciences to a pedagogical approach to education.

The phrase *funds of knowledge* originated in anthropological studies that investigated the sharing of resources and skills found in Latinx communities. In particular, an article by anthropologist Velez-Ibanez (1988) motivated colleagues at the University of Arizona, including Luis Moll, Norma Gonzalez, and James Greenberg, to adapt FoK as an instrument for teaching and learning (Hogg, 2011, p. 668). This group published collaboratively and extensively on FoK in the classroom (Gonzalez et al., 1995; Gonzalez & Moll, 2002; Moll et al., 1989; Moll et al., 1990; Moll & Greenberg, 1990; Moll, 1992; Moll, 2005; Velez-Ibanez & Greenberg, 1992).

Given the number of scholars investigating the applications of FoK for the classroom, Hogg (2011) documented different definitions of FoK. For example, some researchers focused on the "who" or sources of knowledge within a household or community while others wrote about the "what" or area of knowledge (p. 673). For the purposes of this chapter, FoK will refer to the practice "through which educators can approach and document the funds of knowledge of families and represent them on the bases of the knowledge, resources, and strengths they possess" (Moll, 2019, p. 130). This definition focuses narrowly on families rather than communities and advocates for a positive view of learners and their families. It serves as an antidote to deficit views of learners that focus narrowly on teacher-centered, classroom-based learning and performance and fail to account for educational assets that families have, especially working-class families. It encourages teachers to become social scientists and apply qualitative research methods to learn about their students, their families, and the knowledge assets available in their homes and communities for the purpose of using those assets to inform their teaching.

The present research builds on FoK theory and emphasizes the fact that many immigrants who come to the U.S. are more likely to be employed in service industries or are underemployed, despite having earned a high school diploma or more (U.S. Bureau of Labor Statistics, 2021; Migration Policy Institute, 2021). Thus, their knowledge is not limited to skills gleaned from working in agriculture, manufacturing, or construction as early writings on FoK might imply (Moll et al., 1992). Many immigrant families have educational backgrounds that are needed to have informed opinions of the quality of academic instruction received by their children and to supplement perceived gaps. An anecdote sheds light on this phenomenon: An immigrant known by the author who worked as an engineer in his home country and now as a factory foreman in the U.S. was frustrated with the quality of math instruction his son was receiving. He retrieved his own math textbooks during a visit to his homeland to supplement his son's instruction in this subject. If this is the case with mathematics, it may be an even more pronounced problem with language learning. Immigrant families who speak languages that are taught in U.S. schools have valuable insight into the quality of the learning experience, which touches on the subject of heritage language education.

Heritage Language Education

Immigrant families in the U.S. have schooled their children in their home languages almost as long as the nation has been in existence (King, 2008; Schmid, 2001; Valdés et al., 2006, Chapter 2). Most of these opportunities were proffered in parochial schools or were of practical value in homogenous communities. However, the notion of heritage language education (HLE) as "a specific subfield of applied linguistics and language pedagogy" has a shorter history (Leeman, 2015, p. 101). HLE emerged in the last decade of the 20th century and coincided with increasing immigration, the codification of linguistic rights, and federal programs designed to ensure that our nation had the linguistic capital to meet economic and security interests (Brecht & Ingold, 2002, as cited in Carreira & Kagan, 2018). The argument for providing specialized language instruction to this group of learners is that heritage language learners benefit from language pedagogy that accounts for learner identity and their prior knowledge of language and culture.

As defined by Valdés (2000), a heritage language learner is a person reared in a home where a non-English language is spoken. Other definitions of heritage language learners refer to them on the basis of their cultural connections to language through family, community, or country of origin (Kelleher, 2010). The simplicity of these definitions is appealing, implying perhaps that easy language education solutions exist to serve the needs of these learners. While they do serve to bring recognition to the large numbers of second-generation students, these definitions belie the heterogeneity and complexity of learning needs that exists among these students. However, the emergence of Heritage Language Studies as a field has revealed the complexity of designing quality HLE programs (Carreira & Kagan, 2018). HLLs bring different life experiences to the classroom, have varying levels of exposure to and motivations for studying their home languages. The difference among learners who might be called heritage learners may be observed in the definitions above. Some may speak the language at home while others may simply have "cultural connections" to places where the language is spoken. Thus, specific language learning needs may vary according to linguistic skills, especially writing, or language domain, grammar or lexicon. Maria's learning profile fits both definitions. She lives in a home where Spanish is spoken, and she maintains cultural ties to countries where the language is spoken. It was expected that Maria would benefit from pedagogy that accounts for her prior knowledge of Spanish and her ongoing ties with family in Spanish-speaking countries. Given the numbers of students who speak languages other than English at home in the U.S., it makes sense to account for varying degrees of knowledge in the design of language education programs. Teachers who wish to teach language to heritage learners are encouraged to participate in professional development to learn more about HL learner needs and how to develop a responsive curriculum to meet those needs (Gironzetti & Belpoliti, 2021).

Languaging, defined as the "process of making meaning and shaping knowledge and experience through language" (Swain, 2006, p. 98), informed this study. Languaging was derived from Vygotsky's sociocultural theory of learning (Swain & Watanabe, 2013) and emerged from Swain's output hypothesis and her assertion that collaborative dialogues in the classroom could foster the development of linguistic knowledge (Swain, 2000). The linguistic knowledge in Swain's writings account largely for an ability to master grammatical concepts or skills like writing. Indeed, fifteen empirical studies on languaging in the classroom reviewed by Niu and Li (2017) were mostly focused on writing and student mastery of a targeted grammatical form. Despite the focus on skill development in the studies reported, the key idea for the present study is that languaging uses collaborative dialogue as a medium for building knowledge. Collaborative dialogue occurs in two ways: 1) talking or writing with others and 2) talking or writing with oneself. Given Maria's strong relationships with academically motivated peers, it was anticipated that she would describe instances in which she engaged with other students or engaged in self-talk to learn the languages she studied.

FoK, HL and languaging have similarities beyond their ties to Vygotsky's theory of learning. All three have been developed as a pedagogical response to increasing immigration and addressing the needs of diverse learners. All three rely on educational assets beyond what the teacher or curriculum might bring to the classroom. They differ, however, in how they define knowledge and their classroom applications. FoK draws on knowledge acquired by vocation to deliver instruction. For example, one teacher designed a cross-curricular lesson based on selling Mexican candy (Moll et al., 1992). It is a pedagogy based on family economics and enterprise, and not necessarily language or literacy. In contrast, HL pedagogy is focused on leveraging language and literacy practices acquired in the home to help students develop their language skills. Both theories recognize the learning assets that families and communities have and attempt to account for student exposure to and participation in family enterprises or language and literacy activities. Languaging, on the other hand, focuses on the socially mediated learning within the classroom, and in the literature, seems to be associated with second language learning, not necessarily heritage language learning (Swain & Watanabe, 2013). An article by Martin-Beltrán et al. (2020) addresses the gap in research by examining peer interaction and HLLs in world language classrooms. FoK and HL pedagogical approaches attempt to draw upon what learners bring to the classroom whereas languaging uses social interaction in the classroom to shape knowledge. That is, FoK and HL tap prior knowledge whereas languaging facilitates the construction of new knowledge in the classroom. In Maria's case, it was anticipated that all three concepts would influence her learning. Maria's strong relationships with family and academically motivated peers suggested that social interaction would shape her language learning experiences in ways that could inform practice.

RESEARCH DESIGN

It has already been established that the present investigation is an instrumental case study intended to answer three research questions: What are the language learning and literacy development experiences of a second-generation immigrant pursuing studies in Spanish, French, and Japanese? How do sociocultural theories of language learning account for her experiences? How can her experiences inform teaching practice and program design?

This exploratory study proposes to examine the learner experience in light of Vygotsky's sociocultural theory and its derivatives: FoK and Valdés' definition of a heritage language learner. While Maria's story is a rich source for examining these sociocultural theories relevant to language teaching and learning, caution is warranted in the application of this study's conclusions. Again, since this is a single case study, it is generalizable only to theories, not to other groups or individuals (Yin, 2009). Despite this limitation, the researcher developed interview questions with the intent to elicit evidence that these sociocultural theories of language acquisition and pedagogy were evident in this account and were validated by Maria's experiences.

Case study data can be collected through observations, surveys, focus groups, or interviews. For this study, an interview was deemed the most appropriate tool to establish reliability, especially given the sample size of one individual. An observation was not possible, a survey or focus group illogical. Yin (2009) wrote that "case study is preferred in examining contemporary events, when the relevant behaviors cannot be manipulated" (p. 11). Relevant behaviors in this study could neither be manipulated or observed given that Maria's account is a retrospective one.

Internal validity was checked by asking Maria and her mother to read the account and the researcher's interpretations and correct them. The researcher also referenced online sites to better understand the stated goals for the language instruction Maria received. She looked at laws regulating language learning in the state where Maria resides to see how they might have influenced her learning, and she researched the virtual school Maria attended to see how language offerings are described there.

METHODOLOGY

Participant

The individual studied for this case study is Maria, a 17-year-old female high school student living in a large metropolitan city of the southeastern U.S. Maria, who was born in the U.S., is the daughter of legal immigrants. Her mother is from Peru, and her father from Cuba. She and her mother, Ana Maria, maintain close ties with family members who live in Latin America, Spain, and other parts of the U.S. Family members visit on occasion, and they travel to see them as well. Maria's first languages are Spanish, the language of her home, and English. As stated previously, Maria has also studied French and Japanese.

Maria lives with her mother in a rental home in a suburban neighborhood. Ana Maria graduated from high school in her country of origin and has taken some college classes in the U.S. She owns and operates a domestic cleaning service and occasionally brings Maria with her when she cleans homes. Ana Maria's work brought the researcher into contact with Maria three years ago. They have become friends and often talk about raising children and current events.

Maria and the researcher have had informal conversations over the years about her high school experiences and her plans to attend college. A junior, Maria attends a magnet school with a curricular focus on science, technology, engineering, and mathematics. She plans to study biology in college in preparation for her career goal of becoming a physician's assistant. She is a strong student who regularly makes honor roll and associates with other motivated youth. Maria has recounted stories of the positive support Maria and her friends provide one another academically. For example, when Maria and one of her friends recently applied to a selective dual enrollment program, they spent a weekend completing the application together. They push each other to excel on college entrance exams and other academic endeavors, and *se desvelan* or "burn the midnight oil" to study. Given her academic inclinations, one can assume that she has aptitude and motivation to be a successful language learner.

Outside of school, Maria enjoys a strong social network and participates in extracurricular activities that strengthen her mind and body. Maria and her mother attend church where they sing in the choir and perform community service. A student of taekwondo for many years, Maria recently earned a blue belt.

Method

A convenience sampling method was used to select the participant in the study. While the researcher knows many individuals who grew up in households in which Spanish was the predominant language and learned English as second language, Maria stood out as an eager learner of several languages who could speak to the success of her efforts.

When Maria was invited to participate in the interview, she readily agreed, saying that "she is honored to help language teachers become better teachers." Neither Maria nor Ana Maria received compensation for her participation in the study. Informed consent was obtained from mother and daughter for Maria's participation in the research, and she was free to opt in or out of the study at any time. Maria gave consent for the interview to be audio and video recorded. The researcher assured the participant that her confidentiality would be maintained throughout the study. In addition, the final chapter was sent to Maria and her mother for review, correction of biographical facts, and verification of the conclusions reached.

While convenience sampling is susceptible to bias, the method is useful when rapport has already been established. Given the uniqueness of the study participant, the convenience sampling method, and case study approach used, the results are not generalizable to a larger population of language learners.

A semi-structured interview protocol was developed based on an open-ended set of questions. See appendix. After demographic data were collected, questions about experiences particular to each language the participant has studied were asked, yielding rich memories and perspectives on those experiences.

Data Collection

The interview was conducted on Zoom the afternoon of March 8, 2022. The interview was recorded and then transcribed using an online transcription tool, HappyScribe. The transcript was generated by artificial intelligence technology and was then reviewed with the recording and corrected for accuracy.

The transcript of the recording was coded using both deductive and inductive coding methodology. The deductive codes based on a predefined set of codes related to the theoretical frameworks for this study; inductive codes were created as the transcript was analyzed. Pre-selected codes included relationship with family, relationship with teacher, relationship with peers, funds of knowledge, heritage language, and languaging. Additional codes related to learning activity, code switching, age, teacher behavior, and aesthetics were added as the transcript was reviewed. Following the recording, the transcript was reviewed to develop additional questions for follow up.

In retelling Maria's story, her words have been retained as they were spoken in most instances for the purpose of ensuring that her voice comes through.

MARIA'S STORY

Maria grew up speaking two languages: Spanish and English. She associates both languages with specific contexts, home and school: "[A]t school I would be learning English, and then at home I would be studying, well not studying but, like, talking with my mom in Spanish." She considers herself fluent in English and reports having "some troubles, like writing in Spanish." She expressed a desire "to write and to … better my grammar in Spanish as well" and added reflectively, "I could expand my vocabulary."

Like many students during the COVID-19 pandemic, Maria took classes online through a public virtual school to stay on track academically on the advice of her academic counselor, "They said, like, for universities, they want two years of language. So that's why our school was like, yeah, you need to do two years of language, which I did my freshman and sophomore year."

Maria also hoped that the online course would help her to achieve her goals to develop language and literacy in Spanish. She did not find the course helpful to meeting these goals, however, saying that she preferred learning from a physical teacher. When asked how taking class with a physical teacher would help her meet her linguistic goals, she described valuing a face-to-face learning experience, but also lamented:

The program was not good. There were some flaws in it, and it was just Spanglish instead of Spanish. It was a mixture of, like, English, but not written well. And I just didn't like the course. Even though it was mandatory. I didn't like it.

Maria described a specific encounter with confusing content when taking a quiz. She depicted the language as "if they put the English version in like Google translate and then translated it to Spanish. So it didn't sound right. I didn't like that." Maria continued:

I remember reading it and I was like, wait, I'm reading English and Spanish at the same time. What is this? … I would show my mom and then I would be like, mine is correct … the way they wrote was very confusing.

Despite not having formal literacy instruction in Spanish, Maria has internalized the notion of linguistic competence and performance in Spanish and readily identifies awkward constructions. Maria also prefers to avoid code-switching in order to be considered a fluent speaker of both English and Spanish and to be understood by speakers of language in countries where the language is predominantly spoken. She opined:

It's better to learn, like, not Spanglish, because if you're trying to explain something in English like right now, I want to be fluent in English. And then when I'm speaking, like maybe in Spain, I want to be speaking Spanish fluently, not mixing it with another word that is not a whole other language, which other people just don't understand.

When asked if there were contexts in which speaking Spanglish might be appropriate, Maria qualified her view, stating that code mixing could be acceptable, for example, when referring to a specific product or something that is difficult to pronounce:

Sociocultural and Linguistic Assets of a High School Student Named Maria

I feel like growing up, it's good because for me, there are certain words that I'm not able to say in Spanish. Like, I can't pronounce them. For me, I struggle with the word Ibuprofen in Spanish.... But if I want to [ask for one from] my mom, I'll be like, 'me puedes dar Ibuprofen' because I don't want to mispronounce that word.

She observed that when both speakers share the language that code-switching can be an efficient way to communicate. "I guess in certain aspects, if you're trying to talk to a family member that knows it, like my mom, it's really easy."

Social acceptance among extended family plays into Maria's motivations for learning to master Spanish pronunciation. "So, like, when I went to Peru, there weren't a lot of people that spoke English, so it forced me to speak more Spanish, and I didn't want to sound like...[una] gringa." She imagined their thoughts, "So they're like, 'oh, yeah, she's from America.... So she doesn't know how to speak Spanish.'" She remembered thinking, "And so I was like, no, I want to prove myself."

Maria's speaking ability in Spanish improved over time; she associates her English-accented Spanish with her younger self, one that she overcame with maturity and ultimately leveraged to bring humor to her interactions with family:

When I was younger, I did sound like a gringa. I did have an acento. I forgot how to make that accent. But there's this accent that I used to make when I was younger. But now over the time, over years, I've gotten rid of it. But, like, as a joke or something, I ... bring it up.

The idea of age and the desire to be treated as a young adult emerged as topics in Maria's language learning experiences not only with Spanish, but also with the other languages she has studied. The first instance can be seen in her perceptions of how her family views her, "I feel like now as I'm growing up ... they know I'm not a child anymore ... Before they would make fun of me. Again, she imagined her relatives' thoughts of her, "Oh, my gosh, she can't pronounce [the language], but now they're like, 'okay, you can say it like this or like that ... it's not like she's a little gringa.' It's like, 'oh, she's maturing and growing up more.'" Her comments reveal Maria's sophisticated knowledge of language; she understands language to be a tool that strengthens her social network and can serve to entertain others.

Despite her keen interest in sounding like a native speaker, the availability of family to support her language learning, and her own strategic language abilities, Maria did not have the opportunity to use these assets in a meaningful way in her online Spanish class. The little interaction she had with the teacher occurred during brief oral assessments that were conducted by telephone. One conversation she reported was typical of an exchange common in Spanish language classes:

She would be like, "oh, where are you from?" And then I'll be like "from Peru and Cuba." And then she'll be like, "okay, can you tell me some things from there?" I'll be like, "oh, yeah, there's Lima, la capital."

Opportunity for interaction with other students in the online Spanish class was non-existent. "There isn't like a class, a whole group meeting or anything like that. It's just like with the teacher and the student. That's it." She elaborated, "I did not know who had that class either." Maria speculated that knowing other students in the class would have been helpful and observed that knowing more Spanish speakers would have expanded her understanding of the language as a world language:

I would have loved to just be in a class setting, be with friends, because I'll be able to talk with them in Spanish and maybe practice the way I speak to others as well as listening to other people's accents. Because even in Peru, there are certain things that we say from different regions, like we have like La Sierra, and they might be saying a word but in a different accent with a different type of way than the capital. That's why I like to keep an accent as well as, like, just interact with other people instead of just the one-on-one teacher online, which isn't really personal for me.

At 17 years of age and nearing graduation, Maria still sees her mastery of Spanish literacy as a future goal. In other words, the two years of formal language instruction in her heritage language have been of little benefit. She believes the best way to accomplish that goal is by travel or study abroad:

I want to travel to Spain for a little bit or either Peru to travel and study over there for a few months. And I can either ask my grandparents or my uncles or my aunts. I can look [at] abroad programs maybe because I just want to be more involved with the culture as well.

Maria cited her family's plan to immigrate to Spain as a reason to spend time in that country. "Most of my family is actually moving to Spain, so ... I want to see Spain more. That's why this year maybe I might be traveling to Spain in the spring."

Maria also studied French in middle school as a part of the curriculum. She expressed eagerness at the idea of learning a third language and reported being like "everyone when they first start [studying] a new language ... very intrigued, very motivated, very happy in the sense of learning a whole other language." However, she was quickly disappointed as "my teacher left the first week of French when we were learning the basics. So she just came and left. And then we had a substitute for the majority of the year." Toward the end of the academic year, a full-time French teacher was hired, and again Maria felt optimistic about the opportunity. "And so we had an actual teacher. We were actually pretty happy, but that year I did not learn almost anything of French. I learned pronouns at most....So it was just very simple things." Her second year of studying French improved somewhat. Maria reported:

And then in my second year, that's when I started [to learn French]. I guess I can kind of write, understand it a bit, but the teacher was a bit umm spontaneous in a sense and would pick on me and other students and had this attitude towards the class where it brought down my motivation and my passion at the start. And that went downwards as the year progressed.

Maria wished for a dynamic learning opportunity, one in which the teacher made her feel invited to learn. "I was hoping to be treated by a French teacher with open arms and be like very inspired and very happy to be teaching their language. Instead I got a teacher that was very not negative, but she was special." The equivalent for special in Spanish is *especial*; in this context, it means *peculiar* and is not a compliment.

Maria also objected to one of the learning activities the teacher offered, viewing the activity as childish: "She would teach us nursery rhymes and would treat us kind of badly even though we were middle schoolers." The treatment diminished Maria's motivation for learning the language. "The way she would just treat us, it's just like, oh, since you're treating me like that, I'm not going to pay attention. So that's where my motivation went down and why should I bother?"

Sociocultural and Linguistic Assets of a High School Student Named Maria

When asked if the learning activity made her feel childish, Maria agreed and then hedged, noting that instruction did not progress beyond recitation, "Yeah I guess that's nice to listen to nursery rhymes when first learning the language. But she would keep on repeating it throughout the year and we wouldn't really progress." Maria also described an incident in which she observed the teacher acting unprofessionally:

She was such an interesting teacher. She would dance around. I remember this one time she took off her shoes and danced around the classroom, and the whole class was rowdy and loud. I guess it was funny at the time, but it was really like what? That's weird, but okay?

Maria recounted her experiences with this teacher: "I don't think she had much interest in learning personally." Fortunately, Maria had a third French teacher, Madame Laurent, who made a difference in the quality of the learning experience. She said, "Luckily, my last year, I was blessed, and I got one of my favorite teachers … She was just a wonderful teacher. She taught us, like a lot." Maria also commented on the content of the lessons, "I remember that she taught us the same thing from the last few years, but more detailed and more precise." She appreciated the teacher's instruction and learning activities: "She would correct our errors, and she would have oral discussions as well as presentations, so she could hear your accent as well." Maria focused on that rather than "my other teacher who [gave us] nursery rhymes." Maria elaborated on the value of being given meaningful assignments:

Now that I remember, she did a whole lesson on dinner etiquette. So she made us dress up in suits and dresses. That day, we had to come in with high heels, and she was assessing how we looked at a dinner table. And she taught etiquette, to put our hands on the table, but not our elbows. That's wrong. And then how to cut stuff … as well as putting the napkin on your lap. And she would look at our presentation as a whole. And she would assess that and look around at the class. It was pretty.

Madame Laurent gave the students not only instruction in French, but also in another skill, etiquette, that could prepare the students to participate in their future professional lives. She also created an environment that was aesthetically appealing to Maria.

Maria explained how the target language was seamlessly integrated into the lesson, "we [would] all have to greet her in French … She would have little conversations on the side with each individual student to see how well you practiced for that event." Maria went on at length on how she viewed the teacher and the lesson. In contrast to her second French teacher, she saw her as more professional, more skilled, and more caring, and she cited:

It's far more like professional in a sense, and more like more detailed rather than a little song. It's more personalized. And you can tell the effort that the teacher made because she also dressed up and she also made the classroom very pretty. So you can tell that the teacher actually cares and has that passion for teaching. So that's what I like to learn more. And the fact that the way she was so smart … And I just loved her. She was such a great teacher.

The fourth language that Maria has studied is Japanese. She began studying Japanese informally on the language learning application, Duolingo, at the start of the pandemic in 2020. Her motivation for learning Japanese arose out of appreciation for the culture and a desire to live abroad. "I personally really love the culture and I do have a future living in Japan." Aesthetic elements of culture again drew her attention, "the food, the music...I just love everything. It's very pretty." Japanese pop culture, in particular, has played a significant role in her youth, in her words:

I grew up on it ... it influenced me in my daily life... I watched dramas as well as I listen to their music when I go out, I like looking for places where they serve their food because I think it's very tasty. And overall, the difference in culture, the way they dress, like their kimonos, as well as the accents are very pretty to me. And landscapes are very pretty as well.

She added that the Japanese are "very technologically advanced. And those small things built up my interest over the years. I really like that aspect of that culture." Compared to her Spanish and early French studies, Maria was able to observe her own linguistic growth:

After a month, I knew how to say certain phrases. I don't remember, but it was these long phrases that I was able to repeat as they instructed, you would record yourself and then you would hear the other person say it. So you hear the person say it first and then you record yourself and by the sound of it, they would check if it was correct or if it was wrong.

She also bought a little notebook, in which she used to write Kanji or Katakana, but her attention lagged when she had to return to school and her current formal studies. Maria noted that she "wanted something more intensive ... because I feel like if I'm not personally pushed by something, I won't be able to dive in. I need extra little nudge in order to keep on going." That nudge would most likely come from "finding maybe someone that also likes to learn the language." In other words, if Maria were to continue her studies of Japanese, she would look for a study buddy and not necessarily a teacher. Maria imagined possible interactions with her peers, "I can probably go up to them and then say something and then they actually know what I'm saying."

However, Maria speculated that finding a person with sincere interest in language learning might be challenging and that their interests in pop culture do not encompass a commitment to language learning. She expressed the following:

Anime has really increased over the years, especially during the epidemic, a lot of people are watching anime and they're saying, like, these crazy things that are really funny. Like, baka, which is like stupid ... It's not really like they actually enjoy the language. Like they want to learn it. They just use the small little phrases.

She emphasized her desire to have a friend in class, "But I really wanted a friend that enjoys and actually wants to learn. I have other friends that actually want to learn Korean, like Blanca, my best friend." (Blanca is the friend with whom Maria spends time studying together and planning for college.)

Maria hopes that she will be able to find like-minded peers once she goes to college. She also wishes to attend college where she can meet diverse students. "When I'm choosing the college that I'm going to, I'm really looking for a diverse group of people ... I want a mixture of Asians, Whites, Blacks, Hispanics." Central to that vision is her desire to have friends who are also interested in language study. "Hopefully by then when I'm learning it [Japanese], I'll be able to have some Japanese friends or people that are studying at the same level or maybe above me so they can tutor me." Again, travel and study abroad figure into her future vision of language study: "I'll be able to maybe travel with them to Japan or maybe have like go to a Japanese place, meet there or little activities like that would be nice."

DISCUSSION

The research questions investigated for this instrumental case study were: What are the language learning and literacy development experiences of a second-generation immigrant pursuing studies in Spanish, French, and Japanese? How do sociocultural theories of language learning account for her experiences? How can her experiences inform teaching practice and program design?

Many dimensions of Vygotsky's sociocultural theory are evident in Maria's story. Her account is rich with anecdotes in which family and friends positively influenced her language learning. Her sociocultural identity is a primary motivation for her studies of Spanish. Maria wants to show her entire family by showing that she, too, speaks their shared language with a native accent. The learner's view of her cultural identity can be observed in her account. In her case, funds of knowledge might be better described as "funds of identity," a concept termed by Esteban-Guitart and Moll (2014) who offer a theory of identity "inspired by funds of knowledge" (p. 31). Maria has shrugged off the stigma of being "la gringa" by turning the label into a shared joke. Her efforts in this regard have likely encouraged her extended family to teach her more language and to take her efforts seriously. Moreover, Maria sees her relatives as a valuable resource for future learning.

The sociocultural influence of age may also be appreciated in Maria's story. Being recognized as a capable young adult is important to her. Learning activities she deems childish, like the recitation of nursery rhymes, are of instructional value only if instruction progresses and evolves to include situations in which skills—linguistic and social—are combined. A lesson in etiquette, thus, was particularly meaningful to her as she could imagine her future self speaking in French and dining with professional colleagues. Her fascination with Japanese pop culture and its incentive for language study is also a reflection of her age.

Proponents of FoK practices encourage teachers to incorporate the knowledge and skills of families into the classroom. However, there was no evidence of a teacher leveraging family knowledge to teach Maria. Nor did a heritage language pedagogy imparted by the teacher figure into her learning; teacher-student interactions were limited and did not draw upon her prior knowledge of Spanish. The website for the virtual school state where Maria resides no longer offers a heritage language class for Spanish and does not provide an explanation for its discontinuation. When the researcher contacted the school by phone seeking more information, a representative explained that the class may no longer be offered due to low enrollment.

The concept of languaging and collaborative dialogue theorized by Swain was conspicuously absent from Maria's account of classroom interactions, leaving little opportunity for that theory to be explored. However, Maria engaged in languaging frequently with her mother, other family members and friends, and in her self-talk. Maria benefited greatly from her mother as an important source of knowledge and on herself as a reflective learner. Maria recounted several conversations that took place between her and her mother or other family members or were instances of private, inner dialogue.

Languaging may have occurred during the etiquette lesson with the French teacher as there may have been a specific aspect of language that the teacher wished for students to focus on during the lesson. This cannot be discerned from the narrative. If the case study were to be repeated and include classroom observations, the degree to which languaging contributed to her formal language learning experiences could be better explored. Two years of studying French with weak teachers were easily matched and bettered by a single year of instruction with a knowledgeable and passionate teacher. Maria came away from that year with some confidence in French and useful skills.

Similarly with Spanish, two years of online language instruction did not build on the knowledge of Spanish that Maria brought into the classroom in an appreciable way. It was not the instructional mode of online learning that slowed her progress; however, it was the lack of meaningful interaction. She yearned for a chance to engage with other heritage speakers, to hear their accents, and to learn about their cultures. Maria's knowledge of Spanish and that of other second-generation immigrants could be leveraged for the benefit of all learners in her state's virtual language classes. Opportunities to interact with a teacher or peers with collaborative dialogue would likely improve the experience for all students. In Maria's case, she envisions that in the future, she will be learning Spanish from her family and Japanese with college friends.

Other themes emerged in the interview that are worthy of further investigation. The researcher did not examine the research literature pertaining to motivation in language learning in preparing to conduct the study; however, motivation emerged on several occasions during the interview. With respect to Spanish, Maria's motivations were tied to identity and the integrative motivation defined by Gardner (1985) or Dörnyei's (2005) concept of the ideal of the L2 (second language) self. For a second-generation immigrant like Maria, one for whom the L1 (first language) and L2 might be interchangeable, another more nuanced concept of motivation and self could be theorized.

Intrinsic motivation appears to play a role in her study of Japanese language and culture. Japanese popular music, often referred to as J-pop, and anime moved her to study the Japanese language. Apparently, the draw of Japanese cultural products to Japanese language study is not unique to Maria (for a fuller discussion on this phenomenon, see also Fukunaga, 2006; Shintaku, 2022). In terms of the theories explored in this study, this finding points back to the literature review and the observation how human-designed systems—like art, music, math, or language— facilitate human interactions. Not only do these systems facilitate human interactions, but they also motivate them. Students like Maria are buffeted by social influences beyond their respective heritage, including peer groups, technology, and pop culture, as multilingual learners do not exist in a cultural vacuum.

An unexpected finding was the aesthetic value Maria considers important to her learning. Twice during the interview, she mentioned the word "pretty" with respect to the learning opportunities presented to her. She appreciated the extra effort made by the French teacher to create a pleasing classroom environment. Similarly, she finds aesthetic aspects of Japanese culture so captivating that it moved her to study the language independently for a couple of months. Bevilacqua Martello (2017) investigated the relationship between the use of visual arts in world language instruction and student motivation in her dissertation research. While her findings did not find a statistical link between the arts and student motivation in the language classroom, she did find that students enjoyed learning activities that combined the study of content with active participation. Maria's comment that she would need a "nudge" from friends to persist in her study of Japanese seems to support that finding.

CONCLUSION

Maria's story serves as a powerful example for scholars and language teachers who seek to improve their instructional practices through greater understanding of sociocultural theories that can inform classroom practice. Many sociocultural factors such as family, peer relations, and age can contribute to the success of language learners at the individual level.

The sociocultural influence of family and friends in language learning emerged in this study as a critical resource for Maria, a second-generation immigrant. Even though teaching strategies tied to FoK or heritage language pedagogy were not evident in her stories, Maria's anecdotes suggest that she would have benefited from pedagogies that account for her linguistic and cultural assets. Such an approach would likely move students like Maria toward literacy in their heritage languages faster than the two years of foreign language study required by the state where she resides. The regulations do allow an exemption from this requirement for a student whose native language is not English if they can demonstrate proficiency in his/her native language. Authentic opportunities for second-generation, Spanish-speaking immigrants–almost 25% of the school age population in her state–should be abundant (Migration Policy Institute, 2022).

There were few opportunities to engage in languaging in the classroom in Maria's language learning experiences. The devastating impact of COVID-19 on social engagement of any kind may explain its absence in her Spanish studies. As for her studies of Japanese, the language app that Maria used does not feature live human interaction by design. Sociocultural theories of learning were not developed nor systematically researched during global pandemics, which opens up additional avenues of sociocultural research on languaging in virtual classrooms or using language apps. Questions like "Does talking with a chatbot count as languaging?" need to be investigated.

Sociocultural characteristics of the learner, specifically age in Maria's case, should also inform classroom practice. Learners like Maria appreciate learning activities that recognize them as young adults. The use of nursery rhymes in a language classroom of adolescents could serve as an interesting source for a lesson in cultural values or history. For second-generation immigrants in heritage language classes, they could be used in heritage language classes to interview family members about ones that they recall from childhood. Other source texts like popular song lyrics or movies likely hold more appeal for adolescent students.

Future studies of sociocultural influences on teaching and learning of languages for second-generation immigrants should investigate the interplay of motivational and sociocultural factors on second or additional language acquisition. A theory of motivation that expands the definition of identity beyond that of being a native speaker or non-native speaker which accounts for more than an ideal L2 self would be useful for scholars and practitioners alike. Differing definitions of a heritage language learners posit a range of proficiencies, so too might a revised concept of motivation for second-generation immigrants. Finally, the motivational value of human interaction in digital learning whether it be between teacher-student or student-student deserves additional research.

REFERENCES

Annie E. Casey Foundation. (2021, October 21). *Who are children in immigrant families?* https://www.aecf.org/blog/who-are-the-children-in-immigrant-families

Bevilacqua Martello, M. (2017). *Use of visual arts in world language instruction to increase student motivation and attitude* [Doctoral Dissertation, Boise State University]. doi:10.18122/B27Q69

Carreira, M., & Kagan, O. (2018). Heritage language education: A proposal for the next 50 years. *Foreign Language Annals, 51*(1), 152–168. doi:10.1111/flan.12331

Dörnyei, Z. (2005). *The psychology of the language learner: Individual differences in second language acquisition*. Lawrence Erlbaum Associates Publishers.

Esteban-Guitart, M., & Moll, L. C. (2014). Funds of identity: A new concept based on the funds of knowledge approach. *Culture and Psychology, 20*(1), 31–48. doi:10.1177/1354067X13515934

Fahim, M., & Haghani, M. (2012). Sociocultural perspectives on foreign language learning. *Journal of Language Teaching and Research, 3*(4), 693–699. doi:10.4304/jltr.3.4.693-699

Flyvbjerg, B. (2006). Five misunderstandings about case-study research. *Qualitative Inquiry, 12*(2), 219–245. doi:10.1177/1077800405284363

Fukunaga, N. (2006). Those anime students: Foreign language literacy development through Japanese popular culture. *Journal of Adolescent & Adult Literacy, 50*(3), 206–222. doi:10.1598/JAAL.50.3.5

Gardner, R. C. (1985). *Social psychology and second language learning: The role of attitudes and motivation*. Edward Arnold.

Gironzetti, E., & Belpoliti, F. (2021). The other side of heritage language education: Understanding Spanish heritage language teachers in the United States. *Foreign Language Annals, 54*(4), 1189–1213. doi:10.1111/flan.12591

Gonzalez, N., & Moll, L. C. (2002). Cruzando el puente: Building bridges to funds of knowledge. *Educational Policy, 16*(4), 623–641. doi:10.1177/0895904802016004009

Gonzalez, N., Moll, L.C., Floyd Tenery, M. F., Rivera, A., Rendon, P., Gonzales, R., & Amanti, C. (1995). Funds of knowledge for teaching in Latino households. *Urban Education, 29*(4), 443-470. doi:10.1177/0042085995029004005

Gredler, M. E. (2001). *Learning and instruction: Theory into practice*. Pearson.

Hogg, L. (2011). Funds of knowledge: An investigation of coherence within the literature. *Teaching and Teacher Education, 27*(3), 666–677. doi:10.1016/j.tate.2010.11.005

Kelleher, A. (2010). *Who is a heritage language learner?* Heritage Briefs. https://cal.org/heritage/pdfs/brifukuefs/Who-is-a-Heritage-Language-Learner.pdf

King, K. (2008). *Sustaining linguistic diversity: Endangered and minority languages and language varieties*. Georgetown University Press.

Lantolf, P., & Thorne, S. L. (2007). Sociocultural theory and second language learning. In B. VanPatten & J. Williams (Eds.), *Theories in second language acquisition: An introduction* (pp. 693–701). Lawrence Erlbaum Associates Publishers.

Leeman, J. (2015). Heritage language education and identity in the United States. *Annual Review of Applied Linguistics, 35*, 100–119. doi:10.1017/S0267190514000245

Martin-Beltrán, M., Garcia, A. A., & Montoya-Ávila, A. (2020). "I know there's something like that in Spanish": Heritage language learners' multifaceted interactions with linguistically diverse peers. *International Journal of Applied Linguistics, 30*(3), 530–552. doi:10.1111/ijal.12310

Migration Policy Institute. (2021, June 21). *Black and Latino college graduates, immigrant and U.S. born alike, face greater risk of skill underutilization than white counterparts, MPI analysis finds.* https://www.migrationpolicy.org/news/immigrant-skill-underutilization-race-ethnicity-state-analysis

Migration Policy Institute. (2022, May 1). *State language data - FL.* https://www.migrationpolicy.org/data/state-profiles/state/language/FL

Moll, L. C. (1992). Bilingual classroom studies and community analysis: Some recent trends. *Educational Researcher, 21*(2), 20–24. doi:10.3102/0013189X021002020

Moll, L. C. (2005). Reflection and possibilities. In N. Gonzalez, L. C. Moll, & C. Amanti (Eds.), *Funds of knowledge: Theorizing practices in households, communities and classrooms* (pp. 275–287). Lawrence Erlbaum. doi:10.4324/9781410613462-5

Moll, L. C. (2019). Elaborating funds of knowledge: Community-oriented practices in international contexts. *Literacy Research: Theory, Method, and Practice, 68*(1), 130–138. doi:10.1177/2381336919870805

Moll, L. C., Amanti, C., Neff, D., & Gonzalez, N. (1992). Funds of knowledge for teaching: Using a qualitative approach to connect homes and classrooms. *Theory into Practice, 31*(2), 132–141. doi:10.1080/00405849209543534

Moll, L. C., & Greenberg, J. (1990). Creating zones of possibilities: Combining social contexts for instruction. In L. C. Moll (Ed.), *Vygotsky and education* (pp. 319–348). Cambridge University Press. doi:10.1017/CBO9781139173674.016

Moll, L. C., Vélez-Ibáñez, C., Greenberg, J., Whitmore, K., Saavedra, E., Dworin, J., & Andrade, R. (1990). *Community knowledge and classroom practice: Combining resources for literacy instruction: A handbook for teachers and planners* (OBEMLA Contract No. 300-87-0131). University of Arizona College of Education and Bureau of Applied Research in Anthropology.

Moll, L. C., Velez-Ibanez, C., & Greenberg, J. B. (1989). Year one progress report: Community knowledge and classroom practice: Combining resources for literacy instruction (IARP Subcontract No. L-10). Tucson, AZ: University of Arizona, College of Education and Bureau of Applied Research in Anthropology.

National Center for Education Statistics. (2022). *English Language Learners in Public Schools. Condition of Education.* U.S. Department of Education, Institute of Education Sciences. https://nces.ed.gov/programs/coe/indicator/cgf

Niu, R., & Li, L. (2017). A review of studies on languaging and second language learning (2006-2017). *Theory and Practice in Language Studies, 7*(12), 1222–1228. doi:10.17507/tpls.0712.08

Schmid, C. (2001). *The politics of language: Conflict, identity, and cultural pluralism in comparative perspective.* Oxford University Press.

Shintaku, K. (2022). Self-directed learning with anime: A case of Japanese language and culture. *Foreign Language Annals*, *55*(1), 283–308. doi:10.1111/flan.12598

Stake, R. (1995). *The art of case study research*. Sage Publications.

Swain, M. (2000). The output hypothesis and beyond: Mediating acquisition through collaborative dialogue. In J. P. Lantolf (Ed.), *Sociocultural theory and second language learning* (pp. 97–114). Oxford University Press.

Swain, M. (2006). Languaging, agency and collaboration in advanced second language proficiency. In H. Byrnes (Ed.), *Advanced language learning: The contribution of Halliday and Vygotsky* (pp. 95–108). Continuum., doi:10.5040/9781474212113.ch-004

Swain, M., & Watanabe, Y. (2013). Languaging: Collaborative dialogue as a source of second language learning. In C. Chapelle (Ed.), *The encyclopedia of applied linguistics* (pp. 1–8). Blackwell Publishing., doi:10.1002/9781405198431.wbeal0664

U.S. Bureau of Labor Statistics. (2021, May 18). *Foreign-born workers: Labor force characteristics–2020*. https://www.bls.gov/news.release/pdf/forbrn.pdf

U.S. Department of Education. (2016). *ED Facts Data Warehouse, 2014–15. SEA File C141, LEP Enrolled*. Digest of Education Statistics. https://nces.ed.gov/programs/digest/d16/tables/dt16_204.27.asp

Valdés, G. (2000). Introduction. In L. Sandstedt (Ed.), *Spanish for native speakers*. Heinle.

Valdés, G., Fishman, J. A., Chávez, R., & Pérez, W. (2006). *Developing minority language resources: The case of Spanish in California*. Multilingual Matters., doi:10.21832/9781853598999-004

Velez-Ibanez, C. G. (1988). Networks of exchange among Mexicans in the U.S. and Mexico: Local level mediating responses to national and international transformations. *Urban Anthropology*, *17*(1), 27–51.

Velez-Ibanez, C. G., & Greenberg, J. B. (1992). Formation and transformation of funds of knowledge among U.S.-Mexican households. *Anthropology & Education Quarterly*, *23*(4), 313–335. doi:10.1525/aeq.1992.23.4.05x1582v

Vygotsky, L. S. (1978). *Mind in society: The development of higher psychological processes*. Harvard University Press.

Yin, R. K. (2009). *Case study research: Design and methods* (4th ed.). Sage., doi:10.3138/cjpe.30.1.108

APPENDIX

Research Question Protocol

1. Greeting and small talk
2. Establishing parameters of the interview
    a. I will be asking you some questions about your educational experience in general and specific questions studying different languages.
    b. You are welcome to elaborate and, ask questions. I would like for this to be a conversation.
    c. I will be recording the interview. If you want to stop at any point, let me know.
3. Demographics
    a. How old are you?
    b. What grade are you in?
    c. What's your favorite subject in school?
    d. What is your first language? How did you learn it?
    e. What can you do in your first language? (Listen/speak/read/write)
4. Let's talk about language study
    a. At what age did you start learning other languages?
    b. What other languages do you know or have you studied?
    c. Did you study Spanish formally?
    d. Tell me about that experience.
    e. Was the teacher aware that you already knew Spanish?
    f. How did she help you develop your language skills?
    g. What can you do with Spanish?
    h. What more would you like to learn?
5. What language did you learn next? Tell me about that experience.
    a. Was the teacher aware that you already knew xxx?
    b. How did she help you develop your language skills?
    c. What can you do with xxx?
    d. What more would you like to learn?
    e. How did knowledge of other languages help you study this language?
    f. What challenges did you encounter?
6. When did you decide to study other languages?
    a. What interested you then in learning that language?
    b. How did the teacher engage you?
    c. What were some of the challenges you encountered in the class?

Section 7
Language and Society

Chapter 19
Literacy Practices for Peacebuilding

Lina Trigos-Carrillo
https://orcid.org/0000-0003-2297-3906
Universidad del Norte, Colombia

Luzkarime Calle-Díaz
https://orcid.org/0000-0003-1459-8974
Universidad del Norte, Colombia

Jesús Guerra-Lyons
Universidad del Norte, Colombia

ABSTRACT

The effects of the pandemic, natural disasters, wars, and economic distress at the turn of the second decade of the 20th century are a call to strengthen peace education around the world. In this chapter, the authors argue that intentional social practices of critical literacies offer opportunities for peacebuilding, understood as a dynamic process which includes the development of harmony in different life dimensions. After providing an overview of peace research and peace education in the Colombian context, the authors provide a conceptualization of critical literacy and its relation to peacebuilding. Finally, the chapter offers a set of practical strategies to promote peacebuilding through critical literacies based on research experiences across the Americas. The strategies include the use of children's literature to understand social reality and to develop empathy, critical literacies to develop critical intercultural awareness, and connecting with families and communities through literacy practices to make peace.

DOI: 10.4018/978-1-6684-5022-2.ch019

INTRODUCTION

The pandemic has widened inequality gaps around the globe (Schleicher, 2020). Increased poverty, food insecurity, unemployment, and lack of access to quality education have generally been considered as sources of direct and structural violence in different contexts around the world. Colombia is not the exception. After the peace agreement between the government and the FARC-EP guerilla group in 2016, there was a period of lower criminality and a sense of hope (Rico & Barreto, 2022). However, in the last two years, with the pandemic and the lack of governmental commitment with the implementation of the peace agreement, the effects of the armed conflict and structural violence have deepened (ACAPS, 2022). This renewed conflict dynamics represent a backlash in the country's search for durable peace, understood not only as the absence of direct violence, but also as the realization of a more just society, with equity, empathy, and solidarity. Peace starts in the micro interactions among people and the comprehension of how violence, in its multifaceted dimensions, operates to make social transformation possible. Since "reading the word is reading the world" (Freire & Macedo, 1987), in this chapter, we make the connection between critical literacy and peacebuilding. We argue that a peacebuilding pedagogy needs to consider the central role of dialogue and the power of literacy to foster critical citizenship from an early age. We asked, why and how does critical literacy promote peacebuilding? What literacy practices foster peacebuilding?

We will first provide an overview of peace and peace research. Second, we discuss Peace Education in general and in the Colombian context. Next, we provide a conceptualization of critical literacy and its relation to peacebuilding. Finally, we offer a set of strategies to promote peacebuilding through critical literacies from our research experiences working with schools, families, and communities across the Americas.

PEACE STUDIES

The emergence of Peace Studies marked a conceptualization of peace as the absence of war (Wright, 1942). Later, Galtung (1964) incorporated a definition of peace and peace research from two perspectives: *negative peace*, which he described as the absence of violence; and *positive peace*, which is the integration of human society, a state closer to what he also defined as a utopian 'general and complete peace' (GCP). Galtung (1969) further elaborated on his bifocal perspective on peace, by including the notion of absence of *direct violence* in his definition of *negative peace,* and absence of *structural violence* in his positive peace definition. The latter refers to the violence that emerges from society's structural division and problems of race, gender, religion, among other sources of discrimination and unrest.

More recently, Jiménez (2014) contributed a third perspective on peace research: *neutral peace*. He argues that neutrality is the foundation of every social relation, and that respect for 'the other' can help devalue the diverse forms of violence (direct, structural, and cultural and/or symbolic). Neutral peace seeks to neutralize violent elements and scenarios that are embedded in social patterns and relations among individuals, groups (i.e., family, school), and nature. This view of peace recognizes the potential of egalitarian dialogue and acknowledges that violence is rooted in everyday encounters; therefore, neutral peace can be strengthened in everyday relationships by fostering values such as empathy, tolerance, diversity, and solidarity.

Literacy Practices for Peacebuilding

According to Jiménez (2014), neutral peace needs to work changes from the existing scientific and cultural paradigms to *neutralize* univocal and pre-established methods to understand reality with the aim of creating a pacifist paradigm. He goes on to affirm that neutral peace needs to have a polyphonic character; that is, to get past the ethnocentric, hierarchical, and dominant discourse in a meritocratic western society – androcentric and white – with a proposal in which multiple voices can be expressed and heard.

Neutral peace supports two courses of action. Firstly, it favors *empathy* with the 'other' and *dialogue* as the method that aims at using language as the core of conflict resolution, management, and transformation. Communication is key to understanding others' culture, and to tolerate and value differences as something positive. Secondly, neutral peace pays full attention to *language*. Language plays a pivotal role in building structures of interaction (interpersonal, intrapersonal, collective, educational, organizational, and virtual) for a bio-socio-cultural human being that is in constant cognitive, emotional, and behavioral contact with him or herself, with others, and with nature (Jiménez, 2014).

In the search for breaking down the multifaceted nature of peace, Oxford (2013) speaks of multidimensional peace, which she defines as a dynamic, active process which includes the development of harmony in six life dimensions: *intrapersonal (inner) peace*, which refers to harmony in the heart; *interpersonal peace*, which involves caring about family members, friends, acquaintances, and even strangers; *intergroup peace*, which promotes harmony among groups that are classified by race, age, gender, sexual orientation, intelligence, ethnicity, class, religion, (dis)ability, and other criteria; *intercultural peace*, which describes harmony that exists among societies, each of which views itself as internally united by a common history; *international peace*, that is, harmony between nations; and *ecological peace*, which involves reconnecting with nature, actively caring for the environment, and taking positive steps to slow climate change.

FROM PEACE RESEARCH TO PEACE EDUCATION

Understanding the multidimensional nature of peace is fundamental for the emergence and comprehension of Peace Education. The history of Peace Education is difficult to trace. Scholars have found evidence of peacemaking and conflict resolution traditions and informal practices that were transmitted from generation to generation, especially within indigenous communities. Different religions around the world have also promoted ideologies for peacemaking and procedures to solve conflicts (Harris, 2010). According to Harris (2010), formal Peace Education can be traced back to Comenius (1969), who considered that understanding others and sharing knowledge and values could help overcome rivalries that provoke conflict. Comenius posited that "the ultimate goal of education was a world in which men and women would live in harmony with acceptance of diverse cultures" (Harris, 2010, p. 12). Formal peace education programs grew considerably in the 20th century with many women peace educators (e.g., Bertha von Suttner, Jane Adams, and Maria Montessori). Peace education began to spread across the world, first to educate against global conflicts, due to international concerns about the dangers of war, and more recently, to foster understanding and avoid symbolic and structural violence among people, and to reduce the threats of interpersonal and environmental violence (Harris, 2004).

According to Harris and Morrison (2013), Peace Education is both a philosophy and a process that involves "empowering people with the skills, attitudes and knowledge to create a world where conflicts are solved nonviolently and build a sustainable environment" (p. 11). Such skills include listening, reflection, problem solving, cooperation, and conflict resolution. In an era of increasing violence, coming from a myriad of sources and in many forms, there is a pressing need to educate children, from an early age, to be able to process information critically and develop skills that allow them to become active peacemakers and leaders of social transformation. Making sure that peace education is included from the very beginning of schooling will ensure children's development of empathy and solidarity across their lifespan, contributing to better understanding of and responding to social issues.

CONTEXT OF PEACE EDUCATION IN COLOMBIA

Peace Education in Colombia has gained relevance particularly in the last decade as a response to a long-lasting history of conflict and violence, especially during negotiations with the leftist FARC-EP guerrilla group and the signing of the Peace Agreement in 2016. Colombia has been internationally known for its efforts to achieve a school culture that develops "skills, attitudes, actions, and reflections that foster peace and living together, promote democratic participation and responsibility, and strengthen cultural, social, gender differences, among others" (Jaramillo, 2008, p. 66), by promoting citizenship education across the country. In fact, Colombia is considered an example of integration of citizenship education in the school curriculum, together with countries such as Canada, England, Australia, the United States, the Philippines, Brazil, and Costa Rica, among others (Organización de Estados Iberoamericanos para la Educación, la Ciencia y la Cultura, 2014; UNESCO, 2015). Colombian efforts have been concretized, first, with the publication of the Basic Standards for Citizenship Competences (Ministerio de Educación Nacional- MEN, 2004); then, with the issue of Law 1620 (Congreso de la República, 2013), which seeks to promote school living together, education for human rights, sexual education, and prevention of school violence; and more recently with the law enforcing the creation of a Peace Subject (*Cátedra de la Paz*) in 2014.

The Standards for Citizenship Competences aim at developing the necessary knowledge and skills (cognitive, emotional, and communicative) to participate democratically in society, value pluralism, and build peaceful living together (MEN, 2004). Based on the decentralization of the Colombian education system and the schools' autonomy to build their curricula according to the context, implementation of the standards varies from school to school. Some of them have decided to incorporate a separate class called *competencias ciudadanas* (citizenship competences) or *ciudadanía* (citizenship), which is usually placed within the Social Sciences area or department. Some others have incorporated them, as the document suggests, as a cross-curricular endeavor. The *Cátedra de la Paz*, on the other hand, stipulates that schools should develop at least two of the following topics in this class: (a) justice and human rights; (b) sustainable use of natural resources; (c) protection of cultural and natural wealth of the nation; (d) peaceful resolution of conflict; (e) bullying prevention; (f) diversity and plurality; (g) participation in politics; (h) historical memory; (i) moral dilemmas; (j) social impact projects; (k) history of national and international peace agreements; (l) life projects and risk prevention (Ministerio de Educación Nacional, 2015). The variety of topics included in this policy speaks of the multiple dimensions of peace that could be addressed in a peace education program and that could be developed in a school context.

Pedagogies for Peace

As it is evident, Peace Education in Colombia has been emphasized in governmental policies from a top-down approach. However, information about concrete pedagogies for developing peace education

Literacy Practices for Peacebuilding

in the Colombian school context, particularly classroom pedagogies, is still scarce. In a study of teachers' understanding and implementation of peace education in Colombia, Morales and Gebre (2021) found that most Colombian teachers grew up during conflict, therefore, they may not have a clear idea of how peace needs to be conceptualized, fostered or implemented. The study demonstrated that, in the case of *Cátedra de la Paz,* teachers usually turn to four instructional practices: creative engagement, direct instruction, dialogue and collaboration, and use of projects. Findings showed that one of the main challenges of implementing *Cátedra de la Paz* is that teachers do not have a clear set of instructional guidelines, or pedagogical resources at schools, and lack preparation. Calle-Díaz (2020) also found that, when teachers are tasked with teaching peace, they resort to explicit instruction of values (such as respect and responsibility) or the teaching of religion. This resonates with the pressing need for better teacher education programs in peacebuilding pedagogies.

Nevertheless, some initiatives for peace education in Colombia have emerged from individual teachers in the form of school projects, collectives, and university scholars to contribute to peacebuilding across the country. One example of peace education scholarly work that particularly connects universities and schools is that of Enrique Chaux and colleagues, who have not only studied the dynamics of violence and conflict present in different schools in Colombia (Chaux & Velázquez, 2008), but also proposed different programs to foster a more peaceful school environment. *Aulas en paz* (Classrooms in peace), for instance, is a school-based, multi-component, program that seeks to prevent aggression and promote peaceful living together by developing citizenship competences, that is, emotional, cognitive, and communicative skills that, together with knowledge and dispositions, make it possible for people to act in constructive ways in society (Ramos, Nieto & Chaux, 2007). The program includes three components: 1) a curriculum for the development of citizenship competences at school; 2) extracurricular activities with small groups of heterogeneous children (two children with aggressive behavior and four children who have shown prosocial behavior); and 3) workshops, visits, and phone calls with parents. Implementation of this program showed significant improvement in classroom atmosphere, decrease of aggression, increase of prosocial behavior, and enhancement of friendship networks in the classroom.

In an initial review of pedagogies for peacebuilding in Colombia, Adarve et al. (2018) developed the notion of *Pedagogías para la Paz (PpP)*, which they define as a set of pedagogies that emerge from a conscious reflection about why, what for, and through what means to educate for peace. PpP reflect about the act of teaching and learning to build peace, highlighting the balance between contents and methods in the educational process. Adarve et al. (2018) found scholarship (see Cruz, 2012) that classified PpP under three main lines: pedagogies for peace processes, peace pedagogies in culture and formal schooling, and community and non-formal education peace pedagogies. However, the authors recognize that most peace education processes in Colombia emerge in territories affected by internal conflict and fueled by social movements and community practices that have resisted the armed conflict for many decades. This includes pedagogies based on artistic representations (theater, dance, painting), games and sports, and memory-based activities, which are grounded in community organizing: neighborhood, religion, intergenerational, etc. These forms of peace education also resist hegemonic views of Peace education that come from the global North (i.e., focused on human rights, or favoring binary views of peace).

Some other initiatives of peace education in Colombia, particularly at the classroom level, have focused on narratives and storytelling (Montoya et al, 2017; Ruiz et al, 2017) as restorative pedagogical practices to strengthen the social fabric and reconciliation. This is an approach that has been traditionally implemented in communities and that demonstrates the potential of multiliteracies and critical pedagogy for community building, memory repair, and social transformation. This approach puts language, literacy, and dialogue at the core of peacebuilding.

Developing a classroom culture where language, in its entire social and cultural dimensions, is understood and lived as a tool for peacemaking can help achieve the ideal of a peaceful society; one that not only diminishes direct violence, but also fosters dialogue, empathy and solidarity within people, among peoples, and with nature. In this chapter, we argue that educating in critical literacies can promote peace as it holds potential for developing practices for "reading the word and the world" (Freire & Macedo, 1987), critically analyzing a multiplicity of texts, unveiling ideologies hidden in language, understanding the dynamics of power, and developing empathy and solidarity, among others. We argue that critical literacies can and should be a pillar of Peace Education.

THE EMERGENCE OF LITERACY PEDAGOGY

Within the theoretical and programmatic discourse of peace education, the idea that literacy pedagogy is a powerful instrument in peacebuilding has been axiomatic. This tenet applies both in the narrow sense of peace as resolution of violent conflict and in the broader notion of peace as societal transformation. If literacy pedagogy is to serve such far-reaching aims, important questions to be addressed concern the nature of literacy and literacy pedagogy, the type of literacy pedagogy that suits these purposes best, and the experiential/empirical bases upon which we can predicate the success of such a pedagogy in building peace.

In addressing the nature of literacy, the very reference to it as an individual entity is problematic. The use of the term dates to the late 19th century inception of higher education as a massified societal phenomenon. In contrast with elitist schemes dominant in past centuries, the democratization of higher education – initially fueled by the Industrial Revolution- confronted nation states with the problem of ensuring citizens' access to sophisticated written registers constitutive of scientific technological knowledge. The initial answer was to conceive literacy as a modular ability which could be conveniently addressed through language courses, tasked with the mission of teaching students the mechanics of reading and writing so that they could transfer these skills to other contexts. In the second part of the 20th century, this modular conception of literacy faced stern criticism from various perspectives. One important redefinition came from semiologists who, within the multiliteracies movement, questioned the reductionist decontextualized nature of literacy as reading and writing, and argued for a richer definition of literacy as the ability to participate in society through the interpretation of production of various signs and symbols, including writing, fixed and dynamic image, and space (New London Group, 1996). Another major redefinition came from pedagogists' recognition of the socially situated nature of literacy practices (Barton & Hamilton, 2010). Literacies were recognized as being closely intertwined with the meaning making practices of social groups participating in historicized institutional contexts. Importantly, the meaning-making resources of these social groups began to be recognized as discursively differentiated, making the idea of a singular literacy module untenable.

Critical Literacies and the Social Turn

The social turn brought about by these movements redefined litera*cies* as degrees of participation into the meaning making practices of specific social communities, mediated by formal and informal social-

Literacy Practices for Peacebuilding

ization spaces (Gee, 2007). Side by side with this social turn in the conception of literacies, critically oriented commentators have brought attention to the dialectic relationship between literacy practices, social structure, and power (Trigos-Carrillo, Rogers, & Jorge, 2021). This socially oriented conception of critical literacy should be distinguished from the cognitive skills-based framework, which equates it to the ability to derive balanced inferences, detect biases, and apply analytical reasoning skills to texts. In the sociocultural conception of critical literacy, Christie and Maton (2011) draw attention to two major critical persuasions. The social semiotic tradition, drawing on Halliday's and Bernstein's work (Hasan, 2005), assigns central importance to the ideological power of language in maintaining social hegemony and to the reproductive consciousness-shaping nature of educational practices invested in literacy.

The social semiotic conception of critical literacy draws on Systemic Functional Linguistics, a theory of language which emphasizes the relationship between social contexts and their realization by choices in language and other semiotic systems (Eggins, 2007). Critical literacy in the social semiotic tradition is understood as the appropriation of semiotic resources for participating in and transforming social practices. These resources are unequally distributed across social groups on account of hegemonic power relations regulating individuals access to socially valued registers. In a broader sense, social semioticians conceive critical literacy as the ability to deconstruct social meanings from texts and text-engendering practices. As captured in Halliday's (2007) quote:

to be literate is not just to have mastered the written registers (the generic structures and associated modes of meaning and wording), but to be aware of their ideological force: to be aware, in other words, of how society is constructed out of discourse - or rather, out of the dialectic between the discursive and the material. (p. 122)

The dialectic relationship between the material and the discursive constitutes a central theoretical tenet in social semiotic critical theory. Language is not considered to be a neutral reflection of experience, a vehicle for thoughts and emotions produced in a presupposed mental conceptual space. Language engenders and naturalizes ideologized representations and power relations, acting as a powerful organizer of material experience. Language, in other words, both reflects and acts upon the social material environment (Guerra-Lyons & Rosado, 2020). This powerful conception of language makes the social semiotic posture on critical literacy highly compatible with Freire's liberal humanist tradition.

Concerned with the oppressive relations perpetuated by the Brazilian schooling system within a society organized around colonial imperialist values, Freire proposed a breakup from what he called the 'banking' conception of education in favor of a transformative problem-posing orientation which motivates individuals to reclaim their historically situated subjectivities and to bring about societal transformation (Freire, 2018). Freire coined the notion of *conscientização* in referring to the role of education, and literacy in a narrower sense, to problematize naturalized subject positions which objectify and alienate individuals from their humanly vocation to transform the world for the better. This problematization necessarily entails a commitment to continued action and reflection in which educational actors co-participate as peers in subverting unjust social structures inherited from the colonialist imperialist world order. Critical literacy in the liberal humanist tradition thus entails engagement in transformative praxis through increasing freedom of thought and agency.

Based on the Freirean tradition, in Latin America, critical scholars have redefined critical literacy. In this regard, Menezes de Souza (2007) in the first volume of the journal *Critical Literacy: Theories and Practices*, states that if literacy is "a socio-culturally situated practice involving the ongoing negotiation of meaning in continuously contested sites of meaning construction, then all literacy in a certain sense ought to be 'critical'" (p. 4). Nonetheless, the emphasis on the word "critical" relates to a major attention "to literacy in issues relating to citizenship education, development education, foreign-language education and teacher education as sites of various socio-cultural crises in the form of continuously contested meaning construction and negotiation" (p. 4). Menezes de Souza and Monte Mór (2018) propose that "a critique that differs from the Enlightenment and modernity and therefore seeks to promote emancipation is, for Sousa Santos, a critique that is *solidary with difference and plurality* and values the pedagogical need for *translation*" (p. 449). This implies learning to listen to us listening the other (Menezes de Souza, 2011). It also implies

embracing the contradictions and acknowledging the needs of revision in the field of critical literacies; overcoming the dichotomy between the micro and macro levels of spaces for change; exploring the possibilities of social media for new ways of activism; and emphasizing a sense of belonging among language teacher professional communities. (Trigos-Carrillo, Rogers, & Jorge, 2021, p. 22)

With the concepts of peace education and critical literacies in mind, now, we propose some critical literacy practices and strategies to promote peace based on our research experience over 12 years.

CRITICAL LITERACIES TO PROMOTE PEACE

According to Vasquez, Janks, and Comber (2019), "critical literacies can be pleasurable and transformational as well as pedagogical and transgressive" (p. 300). In this sense, critical literacies support peacebuilding through the analysis of social issues and the transformation of local problems that can contribute to the overall peace of communities. In this section, we present strategies to promote peacebuilding through critical literary practices with young children.

Children's Literature to Understand Social Reality and to Develop Empathy

Children's literature is a way to connect with the families and communities' social realities and develop a deeper comprehension of structural violence and peacebuilding. In a social cartography co-constructed with elementary teachers in a small city on the Caribbean Coast in 2022, when schools came back to face-to-face education, teachers identified that increased poverty and instability has contributed to intrafamilial violence, aggressiveness, and a lack of sense of belonging in some families and students. This is interconnected to other community problems such as drug addiction, job informality, lack of public services, food insecurity, and criminality. However, the link between these social realities and curriculum and instruction is not always straightforward, although many scholars have highlighted the potential of critical literacies to understand local realities since an early age (O'Brien & Comber, 2020; Vasquez, 2014).

In complex social contexts, children's literature offers opportunities for peacebuilding by creating a space for empathy, reflection, and transformation. Through picture storybooks, children can reflect on their local realities, and how they connect to other global realities. This reading of the world can be accompanied by the production of written and multimodal texts where children reflect and take part in the transformation of their close environments. Some picture storybooks intentionally address critical

Literacy Practices for Peacebuilding

themes. "Some writers deliberately highlight social issues in books for children and thereby create spaces for critical literacy discussions" (Vasquez, Janks, & Comber, 2019, p. 300). In addition, other texts and pedagogical strategies can be used to frame critical literacies to foster peacebuilding when working with children. Teachers can select and read aloud stories that speak about the students' and communities' social realities to generate conversations and dialogue about them.

Reading-aloud is a pedagogical strategy that can be optimized to nurture critical conversations. Rodriguez Martinez (2017) proposes six stages to design critical literacy read-aloud activities: (1) selecting the books, (2) previewing the books, (3) developing critical questions to use during the activity, (4) activating children's background knowledge, (5) doing a picture walk, and (6) reading the book aloud. From a former study with young children, we add the importance of fostering critical conversations about the stories and generating additional activities where children can create their responses to the stories and take part in social action. Urrea and Trigos-Carrillo (n.d.) found that children in a marginalized rural community in Putumayo, Colombia, developed more empathic interactions among them and with others through a critical literacy intervention.

In recent years, we have seen a rise in children's literature in Spanish that explores Latin American social realities. For example, the picture storybook *Cazucá* talks about the social differences within large cities and the problem of the lack of water in a marginalized neighborhood in an urban setting. A girl must go find the water and bring it home in a bucket. The storybook *Biblioburro*, based on a real-life story, explains how a rural teacher decides to carry books on a donkey for children in distant rural areas in the Colombian mountains. The storybook *Sin agua y sin pan* addresses the problem of human rights for refugees. Children question adult decisions and seek social transformation. The storybook *Narraciones indígenas del desierto* presents narrations of the Wayuu indigenous group in Colombia. Based on their oral history, the book addresses the Wayuu cosmology. *Mapaná* is a crónica about the adventures of a boy in the Amazon jungle. And finally, *Letras al carbón* is a story about learning to read in Palenque, the first town of enslaved Africans in America. Through these picture storybooks, students can see themselves and their communities in literature.

Reading aloud practices can be done along with other critical literacy practices that focus not only on analysis but also on production and praxis. For example, children can produce their own responses to the story, they can also compare the situations in the story with their own, they can role play some solutions to local problems, they can propose action projects or initiatives, or they can imagine transformation or local action.

In sum, critical literacy practices using children's literature are a source to understand the local and global social realities and foster empathy towards peacebuilding.

Critical Literacies and Critical Intercultural Awareness

Critical Intercultural Awareness (CIA) "engages and commits teachers and students to issues of local, national and global citizenship" (Guilherme & Menezes de Souza, 2019, p. 8). CIA includes three dimensions: (1) intercultural attitude, (2) intercultural knowledge, and (3) intercultural skills (Hazaea, 2020). These dimensions are developed through the comprehension and awareness of discourses of difference and diversity. CIA connects to peacebuilding as it relates to the exercise of citizenship and the understanding of difference.

As we already discussed, critical literacy practices offer opportunities to critically analyze local problems and to propose social change and transformation. When reading aloud children's literature and opening spaces for critical dialogue, children learn about difference and understand their role as agents of social transformation. As Vasquez, Janks, and Comber (2019) put it, critical literacy practices

can contribute to changing inequitable ways of being and problematic social practices. This means students who engage in critical literacy from a young age are prepared 1) to make informed decisions regarding issues such as power and control, 2) to engage in the practice of democratic citizenship, and 3) to develop an ability to think and act ethically. (p. 307)

In doing this, critical literacies also contribute to the development of CIA.

For example, in the school community in the Caribbean Coast we mentioned above, the teachers identified a lack of sense of belonging in some students, which translated in students throwing trash on the school and community floors and not taking care of nearby parks. We decided to find children's literature that addressed respectful ways to live in the natural environment. For instance, *Verde fue mi selva* is a picture storybook with 13 stories about the indigenous groups Achuar, Shuar, Huaorani, Secoya, Siona, Quichua, and Cofán from the Ecuadorian Amazon. These stories talk about the ways of living in the jungle, and how the indigenous groups live in respect and harmony with nature. These stories offer opportunities to engage in discussions about other epistemologies (or *Epistemologies of the South* as termed by Boaventura de Sousa Santos) and alternative ways of relating with the world. It also opens spaces to have a dialogue about what we can learn from those epistemologies to improve our own environment. Students can propose solutions to solve their local problems based on the indigenous' understanding of the world.

An important characteristic of CIA is the dialogue with non-traditional knowledge, epistemologies of the South, or *diálogo de saberes*. It consists in decentering Eurocentric knowledge and listening to other ways we can interrelate with ourselves, with others, and with nature. Other children's picture books in Spanish that invite to learn from other worldviews and epistemologies are *La gran canoa* from Venezuela, *La otra orilla* from Chile, and *Jagáiai, narraciones indígenas de la selva* from Colombia.

Connecting With Families and Communities to Build Peace

Families and communities in Latin America possess a rich community cultural wealth (Trigos-Carrillo, 2019); that is, they engage in literacy practices that are often overlooked by research, policy, and media. Connecting to families and communities means that we empathize with their realities and ways of being (Vasquez, 2014) instead of expecting them to fit traditional roles in education. It becomes a strategy to build peace because it allows the school community to listen to the families' and communities' problems, concerns, and dreams. For instance, while engaging with teachers in a curatorship of children's literature for critical literacies in Spanish, one teacher read the book *Un hogar diferente,* by Santiago Briceño, about the challenges of migration. After reading the book silently, she expressed how sometimes she did not consider the realities of the many migrant students from Venezuela that she has in class. While having a dialogue about the book, she realized her students face difficult social and emotional realities that we as teachers often forget. After this critical literacy experience, she was more open to design activities to support immigrant families and children.

In Latin America, teachers and school communities cannot wait for family members, parents, and guardians to reach school. It is important to understand the complex lives of families in marginalized areas and find ways to connect. Teachers can connect their instruction to the families' and community's

Literacy Practices for Peacebuilding

literacy practices. For example, in Mexico, people write *calaveras* during the celebration of the Day of the Death; in Costa Rica and Colombia, women write *recetarios* with the traditional recipes and their procedures (Trigos-Carrillo, 2019). These literacy practices can be used in class to create responses from students and to collaborate with families and communities while recognizing their assets. Another strategy to learn more from families and communities is *community mapping*, where teachers connect the everyday life of the communities around the school to their instruction and curriculum (Clavijo-Olarte & Sharkey, 2019). In this strategy, teachers engage with families and students to articulate their voices in the comprehension of their territory and the identification of their literacy practices and their community cultural wealth.

Another important dimension of peace education is maintaining and honoring historical memory. This can be achieved through literacy events where children and parents co-author their life stories. For instance, working with multilingual and immigrant families, Dorner, Song, Kim, and Trigos-Carrillo (2019) hosted family literacy events where families attended a storytelling workshop, and designed and eventually published their own storybooks with the support of the children and teachers. These events were characterized by sustaining families' languages and cultures, putting families at the center of the design and decision-making, and engaging with families and communities in meaningful and empowering ways.

When connecting with families and communities, we can build peace by developing empathy towards their social and emotional lives, co-constructing strategies to support quality education for all students, and empowering families to have a voice in the school system and advocate for their interests and needs.

CONCLUSION

In this chapter, we argued that peace education can benefit from the central role of dialogue and the power of critical literacies to comprehend local and global social realities and to build peace in educational contexts, particularly with young children. We asked, why does critical literacy promote peacebuilding? What literacy practices foster peacebuilding?

Critical literacies have the potential to promote peace education and peacebuilding because these practices aim at generating reflection and dialogue about local and global social realities that are the seed of direct or structural violence; beyond that, critical literacies provide space for action and transformation to solve conflicts and social injustices that deepen inequality at the micro and at the community level. By connecting radical imaginations found in children's literature to concrete local problems, critical literacies become ways of being and ways of making peace. This conception of peace challenges the idea of peace as the absence of war. Instead, it presents a holistic notion of peace that emerges from the Epistemologies of the South as the ability to live in harmony with others, with oneself and with nature.

The strategies to connect critical literacies to peacebuilding decenter the role of the teacher, encourage children, family, and community voices about local problems, and foster social change and transformation from within the person, the classroom community, and the local community. The strategies presented in this chapter do not intend to be comprehensive, but inspirational. They can serve as a starting point for teachers interested in implementing peace education in their local contexts. They emerged from years of participatory research with students, teachers, and communities across the Americas from a sustaining, asset-based pedagogical approach to education and to community work.

In addition, the chapter offers a selection of picture storybooks in Spanish that embrace critical issues and topics that speak about Latin America and its diversity. These storybooks offer aesthetic and literary opportunities for reflection, dialogue and transformation with young children, youth, adults, and people across the life span. Through storytelling, we and our participants learned about other ways of approaching conflict, hardship, and the effects of violence.

Future research should look at the ways in which digital literacies can bring more variety to the texts and tasks used in pedagogical interventions with critical literacies for peacebuilding. Researchers can further investigate other book genres (fiction, non-fiction), age groups (older children, young adults), and school levels (middle school and high school, university).

We, the three researchers, teachers, and authors of this chapter, are Colombians who have experienced the impacts of violence in our lives. However, we maintain hope in the power of education, language, and literacies to transform social worlds and individual lives. We wish that those who read this chapter enrich these strategies with their experiences, backgrounds, and imagination. Peace is not something that lies on a peace accord, it is something we breathe and embody in our daily interactions and lives.

REFERENCES

ACAPS. (2022, March 31). *COLOMBIA Impact of the armed conflict on children and youth.* ACAPS Thematic Report. https://www.acaps.org/sites/acaps/files/products/files/20220331_acaps_mire_thematic_report_colombia_impact_on_children_and_youth.pdf

Adarve, P., González, S., & Guerrero, M. (2018). Pedagogías para la paz en Colombia: Un primer acercamiento. *Ciudad Paz-ando, 11*(2), 61–71. doi:10.14483/2422278X.13177

Barton, D., & Hamilton, M. (2010). Literacy as a social practice. *Langage & Société*, (3), 45–62. doi:10.3917/ls.133.0045

Calle-Díaz, L. (2020). *School Discourse Practices and their Potential for Peacebuilding and Social Justice* [Unpublished doctoral dissertation]. Universidad del Norte, Barranquilla, Colombia.

Chaux, E., & Velásquez, A. M. (2016). *Orientaciones generales para la implementación de la Cátedra de la Paz.* Ministerio de Educación Nacional.

Christie, F., & Maton, K. (Eds.). (2011). *Disciplinarity: Functional linguistic and sociological perspectives.* Bloomsbury Publishing.

Clavijo-Olarte, A., & Sharkey, J. (2019). Mapping our ways to critical pedagogies: Stories from Colombia. In *International perspectives on critical pedagogies in ELT* (pp. 175–193). Palgrave Macmillan. doi:10.1007/978-3-319-95621-3_9

Comenius, J. A., & Laurie, S. S. (1969). Comenius. Collier-Macmillan.

Dorner, L., Song, K., Kim, S., & Trigos-Carrillo, L. (November/December, 2019). Multilingual family engagement: Shifting the focus from what families need to how they can lead. Literacy Today. International Literacy Association, pp. 30-31.

Eggins, S. (2004). Introduction to systemic functional linguistics. *Continuum*.

Ministerio de Educación Nacional. (2004). Estándares básicos de competencias ciudadanas. Author.

Freire, P. (2018). *Pedagogy of the oppressed.* Bloomsbury Publishing USA.

Freire, P., & Macedo, D. (1987). *Reading the Word and the World.* Routledge.

Galtung, J. (1964). An Editorial. *Journal of Peace Research, 1*(1), 1–4. doi:10.1177/002234336400100101

Galtung, J. (1969). Violence, Peace and Peace Research. *Journal of Peace Research, 6*(3), 167–191. doi:10.1177/002234336900600301

Gee, J. P. (2007). *Social linguistics and literacies: Ideology in discourses.* Routledge. doi:10.4324/9780203944806

Guerra-Lyons, J. D., & Mendinueta, N. R. (2020). On the notion of "owning a forest": Ideological awareness and Genre-based Pedagogy in university critical literacy. *DELTA. Documentação de Estudos em Lingüística Teórica e Aplicada, 36.* Advance online publication. doi:10.1590/1678-460X2020360412

Guilherme, M., & Menezes de Souza, L. M. (Eds.). (2019). *Glocal languages and critical intercultural awareness: The South answers back.* Routledge.

Halliday, M. (2007). [A&C Black.]. *Language and Education, 9.*

Harris, I. (2004). Peace education theory. *Journal of Peace Education Theory, 1*(1), 5–20. doi:10.1080/1740020032000178276

Harris, I. (2010). History of Peace Education. In G. Salomon & E. Cairns (Eds.), Handbook on Peace Education. Taylor & Francis Group.

Harris, I., & Morrison, M. (2013). *Peace Education* (3rd ed.). McFarland & Company, Inc.

Hasan, R. (2005). Semiotic mediation, language and society: Three exotripic theories–Vygotsky, Halliday and Bernstein. *Language, Society and Consciousness, 1,* 55-80.

Hazaea, A. N. (2020). Fostering critical intercultural awareness among EFL students through critical discourse analysis. *Íkala. Revista de Lenguaje y Cultura, 25*(1), 17–33. doi:10.17533/udea.ikala.v25n01a06

Jaramillo, R. (2008). Educación cívica y ciudadana como respuesta a la violencia en Colombia. *Transatlántica de Educación, 4,* 65–76.

Jiménez, F. (2014). Paz neutra: Una ilustración del concepto. *Revista de paz y conflictos, 7,* 19-52.

Congreso de la República. (2013). Ley 1620. Sistema Nacional de Convivencia Escolar y Formación para el Ejercicio de los Derechos Humanos. Sexuales y Reproductivos y la Prevención y Mitigación de la Violencia Escolar.

Menezes de Souza, L. M. (2011). Para uma redefinição de letramento crítico: conflito e produção de significação. In R. F. Maciel & V. A. Araújo (Eds.), *Formação de Professores de Línguas-Ampliando Perspectivas* (1st ed., pp. 128–140). Paco Editorial.

Menezes de Souza, L. M., & Monte Mór, W. (2018). Still Critique? *Revista Brasileira de Lingüística Aplicada, 18*(2), 445–450. doi:10.1590/1984-6398201813940

Ministerio de Educación Nacional. (2015). *Orientaciones Generales para la Implementación de la Catedra de la Paz en los Establecimientos Educativos de Preescolar, Básica y Media de Colombia*. Ministerio de Educación Nacional de Colombia.

Montoya, A., Jaramillo, C., & Correa, A. (2017). *Narrativas de paz en la escuela* [Unpublished master's thesis]. Universidad de Manizales, Manizales.

Morales, E., & Gebre, E. (2021). Teachers' understanding and implementation of peace education in Colombia: The case of Cátedra de la Paz. *Journal of Peace Education, 18*(2), 209–230. doi:10.1080/17400201.2021.1937085

New London Group. (1996). A pedagogy of multiliteracies: Designing social futures. *Harvard Educational Review, 66*(1), 60–92. doi:10.17763/haer.66.1.17370n67v22j160u

O'Brien, J., & Comber, B. (2020). Negotiating critical literacies with young children. In *Literacy learning in the early years* (pp. 152–171). Routledge. doi:10.4324/9781003116325-7

Organización de Estados Iberoamericanos para la Educación, la Ciencia y la Cultura, OEI. (2014). *Miradas sobre la educación en Iberoamérica: avances en las metas educativas 2021*. Author.

Oxford, R. (2013). *The language of peace*. Information Age Publishing Inc.

Ramos, C., Nieto, A. M., & Chaux, E. (2007). Aulas en Paz: Resultados preliminares de un programa multicomponente. *Revista Interamericana de Educación para la Democracia, 1*, 36–56.

Rico, D., & Barreto, I. (2022). Unfreezing of the conflict due to the peace agreement with FARC–EP in Colombia: Signature (2016) and implementation (2018). *Peace and Conflict, 28*(1), 22–33. doi:10.1037/pac0000545

Rodriguez Martinez, A. K. (2017). *An exploration of young English learners' reading experiences in response to critical literacy read-alouds* [Unpublished master's thesis]. Universidad Pontificia Bolivariana, Medellín, Colombia.

Ruiz, D., Mejía, L., Benavides, M., Serna, C., & Villegas, F. (2017). Narrativas de paz al final de la guerra: Experiencia de reconciliación y diálogo en la I.E. San Vicente de Paúl. *La Vicentina, 1*, 38–43.

Schleicher, A. (2020). *The impact of COVID-19 on education: Insights from education at a glance 2020*. https://www. oecd. org/education/the-impact-of-covid-19-on-education-insights-education-at-a-glance-2020. pdf

Trigos-Carrillo, L. (2019). A Critical Sociocultural Perspective to Academic Literacies in Latin America. Íkala, 24(1), 13-26.

Trigos-Carrillo, L., Rogers, R., & Jorge, M. (2021). Critical Literacy: Global Histories and Antecedents. In The Handbook of Critical Literacies (pp. 10-23). Routledge.

UNESCO. (2015). *Global citizenship education: Topics and learning objectives*. Autor.

Urrea, A., & Trigos-Carrillo, L. (Article under review). Fostering Empathy Through Critical Literacies in Early Childhood Education. *Towards Authentic Peace Education*.

Vásquez, V. M. (2014). *Negotiating critical literacies with young children: 10th anniversary edition.* Routledge. doi:10.4324/9781315848624

Vasquez, V. M., Janks, H., & Comber, B. (2019). Critical literacy as a way of being and doing. *Language Arts*, *96*(5), 300–311.

Wright, Q. (1942). *A study of war* (Vols. 1–2). University of Chicago Press.

Chapter 20
Literacy for Democracy

Teresa Lucas
Florida International University, USA

ABSTRACT

The world is more literate than ever, but does this literacy lead to a more thoughtful citizenry? The approach to teaching literacy skills governed by the necessity of choosing the "right" answers on multiple choice assessment instruments has the effect of producing literate and competent workers rather than the critical, creative, and ethical citizens required for functioning democratic societies. The fall of the Soviet Union in 1989 was celebrated as the victory of democratic ideals over authoritarian forms of government in many parts of the globe. However, events in the current century point to a trend towards autocracy. This chapter considers how events in the current century in the United States and Venezuela point to a trend towards autocracy and suggests how strengthening educational practices, especially those for engaging children in thoughtful literacy, can result in a return to democracy.

INTRODUCTION

Literacy is the cornerstone of a democratic society. Preserving the principles of liberty, justice and equality depends on the ability of all citizens to access and comprehend information relevant to their well-being, to think critically about issues, and to participate thoughtfully in the democratic process. This chapter traces the history of the last 50 years during which anti-democratic forces in many countries have worked toward delegitimizing non-political public institutions essential for ensuring the functioning of government and the protection of the citizenry. Especially important in this endeavor is the weakening, controlling and even eliminating of public education, created by Horace Mann (1796-1859) in the United States as the "great equalizer of the conditions of man" (Eakin, 2000). For those with ambitions to govern by fiat, an informed, ethical, and active citizenry is dangerous. Literacy serves only as necessary for instrumental purposes related to following instructions and gaining employment. Literacy as a window to the world, avenue for thinking critically and engaging in debate about the role of government in ensuring the common good of all members of society is antithetical to those who would assume autocratic powers.

The chapter follows the weakening of democratic institutions in Venezuela and the United States as examples of a wider global trend and as context for examining the attacks on public education in the

DOI: 10.4018/978-1-6684-5022-2.ch020

Literacy for Democracy

United States, with the consequent change in focus on promoting literacy for instrumental ends rather than for personal and social enrichment. The Western world that was lulled into a sense of complacency with the disintegration of the Soviet Union in 1989. Historian Francis Fukuyama proclaimed the "end of history" with the victory of democratic ideals over authoritarian forms of government. Elections were held in many former Soviet Bloc countries. The 1980s saw autocratic regimes toppled in Chile, Brazil, Argentina, Haiti, Romania, and the Philippines. The world seemed poised to enter a new era of liberty for all (Fukuyama, 1992).

However, events in the current century point in another direction as autocratic regimes take hold in China, Russia, Poland, Hungary, Venezuela, and Nicaragua, among others. The Russian invasion of Ukraine in February 2022 finally awakened democratic nations to the threat to their systems of government by forces that seek to undermine the principles on which democracy is based. That danger is perhaps most pronounced in the oldest and most powerful of the democratic community of nations. The insurrection at the U.S. Capitol on January 6, 2021, is a stark reminder of Benjamin Franklin's warning, when asked at the conclusion of the Constitutional Convention in 1787, if the United States would be a monarchy or a republic, to which Franklin responded: "A republic, if you can keep it."

FROM DICTATORSHIP TO DEMOCRACY TO AUTOCRACY IN VENEZUELA

Venezuela was my home for nearly 20 years from 1971 to 2000, giving me a first-hand view of the transformation of a country from a democracy to an autocracy in just a few years. The more gradual breakdown of democracy in the U.S. mirrors the process in Venezuela. The narration of the events in Venezuela is instructive for understanding the forces at work in the U.S. and hopefully for taking measures to guard against a total destruction of the democratic system.

Venezuela became independent from Spain in 1821, after which power passed from one dictator to another. In 1908, Juan Vicente Gomez assumed power and ruled with an iron hand until his death in 1935. His successors ruled until 1945 when a popular movement perpetrated a *coup d'etat*, leading to the country's first election with universal suffrage. The political party whose leaders had led the coup, *Acción Democràtica,* easily won the election. The experiment in democracy lasted only three years until 1948 when a military coup deposed the elected leaders, imprisoning some and sending others into exile. The military ruled with Marcos Perez Jimenez at the helm until another coup sent him into exile in 1958.

The leaders of *Acción Democràtica* were released from prison and came back from exile to join with another political party to plan for the transition to democracy. Raul Betancourt was elected president in 1958. Peaceful transitions of power ensued. With an economy bolstered by the discovery and development of vast petroleum resources, the country was free and prosperous. But democratic institutions were new and inexperienced. Poverty continued to affect the majority of the population. When petroleum prices surged in the 1970s, the vast amount of money pouring into government coffers was difficult for politicians to resist. Widespread corruption weakened the already fragile new democracy.

The familiar tactic of the *coup d'etat* raised its head again in 1992 when a young army lieutenant, Hugo Chavez, rose up against the government. The coup failed, but Chavez promised to come back. After receiving a pardon from a prison sentence imposed on him, he returned in style, winning the 1998 presidential election.

Chavez was an army recruit from a lower middle-class family with no experience in politics. Given the rampant corruption in the previous administrations, his outsider status was a plus. He knew how to reach the majority of the population who felt they'd been ignored as the oil money flowed in. He promised to share the wealth. At first, he followed through, thanks to a sharp rise in the price of oil. He spent lavishly on housing projects and food distribution. He held rallies where people aired their grievances and made promises to address their problems. People adored him. They didn't notice that he filled government positions with loyalists who saw the possibility to become rich with the money flowing into their ministries. When career employees of the one institution that had always been off-limits to political maneuvering, the state oil company PDVSA, went on strike to protest the mismanagement of the organization two years after Chavez assumed power, he fired more than 2,000 engineers, scientists, and career administrators. Farms and industries were expropriated, resulting in the flight of foreign investment. Seeing little future, wealthy and middle-class families began to migrate to other countries. With surging unemployment, many lower income people also began to leave. Seven million Venezuelans have made the decision to seek their fortune elsewhere.

INCLUSIVITY TO EXCLUSIVITY IN THE UNITED STATES

The recent history of Venezuela is instructive as an example of the trend toward autocratic regimes in the 21st century. Autocrats come to power not through violent coups, but through the ballot box. After winning a free election, they champion divisive issues such as corruption, immigration, freedom of religion, gender equality, and abortion rights. They restrict freedom of the press, appoint officials loyal to themselves to institutional posts, and campaign to restrict voting laws to manipulate future elections (Snyder, 2017).

Venezuela was a short-lived experiment, but a highly participatory and enthusiastic democracy. I lived there for many of the stable years, bringing up my children in a thriving environment. Shortly after Chavez' election, I returned to the U.S. to pursue graduate studies, on a hiatus to see how the situation in Venezuela would evolve. I came with the self-assurance that the U.S. was an enduring democracy, made so by the strength of its institutions. That confidence was shaken upon arrival in Tallahassee, Florida just in time for the 2000 presidential elections. The delayed results and victory of the candidate who lost the popular vote seemed more an event that would have happened in a less stable democracy.

In the 1960s, shortly before I moved to Venezuela, the United States had taken strides toward implementing the ideals of equality and justice for all enshrined in the Declaration of Independence. President Lyndon Johnson led the effort to pass legislation that included the expansion of civil rights, safeguards for voting rights, the creation of Medicare and Medicaid, the Elementary and Secondary Education Act that expanded opportunities for low-income students, and reform of immigration policies to favor family reunification and provide a program for refugees. Many of these policies were extensions of Franklin Roosevelt's "New Deal" that created Social Security and jobs through government work projects during the 1930s Depression. Johnson called his efforts "The Great Society" (Kearns-Goodwin, 2018). By the time I returned to the U.S. in 2000, there seemed to be a reversal of sentiments and policies.

SEARCHING FOR ANSWERS

There is a law suggested by Robert Michels, a German sociologist in the early 20th century, that explains the workings of power. The "Iron Law of Oligarchy" explains the nature of the institutions that societ-

Literacy for Democracy

ies form to organize themselves in the political and economic spheres. **Inclusive** economic institutions "allow and encourage participation by the great mass of people in economic activities that make best use of their talents and skills and that enable individuals to make choices they wish. To be inclusive, economic institutions must feature secure private property, an unbiased system of law, and a provision of public services that provides a level playing field in which people can exchange and contract; it also must permit the entry of new businesses and allow people to choose their careers" (Acemoglu & Robinson, 2012: 74). **Extractive** economic institutions "are designed to extract incomes and wealth from one subset of society to benefit a different subset" (Ibid: 76). The assumption is that the United States embodies the model of inclusive economic institutions, while North Korea, for example, exemplifies the model of extractive economic institutions. However, the ethics of large corporations have morphed since the 1950s from serving shareholders, employees, and customers to serving only shareholders, creating extractive entities.

Political institutions also can be classified as inclusive and extractive. "Political institutions determine who has power in society and to what ends that power can be used" (Ibid: 80). Extractive absolutist governments concentrate power in a dictator or a small leadership group. They tend to create extractive economic institutions, while inclusive governments, in which power is distributed broadly at all levels of society, permit inclusive economic institutions based on the rule of law.

In Venezuela, the transformation from a society that was imperfectly inclusive politically and somewhat inclusive economically to embodying extractive economic and political institutions occurred rapidly, since the institutions in place when Chavez came to power were relatively new and weak. In the U.S., a similar process is unfolding, but given the strength of the U.S. institutions, it has taken much longer.

The opening of opportunity to all levels of society began with the New Deal of the 1930s and was strengthened with the "Great Society" legislation of the 1960s. The opening of the economic and political institutions to a wide proportion of society resulted in a concerted effort by those who prefer extractive institutions to reverse the inclusive trends and seek to consolidate power in extractive institutions.

THEORETICAL FOUNDATION OF EXTRACTIVE INSTITUTIONS

James Buchanan was an economist who established the Thomas Jefferson Center for Political Economy and Social Philosophy at the University of Virginia in 1956. Its guiding principles were based on 19th century *laissez-faire* economic policies and the 20th century "self-interest" doctrine championed by Milton Friedman of the Chicago School of Economics. Their basic assumption was that "individuals always acted to advance their personal economic self-interest rather than collective goals or common good…. the very terms of their analysis denied such motives as compassion, fairness, solidarity, generosity, justice, and sustainability" (MacLean, 2017: 98). The founding document of the Center "made clear who would 'not be allowed to participate': anyone who, even inadvertently, would value "security" – the New Deal's mantra – above liberty, and who would "replace the role of the individual and of voluntary association by the coercive powers of the collective order" (Ibid: 45). The aim was to convert economic and political institutions in the U.S. that had become increasingly inclusive to ones that would be extractive.

The self-interest doctrine runs contrary to the philosophy of Franklin Roosevelt, who considered "the role of the federal government to regulate the economy and secure the lives of the American people from the bottom to the top. His purpose – to rebuild the social system "on sounder foundations and on sounder lines" – sprang from what Frances Perkins, his Secretary of Labor, called "his general attitude that the people mattered" (Kearns-Goodwin, 2018: 293). Lyndon Johnson's Great Society in the 1960s also ran counter to Buchanan's ideals, with the emphasis on civil rights, safeguards for voting rights, creation of Medicare and Medicaid, immigration policies that eliminated an outdated national quota system and favored family reunification and refugee policies, and the Elementary and Secondary Education Act that provided federal funding to improve education and support for lower-income children (Kearns-Goodwin: 338), as well as gender equality.

The 1960s thrust towards an inclusive society spurred action towards implementation of the self-interest doctrine. Charles Koch provided funding for and served on the board of the Institute for Humane Studies that recruited scholars to engage in the "search for important truths" to guide the pursuit of liberty, as defined by James Buchanan's doctrine. It would do that by "the training in depth of highly talented persons" with "the greatest promise of leadership". That would take time…because "ideas do not bear fruit immediately" (MacLean, 2017: 135).

The Koch brothers also funded the Cato Institute in 1977, with the express purpose of exposing the evil of the leaders of labor unions, those corporations and business associations that continued to seek special benefits through lobbying, and the intellectuals who supported government action in support of social programs to achieve economic and political equality. "The task facing the libertarian cadre who would staff the Cato Institute and related efforts would be to drive home to the populace the parasitic nature of all three groups, exposing every practical instance of it to help larger numbers see the evil of statist corruption – and what must be done to vanquish it" (Ibid: 141). A related think tank, the Reason Foundation, promoted the idea that government bureaucrats were wasting taxpayers' dollars, and that the public would be better served by privatizing the work of the government, including education. Libertarians stoked fear of Communism to encourage Americans to distrust government by equating the pursuit of the common good through government policies with socialism, a term used interchangeably with "communism".

EXTRACTIVE OR INCLUSIVE?

The Federalist Society was founded in 1982 by students at Yale, Harvard and University of Chicago law schools, with the ideals of "checking federal power, protecting individual liberty and interpreting the Constitution according to its original meaning". With funding from the Olin Foundation, the Scaife Foundation, the Koch family foundations, Google, Chevron, Richard Mellon Foundation, and the Mercer family, the Society has assumed the role of vetting judicial candidates to assure their ideological fealty to the doctrine of self-interest (Montgomery, 2019). The Federalist Society assumes the role of proposing candidates for federal judgeships, including for the Supreme Court. In recent years, Leonard Leo, Co-chairman of the Society, has succeeded in the appointment of three conservative Catholic Justices, resulting in six Catholics on the nine-member Court. He is a member of ultra-conservative Roman Catholic organizations Opus Dei and the Order of Malta. The current Court represents an example of an extractive institution that attempts to counter the majority of the population with decisions leading to restrictions on reproductive freedom and voting rights while loosening restrictions on guns and practices harmful to the environment (Mehta & Dorning: 2022).

In the legal campaign furthering the goals of the movement towards extractive institutions that promote minority rule, the American Legislative Exchange Council (ALEC), founded in 1973, is an organization of "conservative state legislators and private sector representatives who draft and share model state-level

Literacy for Democracy

legislation for distribution among state governments in the United States" (ALEC: 2022). Bills advanced by ALEC include ever-broader 2nd amendment protections that include permit-less acquisition of arms, "open-carry" with few restrictions; "stand-your-ground" laws that extend defense of the home to any environment; and the sale of automatic rifles. Bills drafted by ALEC and passed in many state legislatures after the 2020 general election include restrictions on voting rights and immigration. Recently, ALEC has been instrumental in legislation passed in many states restricting abortion rights and the rights of the LBGTQ community, as well as restricting the teaching of the racial history of the U.S.

After the passage of the 1968 Gun Control Act, the movement to establish the self-interest doctrine found a way to attract individuals who accepted some inclusive government policies, such as Social Security and Medicare, attractive. The National Rifle Association (NRA) was transformed from an apolitical organization of sportspersons to a powerful lobbying group funded by Buchanan's disciples. The establishment of the Bureau of Alcohol, Tobacco, and Firearms (ATF), founded in 1972, amplified cries of government interference in individual rights.

Religious freedom was another rallying call to broaden appeal of the self-interest doctrine, now referred to as "individual rights". The Roe vs Wade Supreme Court decision in 1973 that legalized abortion calvinized religious entities. Similar to the NRA's transformation from a largely non-political organization, churches of many denominations shed their adherence to the "separation of church and state" doctrine enshrined in the Constitution to become active in anti-abortion campaigns. The political activism around the issue led to the declaration of religious freedom to permit doctors to deny treatment to women seeking an abortion and for schools to refuse to hire teachers from the LBGTQ community.

The efforts to reverse the opening of society after the 1960s were touted as having come from grassroots efforts. In reality, they were all inspired by powerful groups following the philosophy of John Buchanan and Milton Friedman to retain the economic and political power accumulated over the years. To capture a sizable percentage of the population, organizers suggested that the provision of benefits meant to provide equity in society were harbingers of socialism. Immigration reform would result in people losing their jobs and increased crime. Voting and civil rights would lead to minority groups wresting power from the traditional White majority. Owning a gun was no longer for sport, but to defend one's rights against rampant crime. The sparking of fear in the working-class White majority was key for the wealthy self-interest proponents to gain the support of policies that did not align with the needs of the working-class Whites, such as tax cuts for the wealthy and opposition to universal healthcare.

FOCUS ON EDUCATION

As a sizable majority of the population was becoming convinced of the dangers of the march toward socialism, the effort to grasp control of the political and economic fortunes of the country was very much focused on education. The 1954 Brown vs Board of Education Supreme Court decision reversed the 1896 Plessy vs Ferguson decision upholding the constitutionality of racial segregation under the "separate but equal" doctrine. Orders to integrate public schools caused extreme reactions. Prince Edward County in Virginia closed all its public schools from 1959 to 1964 rather than accepting integration (MacLean, 2017).

Eventually, public schools in Virginia re-opened, but the effort to weaken public education continued, sparked by the 1984 report "A Nation at Risk" that painted a bleak picture of the public education system, a picture that year after year has been shown to be alarmist by the results of the PDK/Gallup national public schools survey consistently showing over 70% of parents give high ratings to their children's schools. In 2018, on the thirty-fifth anniversary of *A Nation at Risk,* NPR reporter Anya Kamenetz interviewed surviving members of the commission that wrote the report. They candidly admitted that the conclusions were predetermined and the data cited were "cherry-picked" to make American public schools look as bad as possible (Ravitch, 2020: 16). The objective of the report was to bolster the argument for privatizing public schools.

Charter schools, originally intended to be laboratory schools within the public school system soon morphed into a structure of privately-owned schools that would extract money from public school budgets and save children from having to attend the "deficient" public schools. The value of neighborhood public schools that serve to solidify the bonds among schools, families, and communities is not considered in the self-interest doctrine (Ibid: 27).

Voucher programs divert public money even more egregiously to private entities from which no accountability is demanded. Privatization of educational institutions tends to transform them into extractive rather than inclusive organizations. Public schools, colleges and universities are meant to level the playing field for all students. The original purpose of public education was defined by the "Father of Public Education" Horace Mann (1796-1859) as the "great equalizer of the conditions of man" (Eakin, 2000). "Cultivating a social spirit in students" was highlighted by John Dewey as the goal of public education (Mason). Both of these goals are lost in the drive to "produce literate and docile workers…(rather than) self-reflective and politically engaged citizens…" (Ibid: 141).

Wresting control of public education from the hands of educators to promote "education for the workforce" impedes the development of literate, self-reflective and engaged citizens. Reaction to the *Nation at Risk* report spawned the *No Child Left Behind* (NCLB 2002), *Race to the Top* (RTT 2009), and *Every Student Succeeds* (ESSA 2015) *Acts*. With minor changes from one act to the next, these policies

> *…locked the nation's public schools into an ironclad regime of annual testing of every student in two basic subjects from grades 3-8. It also locked policymakers at the federal and state levels into a mindset that they could not escape. When they thought about schools, they could only think about accountability, test scores, and the incentives and punishments that they hoped would produce results" (Burns, 2018: 141).*

The goal of producing engaged citizens who would participate in society and uphold democratic values was lost.

The encroachment of private enterprise principles affects higher education, as well, including teacher preparation programs. Already in 1967, California Governor Ronald Reagan assured taxpayers they would "no longer be forced to subsidize intellectual curiosity in the state's public universities" (Berrett, 2015, in Burns, 2018, pp. 55-56). In reallocating public resources to private entities, university policies and programs shift the focus from the development of intellectual curiosity and the cultivation of character attributes, such as integrity, honesty, responsibility, ethics, and compassion, to workforce development.

Undergirding the shift to workforce development is the almost universal acceptance by educators of the concept of "behavioral objectives". As noted by Silberman in 1970, the "insistence on behavioral definition of objectives, as Professor Lee J. Cronbach of Stanford points out, is a prescription for training and not for education" (Silberman 1970: 200). He continues: "Education can, and almost certainly should, include training; in almost every field there are skills that have to be mastered, concepts that have to be learned. But the converse does not hold; education cannot be subsumed under training" (Ibid). The concepts to be learned in history, science, philosophy, economics cannot be reduced to skills. Behavioral

Literacy for Democracy

objectives result in predetermined results for students instead of opening the students' minds to reflect and grasp deeper understandings.

The consequences of valuing test scores and workforce preparation over developing thinking, knowledgeable, ethical, compassionate, reflective citizens is evident in a population that fails to distinguish truth from falsehood, understand the principles of science, and develop basic knowledge of history. At the same time, the acceptance of an ideology that focuses on the individual at the expense of the collective, results in a moral decline that we see in the increasingly virulent attacks on "the other; in the hateful discourse and actions prevalent in society today.

While this chapter describes trends toward societal organization through exclusive institutions in the United States, the tendency toward autocratic government through elections is seen throughout the globe. Vladimir Putin, after disqualifying opposition candidates in a series of elections, used his absolute power to invade Ukraine. Viktor Orban recently was elected to a fourth term as president in Hungary. Nicolas Maduro consolidated his power in Venezuela through manipulated elections.

WHAT CAN WE DO?

To reverse the tide of increasingly extractive institutions the first step is to be aware of the campaign unleashed by measures to create inclusive institutions with the legislation of the 1960s. It is not a coincidence that so many efforts to promote policies that aim to limit power to a determined segment of the population were developed in the period following the 1960s. Aware that the traditional power structure of mostly White, wealthy men is threatened by a diverse, educated population, the organizations (Cato Institute, Federalist Society, ALEC, etc.) created in the latter part of the 20th century create bonds with White people of all social classes by stoking fear of minority populations. Efforts to restrict civil and voting rights, attacks on immigrants and the LGBTQ community, as well as the expansion of gun rights, abortion restrictions and "religious freedom" condoning the denial of services based on religious conviction seek to deepen divisions and weaken democracy.

Understanding the dynamics of the past 50 years offers a window into the steps we might take as we go forward as educators. The individuals and organizations who participated in the various movements to bring the United States to the brink of losing our democracy in favor of an extractive autocracy understand the importance of attacking public education. As the European Parliament has recognized since its founding:

Democracy and tolerance ... are crucial moral values in the European Union...the guiding principles for living together and organizing society, public life and politics." But since the values are not "self-evident; these values need to be cultivated and fostered amongst people, in particular amongst newcomers in society such as youngsters and immigrants (CULT, 2017: 15-16).

Public education in the U.S. has a pivotal role in reclaiming the impetus of the Great Society toward an ever more inclusive society. To do this, we have to gently affirm our right and responsibility to determine how best to educate children and young adults to become thoughtful, enthusiastic, and kind citizens who believe in the concept of the common good.

FOCUS ON LITERACY

When we speak of educating the "newcomers to society" who are "youngsters", our attention turns to the focus of this book – literacy. Guiding students to literacy means opening the eyes and hearts of children to the vast world of knowledge, wisdom, moral clarity, and opportunity afforded by the ability to read. Literacy in all its forms enables people to learn and think about ideas and discriminate among them. Gaining the key to literacy opens myriad worlds to explore. To encourage children to embrace the excitement of knowing how to read, we have to set aside the constraints imposed by the accountability and test scores regime that focuses on skills and strategies in reading, rather than on understanding and knowledge.

Cesar Bona, an educator in Spain recognized as one of the 50 best teachers in the world by the Global Teacher Prize, relates his experience as a child in his book *La Nueva Educación: Los retos y desafíos de un maestro de hoy*. He loved to read, but that love turned to hate when obliged to read an assigned text chosen by the teacher, with instructions to name the characters, context and plot. The delight in reading for pleasure or to discover new worlds was erased the moment the text was obligatory and saddled with exercises that contributed little to gaining meaningful knowledge and wisdom from absorption in the text. As Bona notes: "Young children learn through curiosity, an innate curiosity that we have throughout life, but that many of us leave behind as we grow. But there's more. The schools seem dedicated to teaching instead of inviting us to learn" (Bona, 2016: 20).

What does it mean to invite children to learn? According to Nightengale, Massy and Knowles, "It means to end dependence on pre-packaged curricular programs….A significant component of developing lesson plans is understanding the learning preferences, culture, and students' perspectives….It requires relationship building to develop instruction for individual students" (Nightengale, Massy & Knowles, 2021: 13). The authors suggest we view literacy

"as a cultural process, mediated by lived experiences, cultural identities and linguistic practices. From this perspective, we view all literacy (language, text, words, visual expression) as an interactive exchange, contextualized through the reader's sociocultural lens. Acknowledging literacy from a sociocultural lens maintains that all reading and writing is mediated through social, cultural, political and socio-historic practices, an interpretation characterized by Gee (1996) called "new" literacies studies or socio-literacy studies" (Ibid: 8).

In this view "reading" is not a designated "subject" but is integrated in all aspects of the curriculum dedicated, not to what answers the teacher wants, but "guiding students to think for himself, so that he is dependent on neither the opinions or the facts of others, and that he uses that capacity to think about his own education, which means to think about his own nature and his place in the universe – about the meaning of life and knowledge and of the relation between them" (Silberman 1970: 114).

American schools do not reflect this view of reading but follow the emphasis on behavioral objectives adopted in education generally. The approach to reading is to focus on skills, rather than meaning and understanding. Teachers create objectives, even for reading comprehension, e.g: "Examine text features of informational texts…Ask and answer questions about text type." As Wexler points out, decoding, matching sounds to letters, is a skill, for which behavioral objectives may be appropriate. Understanding and interpreting texts cannot be reduced to observable skills (Wexler, 2020: 19-20).

Literacy for Democracy

The head of a London infant school many years ago asked: "Reading for what?" (Silberman 1970: 241), echoing Pinar's question with regards to curriculum: "What knowledge is of most worth?" (Pinar, 2012: 30). Without denying the importance of teaching certain reading skills and strategies, we suggest the road to literacy in schools runs through the awakening in children of the desire to read by creating an "environment that will make them *want* to read and write. 'Interest can be a driving power, Nora L. Goddard writes, 'and we try to get the child's absorption in what he sees and does to overflow into reading and writing about those things. In this way the driving force of his interest will help him through the first steps of reading" (Silberman, 2012: 241).

Creating the environment in which teachers are cognizant of the child's interests requires establishing relationships with children and their families as the first step to literacy. What is their background? What experiences have they had? What are their interests? What makes them happy or sad? What do they want to learn? As teachers learn about their students, they establish trust, so relationships flourish. Children are open to the world the teacher introduces to them through literacy.

The introduction to literacy does not begin with identifying letters and sounds, but through conversations about topics that interest the children and others the teacher chooses to broaden their world. Field trips and excursions around the school grounds provide fodder for conversations. Frequent and extended reading to the children sparks interest in the reading process itself while building knowledge and vocabulary. Labelling the objects in the classroom provides practice in identifying words with their meaning.

Literacy includes writing as well as reading. The Language Experience Approach is effective in making the link between reading and writing. Children create stories about themselves, or about a field trip the class participated in, or about a topic the class has discussed. The teacher writes the story as the child speaks and then reads it back to the child. Children are excited to tell their stories. They understand the link between reading and writing (Curtain & Dahlberg:: 2004).

Cognitive scientist David Willingham notes that "reading comprehension actually overlaps quite a bit with the comprehension of spoken language." By reading to and conversing with children, teachers prepare the children to read on their own. When children have acquired a "broad vocabulary and a rich base of background knowledge", they are likely to quickly master reading strategies." According to Willingham, "teaching reading strategies gives developing readers a boost, but it should be a small part of a teacher's job" (Willingham, 2007: 45).

In viewing literacy as the means to understanding the world and not as a subject to be learned children are presented with the opportunity to select from a wide variety of materials, literature as well as nonfiction, books as well as paragraphs. Educating for thoughtful literacy is an integral part of developing citizens who work to preserve the values of a democratic society. Schools and teachers in the United States are being targeted by the same forces that have been working to undermine the democratic system for the past 50 years. By controlling what and how children are taught, these forces hope to finalize a victory for extractive institutions and the self-interest doctrine, in other words, autocracy. Educators are called to imitate the courage of the Ukrainian people who understand that their freedom is at stake in the face of the Russian invasion. In the words of a teacher education candidate: "Teachers can make the classroom a place of hope where students and their teachers can get a glimpse of the kind of the society they could live in."

REFERENCES

Acemoglu, D., & Robinson, J. A. (2012). *Why nations fail: The origins of power, prosperity, and poverty.* Crown Publishing Group.

Achenbach, J., Higham, S., & Horwitz, S. (2013). How NRA's true believers converted a marksmanship group into a mighty gun lobby. *The Washington Post.*

Ben-Ghiat, R. (2018). Power, Curriculum, and Embodiment. Palgrave Macmilan.

Curtain, H., & Dahlberg, C. A. (2016). *Languages and learners: Making the match.* Pearson Education, Inc.

Directorate-General for Internal Policies, Policy Department for Structural and Cohesion Policies Culture and Education. (2017). *Research for CULT Committee - Teaching Common Values in Europe.* Author.

Eakin, S. (2000). Giants of American education: Horace Mann. *Technos, 9*(2), 4–7.

Fukuyama, F. (1992). *The end of history and the last man.* Free Press.

Gerhart, A., & Alcantara, C. (2018). How the NRA transformed from marksmen to lobbyists. *The Washington Post.* https://www.washingtonpost.com/graphics/2018/national/gun- control-1968/

Giridharadas, A. (2018). *Winners take all: The elite charade of changing the world.* Vintage Books.

Kearns-Goodwin, D. (2018). *Leadership in turbulent times.* Simon & Schuster.

MacLean, N. (2017). *Democracy in chains: The deep history of the radical right's stealth plan for America.* Viking.

Mason, L. E. (2017). The Significance of Dewey's Democracy and Education for 21st-Century Education. *Education and Culture, 33*(1), 41–57. doi:10.5703/educationculture.33.1.0041

Montgomery, D. (2019). Conquerors of the Courts. *Washington Post Magazine.* https://www.washingtonpost.com/news/magazine/wp/2019/01/02/feature/conquerors-of-the-courts/

Nightengale-Lee, B., Massy, P., & Knowles, B. (2021). Putting Black Boys' Literacies First: Collective Curriculum Development for the Lives & Literacies of Black Boys. *Journal of literacy innovation, 6*(1), 5-22.

Packer, G. (2020, Feb.). How to destroy a government. *Atlantic*, 54–74.

Poll, P. D. K. (2019). *Frustration in the schools: PDK's poll of public's attitudes toward the public schools.* https://pdkpoll.org/results

Ravitch, D. (2020). *Slaying Goliath: The passionate resistance to privatization and the fight to save America's public schools.* Alfred A. Knopf.

Silberman, C. E. (1970). *Crisis in the classroom: The remaking of American education.* Random House.

Snyder, T. (2007). *On Tyranny: Twenty lessons from the 20th century.* Academic Press.

Southern Poverty Law Center Report. (2020). *The year in hate and extremism 2019.* https://www.splcenter.org/news/2020/03/18/year-hate-and-extremism-2019

Chapter 21
Love and Language:
Peace Building in the Foreign Language Classroom

Aixa Pérez-Prado
https://orcid.org/0000-0002-1651-815X
Florida International University, USA

ABSTRACT

Language is a necessary tool to understand the world. It can be used as an instrument of hate, harm, exclusion, and dehumanization or as an instrument of love, help, inclusion, and humanization. Language is a component of peace, and the language classroom can be a place where communicative competence is expressed through communicative peace. This chapter will explore the relationship between language acquisition, emotion, critical thinking, and peace building. It will demonstrate how applied peace linguistics can help teachers create empathetic and equitable foreign language classroom environments. The author will describe the characteristics of a language acquisition classroom that encourages both critical thinking and peace building. Strategies for teaching language learners by centering emotion during language activities, encouraging critical thinking, and creating peaceful connections among diverse learners will be suggested.

INTRODUCTION

In a world burdened with ongoing conflicts among nations, cultures, and diverse linguistic groups, often stemming from prejudice and miscommunication, peace building is an essential component of education. In order to build peace, the ability to communicate in thoughtful and peaceful ways is necessary. Because the foreign language classroom is a place where much more than language and literacy are learned, it is an ideal place for increasing connection, diversity, and peace building.

Language classrooms are often populated with learners from countries or cultures that are in conflict. Yet within the classroom, all learners are striving for similar goals. Language learners interpret, receive, and internalize classroom language through learning activities. Since language learning goes beyond the accumulation of words and grammar, sometimes influencing how a person sees themselves and others,

DOI: 10.4018/978-1-6684-5022-2.ch021

second language and literacy acquisition can influence both personal identity and global perception. Thus, the language classroom can be a place where stereotypes and biases are challenged and eradicated, a place where literacy and peace building are encouraged.

Research indicates that being multilingual impacts language choice and usage in emotionally charged situations. These may occur inside or outside of the classroom and be contained within classroom relationships, and interactions with strangers (Grabois, 1999; Grosjean, 1982; Pavlenko & Lantolf, 2000). Classroom language and literacy activities are important factors in the construction of global competency for multilinguals. Thus, it seems reasonable that language classrooms be places where a new language and the emotions it generates is practiced and used for humanizing and peace building purposes.

To teach a language is to delve into all the areas that are affected by the human condition. Because of this, teachers and learners benefit from being taught not only to communicate about peace, but how to communicate in peaceful ways. Gomes de Matos (2010) suggests that communicative peace is a deeply rooted feature of communicative competence and that adding the language of peace to the language classroom is necessary as part of global human rights. Language teacher education programs that prepare teachers to employ peace building language and literacy practices as part of communicative competence are functioning in globally competent and culturally relevant ways.

This chapter will explore why and how the foreign language classroom should incorporate peace building to provide an environment where language and literacy are developed in humanizing ways. The inclusion of emotion and the valuing of the first language in the classroom will be discussed, and suggestions provided for creating classrooms where critical thinking is encouraged through language acquisition activities that promote literacy through peace building. The goal is for the language classroom to become a place where language is acquired in a context that supports emotional expression, promotes peace, values diverse ways of knowing, and inspires critical thinking about global issues.
Objectives:

- Explore the concept of language classrooms as places that value and welcome the expression of emotion through learning activities centered on emotional topics.
- Discuss how Peace Linguistics can help teachers create culturally responsive classrooms that value diversity and promote literacy through peaceful language practice.
- Consider the language classroom as a context for building both communicative competence and communicative peace through critical and creative thinking.
- Describe how a language acquisition friendly activities are conducive to positive emotional responses, peace building, and increased connection among diverse learners

BACKGROUND

For the language classroom to be a place where not only language is practiced, but also a place that encourages the expression of emotion and peaceful communication, learners and teachers must be aware of the inherent worth of all world languages. While no scientific evidence exists that using a certain linguistic variety correlates with accomplishment or intelligence (Friedrich & Gomes de Matos, 2012), misunderstanding and violence can result from negative attitudes towards users of specific languages and dialects. Accent, vocabulary choice, and regional variation, when questioned or challenged, can lead to negative emotional responses from speakers, affecting classroom learning in harmful ways.

Applying peaceful classroom practices requires respecting dialectal variation within and across languages. Additionally, because language changes over time, variability in language use should continuously be considered in the classroom. Teachers and learners must modify and adapt their language practices and abilities as they are presented with new information. Classroom literacy materials and activities that emphasize the worth of all world languages and cultures, and encompass peace building as a central focus, are beneficial for increasing the global competency of learners.

Language Equity

As part of equitable language practice and culturally responsive teaching, the use of the first language holds value in the language classroom. The classroom cannot be a place where first languages and their speakers are marginalized. In addition to valuing the first language, equitable language pedagogy includes empathy and thoughtfulness in error correction. When learners are overcorrected in the language classroom, they may have a negative emotional response to that correction, resulting in resentment and self-consciousness. When accents are mocked or not tolerated, the identity of a second language learner is affected in detrimental ways. This, in turn, can lead to a lessened inclination to learn the target language because openness to receiving language input is diminished (Krashen, 1986). Depending on the culture of the classroom and school, this may also lead to learners feeling like they are less worthy and competent.

Language, Thought, and Culture

Linguistic relativity, or the idea that our language is integral in how we think and understand the world, is an object of continuous speculation and research. This connection is of relevance when considering the language classroom where language, thought and culture are intricately intertwined. Although many researchers have looked at the connections between these spheres (Boroditsky, 2001; Boroditsky, 2009; Casasanto & Boroditsky, 2008; Gumperz & Levinson, 1996; Ji et al., 2005; Lupyan, 2012; McWhorter, 2014) their conclusions vary widely. Rather than a direct correlation, there appears to be a continuum of how much each sphere is influenced by the other. For language teachers, the concept that language is influenced by thought (and culture) is of great significance as the language classroom is a place where critical thinking and cultural knowledge are essential to the learning. Of interest is acknowledging connections and looking further into how emotion plays a part in all three spheres. When we consider the context of the language classroom, we can design activities that promote peace building by exploring how each area influences the other.

Languaging, Translanguaging, and Multilingualism

Languaging, the act of using language for collaborative problem-solving purposes, is an important aspect of peace building. Cultural knowledge, body language, emotion, identity, and ideology all influence how, when and for what purposes language is used. For multilinguals, the need to understand and negotiate two or more cultures and languages is ever present. Languaging, for multilinguals, is always multilayered and often complex. Without a negotiation of meaning, individual interlocutors may make assumptions that lead to misunderstandings, and create overgeneralizations about others that lead to stereotypes, prejudice, heartbreak, and confusion. These negative emotional outcomes will often be carried beyond the classroom to the wider world and influence how learners interact with members of cultures other than their own. Similarly, perceptions and stereotypes created outside the classroom regarding speakers of other languages can negatively influence the use of language and the quality of interactions within the classroom. This can be seen across the globe in countries where various languages or dialects are spoken, yet only one language is considered 'standard' and holds the most prestige. Examples of this include the Galician, Catalan and Basque languages in Spain, and the numerous indigenous languages that are rarely considered worthy of teaching across North, Central and South America.

To become effective communicators, language learners need recognize that cultural viewpoints can intertwine with thinking and language use. Learners and their teachers must accept that their way of thinking and speaking is not the only way, nor is it necessarily the best way. When individuals are in relationships that cross cultures, whether inside or outside the classroom, these considerations become paramount to harmony, trust, and the attainment of global competency. When language classrooms have peace building as a focus of language practice, the recognition of diversity in ways of understanding the world become part of classroom learning.

Translanguaging, providing space for multilinguals to access their full linguistic repertoire, creates an environment where language is practiced in a dynamic and integrative way. This practice holds the incorporation of both the native and target language in the classroom as natural and just (García & Leiva, 2014). Teachers accept the use of both languages as a legitimate pedagogical practice. Translanguaging can be beneficial when working with developing bilinguals in a context where the target language is the dominant language in the culture. Translanguaging is an empathetic practice that responds to learner emotions. When learners are given access to both their native language, and the language being acquired within the classroom, they may experience an enhanced ability to communicate in peaceful ways.

Language Acquisition

A primary function of the foreign language classroom is to help learners acquire the target language. Learners arrive in the classroom having already acquired a first language in a context that is replete with emotion, the home and family. First language acquisition, a highly successful process, can provide valuable insight into the process that second language learners go through.

Babies need caregivers for food, shelter, company, cleanliness and perhaps most importantly, love. Most caregivers are captivated by the babies in their care and strive to meet all their needs, physical, cultural, emotional, and linguistic. The mutual love that develops between caregivers and babies creates a relationship and an environment that is ideal for language acquisition. It is warm and accepting, repetitive and comforting, personal and meaningful, collaborative, and interactive, engaging and empathetic, contextual and kind. All these characteristics can be brought into the second language classroom.

Without any formal training in a language, babies are able to successfully acquire their first language in a few years of emotionally charged and loving interactions with caregivers. Vygotsky (1978) emphasizes the importance of social interaction as part of language acquisition, positing that early childhood language development depends on a 'zone of proximal development' formed between a child and a more knowledgeable adult engaging in social interaction. In this zone the child can learn from the adult, often repeating what they hear and reinterpreting it.

Second languages are acquired in a process that has many similarities to first language acquisition. This is of relevance when we are considering the role of emotion in language learning. It is natural to take the emotions of a learner into account during first language acquisition, and much of what caretakers do linguistically is responding to emotions, both positive and negative. The first language is acquired in an

Love and Language

environment that is infused with emotion. Words for expressing pleasure, displeasure and acknowledging meaningful relationships are among the earliest aspects of language learned. Yet, in traditional second language classrooms, emotions have been largely absent (Shao et al., 2019)

The need for social interaction and meaningful connection in the classroom have been recognized by second language researchers who have built on Vygotsky's ideas and those of second language researcher, Stephen Krashen. The ideas proposed in Krashen's monitor model hypothesis (Krashen, 1982) are in line with the need for learners' emotional experiences during language acquisition to be considered. Krashen hypothesized that to acquire language, second language learners need only be exposed to comprehensible input in low stress situations, without excessive emphasis on correctness. In essence, Krashen is saying that an important part of language acquisition includes language learners' emotional learning context. Learners should feel calm, peaceful, and confident in the classroom to be open to language input. Krashen's hypothesis recognizes the need for learners to be in an environment in which their emotions are being considered and in which they are free to make mistakes without fear. This is in harmony with the idea that the language classroom should be a place where emotion is relevant, and where communicative peace is taught alongside with communicative competence. The absence of fear is an essential aspect of peace building.

Second language researchers have expanded Krashen's ideas, ascertaining that in addition to comprehensible input, learners also need prolonged social interaction to acquire language. This interaction includes modified input from interlocutors, comprehension checks, repetition, paraphrasing and negotiation of meaning (Gass, 1997; Long, 1996). According to Long (1996) and other researchers, comprehensible input both fosters acquisition and encourages the output that is essential for fluency to develop. Therefore, activities for language learners should not only be comprehensible, but also interactive and include meaningful output (Ellis, 2012; Swain, 2001). Most meaningful interaction includes some aspect of emotional content.

Swain (2001) contends that because language learning demands both cognitive and social interactive elements, learners must pay attention to both form and meaning during interactions. As a socially mediated activity, language eventually becomes internalized through interaction, providing learners with raw linguistic material (Dörnyei, 2009; Lantolf, 2000; Swain, 2010). When the suppression of emotion is present or regulated in the language classroom, learners may experience discomfort, interact less, and express more disfluencies during interactions (Roche & Arnold, 2018). By embracing diverse sociocultural perspectives through interaction, teachers can create a learning environment that provides opportunities for language acquisition and connection around positive emotions that benefit learners (Piniel & Albert, 2018). This type of environment is a place where peace building can take place.

For learners in classrooms to experience the second language as it is used in the real world, a variety of interactions including different interlocutors interacting for varied purposes is necessary. Social status differences give rise to disparity in conversations, causing limits in communicative confidence of some interlocutors (Pica, 1987). To mediate the effects of social status differences in the classroom, and increase communicative competence, connection, and meaningful interaction, teachers can teach the language of inclusion, equity, and connection explicitly while giving learners the time and the space to practice this language without fear. This type of instruction ensures that a peace building environment is created in the language classroom.

While there is still much research to be done on language acquisition, it is generally agreed that interaction in the language classroom that includes comprehensible input and engaged output is valuable. It is also generally accepted that the language classroom should be a safe place for developing language learners to express themselves in a variety of ways, and that all classrooms should be places where stress and anxiety are minimized (Zadina, 2022). This idea, and how to achieve it, is the basis for the peace building language activities offered later in this chapter.

TRANSFORMING THE SECOND LANGUAGE CLASSROOM

Habits of Mind

Fostering critical and creative thinking habits in the language classroom empowers learners to face challenges they will encounter during the learning process. Yet, not all learners respond equally well to even the most well-prepared lessons. Language learners arrive in the classroom with different cultural backgrounds, personalities, capabilities, wants and needs that call for different kinds of language. Teachers must manage the different needs of the classroom with the disposition to think critically and creatively about teaching. Ultimately, language teachers prepare learners not only for the language use that is rewarded in academic settings, but also for being able to negotiate language in all kinds of settings and circumstances.

A 'Habit of Mind' means having a disposition toward behaving in an intelligent and reflective way when faced with a problem, the answer to which is not immediately evident (Costa & Kallick, 2008). Research indicates that certain characteristics of effective thinkers and problem solvers that can be taught; these are grouped under the label 'Habits of Mind' (HoM) as identified by Costa and Kallick (2008). The HoM encourage thoughtful, reflective, and mindful behavior, dispositions necessary for peace building. Teachers of language learners who integrate HoM in their teaching can provide classroom experiences that prepare learners to become capable and skilled problem solvers, to become thinkers that can think in more than one language, and to become persons who are interested in communicative peace.

Peace Linguistics

Curtis (2018) describes Peace Linguistics as a part of Applied Linguistics that is, "based on systematic analyses of the ways in which language is used to communicate and create conflict and to communicate and create peace." Although the idea of Peace Linguistics has been established for over two decades, it remains largely unknown to many teachers and teacher educators and rarely is part of a teacher education programs. Yet, Peace Linguistics can be a fundamentally important concept to bring into the foreign language classroom where learners' emotions, identities, and linguistic backgrounds are valued.

Rebecca Oxford (2013) states that to fully understand peace and to work for peace, we need to know and use its language. Oxford defines the language of peace as, "any form of communication - verbal and nonverbal - that describes, reflects, expresses, or actively expands peace," and that is needed to practice peace in a meaningful way. This involves being aware of the need for peaceful language as well as using active listening strategies, abundant self-reflection, and consistent practice. By incorporating the language of peace in a systematic, intentional way that promotes critical and creative thinking, transformative literacy practices are enabled in the classroom.

Words are never neutral (Oxford, 2013); thus, language is never a neutral practice. In addition to words, body language, in the form of gestures, mannerisms, and proxemics, plays a significant role in meaning construction. Body language can be especially tricky when communicating across cultures, as

Love and Language

is often the case in the foreign language classroom. Thus, it is an essential part of the learning that needs to be integrated into a classroom that promotes both language acquisition and peace building.

If peace has importance in language education, then teacher education programs must strive to expand by including the affective dimension of learning in the classroom with specific regard for the role that emotion has on cross cultural linguistic practices. Teacher education courses for teachers of diverse learners should include discussion and exploration of identity, transformation, and social action. The same courses that prepare teachers to work with language learners can also be courses that encourage contemplative learning and transformative practices. Teacher education courses in this vein would include commitment to keeping an open mind, suspending assumptions, valuing multiple perspectives, cultivating a climate of compassion in the classroom and being willing to self-reflect (Burggraff & Grossenbacher, 2007).

Communicative Peace and Communicative Dignity

Gomes de Matos (2014) explains that Peace Linguistics is embedded in two concepts: *communicative peace* and *communicative dignity*. The author states that all communication can be improved when language is considered and implemented as a peacebuilding force, and when language users are taught to use languages peacefully. Gomes de Matos further sustains that language teachers be educated to understand how to assist their students to communicate in peaceful ways. In doing so, teachers are assisting learners in attaining global competency.

The strong global presence of the English language further determines the necessity for implementing Peace Linguistics as a practice in the training of English language teachers (LeBlanc, 2010). Gomes de Matos proposes principles for Applied Peace Linguistics as well as a series of recommendations for language teaching programs. These recommendations are summarized below.

- Language should have a deeply humanizing function.
- Languages should be taught/learned and used for humanizing purposes
- Language users/learners should learn how to interact and to be interacted with in human-dignifying peace-promoting ways.
- Teachers of English language learners should be educated to communicate about peace and to communicate in peaceful ways
- Teaching English to Speakers of Other Languages (TESOL) teacher education programs should include a methodological component centered on how to prepare teachers to teach English for communicative peace.

ISSUES, CONTROVERSIES, PROBLEMS

Language Status

Both inside and outside of the classroom, conflict has often resulted from negative attitudes towards users or groups of users of specific languages or non-standard dialects. This can be seen in the negative opinions about codeswitching, the manipulation and mixing of two language systems by multilinguals, as well as the prohibition of the use of indigenous languages and local dialects in schools all over the world. When teachers and administrators hold negative views of codeswitching, language mixing, or ideas about superiority of standard language over other forms of a language, this can negatively affect learners in the language classroom.

The concept of language equity is integral to empathetic and compassionate teaching in the language classroom. Dialectal variations, including pronunciation and vocabulary choices, can be accepted, and welcomed in the learning environment. In English language classrooms, all possible forms of English can find a home, including pronunciation variations that reflect the different 'Englishes' spoken around the world (Kachru, 1992). There is no reason that a certain standard form of English that is spoken by a select group from a certain country should be held as superior to any other form of English. The same is true for any other language that is taught. The standard form must, therefore, be recognized simply as one of many forms of the language being studied, but not as the only form that is acceptable in the classroom. However, this is not always the case within the foreign language, the academic institution, and the larger community.

Speakers of non-standard and foreign languages are often criticized for accents, dialect variations, and non-standard word choices. These criticisms are not only unfair but may also lead to some learners developing feelings of marginalization, lowered self-esteem, and self-confidence. The emotions engendered by attitudes that devalue non-standard language use negatively affect learning and hamper peace building. Language classrooms should be places where linguistic discrimination is unacceptable and where awareness is raised about the cause and consequences of linguistic discrimination (Vanegas et al., 2016). The recognition of language equity is an important part of a language acquisition friendly and peace building classroom that will prepare globally competent learners.

Use of the First Language in the Classroom

The extent to which teachers of language learners and the learners themselves hold positive and negative views of the first language (L1) can be problematic. While some historical language teaching practices incorporated the use of a great deal of the first language and relied heavily on translation, many more contemporary classrooms have veered away from those practices and towards a more communicative methodology in which the first language is not used at all. In fact, in many classrooms the first language has been banned in an effort to make practice in the language being learned both necessary and abundant. In these classrooms the use of codeswitching or language mixing is generally not acceptable. However, more recently the question has been raised as to whether this total ban on the first language in the classroom is justifiable, empathetic, and ultimately beneficial for language learners.

It makes sense that the more the new language is used in interactive, uplifting, and meaningful ways, the more likely that the new language will be acquired. However, the banning of the first language completely, and the prohibition of codeswitching, can be troubling in the limits that it can put on learners' abilities to actively engage in thoughtful interaction in the classroom. The complete ban of the first language may also send a message to learners that their native language is less valuable or worthy than the target language. Thus, some teachers have begun to modify their previous bans on the use of the first language and allow learners to use their first language in the classroom as a vehicle towards acquiring the second language.

Translanguaging, a process that encourages the use of bilingual students' languages in a dynamic and integrative way (Cenoz & Gorter, 2017) creates an environment in which the first language and target language are equal partners in the learning process. Many teachers of developing bilinguals have begun to incorporate translanguaging as a legitimate pedagogical practice. According to Lasagabaster and Garcia (2014), translanguaging allows bilingual students to create meaning, "while shaping their experiences and increasing their knowledge by using their linguistic and semiotic repertoire without arbitrary separation." Translanguaging can be an important part of a language classroom that is also a peace building classroom.

However, translanguaging and what it implies about language, bilingualism, and multilingualism has led to some controversy. Some scholars of translanguaging have questioned the idea that discrete languages exist. They argue that multilingualism itself does not exist but rather that the label of 'language' is a product of sociocultural and political power dynamics including colonialism (Makoni & Makoni, 2010; Makoni & Pennycook, 2007; Pennycook, 2006). García and Otheguy (2014) reject the concept of multilingualism in individuals, positing that bilinguals have internally undistinguishable, singular language structures that are uniquely arranged as a single language, or idiolect.

Codeswitching does not exist if two language systems do not exist within the individual (Otheguy et al., 2015). According to MacSwan (2019), the results of denying the existence of multilingualism and thereby codeswitching may be problematic. "If codeswitching does not exist, then neither does the empirical basis for the repudiation of a deficit perspective on language mixing, a critically important and frequently cited body of basic scientific research." (MacSwan, 2019). MacSwan worries that taken from this perspective codeswitching no longer exists as being a talent of bilingualism worthy of study that reinforces the benefits of multilingualism and challenges a deficit model. MacSwan (2019) goes on to propose an alternative view on translanguaging from a multilingual perspective. The idea of what a language is, whether individual multilingualism exists, and how codeswitching and language mixing work (whether they exist at all) are all important considerations for language teachers and worthy of further study.

Teacher Awareness and Acceptance

The question of how much a TESOL teacher education program should prepare teachers for classrooms that include not only language instruction, but also peace building, is not without controversy. Gomes de Matos (2002) states that TESOL programs, "should include a methodological component centered on how to prepare teachers to teach English for communicative peace." However, few programs include such a component, and not all TESOL practitioners feel that this component should be part of a teacher education program. When such a component does not exist, the awareness of what peace language is, and how to apply it in classrooms, may not exist among practitioners.

Language teachers require a reasonable degree of awareness of how language works to be effective instructors (Andrews, 2007). To create classroom environments that foster peace, this awareness must go beyond the structure and components of language and include the sociolinguistic and functional aspects of language that are used in the classroom. These include language mixing and codeswitching as aspects of communicative competence that may be used for communicative peace.

Whereas many would agree that the classroom is a place where violence and the language of violence should be strongly discouraged, others may consider the implementation of Applied Peace Linguistics in the foreign language classroom as the intrusion of a certain subset of political beliefs emphasizing liberalism, social justice, and peace ideology. This is particularly relevant when considering the New Peace Linguistics (NPL) as described by Curtis (2018). NPL is more focused than traditional Peace Linguistics on analyzing the language used by people who have the power to start wars and to bring peace. A central tenet of NPL is that all conflicts start and end with language, and that words can lead to war. Further, it

Love and Language

is posited that when peaceful solutions are found it is because of the use of language in negotiation and mediation that this occurs. Thus, practicing NPL in the language classroom is closely tied to politics and world views that may cause conflicting emotions and distress in some language teachers and learners.

Finally, how the language of peace is to be applied within classroom activities and the practical construction and application of those activities remains unclear for many practitioners. Since teacher education programs in TESOL have rarely focused on teaching peace along with communicative competence, many teachers may feel unprepared to combine these two aspects of learning in the classroom. If teachers feel unprepared to integrate communicative peace with communicative competence in the classroom, they are less likely to attempt to blend the two and therefore less likely to consider global competency for their learners as a language classroom goal.

SOLUTIONS AND RECOMMENDATIONS

Applying Peaceful and Thoughtful Practices to Language Pedagogy

In order to create classroom environments that encourage the expression of emotion, peace building and critical thinking, conscious application of thoughtful pedagogical practices should be integrated into the curriculum. These practices may include the incorporation of Habits of Mind and the use of Language Acquisition Friendly (LAF) Perez-activities that incorporate peace building contexts (Pérez-Prado, 2021). While there are undoubtedly many ways to create thoughtful and peace building language classrooms, the following section will demonstrate how applying the HoM and LAF to the language classroom might be beneficial in the construction of global competency within the language classroom.

The following list links each Habit of Mind to second language acquisition and peace building possibilities in the classroom.

1. **Persistence:** Staying focused and sticking to a task until it is done, reaching a goal, and not giving up when a task becomes challenging. Second language acquisition takes persistence and peace building take sustained practice and persistence.
2. **Managing Impulsivity:** Thinking before reacting, staying calm thoughtful and deliberative. Using the language of peace and remaining open to multiple perspectives demands that impulsivity be managed.
3. **Listening with Understanding and Empathy:** Stepping into the shoes of another person by listening attentively and striving to understand where others are coming from. Language learners thrive in empathetic and understanding environments that include lots of listening. Classroom practices that incorporate empathy and listening are peace building.
4. **Thinking Flexibly:** Finding more than one way to think about a problem and keeping an open mind to new ideas. Creating culturally responsive classroom environments demands that multiple perspectives be valued, and that learners and teachers remain flexible to new ideas.
5. **Metacognition:** Awareness of thought patterns and strategies used while thinking and awareness of how others may think differently. Language acquisition makes learners aware of their own thinking.
6. **Striving for Accuracy:** Accomplishing careful work, checking work, and modifying as needed. Language acquisition requires attention to accuracy.

Love and Language

7. **Applying Past Knowledge:** Tapping into previous cultural and linguistic knowledge to build new knowledge on the foundation of prior knowledge and experience. Second language acquisition builds upon first language knowledge.
8. **Questioning and Problem Posing:** Keeping a questioning attitude; knowing what data are needed and developing questioning strategies. Second language acquisition thrives in an environment of asking and answering questions. Classrooms that encourage peaceful communication inspire curiosity and diversity in problem posing.
9. **Thinking and Communicating with Clarity and Precision:** Clarity in communication, avoiding overgeneralizations or ambiguity when clarity is necessary. Language learners need extensive interactive practice in communicating with clarity. Peace building classrooms demand clarity in communication for better understanding and meaning making.
10. **Gathering Data Through all the Senses:** Tuning into surroundings by using all the senses. Language learners need to learn to use contextual clues including body language and surroundings to clarify meaning when language is not comprehensible. Use of the senses is an essential human trait that transcends cultures and that helps diverse individuals find connection.
11. **Creating, Imagining, and Innovating:** Having the courage and inspiration to try new things and imagine new possibilities, using creative talents to resolve problems and create interesting solutions. Language acquisition and peace building are inherently creative processes where learners create new sociolinguistic identities and connections with others.
12. **Responding with Wonderment and Awe**: Taking the time to marvel at the beauty and wonders that are available in nature and society. A classroom that encourages the expression of emotion and that values emotional responses from learners is culturally responsive and in line with peace building and connection.
13. **Taking Responsible Risks:** Being willing to try new things and participate in new activities, having a sense of adventure and the courage to fail. Language learning and peace building are both risk taking activities. Safe classrooms allow for vulnerability to enter the communicative process.
14. **Finding Humor:** Being able to laugh at oneself and at situations that are difficult or unexpected, using humor to manage the challenging aspects of our lives. Language learners who can find humor in their attempts in the new language are at a distinct advantage for prolonging and initiating interactions with native speakers and creating connections across cultures.
15. **Thinking Interdependently**: Fostering a sense of teamwork and the willingness and ability to accept the ideas and perspectives of others. Language learners can enhance their acquisition of the target language by interacting with others and working together on tasks interdependently. To peace build in the classroom and outside of the classroom people must think interdependently.
16. **Remaining Open to Continuous Learning**: Accepting that we are in a process of learning throughout our lives and that we will never know everything, being open to learning something new every day. Language learning and peace building are lifelong processes.

By integrating the HoM within peace building language activities, teachers are giving learners practice in using creative and critical thinking in the target language. The HoM also take the emotions of learners into account and increase the possibility that a context of communicative peace will be fostered through the teaching of communicative competence.

Creating Language Acquisition Friendly and Peace Building Activities

To ensure that classroom contexts promote communicative competence and communicative peace, certain conditions must be met. These conditions include the creation of an empathetic and stress-reduced learning environment, activities that promote meaningful interaction, and feedback from teachers and peers that is encouraging and uplifting. For these conditions to be present in the classroom, it is recommended that language teachers create activities that are both peace building and favorable to language acquisition (Pérez-Prado, 2021).

Identified conditions and characteristics for language acquisition to take place in the classroom are summarized in the list below under the label 'Language Acquisition Friendly'. These conditions are later fleshed out in more detail with an added layer of purposeful peace building aspects. The acceptance and encouragement of emotional connections to the learning material and relationship building between peers, teachers, and learners, are also essential in each of these classroom characteristics and conditions.

Table 1. Language Acquisition Friendly (LAF) Classroom Characteristics

- Interactivity is present
- Clear directions and modeling are provided
- Authentic language is used
- Critical and creative thinking skills are encouraged
- Classroom activities are personal and meaningful
- Cooperative learning structures are implemented
- Multiple global perspectives are valued and encouraged
- Learning activities are engaging and motivating
- Learning activities are purposeful
- Visuals and graphic organizers are used
- Body language is utilized for clarity and comprehension
- Natural repetition within activities is encouraged
- The first language is welcome, valued, and built on
- Error correction is delivered with empathy

Interactivity

Interaction is essential in a LAF and peace building classroom. We cannot learn language or build peace alone; we need the collaboration of others. In the classroom this can be achieved through active learning activities including information gap, simulation, task-based and other learning structures that promote interaction (Pérez-Prado, 2021). Interactions with negotiation of meaning and encouragement of diverse perspectives promote peace while providing language learners with comprehensible input and the opportunities to produce output in an empathetic and caring environment.

Directions and Modeling

Despite the quality of an activity, if students do not understand what they are meant to do, the activity will not provide any benefit in terms of language acquisition or peace building. When learners understand teacher expectations, they are more likely to follow directions and take risks using the target language.

Love and Language

Making activities clear increases comprehensible input and helps to lower the affective filter while building the confidence and the comfort that learners need to be able to peace build in the classroom.

Authentic Language

Authentic language is the language that native speakers use when they are engaged in oral and written discourse. Using small clips from movies and interviews designed for native speakers can help language teachers provide authentic language to their learners. The selection of the clips, interviews, or other forms of media used can be carefully curated to promote peace building, inspire dialogue, and encourage the expression of multiple perspectives.

Critical and Creative Thinking Skills

The use of higher order thinking skills is imperative in teaching communicative competence and communicative peace. If students are not given access to the vocabulary and grammar that is involved in thinking on a complex level, they cannot verbally engage in complex learning activities. By integrating the HoM into language learning activities, critical and creative thinking will be practiced.

Personal and Meaningful Activities

When learners find that the lessons, they encounter have personal relevance and are meaningful to them, they are engaged, able to retain more, and enjoy learning more (Pérez-Prado, 2021). Making connections between a language lesson and a learner's life encourages that learner, validates that learner and provides a culturally relevant classroom environment where peace building, and emotion are welcome.

Cooperative Learning Structures

Research on the use of cooperative learning structures has demonstrated their effectiveness for language learning (Brown, 2001; Johnson & Johnson, 1989; Kagan, 1993). Cooperative learning goes beyond interaction for the sake of language practice, it creates the need to interact linguistically to complete a given task. When a task is centered on peace building and uses the language of peace, the goals of a peace building and LAF classroom are more readily met.

Valuing Diverse Perspectives

Allowing, validating, and recognizing a variety of global perspectives in every classroom activity is imperative for a peace building classroom. No matter a learner's native language or cultural background, each brings an important perspective to class activities. The classroom that values diversity becomes a safe space to build peace and connection and embrace emotions that are generated while taking risks while practicing the target language.

Engaging and Motivating Activities

The language classroom can be one of the most interesting classes for learners, and a place to express joy. Language is part of virtually all topics and any number of topics may be employed that engage students to want to interact in the target language in peaceful and motivating ways (Richards, 2020). Games, interactive activities, role plays, and simulations designed for peace building can all serve to make language acquisition engaging and motivating.

Activities With a Purpose

When learners come across an activity or that has a clear purpose and end goal or is specifically designed as a Task-Based Language Teaching (TBLT) activity (Pica, 2008) they are more motivated to complete that activity (Ellis, 2003). When language learning is housed within a purposeful activity, learners are using language purposefully to find the 'solution' or accomplish the task. By creating language and literacy activities with a goal that includes peace building, the focus is taken off language and on to solving the task at hand.

Graphic Organizers and Visuals

All learners can benefit from seeing a visual or a graphic organizer to clarify the meaning of text or oral language. Communication is sometimes established through visuals when words are not adequate to express feeling, meaning, or emotion. Visuals and graphic organizers that are created to promote peace and connection within and outside of the classroom function as an important tool in the peace building process.

Gestures and Body Language

Body language provides context, clarity, and a cultural cue during interactions. However, the meaning of gestures varies widely across cultures as does the extent to which gestures are used. Many misunderstandings and miscommunications may be linked to misunderstood gestures. Clarification and understanding of gestures through language classroom activities can lead to increased peace building and connection both inside and outside of the classroom.

Repetition

Repetition is an important part of language acquisition and natural discourse. When repetition is incorporated within classroom activities, learners get to hear things many times and reinforce their understanding. Peace linguistic activities including chants, songs, and poetry, can be valuable part of a culturally responsive classroom.

Building on Prior Knowledge

The first language (L1) is a valuable resource in the second language classroom. In classrooms where learners share the same first language, discussion in the first language during activities to clarify concepts or to expand on understanding may be valuable. First language is also closely linked with emotion (Anooshian & Hertel, 1994; Pavlenko, 2002; Pavlenko & Lantolf, 2000; Schumann, 1999). Allowing for some use of the first language in the second language classroom may promote an environment where learners feel more inclined to peace building.

Error Correction

When second language learners are corrected for every error they commit, the classroom tends to get quieter. With overcorrection of errors, learners may feel intimidated or hopeless and be less likely interact in the target language. Errors can be corrected with empathy and modeling when appropriate, or at specific designated times without singling out particular learners. By taking learner emotions into account during error correction, teachers can create an environment of communicative peace in which corrective feedback is accepted and valued.

Adaptability

A good language activity is adaptable for learners at different levels. Along with modifying linguistic and contextual demands to simplify a lesson or to make it more challenging, teachers can adapt for increasing communicative peace. Activities can be adapted to ensure that peace language is used and that topics discussed, and tasks encountered in the language classroom have a goal that includes peace building.

Language Acquisition Friendly Peace Building Activities

Two LAF activities adapted to include peace building are provided below. These activities can be used in any classroom of language learners from upper elementary grades to adult, and from a high beginner to advanced level. With some adaptation they can also be used with younger learners. The activities have been practiced over the past decade with TESOL students as part of a TESOL teacher education program at Florida International University. TESOL students have participated as learners both in person and remotely, and later led the activities with language learners of their own.

Activity 1: Peace Building Circle

See Table 2.

Table 2.

Language Practice	Listening & Speaking Agreeing, disagreeing, expressing opinions, pondering, commenting, offering alternatives
Grammar/Vocabulary Practiced	Simple present, conditionals, modals Vocabulary: words depend on specific topics and include peace language
LAF aspects	• Personal and meaningful – learners are expressing their own ideas • Engaging – learners are actively engaged in listening throughout the activity • Interactive – learners interact with one another to complete the task • Cooperative – they must cooperate to complete the task as they cannot repeat one another • Repetition – there is natural repetition of sentence starters and forms as the activity progresses around the circle • Higher order thinking – learners must come up new and creative ways to agree and disagree to the prompt • Values Diversity – different ways of thinking are valued and encouraged
Primary HoM Practice	Thinking Flexibly, Thinking Interdependently, Creating, Imagining, and Innovating, Communicating with Clarity and Precision
Peace Building Practice	Topics of discussion are chosen to promote peace and to practice peace language
Materials Needed	Prepared sentences to work from to start the activity. Topics should center on global/peace related topics that are somewhat controversial

Adapted from Agree/Disagree Circle (Pérez-Prado, 2021; based on the ideas of De Bono, 1992)

Steps

- Sit learners in a circle
- Make a statement that offers an opinion on a topic related to global peace. Example sentences are included below.
- Go around the circle three times. Each learner will have three turns.
- Teacher starts round by stating the prompt sentence. E.g.) War is inevitable.
- Go around the circle once <u>clockwise</u> with each student creating a sentence that is in <u>agreement</u> with the initial sentence E.g.) I agree, people are violent.
  - Learners have to listen and come up with a new reason to agree when it is their turn, no repeating what another student has said.
- After everyone has gone, go counter <u>counterclockwise</u> around the circle with every learner <u>disagreeing</u> with the initial sentence. E.g.) I disagree, many countries have never had wars.
- Finally, go around the circle a third time with each student giving a related sentence that is <u>neither in agreement nor in disagreement</u> with the original sentence. E.g.) If war is inevitable, peace is temporary.
- Give learners one 'pass' per topic so they can 'pass' only once in the three times around the circle.
- Once three rounds are over, pair up learners or form small groups to talk about how they felt and what their actual opinions are, then have a general discussion in the large group. Extensions can include a follow up reading or writing activity.
- This activity encourages listening, creative thinking, and connection

Table 3. Possible Sentences for Activity

War is inevitable. People are inherently good. Words are powerful. Actions speak louder than words. Some countries are superior to others. Nationalism is necessary. Racism is taught.

Activity 2: Listening and Imagining: What's Going On?

See Table 4.

Table 4.

Language Practice	Listening & Writing Explaining, describing, listening to others, empathizing, asking, and answering questions
Grammar/Vocabulary Practiced	Simple present tense, present continuous, descriptive adjectives Vocabulary will include words associated with prompt. If using words learners do not know, include a word bank, and teach those words beforehand. Include words used for peace building.
LAF aspects	• Personal and meaningful – learners are expressing their own ideas • Cooperative – when done in pairs or when learners build on one another's ideas during interaction. • Engaging – learners are engaged in the story and listening to complete the task • Interactive – learners share their ideas and interact while being questioned by teacher • Values diversity –learners demonstrate different perspectives with their responses • Higher order thinking – with more than one right answer, learners must think abstractly and consider various possibilities to complete the activity. They can be creative and analytical in their responses.
Primary HoM Practice	Listening with Understanding & Empathy, Thinking Interdependently, Communicating with Clarity & Precision
Peacebuilding Practice	Seeing situations from multiple perspectives, empathizing with others, brainstorming peaceful solutions
Materials Needed	Text that paints a picture with words, paper, and pencil

Adapted from Listening and Imagining (Pérez-Prado, 2021).

Steps

- Ask learners to close their eyes and visualize while you read a descriptive paragraph from a book or make up a scene of your own. [example scene is provided below]
- Tell learners that they will be answering questions about the scene that they imagine. Emphasize that there is <u>more than one right answer</u> to each question.
- Read the paragraph or scene slowly, at least twice.
- Ask learners questions about the passage read.
- Ask questions that can have multiple correct answers. For example, if you are reading a passage about a natural disaster, ask questions about how people react, the noises that can be heard, what will happen next, etc.

- Have learners form pairs, share, and compare their responses for five to ten minutes.
- As a large group debrief the experience with learners sharing responses and contributing personal experiences they have had with cross cultural communication and conflict.
- This activity encourages empathy, seeing things from multiple perspectives, expressing difficult emotions, and brainstorming conflict resolution.

Table 5. Sample Scene and Questions

You are traveling in a country far from home. The language and culture are very different from your own. While on a bus you sit next to a friendly local couple. They ask you many personal questions and seem to find your answers amusing. When you arrive at your destination, they invite you to eat with them and you agree, but once you get to the restaurant you start to feel uncomfortable. You tell them you have to go, but they insist you stay. Soon others approach your table and start arguing loudly with the couple. Questions: 1. Where are you and what language is being spoken? 2. What does the surrounding country look like? 3. Who are the couple on the bus? Write a short description. 4. What kinds of questions do they ask you? 5. How are you feeling when you get off the bus? 6. What makes you uncomfortable in the restaurant? 7. Why do people start arguing with the couple?

The above examples are only two of the countless potential language activities that are used in communicative classrooms that can be adapted to promote both critical thinking and peace building. Thoughtful practitioners who employ Habits of Mind, or other critical and creative thinking strategies, and keep in mind the ideas of Peace Linguistics, can modify their existing activities to create a classroom environment that promotes communicative peace along with communicative competence and thus facilitates the acquisition of global competence.

FUTURE RESEARCH DIRECTIONS

There is still much to research in the areas of emotion, Peace Linguistics, and peace building in the language classroom. Whether TESOL programs should include the possibilities and the benefits of peace building in their curricula and provide new teachers with the tools necessary to integrate this into classroom activities is an area for further study. In addition, the concept of what a language is and how we should study multilinguals, the resources, and possibilities they bring into the language classroom, and how multiple linguistic and cultural identities can affect perception and instruction continues to be an area with much room for exploration.

CONCLUSION

Integrating peace building, the language of peace, and the inclusion of emotion in language classrooms demands critical and creative thinking from both teachers and students. The disposition to foster a climate that welcomes peaceful connection and provides room for multiple perspectives while maintaining language equity and laying the way for global competence is necessary. The stereotyping and prejudices that exist within and across cultures based on linguistic, social, and cultural background can be brought into the classroom and when left unaddressed are harmful and contrary to a climate of empathy and connection. By specifically teaching peace language and integrating peace building literacy practices into language activities, teachers can help prepare learners to use their linguistic tools for good, and to express themselves authentically both inside and outside of the classroom. Integrating positive emotions such as love, acceptance, and a sense of belonging into the classroom can help in creating a culturally responsive teaching climate of communicative peace, connection, and global competence.

REFERENCES

Andrews, S. (2007). *Teacher Language Awareness*. Cambridge University Press.

Anooshian, L., & Hertel, P. (1994). Emotionality in free recall: Language specificity in bilingual memory. *Cognition and Emotion*, *8*(6), 503–514. doi:10.1080/02699939408408956

Boroditsky, L. (2001). Does language shape thought? Mandarin and English speakers' conceptions of time. *Cognitive Psychology*, *43*(1), 1–22. doi:10.1006/cogp.2001.0748 PMID:11487292

Boroditsky, L. (2009). How does our language shape the way we think? *What's Next?* 116-129.

Brown, D. (2001). *Teaching by principles: An interactive approach to language pedagogy* (2nd ed.). Prentice Hall Regents.

Burggraff, S., & Grossenbacher, P. (2007). Contemplative modes of inquiry in liberal arts education. *Liberal Arts Online*. Retrieved from the internet, July 5, 2022 https://www.wabash.edu/news/docs/Jun-07ContemplativeModes1.pdf

Casasanto, D., & Boroditsky, L. (2008). Time in the mind: Using space to think about time. *Cognition*, *106*(2), 579–593. doi:10.1016/j.cognition.2007.03.004 PMID:17509553

Cenoz, J., & Gorter, D. (2017). Translanguaging as a Pedagogical Tool in Multilingual Education. In Language Awareness and Multilingualism. Springer. doi:10.1007/978-3-319-02240-6_20

Costa, A., & Kallick, B. (2008). *Learning and leading with the habits of mind: 16 essential characteristics for success*. Association for Supervision and Curriculum Development.

Curtis, A. (2018). Introducing and defining peace linguistics. *Word*, *27*(3), 11–13.

De Bono, E. (1992). *Six Thinking Hats for Schools: Book 3*. Hawker Brownlow Education.

Dörnyei, Z. (2009). *The Psychology of Second Language Acquisition*. Oxford University Press.

Ellis, J. M. (2003). *Task-based language learning and teaching*. Oxford University Press.

Ellis, R. (2012). Language Teaching Research and Language Pedagogy. Wiley-Blackwell. doi:10.1002/9781118271643

Friedrich, P., & Gomes de Matos, F. (2012). Towards a Non-Killing Linguistics. In Non-Killing linguistics. Practical Applications (pp. 17-38). Center for Global Non-Killing.

García, O., & Leiva, C. (2014). *Theorizing and Enacting Translanguaging for Social Justice*. In A. Creese & A. Blackledge (Eds.), *Heteroglossia as Practice and Pedagogy* (pp. 199–216). Springer. doi:10.1007/978-94-007-7856-6_11

García, O., & Otheguy, R. (2014). Spanish and Hispanic bilingualism. In M. Lacorte (Ed.), *The Routledge handbook of Hispanic applied linguistics* (pp. 639–658). Routledge.

Gass, S. M. (1997). *Input, Interaction, and the Second Language Learner*. Lawrence Erlbaum and Associates.

Gomes de Matos, F. (2002). *Applied Linguistics. A new frontier for TESOLers*. World Federation of Modern Languages Associations.

Gomes de Matos, F. (2010). *Nurturing Nonkilling. A Poetic Plantation*. CGNK Publications.

Gomes de Matos, F. (2014). Peace Linguistics for Language Teachers. D.E.L.T.A, 30(2), 415-424. doi:10.1590/0102-445089915180373104

Grabois, H. (1999). The convergence of sociocultural theory and cognitive linguistics: Lexical semantics and the L2 acquisition of love, fear, and happiness. In Languages of Sentiment: Cultural Constructions of Emotional Substrates. Academic Press.

Grosjean, F. (1982). *Life with Two Languages*. Harvard University Press.

Gumperz, J. J., & Levinson, S. C. (1996). *Rethinking Linguistic Relativity*. Cambridge University Press.

Ji, L., Nisbett, R. E., & Zhang, Z. (2005). Is it culture or is it language: Examination of language effects in cross-cultural research on categorization. *Journal of Personality and Social Psychology*, 87, 57–65. doi:10.1037/0022-3514.87.1.57

Johnson, D., & Johnson, R. (1989). *Cooperation and competition: Theory and research*. Interaction Book Company.

Kachru, B. (1992). *The Other Tongue: English across cultures*. University of Illinois Press.

Kagan, S. (1993). The structural approach to cooperative learning. In D. Daniel (Ed.), *Cooperative learning: A response to linguistic and cultural diversity*.

Krashen, S. (1982). *Principles and Practice in Second Language Acquisition*. Pergamon.

Krashen, S. D. (1986). *Principles and practice in second language acquisiton*. Pergamon Press.

Lantolf, J. P. (Ed.). (2000). *Sociocultural Theory and Second Language Learning*. Oxford University Press.

Lasagabaster, D., & Garcia, O. (2014). Translanguaging: Towards a dynamic model of bilingualism at school [Translanguaging: hacia un modelo dinámico de bilingüismo en la escuela]. Cultura y Educacion, 26(3), 557-572.

LeBlanc, J. (2010). *How ESOL teachers become aware of Communicative Peace*. MA TESOL Collection. Paper 497. Retrieved from https://digitalcollections.sit.edu/cgi/viewcontent.cgi?article=1510&context=ipp_col

Long, M. (1996). 'The role of the linguistic environment in second language acquisition. In W. Ritchie & T. Bhatia (Eds.), *Handbook of Second Language Acquisition* (pp. 413–468). Academic Press.

Lupyan, G. (2012). Linguistically modulated perception and cognition: The label- feedback hypothesis. *Frontiers in Psychology*, *3*, 54. doi:10.3389/fpsyg.2012.00054

MacSwan, J. (2017, February). A Multilingual Perspective on Translanguaging. *American Educational Research Journal*, *54*(1), 167–201.

MacSwan, J. (2019). A multilingual perspective on translanguaging. *Decolonizing Foreign Language Education*, 186–219. doi:10.4324/9780429453113-8

Makoni, S., & Makoni, B. (2010). Multilingual discourse on wheels and public English in Africa: A case for "vague linguistics.". In J. Maybin & J. Swann (Eds.), *The Routledge companion to English language studies* (pp. 258–270). Routledge.

Makoni, S., & Pennycook, A. D. (2007). Disinventing and reconstituting languages. In S. Makoni & A. Pennycook (Eds.), *Disinventing and reconstituting languages* (pp. 1–41). Multilingual Matters.

McWhorter, J. H. (2014). *The Language Hoax. Why the World Looks the Same in Any Language*. Oxford University Press.

Otheguy, R., García, O., & Reid, W. (2015). Clarifying translanguaging and decon- structing named languages: A perspective from linguistics. *Applied Linguistics Review*, *6*(3), 281–307. doi:10.1515/applirev-2015-0014

Oxford, R. L. (2013). *The language of peace. Communicating to create harmony*. Information Age Publishing.

Pavlenko, A. (2002). Bilingualism and emotions. *Multilingua*, *21*, 45–78.

Pavlenko, A., & Lantolf, J. (2000). Second language learning as participation and the (re)construction of selves. In J. Lantolf (Ed.), *Sociocultural Theory and Second Language Learning* (p. 155177). Oxford University Press.

Pennycook, A. (2006). Postmodernism in language policy. In T. Ricento (Ed.), *An introduction to language policy: Theory and method* (pp. 60–67). Blackwell.

Pérez-Prado, A. (2021). *LAF with the Habits of Mind: Strategies and Activities for Diverse Language Learners*. Habits of Mind Institute.

Pica, T. (1987, Spring). Article. *Applied Linguistics*, *8*(1), 3–21. https://doi.org/10.1093/applin/8.1.3

Pica, T. (2008). Task-based instruction. In N. Van Deusen-Scholl & N.H. Hornberger (Eds.), Encyclopedia of language and education (2nd ed., vol. 4, pp. 71-82). New York, NY: Springer Science+Business Media LLC.

Piniel, K., & Albert, A. (2018). Advanced learners' foreign language-related emotions across the four skills. *Studies in Second Language Learning and Teaching*, *8*(1), 127–147. https://doi.org/10.14746/ssllt.2018.8.1.6

Richards, R. (2020). Exploring Emotions in Language Teaching. *RELC Journal.* doi:10.1177/0033688220927531

Roche, J. M., & Arnold, H. S. (2018). The effects of emotion suppression during language planning and production. *Journal of Speech, Language, and Hearing Research: JSLHR, 61*(8), 2076–2083.

Schumann. (1999). *The Neurobiology of Affect in Language Learning.* Blackwell Publishers.

Shao, K., Pekrun, R., & Nicholson, L. J. (2019). Emotions in classroom language learning: What can we learn from achievement emotion research? *System, 86,* 102121. https://doi.org/10.1016/j.system.2019.102121

Swain, M. (2001). Integrating language and content teaching through collaborative tasks. *Canadian Modern Language Review, 58*(1), 44–63.

Swain, M. (2010). 'Talking-it-through': Languaging as a source of learning. In R. Batstone (Ed.), *Sociocognitive perspectives on language use and language learning* (pp. 112–130). Oxford University Press.

Vanegas, M., Fernández, J., González, Y., Jaramillo, G., Muñoz, L., & Ríos, C. (2016). Linguistic discrimination in an English language teaching program: Voices of the invisible others. Íkala, Revista de Lenguaje y Cultura Medellín, 21(2), 133-151.

Vygotsky, L. S. (1978). *Mind in society: The development of higher psychological processes.* Harvard University Press.

Zadina, J. N. (2022). *Engaging The Cognitive Brain, The Emotional Brain, and the Heart of Learners: Science and Strategies.* http://www.brainresearch.us/blog.html?entry=engaging-the-cognitive-brain-the1

ADDITIONAL READING

Benesch, S. (2018). Emotions as agency: Feeling rules, emotion labor, and English language teachers' decision-making. *System, 79,* 60–69. doi:10.1016/j.system.2018.03.015

Freire, P. (1972). *A Pedagogy of the Oppressed.* Herder and Herder.

Pell, M. D., Monetta, L., Paulmann, S., & Kotz, S. A. (2009). Recognizing emotions in a foreign language. *Journal of Nonverbal Behavior, 33*(2), 107–120. doi:10.100710919-008-0065-7

KEY TERMS AND DEFINITIONS

Codeswitching: The practice of switching between two or more languages or varieties of language in conversations among bilinguals and multilinguals.

Communicative Competence: Knowledge of the components of language, as well as knowledge about appropriate and efficient language use.

Communicative Peace: Communication that is thoughtful, humanizing, constructive, and fosters well-being.

Culturally Responsive Teaching: Teaching that encourages student engagement by valuing what students bring with them to the classroom and centering classroom practices around student experiences.

Global Competence: A combination of attitudes, values, knowledge, and abilities applied to intercultural communications and issues of global interest.

Language Equity: The recognition that all languages and all varieties of a language, are equally worthy.

Languaging: A process of meaning making that is collaborative and dialogic, useful in building knowledge interdependently for the purpose of communicative problem solving.

Multilingualism: An individual or group's use of more than one language for communicative purposes.

Peace Education: Educating for peace, social justice, and the prevention of violence.

Peace Linguistics: An interdisciplinary approach of language instruction with the goal of educating learners to be peaceful language users.

Translanguaging: Valuing the use of a person's full linguistic repertoire in the classroom.

Chapter 22
Funds of Perezhivanie:
Creating Cracks in the Walls of Oppression

Fernanda Liberali
https://orcid.org/0000-0001-7165-646X
Pontifical Catholic University of São Paulo, Brazil

Larissa Mazuchelli
https://orcid.org/0000-0002-5253-7593
Federal University of Uberlandia, Brazil

Rafael da Silva Tosetti Pejão
https://orcid.org/0000-0003-0707-0709
Pontifical Catholic University of São Paulo, Brazil

Daniela Vendramini-Zanella
https://orcid.org/0000-0002-0331-545X
University of Sorocaba, Brazil

Valdite Pereira Fuga
Pontifical Catholic University of São Paulo, Brazil

Luciana Modesto-Sarra
https://orcid.org/0000-0002-7597-6484
Pontifical Catholic University of São Paulo, Brazil

ABSTRACT

This chapter discusses the development of funds of perezhivanie in participants of the Brincadas Project, a response to the appalling experiences of COVID-19 in Brazil organized by the Research Group Language in Activities in School Contexts. The project, grounded on critical collaborative research, decolonial studies, and Vygotskian and Freirean's body of works, involves participants' critical, intentional, and engaged actions to individually and collectively recreate ways of "producing life" and research together. The authors focus on two activities for this work: a cine club with the indigenous community Tekoa Pyau and a workshop session on ag(e)ing. Both activities exemplify the development and expansion of participants' funds of perezhivanie while expressing how these resources for "talking back" may significantly impact society.

DOI: 10.4018/978-1-6684-5022-2.ch022

INTRODUCTION

This chapter discusses the development of funds of perezhivanie in participants of the Brincadas Project, organized by the Research Group Language in Activities in School Context (Grupo de Pesquisa Linguagem e Atividade em Contexto Escolar, in Portuguese), as a response to the dreadful living conditions experienced during the COVID-19 pandemic in Brazil.

In Brazil, the pandemic crisis has highlighted the necropolitics[1] (Mbembe, 2003) of a government that despises its population's death. Among several examples, the authors stress the incitement not to use masks and the contempt for adopting distancing measures; the absence of a national policy for buying vaccines and the government's questioning of their efficacy; the encouragement of medication and treatment without scientific evidence; and the lack of financial support for families in need.

In 2022, for example, around 130,000 families are at risk of being evicted. Between March 2020 and February 2022, more than 27,600 families left their homes, representing a rise of circa 300% in the last two years (Despejo Zero, 2022). Data on food insecurity also indicate the increase in despair of families who cannot feed themselves. Although hunger is a historical problem in Brazil, as is access to housing, in the last two years, the number of people experiencing food insecurity has increased from 10.3 million to 19.1 million (Rede PENSSAN, 2021). In this regard, it is worth noting that in 2019 the National Council for Food and Nutrition Security was terminated by the Bolsonaro Government in the form of a Provisional Measure (PM N. 870, Jan 1, 2019). The return of Brazil to the United Nations Hunger Map is not due only to the recent health crisis, but to the political mechanisms that have been annihilating social advances.

In this terrifying political helplessness and health crisis scenario, the authors highlight the struggling experiences to survive of two population groups—indigenous communities and the ag(e)ing[2] population—that live in destitution, suffering from discrimination and systemic violence. The former has been resisting, since the Portuguese colonization, the violence that reduced its population from around 3 million to 250 thousand—currently distributed in only 200 ethnic groups and circa 170 languages. The latter resists being blamed for the "overburden" on the health and pension systems. In the context of the pandemic, besides the health crisis, the indigenous population faces increased hunger and violence in the dispute over land for monoculture and livestock. In turn, the ag(e)ing population was ridiculed and accused of not understanding the gravity of the pandemic. At the same time, their lives were considered disposable by politicians who regard it inconceivable that "now everyone wants to live to 100, 120, 130 years" and doctors who have decided that the lives of older people in Intensive Care Units are not worth the treatment[3].

Alongside other initiatives, the Brincadas Project has responded to this reality by offering financial support, education and play, and psychological aid[4]. As discussed in previous works (Liberali, Mazuchelli & Modesto-Sarra, 2021; Liberali et al., 2021a), the project has involved working with "the disposable lives" of the deaf, the LGBTQIAP+ community, the quilombolas, the indigenous groups, the migrants, the afro-Brazilians, the ag(e)ing people, women, and people with disability so that they can "talk back" (hooks, 1989) and transform their struggling experiences into potent resources to create cracks (Walsh, 2019) in the walls of oppression. As suggested by hooks (1989), talking back involves raising one's voice to speak as an equal to an authority figure in a daring attitude of disagreement, simply having an unsolicited opinion or speaking out, which may be viewed as an act of courage.

In this chapter, the authors focus on two activities developed in 2021 that exemplify how the participants' critical, voluntary, and engaged actions may foster the expansion of their funds of perezhivanie[5], here understood as sets of resources developed from dramatic events (Vygotsky, 1994a) lived with others that can translate into new ways of living and meaning-making (Megale & Liberali, 2020). The first activity was developed with Aldeia Tekoa Pyau, an indigenous community located on the outskirts of São Paulo that suffers from the struggles of living between a rural community and a large city favela. The work with indigenous children, youth, and educators aimed at worshiping their ancestry, traditions, and wisdom and dealing with environmental issues through a cine club on human rights.

The second activity was a Brincada workshop carried out within an outreach course. Designed to enable educators to think about ag(e)ing and their ag(e)ing experiences as a complex multidimensional process, the Brincada "For the right of ag(e)ing" aimed to challenge dominant biomedical frameworks that determine ag(e)ing from a loss and deficit stance in a context of increased violence and neglect of this population. The participants collaboratively elaborated a manifesto in response to the World Health Organization's intention to include "old age" in its 11th review of the International Classification of Diseases.

The two activities are theoretically and methodologically grounded in Critical Collaborative Research (Magalhães, 2011; Magalhães & Fidalgo, 2019) and Engaged Multiliteracy (Liberali, 2022), which informs the praxis of Language in Activities in School Context Group that seeks to transform the historical scenario of inequalities and survival struggle by collaboratively expanding participant's social, cognitive, and affective repertoires, which this chapter now presents. Next, the two activities are introduced and discussed, followed by the chapters' final considerations.

THEORETICAL AND METHODOLOGICAL DISCUSSION: A PRAXIS TO *CRACK* OPPRESSION

The work developed by the Research Group Language in Activities in School Context and the discussion in this chapter are grounded in Critical Collaborative Research (Magalhães, 2011), which involves participants' critical, intentional, and engaged actions to individually and collectively recreate ways of "producing life" and research together. It is also based on a decolonial perspective that, in general terms, underlines the continuous struggle and survival against the colonial matrix of power that affects every dimension of life, forcing groups to become invisible and subaltern (Grosfoguel, 2010; Quijano, 2010; Walsh, 2019). The decolonial view aspires to upend colonial structures through, for example, revisiting past historical events, which implies the recognition of multiple coexisting voices, in the same time-space, with their interconnected histories and trajectories presented in an unrepeatable way.

In this study, the creation of cracks in the walls of oppression is circumscribed to the ethical-political positioning from decolonial stands (Maldonado-Torres, 2016) that can question, challenge, transgress, and displace such a dominant-colonizer system. This activism allows the Research Group Language in Activities in School Context to crack these walls of oppression and create varied ways of being, doing, feeling, thinking, and existing in different spaces, geographies, and times (Walsh, 2019). However, it is noteworthy that such activism and theoretical and methodological stances do not aim at delegitimizing or excluding Western, Global North, Euro-USA-centered views. Rather, it aims at creating opportunities to acknowledge the multiplicities of knowledges and experiences that coexist, which are fundamental for fighting the colonial premise of "reality impartial observation." Such a privileged position, which Castro-Gómez (2003) entitled "ponto zero," refers to the point of view that hides itself by not presenting itself as a point of view (Grosfoguel, 2010). For the Colombian philosopher, placing oneself at point zero

Funds of Perezhivanie

leads to silencing, subalternizing, and hierarchizing the existing epistemologies, favoring universal and neutral thinking. Fighting colonialism and its entrenched system of oppression thus involves "practicing freedom," which stresses and increases the challenges that urge people to respond, evoking new ones followed by new understandings and yet further challenges (Freire, 1970).

For the Language in Activities in School Context Research Group, new, co-existing, and at times conflicting perspectives are central for the development of funds of perezhivanie. According to Vygotsky (1994a), perezhivanie relates to how each subject experiences the same situation uniquely and is affected by them, reiterating the inseparability between emotion, cognition, and environment. In other words, it is a prism that refracts external and internal factors in particular ways. The concept of funds of perezhivanie, as discussed elsewhere (Megale & Liberali, 2020), is a set of resources developed from dramatic events (Vygotsky, 1994a) lived with others that can translate into new ways of living and meaning-making. It thus integrates and highlights the interactive and collaborative nature of mobility (Blommaert, 2016) of individuals' agentive lived experiences with the concepts of repertoire (Blommaert & Backus, 2013) and translanguaging (García, 2009; García & Wei, 2014; García & Voguel, 2017).

Mobility, a central concept in language studies, is "a matter of determining the different orders of indexicality through which communication travels, and their effect on communicative conditions and outcomes" (Blommaert, 2016, p. 246). Repertoires, in turn, are mobility records (Blommaert & Backus, 2011) that include an individual's movement and linguistic and semiotic resources in different time-spaces. Regarding translanguaging, Garcia (2009) explains that the concept encompasses the intersection of different language structures and semiotic systems for meaning-making, allowing expanding repertoires and increasing mobility. From a decolonial perspective, translanguaging offers a social, critical, and transformative space for multilingual speakers and minorities to "talk back" (hooks, 1989), thus collaborating to crack—albeit initially —the hierarchies that delegitimize and invisibilize minority groups by restricting their repertoires and mobility (Garcia & Vogel, 2017).

Thus, funds of perezhivanie refer to the resources agentively (re)developed in the individual's continuous transformation process in a collectivized, collaborative, and dynamic manner that contribute to increasing mobility and expanding repertoires. Their development comes from the dramatic experiences lived in society and from varied ways in which such experiences are refracted by each one from their invoked histories in diverse contexts. In this sense, dramatic experiences may enable expanding various ways of thinking, acting, learning, and producing knowledge, experiences, and feelings. According to Megale & Liberali (2020), the unique ways of living experiences can compose and modify the resources (narratives, multimodal possibilities, and histories, to name a few) that constitute the continuous process of (re)developing the individuals' funds of perezhivanie. Therefore, these may provoke the emergence of new configurations of human lives from dramatic events experienced with each other.

Lived experiences can expand funds of perezhivanie from the availability of resources, which also raises an individual's power of creation and possibilities to make different, new, and at times more potent decisions. In this sense, unfamiliar situations and encounters may allow the creation of new meanings and understandings of the world. In this continuous meaning-making process, individuals can transform the circumstances of their lives and worlds (Stetsenko, 2017) as they are called to be responsive and responsible for the events here, now, and for what is yet to become. In this sense, funds of perezhivanie are expanded and constructed from grounded positioning and informed choices (Liberali, Fuga & Vendramini-Zanella, 2022). A decolonial undertake of funds of perezhivanie requires, therefore, the individual and collective permanent critical positioning, the development of new "means of speaking" (Blommaert & Backus, 2013, p. 3), and ways of "talking back" (hooks, 1989) so that the collective of individuals renders fissures and creates mechanisms of resistance and rebellion (Walsh, 2019) in search of equity and social justice.

In alliance with this theoretical discussion, the work developed by the Language in Activities in School Context Research Group and presented in this chapter is methodologically based on Critical Collaborative Research (Magalhães, 2011; Magalhães & Fidalgo, 2019), whose interventional character seeks shared critical-collaborative alternatives, underlining the premises of co-authorship and co-construction. With Critical Collaborative Research, participants build an understanding of the investigated transforming reality, dialectically transforming it and being transformed by it towards overcoming oppressions, which is the primary concern of Language in Activities in School Context Research Group.

Critical Collaborative Research provides spaces for dialectical confrontation and for participants' co-production of meanings in order to intervene in an unfair world. Theoretically and methodologically, Critical Collaborative Research allows researchers and participants to collaboratively negotiate pervasive senses and meanings while allowing participants to have their voices heard, valued, and open to be questioned and criticized. In this work, these issues—co-authorship and co-construction—are assigned to those involved in the research, in a responsive way, in its process (syllabus design; development), as well as in the data production, selection, and analysis, and this chapter's elaboration. As discussed elsewhere (Liberali et al., 2021b; Liberali et al., 2022), questioning the other is the highest respect one presents towards the centrality of the collectivity once its interests, needs, and desires are acknowledged and emphasized in the production of reality.

The description of the two activities developed, "Playing with Aldeia Tekoa Pyau" and "Playing for the right of ag(e)ing," guides the discussion. Their organization is based on Engaged Multiliteracy (Liberali, 2022), a concept that expands the multiliteracies practices proposed by the New London Group (1996/2000) through a dialogue with Vygotskian and Freirean works, particularly underscoring the immersion and emergence movements and the methodical rigor in search of the "ser mais" (being more, Freire, 2006). The authors understand that Engaged Multiliteracy is an inviting instrument for developing funds of perezhivanie for its design and theoretical foundation since it allows participants to act upon their repertoires in dramatic situations. In this process, they expand repertoires, increase their mobility, and collaborate to create new ways of understanding and transforming themselves and the world.

Engaged Multiliteracy involves three non-hierarchical moments that allow participants to immerse in different experiences with reality and reflect and act on them. First, Immersion in Reality offers a chance for participants to connect and problematize concrete lives in order to develop consciousness of potentials they already have and those they still have to develop or improve to engage in different social contexts fully. The Critical Construction of Generalizations allows participants to foster, criticize, and expand intercultural contact with various forms of knowing, being, thinking, feeling, and acting. Lastly, the Production of Social Change involves developing ways of critically creating new practices and meanings infused with participants' goals and values to act to transform unfair conditions of reality.

Creating Fissures With Aldeia Tekoa Pyau

Aldeia Tekoa Pyau, from the Mbyá Guarani nation, is located in the western area of São Paulo, in a neighborhood called Jaraguá. Surrounded by two important highways, Rodovia dos Bandeirantes and Rodovia Anhanguera, it is near Parque Estadual do Jaraguá, a conservation area of 532 hectares which consists of six villages: Tekoa Pyau, Itakupe, Yvy Porã, Ita Endy, Ita Vera, and Tekoa Ytu. The focus of the project is on one particular aldeia—the ''upper aldeia'' Tekoa Pyau—which is, with Tekoa Ytu ("lower aldeia"), "the smallest and most precarious indigenous lands in the country, and the two do not add up to two hectares in total," according to Motta (2007, p. 11).

The Brazilian Institute of Geography and Statistics estimates that 90 families live in the community (IBGE, 2010). However, in 2022, Fernando da Costa Ramos, one of the community's leaders, stated that 98 families live in around 75 thousand square kilometers despite the land not being a lawful indigenous territory (Figure 1). Although the indigenous peoples have been legally the rightful owners since the 1960s, the struggle and resistance for the official registration of lands do not cease. Indigenous leaders and the community frequently resort to the Brazilian government for this act to meet their rights and needs.

Figure 1. Aerial photography of Aldeia Tekoa Pyau
Source: Google View https://bit.ly/3uozWE0

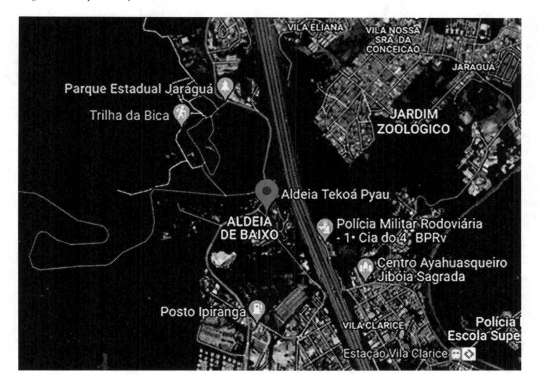

The struggle and resistance of the Guarani Mbyá Nation for the demarcation of these lands aim to preserve the forest and guarantee the indigenous way of life. In 1970, the construction of Rodovia dos Bandeirantes divided the territory and destroyed part of the area. Ten years later, before the enactment of the Brazilian Constitution, part of the land was legally recognized. However, in 2005, the group was removed from the land after a repossession action resulting from an injunction.

The majority of the inhabitants are Guarani, but other ethnicities such as Pataxós, Caingangues, and Potiguaras also live in the region. The predominant languages spoken are Guarani and Portuguese. The humble houses of the aldeia are made of wood and were built intuitively and scattered randomly (Figure 2). Some were renovated in 2021, with financial and material support from Brincada de Apoio. As reported elsewhere (Santos, 2012), the community shares space with native flora, such as coffee trees.

However, the conditions for farming are not viable—an old creek where children played now receives part of the sewage from neighboring communities. Electricity, clean water, and sanitation are in precarious conditions.

Figure 2. Aldeia Tekoa Pyau
Source: Brincadas Project

Since it is an urban aldeia, it lacks typical characteristics that provide for indigenous communities in the forests, which means that Tekoa Pyau people need to find means to adapt and survive in the city. In order to do so, they seek employment, food, health assistance, and other services "in an urban way." As part of this process, many indigenous people leave the aldeia. In this sense, living in such a community translates as quite a challenge for children and teenagers who struggle to find meaning and imagine a future with their people.

To support the aldeia there is a Center for Indigenous Education and Culture (CECI-Jaraguá, a Municipal Public School), a Primary Care Unit, a "Casa de Reza" (a community space used for spiritual and educational activities), and a state school for primary education, the State High School Djekupe Amba Arandy. CECI-Jaraguá develops educational activities respecting the specificities of Guarani Mbyá education and culture to contribute to the community's self-management. The teachings aim to strengthen the Guarani's identity, which is based on the shared knowledge of the elders and the teachings of the family nucleus. CECI-Jaraguá also provides support to the community, such as material aid and the care of almost five hundred children aged 2 to 6 and older.

The partnership of the Brincadas Project with Tekoa Pyau started at the beginning of the COVID-19 pandemic. Through Brincada de Apoio, the community was served with a power generator, winter clothes, baby clothes, wood to recover the houses, and food for the animals. After that, the Brincadas Project initiated its first educational work in the second semester of 2021. Following the interests of the aldeia, the Brincadas Project organized a cine club with the ENTRETODOS team to play with the children and the youth of the community. ENTRETODOS is a renowned organization that offers free short films (up to 25 min) and Human Rights festivals that seek to expand access to debates involving diverse daily life themes in the foundations of Brazilian society through the powerful artistic and pedagogical tools that cine clubs use.

In line with the Engaged Multiliteracy perspective, the researchers organized a session where participants watched short movies as the starting point for reflections and actions regarding ecological and

Funds of Perezhivanie

social issues. Together with the representatives from the aldeia, they decided that this session would be part of the Children's Day festivities (Figure 3).

Figure 3. Tekoa Pyau youth during cine club
Source: Brincadas Project

Indigenous children, teenagers, and educators from the aldeia, the ENTRETODOS team, and the researchers from the Brincadas Project met at the festivity, which lasted a day, to create the cine club activities. These cine clubs were thought of as a means to crack the walls of ecological and social justice destruction. The researchers selected national and international short animations and movies together with educators from the aldeia as prompts for the activities. The selected films were the Iranian short animations "White Paper" (2010, Shakib) and "Game Over" (2012, Shakib), the Spanish short animation "Maisha" (2015, Gómez & Piulachs), and the Brazilian short animations "(Des)matamento" ("(De) forestation," 2020, Guerra), "Menino Pipa" ("Kite Boy," 2018, Kelle), and "Assum Preto" ("Chopi blackbird," 2020, Machado), and short films and documentary "Nós Somos" ("We are," 2018, Bezerra

& Sabatini), "Menino Pipa" ("Kite Boy," 2018, Kelle), and "Mandayaki and Takino" (2020, Yariatu Juruna, Dadyma Juruna).

The activities started in the morning with the younger children (ages varying from 2 to 6) who participated in play activities that connected and engaged them. Next, they watched silent short movies on ecological and social issues as part of the Immersion in Reality. The movies sparked comments by the children. While they drew what was necessary for a better world, they interacted with the researchers—mostly in Guarani but sometimes Portuguese. It is striking that although the movies expressed destructive and protective attitudes towards the environment and human life, the great majority of the drawings represented the positive aspects of the stories. With these drawings, these very young children broke the point zero expressed by situations of silencing, subalternization, and hierarchization expressed in the short movies, which suggests not only these children's meaning-making processes but their engagement with the future of life on Earth. The short films allowed children to understand how much the planet is being devastated by climate crises, the crisis in the demarcation of indigenous lands, the danger of continuous deforestation, and discrimination issues. Engaging in a sustainable future for humanity is evident through the playful resources indigenous children used (Figure 4). Their drawings resonate with mechanisms of resistance and rebellion (Walsh, 2019) to search for ecological justice.

Figure 4. Tekoa Pyau children watching short movies and drawing
Source: Brincadas Project

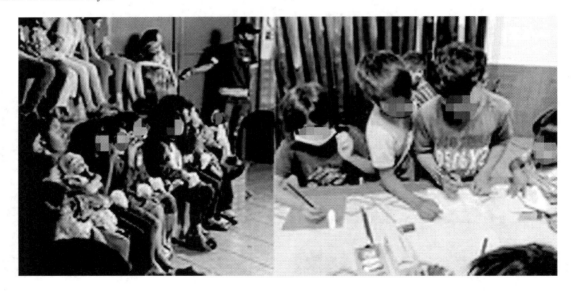

The activity developed is an example of the powerful practice of translanguaging (Gracia & Wei, 2014). Children and researchers used spoken Guarani and Portuguese, drawings, and gestures while interacting to make meaning, understand, express, and share their worlds. Named languages were not, indeed, the unique means of interaction. As a resource for reflection and Immersion in Reality, the movie was recovered and transformed by children's drawings. The children's work from the White Paper (2010, Seed Shakib) movie exemplifies their rich and complex meaning-making process. The movie tells the story of children discriminated against by their families for being colorful and different. They get to-

Funds of Perezhivanie

gether and build a broom with sticks, and with that broom, they sweep the clouds in the sky that make everything gray (no color, no difference). The sun appears, colors everything, including the flowers, and creates a place for the colorful children to hold hands and play happily. As portrayed in figures 5 and 6, it is striking that the children chose to draw elements central to the movie: the cloud swept by the broom designed and a sole multicolored flower representing the diversity of beings. It is indeed indicative of the children's rich and complex meaning-making process.

As presented in figures 4, 5, and 6, the children explained the drawings and reported (sometimes in Guarani, translated by the indigenous leader) liking that the children (in the short movie) cleaned the sky and helped the community. They also mentioned enjoying the movie with "the multicolored flower" because the characters played together despite their differences—their drawings and comments stressed the importance of acceptance. It is also striking how they shared materials and generally created the drawings collaboratively, working together (Figure 4). Such a collaborative stance reflects a Critical Construction of Generalization that involves everyone. It thus opposes traditional individualistic practices that silence children and value the hierarchization of products and knowledges.

Figure 5. White Paper (2010, Seyed Shakib) clouds and children's drawing
Source: Brincadas Project

Figure 6. White Paper (2010, Seyed Shakib) flower and children's drawing
Source: Brincadas Project

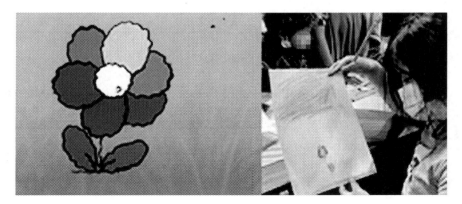

The variety of resources gathered by children and adults was materialized in the different ways of taking part and in the attempts to make meaning with the whole group. The cine club experience provided resources such as using an elaborated broom and the multicolored flower constructed in moments of extreme tension in the movie (Figures 5a and 5b). The unsettling moments in the movies experienced and recreated by children could be seen as a dramatic event that reflects the expansion of participants' funds of perezhivanie (Megale & Liberali, 2020). These were moments in which children were invited to expand dramatic moments with their experiences within the village and their elders, learning traditions, ancestry, and cosmos, being generous and honest with nature and human beings. This Production of Social Change could be triggered by the activity with the short films, prompting them to show epistemologies of resistance, struggle, and voicing of minority groups.

In the afternoon, with the teenagers, similar events took place. They were invited to watch movies and share their understandings and experiences by performing on the issues depicted in the movies with theatrical props (Figure 7) — Immersion in Reality and Critical Construction of Generalization. After watching the short movies, teenagers gathered in smaller groups to discuss the moments and situations which most impacted them. In their conversations, they recovered scenes and mentioned different contradictions and conflicts. They also referenced similarities in their lives and how they could see themselves in the scenes portrayed in the short movies. As depicted in Figure 7, the teenagers expressed their connection to the film with an indigenous child from a forest aldeia who helped her mother with household chores. They also represented and explained the violence (such as prejudice in relation to race, color, and economic situation) they live through in their daily lives as opposed to what the "white people" experienced. Besides, they performed opposite realities, such as playing traditional games *versus* playing with cell phones, and expressed concern that, in their communities, people played more with the latter than the former ("they are addicted," according to them).

Moreover, after one of the groups performed a scene from the one-minute short film "(Des)matamento," the researcher asked, "What do you think about deforestation in Brazil?" Without blinking, an indigenous young man said, "A crime." When the researcher replied, "And why a crime?" He answered, "We have to preserve the forests and trees because they are from all over the world." The researcher insisted, "What do you think of deforestation in Brazilian lands?" Another indigenous youth said, "We have to preserve the land; the land belongs to everyone; the land is our mother; she takes care of us." Notably, in voicing their distress regarding deforestation, these young indigenous youth also voiced the land, daring to bring its perspective into the discussion, a standpoint that "white people" historically have left aside.

These conversations involved creating fissures in the generally silencing, subalternizing, and hierarchizing attitudes normally taken as universal. It is conspicuous that students who typically, according to their teachers, did not participate in the classroom activities engaged in the multiliterate activities (developed within Immersion in Reality, Critical Construction of Generalization, and Production of Social Change), which seemed to be meaningful and provided them with the opportunity to show their skills. Some participants stated that they did not have much experience with performances and "never did it at school." After watching short films that portrayed young people in complex social and ecological situations, and the work of the children and youth in discussing and performing the films, their teachers were surprised with their engagement, how much knowledge about their community and ancestry they shared, and the desire to create and change the world. One of the teachers commented, "Wow, I did not imagine that they could create meaningful work with their peers."

Funds of Perezhivanie

Figure 7. Tekoa Pyau youth's performances
Source: Brincadas Project

Like with the younger children, teenagers lived, through Immersion in Reality, the situations in the short movies and created, in the Critical Constructions of Generalizations, reflections on the movies and conversations, comparing scenes to their life experiences. In this translanguaging process, teenagers collectively overcame boundaries rooted in teachers' visions of who the students are and can be. They increased their mobility and expanded their repertoires while acting intensely in various activities, especially considering the themes in the movies (ecological crisis, discrimination, indigenous culture), thus creating bases for new forms of agency in the Production of Social Change. As Stetsenko (2019) argues, they did not simply "react and respond" but agentively acted in co-realizing the world and themselves. The multiplicities of knowledges, experiences, and voices enabled by the Engaged Multiliteracy activities seem fundamental for expanding their funds of perezhivanie and constructing the viable unheard of (Freire, 1970) to become active agents in the transformation of unfair situations.

In the following section, another example of the activities devised to enable the expansion of funds of perezhivanie is presented. In this case, the focus is on a workshop for teachers aimed at offering educators the resources to live through dramatic experiences and question unfair conditions while creating new possibilities of living and new ways of teaching.

Fissuring for the Right of Ag(e)ing

An important example of the work carried out with educators was the Brincada "For the right of ag(e)ing," held in October 2021 through the Zoom platform. The (trans)formation meeting was attended by about 30 public and private teachers from São Paulo who were enrolled in the Outreach Course "Engaged Multiliteracy: curriculum as (trans)formation," organized by researchers from the Language in Activities in School Context Research Group.

The activity was divided into three main moments (Immersion in Reality, Critical Construction of Generalizations, Production of Social Change) that could be replicated and adapted in the participants' educational praxis. Immersion in Reality allowed participants to approach affectively and cognitively issues in the ag(e)ing universe. Initially, the teachers were welcomed with the song "Conversa de Botas Batidas" (Camelo, 2003) and invited to participate in a game in which they needed to look at each other, observe the wrinkles and changes in each other bodies, and trace the lines on their hands, neck, and face with a pencil while looking at each other through the Zoom camera. In the end, they exaggerated their facial expressions for a picture. Then, the participants played "statues"–they made statues of a baby, an active, healthy child, a busy executive, and an older man. Like the previous activity, the proposal provides a collective immersion in the theme and works with participants' stereotypes about imagined representations of these stages of life (Figure 8), that is, their translanguaging repertoires.

Figure 8. Tracing lines and patterns on the body
Source: Brincadas Project

Finally, the last activity of this first (trans)formative moment was carried out through a padlet entitled "The Wall of the Forgotten" (Figure 9), through which teachers watched short videos and read clippings of posts and memes that circulated on social media. Through this activity, they were able to apprehend oppressions suffered by older people in different time-spaces, such as through the sharing of derogatory memes in WhatsApp groups, domestic violence and older people's neglect, hate speech shared in the public sphere, and the scandal of the health insurer Prevent Senior that allegedly reduced the oxygen level of patients hospitalized in Intensive Care Units (ICUs) to accelerate the release of hospital beds. This maneuver scandalized the country and was summarized in the phrase "death is also hospital discharge"

(Goes, 2021). The welcoming activity and the beginning of the immersion allowed participants to bodily, affectively, and cognitively act upon their repertoires while relating to the theme.

Figure 9. The wall of the forgotten
Source: Brincadas Project
From left to right: video about domestic violence against older women; meme "Black car takes older people to make soap," news about the first death by COVID-19 in Brazil; meme "Selling a cage for stubborn older men"; Tweet from a famous pastor about COVID-19 deaths.

In the second moment of the meeting, the participants were divided into two groups to act on two dilemmas during the Critical Construction of Generalizations. In group 1, integrating Mathematics and Languages, participants prepared to stage a family discussion about adopting care "to alleviate family suffering" for the older mother with COVID-19. Based on the Prevent Senior scandal, the dilemma required participants to build arguments for creating the scene. In preparation, educators read public documents on ag(e)ing in São Paulo, a scientific article on mortality rates among ag(e)ing adults with COVID-19, and watched a video on demographic ag(e)ing. The objective was to consider what information and important issues the texts brought to their attention in order to construct the point of view of each of the characters in the scene (the doctor and the family members).

Based on an account of an older woman who feels "unwanted and helpless" in medical care, participants in group 2, which integrated Science and Health, were invited to perform a scene of medical care with the participation of a younger companion (Figure 10). To create the performance, participants read news about the practice of infantilization and silencing of ag(e)ing people within medical contexts, the roles of geriatricians and gerontologists in promoting well-being, and how varied activities help maintain cognitive health. They also read scientific articles that describe different theories about the biology and the multidimensionality of ag(e)ing. As the activity of group 1, this proposal required reading texts to consider what information and important issues the text brought to the construction of the point of view of each of the characters in the scene (the doctor, the older person, and the companion). It allowed participants to expand their funds of perezhivanie through amplifying understandings of ag(e)ing, challenging dominant social, political, and biomedical frameworks that silence and subalternize older adults.

Figure 10. Performance lead-off text and sharing readings for the scene's design
Source: Brincadas Project

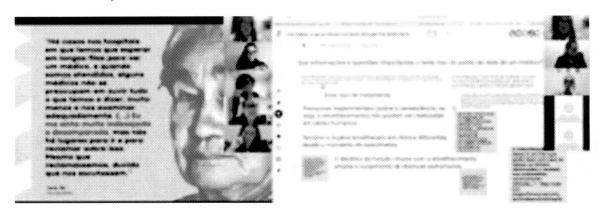

After socializing the performances planned in each group, the participants moved on to the last activity, the Production of Social Change. At that moment, inspired by the discussions and reflections carried out in the previous activities, the educators were invited to prepare a "Manifesto for the Right of Ag(e)ing" (Figure 11) as a response to the revision of the International Classification of Diseases (ICD) that proposed the inclusion of "old age" (code MG2A) as a category within the classification—a change that would increase prejudice and stigma against older people. In the manifesto, the participants presented the ideas they rejected, defended, and supported to guarantee the right of ag(e)ing. These activities generated discussions and demanded positioning from the teachers who engaged in the project and the theme and contributed to disseminating the manifesto, later translated into English and Spanish by the Language in Activities in School Context Group researchers.

Figure 11. Participants write the manifesto for the right to aging
Source: Brincadas Project

Funds of Perezhivanie

The work carried out—part of a broader training project that seeks to support teachers to work critically and collaboratively in different school subjects—allowed participants to identify ageism and discriminatory practices, expanding their repertoires and increasing their mobility on issues and struggles of ag(e)ing and their teaching practices, as well as visualizing possibilities of liberation. Teachers had the opportunity to face the ag(e)ing marks that are socially expected to be erased or hidden. They also challenged universal views on ag(e)ing that subjugates the very possibility of thinking about the complexity, heterogeneity, and potentiality of ag(e)ing and raised their voices, whether while performing older adults being neglected or disrespected or when creating a manifesto to demand respect and equity. In this sense, teachers simultaneously had the chance to develop funds of perezhivanie related to their own experiences and understandings of ag(e)ing and ageism and how to work with ag(e)ing issues in educational contexts through school subjects but also beyond them. As one of the participants commented, "I was moved by each account and identified some situations we witness in the family, and we remember and put ourselves in their places." As Liberali (2019, p. 08) argues, "the suggested idea is that understanding, developing awareness and using multimodal resources build repertoires that create new possible agencies. In other words, they create the possibility of breaking with a certain framework of action and taking the initiative to transform it."

As in the activities with aldeia Tekoa Pyau, the viable unheard of (Freire, 1970) was enabled by the activities, which allowed the collective increase of mobility and expansion of funds of perezhivanie with the construction of knowledges, experiences, and voices. In this sense, the objective of this Brincada goes beyond "educating about" ag(e)ing and ageism. It aims to enable teachers to become responsible for bringing issues regarding those forgotten to school. It is a possibility to break the point zero that silences and subalternizes ag(e)ing lives by determining, for example, those who can live and survive a pandemic. By offering opportunities for the participants to live dramatic experiences, the Brincada contributes to helping teachers and educators not to limit themselves to their syllabus and consider themes such as ag(e)ing and ageism as "side subjects" or "extracurricular activities."

In this sense, the Brincadas Project also provides teachers with instruments to develop mobility as teachers to work and transform realities. As stated by Clavijo-Olarte and Sharkey (2019, p. 179), "there are numerous calls for teachers to develop and enact curricula that reflect students' realities, and there are examples of fully developed critical pedagogy projects (cf., Comber, 2016) but little documentation of how and where teachers learn to do this work (McDonald, Bowman & Brayko, 2013)." The Brincadas Project responds to this call by presenting workshops, courses, lives, and sessions in which educators can experience and reflect on the process of teaching-learning to live while expanding their funds of perezhivanie.

CONCLUSION

The two groups in the examples are characterized as "ungrievable," as Butler (2020) suggested. They may be seen as not valuable, deviating from expected standards, not producing as expected, not consuming as desired, and not acting as established. Like the manuscript journal from July 15th, 1955, by Carolina Maria de Jesus, an Afro-Brazilian poet and writer, would present:

Don't say that I was trash,

that I lived on the margin of life.

Say that I was looking for work,

but I was always slighted.

Tell the Brazilian people

that my dream was to be a writer,

but I did not have money

to pay for a publisher (Jesus, 1960)

In these lines, Jesus (1960) expressed the feelings that many of the wretched ones of the Brazilian society have concerning the unfair conditions of their living today. The necropolitics that sustains those in powerful positions in the country led to the devastation seen during the COVID-19 pandemic and beyond. It reinforces the destruction of persons and the creation of death-worlds, in which vast populations are subjected to conditions of life conferring upon them the status of living dead (Mbembe, 2003).

In the examples, nevertheless, the groups acted upon their funds of perezhivanie, expanded their mobilities, and performed an act of risk and daring, raising their voices in acts of courage to challenge those who might consider indigenous children and youth incapable of "meaningful work" or those who insist in thinking that ag(e)ing is a synonym of a disease that must be "contained" and "resolved." The participants managed to create opportunities of belonging that led to changing the nature and direction of speech. Through the performances and activities developed in the Immersion in Reality, Critical Construction of Generalizations, and Production of Social Change, the participants transformed knowledges of themselves and the world, made themselves heard, seen, and their potency acknowledged. In both cases, critical collaboration was the essence of the organization—it generated a safe space for children, teenagers, adults, and ag(e)ing people to present their ideas, experience varied ways of being, thinking, and feeling (in) the world, thus breaking the point zero (Castro-Gómez, 2003), albeit germinally.

By joining the Engaged Multiliteracy activities, participants could recognize the multiplicities of knowledges and experiences upon which to question, challenge, transgress, and displace. These activities and the work developed thus point to the development of funds of perezhivanie, as they spark reflections, potential new resources, forms of critical and active participation, and meaning-making because of the semiotic, interpersonal, intellectual, cognitive, and affective resources provided by the critical collaborative design of the activities. Engaged Multiliteracy thus offers the possibility for expanding mobility (Blommaert & Backus, 2011) by engaging participants (including those who were part of the design of the meetings, the data selection and analysis, and the elaboration of this chapter) in various possibilities of meaning-making so that they can "talk back" (hooks, 1989) to the unfair situations they might have experienced. They *still rise*, as Maya Angelou, an Afro-American author, actress, screenwriter, dancer, poet, and civil rights activist, reminds us:

You may shoot me with your words,

Funds of Perezhivanie

You may cut me with your eyes,

You may kill me with your hatefulness,

But still, like air, I'll rise (Angelou, 2020)

Like the poem, the oppressed groups who are relentlessly shot, devastated, and destroyed keep finding the energy to survive and strive for social justice. Their strength is fueled and expanded by essential experiences which may provide them with opportunities to recognize their value, their potential, and their collective possibility to overcome. Therefore, it is essential to develop an educational, political, and structural commitment to direct society's resources to benefit all people, particularly those who are economically, socially, politically, or culturally marginalized and oppressed (Stetsenko, 2020).

As educators, the struggle to support children, teenagers, adults, and older people to rethink who they are, what they know, and how they intend to act upon everyone's funds of perezhivanie must be stressed. Developing funds of perezhivanie is seen as a means to evoke new challenges, followed by new understandings and yet further challenges (Freire, 1970), which can spark forms of existing, thinking, and doing that may promote visions of harmonious and whole life. As this chapter ends, the authors acknowledge the limitations of the project in creating lasting transformations and in proving the development of funds of perezhivanie. The authors emphasize, however, that the core of the work developed within the Language and Activity in School Context Research Group is understanding that the change for a more socially just and equitable world depends upon the transformations of conscience. Changing the relations among people inevitably leads to changes in consciousness (Vygotsky, 1994b). In this sense, the Brincadas Project aims to create possibilities for such transformations, albeit blossoming. These are the cracks where the researchers and participants sow in. As Walsh (2019, p. 105) explains, "my bet these days is on small hopes, that is, on these many-other ways of thinking, knowing, being, feeling, doing, and living that are possible and exist despite the system, defying it, transgressing it, making it crack."

In this sense, the authors wish to end this chapter by honoring the lives lost during the Brazilian COVID-19 pandemic and the lives of those who have not lost the desire to continue to *esperançar* so that older people are not discarded at hospitals and the indigenous youth and children are not violated and made disappear. This work leads to the Latin American ancestral perspective of Good Living Sumak Kawsay geared toward a production seen as an ethical and moral framework that produces fairer, balanced, and poverty-free societies (Venegas, 2017; Krenak, 2020).

ACKNOWLEDGMENT

This research was supported by Language and Activity in School Context Research Group and Projeto Brincadas.

This research was supported by the National Council for Scientific and Technological Development—CNPq [grant number 301512/2019-1]; The Postgraduate Internationalization Program—Piprint [grant number 21664]; and the Incentive Plan for Outreach Projects—Pipext [grant number 17377].

REFERENCES

Angelou, M. (2020). *Still I Rise*. Poetry Foundation. htttps://bit.ly/3KqhU9h

Bezerra, T., & Sabatini, G. (2018). *Nós Somos* [We are, Film]. Tereza Bezerra & Giselle Sabatini.

Blommaert, J. (2016). From mobility to complexity in sociolinguistic theory and method. In N. Coupland (Ed.), *Sociolinguistics: Theoretical Debates* (pp. 242–259). Cambridge University Press. doi:10.1017/CBO9781107449787.012

Blommaert, J., & Backus, A. (2011). Repertoires revisited: 'Knowing language'. Superdiversity. *Working Papers in Urban Language and Literacies*, 67, 1-26.

Blommaert, J., & Backus, A. (2013). A. Superdiverse Repertoires and the Individual. Current Challenges for Educational Studies. In I. Saint-Georges & J. J. Weber (Eds.), *Multilingualism and Multimodality* (pp. 11–32). Sense. doi:10.1007/978-94-6209-266-2_2

Brasil. Provisional Measure No. 870, January 1st 2019. Brazilian Official Gazette: section 1, 1-13. Brasília, Federal District.

Butler, J. (2020). *The force of nonviolence*. Verso Books.

Camelo, M. (2003). Conversa de Botas Batidas. In Los Hermanos. In Ventura. BMG.

Castro-Gómez, S. (2003). *La Hybris del Punto Cero: ciencia, raza e ilustración en la Nueva Granada*. Editora Pontifica Universidade Javeriana.

Clavijo-Olarte, A., & Sharkey, J. (2019). Mapping Our Ways to Critical Pedagogies: Stories from Colombia. In M. López-Gopar (Ed.), *International Perspectives on Critical Pedagogies in ELT. International Perspectives on English Language Teaching*. Palgrave Macmillan. doi:10.1007/978-3-319-95621-3_9

Comber, B. (2016). *Literacy, place and pedagogies of possibility*. Routledge.

Despejo Zero. (2022). *Balanço dos dados até fevereiro de 2022* [Data balance until February 2022]. Campanha Despejo Zero. https://bit.ly/3vnCTVV

Freire, P. (1970). *Pedagogy of the Oppressed*. Herder and Herder.

Freire, P. (2006). *Pedagogia da autonomia* [Pedagogy of autonomy]. Paz e Terra.

García, O. (2009). *Bilingual Education in the 21st Century: A Global Perspective*. Basil/Blackwell.

García, O., & Vogel, S. (2017). Translanguaging. In G. Noblit & L. Moll (Eds.), *Oxford Research Encyclopedia of Education*. Oxford University Press., doi:10.1093/acrefore/9780190264093.013.181

García, O., & Wei, L. (2014). *Translanguaging: Language, Bilingualism, and Education*. Palgrave MacMillan. doi:10.1057/9781137385765

Goes, T. (2021, December 16). '*O caso Prevent Senior' exibe o sadismo e a crueldade que contaminaram a operadora*. Folha de São Paulo. https://bit.ly/34tEXku

Gómez, L., & Piulachs, J. (2015). *Maisha* [Film]. Lula Gómez & Jordi Piulachs.

Grosfoguel, R. (2010). Para descolonizar os estudos de economia política e os estudos póscoloniais: transmodernidade, pensamento de fronteira e colonialidade global [To decolonize political economy studies and postcolonial studies: transmodernity, frontier thinking and global coloniality]. In Epistemologias do Sul [Epistemologies of the South] (pp. 378-412). Cortez Editora.

Guerra, G. (2020). *(Des)matamento* [(De)foresting, Film]. Gunga Guerra.

hooks, B. (1989). *Talking Back: Thinking Feminist, Thinking Black*. Between the Lines.

IBGE, Brazilian Institute of Geography and Statistics. (2010). *2010 Brazilian Census*. Author.

Jesus, C. M. (1960). *Quarto de despejo* [Dark room]. Livraria F. Alves.

Juruna, Y., & Juruna, D. (2020). *Mandayaki and Takino* [Film]. Yariato Juruna & Dadyma Juruna.

Kelle, G. (2018). *Menino Pipa* [Kite Boy, Film]. Giovanna Lira.

Krenak, A. (2020). *O amanhã não está à venda* [Tomorrow is not for sale]. Companhia das Letras.

Liberali, F., Fuga, V., & Vendramini-Zanella, D. (2022). O Desenvolvimento Engajado e o teatro-brincar na constituição da coletividade (Engaged Development and play-theatre in the constitution of the collectivity). In P. Marques & A. L. Smolka (Eds.), Desenvolvimento humano, drama e vivências: discussões em torno de 'Sobre a questão da psicologia da criação pelo autor', de L S. Vigotski. Academic Press.

Liberali, F., Fuga, V., Vendramini-Zanella, D., Mazuchelli, L. P., Klen-Alves, V., Modesto-Sarra, L. K., & Oliveira, E. P. (2022). A vivência crítico-colaborativa para construção de uma linguística aplicada decolonial [A critical-collaborative perezhivanie for the construction of a decolonial applied linguistics]. Academic Press.

Liberali, F. C. (2019). Práticas discursivas na construção de patrimônios vivenciais [Discursive practices in the construction of funds of perezhivanie]. Project submitted to the Department of English, Pontifical Catholic University of São Paulo.

Liberali, F. C. (2022). *Multiletramento Engajado na construção de práticas do Bem Viver* [Engaged Multiliteracy in building Good Living practices]. Academic Press.

Liberali, F. C., Magalhães, M. C. C., Meaney, M. C., Sousa, S. S., Pardim, R. P., & Diegues, U. C. C. (2021b). Critically Collaborating to create the viable unheard of - connecting Vygotsky and Freire to deal with a devastating reality. In V. L. T. Souza & G. S. Arinelli (Eds.), *Qualitative research and social intervention: transformative methodologies for collective contexts* (pp. 65–83). Springer.

Liberali, F. C., Mazuchelli, L.P., Modesto-Sarra, L. K. (2021). O brincar no Multiletramento Engajado para a Construção de Práticas Insurgentes [Play in the Engaged Multiliteracy for crafting insurgent practices]. *Revista De Estudos Em Educação E Diversidade, 2*(6), 1-26. doi:10.22481/reed.v2i6.9643

Liberali, F. C., Modesto Sarra, L. K., Mazuchelli, L. P., Amaral, M. F., Medeiros, B. S. F. (2021a). Teatro do oprimido e direitos humanos: estratégia pedagógica para a (trans)formação [Theater of the Oppressed and Human Rights: Pedagogical Strategy for (Trans)Formation]. *Cadernos De Linguagem E Sociedade, 22*(2), 232–252.

Machado, B. (2020). *Assum Preto* [Chopi blackbird, Film]. Bako Machado.

Magalhães, M. C. C. (2011). Pesquisa Crítica de Colaboração: escolhas epistemo-metodológicas na organização e condução de pesquisa de intervenção no contexto escolar [Critical Collaborative Research: epistemic-methodological choices in the organization and conduct of intervention research in the school context]. In M. C. C. Magalhães, & S. S. Fidalgo (Eds.), Questões de método e de linguagem na formação docente [Questions of method and language in teacher education] (pp. 13-39). Mercado de Letras.

Magalhães, M. C. C., & Fidalgo, S. (2019). Reviewing Critical Research Methodologies for Teacher Education in Applied Linguistics. *DELTA. Documentação de Estudos em Lingüística Teórica e Aplicada*, *35*(3), 1–19. doi:10.1590/1678-460X2019350301

Maldonado-Torres, N. (2016). Transdisciplinaridade e decolonialiade [Transdisciplinarity and decoloniality]. *Revista Sociedade e Estado*, *31*(1), 75–97. doi:10.1590/S0102-69922016000100005

Mazuchelli, L. P. (2019). *Stereotypes and Representations: discourses on and in ag(e)ing* [Doctoral dissertation]. State University of Campinas. doi:10.47749/T/UNICAMP.2019.1095209

Mbembe, A. (2003). Necropolitics. *Public Culture*, *15*(1), 11–40. doi:10.1215/08992363-15-1-11

McDonald, M. A., Bowman, M., & Brayko, D. (2013). Learning to see students: Opportunities to develop relational practices of teaching through community-based placements in teacher education. *Teachers College Record*, *115*(4), 1–17. doi:10.1177/016146811311500404

Megale, A. H., & Liberali, F. C. (2020). As implicações do conceito de patrimônio vivencial como uma alternativa para a educação multilíngue [Implications of the concept of funds of perezhivanie as an alternative for multilingual education]. *Revista X*, *15*(1), 55–74. doi:10.5380/rvx.v15i1.69979

Motta, A. V. M. (2007). *Tekoa Pyau: uma aldeia guarani na metrópole* [Master's thesis]. Pontifical Catholic University of São Paulo]. https://tede2.pucsp.br/handle/handle/3834

New London Group. (2000). The Pedagogy of Multiliteracies: Designing Social Futures. *Harvard Educational Review*, *66*(1), 60–92.

Quijano, A. (2010). Colonialidade do poder e classificação social [Coloniality of power and social classification]. In Epistemologias do Sul [Epistemologies of the South] (pp. 68-107). Editora Cortez.

Rede, P. (2021). *National Survey of Food Insecurity in the Context of the Covid-19 Pandemic in Brazil.* https://bit.ly/3ONXlau

Santos, P. C. (2012, July 12). *Aldeia Tekoa Pyau: o desafio de ser vizinha da cidade* [Aldeia Tekoa Pyau: the challenge of being the neighbor of the city]. Portal do Aprendiz. UOL. https://bit.ly/3Kr9tuz

Shakib, S. M. P. (2010). *White Paper* [Film]. Seyed Mohsen Pourmohseni Shakib.

Shakib, S. M. P. (2012). *Game Over* [Film]. Seyed Mohsen Pourmohseni Shakib.

Stetsenko, A. (2017). *The transformative mind: Expanding Vygotsky's approach to development and education.* Cambridge University Press. doi:10.1017/9780511843044

Stetsenko, A. (2019). Radical-Transformative Agency: Continuities and Contrasts With Relational Agency and Implications for Education. *Front. Educ*, *4*(148), 1–13. doi:10.3389/feduc.2019.00148

Stetsenko, A. (2020). Radical-Transformative Agency: Developing a Transformative Activist Stance on a Marxist-Vygotskyan Foundation. In A. Tanzi Neto, F. Liberali, & M. Dafermos (Eds.), *Revisiting Vygotsky for Social Change: Bringing together theory and practice* (pp. 31–63). Peter Lang.

Venegas, H. (2017). Buen Vivir: Indigenous alternative to neoliberalism. *Newscoop*. https://bityli.com/hc0ASM

Vygotsky, L. S. (1994a). The problem of the environment. In R. van der Veer & J. Valsiner (Eds.), *The Vygotsky reader*. Blackwell.

Vygotsky, L. S. (1994b). The socialist alteration of man. In R. van der Veer & J. Valsiner (Eds.), *The Vygotsky reader*. Blackwell.

Walsh, C. (2019). Gritos, gretas e semeaduras de vida: Entreteceres do pedagógico e do colonial [Cries, cracks, and sowings of life: Interweaving the pedagogical and the colonial]. In S. R. M. Souza & L. C. Santos (Eds.), *Entre-linhas: educação, fenomenologia e insurgência popular* [Between the lines: education, phenomenology and popular insurgency] (pp. 93–120). EDUFBA.

KEY TERMS AND DEFINITIONS

Brincadas Project: A project designed as a response to the COVID-19 pandemic. In line with the Global Play Brigade, it brings together students, teachers, and researchers from the LACE Research Group that inform and promote online activities, webinars about education, virtual meetings to play with participants of all ages, and psychological and financial support for those in need.

Coloniality: A structure of principles and practices that founds modernity and engenders forms of exploration and domination of being, seeing, doing, thinking, feeling, and acting.

Cracks: Insurgent stances that challenge, transgress, and crack (fissure) coloniality and its systems of power and oppression.

Critical Collaborative Research: The *praxis* of critically creating zones of mutually and interdependently shared production of meaning to change realities in which participants engage pedagogically to take cognitive and emotional risks to debate concepts, values, ideas, and intervene in an unfair world creatively.

Engaged Multiliteracy: An engaged pedagogical instrument based on the works of Freire and Vygotsky that aims to construct more equitable and fair ways of living the world through education.

Oppression: It is a type of relationship that de-humanize both the person who is oppressed and who oppresses. It prevents subjects from living their lives fully.

Perezhivanie: Usually translated as "lived experience," the Russian term involves life in transformation and is a prism that refracts the unique combination of social and individual characteristics in the process of development.

viable Unheard Of: A term that refers to what is unprecedented, not yet clearly known and experienced, but dreamed. When it starts to be perceived, it allows thinking of alternatives to overcome limiting situations experienced in a given context to create the possible.

ENDNOTES

1. According to Mbembe (2003), necropolitics is the current form of submission of life to the power of death, which contributes to making invisible groups submissive to living conditions that give them the status of living-dead.
2. Ag(e)ing is a neologism to simultaneously index age, aging, and aged (Mazuchelli, 2019).
3. The authors refer to the Minister of Economy, Paulo Guedes, who criticized, in 2021, the Brazilian longevity increase and the Prevent Senior scandal. The private health insurance company focused on the ag(e)ing population is investigated for reducing the oxygen level of patients hospitalized in Intensive Care Units to accelerate the release of hospital beds.
4. Each segment focuses on assisting people with what they most need. The Brincada de Apoio provides financial and material support, including supplying food and hygiene products. At the same time, Brincada do Brincar and Brincada da Educação offer online education and play workshops, and Brincada do Ouvir provides emotional and psychological aid. The Brincadas Project is a segment of the transnational organization of activists, the Global Play Brigade. Find out more here: https://bit.ly/3wWTEIG.
5. Perezhivanie is a Russian word usually translated as "lived experience" (see key terms section at the end of this chapter).

Compilation of References

ACAPS. (2022, March 31). *COLOMBIA Impact of the armed conflict on children and youth.* ACAPS Thematic Report. https://www.acaps.org/sites/acaps/files/products/files/20220331_acaps_mire_thematic_report_colombia_impact_on_children_and_youth.pdf

Acemoglu, D., & Robinson, J. A. (2012). *Why nations fail: The origins of power, prosperity, and poverty.* Crown Publishing Group.

Achenbach, J., Higham, S., & Horwitz, S. (2013). How NRA's true believers converted a marksmanship group into a mighty gun lobby. *The Washington Post.*

Achinstein, B., & Ogawa, R. (2006). (In) Fidelity: What the Resistance of New Teachers Reveals about Professional Principles and Prescriptive Educational Policies. *Harvard Educational Review, 76*(1), 30–63. doi:10.17763/haer.76.1.e14543458r811864

Adarve, M., Santa Cruz, S. N., & Fraga, S. C. (2016). *Tensión entre formación entre formación permanente y prácticas de enseñanza. Desafíos de alfabetización inicial en escenarios de primera infancia. Ponencia presentada en I Jornadas sobre las Prácticas de Enseñanza en la Formación Docente.* Universidad Nacional de Quilmes. https://ridaa.unq.edu.ar/handle/20.500.11807/757

Adarve, P., González, S., & Guerrero, M. (2018). Pedagogías para la paz en Colombia: Un primer acercamiento. *Ciudad Paz-ando, 11*(2), 61–71. doi:10.14483/2422278X.13177

Adichie, C. (2009). *The danger of a single story* [Video]. https://www.ted.com/talks/chimamandangoziadichiethedangerofasinglestory

Adichie, C. N. (2009). *The danger of a single story.* Retrieved June, 2022 from https://www.ted.com/talks/chimamanda_ngozi_adichie_the_danger_of_a_single_story?language=pl

Agar, M. (1996). *Language Shock: Understanding the Culture of Conversation.* Quill.

Ahluwalia, P. (2000). Towards (re)conciliation: The post-colonial economy of giving. *Social Identities, 6*(1), 29–48. doi:10.1080/13504630051345

Aksu-Koc, A., Acarlar, F., Kuntay, A., Mavis, I., Sofu, H., Topbas, S., Turan, F., & Akturk-Ari, B. (2019). *Türkçe İletişim Gelişimi Envanteri (TİGE)* [Turkish Communicative Development Inventory manual]. Detay Publishing.

Albertini, J. A., & Schley, S. (2003). Writing, characteristics, instruction and assessment. In M. Marschark & E. P. Spencer (Eds.), *Oxford handbook of deaf studies, language and education* (pp. 97–109). Oxford University Press, Inc.

Allen, T., Letteri, A., Hoa Choi, S., & Dang, D. (2014). Early visual language exposure and emergent literacy in preschool Deaf children: Findings from a national longitudinal study. *American Annals of the Deaf, 159*(4), 346–358. Advance online publication. doi:10.1353/aad.2014.0030 PMID:25669017

Álvarez Valencia, J. A. (2016a). Social networking sites for language learning: Examining learning theories in nested semiotic spaces. *Signo y Pensamiento, 68*(68), 66–84. doi:10.11144/Javeriana.syp35-68.snsl

Álvarez Valencia, J. A. (2016b). Meaning making and communication in the multimodal age: Ideas for language teachers. *Colombian Applied Linguistics Journal, 18*(1), 98–115. doi:10.14483/calj.v18n1.8403

Álvarez Valencia, J. A. (2021). Practical and theoretical articulations between multimodal pedagogy and an intercultural orientation to second/foreign language education. In J. A. Álvarez Valencia, A. Ramírez, & O. Vergara (Eds.), *Interculturality in Teacher Education: Theoretical and practical considerations*. Programa Editorial Univalle.

Alves, J. (2019). Setting the Tone: Micro/Macro Racial Aggression, Antiblackness and the Outlining of a Trans-National Research Agenda on Community Responses to State Terror. *Currents, 1*(1), 79–94. doi:10.3998/currents.17387731.0001.107

Andrews, S. (2007). *Teacher Language Awareness*. Cambridge University Press.

Andrews, J., & Baker, S. (2019). ASL nursery rhymes: Exploring a support for early language and emergent literacy skills for signing Deaf children. *Sign Language Studies, 20*(1), 5–40. doi:10.1353ls.2019.0007

Angelou, M. (2020). *Still I Rise*. Poetry Foundation. https://bit.ly/3KqhU9h

Annie E. Casey Foundation. (2021, October 21). *Who are children in immigrant families?* https://www.aecf.org/blog/who-are-the-children-in-immigrant-families

Anooshian, L., & Hertel, P. (1994). Emotionality in free recall: Language specificity in bilingual memory. *Cognition and Emotion, 8*(6), 503–514. doi:10.1080/02699939408408956

Antia, S., Lederberg, A., Easterbrooks, S., Schick, B., Branum-Martin, L., Connor, C., & Webb, M.-Y. (2020). Language and reading progress of young Deaf and hard-of-hearing children. *Journal of Deaf Studies and Deaf Education, 25*(3), 334–350. doi:10.1093/deafed/enz050 PMID:32052022

Anti-defamation League. (2020). *Anti-Bias Building Blocks*. Anti-Defamation League.

Apple, M. (1998). The culture and commerce of the textbook. In L. E. Beyer & M. W. Apple (Eds.), *The curriculum: Problems, politics, and possibilities* (2nd ed., pp. 157–176). State University of New York Press.

Asare, M. (1992). *Sosu's call*. Sub-Saharan Publishers.

Bader, L. A., & Pearce, D. L. (2012). *Bader Reading and Language Inventory* (7th ed.). Pearson Education.

Baez, M., & D' Ottavio, M. E. (2020). La diversidad en el aula: el desafío de interpretar la singularidad de los procesos de alfabetización inicial. *Ciencia y Educación, 3*(3), 31-40. doi:10.22206/cyed.2019.v3i3.pp31-40

Bahuchet, S., & Guillaume, H. (1982). Aka-farmer Relations in the Northwest Congo Basin. In E. Leacock & R. B. Lee (Eds.), *Politics and History in Band Societies* (pp. 189–211). Cambridge University Press.

Bajaj, M., Canlas, M., & Argenal, A. (2017). Between rights and realities: Human rights education for immigrant and refugee youth in an urban public high school: Human rights education for newcomer youth. *Anthropology & Education Quarterly, 48*(2), 124–140. doi:10.1111/aeq.12189

Compilation of References

Baker, W. (2011). Intercultural awareness: Modelling an understanding of cultures in intercultural communication through English as a lingua franca. *Language and Intercultural Communication*, *11*(3), 197–214. doi:10.1080/14708477.2011.577779

Ballantyne, K. G., Sanderman, A. R., & McLaughlin, N. (2008). *Dual language learners in early years: Getting ready to succeed in school*. National Clearinghouse for English Language Acquisition.

Banco Interamericano de Desarrollo. (2018). *Profesión: profesor en América Latina ¿Por qué se perdió el prestigio docente y cómo recuperarlo?* Author.

Bandura, A. (1977). *Social learning theory*. Prentice Hall.

Barlette, J. D., Griffin, J., & Thomson, D. (2020). *Resources for supporting children's emotional well-being during the COVID-19 pandemic*. Retrieved from https://www.childtrends.org/publications/resources-for-supporting-childrens-emotional-wellbeing-during-the-covid-19-pandemic

Barton, D., & Hamilton, M. (2000). Literacy practices. In D. Barton, M. Hamilton & R. Ivanic (Eds.), Situated literacies: Reading and writing in context (pp. 7-15). Routledge.

Barton, D., & Hamilton, M. (2010). Literacy as a social practice. *Langage & Société*, (3), 45–62. doi:10.3917/ls.133.0045

Bat-Chava, Y., Martin, D., & Imperatore, L. (2013). Long-term improvements in oral communication skills and quality of peer relations in children with cochlear implants: Parental testimony. *Child: Care, Health and Development*, *40*(6), 870–881. doi:10.1111/cch.12102 PMID:24028465

Bates, E. (1976). *Language and context the acquisition of pragmatics*. Academic Press.

Beattie, R. G., & Kysela, G. M. (1995). A descriptive study of communicative intensions used by hearing teachers and preschool children with hearing loses. *Journal of Childhood Communication Disorders*, *17*(1), 32–41. doi:10.1177/152574019501700106

Beck, I. L., & McKeown, M. G. (2001, September). Text Talk: Capturing the benefits of read aloud experiences for young children. *The Reading Teacher*, *1*(55).

Beck, I. L., & McKeown, M. G. (2007). Increasing young low-income children's oral vocabulary repertoires through rich and focus instruction. *The Elementary School Journal*, *107*(3), 251–271. doi:10.1086/511706

Behrman, E. H. (2006). Teaching about language, power, and text: A review of classroom practices that support critical literacy. *Journal of Adolescent & Adult Literacy*, *49*(6), 490–498. doi:10.1598/JAAL.49.6.4

Beijaard, D., Meijer, P., & Verloop, N. (2004). Reconsidering research on teachers' professional identity. *Teaching and Teacher Education*, *20*(2), 107–128. doi:10.1016/j.tate.2003.07.001

Bell, A., & Houston, K. (2014). Red flags: Barriers to listening and spoken language in children with hearing loss. *Perspectives on Hearing and Hearing Disorders in Childhood*, *24*(1), 11–18. doi:10.1044/hhdc24.1.11

Ben-Ghiat, R. (2018). Power, Curriculum, and Embodiment. Palgrave Macmillan.

Bennett, J. M., & Bennett, M. J. (2004). Developing intercultural sensitivity: An integrative approach to global and domestic diversity. In D. Landis, J. Bennett, & M. Bennett (Eds.), *Handbook of intercultural training* (3rd ed., pp. 147–165). Sage. doi:10.4135/9781452231129.n6

Bennett, M. J. (1993). Towards a developmental model of intercultural sensitivity. In R. M. Paige (Ed.), *Education for the intercultural experience*. Intercultural Press.

Ben-Rafael, E., Shohamy, E., Amara, M. H., & Trumper-Hecht, N. (2006). Linguistic Landscape as Symbolic Construction of the Public Space: The Case of Israel. In D. Gorter (Ed.), *Linguistic landscape: A new approach to multilingualism* (pp. 7–30). Multilingual Matters. doi:10.21832/9781853599170-002

Bentley, D., & Souto-Manning, M. (2019). *Pre-k stories: Playing with authorship and integrating curriculum in early childhood*. Teachers College Press.

Berger, P. L., & Luckman, T. (1996). *The social construction of reality: A treatise in the sociology of knowledge*. Penguin Books.

Berger, R. (2003). *An Ethic of Excellence: Building a Culture of Craftsmanship with Students* (1st ed.). Heinemann.

Berger, R., Rugen, L., Woodfin, L., & Education, E. L. (2014). *Leaders of Their Own Learning: Transforming Schools Through Student-Engaged Assessment* (1st ed.). Jossey-Bass.

Berger, S., & Curato, M. (2018). *What if...?* Little, Brown and Company.

Bergeson-Dana, T. (2014). Spoken language development in infants who are deaf or hard of hearing: The role of maternal infant-directed speech. *The Volta Review*, *112*(2), 171–180.

Bevilacqua Martello, M. (2017). *Use of visual arts in world language instruction to increase student motivation and attitude* [Doctoral Dissertation, Boise State University]. doi:10.18122/B27Q69

Bezemer, J., & Kress, G. (2016). *Multimodality, learning and communication: A social semiotic frame*. Routledge.

Bezerra, T., & Sabatini, G. (2018). *Nós Somos* [We are, Film]. Tereza Bezerra & Giselle Sabatini.

Bhabha, H. K. (2004). *The Location of Culture* (2nd ed.). Routledge.

Bijeikienė, V., & Meškauskienė, A. (2020). The Value of Plurilingualism or What Factors affect the development of plurilingual competences. *Sustainable Multilingualism*, *16*(1), 131–144. doi:10.2478m-2020-0007

Binkley, M., Erstad, O., & Herman, J. (2012). Defining twenty-first century skills. In P. Griffin, B. McGaw, & E. Care (Eds.), *Assessment and Teaching of 21st Century Skills* (pp. 17–66). Springer. doi:10.1007/978-94-007-2324-5_2

Bishop, R. S. (1990). Mirrors, windows and sliding doors. *Choosing and Using Books for the Classroom*, *6*(3).

Bishop, D. V., & Adams, C. (1990). A prospective study of the relationship between specific language impairment, phonological disorders and reading retardation. *Journal of Child Psychology and Psychiatry, and Allied Disciplines*, *31*(7), 1027–1050. doi:10.1111/j.1469-7610.1990.tb00844.x PMID:2289942

Bishop, R. S. (1990). Mirrors, windows, and sliding glass doors. *Perspectives - Gerontological Nursing Association*, *1*(3), ix–xi.

Bishop, R. S. (1990). Walk tall in the world: African American literature for today's children. *The Journal of Negro Education*, *59*(4), 556. Advance online publication. doi:10.2307/2295312

Blackledge, A., & Creese, A. (2010). *Multilingualism: A critical perspective*. Bloomsbury Publishing.

Blanchard, P., Bancel, N., Boëtsch, G., Deroo, É., Lemaire, S., & Forsdick, C. (Eds.). (2008). *Human Zoos: Science and Spectacle in the Age of Colonial Empires*. Liverpool University Press.

Block, D., & Corona, V. (2017). Intersectionality in language and identity research. In K. Rajagopalan (Ed.), *The Routledge handbook of language and identity* (pp. 507–519). Routledge.

Compilation of References

Blommaert, J., & Backus, A. (2011). Repertoires revisited: 'Knowing language'. Superdiversity. *Working Papers in Urban Language and Literacies, 67*, 1-26.

Blommaert, J. (2005). *Discourse: Key topics in sociolinguistics.* Cambridge University Press. doi:10.1017/CBO9780511610295

Blommaert, J. (2016). From mobility to complexity in sociolinguistic theory and method. In N. Coupland (Ed.), *Sociolinguistics: Theoretical Debates* (pp. 242–259). Cambridge University Press. doi:10.1017/CBO9781107449787.012

Blommaert, J., & Backus, A. (2013). A. Superdiverse Repertoires and the Individual. Current Challenges for Educational Studies. In I. Saint-Georges & J. J. Weber (Eds.), *Multilingualism and Multimodality* (pp. 11–32). Sense. doi:10.1007/978-94-6209-266-2_2

Blythe, B., & Associates. (1998). The teaching for understanding guide. Jossey-Bass.

Blythe, T. (2019). *Teaching for Understanding: Ongoing Assessment.* Annenberg Learner. Retrieved August 20, 2021, from https://www.learner.org/wp-content/uploads/2019/02/7.OngoingAssessment.pdf

Blythe, T. (1998). *The teaching for understanding guide.* Jossey Bass.

Boche, B. (2014). ML in the classroom: Emerging conceptions of first-year teachers. *Journal of Language & Literacy Education, 10*(1), 114–135.

Boeckmann, K.-B. (2012). Promoting plurilingualism in the majority language classroom. *Innovation in Language Learning and Teaching, 6*(3), 259–274. doi:10.1080/17501229.2012.725253

Boeckmann, K.-B., Aalto, E., Abel, A., Atanasoska, T., & Lamb, T. (2012). *Promoting plurilingualism: Majority language in multilingual settings.* Council of Europe.

Boghian, I. (2016). A model for teaching cultural awareness in foreign language classes. In I. Boldea (Ed.), *Globalization and national identity. Studies on the strategies of intercultural dialogue* (pp. 967–981). Archipelag XXI Press.

Boix Mansilla, V., & Jackson, A. (2013). Educating for global competence: Learning redefined for an interconnected world. *Mastering Global Literacy*, 1–24. Retrieved from www.pz.harvard.edu/ site/ default/ files/Educating% 20for% 20Global% 20Competence% 20Short% 20HHJ.pdf

Boix Mansilla, V., & Jackson, A. (2011). *Educating for global competence: Preparing our youth to engage in the world.* The Asia Society.

Boix-Mansilla, V. (2015). *Finding our way into each other's worlds: Musings on cultural perspective taking.* Retrieved on April 9, 2022, from http://www.pz.harvard.edu/sites/default/files/FINDING%20OUR%20WAY%20INTO%20EACH%20OTHER%C2%B9S%20WORLDS.pdf

Boix-Mansilla, V. (2016). How to be a Global Thinker: Using global thinking Routines to create classroom cultures that nurture global competence. *Education Leadership, 74*(4), 10-16.

Boix-Mansilla, V. B., Jackson, A., & Jacobs, I. H. (2013). Educating for global competence: Learning redefined for an interconnected world. *Mastering Global Literacy*, 5–27.

Boix-Mansilla, V., Rivard, M., & The ID Global Group. (2014). *The many stories library. Milestone learning experiences: A guide for teachers.* ID-Global, Project Zero. Retrieved April, 2022 from https://pz.harvard.edu/sites/default/files/The%20Many%20Stories%20Library%20Project.pdf

Boix-Mansilla, V. (2016). How to be a global thinker: Using global thinking routines to create classroom cultures that nurture global competence. *Educational Leadership, 74*(4), 10–16.

Boris, B. (2017). *What makes storytelling so effective for learning? Learning the way*. Harvard Business Publishing. Retrieved March 2022 from https://www.harvardbusiness.org/what-makes-storytelling-so-effective-for-learning/#:~:text=Connecting%20learners,them%20more%20open%20to%20learning

Boroditsky, L. (2009). How does our language shape the way we think? *What's Next?* 116-129.

Boroditsky, L. (2001). Does language shape thought? Mandarin and English speakers' conceptions of time. *Cognitive Psychology, 43*(1), 1–22. doi:10.1006/cogp.2001.0748 PMID:11487292

Bortfeld, H., & Oghalai, J. S. (2018). Joint attention in hearing parent-deaf child and hearing parent-hearing child dyads. *IEEE Transactions on Cognitive and Developmental Systems, 12*(2), 243–249. doi:10.1109/TCDS.2018.2877658 PMID:33748419

Botelho, M., Kerekes, J., Jang, E., & Peterson, Sh. (2014). Assessing multiliteracies: Mismatches and opportunities. *Language and Literature, 16*(1), 1–20.

Boyette, A. H., Lew-Levy, S., Jang, H., & Kandza, V. (2022). Social ties in the Congo Basin: insights into tropical forest adaptation from BaYaka and their neighbours. *Philosophical Transactions of the Royal Society B, 377*(1849), 20200490.

Bradford, P. V., & Blume, H. (1992). *Ota Benga: The Pygmy in the Zoo*. St Martin's Press.

Brakermeier, E. L., Wirkner, J., Knaevelsrud, C., Wurns, S., Christiansen, H., & Lueken. (2020). Die Covid-19- Pandemie ais Herausdorderunf fur die pshyschische Gesundheit. *Z. Kiln. Psychol. Psychother. 49*(1).

Brasil. Provisional Measure No. 870, January 1st 2019. Brazilian Official Gazette: section 1, 1-13. Brasília, Federal District.

Bratitsis, T. (2015). Digital Storytelling, Creative Writing and 21st Century Literacy. *Bulletin of Educational Reflection and Communication*, 55.

Bratitsis, T. (2018). Storytelling digitalization as a Design Thinking process in educational context. In A. Moutsios-Rentzos, A. Giannakoulopoulos, M. Meimaris (Eds.), *Proceedings of the International Digital Storytelling Conference - "Current trends in digital storytelling: Research & practices"* (pp. 309-320). Academic Press.

Bratitsis, T. (2018). Storytelling digitalization as a Design Thinking process in educational context. In A. Moutsios-Rentzos, A. Giannakoulopoulos, M. Meimaris (Eds.), *Proceedings of the International Digital Storytelling Conference - "Current Trends in Digital Storytelling: Research & Practices"* (pp. 309-320). Academic Press.

Bratitsis, T. (2021a). Multiliteracy education competences framework. Deliverable O1A1, StoryLogicNet – Collaborative Writing for Children's Multiliteracy Skills Utilising Multimodal Tools, EU PROJECT No. 2018-1-PT01-KA201-047325

Bratitsis, T. (2021b). StoryLogicNet Toolkit. Deliverable O1A4, StoryLogicNet – Collaborative Writing for Children's Multiliteracy Skills Utilising Multimodal Tools, EU PROJECT No. 2018-1-PT01-KA201-047325

Bratitsis, T., Chesi, P., Godio, C., Barroca, A., Fruhmann, P., Broer, Y., Szczygielska, E., Gonzalez, R., Martin, M., Toia, M., & Malita, L. (2014). European educators' training needs for applying digital storytelling in their teaching practice. In *International Conference on Information Communication Technologies in Education - ICICTE 2014* (pp 194-204). Academic Press.

Bratitsis, T., Bardanika, P., & Ioannou, M. (2017). Science education and augmented reality content: The case of the water circle. In M. Kinshuk, D. Chang, D. Sampson, NS. Chen, R. Vasiu, & R. Huang (Eds.), *Proceedings of the 17th IEEE International Conference on Advanced Learning Technologies - ICALT 2017* (pp. 485-489). IEEE. 10.1109/ICALT.2017.64

Bratitsis, T., Kotopoulos, T., & Mandila, K. (2011) Kindergarten children as story Makers: The effect of the digital medium. In F. Xhafa, L. Barolli, & M. Köppen (Eds.), *Proceedings of the IEEE 3rd International Conference On Intelligent Networking and Collaborative Systems - INCoS 2011* (pp. 84-91). 10.1109/INCoS.2011.108

Bratitsis, T., & Ziannas, P. (2015). From early childhood to special education: Interactive digital storytelling as a coaching approach for fostering social empathy. *Computer Science Procedure, 67*, 231–240. doi:10.1016/j.procs.2015.09.267

Braun, V., & Clarke, V. (2006). Using thematic analysis in psychology. *Qualitative Research in Psychology, 3*(2), 77–101. doi:10.1191/1478088706qp063oa

Bronfenbrenner, U. (1977). Toward an experimental ecology of human development. *The American Psychologist, 32*(7), 513–531. doi:10.1037/0003-066X.32.7.513

Brooks, M. (2009). Drawing, visualisation and young children's exploration of "big ideas.". *International Journal of Science Education, 31*(3), 319–341. doi:10.1080/09500690802595771

Brown, C. S. (2014). Language and literacy development in the early years: Foundational Skills that Support Emergent Readers. *The Language and Literacy Spectrum,* (24), 35-48. Retrieved from https://files.eric.ed.gov/fulltext/EJ1034914.pdf

Brown, B. (2012). *Daring greatly: How the courage to be vulnerable transforms the way we live, love, parent, and lead.* Avery Publishing Group.

Brown, D. (2001). *Teaching by principles: An interactive approach to language pedagogy* (2nd ed.). Prentice Hall Regents.

Brown, P., & Watson, L. (2017). Language, play and early literacy for deaf children: The role of parent input. *Deafness & Education International, 19*(3/4), 108–114. doi:10.1080/14643154.2018.1435444

Brown, T. (2009). *Change by design. How Design Thinking Transforms Organizations and Inspires Innovation.* HarperBusiness.

Bruner, J. (1983). *Children's talk: Learning to use language.* Norton & Company.

Bruner, J. (1990). *Acts of meaning.* Harvard University Press.

Bucholtz, M. (2021). Community-centred collaboration in applied linguistics. *Applied Linguistics, 42*(6), 1153–1161. doi:10.1093/applin/amab064

Burggraff, S., & Grossenbacher, P. (2007). Contemplative modes of inquiry in liberal arts education. *Liberal Arts Online.* Retrieved from the internet, July 5, 2022 https://www.wabash.edu/news/docs/Jun07ContemplativeModes1.pdf

Burmark, L. (2004). Visual presentations that prompt, flash & transform. *Media and Methods, 40*(6), 4–5.

Butler, J. (2020). *The force of nonviolence.* Verso Books.

Button, K., Johnson, M., & Furgerson, P. (1996). Interactive Writing in the Primary Classroom. *The Reading Teacher, 49*(6), 446–454.

Byram, M. (1997). *Teaching and assessing intercultural communicative competence.* Multilingual Matters.

Byram, M., Gribkova, B., & Starkey, H. (2002). *Developing the intercultural dimension in language teaching: A practical introduction for teachers.* Council of Europe.

Byrd, S. A., Kileny, S., & Kileny, P. (2011). *The right not to hear: The ethics of parental refusal of hearing rehabilitation.* Academic Press.

Bzoch, R. K., League, R., & Brown, L. V. (2003). *Reel 3 receptive-expressive emergent languages test. Examiner's Manual*. Pro-Ed.

Bzoch, R. K., League, R., & Brown, L. V. (2003). *Reel-3 receptive-expressive emergent languages test*. Pro-Ed.

Cabrejo, E. (2007). Representaciones mentales, acción y construcción. In Lenguaje y saberes infantiles. Universidad Francisco José de Caldas. Cátedra Unesco en Desarrollo del niño.

Cadiero-Kaplan, K. (2002). Literacy ideologies: Critically engaging the language arts curriculum. *Language Arts*, *79*(5), 372–381.

Cahill, M. A., & Gregory, A. E. (2016). "Please let us write!" Sharing writing in the early childhood classroom. *YC Young Children*, *71*(2), 64–69. https://www.proquest.com/scholarly-journals/please-let-us-write-sharing-writing-early/docview/1818310134/se-2?accountid=10901

Caldera, L. A. B. (2008). Concepción sagrada de la naturaleza en la mítica muisca. *Franciscanum. Revista de las ciencias del espíritu, 50*(149), 151-176.

Calle-Díaz, L. (2020). *School Discourse Practices and their Potential for Peacebuilding and Social Justice* [Unpublished doctoral dissertation]. Universidad del Norte, Barranquilla, Colombia.

Cambourne, B. (1988). *The whole story: Natural learning and the acquisition of literacy in the classroom*. Ashton Scholastic.

Cambourne, B. (2009). Revisiting the Concept of "Natural Learning". In J. V. Hoffman & Y. M. Goodman (Eds.), *Changing literacies for changing times* (pp. 125–145). Taylor & Francis.

Camelo, M. (2003). Conversa de Botas Batidas. In Los Hermanos. In Ventura. BMG.

Canagarajah, S. (2002). Reconstructing Local Knowledge. *Journal of Language, Identity, and Education*, *1*(4), 243–259. doi:10.1207/S15327701JLIE0104_1

Canagarajah, S. (2013). *Translingual Practice: Global Englishes and Cosmopolitan Relations*. Routledge. doi:10.4324/9780203120293

Canagarajah, S. (Ed.). (2005). *Reclaiming the local in language policy and practice*. Lawrence Erlbaum. doi:10.4324/9781410611840

Capone, N. C. (2010). Language assessment and intervention: A developmental approach. In B. B. Schulman & N. C. Capone (Eds.), *Language development foundations, processes and clinical applications* (pp. 1–33). Jones and Barlett Publishers.

Carreira, M., & Kagan, O. (2018). Heritage language education: A proposal for the next 50 years. *Foreign Language Annals*, *51*(1), 152–168. doi:10.1111/flan.12331

Carter, N., Bryant-Lukosius, D., DiCenso, A., Blythe, J., & Neville, A. J. (2014). The use of triangulation in qualitative research. *Oncology Nursing Forum*, *41*(5), 545–547. doi:10.1188/14.ONF.545-547 PMID:25158659

Casasanto, D., & Boroditsky, L. (2008). Time in the mind: Using space to think about time. *Cognition*, *106*(2), 579–593. doi:10.1016/j.cognition.2007.03.004 PMID:17509553

Caskey, M., Stephens, B., Tucker, R., & Vohr, B. (2011). Importance of parent talk on the development of preterm infant vocalizations. *Pediatrics*, *128*(5), 910–916. doi:10.1542/peds.2011-0609 PMID:22007020

Castillo, R. (2018). *Teachers' beliefs about critical literacy in early childhood classrooms.* ProQuest Dissertations Publishing.

Castro-Gómez, S. (2003). *La Hybris del Punto Cero: ciencia, raza e ilustración en la Nueva Granada.* Editora Pontifica Universidade Javeriana.

Cazden, C. (2000). *Classroom discourse: The language of teaching and learning.* Heinemann.

Cazden, C. (2004). The value of conversations for language development and reading comprehension. *Literacy, Teaching and Learning, 9*(1), 1–6.

CDC Data and statistics on children's mental health. (2019). CDC. https://www.ncbi.nlm.nih.gov/pmc/articles/PMC7444649/#bib0006

CDC. (2018, April 11). *What is "Early Intervention" and is my child eligible?* Centers for Disease Control and Prevention. https://www.cdc.gov/ncbddd/actearly/parents/states.html

CDC. (2021, June 16). *Summary of diagnostics among infants not passing hearing screening.* Centers for Disease Control and Prevention. https://www.cdc.gov/ncbddd/hearingloss/2019-data/06-diagnostics.html

Cenoz, J., & Gorter, D. (2017). Translanguaging as a Pedagogical Tool in Multilingual Education. In Language Awareness and Multilingualism. Springer. doi:10.1007/978-3-319-02240-6_20

Cenoz, J., & Gorter, D. (2008). The linguistic landscape as an additional source of input in second language acquisition. *IRAL -. International Review of Applied Linguistics in Language Teaching, 46*(3), 257–276. doi:10.1515/IRAL.2008.012

CEPAL. (2014). *El analfabetismo funcional en América Latina y el Caribe. Panorama y principales desafíos de política.* https://repositorio.cepal.org/bitstream/handle/11362/36781/S2014179_es.pdf?sequence=1&isAllowed=y

Cervetti, G., Pardales, M. J., & Damico, J. S. (2001). A tale of differences: Comparing the traditions, perspectives, and educational goals of critical reading and political literacy. *Reading Online, 4*(49). wwwreadingonline.org/articles/art_index.asp?HREF=/articles/cervetti/index.html

Chafel, J., & Neitzel, C. (2012). "I would like to see how they got poor and see what it's like to be poor": An analysis of young children's literacy responses to a critical literacy text about poverty. *Journal of Poverty, 16*(2), 147–170. doi:10.1080/10875549.2012.667058

Chang, P. (2017). Breaking the sound barrier: Exploring parents' decision-making process of cochlear implants for their children. *Patient Education and Counseling, 100*(8), 1544–1551. doi:10.1016/j.pec.2017.03.005 PMID:28291575

Chaudhri, A., & Teale, W. H. (2013). Stories of multiracial experiences in literature for children, ages 9-14. *Children's Literature in Education, 44*(4), 359–376. doi:10.100710583-013-9196-5

Chaux, E., & Velásquez, A. M. (2016). *Orientaciones generales para la implementación de la Cátedra de la Paz.* Ministerio de Educación Nacional.

Chen, Ch.-Y. (2004). *Guji Guji.* Kane/Miller Book Publishers, Inc.

Chen, G. M., & Starosta, W. J. (1998). A review of the concept of intercultural awareness. *Human Communication, 2,* 27–54.

Children, R. (2022). *100 languages: No way, the hundred is there.* Retrieved March 19, 2022 from https://www.reggiochildren.it/en/reggio-emilia-approach/100-linguaggi-en/

Chimamanda Ngozi Adichie: The danger of a single story | TED. (2009, October 7). [Video]. YouTube. https://www.youtube.com/watch?v=D9Ihs241zeg&t=743s

Chiu, M. M., McBride-Chang, C., & Lin, D. (2011). Ecological, Psychological, and Cognitive Components of Reading Difficulties: Testing the Component Model of Reading in Fourth Graders Across 38 Countries. *Journal of Learning Disabilities*, *45*(5), 391–405. doi:10.1177/0022219411431241 PMID:22183193

Chomsky, N. (2002). *Syntactic structures* (2nd ed.). Mouton de Gruyter. doi:10.1515/9783110218329

Christie, F., & Maton, K. (Eds.). (2011). *Disciplinarity: Functional linguistic and sociological perspectives*. Bloomsbury Publishing.

Church, A., Paatsch, L., & Toe, D. (2017). Some trouble with repair: Conversations between children with cochlear implants and hearing peers. *Discourse Studies*, *19*(1), 49–68. doi:10.1177/1461445616683592

Clark, M., Cue, K., Delgado, N., Greene-Woods, A., & Wolsey, J.-L. (2020). Early intervention protocols: Proposing a default bimodal bilingual approach for deaf children. *Maternal and Child Health Journal*, *24*(11), 1339–1344. doi:10.100710995-020-03005-2 PMID:32897446

Clavijo, A. (2000). *Una mirada a la lectura y la escritura desde la práctica de los docentes en la escuela. Revista Científica. No. 2*. Universidad Distrital.

Clavijo, A. (2007). *Prácticas innovadoras en lectura y escritura* [Innovative practices in reading and writing]. Universidad Distrital.

Clavijo, A., & Ramírez-Galindo, L. (2019). *Las pedagogías de la comunidad a través de investigaciones locales en el contexto urbano de Bogotá* [Community pedagogies through local research in the urban context of Bogotá]. Editorial UD.

Clavijo-Olarte, A., & Austin, T. (2022). Crossing linguistic boundaries with community literacies: A collaborative, place-based ethnography in two urban localities in Bogotá. In Language Education in Multilingual Colombia. Critical Perspectives and Voices from the Field. Multilingual Matters.

Clavijo-Olarte, A., Medina, R. A., Calderón, D., Rodríguez, A., Prieto, K., & Nader, M. C. (2021). *Investigating the social, cultural, linguistic and literacy practices to construct Bogotá as a multicultural place: Final Research Report*. Universidad Distrital Francisco José de Caldas.

Clavijo-Olarte, A., & Sharkey, J. (2019). Mapping our ways to critical pedagogies: Stories from Colombia. In *International perspectives on critical pedagogies in ELT* (pp. 175–193). Palgrave Macmillan. doi:10.1007/978-3-319-95621-3_9

Cochran-Smith, M., & Zeichner, K. M. (2005). *Studying Teacher Education: The Report of the AERA Panel on Research and Teacher Education*. Retrieved from: https://mjcoonkitt.wordpress.com/2013/01/17/cochran-smith-zeichner-2005/

Cochran-Smith, M. (2005). Teacher Educators as Researchers: Multiple Perspectives. *Teaching and Teacher Education*, *21*(2), 219–225. doi:10.1016/j.tate.2004.12.003

Cochran-Smith, M. (2021). Rethinking teacher education: The trouble with accountability. *Oxford Review of Education*, *1*(47), 8–24. doi:10.1080/03054985.2020.1842181

Coffey, H. (2010). *Critical literacy*. LEARN NC: University of North Carolina at Chapel Hill School of Education. Retrieved from www.learnc.org/lp/pages/4437

Coggins, T. E., & Carpenter, R. L. (1981). The communicative intention inventory: A system for observing and coding children's early intentional communication. *Applied Psycholinguistics*, *2*(3), 235–251. doi:10.1017/S0142716400006536

Cohen, N. (2003). Cochlear implant candidacy and surgical considerations. *Audiology & Neurotology*, *9*(4), 197–202. doi:10.1159/000078389 PMID:15205547

Cole, E. B. (1992). *Listening and talking a guide to promoting spoken language in young hearing-impaired children*. Alexander Graham Bell Association for the Deaf.

Collins, B. A., O'Connor, E. E., Suárez-Orozco, C., Nieto-Castañon, A., & Toppelberg, C. O. (2014). Dual language profiles of Latino children of immigrants: Stability and change over the early school years. *Applied Psycholinguistics*, *35*(3), 581–620. doi:10.1017/S0142716412000513 PMID:24825925

Collins, F., & Safford, K. (2008). The right book to the right child at the right time: Primary teaching knowledge of children's literature. *Changing English*, *15*(4), 415–422. doi:10.1080/13586840802493068

Comber, B. (2011). Critical literacy in the early years: Emergence and sustenance in an age of accountability. In J. Larson & J. Marsh (Eds.), Handbook of research in early childhood literacy. Academic Press.

Comber, B. (2000). What really counts in early literacy lessons. *Language Arts*, *78*(1), 39–49.

Comber, B. (2001). Critical inquiry or safe literacies: Who's allowed to ask which questions? In S. Boran & B. Comber (Eds.), *Critiquing whole language and classroom inquiry* (pp. 81–102). NCTE.

Comber, B. (2003). Critical literacy: Power and pleasure with language in the early years. *Australian Journal of Language and Literacy*, *24*(3), 168–181.

Comber, B. (2014). Literacy, poverty and schooling: What matters in young people's education? *Literacy*, *48*(3), 115–123. doi:10.1111/lit.12041

Comber, B. (2016). *Literacy, place and pedagogies of possibility*. Routledge.

Comber, B., Nixon, H., & Reid, J. A. (2007). *Literacies in place: Teaching environmental communications*. Primary English Teaching Association.

Comber, B., & Simpson, A. (2007). *Negotiating critical literacies in the classroom*. Taylor and Francis.

Comber, B., & Simpson, A. (Eds.). (2001). *Negotiating critical literacies in classrooms*. Erlbaum. doi:10.4324/9781410600288

Comber, B., Thomson, P., & Wells, M. (2001). Critical literacy finds a "place": Writing and social action in a low-income Australian grade 2/3 classroom. *The Elementary School Journal*, *101*(4), 451–464. doi:10.1086/499681

Comenius, J. A., & Laurie, S. S. (1969). Comenius. Collier-Macmillan.

Congreso de la República. (2013). Ley 1620. Sistema Nacional de Convivencia Escolar y Formación para el Ejercicio de los Derechos Humanos. Sexuales y Reproductivos y la Prevención y Mitigación de la Violencia Escolar.

Cooper, K. (2020). *Don't let children be the hidden victims of COVID-19 pandemic*. UNICEF. https://www.unicef.org/press-releases/dont-let-children-be-hidden-victims-covid-19-pandemic.

Cope, B., & Kalantzis, M. (2000). *Multiliteracies: Literacy learning and the design of social futures*. Psychology Press.

Cope, B., & Kalantzis, M. (2000). Multiliteracies: The beginnings of an idea. In B. Cope & M. Kalantzis (Eds.), *Multiliteracies: Literacy learning and the design of social futures* (pp. 3–8). Routledge.

Cope, B., & Kalantzis, M. (2006). *The Learning by Design Guide*. Common Ground.

Cope, B., & Kalantzis, M. (2009). Multiliteracies: New literacies, new learning. *Pedagogies*, *4*(3), 164–195. doi:10.1080/15544800903076044

Cope, B., & Kalantzis, M. (2015). The Things You Do to Know: An Introduction to the Pedagogy of Multiliteracies. In B. Cope & M. Kalantzis (Eds.), *A Pedagogy of Multiliteracies: Learning By Design* (pp. 1–36). Palgrave. doi:10.1057/9781137539724_1

Coppens, K., Tellings, A., Van der Veld, W., Schreuder, R., & Verhoeven, L. (2012). Vocabulary development in children with hearing loss: The role of child, family, and educational variables. *Research in Developmental Disabilities*, *33*(1), 119–128. doi:10.1016/j.ridd.2011.08.030 PMID:22093656

Córdova Hernández, L., López-Gopar, M. E., & Sughrua, W. M. (2017). From linguistic landscape to semiotic landscape: indigenous language revitalization and literacy. *Studie z aplikované lingvistiky-Studies in Applied Linguistics*, *8*(2), 7-21.

Coronel-Molina, S. M., & McCarty, T. L. (2016). *Indigenous Language Revitalization in the Americas*. Routledge. doi:10.4324/9780203070673

Costa, A. (2001). *Developing minds: A resource book for teaching thinking*. Association for Supervision and Curriculum Development.

Costa, A., & Kallick, B. (2008). *Learning and leading with the habits of mind: 16 essential characteristics for success*. Association for Supervision and Curriculum Development.

Coste, D., Moore, D., & Zarate, G. (2009). *Plurilingual and pluricultural competence. Language Policy Division*. Council of Europe. https://www.coe.int/t/dg4/linguistic/Source/SourcePublications/CompetencePlurilingue09web_en.pdf

Coulby, D. (2006). Intercultural education: Theory and Practice. *Intercultural Education*, *17*(3), 245–257. doi:10.1080/14675980600840274

Crafton, L., Brennan, M., & Silvers, P. (2007). Critical inquiry and multiliteracies in a first-grade classroom. *Language Arts*, *84*(6), 510–518.

Crehan, L. (2016). *Exploring the impact of career models on teacher motivation*. International Institute of Educational Planning. http://repositorio.minedu.gob.pe/bitstream/handle/123456789/4889/Exploring%20the%20impact%20of%20career%20models%20on%20teacher%20motivation.pdf?sequence=1&isAllowed=y

Crenshaw, K. (1989). Demarginalizing the intersection of race and sex: A black feminist critique of antidiscrimination doctrine, feminist theory, and antiracist politics. *University of Chicago Legal Forum*, *1*, 139–167.

Crenshaw, K. W. (2017). *On intersectionality: Essential writings*. The New Press.

Creswell, J. W., & Poth, C. N. (2018). Qualitative Inquiry & Research Design. *Sage (Atlanta, Ga.)*.

Cross, N. (2011). *Design Thinking: Understanding How Designers Think and Work*. Berg Publishers. doi:10.5040/9781474293884

Crouch, D., & Cambourne, B. (2020). *Made for learning: How the conditions of learning guide teacher decisions*. Richard C. Owen Publishers, Inc.

Cummins, J. (2001). *Bilingual children's mother tongue: Why is it important for education*. http://iteachilearn.org/cummins/mother.htm

Curtain, H., & Dahlberg, C. A. (2016). *Languages and learners: Making the match*. Pearson Education, Inc.

Curtis, A. (2018). Introducing and defining peace linguistics. *Word*, *27*(3), 11–13.

Curtis, J., & Cornell, L. (2016). *This Is Me: A Story of Who We Are & Where We Came From*. Workman Publishing.

Curtiss, S., Prutting, C. A., & Lowell, E. L. (1979). Pragmatic and semantic development in young children with impaired hearing. *Journal of Speech and Hearing Research*, *22*(3), 534–552. doi:10.1044/jshr.2203.534 PMID:502512

Cutrim Schmid, E. (2021). A classroom-based investigation into pre-service EFL teachers' evolving understandings of a plurilingual pedagogy to foreign language education. *Landscape Journal*, *4*. Advance online publication. doi:10.18452/23383

Cutrim Schmid, E. (2022). 'I think it's boring if you now only speak English': Enhancing learner investment in EFL learning through the use of plurilingual tasks. *Innovation in Language Learning and Teaching*, *16*(1), 67–81. doi:10.1080/17501229.2020.1868476

Darling-Hammond, L., Hyler, M. E., & Gardner, M. (2017). *Effective Teacher Professional Development*. Learning Policy Institute. https://files.eric.ed.gov/fulltext/ED606743.pdf

Darling-Hammond, L. (2006). *Powerful Teacher Education: Lessons from Exemplary Programs*. Jossey Bass.

Darling-Hammond, L., & Oakes, J. (2019). *Preparing Teachers for Deeper Learning*. Harvard Education Press.

Datta, R. (2018). Decolonizing both researcher and research and its effectiveness in Indigenous research. *Research Ethics Review*, *14*(2), 1–24. doi:10.1177/1747016117733296

Davis, J. R., & Arend, B. (2013). Seven ways of learning: A resource for more purposeful, effective, and enjoyable college teaching. Sterling, VA: Stylus Publishing.

Day, P. S. (1986). Deaf children's expression of communicative intentions. *Journal of Communication Disorders*, *19*(5), 367–385. doi:10.1016/0021-9924(86)90027-4 PMID:3771827

De Bono, E. (1992). *Six Thinking Hats for Schools: Book 3*. Hawker Brownlow Education.

de Sousa Santos, B. (2008). *Another knowledge is possible: Beyond northern epistemologies*. Verso.

de Sousa Santos, B. (2010). *Descolonizar el saber, reinventar el poder*. Ediciones Trilce.

de Sousa Santos, B. (2014). *Epistemologies of the south: Justice against epistemicide* (1st ed.). Paradigm Publishers.

de Sousa Santos, B. (2018). *The end of the cognitive empire: The coming of age of epistemologies of the south*. Duke University Press. doi:10.1215/9781478002000

de Villiers, P., & Pomerantz, S. (1992). Hearing impaired students learning new words from written context. *Applied Psycholinguistics*, *13*(4), 409–431. doi:10.1017/S0142716400005749

DeAngelis, T. (2015). *In Search of Cultural Competence*. Monitor on Psychology. Retrieved August 20, 2021, from http://www.apa.org/monitor/2015/03/cultural-competence

Deardorff, D. K. (2006). Intercultural competence model. *Journal of Science in International Education*, *10*, 241–266.

Dede, C. (2010). Comparing frameworks for 21st century skills. In J. Bellanca & R. Brandt (Eds.), 21st Century Skills: Rethinking How Students Learn (pp. 51-76). Solution Tree Press.

Dehaene, S. (2017). *El cerebro lector*. Siglo XXI.

Demoiny, S. B. (2016, November 30). *ERIC - EJ1150569 - Are You Ready? Elementary*. Academic Press.

Deng, Q., & Tong, S. (2021). Linguistic but not cognitive weaknesses in Deaf or hard-of-hearing poor comprehenders. *Journal of Deaf Studies and Deaf Education*, *26*(3), 351–362. doi:10.1093/deafed/enab006 PMID:33824969

Dervin, F. (2006). *Quality in intercultural education: The development of proteophilic competence*. University of Turku.

Dervin, F., & Jacobsson, A. (2021). What is interculturality? In F. Dervin & A. Jacobsson (Eds.), *Teacher Education for Critical and Reflexive Interculturality* (pp. 11–21). Springer International Publishing. doi:10.1007/978-3-030-66337-7_2

Despejo Zero. (2022). *Balanço dos dados até fevereiro de 2022* [Data balance until February 2022]. Campanha Despejo Zero. https://bit.ly/3vnCTVV

Dewart, H., & Summers, S. (1995). *The pragmatics profile of everyday communication skills in children.* Nfer-Nelson.

Díaz, A. (2009). *Pensar la didáctica.* Amorrortu editores.

Directorate-General for Internal Policies, Policy Department for Structural and Cohesion Policies Culture and Education. (2017). *Research for CULT Committee - Teaching Common Values in Europe.* Author.

Do, E. Y.-L., & Gross, M. D. (2001). Thinking with diagrams in architectural design. *Artificial Intelligence Review, 15*(1/2), 135–149. doi:10.1023/A:1006661524497

Dore, J. (1974). A pragmatic description of early language development. *Journal of Psycholinguistic Research, 3*(4), 343–351. doi:10.1007/BF01068169

Dorner, L., Song, K., Kim, S., & Trigos-Carrillo, L. (November/December, 2019). Multilingual family engagement: Shifting the focus from what families need to how they can lead. Literacy Today. International Literacy Association, pp. 30-31.

Dörnyei, Z. (2005). *The psychology of the language learner: Individual differences in second language acquisition.* Lawrence Erlbaum Associates Publishers.

Dörnyei, Z. (2009). *The Psychology of Second Language Acquisition.* Oxford University Press.

Dotger, B. H. (2013). *"I had no idea!" Clinical Simulations for Teacher Development.* Information Age Publishers.

Drewry, R. J., Cumming-Potvin, W. M., & Maor, D. (2019). New Approaches to Literacy Problems: Multiliteracies and Inclusive Pedagogies. *The Australian Journal of Teacher Education, 44*(11), 61–78. doi:10.14221/ajte.2019v44.n11.4

Drew, S. V. (2013). Open up the ceiling on the common core state standards: Preparing students for 21st-century literacy--now. *Journal of Adolescent & Adult Literacy, 56*(4), 321–330. doi:10.1002/JAAL.00145

Duchêne, A., & Heller, M. (2012). *Language in late capitalism: Pride and profit.* Routledge. doi:10.4324/9780203155868

Duffy, G. G., Webb, S. M., & Davis, S. (2009). Literacy Education at Crossroads. In J. V. Hoffman & Y. M. Goodman (Eds.), *Changing literacies for changing times* (pp. 189–197). Routledge.

Duncan, M., & Lederberg, A. (2018). Relations between teacher talk characteristics and child language in spoken-language Deaf and hard-of-hearing classrooms. *Journal of Speech, Language, and Hearing Research: JSLHR, 61*(12), 2977–2995. doi:10.1044/2018_JSLHR-L-17-0475 PMID:30458501

Duncan, S. E., & Ávila, E. A. (2000). *PreLAS 2000 Assessment Kit.* CTM Mc Graw Hill.

Dunn, M. L., Padilla, R. L., Lugo, E. D., & Dunn, M. L. (1986). *TVIP: Test de Vocabulario en Imagenes Peabody. Adaptación Hispanoamericana.* Pearson.

Dyson, A. H. (2007). Relational sense and textual sense in a U.S. urban classroom: The contested case of Emily, girlfriend of a ninja. In B. Comber & A. Simpson (Eds.), *Negotiating critical literacies in the classroom* (pp. 3–18). Taylor and Francis.

Dyson, A. H. (2013). *Rewriting the basics: Literacy learning in children's cultures.* Teachers College Press.

Dyson, A. H. (2020). "We're Playing Sisters, on Paper!": Children composing on graphic playgrounds. *Literacy*, *54*(2), 3–12. doi:10.1111/lit.12214

EACEA. (2012). *Citizenship Education in Europe*. Education, Audiovisual and Culture Executive Agency P9 Eurydice. Retrieved on April 15, 2022, from https://eacea.ec.europa.eu/education/eurydice

Eakin, S. (2000). Giants of American education: Horace Mann. *Technos*, *9*(2), 4–7.

Easterbrooks, S., & Lederberg, A. (2021). Reading fluency in young elementary school age deaf and hard-of-hearing children. *Journal of Deaf Studies and Deaf Education*, *26*(1), 99–111. doi:10.1093/deafed/enaa024 PMID:32909026

Edwards, C. (1986). *Promoting social and moral development in young children: Creative approaches for the classroom*. Teachers College Press.

Edwards, C., Gandini, L., & Forman, G. (1998). *The hundred languages of children: The Reggio Emilia approach, advanced reflections*. Ablex Publishing Corporation.

Edwards, C., Gandini, L., & Forman, G. (2012). *The hundred languages of children. The Reggio Emilia experience in transformation* (3rd ed.). Praeger.

Egan, K. (1989, Spring). Memory, imagination, and learning: connected by the story. *The Docket: Journal of the New Jersey Council for the Social Studies*, 9-13.

Ege, P., Acarlar, F., & Turan, F. (2004). *Ankara Artikülasyon Testi (AAT)* [Ankara Articulation Test]. Ankara University, Scientific Research Project Publication.

Eggins, S. (2004). Introduction to systemic functional linguistics. *Continuum*.

Eisenberg, L., Iler Kirk, K., Schaefer Martinez, A., Ying, E., & Miyamoto, R. (2004). Communication abilities of children with aided residual hearing. *Archives of Otolaryngology—Head & Neck Surgery*, *130*(5), 563–569. doi:10.1001/archotol.130.5.563 PMID:15148177

Ellis, R. (2012). Language Teaching Research and Language Pedagogy. Wiley-Blackwell. doi:10.1002/9781118271643

Ellis, J. M. (2003). *Task-based language learning and teaching*. Oxford University Press.

Elo, S., & Kyngäs, H. (2008). The qualitative content analysis process. *Journal of Advanced Nursing*, *62*(1), 107–115. doi:10.1111/j.1365-2648.2007.04569.x PMID:18352969

Enriquez, G., Johnson, E., Kontovourki, S., & Mallozi, C. A. (2016). *Literacies, learning and the body: Putting theory and research into pedagogical practice*. Routledge.

Erickson, M. (1987). Deaf readers reading beyond literal. *American Annals of the Deaf*, *132*(4), 291–294. doi:10.1353/aad.2012.0711 PMID:3442290

Erikson, E. H. (1980). *Identity and the life cycle*. Norton.

Eslava, J. (2014). *Entre el Amor y los Límites: Ayudando a los hijos a alcanzar la autorregulación e la conducta*. Panamericana Editorial Ltda.

Espinosa, M. (2015). *Getting it right: For children from diverse backgrounds*. Pearson Education.

Esteban-Guitart, M., & Moll, L. C. (2014). Funds of identity: A new concept based on the funds of knowledge approach. *Culture and Psychology*, *20*(1), 31–48. doi:10.1177/1354067X13515934

European Commission. (2013). *Co-creating European citizenship*. Policy review. Publications Office of the European Union, EUR 25948.

Evans, S. (2010). The role of multicultural literature and interactive read-alouds on student perspectives toward diversity. *Journal of Research in Innovative Teaching*, *3*(1), 92–104.

Exley, B., Woods, A., & Dooley, K. (2014) Thinking critically in the land of princesses and giants: The affordances and challenges of critical approaches in the early years. In J. Z. Pandya & J. Ávila (Eds.) Moving critical literacies forward: A new look at praxis across contexts (pp. 59-70). Routledge.

Fahim, M., & Haghani, M. (2012). Sociocultural perspectives on foreign language learning. *Journal of Language Teaching and Research*, *3*(4), 693–699. doi:10.4304/jltr.3.4.693-699

Fain, J. G., & Horn, R. (2011). Valuing home language to support young children's talk about books. In R. J. Meyer & K. F. Whitmore (Eds.), *Reclaiming literacy: Teachers, students and researchers regaining spaces for thinking and action* (pp. 209–218). Routledge.

Fairclough, N. (2014). *Power and language*. Routledge.

Falk, J., Anderson Di Perri, K., Howerton-Fox, A., & Jezik, C. (2020). Implications of a sight word intervention for Deaf students. *American Annals of the Deaf*, *164*(5), 592–607. doi:10.1353/aad.2020.0005 PMID:32089538

Fanon, F. (2004). *The Wretched of the Earth. 1961* (R. Philcox, Trans.). Grove Press.

Farrell, T. (2015). Second language teacher education: A reality check. In *International perspectives of English language teacher education* (pp. 1–15). Palgrave Macmillan. doi:10.1057/9781137440068_1

Farrell, T. S. C. (2015). *Reflective language teaching: From research to practice*. Bloomsbury Publishing.

Fernandez, E. S. (2014). *Teaching for a Culturally Diverse and Racially Just World*. Cascade Books.

Ferrão Candau, V. M. (2019). Educación intercultural crítica: Construyendo caminos. In C. Walsh (Ed.), *Pedagogías decoloniales: Prácticas insurgentes de resistir, (re)existir y (re)vivir (Pensamiento decolonial)- Tomo I* (1st ed., pp. 145–164). Editorial Abya-Yala.

Ferreiro, E. (1998). *Alfabetización. Teoría y práctica*. Siglo XXI Editores.

Ferreiro, E., & Teberosky, A. (2007). *Los sistemas de escritura del niño*. Siglo XXI México.

Fitzpatrick, E., Squires, B., & Kay-Raining Bird, E. (2020). What's that you say? Communication breakdowns and their repairs in children who are deaf or hard of hearing. *Journal of Deaf Studies and Deaf Education*, *25*(4), 490–504. doi:10.1093/deafed/enaa010 PMID:32463866

Flores, M. A. (2016). Teacher Education Curriculum. In J. Loughran & M. L. Hamilton (Eds.), *International Handbook of Teacher Education* (pp. 187–230). Springer. doi:10.1007/978-981-10-0366-0_5

Flórez, R., Restrepo, M. & Schwanenflugel, P. (n.d.). *Alfabetismo emergente. Investigación, teoría y práctica. El caso de la lectura*. Universidad Nacional de Colombia.

Flyvbjerg, B. (2006). Five misunderstandings about case-study research. *Qualitative Inquiry*, *12*(2), 219–245. doi:10.1177/1077800405284363

Foster, S. H. (1986). Learning discourse topic management in the preschool years. *Journal of Child Language*, *13*(2), 231–250. doi:10.1017/S0305000900008035 PMID:3745330

Compilation of References

Foundation, The Hawn. (2011). *The MindUP Curriculum: Grades PreKh2: Brain-Focused Strategies for Learning and Living* (Illustrated ed.). Scholastic Teaching Resources.

Franco Rodríguez, J. M. (2013). An alternative reading of the linguistic landscape: The case of Almería. *Revista Internacional de Lingüística Iberoamericana, 21*(1), 109–134.

Francois, C. (2013). Reading is about relating: Urban youths give voice to the possibility for school literacy. *Journal of Adolescent & Adult Literacy, 57*(2), 141–149. doi:10.1002/JAAL.218

Freire, P. (2006). Pedagogy of the Oppressed (30th ann. ed.). Continuum International Publishing Group.

Freire, P. (2018). *Pedagogy of the oppressed.* Bloomsbury Publishing USA.

Freire, P. (1970). *Pedagogy of the Oppressed.* Herder and Herder.

Freire, P. (1970). *Pedagogy of the oppressed.* Seabury Press.

Freire, P. (1987). The importance of the act of reading. In P. Freire & D. Macedo (Eds.), *Literacy: Reading the word and the world* (pp. 29–36). Bergin & Garvey.

Freire, P. (2000). Pedagogy of the oppressed. *Continuum*.

Freire, P. (2006). *Pedagogia da autonomia* [Pedagogy of autonomy]. Paz e Terra.

Freire, P., & Macedo, D. (1987). *Literacy: Reading the word and the world.* Bergin & Garvey.

Freire, P., & Macedo, D. (1987). *Reading the Word and the World.* Routledge.

Friedrich, P., & Gomes de Matos, F. (2012). Towards a Non-Killing Linguistics. In Non-Killing linguistics. Practical Applications (pp. 17-38). Center for Global Non-Killing.

Fukunaga, N. (2006). "Those anime students": Foreign language literacy development through Japanese popular culture. *Journal of Adolescent & Adult Literacy, 50*(3), 206–222. doi:10.1598/JAAL.50.3.5

Fukuyama, F. (1992). *The end of history and the last man.* Free Press.

Gakhar, S., & Thompson, A. (2007). Digital storytelling: Engaging, communicating, and collaborating. In R. Carlsen, & DA. Willis (Eds.), *Proceedings of the Society for Information Technology and Teacher Education International Conference 2007* (pp. 607-612). Chesapeake, VA: AACE.

Galante, A. (2020). Plurilingual and pluricultural competence (PPC) scale: The inseparability of language and culture. *International Journal of Multilingualism, 0*(0), 1–22. doi:10.1080/14790718.2020.1753747

Galda, L., Sipe, L., Liang, L. & Cullinan, B. (2013). *Literature and the child.* Cengage Learning.

Gallingane, C., & Sophia Han, H. (2015, September 11). Words can help manage emotions: Using based strategies for vocabulary instruction to teach emotional words to young children. *Childhood Education, 91*, 351–362.

Galtung, J. (1964). An Editorial. *Journal of Peace Research, 1*(1), 1–4. doi:10.1177/002234336400100101

Galtung, J. (1969). Violence, Peace and Peace Research. *Journal of Peace Research, 6*(3), 167–191. doi:10.1177/002234336900600301

García, M. (2014). Estrategias didácticas. Modos de enseñar y aprender. In I. Hurtado & F. García (Eds.), *Manual de didáctica: aprender a enseñar* (pp. 97–119). Pirámide.

García, O. (2009). *Bilingual Education in the 21st Century: A Global Perspective.* Basil/Blackwell.

García, O., & Leiva, C. (2014). *Theorizing and Enacting Translanguaging for Social Justice*. In A. Creese & A. Blackledge (Eds.), *Heteroglossia as Practice and Pedagogy* (pp. 199–216). Springer. doi:10.1007/978-94-007-7856-6_11

García, O., & Otheguy, R. (2014). Spanish and Hispanic bilingualism. In M. Lacorte (Ed.), *The Routledge handbook of Hispanic applied linguistics* (pp. 639–658). Routledge.

García, O., & Vogel, S. (2017). Translanguaging. In G. Noblit & L. Moll (Eds.), *Oxford Research Encyclopedia of Education*. Oxford University Press., doi:10.1093/acrefore/9780190264093.013.181

García, O., & Wei, L. (2014). *Translanguaging: Language, Bilingualism, and Education*. Palgrave MacMillan. doi:10.1057/9781137385765

Gardner, H. (1980). *Artful scribbles: The significance of children's drawings*. Basic Books, Inc.

Gardner, R. C. (1985). *Social psychology and second language learning: The role of attitudes and motivation*. Edward Arnold.

Garvin, R. (2010). Responses to the Linguistic Landscape in Memphis, Tennessee: An Urban Space in Transition. In Linguistic Landscape in the City (pp. 252-272). Blue Ridge Summit: Multilingual Matters.

Gascon-Ramos, M., Campbell, M., Bamford, J., & Young, A. (2010). Influences on parental evaluation of the content of early intervention following early identification of deafness: A study about parents' preferences and satisfaction. *Child: Care, Health and Development*, *36*(6), 868–877. doi:10.1111/j.1365-2214.2010.01092.x PMID:20666784

Gass, S. M. (1997). *Input, Interaction, and the Second Language Learner*. Lawrence Erlbaum and Associates.

Gee, J. (1996). *Social linguistics and literacies: Ideology in discourses*. Routledge Falmer.

Geers, A., Moog, J., & Rudge, A. (2019). Effects of frequency of early intervention on spoken language and literacy levels of children who are deaf or hard of hearing in preschool and elementary school. *Journal of Early Hearing Detection and Intervention*, *4*(1), 15–27.

Genc, E., Uzuner, Y., & Genc, T. (2017). A study on the communicative functions used in various contexts by a child with hearing loss. Ankara University Faculty of Educational Sciences Journal of Special Education, 18(3), 355-381.

Gerhart, A., & Alcantara, C. (2018). How the NRA transformed from marksmen to lobbyists. *The Washington Post*. https://www.washingtonpost.com/graphics/2018/national/gun- control-1968/

Giridharadas, A. (2018). *Winners take all: The elite charade of changing the world*. Vintage Books.

Gironzetti, E., & Belpoliti, F. (2021). The other side of heritage language education: Understanding Spanish heritage language teachers in the United States. *Foreign Language Annals*, *54*(4), 1189–1213. doi:10.1111/flan.12591

Given, L. (2008). Virtual Ethnography. In *The SAGE encyclopedia of qualitative research methods*. SAGE Publications, Inc. doi:10.4135/9781412963909.n484

Global competence is a 21st century imperative. (n.d.). National Education Association. Retrieved June 20, 2021, from https://citeseerx.ist.psu.edu/viewdoc/download?doi=10.1.1.184.8517&rep=rep1&t

Goberis, D., Beams, D., Dalpes, M., Abrisch, A., Baca, R., & Yoshinaga-Itano, C. (2012). The missing link in language development of Deaf and hard of hearing children: Pragmatic language development. *Seminars in Speech and Language*, *33*(04), 297–309. doi:10.1055-0032-1326916 PMID:23081790

Goes, T. (2021, December 16). '*O caso Prevent Senior' exibe o sadismo e a crueldade que contaminaram a operadora*. Folha de São Paulo. https://bit.ly/34tEXku

Goldin-Meadow, S., & Mayberry, R. (2001). How do profoundly deaf children learn to read? *Learning Disabilities Research & Practice, 16*(4), 222. doi:10.1111/0938-8982.00022

Goldstein, S. B. (2021). Ground rules for discussing diversity: Complex considerations. In M. E. Kite, K. A. Case, & W. R. Williams (Eds.), *Negotiating difficult moments in teaching diversity and social justice* (pp. 17–29). American Psychological Association. doi:10.1037/0000216-002

Goleman, D. (2008). *Emotional intelligence.* Retrieved from: https://danielgoleman.info/topics/emotional-intelligence

Gomes de Matos, F. (2014). Peace Linguistics for Language Teachers. D.E.L.T.A, 30(2), 415-424. doi:10.1590/0102-4450899151803731 04

Gomes de Matos, F. (2002). *Applied Linguistics. A new frontier for TESOLers.* World Federation of Modern Languages Associations.

Gomes de Matos, F. (2010). *Nurturing Nonkilling. A Poetic Plantation.* CGNK Publications.

Gómez, L., & Piulachs, J. (2015). *Maisha* [Film]. Lula Gómez & Jordi Piulachs.

Gómez-Rodríguez, L. F. (2015). Critical intercultural learning through topics of deep culture in an EFL Classroom. *Ikala, 20*(1), 43–59.

Gonzalez, N., Moll, L.C., Floyd Tenery, M. F., Rivera, A., Rendon, P., Gonzales, R., & Amanti, C. (1995). Funds of knowledge for teaching in Latino households. *Urban Education, 29*(4), 443-470. doi:10.1177/0042085995029004005

Gonzalez, N., & Moll, L. C. (2002). Cruzando el puente: Building bridges to funds of knowledge. *Educational Policy, 16*(4), 623–641. doi:10.1177/0895904802016004009

Gonzalez, N., Moll, L. C., & Amanti, C. (Eds.). (2005). *Funds of knowledge: Theorizing practices in households, communities, and classrooms.* Erlbaum.

González-Novoa, A. & Perera-Méndez, P. (2021). Panglotia, pampedia y pansofía: el realismo pedagógico en Comenio. *Pedagogía y Saberes*, (54), 23-36. doi:10.17227/pys.num54-11286

Goodman, K. S. (2014). *What's whole in Whole Language in the 21st century?* Garn Press.

Gore, J. M. (2021). The Quest for Better teachers. *Oxford Review of Education, 1*(47), 45–60. doi:10.1080/03054985.2020.1842182

Grabois, H. (1999). The convergence of sociocultural theory and cognitive linguistics: Lexical semantics and the L2 acquisition of love, fear, and happiness. In Languages of Sentiment: Cultural Constructions of Emotional Substrates. Academic Press.

Grant, N. S., & Bolin, B. L. (2016). Digital Storytelling: A Method for Engaging Students and Increasing Cultural Competency. *The Journal of Effective Teaching, 16*, 44–61.

Gratier, M., & Devouche, E. (2011). Imitation and repetition of prosodic contour in vocal interaction at 3 months. *Developmental Psychology, 47*(1), 67–76. doi:10.1037/a0020722 PMID:21244150

Graves, D., & Hansen, J. (1983). The author's chair. *Language Arts, 60*(2), 176–183. https://www.jstor.org/stable/41961448

Gredler, M. E. (2001). *Learning and instruction: Theory into practice.* Pearson.

Gregory, A. E., & Cahill, M. A. (2009). Constructing critical literacy: Self-reflexive ways for curriculum and pedagogy. *Critical Literacy: Theories and Practices, 3*(2), 6–16.

Grinker, R. R. (1994). *Houses in the Rainforest: Ethnicity and Inequality among Farmers and Foragers in Central Africa*. University of California Press. doi:10.1525/9780520915664

Grinker, R. R. (2001). *In the Arms of Africa: The Life of Colin M*. Turnbull.

Grosfoguel, R. (2010). Para descolonizar os estudos de economia política e os estudos póscoloniais: transmodernidade, pensamento de fronteira e colonialidade global [To decolonize political economy studies and postcolonial studies: transmodernity, frontier thinking and global coloniality]. In Epistemologias do Sul [Epistemologies of the South] (pp. 378-412). Cortez Editora.

Grosfoguel, R. (2019). Knowledges born in the struggle: Constructing the epistemologies of the Global South. In B. de Sousa Santos & M. P. Meneses (Eds.), *Epistemic Extractivism: A Dialogue with Alberto Acosta, Leanne Betasamosake Simpson, and Silvia Rivera Cusicanqui* (pp. 203–218). Routledge. doi:10.4324/9780429344596-12

Grosjean, F. (1982). *Life with Two Languages*. Harvard University Press.

Guba, E. G., & Lincoln, Y. S. (2005). Paradigmatic Controversies, Contradictions, and Emerging Confluences. In N. K. Denzin & Y. S. Lincoln (Eds.), *The Sage handbook of qualitative research* (pp. 191–215). Sage Publications Ltd.

Guerra, G. (2020). *(Des)matamento* [(De)foresting, Film]. Gunga Guerra.

Guerra-Lyons, J. D., & Mendinueta, N. R. (2020). On the notion of "owning a forest": Ideological awareness and Genre-based Pedagogy in university critical literacy. *DELTA. Documentação de Estudos em Lingüística Teórica e Aplicada, 36*. Advance online publication. doi:10.1590/1678-460X2020360412

Guilherme, M., & Menezes de Souza, L. M. (Eds.). (2019). *Glocal languages and critical intercultural awareness: The South answers back*. Routledge.

Gumperz, J. J., & Levinson, S. C. (1996). *Rethinking Linguistic Relativity*. Cambridge University Press.

Guzmán, R. (2017). Aprendizaje de los profesores sobre alfabetización y métodos de enseñanza. *Revista Folios, 46*(46), 105–116. doi:10.17227/01234870.46folios105.116

Guzmán, R., & Chocontá, J. (2018). *Desarrollo infantil y escritura. Vínculos entre infancia, cultura y pensamiento*. Universidad de La Sabana. doi:10.5294/978-958-12-0476-2

Guzmán, R., & Ecima, I. (2011). Conocimiento práctico y conocimiento académico en los profesores del nivel inicial. Seis preguntas. *Revista Folios, 34*(34), 3–14. doi:10.17227/01234870.34folios3.13

Haas Dyson, A., & Genishi, C. (Eds.). (1994). *The need for story: Cultural diversity in classroom and community*. Teachers College Press.

Hall, A. H. (2014). Beyond the author's chair. *The Reading Teacher, 68*(1), 27–31. doi:10.1002/trtr.1297

Halliday, M. (2007). [A&C Black.]. *Language and Education, 9*, •••.

Halliday, M. A. K. (1975). *Learning how to mean: Explorations in the development of language*. Edward Arnold. doi:10.1016/B978-0-12-443701-2.50025-1

Hall, M., Hall, W., & Caselli, N. (2019). Deaf children need language, not (just) speech. *First Language, 39*(4), 367–395. doi:10.1177/0142723719834102

Hall, W. C. (2017). What you don't know can hurt you: The risk of language deprivation by impairing sign language development in deaf children. *Maternal and Child Health Journal, 21*(5), 961–965. doi:10.100710995-017-2287-y PMID:28185206

Compilation of References

Hammerness, K., Darling-Hammond, L., & Bransford, J. (2005). How teachers learn and develop. In L. Darling-Hammond & J. Bransford (Eds.), *Preparing teachers for a changing world* (pp. 359–389). Josey Bass.

Hands and Voices. (2020). *Communication considerations: Total Communication*. Hands and Voices. https://www.handsandvoices.org/comcon/articles/totalcom.htm

Haneda, M. (2006). Becoming literate in a second language: Connecting home, community, and school literacy practices. *Theory into Practice*, *45*(4), 337–345. doi:10.120715430421tip4504_7

Harris, I. (2010). History of Peace Education. In G. Salomon & E. Cairns (Eds.), Handbook on Peace Education. Taylor & Francis Group.

Harris, I. (2004). Peace education theory. *Journal of Peace Education Theory*, *1*(1), 5–20. doi:10.1080/1740020032000178276

Harris, I., & Morrison, M. (2013). *Peace Education* (3rd ed.). McFarland & Company, Inc.

Harris, M. (2015). The impact of new technologies on the literacy attainment of deaf children. *Topics in Language Disorders*, *35*(2), 120–132. doi:10.1097/TLD.0000000000000052

Harro, B. (2000). The Cycle of Socialization. In M. Adams (Ed.), *Readings for diversity and social justice* (pp. 15–20). Routledge.

Hart, B., & Risley, T. R. (1995). *Meaningful differences in the everyday experience of young American children*. Paul H Brookes Publishing.

Harvard Graduate School of Education. (2016). *Project Zero*. Retrieved March 7, 2021, from http://www.pz.harvard.edu/

Harvard Graduate School of Education. (2020). *Project Zero's Thinking Routines Toolbox*. http://www.pz.harvard.edu/thinking-routines

Harvard on The Developing Child. (n.d.). *How to support children (and yourself) during COVID-19 outbreaks*. https://developingchild.harvard.edu/resources/how-to-support-children-and-yourself-during-the-covid-19-outbreak/

Harwood, D. (2008). Deconstructing and reconstructing Cinderella: Theoretical defense of critical literacy for young children. *Language and Literature*, *10*(2), 1–13.

Hasan, R. (2005). Semiotic mediation, language and society: Three exotripic theories–Vygotsky, Halliday and Bernstein. *Language, Society and Consciousness*, *1*, 55-80.

Hasson, U., Ghazanfar, A. A., Galantucci, B., Garrod, S., & Keysers, Ch. (2012). Brain-to-brain coupling: A mechanism for creating and sharing a social world. *Trends in Cognitive Sciences*, *16*(2), 114–121. doi:10.1016/j.tics.2011.12.007 PMID:22221820

Hayes, H., Geers, A., Treiman, R., & Moog, J. (2009). Receptive vocabulary development in deaf children with cochlear implants: Achievement in an intensive auditory-oral educational setting. *Ear and Hearing*, *30*(1), 128–135. doi:10.1097/AUD.0b013e3181926524 PMID:19125035

Hazaea, A. N. (2020). Fostering critical intercultural awareness among EFL students through critical discourse analysis. *Íkala. Revista de Lenguaje y Cultura*, *25*(1), 17–33. doi:10.17533/udea.ikala.v25n01a06

Heath, S. B. (1982). What no bedtime story means: Narrative skills at home and school. *Language in Society, 11*, 49-76. https://www.jstor.org/stable/4167291

Heath, S. B., & Street, B. (2008). *On ethnography: Approaches to language and literature*. Teachers College Press.

Heller, M. (2003). Globalization, the new economy, and the commodification of language and identity. *Journal of Sociolinguistics*, 7(4), 473–492. doi:10.1111/j.1467-9841.2003.00238.x

Heller, M. (2011). Language as resource in the globalized new economy. In N. Coupland (Ed.), *Handbook of language and globalization*. Blackwell Publishing.

Heller, M., & McElhinny, B. (2017). *Language, capitalism, colonialism: Toward a critical history*. University of Toronto Press.

Henkes, K. (2010). Prudencia se preocupa. Harper Collins Publishers.

Hepple, E., Sockhill, M., Tan, A., & Alford, J. (2014). ML pedagogy: Creating claymations with adolescent, post-beginner English language learners. *Journal of Adolescent & Adult Literacy*, 58(3), 219–229. doi:10.1002/jaal.339

Hewlett, S. B. (2000). Central African Government's and International NGOs' perceptions of Baka Pygmy development. In Hunter-Gatherers in the modern world (pp. 381–390). New York: Berghahn.

Hewlett, B. (2021). Social learning and innovation in adolescence: A comparative study of Aka and Chabu hunter-gatherers of Central and Eastern Africa. *Human Nature (Hawthorne, N.Y.)*, 32(1), 239–278. doi:10.100712110-021-09391-y PMID:33881734

Hewlett, B. S., & Lamb, M. E. (2009). *Hunter-Gatherer Childhoods. Evolutionary, Developmental & Cultural Perspectives*. Transaction.

Hillegass, M. M. (2005). Early childhood studies. In S. Frost & F. Sibberson (Eds.), School Talk (Vol. 10, pp. 1–3). Academic Press.

Hilton, A. (2011). *Educating for Global Competence*. Asia Society. Retrieved March 10, 2021, from https://asiasociety.org/education/educating-global-competence

Hinton, L., & Hale, K. (2013). *The Green Book of Language Revitalization in Practice*. BRILL.

Hinton, L., Huss, L., & Roche, G. (Eds.). (2018). *The routledge handbook of language revitalization* (1st ed.). Routledge. doi:10.4324/9781315561271

Hirsh-Pasek, K., Adamson, L. B., Bakerman, R., Tresch Owen, M., Michnick Golinkoff, R., Pace, A., Yust, P. K. S., & Suma, K. (2015). The contribution of early communication quality to low-income children's language success. *Psychological Science*, 26(7), 1071–1083. doi:10.1177/0956797615581493 PMID:26048887

Hoffmeister, R., Henner, J., Caldwell-Harris, C., & Novogrodsky, R. (2022). Deaf children's ASL vocabulary and asl syntax knowledge supports English knowledge. *Journal of Deaf Studies and Deaf Education*, 27(1), 37–47. doi:10.1093/deafed/enab032 PMID:34788799

Hogg, L. (2011). Funds of knowledge: An investigation of coherence within the literature. *Teaching and Teacher Education*, 27(3), 666–677. doi:10.1016/j.tate.2010.11.005

Holcomb, L., Golos, D., Moses, A., & Broadrick, A. (2022). Enriching Deaf children's American Sign Language phonological awareness: A quasi-experimental study. *Journal of Deaf Studies and Deaf Education*, 27(1), 26–36. doi:10.1093/deafed/enab028 PMID:34392343

Honebein, P. C. (1996). Seven goals for the design of constructivist learning environments. In B. G. Wilson (Ed.), *Constructivist learning environments: Case studies in instructional design*. Educational Technology Publications.

hooks, B. (1989). *Talking Back: Thinking Feminist, Thinking Black*. Between the Lines.

Hua, Z. (2016). Identifying research paradigms. In Z. Hua (Ed.), *Research methods in intercultural communication* (pp. 3–22). Wiley-Blackwell.

Hua, Z., Otsuji, E., & Pennycook, A. (2017). Multilingual, multisensory and multimodal repertoires in corner shops, streets and markets: Introduction. *Social Semiotics*, *27*(4), 383–393. doi:10.1080/10350330.2017.1334383

Human Development Report. (2020). Retrieved June, 2022 from https://hdr.undp.org/sites/default/files/Country-Profiles/CAF.pdf

Human Rights Watch. (2014). *25th Anniversary of the Convention on the Rights of the Child*. Humanrightswatch.org.

Humphries, T., Kushalnagar, P., Mathur, G., Napoli, D. J., Padden, C., Rathmann, C., & Smith, S. (2016). Avoiding linguistic neglect of deaf children. *The Social Service Review*, *90*(4), 589–619. doi:10.1086/689543

Humphries, T., Kushalnagar, P., Mathur, G., Napoli, D., Padden, C., Rathmann, C., & Smith, S. (2012). Language acquisition for deaf children: Reducing the harms of zero tolerance to the use of alternative approaches. *Harm Reduction Journal*, *9*(1), 16. doi:10.1186/1477-7517-9-16 PMID:22472091

Huser, C. (2019). 'I want to share this video with you today.' Children's participation rights in childhood research. *Human Rights Education Review.*, *2*(2), 45–63. doi:10.7577/hrer.3322

Huysmans, A. J. (2014). *Guide Lecture ORA* [copies of materials from SMA's Monasao mission library]. Central African Republic.

Ibagón, N. (2015). La educación, un derecho que cuesta: Dimensión fiscal y su relación con la política educativa en América Latina. *Revista Educación y Humanismo.*, *17*(28), 29–37. doi:10.17081/eduhum.17.28.1164

IBGE, Brazilian Institute of Geography and Statistics. (2010). *2010 Brazilian Census*. Author.

Ichikawa, M. (1996). The co-existence of man and nature in the African rain forest. In R. Ellen & K. Fukui (Eds.), *Redefining Nature. Ecology, Culture and Domestication* (pp. 467–492). Berg.

Iddings, A. C. D., McCafferty, S. G., & Da Silva, M. L. T. (2011). Conscientização through graffiti literacies in the streets of a São Paulo neighborhood: An ecosocial semiotic perspective. *Reading Research Quarterly*, *46*(1), 5–21. doi:10.1598/RRQ.46.1.1

Immordino-Yang, M. (2015). *Emotions, Learning, and the Brain: Exploring the Educational Implications of Affective Neuroscience*. W.W. Norton and Company.

Immordino-Yang, M. H. (2016). *Emotions, learning, and the brain: Exploring the educational implications for affective neuroscience*. W.W. Norton & Company.

Immordino-Yang, M. H. (2016). *Emotions, learning, and the brain: Exploring the educational implications of affective neuroscience*. W.W. Norton.

Immordino-Yang, M. H., & Damasio, A. R. (2007). We Feel therefore we learn: The relevance of affective and social neuroscience to education. *Mind, Brain and Education: The Official Journal of the International Mind, Brain, and Education Society*, *1*(1), 3–10. doi:10.1111/j.1751-228X.2007.00004.x

Ivey, G. (2014). The social side of engaged reading for young adolescents. *The Reading Teacher*, *68*(3), 165–171. doi:10.1002/trtr.1268

Ivey, G., & Broaddus, K. (2001). "Just plain reading": A survey of what makes students want to read in middle school classrooms. *Reading Research Quarterly*, *36*(4), 36350–36377. doi:10.1598/RRQ.36.4.2

Ivey, G., & Johnston, P. H. (2013). Engagement with young adult literature: Outcomes and practices. *Journal of Literacy Research, 47*, 297–327. doi:10.1177/1086296X15619731

Jabr, F. (2019). The story of storytelling. *Harper's Magazine*. Retrieved March 2022. https://harpers.org/archive/2019/03/the-story-of-storytelling/

Janks, H. (2013). Critical literacy in teaching and research. *Education Inquiry, 4*(2), 225–242. doi:10.3402/edui.v4i2.22071

Jaramillo, R. (2008). Educación cívica y ciudadana como respuesta a la violencia en Colombia. *Transatlántica de Educación, 4*, 65–76.

Jaworski, A., & Thurlow, C. (Eds.). (2010). *Semiotic landscapes: Language, image, space*. A&C Black.

Jesson, J., Matheson, L., & Lacey, F. M. (2011). Doing your literature review: Traditional and systematic techniques. *Sage (Atlanta, Ga.)*.

Jesus, C. M. (1960). *Quarto de despejo* [Dark room]. Livraria F. Alves.

Jiao, W. Y., Wang, L. N., Liu, J., Fang, S. F., Jiao, F. Y., Pettoello-Mantovani, M., & Somekh, E. (2020, June). Behavioral and Emotional Disorders in Children during the COVID-19 Epidemic. *The Journal of Pediatrics, 221*, 264–266.e1. doi:10.1016/j.jpeds.2020.03.013 PMID:32248989

Ji, L., Nisbett, R. E., & Zhang, Z. (2005). Is it culture or is it language: Examination of language effects in cross-cultural research on categorization. *Journal of Personality and Social Psychology, 87*, 57–65. doi:10.1037/0022-3514.87.1.57

Jiménez, F. (2014). Paz neutra: Una ilustración del concepto. *Revista de paz y conflictos, 7*, 19-52.

Jiménez, R., Smith, P., & Teague, B. (2009). Transnational and Community Literacies for Teachers. *Journal of Adolescent & Adult Literacy, 53*(1), 1–16. doi:10.1598/JAAL.53.1.2

Johns Hopkins Medicine. (n.d.). *What is Coronavirus?* https://www.hopkinsmedicine.org/health/conditions-and-diseases/coronavirus

Johnson, D., & Johnson, R. (1989). *Cooperation and competition: Theory and research*. Interaction Book Company.

Joint Committee on Infant Hearing. (2007). Year 2007 position statement: Principles and guidelines for early hearing detection and intervention programs. *Pediatrics, 120*(4), 898–921. doi:10.1542/peds.2007-2333 PMID:17908777

Jonkman, J. (2020). Underground multiculturalism: Contentious cultural politics in gold-mining regions in Chocó, Colombia. *Journal of Latin American Studies, 53*(1), 1–28. doi:10.1017/S0022216X2000098X

Juruna, Y., & Juruna, D. (2020). *Mandayaki and Takino* [Film]. Yariato Juruna & Dadyma Juruna.

JUST. (2019). *Aligned Professional Development Systems Planning and Implementation Guide*. JUST.

Kachru, B. (1992). *The Other Tongue: English across cultures*. University of Illinois Press.

Kagan, S. (1993). The structural approach to cooperative learning. In D. Daniel (Ed.), *Cooperative learning: A response to linguistic and cultural diversity*.

Kalantzis, M., & Cope, B. (2016). New media and productive diversity in learning. In S. Barch & N. Glutsch (Eds.), *Diversity in der LehrerInnenbildung* (pp. 310–325). Waxmann.

Katz, J., Onen, F., Demir, N., Uzlukaya, A., & Uludağ, P. (1974). Peabody Picture Vocabulary Test Form B. *Hacettepe Bulletin of Social Sciences and Humanities, 6*, 129–140.

Compilation of References

Kazak-Berument, S., & Güven, A. G. (2013). Turkish expressive and receptive language test: I. Standardization, reliability and validity study of the receptive vocabulary sub-scale. *Turkish Journal of Psychiatry*, *24*(3), 192–201. PMID:24049009

Kearns-Goodwin, D. (2018). *Leadership in turbulent times*. Simon & Schuster.

Keenan, E. O. (1974). Conversational competence in children. *Journal of Child Language*, *1*(2), 163–183. doi:10.1017/S0305000900000623

Kelle, G. (2018). *Menino Pipa* [Kite Boy, Film]. Giovanna Lira.

Kelleher, A. (2010). *Who is a heritage language learner?* Heritage Briefs. https://cal.org/heritage/pdfs/brifukuefs/Who-is-a-Heritage-Language-Learner.pdf

Khan, F. R., Westwood, R., & Boje, D. M. (2010). 'I feel like a foreign agent': NGOs and corporate social responsibility interventions into Third World child labor. *Human Relations*, *63*(9), 1417–1438. doi:10.1177/0018726709359330

Kim, G. M., & Omerbašić, D. (2017). Multimodal literacies: Imagining lives through Korean dramas. *Journal of Adolescent & Adult Literacy*, *60*(5), 557–566. doi:10.1002/jaal.609

Kim, J. H. (2015). *Understanding narrative inquiry: The crafting and analysis of stories as research*. Sage Publications.

Kim, S. J. (2016). Opening up spaces for early critical literacy: Korean kindergarteners exploring diversity through multicultural picture books. *Australian Journal of Language and Literacy*, *39*(2), 176–187.

King, K. (2008). *Sustaining linguistic diversity: Endangered and minority languages and language varieties*. Georgetown University Press.

Kiramba, L. K. (2017). Multilingual literacies: Invisible representation of literacy in a rural classroom. *Journal of Adolescent & Adult Literacy*, *61*(3), 267–277. doi:10.1002/jaal.690

Kirk Thagard, E., Strong Hilsmier, A., & Easterbrooks, S. (2011). Pragmatic language in Deaf and hard of hearing students: Correlation with success in general education. *American Annals of the Deaf*, *155*(5), 526–534. doi:10.1353/aad.2011.0008 PMID:21449250

Kite, M. A., Case, K. A., & Williams, W. R. (Eds.). (2021). *Navigating difficult moments in teaching diversity and social justice*. American Psychological Association. doi:10.1037/0000216-000

Knobel, M., & Lankshear, C. (2007). *The new literacies sampler*. Peter Lang.

Kohler, A. (2005). Of Apes and men: Baka and Bantu attitudes to wildlife and the making of eco-goodies and baddies. *Conservation & Society*, *3*(2), 407–435.

Köhler, A., & Lewis, J. (2002). Putting Hunter-Gatherer and Farmer Relations in Perspective. A Commentary from Central Africa. In S. Kent (Ed.), *Ethnicity, Huntergatherers, and the "Other": Association or Assimilation in Southern Africa?* (pp. 276–305). Smithsonian Institute.

Kondaurova, M. V., Fagan, M. K., & Zheng, Q. (2020). Vocal imitation between mothers and their children with cochlear implants. *Infancy*, *25*(6), 827–850. doi:10.1111/infa.12363 PMID:32799404

Kondaurova, M. V., Smith, N. A., Zheng, Q., Reed, J., & Fagan, M. K. (2020). Vocal turn-taking between mothers and their children with cochlear implants. *Ear and Hearing*, *41*(2), 362–373. doi:10.1097/AUD.0000000000000769 PMID:31436755

Korthagen, F. A. (2003). In search of the essence of a good teacher: Towards a more holistic approach in teacher education. *Teaching and Teacher Education*, *20*(1), 77–97. doi:10.1016/j.tate.2003.10.002

Korthagen, F., Loughran, J., & Russel, T. (2006). Developing fundamental principles for teacher education programs and practices. *Teaching and Teacher Education*, *22*(8), 1020–1041. doi:10.1016/j.tate.2006.04.022

Koulaninga, A. (2009). *L'Education chez les pygmées de Centrafrique*. L'Harmattan.

Kozinets, R. V. (2006). Netnography. In V. Jupp (Ed.), *The SAGE Dictionary of Social Research Methods* (p. 193). SAGE Publications, Ltd. doi:10.4135/9780857020116.n127

Kozinets, R. V. (2010). *Netnography: Doing Ethnographic Research Online*. SAGE Publications.

Kramsch, C. (1993). *Context and culture in language teaching*. Oxford University Press.

Kramsch, C. (1998). *Language and Culture* (H. G. Widdowson, Ed.). OUP Oxford.

Kramsch, C. (2009). *The multilingual subject: What foreign language learners say about their experience and why it matters*. Oxford University Press.

Kramsch, C. (2013). Culture in foreign language teaching. *Iranian Journal of Language Teaching Research.*, *1*(1), 57–78.

Kramsch, C. (2018). Is there still a place for culture in a multilingual FL education? Language Education and Multilingualism. *Landscape Journal*, *1*, 16–33. doi:10.18452/19039

Krashen, S. (1982). *Principles and Practice in Second Language Acquisition*. Pergamon.

Krashen, S. (2016). The purpose of education, free voluntary reading, and dealing with the impact of poverty. *School Libraries Worldwide*, *22*(1), 1–7. doi:10.29173lw6901

Krashen, S. D. (1985). *The input hypothesis: Issues and implications*. Longman.

Krashen, S. D. (1986). *Principles and practice in second language acquisiton*. Pergamon Press.

Krechevsky, M., Mardell, B., Rivard, M., & Wilson, D. (2013). *Visible learners: Promoting Reggio inspired approaches in all schools*. Jossey-Bass.

Krechevsky, M., Mardell, B., & Romans, A. N. (2014). Engaging city hall: Children as citizens. *New Educator*, *10*(1), 10–20. doi:10.1080/1547688X.2014.868212

Krenak, A. (2020). *O amanhã não está à venda* [Tomorrow is not for sale]. Companhia das Letras.

Kress, G. (2000). Multimodality. In B. Cope & M. Kalantzis (Eds.), *ML: Literacy learning and the design of social futures* (pp. 182–202). Routledge.

Krippendorff, K. (2004). Content Analysis: An introduction to its methodology. *Sage (Atlanta, Ga.)*.

Kuby, C. (2011). Humpty Dumpty and Rosa Parks: Making space for critical dialogue with 5- and 6- year-olds. *YC Young Children*, *66*(5), 36–40, 42–43.

Kuby, C. R. (2013). 'OK this is hard': Doing emotions in social justice dialogue. *Education, Citizenship and Social Justice*, *8*(1), 29–42. doi:10.1177/1746197912448714

Kuby, C. R. (2013). *Critical literacy in the early childhood classroom: Unpacking histories, unlearning privilege*. Teachers College Press.

Kuby, C. R., & Rucker, T. G. (2020). (Re)Thinking children as fully (in)human and literacies as otherwise through (re)etymologizing intervene and inequality. *Journal of Early Childhood Literacy*, *20*(1), 13–43. doi:10.1177/1468798420904774

Kumaravadivelu, B. (2001). Towards a postmethods pedagogy. *TESOL Quarterly*, *35*(4), 537–560. doi:10.2307/3588427

Compilation of References

Labadie, M., Mosley Wetzel, M., & Rogers, R. (2012). Opening spaces for critical literacy: Introducing books to young readers. *The Reading Teacher*, *66*(2), 117–127. doi:10.1002/TRTR.01097

Laevers, F. (2011). *Experiential Education: Making Care and Education More Effective Through Well-Being and Involvement*. Leuven University / Centre for Experiential Education, Belgium. Retrieved March 1, 2022 from https://www.child-encyclopedia.com/sites/default/files/textes-experts/en/857/experiential-education-making-care-and-education-more-effective-through-well-being-and-involvement.pdf

Laevers, F., & Declercq, B. (2018). How well-being and involvement fit into the commitment to children's rights. *European Journal of Education Research Development and Policy, Special Issue: Learner agency at the confluence between rights-based approaches and well-being*, *53*(3), 325-335.

Laevers, F., Moons, J., & Declercq, B. (2013). *A process-oriented monitoring system for the arly years* [POMS]. CEGO Publishers.

Lambert, J. (2013). *Digital Storytelling. Capturing lives, creating community*. Routhledge. doi:10.4324/9780203102329

Landry, R., & Bourhis, R. Y. (1997). Linguistic Landscape and Ethnolinguistic Vitality: An Empirical Study. *Journal of Language and Social Psychology*, *16*(1), 23–49. doi:10.1177/0261927X970161002

Lantolf, J. P. (Ed.). (2000). *Sociocultural Theory and Second Language Learning*. Oxford University Press.

Lantolf, P., & Thorne, S. L. (2007). Sociocultural theory and second language learning. In B. VanPatten & J. Williams (Eds.), *Theories in second language acquisition: An introduction* (pp. 693–701). Lawrence Erlbaum Associates Publishers.

Lapp, D., Flood, J., Head, S. B., & Langer, J. (2009). The communicative, visual, and performative arts: Core components of literacy education. In J. V. Hoffman. & Y.M. Goodman (Eds.), Changing literacies for changing times: An historical perspective on the future of reading, public policy and classroom practices (pp. 3-16). Routledge.

Lapp, D., Flood, J., Brice Heath, S., & Langer, J. (2009). The Communicative, Visual and Performative Arts: Core Components of Literacy Education. In J. V. Hoffman & Y. M. Goodman (Eds.), *Changing literacies for changing times* (pp. 3–16). Taylor & Francis.

Lasagabaster, D., & Garcia, O. (2014). Translanguaging: Towards a dynamic model of bilingualism at school [Translanguaging: hacia un modelo dinámico de bilingüismo en la escuela]. Cultura y Educacion, 26(3), 557-572.

Lassiter, L. (2005). Collaborative Ethnography and Public Anthropology. *Current Anthropology*, *46*(1), 83–106. doi:10.1086/425658

Lassiter, L. (2005). *The Chicago guide to collaborative ethnography*. University of Chicago Press. doi:10.7208/chicago/9780226467016.001.0001

Lasso, M. D. (2018). Letting Go of Teacher Power: Innovative Democratic Assessment. In E. Jean Francois (Ed.), *Transnational Perspectives on Innovation in Teaching and Learning Technologies* (pp. 200–224). Brill Sense.

Lau, S. M. C., & Viegen, S. V. (2020). *Plurilingual pedagogies: Critical and creative endeavors for equitable language in education*. Springer International Publishing. doi:10.1007/978-3-030-36983-5

Lazar, A. M., Edwards, P. A., & Thompson McMillon, G. (2012). *Bridging literacy and equity: The essential guide to social equity teaching*. Teachers College Press.

Le Guin, U. K. (2004). *The wave in the mind: Talks and essays of the writer, the reader, and the imagination*. Shambhala.

Leander, K., & Boldt, G. (2013). Rereading "A pedagogy of multiliteracies" bodies, texts, and emergence. *Journal of Literacy Research*, *45*(1), 22–46. doi:10.1177/1086296X12468587

LeBlanc, J. (2010). *How ESOL teachers become aware of Communicative Peace*. MA TESOL Collection. Paper 497. Retrieved from https://digitalcollections.sit.edu/cgi/viewcontent.cgi?article=1510&context=ipp_col

Lederberg, A. R., Schick, B., & Spencer, P. E. (2013). Language and literacy development of deaf and hard-of-hearing children: Successes and challenges. *Developmental Psychology*, 49(1), 15–30. doi:10.1037/a0029558 PMID:22845829

Leeman, J. (2015). Heritage language education and identity in the United States. *Annual Review of Applied Linguistics*, 35, 100–119. doi:10.1017/S0267190514000245

Leland, H. C., Lewison, M., & Harste, J. C. (2018). Teaching children's literature. Academic Press.

Leland, C., Lewison, M., & Harste, J. (2018). *Teaching Children's Literature: It's critical*. Routledge.

Lesaux, N., & Harris, J. (2015). *Cultivating knowledge, building language: Literacy instruction for English Learners in Elementary School*. Heinemann.

Lewis, J. (2017). Egalitarian social organization: The case of the Mbendjele BaYaka. In B. S. Hewlett (Ed.), *Hunter-Gathers of the Congo Basin* (pp. 219–244). Routledge. doi:10.4324/9780203789438-8

Lewison, M., Flint, A., & Van Sluys, K. (2002). Taking on critical literacy: The journey of newcomers and novices. *Language Arts*, 79(5), 382–392.

Lewison, M., Leland, C., & Harste, J. C. (2015). *Creating critical literacy classrooms: Reading and writing with an edge* (2nd ed.). Routledge.

Lew-Levy, S., Reckin, R., Lavi, N., Cristóbal-Azkarate, J., & Ellis-Davies, K. (2017/28). How Do Hunter-Gatherer Children Learn Subsistence Skills? *Human Nature (Hawthorne, N.Y.)*, 28(4), 367–394. doi:10.100712110-017-9302-2 PMID:28994008

Li, J., Akiva, T., & Winters, D. (2018). *Simple Interactions tool*. Simple Interactions. https://www.simpleinteractions.org/the-sitool.html

Liberali, F. C. (2019). Práticas discursivas na construção de patrimônios vivenciais [Discursive practices in the construction of funds of perezhivanie]. Project submitted to the Department of English, Pontifical Catholic University of São Paulo.

Liberali, F. C., Mazuchelli, L.P., Modesto-Sarra, L. K. (2021). O brincar no Multiletramento Engajado para a Construção de Práticas Insurgentes [Play in the Engaged Multiliteracy for crafting insurgent practices]. *Revista De Estudos Em Educação E Diversidade*, 2(6), 1-26. doi:10.22481/reed.v2i6.9643

Liberali, F. C., Modesto Sarra, L. K., Mazuchelli, L. P., Amaral, M. F., Medeiros, B. S. F. (2021a). Teatro do oprimido e direitos humanos: estratégia pedagógica para a (trans)formação [Theater of the Oppressed and Human Rights: Pedagogical Strategy for (Trans)Formation]. *Cadernos De Linguagem E Sociedade*, 22(2), 232–252.

Liberali, F., Fuga, V., & Vendramini-Zanella, D. (2022). O Desenvolvimento Engajado e o teatro-brincar na constituição da coletividade (Engaged Development and play-theatre in the constitution of the collectivity). In P. Marques & A. L. Smolka (Eds.), Desenvolvimento humano, drama e vivências: discussões em torno de 'Sobre a questão da psicologia da criação pelo autor', de L S. Vigotski. Academic Press.

Liberali, F., Fuga, V., Vendramini-Zanella, D., Mazuchelli, L. P., Klen-Alves, V., Modesto-Sarra, L. K., & Oliveira, E. P. (2022). A vivência crítico-colaborativa para construção de uma linguística aplicada decolonial [A critical-collaborative perezhivanie for the construction of a decolonial applied linguistics]. Academic Press.

Liberali, F. C. (2022). *Multiletramento Engajado na construção de práticas do Bem Viver* [Engaged Multiliteracy in building Good Living practices]. Academic Press.

Liberali, F. C., Magalhães, M. C. C., Meaney, M. C., Sousa, S. S., Pardim, R. P., & Diegues, U. C. C. (2021b). Critically Collaborating to create the viable unheard of - connecting Vygotsky and Freire to deal with a devastating reality. In V. L. T. Souza & G. S. Arinelli (Eds.), *Qualitative research and social intervention: transformative methodologies for collective contexts* (pp. 65–83). Springer.

Lickteig, M. J., & Russell, J. F. (1993). Elementary teachers' read-aloud practices. *Reading Improvement, 30*(4), 202–208.

Liddicoat, A., & Scarino, A. (2013). *Intercultural language teaching and learning*. Wiley-Blackwell. doi:10.1002/9781118482070

Lin, A. M. (2018). Theories of trans/languaging and trans-semiotizing: Implications for content-based education classrooms. *International Journal of Bilingual Education and Bilingualism, 22*(1), 5–16. doi:10.1080/13670050.2018.1515175

Litwin, E. (2008). El campo de la didáctica: la búsqueda de una nueva agenda. In A. Camilloni, A. Davini, G. Edelstein, E. Litwin, M. Souto, & S. Barco (Eds.), *Corrientes didácticas contemporáneas* (pp. 91–115). Paidós.

Litwin, E. (2016). *El oficio de enseñar. Condiciones y contextos*. PAIDÓS.

Liu, C. (2016). Cultivation of intercultural awareness in EFL teaching. *Journal of Language Teaching and Research, 7*(1), 226–232. doi:10.17507/jltr.0701.26

Liu, Y.-T. (1996). Is designing one search or two? A model of design thinking involving symbolism and connectionism. *Design Studies, 17*(4), 435–449. doi:10.1016/S0142-694X(96)00018-X

Livermore, D. (2011). *The Cultural Intelligence Difference*. American Management Association.

Llenas, A. (2012). *The Color Monster: A Story About Emotions*. Little, Brown and Company.

Lloyd, P., & Scott, P. (1995). Difference in similarity: Interpreting the architectural design process. *Planning and Design, 22*(4), 383–406. doi:10.1068/b220383

Long, M. (1996). 'The role of the linguistic environment in second language acquisition. In W. Ritchie & T. Bhatia (Eds.), *Handbook of Second Language Acquisition* (pp. 413–468). Academic Press.

López Sáenz, M. C., & Penas Ibáñez, B. (2006). *Interculturalism: Between identity and diversity*. Lang.

Lopez, L. M., & Greenfield, D. B. (2004). The cross-language transfer of phonological skills of Hispanic Head Start children. Early Childhood Science Education Research Trends in Learning and Teaching. *Bilingual Research Journal, 28*.

Losada, J., & Suaza, D. (2018). Video-mediated listening and Multiliteraces. *Colombian Applied Linguistics Journal, 20*(1), 11–24. doi:10.14483/22487085.12349

Loughran, J., & Hamilton, M. L. (2016). Developing an Understanding of Teacher Education. In J. Loughran & M. L. Hamilton (Eds.), *International Handbook of Teacher Education* (pp. 3–22). Springer. doi:10.1007/978-981-10-0366-0_1

Lozano, M. E., Jiménez-Caicedo, J. P., & Abraham, L. B. (2020). Linguistic Landscape Projects in Language Teaching: Opportunities for Critical Language Learning Beyond the Classroom. In *Language Teaching in the Linguistic Landscape* (pp. 17–42). Springer. doi:10.1007/978-3-030-55761-4_2

Luft, P. (2008). Examining educators of the Deaf as "Highly Qualified" teachers: Roles and responsibilities under IDEA and NCLB. *American Annals of the Deaf, 152*(5), 429–440. doi:10.1353/aad.2008.0014 PMID:18488531

Luke, A., & Freebody, P. (1997). Shaping the social practices of reading. In S. Muspratt, A. Luke, & P. Freebody (Eds.), *Constructing critical literacies: Teaching and learning textual practice* (pp. 185–225). Hampton Press.

Luke, A., & Freebody, P. (1999). Further notes in the four resource model. *Practically Primary, 4*(2), 5–8.

Luke, C. (2000). Cyber-schooling and technological change: ML for new times. In B. Cope & M. Kalantzis (Eds.), *ML: Literacy learning and the design of social futures* (pp. 3–8). Routledge.

Lupyan, G. (2012). Linguistically modulated perception and cognition: The label- feedback hypothesis. *Frontiers in Psychology*, *3*, 54. doi:10.3389/fpsyg.2012.00054

Macedo, D. (2019). *Decolonizing foreign language education: The misteaching of English and other colonial languages*. Routledge.

MacGowan, T. L., Tasker, S. L., & Schmidt, L. A. (2021). Differences in established joint attention in hearing-hearing and hearing-deaf mother-child dyads: Associations with social competence, settings, and tasks. *Child Development*, *92*(4), 1388–1402. doi:10.1111/cdev.13474 PMID:33325060

Machado, B. (2020). *Assum Preto* [Chopi blackbird, Film]. Bako Machado.

MacLean, N. (2017). *Democracy in chains: The deep history of the radical right's stealth plan for America*. Viking.

MacSwan, J. (2019). A multilingual perspective on translanguaging. *Decolonizing Foreign Language Education*, 186–219. doi:10.4324/9780429453113-8

MacSwan, J. (2017, February). A Multilingual Perspective on Translanguaging. *American Educational Research Journal*, *54*(1), 167–201.

Magalhães, M. C. C. (2011). Pesquisa Crítica de Colaboração: escolhas epistemo-metodológicas na organização e condução de pesquisa de intervenção no contexto escolar [Critical Collaborative Research: epistemic-methodological choices in the organization and conduct of intervention research in the school context]. In M. C. C. Magalhães, & S. S. Fidalgo (Eds.), Questões de método e de linguagem na formação docente [Questions of method and language in teacher education] (pp. 13-39). Mercado de Letras.

Magalhães, M. C. C., & Fidalgo, S. (2019). Reviewing Critical Research Methodologies for Teacher Education in Applied Linguistics. *DELTA. Documentação de Estudos em Lingüística Teórica e Aplicada*, *35*(3), 1–19. doi:10.1590/1678-460X2019350301

Magnat, V. (2020). Towards a Performative Ethics of Reciprocity. In N. K. Denzin & M. D. Giardina (Eds.), *Qualitative Inquiry and the Politics of Resistance Possibilities, Performances, and Praxis* (pp. 115–129). Routledge. doi:10.4324/9780429316982-8

Makoni, S., & Makoni, B. (2010). Multilingual discourse on wheels and public English in Africa: A case for "vague linguistics.". In J. Maybin & J. Swann (Eds.), *The Routledge companion to English language studies* (pp. 258–270). Routledge.

Makoni, S., & Pennycook, A. D. (2007). Disinventing and reconstituting languages. In S. Makoni & A. Pennycook (Eds.), *Disinventing and reconstituting languages* (pp. 1–41). Multilingual Matters.

Malaguzzi, L. (1987). *Reggio Emilia Approach*. Retrieved from https://www.reggiochildren.it/en/reggio-emilia-approach/100-linguaggi-en/

Maldonado-Torres, N. (2016). Transdisciplinaridade e decolonialiade [Transdisciplinarity and decoloniality]. *Revista Sociedade e Estado*, *31*(1), 75–97. doi:10.1590/S0102-69922016000100005

Mansilla, V. B., & Chua, F. S. (2017). Signature Pedagogies in Global Competence Education: Understanding Quality Teaching Practice. In S. Choo, D. Sawch, A. Villanueva, & R. Vinz (Eds.), *Educating for the 21st Century*. Springer., doi:10.1007/978-981-10-1673-8_5

Compilation of References

Markowska-Manista, U. (2012). Obszary dyskryminacji i marginalizacji Pigmejów w Afryce Środkowej. In K. Jarecka-Stępień & J. Kościółek (Eds.), *Problemy współczesnej Afryki. Szanse i wyzwania na przyszłość* (pp. 83–97). Wyd. Księgarnia Akademicka.

Markowska-Manista, U. (2014). Kolonialne i postkolonialne uwikłania łowców-zbieraczy w Afryce Środkowej. *Przegląd Humanistyczny*, *446*(05), 33–45.

Markowska-Manista, U. (2016). "Invisible" and "unheard" children in fragile contexts–reflections from field research among the Ba'Aka in the Central African Republic. *Problemy Wczesnej Edukacji*, *35*(4), 39–50. doi:10.5604/01.3001.0009.7629

Markowska-Manista, U. (2017). The Written and Unwritten Rights of Indigenous Children in Central Africa – Between the Freedom of "Tradition" and Enslavement for "Development". In A. Odrowąż-Coates & S. Goswami (Eds.), *Symbolic Violence in Socio-educational Contexts* (pp. 127–142). Wydawnictwo Akademii Pedagogiki Specjalnej.

Markowska-Manista, U. (2018). The ethical dilemmas of research with children from the countries of the Global South. Whose participation? *Polish Journal of Educational Studies*, *71*(1), 51–65. doi:10.2478/poljes-2018-0005

Markowska-Manista, U. (2019). Postcolonial dimensions of social work in the Central African Republic and its impact on the life of hunter-gatherer children and youth–a critical perspective. In T. Kleibl, R. Lutz, N. Noyoo, B. Bunk, A. Dittmann, & B. Seepamore (Eds.), *The Routledge Handbook of Postcolonial Social Work* (pp. 286–301). Routledge.

Markowska-Manista, U. (2020). The life of Ba'Aka children and their rights: Between the processes of poverty and deprivation. In D. Lawson, D. Angemi, & I. Kasirye (Eds.), *What Works for Africa's Poorest Children: From measurement to action* (pp. 287–301). Practical Action Publishing.

Marschark, M., Sapere, P., Convertino, C., Mayer, C., Wauters, L., & Sarchet, T. (2009). Are Deaf students' reading challenges really about reading? *American Annals of the Deaf*, *154*(4), 357–370. doi:10.1353/aad.0.0111 PMID:20066918

Marshall, C., Jones, A., Fastelli, A., Atkinson, J., Botting, N., & Morgan, G. (2018). Semantic fluency in deaf children who use spoken and signed language in comparison with hearing peers. *International Journal of Language & Communication Disorders*, *53*(1), 157–170. doi:10.1111/1460-6984.12333 PMID:28691260

Marshall, E., & Toohey, K. (2010). Representing family: Community funds of knowledge, bilingualism, and multimodality. *Harvard Educational Review*, *80*(2), 221–241. doi:10.17763/haer.80.2.h3446j54n608q442

Martin-Beltrán, M., Garcia, A. A., & Montoya-Ávila, A. (2020). "I know there's something like that in Spanish": Heritage language learners' multifaceted interactions with linguistically diverse peers. *International Journal of Applied Linguistics*, *30*(3), 530–552. doi:10.1111/ijal.12310

Mason, L. E. (2017). The Significance of Dewey's Democracy and Education for 21st-Century Education. *Education and Culture*, *33*(1), 41–57. doi:10.5703/educationculture.33.1.0041

Maturana, H. R. (1978). Biology of language: The epistemology of reality. In G. Miller & E. Lenneberg (Eds.), *Psychology and Biology of Language and Thought*. Academic Press.

Mayer, C. (2007). What really matters in the early literacy development of Deaf children. *Journal of Deaf Studies and Deaf Education*, *12*(4), 411–431. doi:10.1093/deafed/enm020 PMID:17566067

Mayer, R. (2002). *Artificial Africa's: Colonial Images in the Times of Globalization*. University Press of New England.

May, S. (2009). Critical Multiculturalism and Education. In J. A. Banks (Ed.), *The Routledge International Companion to Multicultural Education* (pp. 33–48). Routledge.

Mazuchelli, L. P. (2019). *Stereotypes and Representations: discourses on and in ag(e)ing* [Doctoral dissertation]. State University of Campinas. doi:10.47749/T/UNICAMP.2019.1095209

Mbembe, A. (2003). Necropolitics. *Public Culture*, *15*(1), 11–40. doi:10.1215/08992363-15-1-11

McCallister, C. A. (2008). "The author's chair" revisited. *Curriculum Inquiry*, *38*(4), 455–471. doi:10.1111/j.1467-873X.2008.00424.x

McCarty, T. L., Nicholas, S. E., & Wigglesworth, G. (Eds.). (2019). *A world of Indigenous languages: Politics, pedagogies and prospects for language reclamation*. Multilingual Matters., doi:10.21832/MCCART3064

McCloskey, E. (2012). Conversations about jail: Inclusive settings for critical literacy. *Early Childhood Education Journal*, *40*(6), 369–377. doi:10.100710643-012-0528-7

McDonald, M. (1998). Traditional storytelling today: An international sourcebook. Fitzroy Dearborn.

McDonald, M. A., Bowman, M., & Brayko, D. (2013). Learning to see students: Opportunities to develop relational practices of teaching through community-based placements in teacher education. *Teachers College Record*, *115*(4), 1–17. doi:10.1177/016146811311500404

McDrury, J., & Alterio, M. (2003). *Learning through storytelling in higher education: using reflection and experience to improve learning*. Kogan Page.

McLaughlin, M., & DeVoogd, G. L. (2004). *Critical literacy: Enhancing students comprehension of text*. Scholastic.

McLean, J., & Snyder-McLean, L. (1999). *How children learn language*. Singular Publishing.

McLoughlin, J. A., & Lewis, R. B. (2005). *Assessing students with special needs* (6th ed.). Prentice Hall.

McNiff, J. (2016). *You and your action research project*. Routledge Taylor & Francis Group. doi:10.4324/9781315693620

McWhorter, J. H. (2014). *The Language Hoax. Why the World Looks the Same in Any Language*. Oxford University Press.

Medina, R., Ramírez, M., & Clavijo, A. (2015). Reading the community critically in the digital age: A ML approach. In P. Chamness Miller, M. Mantero, & H. Hendo (Eds.), *ISLS Readings in Language Studies* (Vol. 5, pp. 45–66). International Society for Language Studies.

Medrano, C. A. (2015). *The effects of implementing a Spanish language program for young children of Hispanic Background* [Doctoral dissertation]. Nova Southeastern University.

Megale, A. H., & Liberali, F. C. (2020). As implicações do conceito de patrimônio vivencial como uma alternativa para a educação multilíngue [Implications of the concept of funds of perezhivanie as an alternative for multilingual education]. *Revista X*, *15*(1), 55–74. doi:10.5380/rvx.v15i1.69979

Meier, N. (2009). Reading first? *Critical Literacy: Theories and Practices*, *3*(2), 69–83.

Melliou, K., Moutafidou, A., & Bratitsis, T. (2014). Children's Rights: A narrative video using Digital Storytelling and Visible Thinking approach created by kindergarteners. *International Digital Storytelling Conference Digital Storytelling in Times of Crisis*.

Meltzoff, A. N., & Moore, M. K. (1989). Imitation in newborn infants: Exploring the range of gestures imitated and the underlying mechanisms. *Developmental Psychology*, *25*(6), 954–962. doi:10.1037/0012-1649.25.6.954 PMID:25147405

Meltzoff, A. N., & Moore, M. K. (1997). Explaining facial imitation: A theoretical model. *Infant and Child Development*, *6*(3-4), 179–192. PMID:24634574

Menezes de Souza, L. M. (2011). Para uma redefinição de letramento crítico: conflito e produção de significação. In R. F. Maciel & V. A. Araújo (Eds.), *Formação de Professores de Línguas-Ampliando Perspectivas* (1st ed., pp. 128–140). Paco Editorial.

Menezes de Souza, L. M., & Monte Mór, W. (2018). Still Critique? *Revista Brasileira de Lingüística Aplicada*, *18*(2), 445–450. doi:10.1590/1984-6398201813940

Meng, X. (2016). *A pedagogy of ML into practice: A case study in one grade one literacy classroom* [Doctoral thesis, University of West Ontario, Canada]. https://ir.lib.uwo.ca/cgi/viewcontent.cgi?article=5409&context=etd

Mentha, S., Church, A., & Page, J. (2015). Teachers as brokers: Perceptions of 'participation' and agency in early childhood education and care. *International Journal of Children's Rights*, *23*(3), 622–637. doi:10.1163/15718182-02303011

Mertens, D. (2017). Transformative Research: Personal and Societal. *International Journal for Transformative Research*, *4*(1), 18–24. doi:10.1515/ijtr-2017-0001

Meyer, J. R., & Whitmore, K. F. (2011). Reclaiming joy: Spaces for thinking and action. In R. J. Meyer & K. F. Whitmore (Eds.), *Reclaiming literacy: Teachers, students and researchers regaining spaces for thinking and action* (pp. 279–288). Routledge.

Michelson, K. (2018). Teaching culture as a relational process through a ML-based global simulation. *Language, Culture and Curriculum*, *31*(1), 1–20. doi:10.1080/07908318.2017.1338295

Michelson, K., & Dupuy, B. (2014). Multi-storied lives: Global simulation as an approach to developing ML in an intermediate French course. *Journal of Linguistics and Language Teaching*, *6*(1), 21–49. doi:10.5070/L26119613

Mignolo, W. D., & Escobar, A. (Eds.). (2013). *Globalization and the decolonial option*. Routledge. doi:10.4324/9781315868448

Migration Policy Institute. (2021, June 21). *Black and Latino college graduates, immigrant and U.S. born alike, face greater risk of skill underutilization than white counterparts, MPI analysis finds*. https://www.migrationpolicy.org/news/immigrant-skill-underutilization-race-ethnicity-state-analysis

Migration Policy Institute. (2022, May 1). *State language data - FL*. https://www.migrationpolicy.org/data/state-profiles/state/language/FL

Mikkelsen, N. (1990). Toward greater equity in literacy education: Storymaking and non-mainstream students. *Language Arts*, *67*(6), 556–566.

Miller, D., & Sharp, C. (2018). *Game changer! Book access for all kids*. Scholastic.

Mills, G. E., & Gay, L. R. (2019). *Educational research: Competencies for analysis and application* (12th ed.). Pearson.

Mills, K. A. (2015). Doing digital composition on the social web: Knowledge processes in literacy learning. In *A Pedagogy of Multiliteracies* (pp. 172–185). Palgrave Macmillan. doi:10.1057/9781137539724_10

Ministerio de Educación Nacional. (2004). Estándares básicos de competencias ciudadanas. Author.

Ministerio de Educación Nacional. (2015). *Orientaciones Generales para la Implementación de la Catedra de la Paz en los Establecimientos Educativos de Preescolar, Básica y Media de Colombia*. Ministerio de Educación Nacional de Colombia.

Moeller, M. (2000). Early intervention and language development in children who are Deaf and hard of hearing. *Pediatrics*, *106*(3), e43–e43. doi:10.1542/peds.106.3.e43 PMID:10969127

Moje, E. B., Overby, M., Tysvaer, N., & Morris, K. (2008). The complex world of adolescent literacy: Myths, motivations, and mysteries. *Harvard Educational Review*, *78*(1), 107–154. doi:10.17763/haer.78.1.54468j6204x24157 PMID:19756223

Moll, L. C., Velez-Ibanez, C., & Greenberg, J. B. (1989). Year one progress report: Community knowledge and classroom practice: Combining resources for literacy instruction (IARP Subcontract No. L-10). Tucson, AZ: University of Arizona, College of Education and Bureau of Applied Research in Anthropology.

Moll, L. C., Vélez-Ibáñez, C., Greenberg, J., Whitmore, K., Saavedra, E., Dworin, J., & Andrade, R. (1990). *Community knowledge and classroom practice: Combining resources for literacy instruction: A handbook for teachers and planners* (OBEMLA Contract No. 300-87-0131). University of Arizona College of Education and Bureau of Applied Research in Anthropology.

Moll, L. (2019). Elaborating funds of knowledge: Community-oriented practices in international contexts. *Literacy Research: Theory, Method, and Practice*, *68*(1), 130–138. doi:10.1177/2381336919870805

Moll, L. C. (1992). Bilingual classroom studies and community analysis: Some recent trends. *Educational Researcher*, *21*(2), 20–24. doi:10.3102/0013189X021002020

Moll, L. C. (2005). Reflection and possibilities. In N. Gonzalez, L. C. Moll, & C. Amanti (Eds.), *Funds of knowledge: Theorizing practices in households, communities and classrooms* (pp. 275–287). Lawrence Erlbaum. doi:10.4324/9781410613462-5

Moll, L. C., Amanti, C., Neff, D., & Gonzalez, N. (1992). Funds of knowledge for teaching: Using a qualitative approach to connect homes and classrooms. *Theory into Practice*, *31*(2), 132–141. doi:10.1080/00405849209543534

Moll, L. C., & Greenberg, J. (1990). Creating zones of possibilities: Combining social contexts for instruction. In L. C. Moll (Ed.), *Vygotsky and education* (pp. 319–348). Cambridge University Press. doi:10.1017/CBO9781139173674.016

Montessori, M. (1949). *Education and peace* (H. R. Lane, Trans.). Henry Regnery.

Montgomery, D. (2019). Conquerors of the Courts. *Washington Post Magazine*. https://www.washingtonpost.com/news/magazine/wp/2019/01/02/feature/conquerors-of-the-courts/

Montgomery, S. E., Miller, W., Foss, P., Tallakson, D. & Howard, M. (2017). *Banners for books: "Mighty-hearted" kindergartners take action through arts-based service learning*. Academic Press.

Montoya, A., Jaramillo, C., & Correa, A. (2017). *Narrativas de paz en la escuela* [Unpublished master's thesis]. Universidad de Manizales, Manizales.

Morales, E., & Gebre, E. (2021). Teachers' understanding and implementation of peace education in Colombia: The case of Cátedra de la Paz. *Journal of Peace Education*, *18*(2), 209–230. doi:10.1080/17400201.2021.1937085

Mora, R. A. (2011). Tres retos para la investigación y formación de docentes en inglés: Reflexividad sobre las creencias y prácticas en literacidad. *Revista Q*, *5*(10), 1–20.

Mora, R. A., Pulgarín, C., Ramírez, N., & Mejía-Vélez, M. C. (2018). English literacies in Medellin: The city as literacy. In *Learning Cities* (pp. 37–60). Springer. doi:10.1007/978-981-10-8100-2_4

Morgan, B. D. (2002). Critical practice in community-based ESL programs: A Canadian perspective. *Journal of Language, Identity, and Education*, *1*(2), 141–162. doi:10.1207/S15327701JLIE0102_03

Moroe, N. (2018). Why fix it if it's not broken! The role of audiologists in families of hearing children born to deaf parents. *Hearing, Balance and Communication*, *16*(3), 173–181. doi:10.1080/21695717.2018.1499990

Morra, S. (n.d.). *8 steps to great digital storytelling*. Retrieved August 15, 2018 https://edtechteacher.org/8-steps-to-great-digital-storytelling-from-samantha-on-edudemic/

Mortari, L. (2015). Reflectivity in research practice: An overview of different perspectives. *International Journal of Qualitative Methods*, *14*(5). doi:10.1177/1609406915618045

Most, T. (2002). The use of repair strategies by children with and without hearing impairment. *Language, Speech, and Hearing Services in Schools*, *33*(2), 112–123. doi:10.1044/0161-1461(2002/009) PMID:27764464

Most, T., Shina-August, E., & Meilijson, S. (2010). Pragmatic abilities of children with hearing loss using cochlear implants or hearing aids compared to hearing children. *Journal of Deaf Studies and Deaf Education*, *15*(4), 422–437. doi:10.1093/deafed/enq032 PMID:20624757

Moszkowski, A. (1921). *Conversations with Einstein*. Horizon Press.

Motta, A. V. M. (2007). *Tekoa Pyau: uma aldeia guarani na metrópole* [Master's thesis]. Pontifical Catholic University of São Paulo]. https://tede2.pucsp.br/handle/handle/3834

Moutafidou, A., & Bratitsis, T. (2013). Digital Storytelling and Creative Writing: Two Parallel Worlds with a Common Place. *Proceedings of the 1st International Conference on Creative Writing*.

Mowforth, M., & Munt, I. (2009). *Tourism and Sustainability. Development, globalisation and new tourism in the Third World*. Routledge.

Munn, P. (2010). Children as active participants in their own development and ECE professionals as conscious actors. *International Journal of Early Years Education*, *18*(4), 281–282. doi:10.1080/09669760.2010.535325

Munsch, R., & Martchenko, M. (1995). *From Far Away*. Annick Press.

Murillo, J., & Román, M. (2013). Docentes de Educación primaria en América Latina con más de una actividad laboral. Situación e implicaciones. *Revista Mexicana de Investigación Educativa – RMIE*, *18*(58), 893-924.

Murrell, P. (2001). *The community teacher: A new framework for effective urban teaching*. Teachers College Press.

National Association for the Education of Young Children. (1995). *Responding to Cultural diversity. Recommendations for effective early childhood education. A position statement of the National Association of Young Children*. Author.

National Association for the Education of Young Children. (2019). *A position statement of the National Association for the Education of Young Children: Advancing equity in early childhood education*. Author.

National Association of the Deaf. (2016). *Bill of rights for Deaf and hard of hearing children*. National Association of the Deaf. https://www.nad.org/resources/education/bill-of-rights-for-deaf-and-hard-of-hearing-children/

National Association of the Deaf. (2021). *Early intervention services*. National Association of the Deaf. https://www.nad.org/resources/early-intervention-for-infants-and-toddlers/information-for-parents/early-intervention-services/

National Association of the Deaf—NAD. (n.d.). Retrieved October 10, 2021, from https://www.nad.org/resources/american-sign-language/community-and-culture-frequently-asked-questions/

National Center for Education Statistics. (2022). *English Language Learners in Public Schools. Condition of Education*. U.S. Department of Education, Institute of Education Sciences. https://nces.ed.gov/programs/coe/indicator/cgf

National Institute of Child Health and Human Development. (2000). *Report of the National Reading Panel. Teaching children to read: An evidence-based reading instruction: Report of the subgroups* (NIH, Publication No.00-4754). Washington, DC: US. Government Printing Office.

National Institute on Deafness and Other Communication Disorders. (2019). *American Sign Language*. NIDCD. https://www.nidcd.nih.gov/health/american-sign-language

National Reading Panel. (2000). *Teaching children to read: An evidence-based assessment of the scientific research literature on reading and its implications for reading instructions.* Rockville, MD: National Institutes of Child Health and Human Development. Retrieved from www. Nationalreadingpanel.org/publications/summary.htm

NCTE. (2013). *NCTE framework for 21st century curriculum and assessment.* Retrieved March 22, 2022 from https://cdn.ncte.org/nctefiles/resources/positions/framework_21stcent_curr_assessment.pdf

NEA. (2012). *Preparing 21st century students for a global society.* National Education Association.

New London Group. (2000). The Pedagogy of Multiliteracies: Designing Social Futures. *Harvard Educational Review, 66*(1), 60–92.

Newkirk, T. (1989). *More than stories—The range of children's writing.* Heinemann.

Nicholas, J., & Geers, A. (1997). Communication of oral deaf and normally hearing children at 36 months of age. *Journal of Speech, Language, and Hearing Research: JSLHR, 40*(6), 1314–1327. doi:10.1044/jslhr.4006.1314 PMID:9430751

Nickbakht, M., Meyer, C., Scarinci, N., & Beswick, R. (2021). Family-centered care in the transition to early hearing intervention. *Journal of Deaf Studies and Deaf Education, 26*(1), 21–45. doi:10.1093/deafed/enaa026 PMID:32783059

Nicoladis, & Secco, G. (2000). The role of a child's productive vocabulary in the language choice of a bilingual family. *First Language, 20*(58), 3–28. doi:10.1177/014272370002005801

Nightengale-Lee, B., Massy, P., & Knowles, B. (2021). Putting Black Boys' Literacies First: Collective Curriculum Development for the Lives & Literacies of Black Boys. *Journal of literacy innovation, 6*(1), 5-22.

Niu, R., & Li, L. (2017). A review of studies on languaging and second language learning (2006-2017). *Theory and Practice in Language Studies, 7*(12), 1222–1228. doi:10.17507/tpls.0712.08

Notari-Syverson, A., & Losardo, A. (1996). Assessing children's language in meaningful contexts. In K. N. Cole, P. S. Dale, & D. J. Thal (Eds.), *Assessment of communication and language* (pp. 257–280). Brookes.

NRC. (2013). *Education for life and work: Developing transferable knowledge and skills in the 21st century.* National Academies Press. National Research Council.

O'Brian, J. (2007). Children reading critically: A local history. In B. Comber & A. Simpson (Eds.), *Negotiating critical literacies in the classroom* (pp. 37–54). Taylor and Francis.

O'Brien, J., & Comber, B. (2020). Negotiating critical literacies with young children. In *Literacy learning in the early years* (pp. 152–171). Routledge. doi:10.4324/9781003116325-7

O'Neil, K. (2010). Once upon today: Teaching for social justice with Postmodern picture books. *Children's Literature in Education, 41*(1), 40–51. doi:10.100710583-009-9097-9

Objective 1: Increase Global and Cultural Competencies of All U.S. Students. (2000). International Affairs Office. Retrieved March 15, 2021, from https://sites.ed.gov/international/objective-1-increase-global-and-cultural-competencies-of-all-u-s-students/

Ocampo, J. (2013). *Mitos y Leyendas Indígenas de Colombia – Indigenous Myths and Legends of Colombia.* Plaza & Janes Editores.

OECD. (2019). *OECD Future of Education and Skills 2030: OECD Learning Compass 2030.* OECD Publishing. Retrieved on April 12, 2022, from https://www.oecd.org/education/2030-project/teaching-and-learning/learning/learning-compass-2030/OECD_Learning_Compass_2030_concept_note.pdf

Compilation of References

Okoth, A. A. (2006). *History of Africa: African societies and the establishment of colonial rule, 1800-1915* (Vol. 1). East African Publishers Ltd.

Oosterhof, A. (2003). *Developing and using classroom assessments* (3rd ed.). Prentice Hall.

Organización de Estados Iberoamericanos para la Educación, la Ciencia y la Cultura, OEI. (2014). *Miradas sobre la educación en Iberoamérica: avances en las metas educativas 2021*. Author.

Orr, C. (1998). Improving oral imitation in preschool children with and without hearing impairment. *Physical & Occupational Therapy in Pediatrics*, *18*(3-4), 97–107. doi:10.1300/J006v18n03_07

Ortega, Y. (2021a). *Pedagogies of be[ing], be[longing] and be[coming]: Social justice and peacebuilding in the English curriculum of a marginalized Colombian public high school* [Thesis]. https://tspace.library.utoronto.ca/handle/1807/109308

Ortega, Y. (Director). (2021c, December 14). *Onto epistemological oneness for teaching and research*. https://youtu.be/SJ-B6JemzkU

Ortega, L. (2017). New CALL-SLA Research Interfaces for the 21st Century: Towards Equitable Multilingualism. *CALICO Journal*, *34*(3), 283–316. doi:10.1558/cj.33855

Ortega, Y. (2019). "Teacher, ¿Puedo hablar en Español?" A reflection on plurilingualism and translanguaging practices in EFL. *Profile: Issues in Teachers' Professional Development*, *21*(2), 155–170.

Ortega, Y. (2021b). Transformative Pedagogies for English teaching: Teachers and students building social justice together. *Applied Linguistics*, *42*(6), 1144–1152. doi:10.1093/applin/amab033

Osoria, C. (2020). *Rosalia - The Honduran American*. Christine Osoria.

Otheguy, R., García, O., & Reid, W. (2015). Clarifying translanguaging and decon- structing named languages: A perspective from linguistics. *Applied Linguistics Review*, *6*(3), 281–307. doi:10.1515/applirev-2015-0014

Otsuji, E., & Pennycook, A. (2010). Metrolingualism: Fixity, fluidity and language in flux. *International Journal of Multilingualism*, *7*(3), 240–254. doi:10.1080/14790710903414331

Otto, B. (2006). *Language development in early childhood* (2nd ed.). Pearson Prentice Hall.

Owens, R. E. (2008). *Language development an introduction* (7th ed.). Pearson.

Oxford, R. (2013). *The language of peace*. Information Age Publishing Inc.

Oxford, R. L. (2013). *The language of peace. Communicating to create harmony*. Information Age Publishing.

Packer, G. (2020, Feb.). How to destroy a government. *Atlantic*, 54–74.

Padden, C., & Humphries, T. (1990). *Deaf in America: Voices from a Culture*. Harvard University Press.

Palpacuer, L., & Christelle, J. L. (2018). Multiliteracies in action at the Art Museum. *Journal of Linguistics and Language Teaching*, *10*(2), 134–157. doi:10.5070/L210235237

Pantaleo, S. (2005). Young children engage with the metafictive in pictures books. *Australian Journal of Language and Literacy*, *28*(1), 19–37.

Paris, D. (2011). "A friend who understand fully:" Notes on humanizing research on a multiethnic youth community. *International Journal of Qualitative Studies in Education: QSE*, *24*(2), 137–149. doi:10.1080/09518398.2010.495091

Paris, D., & Winn, M. T. (2014). Humanizing research: Decolonizing qualitative inquiry with youth and communities. *Sage (Atlanta, Ga.)*. Advance online publication. doi:10.4135/9781544329611

Paul, P. V. (2001). *Language and deafness* (3rd ed.). Singular Thomson Learning.

Pavlenko, A. (2002). Bilingualism and emotions. *Multilingua*, *21*, 45–78.

Pavlenko, A. (2014). *The bilingual mind and what it tells us about language and thought*. Cambridge University Press. doi:10.1017/CBO9781139021456

Pavlenko, A., & Lantolf, J. (2000). Second language learning as participation and the (re)construction of selves. In J. Lantolf (Ed.), *Sociocultural Theory and Second Language Learning* (p. 155177). Oxford University Press.

Pedersen, E. (1995). Storytelling and the art of teaching. *English Teaching Forum*, *33*(1), 2-5.

Peek-a-Book Language and Literacy Program. (2021a). *Prudencia se preocupa Círculos de puntos de vista*. https://youtu.be/AKnQwiZYKpE

Peek-a-Book Language and Literacy Program. (2021b). *Prudencia se preocupa: Generar, clasificar, conectar, elaborar mapas conceptuales*. https://youtu.be/_5lrvL9SOZ0

Pemunta, N. V. (2013). The governance of nature as development and the erasure of the Pygmies of Cameroon. *GeoJournal*, *78*(2), 353–371. doi:10.100710708-011-9441-7

Pence, K., & Justice, L. M. (2008). *Language development from theory to practice*. Pearson Prentice Hall.

Pennycook, A. (2006). Postmodernism in language policy. In T. Ricento (Ed.), *An introduction to language policy: Theory and method* (pp. 60–67). Blackwell.

Pérez-Prado, A. (2021). *LAF with the Habits of Mind: Strategies and Activities for Diverse Language Learners*. Habits of Mind Institute.

Perez-Prado, A. (2021). *LAF with the habits of mind: Strategies and activities for teaching diverse language learners*. Institute for Habits of Mind.

Perkings, D. N. (2014). *Future wise: Educating our children for a changing world*. Jossey-Bass.

Perkins, D. (2001). Thinking for understanding. In A. Costa (Ed.), *Developing minds: A resource book for teaching thinking* (pp. 446–450). Association for Supervision and Curriculum Development.

Perkins, D. (2009). *Making learning whole: How seven principles of teaching can transform education*. Jossey-Bass.

Perkins, D. N. (2016). Lifeworthy learning. *Educational Leadership*, *73*(6), 12–17.

Perkins, D. N., Tishman, S., Ritchhart, R., Donis, K., & Andrade, A. (2000). Intelligence in the wild: A dispositional view of intellectual traits. *Educational Psychology Review*, *12*(3), 269–293. doi:10.1023/A:1009031605464

Perry, G., Moore, H., Edwards, C., Acosta, K., & Frey, C. (2009). Maintaining credibility and authority as an instructor of color in diversity-education classrooms: A Qualitative inquiry. *The Journal of Higher Education*, *80*(1), 80–105. doi:10.1080/00221546.2009.11772131

Perry, K. (2012). What is literacy? A critical overview of sociocultural perspectives. *Journal of Language & Literacy Education*, *8*(1), 50–71.

Petersen, M. J. (2021). *Human rights education what works?* The Danish Institute for Human Rights. https://www.humanrights.dk/publications/human-rights-education-what-works

Compilation of References

Piaget, J. (1951). *Play, dreams, and imitation in childhood* (C. Gattegno & F. M. Hodgson, Trans.). Routledge and Kegen Paul, Ltd.

Piaget, J. (1952). *The origins of intelligence in children.* International University Press.

Piaget, J. (1956). *The child's conception of space.* Routledge & K. Paul.

Pica, T. (2008). Task-based instruction. In N. Van Deusen-Scholl & N.H. Hornberger (Eds.), Encyclopedia of language and education (2nd ed., vol. 4, pp. 71-82). New York, NY: Springer Science+Business Media LLC.

Pica, T. (1987, Spring). Article. *Applied Linguistics*, *8*(1), 3–21. https://doi.org/10.1093/applin/8.1.3

Piccardo, E., & North, B. (2019). *The Action-Oriented Approach: A Dynamic Vision of Language Education.* Multilingual Matters.

Pieterse, M., Treloar, R., & Cairns, S. (1989). *Small steps: An early intervention program for children with developmental delays.* Macquire University Press.

Pimperton, H., Kreppner, J., Mahon, M., Stevenson, J., Terlektsi, E., Worsfold, S., Yuen, H. M., & Kennedy, C. R. (2017). Language outcomes in Deaf or hard of hearing teenagers who are spoken language users: Effects of Universal Newborn Hearing Screening and early confirmation. *Ear and Hearing*, *38*(5), 598–610. doi:10.1097/AUD.0000000000000434 PMID:28399063

Piniel, K., & Albert, A. (2018). Advanced learners' foreign language-related emotions across the four skills. *Studies in Second Language Learning and Teaching*, *8*(1), 127–147. https://doi.org/10.14746/ssllt.2018.8.1.6

Pink, S. (2008). An urban tour: The sensory sociality of ethnographic place-making. *Ethnography*, *9*(2), 175–196. doi:10.1177/1466138108089467

Pittas, P. (2011). Questioning Who We Are While Reading Ota Benga, The Pygmy in the Zoo and Joseph Conrad's Heart of Darkness. *Ágora*, *20*, 1–2.

Pizzo, L., & Chilvers, A. (2019). Assessment of language and literacy in children who are d/deaf and hard of hearing. *Education Sciences*, *9*(3), 223. doi:10.3390/educsci9030223

Poll, P. D. K. (2019). *Frustration in the schools: PDK's poll of public's attitudes toward the public schools.* https://pdkpoll.org/results

Poveda, D. (2012). Literacy artifacts and the semiotic landscape of a Spanish secondary school. *Reading Research Quarterly*, *47*(1), 61–88. doi:10.1002/RRQ.010

Premack, D., & Woodruff, G. (1978). Does the chimpanzee have a theory of mind? *Behavioral and Brain Sciences*, *1*(4), 515–526. doi:10.1017/S0140525X00076512

Prensky, M. (2001). Digital Natives, Digital Immigrants Part 2: Do They Really Think Differently? *On the Horizon*, *9*(6), 1–6. doi:10.1108/10748120110424843

Pre-Service Teachers' Perceptions about Discussing Race in Social Studies, Multicultural Education. (2017). Retrieved February 12, 2021, from https://eric.ed.gov/?id=EJ1150569

Probyn, M. (2015). Pedagogical Translanguaging: Bridging discourses in South African science classrooms. *Language and Education*, *29*(3), 218–234. doi:10.1080/09500782.2014.994525

Project Zero. (2016). Retrieved December 12, 2016, from www.pz.harvard.edu/ projects/

Przybylski, L. (2020). *Hybrid ethnography: Online, offline, and in between.* SAGE Publications.

Quennerstedt, A. (2019). Teaching about and through children's human rights in early school years. In A. Quennerstedt (Ed.), Teaching children's human rights in early childhood education and school: Educational aims, content and processes (pp. 56-73). Utgivare: Örebro University.

Quijano, A. (2010). Colonialidade do poder e classificação social [Coloniality of power and social classification]. In Epistemologias do Sul [Epistemologies of the South] (pp. 68-107). Editora Cortez.

Quintero, E. (2008). La pedagogía crítica y los mundos de niños y niñas. In P. McLaren & J. L. Kincheloe (Eds.), Pedagogía Crítica: De qué hablamos, dónde estamos (pp. 277-286). Graó.

Ramírez, J. P. (2021, January 4). Playing the 'Green Lottery': Life Inside Colombia's Emerald Mines. *The New York Times*. https://www.nytimes.com/2021/01/04/travel/colombia-emerald-mines.html

Ramos, C., Nieto, A. M., & Chaux, E. (2007). Aulas en Paz: Resultados preliminares de un programa multicomponente. *Revista Interamericana de Educación para la Democracia, 1*, 36–56.

Rappel, L. J. (2009). *International awareness in second language education: Reflecting on my practice of ELT* [Unpublished master thesis]. Athabasca University, Canada.

Ravitch, D. (2020). *Slaying Goliath: The passionate resistance to privatization and the fight to save America's public schools*. Alfred A. Knopf.

Rede, P. (2021). *National Survey of Food Insecurity in the Context of the Covid-19 Pandemic in Brazil*. https://bit.ly/3ONXlau

Reimagining Migration. (2022). Retrieved on March 26, 2022, from http://www.pz.harvard.edu/projects/re-imagining-migration

Resnick, L., & Snow, C. (2009). *Speaking and listening for preschool through third grade*. University of Pittsburg and The National Center on Education and the Economy.

Retherford, K. S. (1993). *Guide to analysis of language transcripts* (2nd ed.). Thinking Publication.

Rex, L., Murnen, T., Hobbs, J., & McEachen, D. (2002). Teachers' Pedagogical Stories and the Shaping of Classroom Participation: "The Dancer" and "Graveyard Shift at the 7-11". *American Educational Research Journal, 39*(3), 765–796. doi:10.3102/00028312039003765

Reyes, C. C., Haines, S. J., & Clark, K. (2021). *Humanizing methodologies in educational research: Centering non-dominant communities*. Teachers College Press.

Richards, R. (2020). Exploring Emotions in Language Teaching. *RELC Journal*. doi:10.1177/0033688220927531

Rico, D., & Barreto, I. (2022). Unfreezing of the conflict due to the peace agreement with FARC–EP in Colombia: Signature (2016) and implementation (2018). *Peace and Conflict, 28*(1), 22–33. doi:10.1037/pac0000545

Riessman, C. K. (2008). Narrative methods for the human sciences. Sage Publishing.

Rinaldi, C., Reggio Children, & Project Zero. (2001). Documentation and assessment: What is the relationship? In Making learning visible: Children as individual and group learners. Reggio Children srl.

Rincón, J., & Clavijo, A. (2016). Fostering EFL learners' literacies through local inquiry in a multimodal experience. *Colombian Applied Linguistics Journal, 18*(2), 67–82. doi:10.14483/calj.v18n2.10610

Ritchhart, R. (2015). *Creating cultures of thinking: the 8 forces we must master to truly transform our schools*. Jossey Bass.

Ritchhart, R. (2015). *Creating cultures of thinking: The 8 forces we must master to truly transform our schools*. Jossey-Bass.

Ritchhart, R. (2015). *Creating cultures of thinking: The 8 forces we must master to truly trasform our schools*. Jossey-Bass.

Ritchhart, R., Church, M., & Morrison, K. (2011). *Making thinking visible: How to promote engagement, understanding, and independence for all learners*. Jossey-Bass.

Ritchhart, R., Church, M., & Morrison, K. (2011). *Making Thinking Visible: How to Promote Engagement, Understanding, and Independence for All Learners*. Jossey-Bass.

Ritchhart, R., & Perkins, D. N. (2008). Making thinking visible. *Educational Leadership*, 65(5), 57–61.

Ritchhart, R., & Perkins, D. N. (2008). Making Thinking Visible. *Educational Leadership*, 65(5), 57–61.

Rithchhart, R. (2019). *Intellectual character: What it is, why it matters and how to get it*. Jossey Bass.

Rithchhart, R., Church, M., & Morrison, K. (2011). *Making Thinking Visible*. Jossey Bass.

Robin, B. (2006). The educational uses of digital storytelling. In *Proceedings of Society for Information Technology & Teacher Education International Conference* (pp.709-716). Chesapeake, VA: AACE.

Robin, B. (2006). The educational uses of digital storytelling. In *Proceedings of Society for Information Technology & Teacher Education International Conference*. Chesapeake, VA: AACE.

Robin, B. R., & McNeil, S. G. (2012). What educators should know about teaching digital storytelling. *Digital Education Review*, 22, 37–51.

Robson, M. (2002). "Brainstorming". Problem-solving in groups. Gower.

Robson, S. (2012). *Developing thinking and understanding in Young children; an introduction for students*. Routledge. doi:10.4324/9780203133354

Roche, J. M., & Arnold, H. S. (2018). The effects of emotion suppression during language planning and production. *Journal of Speech, Language, and Hearing Research: JSLHR*, 61(8), 2076–2083.

Rodriguez Martinez, A. K. (2017). *An exploration of young English learners' reading experiences in response to critical literacy read-alouds* [Unpublished master's thesis]. Universidad Pontificia Bolivariana, Medellín, Colombia.

Rogers, S. J., Young, G. S., Cook, I., Giolzetti, A., & Ozonoff, S. (2008). Deferred and immediate imitation in regressive and early onset autism. *Journal of Child Psychology and Psychiatry, and Allied Disciplines*, 49(4), 449–457. doi:10.1111/j.1469-7610.2007.01866.x PMID:18221343

Romeo, R. R., Leonard, J. A., Robinson, S. T., West, M. R., Mackey, A. P., Rowe, M. L., & Gabrieli, J. D. E. (2018). Beyond the 30-Million-Word Gap: Children's Conversational Exposure Is Associated with Language-Related Brain Function. *Psychological Science*, 29(5), 700–710. doi:10.1177/0956797617742725 PMID:29442613

Rosenblatt, L. M. (2005). *Making meaning with texts*. Heinemann.

Rosen, R. (2000). Perspectives of the Deaf community on early identification and intervention: A case for diversity and partnerships. *Seminars in Hearing*, 21(04), 327–342. doi:10.1055-2000-13468

Roth, F. P., & Spekman, N. J. (1984). Assessing the pragmatic abilities of children: Part 1. Organizational framework and assessment parameters. *The Journal of Speech and Hearing Disorders*, 49(1), 2–11. doi:10.1044/jshd.4901.02 PMID:6700199

Rouget, G., & Buckner, M. (2011). Musical efficacy: Musicking to survive — The case of the pygmies. *Yearbook for Traditional Music*, 43, 89-121.

Ruddell, R. B., & Unrau, N. J. (2013). Reading as a motivated meaning-construction process: The reader, the text, and the teacher. In D. A. Alvermann, N. J. Unrau, & R. B. Ruddell (Eds.), *Theoretical models and processes of reading* (6th ed., pp. 1015–1068). International Reading Association.

Ruiz, D., Mejía, L., Benavides, M., Serna, C., & Villegas, F. (2017). Narrativas de paz al final de la guerra: Experiencia de reconciliación y diálogo en la I.E. San Vicente de Paúl. *La Vicentina*, *1*, 38–43.

Rushton, S. P., Eitelgeorge, J., & Zickafoose, R. (2003). Connecting Brian Cambourne's conditions of learning theory to brain/mind principles: Implications for early childhood educators. *Early Childhood Education Journal*, *31*(1), 11–21. doi:10.1023/A:1025128600850

Sacks, H., Schegloff, E. A., & Jefferson, G. (1974). A simplest systematics for the organization of turn taking for conversation. *Language*, *50*(4), 696–735. doi:10.1353/lan.1974.0010

Sahli, A. S., & Belgin, E. (2017). Adaptation, validity, and reliability of the Preschool Language Scale-Fifth Edition (PLS-5) in the Turkish context: The Turkish Preschool Language Scale-5 (TPLS-5). *International Journal of Pediatric Otorhinolaryngology*, *98*, 143–149. doi:10.1016/j.ijporl.2017.05.003 PMID:28583491

Sahni, U. (2007). Children's appropriate literacy: Empowering pedagogy from young children's perspective. In B. Comber & A. Simpson (Eds.), *Negotiating critical literacies in the classroom* (pp. 19–37). Taylor and Francis.

Said, E. W. (1995). *Orientalism*. Penguin.

Salali, G. D., Chaudhary, N., Bouer, J., Thompson, J., Vinicius, L., & Migliano, A. B. (2019). Development of social learning and play in BaYaka hunter-gatherers of Congo. *Scientific Reports*, *9*(1), 1–10. doi:10.103841598-019-47515-8 PMID:31367002

Salmon, A. K. (2010). Making thinking visible through action research. *Early Childhood Education*, *39*(1), 15-21.

Salmon, A., & Melliou, K. (2021). Understanding and facing migration through stories for influence. In *Handbook of research on promoting social justice for immigrants and refugees through active citizenship and intercultural education*. IGI Global. https://www.igi-global.com/chapter/understanding-and-facing-migration-through-stories-for-influence/282314

Salmon, A. (2016). Learning by thinking during play: The power of reflection to aid performance. *Early Child Development and Care*, *186*(3), 480–496. doi:10.1080/03004430.2015.1032956

Salmon, A. (2018). *Frameworks That Promote Authentic Learning. Authentic Teaching and Learning for PreK-Fifth Grade: Advice from Practitioners and Coaches*. Routledge. doi:10.4324/9781351211505

Salmon, A. K. (2010). *Tools to enhance young children's thinking*. Young Children's. NAEYC.

Salmon, A. K., & Barrera, M. X. (2021). Intentional questioning to promote thinking and learning thinking skills and creativity. *Thinking Skills and Creativity*, *40*, 1–10. doi:10.1016/j.tsc.2021.100822

Salmon, A. K., Gangotena, M. V., & Melliou, K. (2017). Becoming Globally Competent Citizens: A Learning Journey of Two Classrooms in an Interconnected World. *Early Childhood Education Journal*, *46*(3), 301–312. https://doi.org/10.1007/s10643-017-0860-z

Salmon, A., & Lucas, T. (2011). Exploring young children's conceptions about thinking. *Journal of Research in Childhood Education*, *25*(4), 364–375. doi:10.1080/02568543.2011.605206

Salmon, A., & Melliou, K. (2021). Understanding and Facing Migration Through Stories for Influence. In I. M. Gómez Barreto (Ed.), *Handbook of Research on Promoting Social Justice for Immigrants and Refugees Through Active Citizenship and Intercultural Education* (pp. 205–231). IGI Global. doi:10.4018/978-1-7998-7283-2.ch011

Compilation of References

Sanders, D. A. (1982). *Aural rehabilitation: A management model* (2nd ed.). Prentice-Hall.

Santamaría, J. I. (2017). Red de escuelas Ruk'u'x Qatinamït y revitalización del idioma kaqchikel. *Onomázein, NE, 3*(3), 115–136. doi:10.7764/onomazein.amerindias.07

Santos Alves, S., & Mendes, L. (2006). Awareness and Practice of Plurilingualism and Intercomprehension in europe. *Language and Intercultural Communication, 6*(3–4), 211–218. doi:10.2167/laic248.0

Santos, P. C. (2012, July 12). *Aldeia Tekoa Pyau: o desafio de ser vizinha da cidade* [Aldeia Tekoa Pyau: the challenge of being the neighbor of the city]. Portal do Aprendiz. UOL. https://bit.ly/3Kr9tuz

Sarno, L. (1993). *Song from the forest. My life among the Ba-Benjellé Pygmies*. Bantam Press.

Saunders, R. A. (2019). Reimagining the colonial wildersness: 'Africa', imperialism and the geographical legerdemain of the Vorrh. *Cultural Geographies, 26*(2), 177–194. doi:10.1177/1474474018811669

Savasir, I., Sezgin, N., & Erol, N. (1994). *Ankara Gelişim Tarama Envanteri (AGTE)* [Ankara Developmental Screening Inventory]. Turkish Psychological Association.

Sayer, P. (2010). Using the Linguistic Landscape as a pedagogical resource. *ELT Journal, 64*(2), 143–154. doi:10.1093/elt/ccp051

Scalise Sugiyama, M. (2017). Oral storytelling as evidence of pedagogy in forager societies. *Frontiers in Psychology, 8*, 1–11. doi:10.3389/fpsyg.2017.00471 PMID:28424643

Scarborough, H. (2001). *Connecting early language and literacy to later reading (dis)abilities: Evidence, theory, and practice*. Guilford Press, Handbook for research in early literacy.

Schank, R. (1990). *Tell me a story: Narrative and intelligence*. Northwestern University Press.

Schank, R. C. (1999). *Dynamic memory revisited*. Cambridge University Press. doi:10.1017/CBO9780511527920

Schirmer, R. B. (2000). *Language and literacy development in children who are deaf*. Allyn and Bacon, Inc.

Schleicher, A. (2020). *The impact of COVID-19 on education: Insights from education at a glance 2020*. https://www.oecd.org/education/the-impact-of-covid-19-on-education-insights-education-at-a-glance-2020.pdf

Schmid, C. (2001). *The politics of language: Conflict, identity, and cultural pluralism in comparative perspective*. Oxford University Press.

Schneider, C. (2016). Talking around the texts: Literacy in a multilingual Papua New Guinean community. *Written Language and Literacy, 19*(1), 1–34. doi:10.1075/wll.19.1.01sch

Schumann. (1999). *The Neurobiology of Affect in Language Learning*. Blackwell Publishers.

Secretaría de Educación Pública de México. (2014). *Estrategias y técnicas didácticas*. Recuperado de http://iteatlaxcala.inea.gob.mx/SEducativos/Formacion/ESTRATEGIAS%20Y%20TECNICAS%20DIDACTICAS.pdf

Sehyr, Z., & Emmorey, K. (2022). Contribution of lexical quality and sign language variables to reading comprehension. *Journal of Deaf Studies and Deaf Education, 27*(4), 1–18. doi:10.1093/deafed/enac018 PMID:35775152

Shafi, S., Kazmi, S. H., & Asif, R. (2020). Benefits of code-switching in language learning classroom at University of Education Lahore. *International Research Journal of Management. IT and Social Sciences, 7*(1), 227–234. doi:10.21744/irjmis.v7n1.842

Shakib, S. M. P. (2010). *White Paper* [Film]. Seyed Mohsen Pourmohseni Shakib.

Shakib, S. M. P. (2012). *Game Over* [Film]. Seyed Mohsen Pourmohseni Shakib.

Shao, K., Pekrun, R., & Nicholson, L. J. (2019). Emotions in classroom language learning: What can we learn from achievement emotion research? *System*, *86*, 102121. https://doi.org/10.1016/j.system.2019.102121

Sharkey, J., Clavijo Olarte, A., & Ramírez, L. M. (2016). Developing a Deeper Understanding of Community-Based Pedagogies with Teachers: Learning with and From Teachers in Colombia. *Journal of Teacher Education*, *67*(4), 306–319. doi:10.1177/0022487116654005

Shintaku, K. (2022). Self-directed learning with anime: A case of Japanese language and culture. *Foreign Language Annals*, *55*(1), 283–308. doi:10.1111/flan.12598

Shohamy, E., & Gorter, D. (Eds.). (2009). *Linguistic Landscape: Expanding the Scenery*. Routledge.

Short, K. G. (2018). Globalizing literature in the English Language Arts classroom. *English Journal*, *108*(2), 108–110.

Short, K. G., Lynch-Brown, C., & Tomlinson, C. M. (2014). *Essentials of children's literature*. Pearson.

Short, K., Day, D., & Schroeder, J. (Eds.). (2016). *Teaching globally: Reading the world through literature*. Stenhouse Publishers.

Silberman, C. E. (1970). *Crisis in the classroom: The remaking of American education*. Random House.

Silvers, P., Shorey, M., & Crafton, L. (2010). Critical literacy in a primary multiliteracies classroom: The Hurricane Group. *Journal of Early Childhood Literacy*, *10*(4), 379–409. doi:10.1177/1468798410382354

Silvestri, J., & Wang, Y. (2018). A grounded theory of effective reading by profoundly Deaf adults. *American Annals of the Deaf*, *162*(5), 419–444. doi:10.1353/aad.2018.0002 PMID:29478997

Skinner, B. F. (1957). *Verbal behavior*. Copley Publishing Group. doi:10.1037/11256-000

Sleeter, C. E. (2005). *Un-standardizing curriculum: Multicultural teaching in the standards based classroom*. Teachers College Press.

Sleeter, C. E., & Grant, C. A. (2009). *Making Choices for Multicultural Education: Five Approaches to Race, Class and Gender* (6th ed.). Wiley & Sons, Inc. (Original work published 1999)

Sleeter, C., & Flores Carmona, J. (2017). *Un-standardizing Curriculum. Multicultural Teaching in the Standards Based-Classroom*. Teachers College Press.

Smith, F. (1987). *Joining the literacy club: Further essays in education*. Heineman.

Snyder, T. (2007). *On Tyranny: Twenty lessons from the 20th century*. Academic Press.

Song, S. (2020). Multiculturalism. *The Stanford Encyclopedia of Philosophy*. Available at https://plato.stanford.edu/archives/fall2020/entries/multiculturalism

Sorrels, B. (2017). *Reaching and teaching children exposed to trauma*. Gryphon House Inc.

Southern Poverty Law Center Report. (2020). *The year in hate and extremism 2019*. https://www.splcenter.org/news/2020/03/18/year-hate-and-extremism-2019

Spencer-Oatey, H. (2008). *Culturally Speaking: Culture, communication and politeness theory*. Bloomsbury Publishing.

Stake, R. (1995). *The art of case study research*. Sage Publications.

Compilation of References

Star, S., & Griesemer, J. (1989). Institutional ecology, translations and boundary objects: Amateurs and professionals in Berkeley's Museum of Vertebrate Zoology, 1907-39. *Social Studies of Science*, *3*(19), 387–420. doi:10.1177/030631289019003001

Steffensen, S. V., & Kramsch, C. (2017). The ecology of second language acquisition and socialization. In P. Duff & S. May (Eds.), *Language Socialization* (3rd ed., pp. 17–32). Springer., doi:10.1007/978-3-319-02255-0_2

Stetsenko, A. (2017). *The transformative mind: Expanding Vygotsky's approach to development and education*. Cambridge University Press. doi:10.1017/9780511843044

Stetsenko, A. (2019). Radical-Transformative Agency: Continuities and Contrasts With Relational Agency and Implications for Education. *Front. Educ*, *4*(148), 1–13. doi:10.3389/feduc.2019.00148

Stetsenko, A. (2020). Radical-Transformative Agency: Developing a Transformative Activist Stance on a Marxist-Vygotskyan Foundation. In A. Tanzi Neto, F. Liberali, & M. Dafermos (Eds.), *Revisiting Vygotsky for Social Change: Bringing together theory and practice* (pp. 31–63). Peter Lang.

Stone, P. (1988). *Blueprint for developing Conversational competence: A planning / instruction model with detailed scenarios*. Alexander Graham Bell Association for the Deaf.

Storbeck, C., & Calvert-Evans, J. (2008). Towards integrated practices in early detection of and intervention for Deaf and hard of hearing children. *American Annals of the Deaf*, *153*(3), 314–321. doi:10.1353/aad.0.0047 PMID:18807406

Strauss, V. (2022, March 22). Teachers to cult warriors: Stop treating us as enemies. *The Washington Post*. https://www.washingtonpost.com/education/2022/03/22/teachers-demand-freedom-to-teach/?fbclid=IwAR1MfM78LuuDeARr3nZ-yPYDDzRotPYgwn84kP9DeMOz7O2ekmQDXJUfCdc

Street, B. (2013, September 27). *Multimodality and new literacy studies: What does it mean to talk about 'texts' today?* [Conference session]. Online Talk for Universidad Pontificia Bolivariana: Medellín-Colombia, King's College London.

Street, B. (1984). *Literacy in theory and practice*. Cambridge University Press.

Street, B. (2003). What's new in new literacies studies? Critical approaches to literacy in theory and practice. *Current Issues in Comparative Education*, *5*(2), 77–91.

Street, B. (2012). Society Reschooling. *Reading Research Quarterly*, *2*(47), 216–227. doi:10.1002/RRQ.017

Stribling, S. M. (2014). Creating a critical literacy milieu in a kindergarten classroom. *Journal of Language & Literacy Education*, *10*(1), 45–63.

Strickland, D., & Schickedanz, J. A. (2009). *Learning about print in preschool: Working with letters, words and beginning links with phonemic awareness* (2nd ed.). International Reading Association.

Strom, A. (2021, October 15). *Thinking Routines for a World on the Move. Re-Imagining Migration*. Retrieved January 4, 2021, from https://reimaginingmigration.org/thinking-routines-for-learning-to-live-in-a-world-on-the-move/

Suárez-Orozco, C., Motti-Stefanidi, F., Marks, A., & Katsiaficas, D. (2018). An integrative risk and resilience model for understanding the adaptation of immigrant-origin children and youth. *The American Psychologist*, *73*(6), 781–796. doi:10.1037/amp0000265 PMID:30188166

Suárez-Orozco, M., & Suárez-Orozco, C. (2013, Fall). Taking perspective: Context, culture, and history. In M. G. Hernández, J. Nguyen, C. L. Saetermoe, & C. Suárez-Orozco (Eds.), *Frameworks and ethics for research with immigrants: New directions for child and adolescent development* (Vol. 141, pp. 9–23). Jossey-Bass.

Subbiah, K., Mason, C., Gaffney, M., & Grosse, S. (2018). Progress in documented early identification and intervention for deaf and hard of hearing infants: CDC's hearing screening and follow-up survey, united states, 2006–2016. *Journal of Early Hearing Detection and Intervention*, *3*(2), 1–7. PMID:31745502

Swain, M. (2000). The output hypothesis and beyond: Mediating acquisition through collaborative dialogue. In J. P. Lantolf (Ed.), *Sociocultural theory and second language learning* (pp. 97–114). Oxford University Press.

Swain, M. (2001). Integrating language and content teaching through collaborative tasks. *Canadian Modern Language Review*, *58*(1), 44–63.

Swain, M. (2006). Languaging, agency and collaboration in advanced second language proficiency. In H. Byrnes (Ed.), *Advanced language learning: The contribution of Halliday and Vygotsky* (pp. 95–108). Continuum., doi:10.5040/9781474212113.ch-004

Swain, M. (2010). 'Talking-it-through': Languaging as a source of learning. In R. Batstone (Ed.), *Sociocognitive perspectives on language use and language learning* (pp. 112–130). Oxford University Press.

Swain, M., & Watanabe, Y. (2013). Languaging: Collaborative dialogue as a source of second language learning. In C. Chapelle (Ed.), *The encyclopedia of applied linguistics* (pp. 1–8). Blackwell Publishing., doi:10.1002/9781405198431.wbeal0664

Swedberg, R. (2020). Exploratory research. In C. Elman, J. Mahoney, & J. Gerring (Eds.), *The production of knowledge: Enhancing progress in social science* (pp. 17–41). Cambridge University Press. doi:10.1017/9781108762519.002

Swennen, A., & White, E. (Eds.). (2021). *Being a Teacher Educator*. Routledge.

Syverud, S., Guardino, C., & Selznick, D. (2009). Teaching phonological skills to a Deaf first graders: A promising strategy. *American Annals of the Deaf*, *154*(4), 382–388. doi:10.1353/aad.0.0113 PMID:20066920

Szarfenberg, R. (2006). *Marginalizacja i wykluczenie społeczne. Wykłady*. Retrieved June, 2022 from http://www.owes.info.pl/biblioteka/wyklad_wykluczenie_spoleczne.pdf

Tait, M., De Raeve, L., & Nikolopoulos, T. P. (2007). Deaf children with cochlear implants before the age of 1 year: Comparison of preverbal communication with normally hearing children. *International Journal of Pediatric Otorhinolaryngology*, *71*(10), 1605–1611. doi:10.1016/j.ijporl.2007.07.003 PMID:17692931

Tan, P. L., & McWilliam, E. (2009). From literacy to multiliteracies: Diverse learners and pedagogical practice. *Pedagogies*, *4*(3), 213–225. doi:10.1080/15544800903076119

Tasker, S. L., Nowakowski, M. E., & Schmidt, L. A. (2010). Joint attention and social competence in deaf children with cochlear implants. *Journal of Developmental and Physical Disabilities*, *22*(5), 509–532. doi:10.100710882-010-9189-x

Tatto, M. A., & Coupland, D. B. (2003). Teacher education and teachers' beliefs": Theoretical and measurement concerns. In J. Raths & A. McAninch (Eds.), *Teacher beliefs and classroom performance: The impact of teacher education* (pp. 123–182). Information Publishing Age.

Taylor, S. K., & Mohanty, A. K. (2020). A multi-perspective tour of best practices: Challenges to implementing best practices in complex plurilingual contexts—The case of South Asia. In E. Piccardo, A. Germain-Rutherford, & G. Lawrence (Eds.), Routledge Handbook of Plurilingual Language Education. Routledge.

Taylor, F. (2003). Content analysis and gender stereotypes in children's books. *Teaching Sociology*, *31*(3), 300–311. doi:10.2307/3211327

Compilation of References

Teaching hard history: A framework for teaching American slavery. (n.d.). Learning for Justice. Retrieved March 10, 2021, from https://www.learningforjustice.org/sites/default/files/2021-11/LFJ-2111-Teaching-Hard-History-K-5-Framework-November-2021-11172021.pdf

Teale, W. H., Hoffman, J., Paciga, K., Garrete, L. J., Richardson, S., & Berkel, C. (2009). Early literacy: Then and now. In J. V. Hoffman & Y.M., Goodman (Eds.), Changing literacies for changing times: An historical perspective on the future of reading, public policy and classroom practices (pp. 76-97). Routledge.

Temel, Z. F., Ersoy, O., Avcı, N., & Turla, A. (2004). *Gazi Erken Çocukluk Değerlendirme Aracı (GEÇDA)* [Gazi early childhood assessment tool]. Matsa.

Temple, C., Martinez, M., & Yokota, J. (2019). *Children's books in children's hands: An introduction to their literature.* Pearson.

Terrell, P., & Watson, M. (2018). Laying a firm foundation: Embedding evidence-based emergent literacy practices into early intervention and preschool environments. *Language, Speech, and Hearing Services in Schools, 49*(2), 148–164. doi:10.1044/2017_LSHSS-17-0053 PMID:29621796

Texas Education Association. (2021). *Annual Statewide Report on Language Acquisition for Deaf and Hard of Hearing and Deafblind Students 0-8 Years of Age.* https://tea.texas.gov/reports-and-data/legislative-reports

The New London Group. (1996). A pedagogy of multiliteracies: Designing social futures. *Harvard Educational Review, 66*(1), 60–93. doi:10.17763/haer.66.1.17370n67v22j160u

The United Nations. (1948). *Universal Declaration of Human Rights.* Author.

The United Nations. (1989). Convention on the Rights of the Child. *Treaty Series, 1577,* 3.

Thurlow, C., & Jaworski, A. (2011). Tourism discourse: Languages and banal globalization. *Applied Linguistics Review, 2*(2011), 285–312. doi:10.1515/9783110239331.285

Tibbitts, F. (2017). Evolution of human rights education models. In M. Bajaj (Ed.), *Human rights education: Theory, research, praxis* (pp. 69–95). University of Pennsylvania Press. doi:10.9783/9780812293890-005

Tishman, S., & Palmer, P. (2006). *Artful Thinking. Stronger Thinking and Learning through the power of Art. Final Report.* Project Zero-Harvard Graduate School of Education.

Tishman, S., Jay, E., & Perkins, D. (1993). Teaching thinking dispositions: From transmission to enculturation. *Theory into Practice, 32*(3), 147–153. doi:10.1080/00405849309543590

Toe, D. M., & Paatsch, L. E. (2013). The conversational skills of school-aged children with cochlear implants. *Cochlear Implants International, 14*(2), 67–79. doi:10.1179/1754762812Y.0000000002 PMID:23453220

Toe, D., Beattie, R., & Barr, M. (2007). The development of pragmatic skills in children who are severely and profoundly deaf. *Deafness & Education International, 9*(2), 101–117. doi:10.1179/146431507790560011

Tomaszewski, P., Krzysztofiak, P., & Moron, E. (2019). From sign language to spoken language? A new discourse of language development in Deaf children. *Psychology of Language and Communication, 23*(1), 48–84. doi:10.2478/plc-2019-0004

Topbaş, S. (2006). Turkish articulation and phonology test (SST): Validity, reliability and standardization. *Turkish Journal of Psychology, 21*(58), 39–58.

Topbaş, S., & Güven, S. (2011). *Türkçe Erken Dil Gelişimi Testi (TEDİL)* [Test of Early Language Development-Third Edition: Turkish]. Detay Publishing.

Topbaş, S., & Güven, S. (2013). *Türkçe Okul Çağı Dil Gelişimi Testi (TODİL)* [Test of Language Development-Fourth Edition: Turkish]. Detay Publishing.

Tough, J. (1981). *Talk for teaching and learning* (2nd ed.). Ward Lock Educational.

Traxler, C. (2000). The Stanford Achievement Test, 9th Edition: National norming and performance standards for Deaf and hard-of-hearing students. Journal of Deaf Studies & Deaf Education, 5(4), 337. doi:10.1093/deafed/5.4.337

Trigos-Carrillo, L. (2019). A Critical Sociocultural Perspective to Academic Literacies in Latin America. Íkala, 24(1), 13-26.

Trigos-Carrillo, L., Rogers, R., & Jorge, M. (2021). Critical Literacy: Global Histories and Antecedents. In The Handbook of Critical Literacies (pp. 10-23). Routledge.

Trillos, M., & Etxebarria, M. (2002). Legislación, política lingüística y multilingüismo en Colombia. In Ponencia presentada en el Congreso Mundial sobre Políticas Lingüísticas Linguapax IX, celebrado en Barcelona, España, del (Vol. 16). Academic Press.

Tuck, E., & Yang, K. W. (2012). Decolonization is not a metaphor. *Decolonization*, *1*(1), 1–40.

Tuckwiller, E., Pullen, P., & Coyne, M. (2010). The use of regression discontinuity design in tiered intervention research: A pilot study exploring vocabulary instruction for at-risk kindergartners. *Learning Disabilities Research & Practice*, *25*(3), 137–150. doi:10.1111/j.1540-5826.2010.00311.x

Turnbull, M. C. (1974). *The Forest People*. Book Club Associates.

U.S. Bureau of Labor Statistics. (2021, May 18). *Foreign-born workers: Labor force characteristics–2020.* https://www.bls.gov/news.release/pdf/forbrn.pdf

U.S. Department of Education. (2016). *ED Facts Data Warehouse, 2014–15. SEA File C141, LEP Enrolled.* Digest of Education Statistics. https://nces.ed.gov/programs/digest/d16/tables/dt16_204.27.asp

UNESCO. (2015). *Global citizenship education: Topics and learning objectives.* Autor.

UNESCO. (2021). *Alfabetización para el desarrollo Febrero 19 de 2021.* https://es.unesco.org/news/alfabetizacion-desarrollo

UNICEF. (2020). *UNews.* https://news.un.org/en/tags/unicef

United Nations. (2022). *Sustainable Development Goals* https://www.un.org/sustainabledevelopment/

Uribe Mendoza, C. (2016). *El arte urbano y la producción de sentidos políticos juveniles. In Democracia y Participación Política.* Ibañez.

Urrea, A., & Trigos-Carrillo, L. (Article under review). Fostering Empathy Through Critical Literacies in Early Childhood Education. *Towards Authentic Peace Education.*

US Census Bureau. (2020). Retrieved in July 2022. https://usafacts.org/data/topics/people-society/population-and-demographics/our-changing-population/state/florida/county/miami-dade-county?endDate=2020-01-01&startDate=2010-01-01

Valdés, G. (2000). Introduction. In L. Sandstedt (Ed.), *Spanish for native speakers.* Heinle.

Valdés, G., Fishman, J. A., Chávez, R., & Pérez, W. (2006). *Developing minority language resources: The case of Spanish in California.* Multilingual Matters., doi:10.21832/9781853598999-004

Compilation of References

Van Sluys, K., Flint, A. S., & Lewison, M. (2005). Researching critical literacy: A critical study of analysis of classroom discourse. *Journal of Literacy Research*, *38*(2), 197–233. doi:10.120715548430jlr3802_4

Vanegas, M., Fernández, J., González, Y., Jaramillo, G., Muñoz, L., & Ríos, C. (2016). Linguistic discrimination in an English language teaching program: Voices of the invisible others. Íkala, Revista de Lenguaje y Cultura Medellín, 21(2), 133-151.

Vásquez, V. M. (November 1, 2017). Critical literacy. *Oxford Research Encyclopedia of Education,* 1-17.

Vasquez, V. M. (2004). *Negotiating critical literacy with young children.* Erlbaum. doi:10.4324/9781410611109

Vásquez, V. M. (2007-a). Constructing a critical literacy curriculum with young children. In B. Comber & A. Simpson (Eds.), *Negotiating critical literacies in the classroom* (pp. 55–67). Taylor and Francis.

Vásquez, V. M. (2007-b). Using the everyday to engage in critical literacy with young children. *The NERA Journal*, *43*(2), 6–11.

Vásquez, V. M. (2014). *Negotiating critical literacies with young children.* Routledge. doi:10.4324/9781315848624

Vásquez, V. M. (2016). *Critical literacy across the k-6 curriculum.* Routledge. doi:10.4324/9781315642277

Vasquez, V. M., & Felderman, C. B. (2012). *Technology and critical literacy in early childhood.* ProQuest Ebook Central. doi:10.4324/9780203108185

Vasquez, V. M., Janks, H., & Comber, B. (2019). Critical Literacy as a Way of Being and Doing. *Language Arts*, *96*(5), 13.

Vasquez, V. M., Janks, H., & Comber, B. (2019). Critical literacy as a way of being and doing. *Language Arts*, *96*(5), 300–311.

Vásquez, V. M., Muise, M. R., Adamson, S. C., Chiola-Nakai, D., & Shear, J. (2003). *Getting beyond "I like the book": Creating space for critical literacy in K-6 classrooms.* International Reading Association.

Vásquez, V. M., Tate, S. L., & Harste, J. C. (2013). *Negotiating critical literacies with teachers: Theoretical foundations and pedagogical resources for pre-service and in-service contexts.* Routledge. doi:10.4324/9780203081778

Velez-Ibanez, C. G. (1988). Networks of exchange among Mexicans in the U.S. and Mexico: Local level mediating responses to national and international transformations. *Urban Anthropology*, *17*(1), 27–51.

Velez-Ibanez, C. G., & Greenberg, J. B. (1992). Formation and transformation of funds of knowledge among U.S.-Mexican households. *Anthropology & Education Quarterly*, *23*(4), 313–335. doi:10.1525/aeq.1992.23.4.05x1582v

Venegas, H. (2017). Buen Vivir: Indigenous alternative to neoliberalism. *Newscoop.* https://bityli.com/hc0ASM

Vigotsky, L. (1979). El desarrollo de los procesos psicológicos superiores. *Critica*.

Viner, R. M., Russell, S. J., Croker, H., Packer, J., Ward, J., Stansfield, C., Mytton, O., Bonell, C., & Booy, R. (2020). School closure and management practices during coronavirus outbreaks including COVID-19: A rapid systematic review. *The Lancet. Child & Adolescent Health*, *4*(5), 397–404. doi:10.1016/S2352-4642(20)30095-X PMID:32272089

Visible Thinking. (2009). Visible Thinking Resource Book for Making Thinking Visible. Cambridge MA: Harvard University Press.

Vygotsky, LS (1978). *Mind in society: The development of higher psychological processes.* Academic Press.

Vygotsky, L. (1962). *Thought and language* (E. Hanf-Mann & G. Vakar, Trans.). MIT Press. doi:10.1037/11193-000

Vygotsky, L. (1978). *Mind in Society: The Development of Higher Psychological Processes*. Harvard University Press.

Vygotsky, L. S. (1978). *Mind in society: The development of higher psychological processes*. Harvard University Press.

Vygotsky, L. S. (1994a). The problem of the environment. In R. van der Veer & J. Valsiner (Eds.), *The Vygotsky reader*. Blackwell.

Vygotsky, L. S. (1994b). The socialist alteration of man. In R. van der Veer & J. Valsiner (Eds.), *The Vygotsky reader*. Blackwell.

Walsh, C. (2019). Gritos, gretas e semeaduras de vida: Entreteceres do pedagógico e do colonial [Cries, cracks, and sowings of life: Interweaving the pedagogical and the colonial]. In S. R. M. Souza & L. C. Santos (Eds.), *Entre-linhas: educação, fenomenologia e insurgência popular* [Between the lines: education, phenomenology and popular insurgency] (pp. 93–120). EDUFBA.

Walsh, C. (2019). *Pedagogías decoloniales: Prácticas insurgentes de resistir, (re)existir y (re)vivir (Pensamiento decolonial)- - Tomo II* (1st ed.). Editorial Abya-Yala.

Walsh, C. E. (2012). *Interculturalidad crítica y (de)colonialidad: Ensayos desde Abya Yala*. Abya-Yala.

Walsh, S. (2013). *Classroom Discourse and Teacher Development*. Edinburg University Press. doi:10.1515/9780748645190

Wang, Y. (2014). *Views and attitudes of staff and students towards the significance of intercultural awareness in foreign language teaching and learning in an Australian university context*. [Doctoral thesis, University of Tasmania]. https://eprints.utas.edu.au/18238/1/front-wang-2014-thesis.pdf

Wang, D. J., Trehub, S. E., Volkova, A., & Van Lieshout, P. (2013). Child implant users' imitation of happy-and sad-sounding speech. *Frontiers in Psychology*, *4*, 351. doi:10.3389/fpsyg.2013.00351 PMID:23801976

Wang, Y., Spychala, H., Harris, R., & Oetting, T. (2013). The effectiveness of phonics-based early intervention for deaf and hard of hearing preschool children and its possible impact on reading skills in elementary school: A case study. *American Annals of the Deaf*, *158*(2), 107–120. doi:10.1353/aad.2013.0021 PMID:23967767

Wang, Y., & Williams, C. (2014). Are we hammering square pegs into round holes?: An investigation of the meta-analyses of reading research with students who are D/deaf or hard of hearing and students who are hearing. *American Annals of the Deaf*, *159*(4), 323–345. doi:10.1353/aad.2014.0029 PMID:25669016

Wang, Z., Zhu, X., Fong, F. T., Meng, J., & Wang, H. (2020). Overimitation of children with cochlear implants or hearing aids in comparison with children with normal hearing. *Infants and Young Children*, *33*(1), 84–92. doi:10.1097/IYC.0000000000000157

Wargo, J. (2019). Sounding the garden, voicing a problem: Mobilizing critical literacy through personal digital inquiry with young children. *Language Arts*, *96*(5), 275–285.

Webb, M., Patton-Terry, N., Bingham, G., Puranik, C., & Lederberg, A. (2018). Factorial validity and measurement invariance of the Test of Preschool Early Literacy-Phonological Awareness Test among Deaf and hard-of-Hearing children and hearing children. *Ear and Hearing*, *39*(2), 278–292. doi:10.1097/AUD.0000000000000485 PMID:28837426

Wetherby, A. M., & Rodriguez, G. P. (1992). Measurement of communicative intentions in normally developing children during structured and unstructured contexts. *Journal of Speech and Hearing Research*, *35*(1), 130–138. doi:10.1044/jshr.3501.130 PMID:1735961

Whitehurst, G. J., & Lonigan, C. J. (1998). Child development and emergent literacy. *Child Development*, *68*(3), 848–872. doi:10.1111/j.1467-8624.1998.tb06247.x PMID:9680688

Compilation of References

Whitmore, K. F., Martens, P., Goodman, Y., & Owocki, G. (2005). Remembering critical lessons in early literacy research: A transactional perspective. *Language Arts*, *82*(4), 296–307.

Williams, H. M. A., & Bermeo, M. J. (2020). *A Decolonial Imperative: Pluriversal Rights Education*. Academic Press.

Willinksy, K. (2008). Of critical theory and critical literacy: Connections to the legacy of critical theory. In K. Cooper & R. E. White (Eds.), *Critical literacies in action: Social perspectives and teaching practices* (pp. 3–20). Sense Publishers.

Wiske, M. S. (Ed.). (1998). *Teaching for understanding: Linking research with practice*. Jossey-Bass.

Wisneski, D. (2019). Playing well with others: Collaborating on children's right to play. *Childhood Education*, *95*(6), 50–55. doi:10.1080/00094056.2019.1689060

Woodin, J. (2016). How to research interculturally and ethically. In Z. Hua (Ed.), *Research methods in intercultural communication: A practical guide* (pp. 103–119). Wiley Blackwell.

World Health Organization. (2021). *Deafness and hearing loss*. World Health Organization. https://www.who.int/news-room/fact-sheets/detail/deafness-and-hearing-loss

Wright, Q. (1942). *A study of war* (Vols. 1–2). University of Chicago Press.

Yalaz, K., Anlar, B., & Bayoğlu, B. (2009). *Denver II Developmental Screening Test, standardization for Turkish children*. Developmental Child Neurology Association.

Yasir, M. (2019). *Intercultural communication in a world of diversity*. [Doctoral thesis, Cape Breton University]. https://www.researchgate.net/publication/336769181_Intercultural_Communication_in_a_World_of_Diversity

Yin, R. K. (2009). *Case study research: Design and methods* (4th ed.). Sage., doi:10.3138/cjpe.30.1.108

Yont, K. M., Snow, C. E., & Vernon-Feagans, L. (2003). The role of context in mother-child interactions: An analysis of communicative intents expressed during toy play and book reading with 12-month-olds. *Journal of Pragmatics*, *35*(3), 435–454. doi:10.1016/S0378-2166(02)00144-3

Yoshinaga-Itano, C. (2003). From screening to early identification and intervention: Discovering predictors to successful outcomes for children with significant hearing loss. *Journal of Deaf Studies and Deaf Education*, *8*(1), 11–30. doi:10.1093/deafed/8.1.11 PMID:15448044

Yoshinaga-Itano, C. (2014). Principles and guidelines for early intervention after confirmation that a child is deaf or hard of hearing. *Journal of Deaf Studies and Deaf Education*, *19*(2), 143–175. doi:10.1093/deafed/ent043 PMID:24131505

Yoshinaga-Itano, C., Sedey, A., Coulter, D., & Mehl, A. (1998). Language of early- and later-identified children with hearing loss. *Pediatrics*, *102*(5), 1161–1171. doi:10.1542/peds.102.5.1161 PMID:9794949

Young, A. (2018). Deaf children and their families: Sustainability, sign language, and equality. *American Annals of the Deaf*, *1631*(1), 61–69. doi:10.1353/aad.2018.0011 PMID:29731473

Young, A., & Tattersall, H. (2007). Universal newborn hearing screening and early identification of deafness: Parents' responses to knowing early and their expectations of child communication development. *Journal of Deaf Studies and Deaf Education*, *12*(2), 209–220. doi:10.1093/deafed/enl033 PMID:17277310

Zadina, J. N. (2022). *Engaging The Cognitive Brain, The Emotional Brain, and the Heart of Learners: Science and Strategies*. http://www.brainresearch.us/blog.html?entry=engaging-the-cognitive-brain-the1

Zaghlawan, H. (2011). *A parent-implemented intervention to improve spontaneous imitation by young children with autism* [Unpublished doctoral dissertation]. University of Illinois, Urbana, IL, United States.

Zhao, Y., Wu, X., Sun, P., & Chen, H. (2021). Relationship between vocabulary knowledge and reading comprehension in Deaf and hard of hearing students. *Journal of Deaf Studies and Deaf Education*, *26*(4), 546–555. doi:10.1093/deafed/enab023 PMID:34265846

Zorfass, J., & Urbano, C. (2008). A description of foundation skills interventions for struggling middle-grade readers in four urban Northeast and Island Regions school district (Issues &Answers Repot, REL 2008-No.042). Washington, DC: U.S. Department of Education, Institute of Education Sciences, National Center for Education.

Zuk, J., Yu, X., Sanfilippo, J., Figuccio, M. J., Dunstan, J., Carruthers, C., Sideridis, G., Turesky, T. K., Gagoski, B., Grant, P. E., & Gaab, N. (2021). White matter in infancy is prospectively associated with language outcomes in kindergarten. *Developmental Cognitive Neuroscience*, *50*, 100973. doi:10.1016/j.dcn.2021.100973 PMID:34119849

About the Contributors

Angela K. Salmon is a researcher and educational entrepreneur recognized for building learning communities of practice and empowering teachers to gain ownership and agency in their teaching to advance early childhood education. She is an Associate Professor in Early Childhood Education at Florida International University and the founder of Visible Thinking South Florida initiative, a learning community of practice in Miami, Florida, United States. Dr. Salmon is Certified in Habits of Mind, leading trainings, and capacity building. Her research interests focus on the interplay between cognition, language, and literacy development embedded in global learning approaches. Dr. Salmon embraces children's learning with habits of mind, executive functions, metacognition, and teacher's discourse in the classroom. She draws from progressive ideas that lead to authentic and meaningful learning experiences including play and music. Angela was a former kindergarten teacher; founder of a Reggio Emilia inspired preschool in Miami and two preschools in her home country Ecuador. Her research emerges from insights gained through coaching teachers on the implementation of cutting-edge research-based ideas in the classroom. She is currently exploring the concept of collective stories for influence and multiliteracies to promote global competencies and inclusion. Dr. Salmon is a recognized international consultant, lecturer, and keynote speaker with engagements throughout USA, Canada, Central and South American countries, France, Greece, Spain, New Zealand, and Australia. She served as a faculty member at Harvard Project Zero (PZ) institute for 18 years. Through her long-standing partnership with PZ and the Institute Habits of Mind she developed numerous research initiatives and authored over 50 refereed publications and three books. In 2016 Dr. Salmon was invited as "Thinker in Residence" by the Independent Schools of Victoria in Melbourne Australia. She chaired seven editions of the International Visible Thinking Conference and was chair of the 18th edition of the International Conference on Thinking (ICOT18).

Amparo Clavijo-Olarte is Full Professor in the department of Applied Linguistics to TEFL at Universidad Dr. Amparo Clavijo-Olarte is Full Professor in the department of Applied Linguistics to TEFL at Universidad Distrital Francisco José de Caldas in Bogotá. Colombia. She is the founder of the research group Lectoescrinautas devoted to doing research with public school teachers in the different School Districts of Bogotá to expand the literacy practices inside the classrooms with the rich cultural and linguistic resources present in local communities. Her research interests focus on urban literacies, cultures, and pedagogies for language education. Dr. Clavijo was former editor of the Colombian Applied Linguistics Journal and director of the M.A. in Applied Linguistics at Universidad Distrital Francisco José de Caldas. She has published books with and for teachers in Spanish in Colombia, and book chapters and articles in English in the USA and Australia. She has been invited as visiting professor at the University of Arizona, Universidad de Santiago de Chile, Universidad Nacional de Costa Rica,

Pontificia Universidade Catolica São Paulo, and Universidad Autónoma de Baja California. She was a Fulbright guest researcher at University of New Hampshire 2016-2017. Dr. Clavijo has presented in international conferences of the International Research Association, The American Education Research Association and in local and national conferences. She is currently participating in a research project on Global change, local action: an ethnography of literacies for active citizenship with colleagues from Australia, Brasil, Colombia, and USA. She is part of a collective on Latin American Language Teacher Education for the Global South with colleagues from Brasil, Chile, and Colombia.

* * *

Myles Bittner in a PhD Student in the department of Language, Literacy & Culture at the University of Massachusetts Amherst. His research centers around literacy practices and how educators support and engage with global issues in early childhood education settings.

Tharrenos Bratitsis is a Full Professor at the Early Childhood Education Department, University of Western Macedonia, Greece and a director of the Creativity, Innovation and Technology in Education (CrInTE) Laboratory. He has participated in over 250 international conferences' scientific committees; is a member of the reviewers' board of 47 scientific journals (3 as an associate editor) and publishes regularly, having over 220 scientific papers with over 1000 citations on his work. He has participated in over 45 research funded projects, 23 as a coordinator (global or for UOWM). His research interests include Technology Enhanced Learning, Game-based Learning, Digital Storytelling, STEAM Education, Educational Robotics, Computer Supported Collaborative Learning and Learning Analytics.

Daniel Calderon-Aponte is an English teacher and researcher at Universidad Distrital in Bogotá, Colombia. He holds an MEd in English Teaching and Learning at Loyola University Chicago and an MA in Applied Linguistics at Universidad Distrital. His research interests encompass teacher education, culturally relevant literature, critical literacies, and teachers' identities.

Luzkarime Calle-Díaz holds a PhD in Education from Universidad del Norte, Colombia. Her research interests revolve around the role of language in peacebuilding in school and community contexts as well as the use of children's literature as a tool for citizenship and social justice education. She has ample experience in language teaching and teacher education in the Colombian Caribbean region.

Paula Renata Castillo is the Coordinator and Professor at the Education program in Universidad San Francisco de Quito. She holds a Ph.D. in Curriculum and Instruction from New Mexico State University. She was an early childhood teacher for ten years. Her research interests are children's literature, critical literacy, and bilingual education.

Johanna Choconta is a doctoral student in Education at the Universidad de La Sabana. Master in Early Childhood Studies from the University of Roehampton, London - England, Graduate in Child Pedagogy from the Universidad de La Sabana.

Sarah Evans is the Lower School Assistant Principal at North Broward Preparatory School. She is a National Board Certified Teacher and holds a Bachelor's Degree in Elementary Education and a Master's

About the Contributors

Degree in Languages Arts. Sarah is also a Thinking Maps Trainer and Write from the Beginning Trainer. Before joining the North Broward Preparatory School family, Sarah taught third grade at both a public and a private school. In addition, Sarah served as a kindergarten to 5th grade writing specialist where she designed writing curriculum, delivered professional development in the area of writing instruction, and worked with k-5 students to develop their writing skills. Sarah is most passionate about providing students with rich project-based learning experiences in which students have the opportunity to have an impact on their community and the world. Her work has been published in the book Authentic Teaching and Learning for PreK-Fifth Grade: Advice From Practitioners and Coaches and in several editions of the international magazine, Teachers Matter.

Joyce Fine is an associate professor in the Department of Teaching and Learning in the School of Education and Human Development in the College of Arts, Sciences, & Education at Florida International University. She teaches undergraduate and graduate courses in Reading and Language Arts. She was the Chair of the American Reading Forum, the President of the Organization of Teacher Educators in Literacy, and researched with the International Literacy Association. She has authored many articles and chapters on strategies for improving reading and writing for elementary and secondary students.

Esra Genc graduated from Karadeniz Technical University, department of special education, hearing impaired teaching program in 2012. She received her master's degree in 2016 and doctorate in 2022 at Anadolu University, special education department, education of the hearing impaired. Dr. Genc works as a research assistant at Tokat Gaziosmanpasa University, in Turkey. Her research interests include language and communication skills, measurement and evaluation of language and communication skills in children with hearing loss and qualitative research methods.

Jesús Guerra-Lyons is Assistant Professor at the Department of Spanish, Universidad del Norte (Colombia). He holds a Ph.D. in Applied Linguistics from the Hong Kong Polytechnic University. His research areas include functional linguistics, language pedagogy and critical literacies.

Rosa Julia Guzmán is a Postdoctorate in Social Sciences, Childhood and Youth, Catholic University of Sao Paulo - CLACSO Buenos Aires. Doctorate in Education, Nova University, Fort Lauderdale, Florida, United States. Master in Educational Research and Development, International Center for Education and Human Development (CINDE). Educational Psychology, Universsdad de La Sabana.

Kelly Hernandez currently works as an Academic Writing Coach at the Medical Campus of Miami Dade College (MDC). She also worked ten years at MDC in both student recruitment and curriculum/assessment design for English language learners. Prior to working at MDC, Dr. Hernandez taught workplace English and conducted multicultural communication workshops in Grand Rapids, MI. Kelly was credentialed as a Certified Diversity Professional from Cornell University in 2009. She received a Bachelor of Science in Foreign Service from Georgetown University and a Master of Arts in Teaching English as a Second Language from Michigan State University, and her doctorate is from the University of Miami in Higher Education Leadership. Dr. Hernandez has extensive experience in work and study abroad in South America and the Middle East. Kelly has served as a Women of Tomorrow mentor, Ronald McDonald House meal organizer, adult literacy tutor with the Miami Dade County public library system, and Crossroads Prison Ministry volunteer. She also serves on the Board of Directors of Many Hands International, an organization which sponsors an elementary school in Haiti.

Leanna Hodges is an experienced Teacher of the Deaf and hard of hearing. She is an educator who passionately loves and desires for the world to be a better place for her students. Leanna is an advocate for Deaf and hard of hearing students and their families to have the necessary supports so their child will have reading success. She also has her Bachelor's in Deaf Education from Baylor University, Master's in Deaf Education from Texas Woman's University, and is a Doctoral Candidate at Baylor University who will graduate with her Doctorate of Education in Learning and Organizational Change in May 2023.

Luciana Kool Modesto-Sarra is a Master's student in Applied Linguistics at the Pontifical Catholic University of São Paulo. She holds undergraduate degrees in Physical Education, Education, Language Arts (Portuguese and English), and Mathematics. She has a post-baccalaureate degree in Literacy, Bilingual Education, and Didactics to implement the National Common Curriculum Base and the International Baccalaureate program. She is a teacher at a bilingual and international school and a member of various research groups in Education, including the Research Group on Language and Activity in School Context (LACE), the Brincadas Project, and the Global Play Brigade. She has been working in Education since 1995.

Maria Dolores Lasso is currently appointed as Dean of Undergraduate Studies and Academic Affairs and full-time Education professor at Universidad San Francisco de Quito-USFQ a Liberal Arts university in Ecuador, South America. She teaches at USFQ's Education undergraduate (face to face and online) and graduate programs. She obtained her PhD degree in Education at New Mexico State University, her dissertation focuses on educational leadership and teacher education. She obtained her Master in Education degree from Boston University and an undergraduate degree in Elementary Education from the Pontifical Catholic University of Ecuador. She has been a teacher in Ecuador for more than two decades, focusing on higher education curriculum design, teacher education and educational improvement. She is currently responsible for implementing academic interventions and processes within all USFQ creating several opportunities for continuous improvement in all academic areas at USFQ.

Fernanda Liberali holds a Ph.D. in Applied Linguistics and Language Studies from the Pontifical Catholic University of São Paulo, having postdoctoral experience from the University of Helsinki, the Free University of Berlin, and Rutgers University. She is a professor-researcher at the Pontifical Catholic University of São Paulo, in the Department of Language Sciences and Philosophy and in the Graduate Programs of Applied Linguistics and Language Studies, Education of Teacher Educator, and Education and Curriculum. Fernanda also holds CNPq Productivity Scholarship, is the Research Groups Language in Activity Group in the School Context (LACE) leader, general coordinator of the Digitmed Program and the Brincadas Project, and co-founder of the Global Play Brigade.

Silvia López Angel, M.ED., is the founder and director at BaBidiBu preschool in Bogotá Colombia. She holds a degree in Psychology along with a Master's degree in Education focusing on Curriculum and Instruction in Early Childhood. In 2013 after attending Project Zero (PZ) summer institutes at the Harvard Graduate School of Education, she was nominated as a fellow of PZ Classroom. She has adopted Project Zero ideas into the school's curriculum particularly Visible Thinking, Teaching for Understand-

About the Contributors

ing, and Global Competency frameworks. As a passionate practitioner of PZ's ideas, Silvia collaborated with a book chapter around Pz's ideas and has presented globally at International Conference, most of them organized by CASIE and PZ. She is the co-creator and director of a Global Competency project and blog entitled mini-reporters with the world in mind.

Teresa Lucas holds a doctoral degree in Multilingual/Multicultural Education from Florida State University. She is a Teaching Professor of Foreign Language Education/TESOL at Florida International University.

Urszula Markowska-Manista conducts field research on migration and education in culturally diverse environments, childhood, and youth studies in the field of children's rights. She was director (FU Berlin 2016) and co-director (2017-2021 FH Potsdam) of the international MA Childhood Studies and Children's Rights (MACR) programme and is an assistant professor at the University of Warsaw (Faculty of Education). Markowska-Manista has conducted ethnographic research on children's rights in education in different contexts (Horn of Africa Central Africa, Central and Eastern Europe, and South Caucasus). Her work draws on inclusive and participatory approaches, indigenous and decolonial methodologies, ethical symmetry and the children's rights pedagogy of Janusz Korczak.

Larissa Mazuchelli is an Assistant Professor of English and Applied Linguistics at Federal University of Uberlandia in Brazil with research and teaching experience in language, culture, and cognition, language education, and aging. She holds a Ph.D. in Linguistics from the State University of Campinas and has received two Fulbright scholarships (Foreign Language Teaching Assistant 2013-2014 and Doctoral Dissertation Research Award 2018-2019). She is a member of the Research Group on Language and Activity in School Context (GP LACE) and an associate coordinator of the Study Group on Language in Aging and Pathologies (GELEP) and the Observatory of Ageism, which promotes interventions to raise awareness, combat ageism, and promote the health of aging people.

Rosa A. Medina-Riveros, Ph.D., is a member of LECTOESCRINAUTAS research Group at Universidad Distrital Francisco José de Caldas in Colombia. She is also a lecturer in the Language, Literacy, and Culture concentration at the University of Massachusetts-Amherst. Her interests are literacies and multilingualism.

Carmen Medrano has been in the field of early childhood education for over 30 years. She is graduated from Externado de Colombia University in Education in Bogotá Colombia, and holds a Master's and Doctorate degree in Education with concentration in Reading Education from Nova Southeastern University in Fort Lauderdale, Florida. She has been teaching at Florida International University, for over 17 years, and is also currently teaching at Nova Southeastern University, The focus of her research is language development particularly working with Hispanic children. Dr. Medrano is currently developing curriculum to help teachers in the early childhood field to improve young children´s vocabulary, and thinking skills. She conducted a research study in 2015 on language development of bilingual infant and toddlers from various family childcare homes in Miami. This work has been presented at various conferences including the National Association of Education of Young Children in Orlando, Florida in 2015. She is currently conducting an action research as a continuation of this work.

Kiriaki Melliou is an Education Coordinator at the 6th Peripheral Center of Educational Planning of Attica and among the authors of the new national curriculum (2021) of Early Childhood Education in Greece. She holds a doctoral degree (PhD) with honors from University of Western Macedonia in Early Childhood Education and a Masters of Educational Leadership with Distinction from Rhodes Aegean University. Her research interests focus on the use of Harvard's Project Zero frameworks and ideas to provide all students with powerful opportunities to thrive in the 21st century. In 2014, she became the first Greek educator who joined Harvard's "Out of Eden Learn" online learning community and was featured in the second OOEL "glimpses" video about exemplary classroom practice. She established and now mentors a vibrant OOEL teacher community with more than 1500 active members in Greece. In 2019 she was invited to serve as a Fellow at Project Zero's renowned annual conference at Harvard University—an indicator of the extremely high regard in which she is held at Project Zero. Kiriaki has contributed as an expert to national and international scientific projects awarded by the Ministry of Education and the Council of Europe, to develop methodology and electronic learning scenarios that use PZ's ideas to promote 21st century skills. She has published more than 30 research papers and presented in several international conferences. Since 2020 she has been teaching three graduate courses at the University of Western Macedonia under the topic of learning and thinking strategies for 21st century education.

María Clara Nader holds a degree in Humanities and Spanish Language. She was part of the collective Ciudad Narrada (A Narrated City) and the Lectoescrinautas Research Group at Universidad Distrital (Bogotá, Colombia). Her research has focused on the semantic reading of the city and the literacy practices of university students.

Kenia Najera's experience as a classroom mentor, coach, and assessor over the past twenty-five years has provided her with the opportunity to play multiple hats. She holds a master's degree in education and works as an adjunct professor motivating students to practice visible thinking skills and promote problem solving. Currently, Kenia is a Ph.D candidate interested in researching more about immigrant children's identity development.

Yecid Ortega completed his doctoral program in Language and Literacies Education (LLE) with a collaborative specialization in Comparative International, and Development Education (CIDE) at the Ontario Institute for Studies in Education (OISE) at the University of Toronto. His general research interests are within decolonial critical ethnographic and case study approaches to research. Yecid explores how globalization, capitalism and neoliberalism influence educational policy decision-making processes and their effects on classroom practices and students' lived experiences. He advocates for other forms of knowledge creation and knowledge mobilization as a way to reach out to marginalized communities who cannot have easy access to information.

Rafael da Silva Tosetti Pejão is a Master's student in Applied Linguistics at the Pontifical Catholic University of São Paulo and a member of the Research Group on Language and Activity in School Context (LACE) and the Brincadas Project. His research's primary focus is on indigenous issues and language education. Since 2012, he has worked at the Municipal Department of Education of São Paulo as an Elementary and High School language teacher.

About the Contributors

Aixa Pérez-Prado is a Teaching Professor at Florida International University in Miami, Florida. She has a Bachelor of Arts in English/Creative Writing, a Master of Arts in Teaching English to Speakers of Other Languages (TESOL), and a PhD in Social Science and Education. Aixa began her teaching career as a bilingual Kindergarten teacher in California and has since worked as a cross cultural trainer and teacher of teachers in pedagogy for linguistic and cultural minority students in the U.S., Costa Rica and Morocco. Her teaching and research interests include multilingualism and identity, critical/creative pedagogy, emotion and language learning, peace linguistics, and diversity studies. Aixa's latest academic book is LAF with the Habits of Mind: Strategies and Activities for Diverse Language Learners. She also writes and illustrates books for children that highlight issues of identity, belonging, diversity and communication across cultures. She has two picture books currently in production, City Feet (Reycraft, 2023) and Mercedes Sosa: Voice of the People (Lee & Low, 2024). Aixa writes in Spanish and English, and translates in Spanish, English and Portuguese. Her author/illustrator website is aixaperezprado.com.

Michelle Ploetz is an experienced and energetic educator with documented success leading cross-disciplinary teams in diverse settings, from reservation communities in the southwestern United States to a study abroad program in Spain and two-year colleges in Texas, Arizona, and Minnesota. She worked at Miami Dade College for more than ten years, serving most recently as Dean of Faculty at the Hialeah campus. She is the co-developer of the award-winning Project ACE (Accelerated Content-Based English for Academic Purposes) program, which serves English language learners with strong academic backgrounds. She currently teaches English as a second language at Atlanta College and Career Academy in Atlanta, Georgia and TESOL courses as an adjunct professor with the University of West Florida. Dr. Ploetz holds a Ph.D. in Teaching and Learning from the University of North Dakota and a Master's degree in Interdisciplinary Studies (Applied Linguistics) from Texas Tech University. She serves as a volunteer with the Parkinson's Foundation.

Kewin Prieto is an English teacher researcher at Centro Colombo-Americano in Bogotá, Colombia. He is currenlty a student of the Master's in Applied Linguistics at Universidad Distrital. His work focuses on the potential of local literacies for language pedagogy. His upcoming research is related to local youths citizenship and its relation with EFL curriculum and pedagogy.

Alejandra Rodríguez-Benavides is a Spanish teacher at Northside High School in Jacksonville, NC. She was an EFL teacher at Universidad Pedagógica Nacional language center. She holds a B.A. in Spanish and Foreign Languages at UPN and an M.A. in Applied Linguistics to TEFL at Universidad Distrital Francisco José de Caldas.

Lina Trigos-Carrillo is a professor in the Department of Spanish at Universidad del Norte. She has worked in education for more than 20 years. Her areas of expertise are teacher professional development, intercultural and multilingual education, popular education, critical literacy, reading and writing, and education with families and communities. In Colombia, she has participated in educational projects with teachers and communities in the context of peacebuilding. She has also conducted ethnography with teachers and students in Mexico, Costa Rica, and the United States. She obtained a Ph.D. in Learning, Teaching, and Curriculum with an emphasis on Reading and Literacy from the University of Missouri. In the U.S., Professor Trigos-Carrillo worked with schools and teachers in multilingual and immigrant communities for seven years. She is the author of the book Teaching Math to Multilingual Students PK-8: Positioning English Learners for Success, published in 2021.

Yıldız Uzuner received her PhD in Special Education Division of Hearing Impairment from the University of Cincinnati in the United States. In 1993, she completed her doctoral dissertation titled " An Investigation of A Hearing Mother's Reading Aloud Efforts to Her Preschool Age Hearing And Hearing Impaired Children Before Bedtime ". She works as a lecturer (also researcher) at Anadolu University, Faculty of Education, Department of Special Education, Department of Hearing Impaired Education. In addition to her thirty-seven years of experience in the language development and education of children with hearing loss, she is also an expert in qualitative research methods.

Daniela Vendramini-Zanella holds a Ph.D. in Applied Linguistics and Language Studies from the Pontifical Catholic University of São Paulo, having postdoctoral experience from this same university. She also holds a Master's in Education from the University of Sorocaba (Uniso). She is the coordinator and professor of the Portuguese and English Languages and Literatures undergraduate program at Uniso. She is a member of the Research Group on Language and Activity in School Context (LACE) and the leader of the Research Group "Teaching education from the perspective of SHCAT and language."

Jiamin Xu is a doctoral student in the department of teaching and learning at Florida International University (FIU), concentrating on Early Childhood Education. She also works as a research assistant and/or teaching assistant during the Ph.D. program. She holds a master's degree in Teaching English to Speakers of Other Languages (TESOL) from Florida International University (FIU). Her research focus is on creating a language-acquisition-friendly environment that provides interactive and engaging multicultural learning experiences for young children to develop their language skills, social-emotional skills, and thinking skills.

Index

A

Abya Yala 222, 227-228, 231, 237-238
Activity 15, 26, 30, 39, 52-53, 75, 80, 113, 132, 137-138, 147, 207, 225, 290-291, 293, 315, 329, 349, 352-353, 371, 393, 400-406, 414, 420, 422, 424-426, 429
Affective Filter 321, 401
Aging 412, 426, 434
Analysis of Students' Cultural and Linguistic Background 103
Anglo 224, 237-238
Attachment 91
Author's Chair 129, 135-137, 142, 146, 152, 302-304, 306-308, 311, 313-315, 319-321
Authoring 111, 169, 321
Autocracy 378-379, 385, 387

B

Beliefs 26, 41-42, 45-51, 55-56, 58, 101, 117, 134, 148, 154-156, 222-223, 246, 267, 283, 290, 302, 324, 397
Boundary Objects 129, 138-139, 146-147, 151-152
Brincadas Project 412-413, 418-421, 423-427, 429, 433-434

C

Case Study 187, 281-282, 299-300, 344, 347-349, 355, 360
CATO Institute 382, 385
Cesar Bona 386
Childhood Studies 90, 265
Children 1-7, 9-17, 19-24, 26-27, 30-39, 41-59, 61, 66, 68-69, 71-104, 107, 112-114, 116-117, 119-126, 129-152, 155-156, 158, 160, 162, 164, 171-200, 206, 208-214, 231, 265-275, 277-279, 299, 302-315, 317-321, 323-326, 328-330, 332, 334, 338-339, 344, 346, 348, 357, 363, 366-367, 370-374, 376-378, 380, 382-387, 414, 418-423, 428-429
Children´s Literature 41, 55
Children's Literature 7, 41, 48, 51, 56, 58, 75, 88, 90-91, 93-104, 132-133, 136, 139, 142, 150, 162, 304, 363, 370-373
Children's Literature Folio 93, 96-99, 102-103
Citizenship Education 60, 109, 124, 366, 370, 376
Classroom Diversity Chart 103
Classroom Library 93, 95-96, 103
Classroom Library Survey 103
Codeswitching 395-397, 410
Cognitive Development 73-74, 138, 193, 197, 305
Collaborative Ethnography 239-240, 244, 246-247, 262, 264
Collaborative Story-Writing 106, 112
Collective Stories for Influence 137, 152
Coloniality 250, 431-433
Communication Skills 182, 190-194, 196, 198-200, 205-210, 213-214, 290
Communicative Competence 223, 282, 296, 389-390, 393, 397-401, 406, 410
Communicative Peace 389-390, 393-395, 397-401, 403, 406-408, 410
Communicative Purposes 190, 193, 195, 199, 203, 213, 411
Communities 27, 41, 44, 54-55, 68, 88, 94, 102, 117, 131, 137, 141, 147, 155, 217-222, 225-226, 228, 230-234, 236, 239-240, 242, 244-247, 249-251, 254, 266-268, 270, 273-275, 278-279, 283, 293, 300, 305, 324, 326, 330, 345-347, 359, 363-365, 367-368, 370-373, 384, 413, 418, 422
Community 32, 43, 46, 50, 53-54, 56-57, 62, 67-68, 88, 98, 101, 108-109, 112, 114, 125, 127-128, 140, 147-148, 163, 173, 179, 182, 186, 189, 191, 216, 218-219, 222, 224-232, 234, 239-242, 244-247, 258-270, 273-274, 278-279, 281, 285-286, 293, 297, 299, 305, 307, 309, 311, 315, 319-320, 322, 343, 345-346, 349, 359, 368, 370-373, 379, 383,

385, 396, 412-414, 417-418, 421-422
Community of Learners 322
Community-Oriented Research 265
Conditions of Learning 134, 146, 149, 306, 321-322
Constructivism 31-32, 284
Conversation 5, 10, 15, 61, 75, 77, 79-80, 84-87, 98, 134-135, 140, 144, 193-196, 198-200, 202, 204, 206, 212-213, 237, 306, 308, 310, 319, 351, 361
Cracks 412-414, 429, 433
Critical Collaborative Research 412, 414, 416, 432-433
Critical Intercultural Awareness 363, 371, 375
Critical Literacies 44, 47, 52, 57-67, 69-72, 102, 241, 363-364, 368, 370-374, 376-377
Critical Literacy 41-42, 44-50, 52-59, 61-62, 65-67, 69-72, 93-96, 101-104, 129, 132-133, 136, 140, 145-146, 148, 152, 248, 254, 258-260, 264, 363-364, 369-373, 375-377
Critical Literacy Discussions 93-96, 104, 371
Critical Pedagogy 42, 363, 367, 427
Cultural Competence 300, 323-330, 334, 339-340
Cultural Forces 8
Cultural Pride 93, 98, 104
Culturally Responsive Teaching 389, 391, 407, 411
Culture 3-4, 8-10, 15-16, 18, 27, 35, 37, 41, 45-46, 48, 50-51, 55-56, 60, 87, 94, 97-98, 119, 124, 128, 130, 132-135, 144, 148, 152, 155-156, 173, 186, 189, 191, 193, 216-218, 222, 225-226, 228-229, 231, 234-237, 240, 243, 262, 266, 269, 272-275, 277, 283-285, 293-295, 297-300, 302-305, 308, 311-312, 319, 321, 323-325, 329-330, 335, 339-340, 343, 346, 352-356, 358, 360, 365-368, 386, 388, 391-392, 408, 418, 423, 432
Cultures of Thinking 1, 24, 90

D

Deaf 172-175, 179, 181-189, 209-212, 413
Deaf and Hard of Hearing (DHH) 171-172, 189
Deaf Education 171, 182-188, 210-211
Deaf Students 184-185, 188
Decolonial Studies 412
Democracy 27, 36, 42, 53, 69, 133, 161, 378-380, 385, 388
Design Thinking 115, 123-125, 128, 149, 323, 332
Dialogic Reading 75, 79, 91, 140
Dialogic Thinking 129, 137, 146-147, 152
Didactic 26-30, 32-37, 39, 101, 110, 283
Digital Collective Stories of Voice and Influence 137
Digital Storytelling 106-109, 111, 122-129, 132, 137, 144-149, 152, 302, 307, 313, 318-319
Directing Attention 190, 193, 199-201, 206, 213-214
Directing Attention Skills 193, 199, 201, 214
Discussion 9, 15-16, 50, 69-70, 84, 93, 95-96, 99-101, 104, 107, 117, 122, 129, 140, 155, 194, 286-287, 289, 295, 328, 334, 355-356, 395, 402, 404, 414, 416, 422, 425
Dispositions 2, 10-11, 25, 106-108, 117-119, 121-122, 127-128, 160, 303, 327-328, 367, 394
Dispositions for a World on the Move 118, 121, 128
Diversity Chart 93, 95-96, 103
Documentation 8, 12-13, 24, 78-79, 81, 83, 91, 157, 164, 222, 427
Draw and Tell Technique 302, 304, 306-308, 313, 317, 319
Dual Language Learners 23, 91

E

Early Childhood 1, 3-4, 23, 41, 46-49, 52-53, 55-58, 63, 71-73, 76, 87-88, 90, 98, 107, 117, 119-121, 124, 127, 131, 149, 193, 211-212, 265, 272, 302, 305-307, 319, 321, 340, 376, 392
Early Childhood Education 1, 48, 58, 72, 76, 90, 107, 117, 120, 127, 265, 272, 307, 321, 340, 376
Early Intervention 59, 143, 171, 173-176, 178, 182-187, 212
Early Literacy 42, 55-56, 59, 87, 91, 183, 185-186, 188
Early Years Education 60-61, 63, 65-66, 68, 70, 278
Early Years Learning Environments 1
Early Years Literacy 1
Education 1, 3-5, 10, 16, 18, 23-29, 31, 41-49, 56-63, 65-72, 74, 76, 87-90, 102-103, 106-109, 115, 117, 120, 122-127, 132, 139, 149-154, 156-169, 171, 177-178, 181-188, 190, 196, 198, 200, 209-212, 216-219, 223, 228-229, 231-237, 239-246, 248-249, 258-264, 266-267, 269-279, 282-283, 289, 291, 293, 295-297, 299-300, 303, 305, 307, 319, 321, 324-329, 339-341, 344-347, 358-360, 363-370, 372-376, 378, 380, 382-390, 394-395, 397-398, 403, 407, 409, 411-413, 418, 430, 432-434
Emotional Development 73, 95
Emotions 3-5, 15, 23, 67, 72-73, 86, 110, 129-132, 139, 143, 147, 150, 217, 219, 221, 223, 225, 230, 290, 305, 307, 320, 340, 345, 369, 390, 392-394, 396, 398-399, 401, 403, 406-407, 409-410
Empathy 4-5, 19, 23, 51, 56, 115-118, 124, 132, 136, 140, 142, 149, 303, 323, 325-326, 330, 332, 363-366, 368, 370-371, 373, 376, 391, 398, 403, 406-407
Enculturation 10, 25
Engaged Multiliteracy 414, 416, 418, 423, 428, 431, 433
Extractive Institutions 378, 381-382, 385, 387

Index

F

Family Literacy 101, 373
Foreign Language 161-162, 229, 232-234, 236, 281-283, 293, 296-298, 300, 343, 357-358, 360, 389-390, 392, 394-397, 409-410
Forest Alphabet 265-266, 269-270, 273, 279
Forest Education 266, 269-270, 273, 275, 279
Fragile Context of Everyday Life 279
Freedom to Teach 93-95, 104
Funds of Knowledge 49, 94, 102, 133, 148, 150, 262, 344-345, 349, 355, 358-360
Funds of Perezhivanie 412-413, 415-416, 422-423, 426-429, 431-432
Future Teachers 153-156, 160, 164-166

G

Generative Topics 2, 76, 91
Genre 96, 104, 256
Genres 52, 100, 374
Global Competence 23, 119, 123, 149, 303, 319, 323-328, 334, 336, 338-340, 406-407, 411
Global Competency 1, 19, 22-23, 390-392, 395, 398
Global Literacies 281, 289-292, 300

H

Habits of Mind 320, 323-324, 394, 398, 406-407, 409
Hearing Difference 171-172, 174-178, 189
Hearing Loss 176, 183, 187-188, 190-196, 200, 209-211, 214
Heritage Language 216-217, 343-344, 346-349, 352, 355, 357-359
Human Rights 60, 62-63, 65, 67-72, 133, 273, 366-367, 371, 390, 414, 418, 431

I

Identity 41, 43, 45, 50-52, 55, 62, 66-67, 70, 95, 101, 140-141, 153-155, 163, 166, 168-169, 173, 216-217, 222, 228-229, 234-236, 243-245, 251, 258, 260, 262, 268, 273-275, 279, 282, 285-287, 289, 292-293, 296, 300, 302-305, 307-308, 312, 318-320, 322, 345-346, 355-359, 390-391, 395, 418
Ideology 41-43, 49, 55, 269-270, 297, 375, 385, 391, 397
Imitation 151, 190, 193-194, 199-201, 206, 210-214
Inclusion of Disabilities 104
Inclusive Institutions 378, 385
Indigenous Community Social Learning 279
Indigenous Education 267, 412, 418
Informal Communication Skills Inventory 190-191, 199-200, 205, 214
Interaction 1, 3, 5, 37, 68, 73, 77, 84, 92, 107, 109-111, 131, 133-134, 136, 144, 191-195, 207, 210, 213-214, 216-217, 221-222, 237, 256, 264, 267, 281, 283, 289, 292-293, 302, 305-306, 313, 347, 351, 356-357, 365, 392-393, 396, 400-401, 408, 420
Interactions 3, 5-6, 10-11, 22, 24, 32, 55, 73-74, 77, 88, 110, 121, 131, 134, 145, 156-157, 162, 191, 194-196, 198-200, 205-207, 213-214, 221, 223, 230, 247, 260, 267-268, 270, 272, 287, 305, 308, 314-315, 319, 323, 328, 330, 334, 339, 343, 345, 351, 354-356, 359, 364, 371, 374, 390, 392-393, 399-400, 402
Intercultural Adroitness 300
Intercultural Awareness 281-286, 289, 291-298, 300-301, 363, 371, 375
Intercultural Communication 236, 281-284, 290, 292, 296, 298, 300-301
Intercultural Sensitivity 296, 301
Interculturality 216-217, 231, 235, 237, 260, 292-293, 296

J

James Buchanan 378, 381-382

K

Knowledge Processes 262, 281-283, 285-286, 294-295, 301

L

Language 1-10, 13-19, 22-23, 25, 31-33, 35, 37, 41-43, 45-46, 48, 52, 55-59, 71-75, 77, 86-88, 90-92, 94-95, 97, 102-103, 109, 113, 129-132, 134-137, 139-141, 145, 147-150, 155-156, 158-162, 164-167, 171-200, 208-214, 216-219, 221-237, 239-240, 242-246, 249, 254-256, 258-264, 269, 271, 276, 279, 281-284, 287, 289, 293, 295-308, 311-315, 318-322, 332-334, 339, 343-345, 347-361, 365, 368-370, 374-377, 386-387, 390-403, 406-416, 423, 426, 429-430, 432
Language Acquisition 3, 5, 10, 23, 74, 131, 136, 162, 164, 176, 179, 185, 187, 190-192, 261, 263, 305-306, 321-322, 345, 348, 357-358, 389-390, 392-393, 395-396, 398-400, 402-403, 407-409
Language Acquisition Device (LAD) 305, 322
Language Development 6, 73-75, 86, 88, 91, 133-134,

497

149, 159, 164, 172, 174, 176, 178, 183-185, 187-188, 190-191, 193, 195, 198, 209-212, 302, 306, 308, 312-313, 315, 318, 392

Language Equity 389, 391, 396, 406, 411

Language Learning 74, 109, 130, 134, 159, 216-217, 224, 234, 262, 282-284, 287, 295-296, 302, 304, 306-307, 314-315, 318-319, 321-322, 343-348, 351, 353-360, 389, 392-393, 399, 401-402, 407-410

Language Teaching 164, 216-217, 221, 229, 231, 233, 235, 237, 261-262, 281-282, 284, 296, 298-300, 343, 348, 358, 395-396, 402, 407, 410, 430

Languaging 223, 262, 344, 347, 349, 355-357, 359-360, 389, 391, 410-411

Learning 1-6, 8-18, 22-37, 39, 42-45, 48-49, 55, 57-58, 63, 66, 70-72, 74, 79, 87-88, 90-91, 98, 101, 106-111, 117-119, 121-128, 130-132, 134, 139-140, 142, 145-146, 148-152, 154, 156, 158-162, 165-168, 174, 176, 179-181, 184, 187, 193-194, 198, 200, 210, 212-213, 216-219, 221-222, 224-226, 229-234, 240, 242, 247, 249, 262-263, 265-266, 268-270, 272-273, 276, 278-279, 281-284, 287, 289, 291, 295-300, 302, 304-309, 313-315, 318-323, 325-330, 332-335, 338-340, 343-361, 367, 370-371, 376, 386, 389-396, 398-402, 407-410, 415, 422, 432

Lesson Plans 87-88, 99, 181, 386

Linguistic Landscape 239-240, 242, 244-246, 248, 258-264

Literacies 44, 47, 52, 54, 56-67, 69-72, 102, 108-109, 118, 122, 130, 137, 139-140, 153-154, 157-168, 218, 239-242, 244-245, 258-262, 264, 281, 283, 289-301, 312, 363-364, 368-377, 386, 388, 430

Literacy 1-7, 14-15, 17-19, 22-23, 26-29, 32-33, 35, 37, 39, 41-50, 52-59, 61-62, 65-67, 69-75, 87-88, 90-91, 93-96, 101-104, 106-108, 110-112, 117-118, 123-124, 127, 129-133, 136-140, 145-154, 156-158, 160-165, 167-168, 171, 173, 175-178, 182-186, 188, 191-192, 196, 212, 232, 239-242, 244-246, 248, 254, 258-264, 273, 281-284, 291, 293-294, 296-299, 301, 307, 319-320, 339, 343-345, 347, 350, 352, 355, 357-359, 363-364, 368-371, 373-379, 386-391, 394, 402, 407, 430

Literacy Education 41, 44, 46, 57-58, 150, 153-154, 156-165, 167-168, 239-242, 246, 248, 296, 299, 345

Literacy Events 130, 294, 373

M

Method 26, 29, 33, 39, 42, 45, 78, 112, 125, 150, 157, 197-198, 200, 207, 266, 271-273, 279, 308, 321, 323, 340, 349, 359, 365, 409, 430, 432

Minecraft Education 325, 329

Multilingual Education 216, 240, 407, 432

Multilingualism 234-235, 240-246, 248, 254, 258-260, 262-263, 391, 397, 407, 411, 430

Multiliteracies 54, 71-72, 106-109, 112-113, 117, 119, 121-122, 124, 127, 129-130, 136, 156, 262, 264, 281-284, 297, 299-301, 367-368, 376, 416, 432

Multiliteracy 106-109, 112-116, 122-123, 127-128, 138, 146, 152, 414, 416, 418, 423, 428, 431, 433

Multimodal Texts 109, 239-240, 246, 259, 264, 285, 289, 370

Multimodalities 106-107

Multiple Literacies 118, 122, 139-140, 312

N

Narrative Approach 322

New Literacies 58, 153-154, 157-166, 293, 297-298

North Broward Preparatory School 323, 325

O

Ongoing Assessment 2, 10, 12, 14, 16, 76, 91, 339

Oppression 41, 46-47, 50, 52-56, 155, 231-232, 267, 412-415, 433

ORA Method 266, 271-273, 279

Oral Language Development 88, 91, 193

Overreaching Understanding Goals 92

P

Pachamama 237

Peace Education 62, 363-368, 370, 373, 375-376, 411

Peace Linguistics 389-390, 394-395, 397, 406-408, 411

Peacebuilding 236, 363-364, 367-368, 370-371, 373-374, 395

Pedagogical Impacts 1, 7, 11-12, 22

Pedagogy 26, 30-31, 42, 57-58, 61, 64, 101, 106, 108-109, 112, 117, 122, 124, 127, 129, 152, 155-156, 160, 166, 168, 232-235, 245, 262, 272, 276, 278, 281-285, 287, 289, 291-299, 301, 304, 344, 346-348, 355, 357, 363-364, 367-368, 375-376, 391, 398, 407-408, 410, 427, 430, 432

Pedagogy of Multiliteracies 117, 122, 124, 127, 129, 262, 281-282, 284, 301, 376, 432

Perception 26-27, 31, 37, 39, 100, 152, 268, 274, 291, 390, 406, 409

Perezhivanie 412-413, 415-416, 422-423, 426-429, 431-434

Index

Performances for Understanding 92
Place-Based Pedagogies 264
Plurilingualism 216, 222-224, 226, 234, 236-237
Project-Based Learning 1, 323, 340
Public Education 29, 378, 383-385

Q

Quechua Language 216-219, 221-224, 227-234, 237

R

Reading 4, 6-7, 10, 15, 17-19, 23-37, 39, 41-44, 47-48, 51-55, 57-59, 62, 75, 79, 87, 89, 91, 93-96, 101-103, 124, 127, 130-131, 134, 136-137, 140, 142, 144-146, 149-151, 154, 158-160, 162, 164, 168, 171-183, 185-188, 192, 195, 199, 209-210, 213, 229, 242, 250, 252, 254, 258-259, 261, 263-264, 271, 275, 278, 282-287, 289, 292-294, 296-297, 299-301, 306-307, 314-315, 320, 330, 332, 339, 350, 364, 368, 370-372, 375-376, 386-387, 404-405, 410, 425
Receptive Language 92, 211
Reflection 16, 26, 28, 30-37, 39, 41, 48, 50, 52-53, 66-67, 75, 123, 125, 138, 151, 155, 219, 221, 236, 258-259, 281, 283, 293, 301, 338, 355, 359, 365, 367, 369-370, 373-374, 420
Reimagining Migration 118, 126, 128
Re-Imagining Migration 117, 340
Representation 26, 31-32, 34-35, 37, 39, 63-64, 70, 243, 251, 269, 284, 298, 301, 311, 314
Revitalization 216-218, 221, 227-228, 230-235, 237, 245, 261
Runasimi 237

S

Scarborough 171-172, 174, 178, 186
School 3, 5, 7-8, 10, 12, 15-16, 18, 23, 25-27, 32-34, 36, 46, 48, 50, 53, 57, 63, 65, 71-72, 74-75, 82, 86-87, 89-91, 94, 98, 101-102, 109, 117-118, 122-123, 127, 130, 138-140, 143, 147-148, 150, 156, 158-161, 163, 174, 177, 179-181, 183-184, 187, 191, 195, 199, 219, 236, 245-247, 253, 258-260, 263, 271-275, 279, 283, 286-287, 303-304, 314, 320, 323, 325-330, 332, 334, 338-339, 343-344, 346, 348-350, 352, 354-355, 357, 361, 364, 366-367, 372-374, 381, 384, 387, 391, 408, 412-416, 418, 422-423, 426-427, 429, 432
Secondary Students 343
Self-Efficacy 133, 310-311, 319, 322

Self-Interest 378, 381-384, 387
Semiotic Landscapes 239-240, 244, 247-250, 254, 259, 261, 264
Skilled Reading 171-172, 174, 176-178
Social Learning 265-266, 269-270, 273, 276, 278-279, 305, 319
Standardized Test 214
Story 1, 5, 12, 14-15, 18, 51-54, 56, 75, 87, 91, 98, 106, 108, 110-112, 114-116, 121, 124-126, 128-135, 137-138, 140-147, 149-152, 178, 252, 267, 269, 276, 285-287, 289-292, 294-295, 302, 308, 310-312, 314-315, 318-320, 323-324, 339, 343-345, 348-350, 355, 357, 371, 387, 420
StoryLogicNet 106, 108, 113-114, 123, 127
Stress 73-74, 76-77, 86-88, 156, 305, 393-394, 413
Structural Violence 364-365, 370, 373
Sustainable Development Goals 27, 39, 332-333, 340

T

Teacher Education 49, 56, 58, 124-126, 153-161, 163-169, 235, 245-246, 258, 261, 263, 282, 289, 296-297, 358, 367, 370, 387, 390, 394-395, 397-398, 403, 432
Teacher Education Programs 49, 56, 153-157, 163-167, 246, 367, 390, 394-395, 398
Teacher Educators 153, 155, 166, 168, 261, 394
Teaching 2, 4, 10, 23-29, 31-37, 39, 41-44, 46-50, 54-59, 61, 69, 71-73, 75-76, 78-79, 81, 83, 85, 88-91, 93, 95-96, 99-103, 106-110, 112, 123-126, 128, 133, 140, 142, 149-150, 152, 154-156, 158-159, 161-162, 164, 166-168, 175, 180-181, 187, 191, 213, 216-224, 226, 229-237, 240, 259, 261-262, 264, 271-272, 281-284, 288-289, 294, 296, 298-300, 320-321, 326-328, 339-340, 344-345, 348, 352-353, 355, 357-359, 367-368, 378, 383, 386-389, 391-392, 394-396, 398-399, 401-402, 407, 409-411, 423, 427, 430, 432
Teaching for Understanding 2, 23, 25, 73, 75-76, 78-79, 81, 83, 85, 89, 339
The Viable Unheard of 423, 427, 431
Thinking Map 331, 340
Thinking Routine 15, 19, 81, 86, 140, 328, 334, 340, 342
Thinking Routines 11-12, 14, 20, 73, 75, 88-89, 92, 106, 108, 119-120, 122-123, 128, 140, 146, 149, 340
Trans[cultura]linguación 216-217, 224, 226, 237
Translanguaging 223-224, 226, 236-237, 254, 256-258, 264, 321, 391-392, 396-397, 407-409, 411, 415, 420, 423-424, 430
Turn-Taking 134-135, 190, 193-195, 199-200, 202, 206, 208, 211, 213-214

Turtle Island 231, 237
Twenty-Six Letters of the Forest Alphabet 265, 279

U

Urban Literacies 239-242, 244, 259-260, 264

V

Verbocentricity 301
viable Unheard Of 423, 427, 431, 433
Visible Thinking 73, 92, 117, 125, 127-128, 148, 323
Visible Thinking Routines 73, 92
Vivian Vásquez 41

W

Writing 6-7, 10, 12, 15-17, 20, 26-37, 39, 43-44, 47, 58, 62, 71, 84-85, 110-114, 123-125, 127, 130-131, 134, 136-137, 145, 147, 152, 154, 160-161, 174, 206, 209, 229, 271, 275, 279, 282-283, 286, 293-294, 296-297, 301, 304, 306-307, 313-315, 319-321, 330, 332, 335, 339, 346-347, 350, 368, 386-387, 404

Z

Zone of Proximal Development (ZPD) 133, 306, 322

Recommended Reference Books

IGI Global's reference books are available in three unique pricing formats:
Print Only, E-Book Only, or Print + E-Book.

Shipping fees may apply.

www.igi-global.com

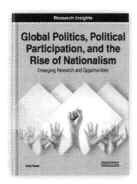

ISBN: 9781799873433
EISBN: 9781799873457
© 2021; 213 pp.
List Price: US$ 175

ISBN: 9781799841562
EISBN: 9781799841579
© 2021; 374 pp.
List Price: US$ 195

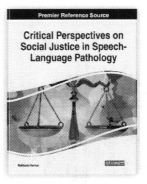

ISBN: 9781799871347
EISBN: 9781799871361
© 2021; 355 pp.
List Price: US$ 195

ISBN: 9781799837299
EISBN: 9781799837312
© 2021; 301 pp.
List Price: US$ 185

ISBN: 9781799870043
EISBN: 9781799870067
© 2021; 290 pp.
List Price: US$ 195

ISBN: 9781799836650
EISBN: 9781799836674
© 2021; 301 pp.
List Price: US$ 195

Do you want to stay current on the latest research trends, product announcements, news, and special offers?
Join IGI Global's mailing list to receive customized recommendations, exclusive discounts, and more.
Sign up at: **www.igi-global.com/newsletters**.

Publisher of Timely, Peer-Reviewed Inclusive Research Since 1988

www.igi-global.com   Sign up at www.igi-global.com/newsletters   facebook.com/igiglobal   twitter.com/igiglobal   linkedin.com/igiglobal

Ensure Quality Research is Introduced to the Academic Community

Become an Evaluator for IGI Global Authored Book Projects

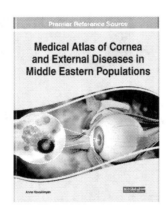
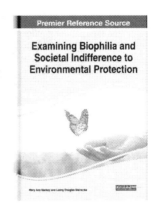
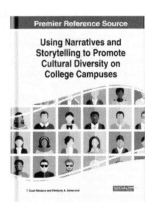

The overall success of an authored book project is dependent on quality and timely manuscript evaluations.

Applications and Inquiries may be sent to:
development@igi-global.com

Applicants must have a doctorate (or equivalent degree) as well as publishing, research, and reviewing experience. Authored Book Evaluators are appointed for one-year terms and are expected to complete at least three evaluations per term. Upon successful completion of this term, evaluators can be considered for an additional term.

If you have a colleague that may be interested in this opportunity, we encourage you to share this information with them.

Easily Identify, Acquire, and Utilize Published Peer-Reviewed Findings in Support of Your Current Research

IGI Global OnDemand

Purchase Individual IGI Global OnDemand Book Chapters and Journal Articles

For More Information:
www.igi-global.com/e-resources/ondemand/

Browse through 150,000+ Articles and Chapters!

Find specific research related to your current studies and projects that have been contributed by international researchers from prestigious institutions, including:

- Accurate and Advanced Search
- Affordably Acquire Research
- Instantly Access Your Content
- Benefit from the InfoSci Platform Features

"It really provides an excellent entry into the research literature of the field. It presents a manageable number of highly relevant sources on topics of interest to a wide range of researchers. The sources are scholarly, but also accessible to 'practitioners'."

- Ms. Lisa Stimatz, MLS, University of North Carolina at Chapel Hill, USA

Interested in Additional Savings?

Subscribe to
IGI Global OnDemand Plus

Learn More

Acquire content from over 128,000+ research-focused book chapters and 33,000+ scholarly journal articles for as low as US$ 5 per article/chapter (original retail price for an article/chapter: US$ 37.50).

6,600+ E-BOOKS. ADVANCED RESEARCH. INCLUSIVE & ACCESSIBLE.

IGI Global e-Book Collection

- **Flexible Purchasing Options** (Perpetual, Subscription, EBA, etc.)
- Multi-Year Agreements with **No Price Increases** Guaranteed
- **No Additional Charge** for Multi-User Licensing
- No Maintenance, Hosting, or Archiving Fees
- Transformative **Open Access Options** Available

Request More Information, or Recommend the IGI Global e-Book Collection to Your Institution's Librarian

Among Titles Included in the IGI Global e-Book Collection

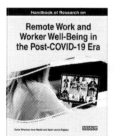

Research Anthology on Racial Equity, Identity, and Privilege (3 Vols.)
EISBN: 9781668445082
Price: US$ 895

Handbook of Research on Remote Work and Worker Well-Being in the Post-COVID-19 Era
EISBN: 9781799867562
Price: US$ 265

Research Anthology on Big Data Analytics, Architectures, and Applications (4 Vols.)
EISBN: 9781668436639
Price: US$ 1,950

Handbook of Research on Challenging Deficit Thinking for Exceptional Education Improvement
EISBN: 9781799888628
Price: US$ 265

Acquire & Open

When your library acquires an IGI Global e-Book and/or e-Journal Collection, your faculty's published work will be considered for immediate conversion to Open Access *(CC BY License)*, at no additional cost to the library or its faculty *(cost only applies to the e-Collection content being acquired)*, through our popular **Transformative Open Access (Read & Publish) Initiative**.

For More Information or to Request a Free Trial, Contact IGI Global's e-Collections Team: eresources@igi-global.com | 1-866-342-6657 ext. 100 | 717-533-8845 ext. 100

Have Your Work Published and Freely Accessible
Open Access Publishing

With the industry shifting from the more traditional publication models to an open access (OA) publication model, publishers are finding that OA publishing has many benefits that are awarded to authors and editors of published work.

| Freely Share Your Research | Higher Discoverability & Citation Impact | Rigorous & Expedited Publishing Process | Increased Advancement & Collaboration |

Acquire & Open

When your library acquires an IGI Global e-Book and/or e-Journal Collection, your faculty's published work will be considered for immediate conversion to Open Access *(CC BY License)*, at no additional cost to the library or its faculty *(cost only applies to the e-Collection content being acquired)*, through our popular **Transformative Open Access (Read & Publish) Initiative**.

- Provide Up To **100%** OA APC or CPC Funding
- Funding to Convert or Start a Journal to **Platinum OA**
- Support for Funding an **OA Reference Book**

IGI Global publications are found in a number of prestigious indices, including Web of Science™, Scopus®, Compendex, and PsycINFO®. The selection criteria is very strict and to ensure that journals and books are accepted into the major indexes, IGI Global closely monitors publications against the criteria that the indexes provide to publishers.

WEB OF SCIENCE™   **Compendex**   **Scopus**
PsycINFO®   **IET Inspec**

Learn More Here: For Questions, Contact IGI Global's Open Access Team at openaccessadmin@igi-global.com

www.igi-global.com